WHEN THE SPIRIT CALLS

When the Spirit Calls

The Killings at Hannah Bay

EDWARD J. HEDICAN

UNIVERSITY OF TORONTO PRESS
Toronto Buffalo London

© University of Toronto Press 2023
Toronto Buffalo London
utorontopress.com

ISBN 978-1-4875-4666-3 (cloth)   ISBN 978-1-4875-4669-4 (EPUB)
ISBN 978-1-4875-4668-7 (paper)   ISBN 978-1-4875-4671-7 (PDF)

Library and Archives Canada Cataloguing in Publication

Title: When the spirit calls : the killings at Hannah Bay / Edward J. Hedican.
Names: Hedican, Edward J., author.
Description: Includes bibliographical references and index.
Identifiers: Canadiana (print) 20220481016 | Canadiana (ebook) 20220481083 |
    ISBN 9781487546687 (softcover) | ISBN 9781487546663 (hardcover) |
    ISBN 9781487546694 (EPUB) | ISBN 9781487546717 (PDF)
Subjects: LCSH: Cree Indians – James Bay Region. | LCSH: Indigenous
    peoples – James Bay Region. | LCSH: Hudson's Bay Company –
    Employees. | LCSH: Murder – James Bay Region. | LCSH: Massacres –
    James Bay Region. | LCSH: Oral history – James Bay Region.
Classification: LCC E99.C88 H43 2023 | DDC 364.152/30916327–dc23

We wish to acknowledge the land on which the University of Toronto Press operates. This land is the traditional territory of the Wendat, the Anishnaabeg, the Haudenosaunee, the Métis, and the Mississaugas of the Credit First Nation.

This book has been published with the help of a grant from the Federation for the Humanities and Social Sciences, through the Awards to Scholarly Publications Program, using funds provided by the Social Sciences and Humanities Research Council of Canada.

University of Toronto Press acknowledges the financial support of the Government of Canada, the Canada Council for the Arts, and the Ontario Arts Council, an agency of the Government of Ontario, for its publishing activities.

Canada Council   Conseil des Arts
for the Arts   du Canada

ONTARIO ARTS COUNCIL
CONSEIL DES ARTS DE L'ONTARIO
an Ontario government agency
un organisme du gouvernement de l'Ontario

Funded by the   Financé par le
Government   gouvernement
of Canada   du Canada

Contents

Preface

History is written by the victors.

– Winston Churchill

Winston Churchill is probably known most notably for his "We shall fight on the beaches" speech of 1940; however, another rhetorical quote, "history is written by the victors," is often attributed to him as well. Some may see in these words a cynical dismissal of the role of objectivity in historical discourse. Remember that Napoleon is reputed to have said, "What is history, but a fable agreed upon?"

Is it true, then, that historical writings are simply fables; that there is no "reality" to the recounting of past events? There are many who would disagree with this assertion; however, it is difficult to refute the idea that the "winners" in history exploit their power to achieve their own ends, or that those in power have a vested self-interest in maintaining their power and influence. In turn, the power of the victors can serve to function as a strong tool in upholding the status of those possessing positions of ascendency in a society. In other words, the victors are in a privileged position to write their own histories, which can glorify their individual causes and disparage those of a subjugated people. The "losers" of history do not usually have access to the venues, such as a sympathetic press, that can be utilized to promote their own view of historical reality. The "truth" of the past is in large part shaped by the might of political and cultural leaders on the "winning" side of history who have the power to craft historical narratives through a range of media, such as a compliant press, to their own benefit. These media are powerful venues for establishing political ideologies and shaping personal assumptions.

This, then, is my prelude to a discussion of Canada's early history in the James Bay area involving the interaction of the members of the

Hudson's Bay Company and the Indigenous population of mainly Cree-speaking people. This book is primarily focused on what the British have termed the "Hannah Bay Massacre" of 1832, and the interpretation of this event as gleaned from the Company's archival records and possible elucidations by the Cree themselves in their oral traditions. As such, in the larger macrocosm of Canadian history itself, we can see in this event the early beginnings of colonial "winners" attempting to manipulate a historical discourse that portrays them in a favourable position vis-à-vis their Indigenous counterparts in any dispute involving the two groups. I also wish to promote the idea that the very foundation of the Hudson's Bay Company in the James Bay area was flawed from the very beginning because of adverse ecological conditions and that these inauspicious settings were bound to lead to "catastrophes in the making" with disastrous results for all involved. The term "catastrophe," I should note, is the one used by John McLean (1932 [1849]: 99), long-time Hudson's Bay Company employee, to describe the Hannah Bay incident.

Disclaimer

From the outset, let me make one point perfectly clear. In the following book I do not condone the killing of Hannah Bay post manager William Corrigal, his family, or others who met their untimely end at the hands of the Cree elder named Quapakay and his sons. Nor, on the other hand, should we condone the killing of Quapakay and his sons by a Hudson's Bay Company posse who, without so much as an enquiry of any kind and administering a rough form of "country justice" amounting to not much more than a lynch mob, took their revenge. However, as we shall see, there were many extenuating circumstances involving starvation, colonial discrimination against Indigenous peoples, breaches of reciprocal obligations, and so on, which complicated the matter. Unfortunately, it is circumstances such as the Hannah Bay killings which formed the fundamental foundations of Indigenous-settler relationships that continue into present day Canada.

Edward J. Hedican
Professor Emeritus
University of Guelph

Acknowledgments

I am particularly indebted to Liana Haapalehto, a former student at the University of Guelph, for all her diligent work in transcribing fur-trader journals and other pertinent accounts, and to Mallory Richard of Winnipeg, Manitoba, for providing her invaluable service by researching the Hudson's Bay Company archives. I am sure that very little, if anything, relating to the Hannah Bay murders would have escaped their scrutiny. For my son Shaun Hedican who resides on the Rocky Bay Anishinaabe Reserve in northern Ontario, I am grateful for his insights and perspectives on life in the Lake Nipigon area. Thanks to Karen Hurson who helped me with proofreading and attempting to decipher the Hudson's Bay Company documents that were used in this study. My long-time friend and colleague of more than forty years, Stan Barrett, professor emeritus at the University of Guelph, has always been very supportive of my research and writing projects, often lending encouragement and advice, and to him I am very grateful. Also at the University of Guelph, Tad McIlwraith has been very helpful sharing his ideas with me on current Indigenous issues. I am also indebted to the late Peter, Donald, and Hamish Patience, formerly of Collins, Ontario, who were all born at Eabametoong First Nation (formerly Fort Hope) on the Albany River. Their father, John Patience, was a long-time Scottish post manager for the Hudson's Bay Company at Fort Hope, and I am therefore grateful for their many insights into the fur trade and the life of a fur-trade family. Elizabeth Patience, their mother and the wife of John Patience, was the daughter of John Yesno, a famous chief who signed the 1905 James Bay Treaty. She provided me with a treasure trove of interesting information about the life of the Anishinaabe people of northern Ontario and their interaction with the British fur traders.

My field research in northern Ontario began in 1974 and extended for at least three decades. This ongoing research, albeit in a different form, actually continues to this day on Facebook with the children of Peter Patience and other former Anishinaabe residents of northern Ontario. For all the Anishinaabe people who provided me with assistance in my research I am particularly indebted to Jaimie Mishibinijima, Ann-Margaret Patience, Anita Patience, Dorothy (Goodwin) Patience, Tom Wastaken, Steve Goodwin, Anne and Samson Basketwang, Sogo Sabosans, Linda Staats, Raymond Wabasons, Harry Achnepeneeskum, and Elijah Yellowhead. And last but not least, my gratitude to the years I spend with McGill anthropologists Philip Salzman, Carmen Lambert, Bruce Trigger, and Richard Salisbury for all they taught me about research and academic life.

Characters

Cree

Bolland: son-in-law of Quapakay; father Artawayham; killed in 1832
Quapakay: Cree elder; shaking tent specialist; killed in 1832
Shaintoquaish: son of Quapakay; killed in 1832
Stacemow: son of Quapakay; killed in 1832

Hudson's Bay Company

Anderson, James (1812–1867): wrote *A Fur Trader's Story*
Beioley, Joseph (1785–1859): Rupert House post master
Corrigal, William (1774–1832): killed at Hannah Bay Post in 1832
McLean, John (1799–1890): disaffected HBC employee; discovered Churchill Falls
McTavish, John (1778–1847): Moose Factory post master
Simpson, Sir George (1787–1860): governor of Hudson's Bay Company (1826–1860)
Swanson, William (1794–1847): leader of HBC party who killed Quapakay and his sons

WHEN THE SPIRIT CALLS

Chapter One

Introduction

Men make their own history, but they do not make it just as they please; they do not make it under circumstances chosen by themselves, but under given circumstances directly encountered and inherited from the past.
 – Karl Marx, *The Eighteenth Brumaire of Louis Bonaparte* (1978 [1852]: 9)

Early Euro-American ethnohistories are often based on those blatantly ethnocentric and racist assumptions formulated by said groups to legitimize the expansion of Western powers in the Americas.
 – R.J. Chacon and R.G. Mendoza, *North American Indigenous Warfare and Ritual Violence* (2007: 224–5)

This book is not a whodunit. There's no mystery here or bodies to uncover. Also, we don't need to ask about the "how" either. But it's the "why" that bothers us. When people are killed, everyone wants to know, why did it happen? There hardly ever seems to be an easy answer. The "why" just seems to seep out, like ink poured in a pool of water, trickling out, farther and farther, in ever increasing concentric rings away from the actual event itself. Before you know it, you are farther and farther away from the scene of the crime, still asking why, and an answer never seems to come.

This pebble in the pond analogy suggests a major point of this book – that there are no fortuitous, isolated incidents. Everything that happens on this Earth has repercussions. What happens in life has a cause and, in turn, causes other events, behaviours, and situations. Of course, what I am telling you is nothing new; it is simply Sir Isaac Newton's third law of motion, which states that for every action there is an equal and opposite reaction. Given this basic principle of life, a murderous event which happened in James Bay in 1832 was caused precipitously by prior events and, after, sent out ripples that influenced, in turn, other events to occur. The goal of this book is to uncover as best as we are able the various circumstances, behaviours, and attitudes that led to the killing of fur trader William Corrigal and similar future occurrences. Principal among these is the racist attitudes held by the white settler population towards Indigenous people that was so very prevalent in the colonial past and apparently continues unabated to this very day.

Respectful Language: Names and Terminology

There are few people, I suspect, who feel confident enough to define precisely the myriad names applied to Indigenous people in North America with any degree of confidence. While there are many terms associated with the First Nations, Inuit, and Métis peoples, and a diverse terminology for Indigenous peoples living in the United States, it is nonetheless important to be respectful of this diversity and refer to the original peoples of North America in a deferential manner and, where possible, to closely use the terms that they themselves would prefer to be identified by and in a manner reflecting their own linguistic usages. Since the discussion that follows in this book covers many areas of North America, some clarification of this matter of definitions and terminology would therefore be a useful place to start. On another matter, there is a significant difference in usage of terminology between Canada and the United States so that these countries will be discussed separately. Let us start with language.

Language: The literature on Indigenous people contains a wide variety of terms used in the past which at times have continued into current usage, while other terms have a more limited usage today. In keeping with the idea of using respectful language, an attempt is made in this book to use terms that most closely describe how Indigenous people wish to be identified. As such, in order to standardize certain terminology for the First Nations of Canada, the following designations will be used in the subsequent text:

1. *Anishinaabe* (pl. *Anishinaabek*) for Ojibwa, Chippewa, or Anishenaabe;
2. *Haudenosaunee* for the Iroquois Six Nations; however, specific names may be used for each society, such as Seneca or Mohawk;
3. *Wendat* for Huron, but not for other related Nations, such as Petun.

Note also that the names of specific historical designations have not been altered as used in the original texts.

In all there are about six Indigenous language families in Canada. One of the largest of these is the Algonquian (or Algonkian) group, which is spread out over the eastern part of North America (Pentland and Wolfart 1982; Rhodes and Todd 1981). In the 1700s members of this family, mainly the Anishinaabe and the Cree, moved into the Plains area with the spread of the fur trade and the availability of horses. Other members of this family, the Micmac and Malecite, live in New Brunswick and Nova Scotia, while the Blackfoot, Blood, and Peigan live in southern Alberta. The five nations of the Iroquoian family, also called the Haudenosaunee – namely, the Mohawk, Oneida, Cayuga, Onondaga, and Seneca – moved into southern Ontario in the late 1700s when Joseph Brant and his followers received a parcel of land, called the "Haldimand Tract," in compensation for their aid to the British during the American Revolution (Triger 1987 [1976]; Weaver 1972).

The Dene, or Athabascan, live mostly in the western part of the Northwest Territories and are northern relatives of the Navajo and Apache. Some representatives of this family include the Chipewyan, Dogrib, Tutchone, and Kutchin. The Inuit belong to the Eskimo-Aleut language family and comprise the Netsilik, or "people of the seal," the Iglulik, and Caribou Inuit. In British Columbia the Salish are the largest language family comprising such groups as the Cowichan of Vancouver Island, the Squamish near Vancouver, and the Bella Coola farther up the Pacific coast (LaViolette 1973; Mcllwraith 1948). Thus, one can readily see that a term for all Indigenous people in Canada tends to gloss over an extensive cultural and linguistic diversity. In this regard, the use of one large cover term, such as "Indian," implies a certain measure of homogeneity that clearly does not apply to the Indigenous people of Canada and North America as a whole.

Canada: Until recently the term *Aboriginal* has been used in Canada to refer to Native peoples in the widest sense of the word; however, more recently the term "Indigenous" has largely supplanted it, in the same manner that the term "Aboriginal" supplanted the term "Native peoples." The term "Indigenous Peoples" is an inclusive term since it is used as a collective phrase to refer to First Nations, Inuit, and Métis peoples. As such, it is important to recognize that there has been an historical sequence of change happening for a considerable period in terms and definitions, with some newer terms replacing older ones. Another point is that some of the older terms, such as Indian, still have relevance in certain contexts.

The term "Aboriginal," for example, has some continuing relevance since it was used in Section 35 of the Constitution Act of 1982, which states, "In this act 'aboriginal peoples of Canada' include the Indian,

Inuit, and Métis peoples of Canada." In the Constitution Act there is clearly a concern with Aboriginal rights, which is to say, "The existing aboriginal and treaty rights of the aboriginal peoples of Canada are hereby recognized and affirmed." My preference departs somewhat from that given here in that I prefer to capitalize the term Aboriginal (and Indigenous) even though a capital letter is not used in most instances because the word most often appears as an adjective. The capitalized form of Aboriginal (and Indigenous) is my preferred usage because it shows deference to the wishes of Aboriginal peoples themselves, as a way of showing respect to their identity as distinct peoples.

Of course, there are also political connotations with the use of any of the terms discussed here. As an example, in my *Oxford* dictionary, "Aboriginal" is defined as "indigenous, existing in a land at the dawn of history, or before the arrival of colonists." In this sense it is clearly recognized that Aboriginal peoples have an inherent right to their ancestral lands which could be an important factor in land claims litigation. Another term, "Aboriginal nations," was used in the final report of the Royal Commission on Aboriginal Peoples (RCAP) in 1996, which referred to "a sizeable body of Aboriginal people with a shared sense of national identity that constitutes the prominent population in a certain territory or collection of territories" (see Frideres1996; Hedican 2008a: 140–3).

In Canada, the term "Indian" was once widely used but has fallen into disfavour today. Many people feel that there is a certain pejorative connotation in the use of the term, and many now regard it as having a discriminatory usage. In any event, the term is an incorrect usage of Christopher Columbus's mistaken identity. However, despite these negative associations the term today nonetheless has a rather specific definition in Canadian law. For example, in the Indian Act, under Section 2 (1), the following definition is given: "'Indian' means a person who pursuant to this Act is registered as an Indian or is entitled to be registered as an Indian." In this context the term "Indian" refers to a Canadian who has specific legal rights and who is entitled to certain benefits according to federal law, such as possibly living on a reserve, special hunting and fishing privileges, or receiving annual payments. The term *reserve* is also becoming another problematic word, meaning the land set aside by the Crown for the benefit and use of an Indian band; however, reserve retains a prominent place in the Indian Act. (For further details see https://laws-lois.justice.gc.ca/eng/acts/i-5/).[1]

Thus, the term "Indian" is contrasted with someone who does not have these special legal rights, referred to as a non-status Indian, and is synonymous with the terms *registered*, *legal*, and *status* referring to

Indian people who are a federal government responsibility. In turn, status Indians are entitled to belong to a national organization of people with special legal status under the Indian Act, called the Assembly of First Nations, formerly known as the National Indian Brotherhood (AFN), and its provincial affiliates (consult their web page for further information: https://www.afn.ca/Home/). In addition, the term "Treaty Indian" refers to descendants of Indians who signed treaties with the Canadian government or, earlier, the British Crown and who have a contemporary connection with a treaty band.

The term "Native" has also fallen into disuse today, although it was widely used in the past. Formerly, it was used in an organization called the Native Council of Canada, now known as The Congress of Aboriginal Peoples (CAP), which is one of five national Indigenous organizations recognized by the government of Canada. Founded in 1971 as the Native Council of Canada (NCC), the organization was originally established to represent the interests of Métis and non-status Indians. Reorganized and renamed in 1993, CAP has extended its constituency to include all off-reserve status and non-status Indians, Métis, and Southern Inuit Aboriginal Peoples, and serves as the national voice for its provincial and territorial affiliate organizations (for further information see http://www.abo-peoples.org/en/).

Several other terms have become popular in recent years, such as "First Nation community," which has mostly replaced "Indian band." In the same manner "First Nation" has begun to be more widely used in Canada, however this term does not encompass the Métis and Inuit people. The term "First Nations" includes both status and non-status Indians. The Canadian Constitution Act makes special mention of the "Métis People of Canada" as one of the three Indigenous peoples in this country and therefore suggests that they have special "Aboriginal rights." The Métis have a unique history and culture in this country, especially in northern Ontario, Manitoba, and several other western provinces (see Redbird 1980; Sawchuck 1978; Slobodin 1966). In March 1983, the Métis Nation separated from the Native Council of Canada to form the Métis National Council (MNC, see their webpage at https://www.metisnation.ca/index.php/who-are-the-metis/mnc).

The Constitution Act also includes a reference to *Inuit* who are people who speak the Inuktitut language (see Balikci 1970; Boas 1888; Graburn 1969; Purich 1992)). *Inuk* is the singular form of Inuit. Since the term Inuit means "the People," as such, to say "Inuit People" is seen as redundant. Inuit also now replaces the term "Eskimo" which is thought to be an Algonquian word meaning "eaters of raw meat." In 1939 the Supreme Court of Canada decided to interpret the federal government's power to make laws affecting "Indians, and Lands Reserved for Indians" as extending to the Inuit as well. The Inuit Tapiriit Kanatami is a national organization representing over 65,000 Inuit. It was founded in 1971 as the Inuit Tapirisat of Canada; initially, it grew out of the Indian and Eskimo Association, which was founded in the 1960s (see https://www.itk.ca/national-voice-for-communities-in-the-canadian-arctic/).

United States: According to Palmer and Rundstrom (2013: 1142–59) the preferred usage in the United States is the term "Indian" instead of "Native American" and other similar labels.[2] They suggest that the term "Indian" is preferred because it is far more widely used, even by Indian people themselves as a supra-tribal identity. They also indicate that the term is used in the Commerce Clause of the US Constitution and by 1846 had become embedded as a specific legal status that people on American soil can have, or be denied, as a matter of course of federal law. In addition, Biolsi (2007: 7) indicates that as far as the term "Indian" is concerned, "entire volumes of the United States Code are consumed with the term." "Tribe" has a similar legal status since it was first defined by the US Supreme Court in 1901 in *Montoya v. United States* (Cramer 2005). It is also claimed, by Palmer and Rundstrom (2013:1155), that the term "Indian Country" is "the epitome of a discontinuous region. It includes reservations, Rancherias, allotments, other trust lands, isolated dwellings and businesses, and other Indian lands of all kinds. It also has legal standing in all US court systems." The phrase apparently originated with the British Royal Proclamation of 1763.[3]

Anthropology and Violence: Doves vs. Hawks

Anthropologists have been in a rather vociferous debate over at last the last eighty years concerning the essential nature of human beings: Are we fundamentally violent creatures, or are we basically peaceful beings? Of course, when we frame the matter in such extreme terms we lose much of the nuances of human life, yet given the nature of scholarly debates, academic opinions often coalesce at the extremities. It is also possible to engage this whole book about such a debate, which is not our purpose here, but violence is nonetheless a central theme. For this reason, it is important to outline the contextual material discussed here in terms of a wider framework of research and thoughtful consideration of human nature as it impinges on the subject of interpersonal violence. However, as Salzman reminds everyone, "No anthropologist wants to appear to be disparaging the people and culture that he or she is studying and discussing" (2008: 17). Nonetheless, people are entitled to their opinions, if expressed in a respective manner, so that the sensitive topics discussed in this book on the subjects of intercultural murders, violence, and societal conflict should be seen as an opportunity to share one's views even in a critical manner.

There is no space here to trace the theme of violence in human societies back to the time of Rousseau, as some (as in Otterbein 2000:841) have suggested. For our purposes it will be sufficient to begin this discussion with the thoughts of one of the founders of modern anthropology, Bronislaw Malinowski.[4] In the 1930s Malinowski embarked on a lecture tour of the United States to alert the American public to the threat posed by the rise of fascism in Germany during the period just prior to the Second World War. This tour was all part of Malinowski's attempt to apply anthropological knowledge to the understanding of public issues. From Malinowski's (1941) perspective, as set out in his seminal paper about human conflict, he suggested that war was not biologically determined. Rather, violence among human beings, he argued, was an abnormal phenomenon among the members of the human species. In a lecture at Oxford in 1933, Malinowski made the following point:

> The hero of the next war, the man who from the air destroys a whole peaceful township in its sleep with poison gas, is not expressing any biological characteristics of his organism, not showing any moral virtues [but] kills them ruthlessly, without discrimination and without personal feelings (cited in Stone 2003: 206).

When fighting begins on a large scale, this signalled to Malinowski that "a breakdown of personality and culture" was occurring (ibid.). Such cases, he believed, was not the result of some built-in aggressive impulse in humans, but the consequence of the indoctrination of certain cultural values, such as aggressive patriotism and certain collective hatred, which leads to the eventual assaults and killings (ibid., 206–7). Thus, according to his argument, violence is "artificially manufactured" and as such could just as easily be prevented.

In terms of the history of human violence in anthropology is concerned, Malinowski's position – that we are basically peaceful creatures who are "tricked" or otherwise manipulated into vicious acts – can be characterized as supporting the "dove" side of the debate. This position, Otterbein (1999a, 1999b, 2000) has categorized as the "myth of the peaceful savage," derived from an earlier monograph by Lawrence Keeley (1996). This idea, then, as one would expect from the Hegelian dialectic, was bound to spawn its opposite, which is to say, that humans are fundamentally violent creatures and that periods of peace in human history are not only relatively rare but abnormal. Thus, anthropologists became pitted against each other, between "those who believed that band and tribal peoples were warlike and those who believed they were not," resulting into two oppositional camps, "hawks" and "doves" (Otterbein 1997: 251–2, 266–70). Sponsel (1996) is one who suggests that Malinowski was responsible for creating these two camps, with one group believing in the "primeval pacifism of man," and the other holding to the view that "war was an essential heritage of man."

No matter how one might view the history of this debate, two sides began to line up, each supporting one position or another, with their individual research and supporting theoretical arguments. As an example, at one extreme, for those who believe human nature to be peaceable, we have Robert Dentan's *The Semai: A Non-Violent People of Malaya* (1968), which supplied the doves with their prime ethnographic example of a peaceful society. On the other side, the favourite would almost certainly be Napoleon Chagnon's *Yanomamö: The Fierce People* (1968) or, perhaps for an earlier generation, Robert Lowie's studies of Crow warfare in *Social Life of the Crow Indians* (1912). However, the problem with these examples, in ethnographic terms, is that the Yanomamö situation could hardly be called warfare, at least in any sense that we would commonly understand the term. A more appropriate description of their conflict situations would probably be "feuding" or "raiding" (Sponsel 1998). Lowie's classic study of the Crow has similar problems of interpretation. As Marvin Harris suggests, "For the interpretation of warfare, Lowie was not the victim of other people's ethnographic biases. He had himself to blame, largely as a result of the peculiar methods of research which he was obliged to maintain in his study of the Crow" (1968: 364).[5]

What Harris is probably suggesting is that Lowie, following the Boasian methodology of historical particularism, led him to rely too much on the selective memories of old Crow warriors who were preoccupied with the "vainglory of counting coup," to use Harris's (1968: 365) phrase, and on their skills as buffalo hunters and marauding horse thieves. As Lowie himself explains, "the Plains Indian fought not for territorial aggrandizement nor for the victor's spoils, but above all because fighting was a game worthwhile because of the recognition it brought when played according to the rules" (1920: 356). Accordingly, it is difficult to characterize such a "game" as warfare when the warriors' principal strategies involve merely touching the body of his opponent (i.e.., "counting coup") and, as a result, as Harris indicates, is bound "from our own experience with warfare [to make us] profoundly skeptical" (1968: 366).

Another perspective on conflict and violence is to attempt to situate such phenomena in the cultural context in which they are embedded. Salzman, for example, in his study *Culture and Conflict in the Middle East*, suggest that violence is restricted to a certain extent by the parameters of the cultural systems in which it takes place:

> A decentralized system of defence based upon self-help, such as balance opposition,[6] relies on each individual to make judgments and act on his own or freely in collaboration with his fellow group members. Acting in defence and retaliation means engaging in violence, for which skill and courage are desirable. In tribal societies based on balanced opposition, male children are raised to be independent, to take responsibility for themselves, and to be ready and able to engage in sanctioned violence against designated enemies. (2008:16)

Thus, Salzman's argument is that certain patterns of violence are constrained by the cultural systems and traditions characteristic of a certain category of societies (hunters and gatherers, pastoralists, or horticulturalists, for example) so that people have expectations about what sorts of violence one can presume to occur from those with whom one acts in opposition. In turn, these expectations tend to be shared in a mutual manner between conflicting parties, as one might come to expect in a duel, so that there are patterns in place that are not necessarily explicit but nonetheless are understood in broad parameters by the participants. Of course, the problem occurs when the conflicting parties do not share mutual cultural expectations about the manner by which the conflict is carried on and eventually resolved. In this regard anthropologists can play a useful role in analyzing these mutually held expectations, or the lack of them, when conflict occurs, as anthropologists can perceive patterns that participants themselves cannot readily recognize because they are too close to the action.

It is apparent that eminent anthropologist Walter Goldschmidt would tend to agree with Salzman's assessment of the role of the cultural underlay of conflict. In a special edition of *Anthropology Today*, entitled "Anthropology and Conflict," Goldschmidt suggests that "there are many ways in which anthropology can contribute to an understanding of conflicts and their resolution" (1986: 12). In the first instance, he suggests, the ethnographic literature on conflict demonstrates that conflict "is a *cultural* phenomenon [italics in original], that it is a form of institutionalized behavior given definition by consensus, and that the definition varies from society to society" (ibid.).[7]

Yet, culture is a malleable concept. Even though cultural norms and values, as learned behaviour, are passed down from generation to generation, each new generation does not necessarily share the views of their generational predecessors. As such, as far as "the textbook rendition of culture as shared, learned, and transmitted by socialization from one generation to another, the world has become too complex, to accommodate that neat formula" (Barrett 2002: 10). Probably this tidy formula has always had problems dealing with the complexities of social change. One generation's views about conflicts with their neighbour's is not necessarily those that were held by their parents, or that will be adopted by their children. As Appadurai (1991: 191) has explained: "The landscape of group identity – the ethnoscapes – around the world are no longer familiar anthropological objects, insofar as groups are no longer tightly territorialized, spatially bounded, historically unselfconscious, or culturally homogeneous." One wonders, though, if this was ever the case, or whether we should regard the classic definition of culture as an ideal-type model, in Weberian terms, without the full array of all the characteristics normally associated with the concept. As an example, societies often offer a complex mix of opinions on many subjects, and the same is probably also true of how members of the Cree population might view conflict with the Hudson's Bay Company.

It should come as no surprise to anybody, then, given the centrality of the culture concept in anthropology, that Salzman, Goldschmidt, and probably many others would see violence in the cultural terms of learned behaviour, although acknowledging at the same time the variability that can occur among members of the same society. Schmidt and Schröder have attempted to explain the compelling logic of elucidating conflict in cultural terms. Violence, they assert,

> has everything to do with cultural factors. Conflicts are mediated by a society's cultural perception that gives specific meaning to the situation, evaluating it on the basis of the experience of past conflicts, [and] stored as objectified knowledge in a group's social memory ... conflicts are caused by structural conditions [in society] like the unequal access to resources. (2001: 4)

In Goldschmidt's case, he not only supports an interpretation of violence in cultural terms, but also rejects two commonly held assumptions about human conflict, the first of which is that such conflicts as warfare are functional, that they are a means of population control, or an integration device. The second view that he rejects is that conflict is a product of natural human aggressiveness. "If aggression must be carefully nurtured and rewarded," Goldschmidt argues, then "such a position is doubtful" (ibid., 12–13).

In opposition to these ideas, he then suggests that his own investigations would indicate that (1) conflict of various sorts usually could be interpreted in terms of vengeance, which is to say, "the desire to protect the sense of dignity of the person or his group," and (2) "is the concomitant sense of group identification." Goldschmidt's conclusion, then, is that in terms of an understanding of conflict and violence, in his opinion, "The human characteristics that underlie pride and sympathy, paradoxically, must be viewed as more important that those underlying hostility and aggression" (ibid., 13). Obviously, as one reads through the following book, there is a wide diversity of viewpoints expressed by various researchers in anthropology but also in history, sociology, psychology, and economics, that are seen to account for the etiology of human conflict. As such, the reader is invited to engage in an assessment of their own thoughts on the matter.[8]

In a countervailing approach, rather than view conflict in terms of the broad brushstrokes of culture and history, the individual actor has returned to centre stage. As an example, in the *Anthropology of Violence and Conflict*, it is noted that "the modern anthropological study of violent confrontations ... views them as social action relative to the interests and convictions of conscious actors" (Schmidt and Schröder 2001: 1).[9] It is, however, a fact of life that individual actions are constrained in a multiplicity of way, but there are nonetheless idiosyncratic impulses that go against the grain of society and thus become difficult to interpret. This is the point made by Appadurai when he indicates that many of today's "ethnic conflicts" seem completely irrational at first sight. Yet, as he suggests, there may be a certain logic behind these efforts to create a "macabre form of certainty" (1998: 229). Even so, many studies of violence tend to focus on the victim's perspective, often missing out on the perpetrator's views altogether, as suggested by Krohn-Hansen, who further points out that "if we are to understand violence ... we must look at the motives and the values of the uses of violence" (1994: 367). This was especially the case with the murders at Hannah Bay – few people at the time gave any thought at all as to the reasons this Cree family killed so many peoples, aside from a form of inscrutable Native irrationality, or an act of fanaticism inspired by esoteric primitive idolatry.[10]

Understanding individual decision-making as an important factor in comprehending violence is also a central theme in Jochim's study, entitled *Strategies of Survival* (1981). As Bettinger points out, Jochim's approach "is clearly a departure from mainstream cultural ecology, which tends to regard individual perceptions and motives as incidental to the problem of human adaptation" (1983: 720). In Jochim's case, a central argument is that violence may be a necessary "strategy for survival" when the resources required in an environment are insufficient for the maintenance of life. Humans will do just about anything to stay alive, to feed themselves and the members of their group, and in these cases violent action made be perceived to be the only path to secure the food needed to survive, especially when there are others in the vicinity with relative abundance who are not willing to share what they have. Or, as Schmidt and Shröder (2001: 3) suggest, "violence ... has shown to confer clear adaptive benefits to the successful party," especially when it replenishes a group's resource base and allows its members to survive a bit longer.

There are also scholars in academic circles, sometimes referred to as "revisionist historians," who claim that anthropologists are responsible for exaggerating violence among the Indigenous people of North America (Biolsi and Zimerman 1997; Deloria 1995). Russell Means and Marvin Wolf, for example, tend to describe pre-contact Indigenous violent conflicts in idealized terms, arguing that "Before the whites came, our conflicts were brief and almost bloodless, resembling far more a professional football game than the lethal annihilations of European conquest" (1995: 16). Similarly, Stephen Reyna states his view that "regardless of how much fighting there was in bands, it was relatively harmless" (1994: 37–8). Paul Sillitoe also supports this point of view that the results of Indigenous violence "pales into insignificance compared to the horror and carnage when industrial nations fight with their technologically awesome arsenals" (1985: 890).[11]

Means and Wolf also contend that documenting Indigenous warfare and other forms of violence only serves to promulgate further violence and aggression directed against the Aboriginal peoples of North America. Similarly, as Keith Otterbein describes, the consequences of "classifying people as non-violent could position them to be victimized as easily as calling a people fierce could make them a target of attack" (2000: 843). In a further commentary of this issue of human violence and the way it is studied, Chacon and Mendoza (2007b: 222) state that

> Despite the evidence for conflict and violence in aboriginal America, revisionist historians argue that anthropologists have conspired to invent a "bloody world" by exaggerating the scale of warfare and ritual violence identified with Amerindian societies. Some elements of this revisionist school of thought argue that scholarly misrepresentation is but one facet of a malicious colonialist legacy determined to denigrate and dehumanize indigenous cultures, societies, and histories.

These are serious charges indeed to make of scholars in another academic discipline, but are they true? Since the present book is about Indigenous (Cree) violence and I am an anthropologist, the charges of "revisionist historians" are worth considering because they bear on the points of view and overall analyses that are studied here. First, consider the arguments presented by Victor Montijo in his article subtitled "An Exposé of Anglo Anthropologists Obsessions." He claims, with reference to the Mayans, that "the anthropological image ... past and present, has been 'too bloody' to deserve credibility" (1993: 15). With all due respect, the image of a Mayan priest on top of his temple holding a still-beating heart with blood dripping down his arm and the hapless victim kicked down the steps with his rib cage torn apart by an obsidian knife is hard to forget. Is Montijo claiming that such tortures never happened? No, he only insists that "those distorted images imposed upon our people by others" be challenged (ibid., 16).[12]

Montijo's request seems eminently fair – scholars need to rely on factual evidence and not on suppositions based on distorted images imposed by colonial powers. Nonetheless, as Chacon and Mendoza argue, "it is a mistake to deny the fact that native peoples are equally capable of lethal engagements with one another and with outsiders" (2007b: 226) any more than it would be a mistake to deny that there existed "patterns of wholesale genocide conducted by some European groups through the course of the colonial era" (ibid., 224). All and all, one may conclude that the revisionists' argument that the very act of reporting research findings on Indigenous violence only serves to justify further aggression against Native peoples is a proposal that lacks any sort of factual evidence. If such were the case, then on what data is there confirmation that this claim has been verified by credible research findings? Furthermore, choosing one side of the violence argument based on emotion or any other faulty assumption does a disservice to the accumulation of valid knowledge as whole. Or, as Beth Conklin asks, should anthropologists tailor their research findings "to produce the images that certain activists or advocacy groups want?" (2003: 5).

In conclusion, the position that seems most reasonable to adopt is not at the extremities of the hawk-dove debate but at a point somewhere in-between, "*depending on the specific circumstances* [emphasis in orig.]" as Otterbein (2000: 843) suggests. Relatively peaceful people can engage in violence for any number of reasons, such as when they need to defend themselves from life-threatening situations, or when so-called warlike people find peace when the circumstances engendering their violence disappear. It is obvious, then, that adopting one polar position or another does little to create the conditions conducive to furthering our understanding of group and interpersonal conflict.

What is needed most are empirical studies documenting the actions of groups that erupt into violent situations, and the *specific circumstances* that could be seen to be responsible for such phenomena. All in all, such is the goal of the present study concerning the unpredictable and unusual murders at Hannah Bay. The circumstances of violent acts cannot be ignored and, as said previously, there are no isolated incidences, leading one therefore to strongly agree with Schmidt and Schröder's position on studying violence and conflict:

"We argue that no violent act can be fully understood without viewing it as one link in the chain of a long process of events, each of which refers to a system of cultural and material structures that can be compared to similar structural conditions anywhere else" (2001: 7). The goal of the present study could not be stated in stronger terms.

Were the Cree Doves or Hawks?

Such a question, phrased in an all-or-nothing manner is not likely to provide a reasonable answer. The reason, as Otterbein (2000: 843) has indicated, is that whether a society is warlike or peaceful is largely dependent upon specific circumstances of time, place, and conditions. What we are interested in here is to attempt to determine if the Cree could be characterized by a "culture of violence," or how they might react to conflicts with competing groups. What, then, would these specific circumstances be, temporally, spatially, or otherwise?

There can be no doubt that the arrival of Europeans in North America exacerbated existing Indigenous conflicts, although they probably did not initiate them, and Europeans played a role in upsetting the existing balance of power. The French were interested in gaining control of the fur trade, especially in controlling the trade routes into the interior, and so formed alliances with the First Nations along the St. Lawrence, such as the Wendat (Huron). In a counter move, the Dutch began supplying the Haudenosaunee (Iroquois) with firearms, probably because the French were attempting to divert the fur trade away from their European rivals. As (Bailey 1969: 12) suggests, "The search for furs led to an economic and political pressure on the tribes of the interior and was an important cause of the revival of inter-tribal warfare." In addition, Trigger (1987: 416) commented that "the traditional prestige system of the Huron and Iroquois made endemic warfare." Eventually, in 1649, the Haudenosaunee routed the Wendat of southern Ontario, leaving a lacuna in southern Ontario, eventually filled by other groups, such as the Mississauga.

The Hudson's Bay Company began to build trading posts, or "factories" as they were called, on the Hudson and James Bay coasts after 1670, such as Fort Albany (1677), Moose Factory (1677), and Fort Severn (1759). Prior to this period the area of northern Ontario referred to as the Hudson Bay Lowlands does not appear to have been occupied on any sort of consistent basis. As Wright (1981: 86) suggests, "without the caribou and fish it is very unlikely that humans could have occupied the total area on any permanent basis ... the limitations imposed by the boreal environment on the subsistence patterns and attendant social organization [small, mobile hunting groups] inhibited ... incursions of peoples and ideas from adjacent regions." While there is still some debate about the location of various Indigenous groups at the time of European contact (see Greenberg and Morrison 1982; Smith 1987), there appears to be fairly solid historical evidence, based on maps and other contemporary documents, that the Cree during the 1640–70 period were situated just north of Lake Superior, around the Lake Nipigon area, but probably no farther north than the Albany River. The Anishinaabe (Ojibwa) were prominent around the Sault Ste. Marie area, from the north shore of Lake Huron north to the Michipicoten region of Lake Superior. The subsequent period (1670–1730) saw a gradual movement northward of both the Cree and the Anishinaabe who took over the territory previously occupied by the Cree, such that "the Ojibwa [Anishinaabe] began to occupy permanently the central Shield region of the Subarctic during the 1730s, settling in the upper Albany River area west of the Cree in the James Bay Lowlands" (Bishop 1981: 160). At this time the Assiniboine were in the Lake of the Woods area near present day Kenora.[13]

In due course, "soon after 1800, the depletion of fur and large game resources resulting from the fur trade competition forced all groups into greater dependence on the trading post, a condition already well advance among those Cree who had early attached themselves to the bayside posts" (Bishop, ibid.). As the Cree moved farther north, closer to the HBC trading posts on the coast, they left a vacated territory in northern Ontario. In turn, as "the Ojibwa [Anishinaabe] took over this territory, they came into contact with the Cree who occupied most of the shield uplands of northern Ontario, and the Assiniboine who lived in the boundary waters area of Minnesota and Ontario in the late seventeenth century. [These three groups] lived in comparative peace most of the time and were often formally allied against their common enemy, the Dakota Sioux" (Ray 1978: 42). One of the reasons for this détente was that "The Ojibwa [Anishinaabe] did not ... come to occupy the [Hudson Bay] Lowlands, since the Cree of this area were well adapted to the less-productive conditions prevailing there" (Bishop 1975: 160).

With the relative depletion of game and furs in the Hudson Bay Lowlands, however, the Cree began to relinquish their lives on the trap lines. Instead, they began to purchase goods at the trading posts and barter these for a profit with other Indigenous groups, thus also saving them a trip to the Bay. This middleman position gave the Cree much influence over more interior groups. As the northern fur trade became established, as Hanks (1982: 103) describes conditions at Oxford House, "a symbiotic relationship developed between the HBC and the local Cree population which grew around the post. This relationship then slowly shifted from one based upon mutual dependence to an association dominated by the traders." Even so, a relative proximity to the trading posts gave the Cree direct access by virtue of their monopoly to the best trade goods that the Hudson's Bay Company had to offer, such as superior firearms, which the Cree could use to defend their intercalary role, even fighting off competitors if necessary. As Yerbury notes, "There is no doubt that firearms were used as weapons of war, and there is historical evidence of warfare between the Cree and the Chipewyan" (1986: 21).[14]

Furthermore, the HBC, recognizing the influential role of the Cree vis-à-vis other Indigenous groups, nominated some of the more dominant Cree as "trading Captains," outfitting them with special coats and giving them special privileges about the trading post, while others were designated as "homeguards," who led hunting parties and provided food for the posts (Francis and Morantz 1983: 41–5, 81–3). So influential were the Cree that their language became a lingua franca, or a language adopted as a common language of the fur trade era. Since their economic position between interior Indigenous groups and the Hudson's Bay Company allowed the Cree to wield much influence, and thereby gain materially from this role, they were unlikely to give up their location without a fight. As far as the European traders were concerned, when Indigenous people such as the Cree acted as middlemen on their behalf it also assisted the Europeans' needs as well:

> It served the European traders to cultivate a middleman status among Indians living near the main posts whose own country had become depleted [as in the case of the Cree]. By utilizing Indian middlemen, the expenses of transporting goods into and out of interior areas and the necessity of maintaining garrisons and other establishments were avoided. (Hickerson 1973: 25)

The middleman role, however, was a precarious one, and every effort was necessary to maintain the position, which often meant that the "middleman traders opposed by force or diplomacy the penetration of Europeans into areas where they held a monopoly of the trade" (Hickerson 1973: 26).[15] In turn, the Indigenous trappers in the hinterland attempted whenever possible to circumvent the middlemen and establish, where possible, direct contact with the traders, realizing that by cutting out the middlemen they would, in turn, probably obtain European goods at a reduced cost. In such situations, when interior groups attempted to sidestep the middlemen, violent conflicts were likely to develop. This was particularly the case with the Cree, who attempted to protect their valuable position at all costs. As an example,

> During the early decades of the fur trade along Hudson Bay ... the Cree and some of the Canadian Athapaskan peoples too were involved in protracted warfare. They fought over access to York Fort and its trade routes and over retention of fur-bearing grounds extending as far west as Lake Athabasca. Inter-tribal conflict resulted in considerable bloodshed, mostly of the unarmed Athapaskans by the gun-bearing Cree, who were able to gain exclusive control over the inland trade of York Fort during these years. (Yerbury 1986: 18)

As a result, "Few Athapaskans could be persuaded to bring their furs past the Cree down to the factory" (ibid., 21).

During the initial period of the European fur trade the Chipewyan lived in a large area in the vicinity of the Churchill River in the present-day Northwest Territories. Soon after the Cree moved into the area of the Hudson Bay Lowlands, they began to conduct an extensive period of warfare with the Chipewyan. The term "warfare," although used extensively in the ethno-historical literature, can probably be regarded as a misnomer since most of this activity involved raiding parties on the part of the Cree into Chipewyan territory, which was situated hundreds of kilometres away from the lowlands inhabited by the Cree. During this period of revenge-raiding, the Chipewyan were at a particular disadvantage because the Cree came to possess firearms from the Hudson's Bay Company, while the Chipewyan were still using their traditional weapons of bows, arrows, and spears.

With the re-establishment of York Factory in 1714, the HBC was anxious to resolve this ongoing conflict in order to facilitate Chipewyan involvement in the fur trade. Lytwyn (2002: 70), for example, commented that "the company had economic motivations for encouraging such a peace initiative; it planned to establish a trading post at the mouth of the Churchill River to collect furs from the Chipewyan. There were also rumours of precious metals in the Chipewyan territory, and the company wanted to develop a friendly relationship to exploit these mineral resources." As far as the Cree were concerned, it is difficult to see what advantage there would be from their perspective to engage in any peace initiates since such a truce would eventually compromise their middleman role between the HBC traders and the far-reaching interior tribes to the west of Hudson Bay. However, the Cree were also anxious to maintain friendly relations with the HBC personnel. The strategy of the Cree in this situation was to take a leading role in the peace mission, thus keeping intact their middleman role and circumventing too close a relationship between the Chipewyan and the HBC traders.[16]

This tactic on the part of the Cree involved a difficult business of inter-tribal diplomacy, yet nonetheless illustrated their business acumen in managing their relationships between interior Indigenous groups and the traders of the Hudson's Bay Company. In the meantime, the HBC's economic interests were also satisfied since peaceful relationships between the Cree and interior Athapaskan groups contributed to an increase in the company's profit margin. As Smith (1981: 139) summarized:

> If the HBC was to profitably carry on the trade, peaceful relations among the Native peoples was essential. Time diverted from hunting fur bearers to war parties was time lost and fears of trading parties required to travel through enemy lands was inhibiting. Therefore, peace was the most desirable state of affairs but an otherwise only slightly altered culture was ideal.

As the old expression relates, and one that is particularly relevant here in the Cree case, "the better part of valour is discretion."[17]

Also in the Hudson Bay region, the Cree conducted an extended period of violent conflict with the Inuit, about which Bishop and Lytwyn (2002: 36) relate, according to the Lowland Cree oral history, Inuit attacks predated the arrival of Europeans. The etiology of these attacks has been obscured by history, although "early European accounts indicate that Inuit raids ceased within a few years after fur-trade posts were constructed by the HBC in the 1670s and 1680s along the coasts of Hudson and James Bay. Instead, the Lowland Cree became the aggressors, often raiding deep into Inuit territory along the northern coasts of Hudson Bay" (ibid., 38). No doubt a deciding factor in this reversal of aggression was that the Cree had obtained guns from the HBC posts shortly after these posts were established in the 1670s, while "historical evidence indicates that they [Inuit] did not know how to use guns until taught by the fur traders in the late eighteenth century" (ibid., 41). One can rule out territorial expansion as a reason for the conflict since the Cree had no intention of occupying Inuit territory. Daniel Francis, in his research, states that he was also puzzled by the possible reasons for the Cree-Inuit conflict, suggesting that it was "motivated by a complex of psychological and cultural needs" (1979: 3). He even put forward the suggestion that the Cree feared Inuit magical powers, which were thought to be the causes of sickness, game shortages, or other calamities.

One could conclude from the preceding discussion that the Cree were no strangers to violent conflict. In fact, it could be argued with considerable justification that the Cree were the most prominent and influential society during the fur trade era. They no doubt would have felt a certain sense of ascendency in their profitable position between the Hudson's Bay Company and other Indigenous groups who were attempting to trade furs in the James Bay area. When it came to conflict, then, the Cree were willing to assert themselves and not back down whatever the opposition. Indeed, one might call them hawks, but certainly they were no timid minions when it came to protecting their rights as they might see them, responding with considerable force if necessary to assert themselves.

The implication is that if the Cree were given sufficient reason, they might even attack their benefactors, the Hudson's Bay Company personnel, if the Cree perceived that they were being taken advantage of in certain ways. It is perhaps a truism, but friendships and alliances could undergo a sudden reversal during the fur trade era. By the early 1800s the Cree in the Hudson Bay region were suffering a reversal in their fortunes. For the most part they had lost the economic advantages of their former middlemen position since the HBC traders were insisting on trading directly with interior tribes such as the Chipewyan, even building a series of interior post, such as Henley House on the Albany River. In fact, Henley House, constructed in 1743, was attacked in 1755, although the instigators were probably Anishinaabe, rather than the Cree, and the reason(s) appeared to have more to do with a dispute over Indigenous women kept at the post rather than fur trade issues per se, although it has also been suggested that French traders were involved in the attacks as instigators (see Bishop 1976b).

Thus, one can suggest based on the historical records that attacks on European fur traders by Indigenous groups had occurred for at least a century before the Hannah Bay incident. In 1697, for example, York Factory was attacked by a French naval force, which caused the English to surrender. It was during this period that seven French traders were killed by a group of Cree near the vicinity of Fort Bourbon at the mouth of the Hayes River. According to Hudson Bay Company historian Edwin Rich (1960), the killings were the result of Cree's lack of food and subsequent starvation. "The killings," Lytwyn (2002: 132) further suggests, "were caused by the refusal of the French traders to share food with the Lowland Cree." Also, according to Nicolas Jeremie, a contemporary observer, "These natives [the Cree], considering themselves dared by the reckless way my men were shooting every kind of game, and feasting before their eyes without sharing anything made a plot to kill them, and seize what they had" (Jeremie 1926: 39; see also Lytwyn 2002: 130–3). It is therefore sufficient to end this section, and to introduce the following one, with the suggestion that the Cree of the Hudson Bay Lowlands were suffering periodically from severe food shortages and that they were not averse to killing Europeans to obtain the necessary sustenance, especially when they considered that the French or English were guilty of breaching the etiquette of sharing their extra provisions in the Cree's time of need.

Narratives of Colonial History

We start this tale with a look at the history of the Hudson's Bay Company; indeed, much of the colonial history of early Canada is presented in terms of a narrative in which Europeans are on a heroic quest, a company of adventurers, of men forming an Honourable Company (as in Douglas MacKay 1966 [1936]). However, there is also another narrative, one that might be termed a counter storyline, that sees this honourable company as crass exploiters who spread disease, abandoned their Indigenous wives and families, and plied their Indigenous clients with liquor to advance their avaricious ends.

When Indigenous people kill Europeans, the Native are called bloody murderers and their act termed a massacre. When Europeans kill Indigenous people, they are likely to receive a reprimand. In other words, there are two counter-posed narratives that make up the history of the fur trade in Canada. It is not the position taken here that one version is right and the other wrong; it is certainly difficult to justify the killing of other human beings; however, there are always extenuating circumstances as well.

What is evident is that both versions need to be told, to be welded together in terms of one coherent narrative, if that is even possible. This book, therefore, is seen as contributing to the narrative that has been suppressed for far too long in the interest of the colonial powers who write the history that school children read and thus come to believe is true. As Feagin (2010: 3) suggests in his comments on systemic racism, "Few mainstream media presentations or school text books provide full and accurate accounts of the history or current status of racist oppression," which, in turn, provide the basis for the alternative narrative of colonial oppression in Canada that was experienced by the Indigenous population.[18] Or, as Rudyard Griffiths writes in the preface to *Our Story: Aboriginal Voices on Canada's Past*, "Even this most cursory look at the traditional narrative of the history of Aboriginal peoples confirms that we read their story through our systems of understanding. It is difficult, if not impossible, for one culture to capture the historical reality of another culture that it has displaced" (2004: 2). Yet we try, nonetheless.

In the James Bay region, as the traders and the missionaries were crafting their own narratives of romantic notions of wilderness, of adventure and of conservation, "all these narrative creations," Carlson (2008, 134) suggests, "had little relevance to everyday life in the region." The traders were taking furs to fulfill the profit motive of predatory capitalist companies whose shareholders had little interest in the James Bay region or its Indigenous people side from the area's economic potential, while the missionaries sought to fulfill their commitment to external religious institutions. Nonetheless, all were drawn together with the Cree into reciprocal relationships based on their individual subsistence needs and co-operative requirements, although the Europeans could do so at a much greater distance from the surrounding environment than the Cree. As Carlson explains further, "This ability to live at a distance from Cree subsistence and to interpret the region apart from any Cree context only increased as the environment degraded, as sickness increased, and as the Cree were less able to feed themselves from the land (ibid.)."

The outsiders were always shielded from the misery that the Cree were forced to endure by their relative wealth and white privilege, shielded from the rapacious effects of market-driven colonial capitalism and demeaning proselytism, as they consoled themselves with their self-serving ethnocentric narratives of honour, adventure, and respectability. The Cree could not rely on the Europeans' outside world, which had done them more harm than good; all they could do was depend upon their own knowledge systems that had sustained them through the centuries and had emanated from an imponderable past, one populated by human beings but also inhabited by the intangible entities in their spirit world. There was perhaps no better way to communicate with this spirit world than through the conjuring tent, by which instructions were received, trusted, and relied upon. British apologists and Christian evangelists would no doubt denigrate such an

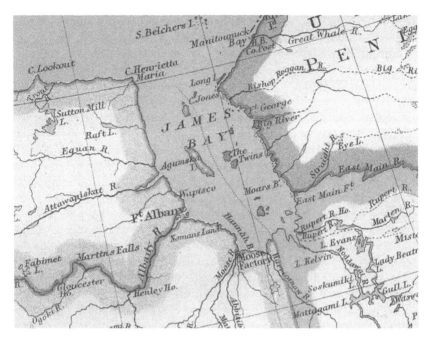

Map 1. James Bay and surrounding territory in the fur trade era. Note the location of Hannah Bay in the southern portion of James Bay.
Source: Public domain

interpretation, but the Cree could not rely on them to provide salvation from starvation.

James Bay: The Winter of 1832

Monday, April 9, 1832

At 11 ½ AM Mess W. Swanson, J. Anderson and John Geo McKenzie – with their party returned all safe, having found the murderers, and inflicted that punishment their Crimes merited ...
— Moose Factory Post Journal (B.135/a/137 f. 27)

In late January of 1832, in the most southern part of James Bay, an elderly Cree man by the name of Quapakay sat by his campfire, deep in thought. He slowly used an index finger to draw back the long grey hair on the side of his face and tucked it behind his ear as he bent forward to blow into the flames. His thoughts were taking hold of his conscious mind, and as a result he was profoundly troubled. Several days ago, the spirits of the shaking tent had told him that to survive the winter he was required to "spoil" the post at Hannah Bay, a relatively insignificant Hudson's Bay Company goose hunting station, more than an actual fur-trading post. Seeking confirmation at this directive, Quapakay then instructed his sons, Stacemow and Shaintoquaish, to contact the spirits again, which resulted in the same message.

The source of Quapakay's mental anguish, at least partly, was that his people had relied on the spirits of the shaking tent for guidance for as far back as he could remember. As Tanner (2005: 211) explains based on his fieldwork among the Cree, "religious actions involve the mediation of non-human persons. These persons are usually said to be located away from human habitation, in a far-off land, under the water, on top of a mountain, or in the bush, and they usually tend also to appear in the myths. Those which play a role in hunting may also appear in the 'Shaking Tent.'" "The Anglican and Pentecostal missionaries were not tolerant of these beliefs and regarded Cree traditional religious practices as examples of 'devil worship' and who treat [Cree religion] as mere superstition that will die out in time" (ibid.). However, for an elder such as Quapakay, the spirits must be relied upon for survival, as they provide precise details on the location of game, on the location of lost relatives, and other such matters that are beyond human comprehension.

If the spirits indicated that caribou where to be found beyond a certain mountain or lake, for example, it would be unthinkable that one would not follow the instructions given in the shaking tent ceremony. To intercede with human will, such as saying that the caribou were too far away, or one had to cross too many lakes to get to them, was not even considered. The spirits were regarded as infallible. There was always the possibility that the spirits, if their suggestions were not followed, would abandon the people to their own unfortunate fate. So, the quandary for Quapakay in this case was a stark one: either forsake the direction of the spirits who provided direction in life from time immemorial and risk certain catastrophe or follow the directions of the spirits and face almost assured retaliation from the Hudson's Bay Company employees.

Quapakay's son Shaintoquaish later explained to Joseph Beioley, the postmaster of Rupert House on the east side of James Bay, that they had been

> ordered by the "Spirit above" to do what they had done; that they had striven hard to get the "Spirit above" not to enforce the task on them,

because they had a disinclination to do what they thought to be wrong
but that the "Spirit above" threatened and assured them that except they
obeyed they should have all their children taken from them (B135/a/138).

As most parents would agree, the threat of losing one's children would
provide a strong incentive to follow through with the directions of the
"Spirit above," regardless of how conflicted one would be about this
potentially calamitous task.

In any event, this ill-fated task was carried out, and the occupants of
the Hannah Bay post were "spoiled" as the Spirit directed, resulting in
the death of post master William Corrigal, his wife, and seven other Indigenous people. Four survivors managed to escape and fled to Moose
Factory, arriving the following day. A posse of Hudson's Bay Company
men was soon organized and dispatched to Hannah Bay, but the men
returned without finding the perpetrators of the crime. Later, in March,
news of the fugitives reached Moose Factory, and a renewed party set
out in early April. Apparently Quapakay and his family, for whatever
reason, had not ventured far from Hannah Bay and were readily found
by the search party. Under the direction of William Swanson, the posse's
leader, all the males, including a fifteen-year-old, numbering five in all,
were summarily shot and killed where they were found. The women
and children were given provisions. In all, the Hannah Bay catastrophe
resulted in the death of sixteen individuals. Ultimately, we are led to
ask, "How could such a disastrous catastrophe have happened?"[19]

Background Research

The research on which this book is based is the culmination of over
forty years of investigation on my part into the various aspects of the
social, historical, economic, and political characteristics of the Indigenous people of Ontario, from the mid-1970s to the present day (Hedican
1976, 1986, 2001, 2008a, 2013, 2017). To give a summary of this activity,
I have conducted first-hand ethnographic research in the Indigenous
communities of Ontario, principally among the Anishinaabe in the relatively remote areas northwest of Lake Nipigon.

This research involved living in a log cabin for almost two years in an
Anishinaabe (Ojibwa First Nation) community that was situated in the
boreal forest region some 200 kilometres north of Thunder Bay. During
this time, from about 1974 to 1990, the First Nation people who lived
there did not have electricity, cars, trucks, or outside electronic communication. Later, when satellite television became available, and with the
use of gasoline generators, people began to establish some connection

Image 1. Photo of log cabin home, Collins, Ontario (1974). This photograph was taken by the author during his fieldwork in northern Ontario in the mid-1970s. At this time almost every residence in the community was made of log construction and did not have running water or electricity.
Photo by Edward Hedican

with the outside world. Television brought some detrimental effects, I thought, because visiting in the community became greatly diminished and reduced outside activities, especially among the younger generation. However, for the most part, people continued to speak their ancestral language and continued to hunt and fish and engage, for the most part, in their traditional subsistence pursuits that had been carried on for many generations.

My research interests during this time were focused on the study of the local Anishinaabe leadership and the economic changes in the community as a result of new interactions with government agencies who were offering make-work programs, such as the Local Initiative Program (LIP) Grants. As local workers began to participate at an increased level in the cash economy of the outside world, traditional country food production declined; however, what resulted was an amalgam of traditional-modern economic areas. After all, people needed cash from the outside world to buy much needed hunting equipment, such as steel traps, rifles, ammunition, snow machines, and so on. In other words, an increased interaction with the outside cash economy did not obliterate the local subsistence economy of hunting and fishing; rather, it caused a merger of the two.

During my tenure of field work a major economic project was initiated that involved the construction of a tourist lodge in the Ogoki River area of Whitewater Lake, situated just south of the Albany River in northern Ontario. With this project, much more cash entered the community, and traditional hunting and fishing began to decline because of the increased demands of the construction cycle. This change caused a ripple effect throughout the local economy, with the result that the people began to rely to a much greater extent on store-bought foods, which were primarily low-quality carbohydrates in contrast to the higher quality protein that was earlier secured from the bush.

I returned to the community to study these socio-economic changes over the next 15 years. Eventually the three brothers who had operated the local store after their fur-trader father's death, moved to Thunder Bay, where they retired. Soon others from the community followed, lured by accessibility of the internet, large department stores, and a greater variety of wage work opportunities. I found it interesting that the children of my earlier field work were now grandparents or were elders in their own right. Many of these former residents have recently contacted me via Facebook, asking for photos and other information from my research days, so modern technology has allowed us to maintain social connections, although not necessarily face to face.

For over four decades I have taught Indigenous studies courses at the University of Guelph with brief teaching stints at Brandon, Lakehead, and York Universities. During this time, I have endeavoured to make intelligible to students the various issues that Indigenous people encounter today. To a large extent this study agenda has been based on using the lessons of applied or "public" anthropology (see Hedican 2016) to better understand the transitions that Indigenous people are making today in the modern world. Contrary to what some Canadians may think, Indigenous people are not left-over anachronisms from the past, or incapable of adjusting to modern conditions. In some cases, deep-rooted prejudices place them at a disadvantage as far as employment or housing in urban environments is concerned. These prejudices have a long history that extends back to the early arrival of Europeans in this country.

This topic of prejudice and discrimination, then, provides a link between current social issues in this country and the focus of the present book. Even though the killings of the Indigenous people and the Europeans in Hannah Bay happened almost two hundred years ago, similar themes were initiated back then that continue to be prevalent today. For example, in 1832 the family of Cree hunters accused of shooting a fur trader, his wife, and several others at the Hannah Bay post were tracked down by a posse of Hudson's Bay men. Without so much as a hearing, let alone a trial of any sort, the male members of this family were shot dead on the spot. Altogether 16 individuals lost their lives because of this tragic situation.

So, one might ask, how have matters changed in Canada over these nearly two centuries? My suggestion, as an answer to this question, is hardly at all.

To illustrate my point – that there exists a continued, unabated discrimination in Canada of Indigenous people extending from the early colonial period to today – let us use as an example the relatively recent (2007) release in Ontario of Linden Report of the Provincial Ipperwash Inquiry (Linden 2007). This report pertains to the shooting and death of an unarmed protester of the Stoney Point First Nation named Dudley George by OPP Officer Kenneth "Tex" Deane on September 6, 1995. When Dudley George was shot and killed by Officer Deane, he had been participating in a protest over land claims in Ipperwash Provincial Park (Hedican 2008b, 2012b). Officer Deane was part of the OPP's Emergency Response Team (ERT) which, under the orders of Ontario's Premier Mike Harris, had been instructed to use all necessary force to disband the protest.

The reader might ask what the Ipperwash protest has to do with the Hannah Bay killings. It is true that these two events were separated by many years – 163 years, to be precise. In certain aspects the two events are not commensurable occurrences, not only because of the time separating them but also because of the different regimes involved and the historical norms and values of each period. They are also incommensurate events because Dudley George was not accused of killing anyone, in contrast to the Cree perpetrators of the killings at Hannah Bay. However, I would suggest, the fundamental issues are much the same. In both cases Indigenous people were shot and killed with apparent impunity, without so much as a hearing or trial being held.

Officer Deane was found guilty of criminal negligence causing death, yet he never served a day in jail; instead, he was sentenced to community service hours in lieu of jail time. This issue of the killing of Indigenous people without due process of law, which has gone on virtually unabated since well before Confederation, will be revisited in this book in greater detail. Certainly, British citizens would not be the subject of such discriminatory "country justice." Have the British, and later Canadians upon which this country of Canada has been founded, really shown much advancement in their treatment of Indigenous people, or is Canada really the paragon of justice and liberty that its citizens imagine it to be?

One has to wonder about the fascination that people have for murder and the countless novels about murder mysteries. Partly, one suspects, the answer has to do with our own mortality and how easily one's life can end. Another reason could pertain to the curious fate of people who, for whatever reason, are prone to kill their fellow citizens. What drives such people to commit such inhumane acts? Our own mortality is a fact of life that we cannot do much about, but for most of us we do not want it to end any sooner than it must. There is certainly a tragedy of immense proportions, even a catastrophe, for those who are murdered, of course, but also for those who engage in such acts.

We will probably never know the reasons why humans are so prone to killing each other, but we can be certain of one thing: Murder does not happen in isolation from other events. Every action, physicists tell us, has a corresponding reaction. Each human act is the result of a set of preceding circumstances and activities that are linked inexorably to wider issues, circumstances, and trends.

Take for example the shooting of Dudley George, mentioned above, by Officer Kenneth Deane. The act itself happened in a matter of seconds, yet the series of events preceding it took decades, possibly centuries. One might conceive of any event as likened to a pebble tossed into a pond, with ripples or rings emanating outwards in successive waves. Dudley George had been a protester at the Ipperwash Provincial Park on that fateful day. What was Dudley George protesting, and why was he shot for what was apparently a simple act of civil disobedience?

The answer lies in a complicated set of historical circumstances. For one thing, Ipperwash Provincial Park had at one time been part of the Stoney Point territory, but it was sold in 1927 without the Stoney Pointers' permission to land developers by an unscrupulous Indian agent. Prior to this, in 1827, millions of Indigenous people's territory in southern Ontario was basically taken away from them by the British Crown under what was termed the Huron Tract Treaty. And then there was another large tract of land that had been "given" to the Stoney Point Band under the terms of this 1827 treaty that was removed from their possession under the War Measures Act of 1942. This tract of land, later designated as Camp Ipperwash, was supposed to aide in the war effort as a training base for Canadian soldiers. However, no soldiers ever trained there. Under the provisions of the land transfer to the Canadian government, this land was supposed to be handed back to the Stoney Point band after the Second World War, but this never happened.[20]

So, one can begin to see a set of grievances that preceded the shooting of Dudley George. Other important factors were important contextual circumstances to the Ipperwash protest, such the discriminatory attitude of Ontario's premier at the time, Mike Harris, who ordered the OPP "to get the f...kin Indians out of the park."[21] Add to this the negative attitudes of some of the OPP officers who saw Indigenous people as "wagon-burners," or the local press who portrayed the Stoney Pointers as "lawless hooligans" who were just after publicity. Other circumstances go back into history with all the suppressive acts, such as various pieces of government legislation that prejudiced Indigenous people in Canada.[22]

What all this means is that while the murders at Hannah Bay may appear to have been a solitary incident, it also is set in a complex series of events. As such, the purpose of this book is to unravel these intertwined circumstances, to provide nuances to the event itself, and to possibly comprehend the interrelated factors that led to the killing of William Corrigal, his family, and several others at the Hannah Bay trading post. In order to understand the killings at Hannah Bay it is necessary to unpack the underlying factors responsible for this act, such as the racist attitudes held by Governor George Simpson, head of the Hudson's Bay Company, and his fellow fur traders towards the Indigenous people of northern Canada, the ecological conditions of the Hudson Bay Lowlands that led to serious conditions of food deprivation and probably also starvation, the breaches of reciprocal obligations and cultural expectations, and the stinginess of the British fur traders who were more interested in wealth and economic gain than they were in extending any humanitarian gestures that would have relieved the Indigenous peoples' suffering.

So here is an important question for all Canadians who believe in equality and social justice: The Ipperwash protest happened almost two centuries after the Hannah Bay incident. What has changed since?

Central Questions Raised by the Hannah Bay Tragedy

1. *To what length would you go to save yourself and your children from starvation?*

Note: The information provided below each question is not meant as an answer per se but as contextual material on which discussions could begin relating to the issues raised in these queries.

Starvation is a horrible way to die. It is a slow, agonizing, and tortuous way to end life. Hopefully none of us will ever face this unthinkable situation. And certainly, very few, if any of us, have ever been in the situation of the Hannah Bay Cree families who were facing death by starvation. As a father of four children, I wonder, as I review the Hannah Bay catastrophe, if I would ever do what the Cree family did to apparently save themselves. Morality becomes a moot point when the lives of your children are at stake – if rationalization takes over it is hard to predict the outcome.

2. *To what extend was the Hudson's Bay Company and, by extension, the British government culpable in the death by starvation of Indigenous people in the James Bay area during the fur-trade era?*

It is ironic that I have just finished writing a book on the Irish Famine of 1847, and now encounter a somewhat similar situation during about the same period (Hedican 2020). Here again, colonial apologists might suggest that the Irish Famine is not comparable in any way with the Hannah Bay situation. However, the British government was in charge as the controlling power in both situations. In both cases not enough food was made available to provide for the necessities of life for the Cree and the Irish. One could argue that the British government was culpable in the deaths of many Indigenous people in the James Bay area as well as that of the Irish population that perished in the 1840s. The Hudson's Bay Company did not keep records of the James Bay Cree who died of starvation. In Ireland, the population of 8.5 million before the famine decreased to under 4 million through death, disease, and emigration. It is also noteworthy that under British rule in India about 85 million people died of starvation between 1760 and 1943. One of the worst famines occurred in Bengal in 1770, in which two million Indians died before the British secretary of state took any action; about one-third to one-half of the Bengali population died of starvation at this time. As such, the starvation endured by the Cree of James Bay and the Irish was not an atypical situation under British rule.

3. *What role does discrimination and prejudice play in the deleterious treatment of Indigenous people not only in an historical context but today as well?*

There is a large body of social scientific evidence to support the contention that discrimination against the Indigenous people of Canada continues in this country in an unabated fashion. One just has to look at the facts, which answer for themselves:

   a. The unemployment rate for all Indigenous people (12.6 per cent) is twice that of the national average (6.6 per cent).
   b. Employment income for Indigenous people ($41,907) is 20 per cent lower than the national average ($51,221). The average income for Indigenous women ($8,902) is nearly $9,000 below the National Council of Welfare's poverty line.
   c. Educational achievement, in terms of higher education, for all Canadians (15.7 per cent) is twice that of the Indigenous population (7.1 per cent).

To these figures we can add an incarceration rate significantly above the national average for Indigenous people, who tend to be arrested with much greater frequency than other Canadians. Many more such trends and statistics could be added to illustrate the extent to which the Indigenous people of Canada are an extremely disadvantaged population in this country. The question is, why?

4. *Are there governmental policies, both implicit and explicit, that have served to disadvantage Indigenous populations?*

Fact: Throughout the history of Canada there have been numerous policies that have attempted to assimilate the Indigenous population or erode Aboriginal rights. For example, in 1969 Prime Minister Pierre Elliot Trudeau unveiled a policy with Jean Chrétien, the minister of Indian affairs, in a white paper entitled "Statement of the Government of Canada on Indian Affairs, 1969," which proposed to eliminate reserves and all special status of Indigenous people despite existing treaty obligations (see Weaver1981). If it was not for the "Citizens Plus" backlash a few years later, this assimilationist policy would undoubtedly have been carried out (see Hawthorn 1966–7; Cairns 2000). Cree leader Harold Cardinal called the Trudeau plan to disband the Indian Affairs Department and disband reserves "a thinly disguised programme of extermination through assimilation" (1969:1). Fortunately, the 1982 Charter of Rights and Freedoms made explicit mention of Indigenous rights in Article 35, indicating that "The existing aboriginal and treaty rights of the aboriginal people of Canada are hereby recognized and affirmed." Even so, Aboriginal rights in Canada are not clearly entrenched in the Canadian Constitution. Certain provincial governments, such as British Columbia, have historically not recognized the right of Indigenous people to claim land in the province. In addition, in 2007, the United Nations Declaration on the Rights of Indigenous Peoples was passed by a vote of 143 to 4, but Canada was one of the few countries to vote against this UN Declaration.

5. *What role does power play in the control of historical discourse and the crafting of narratives of disenfranchisement in the rationalization of Indigenous peoples' treatment by colonial regimes?*

There can be no doubt in Winston Churchill's dictum that victors write the history they prefer, or the one that puts them in the best possible light for posterity. In other words, power rules the day and shapes our interpretation of history by the narratives that are created in the interests of the more powerful society. In turn, power is often associate with racism. Less powerful people become victimized not just by discriminatory acts but also by narratives of disentitlement that portray them as deserving their disadvantaged fate. One is reminded, as an example, of the reference by George Simpson, the governor of the Hudson's Bay Company, to the Chipewyan as "indolent and simple" and that their character is "disgraceful to human nature." He also described Indigenous women in British Columbia as "monkeys," suggesting that they were less than human (Galbraith 1976: 62). On the other hand, the Hudson's Bay Company describes itself in a self-serving manner as "the Honourable Company," as a company of adventurers and explorers (as in MacKay 1966 [1936]). There is an old saying that power corrupts, which means that minorities tend to be vilified for the mere fact that they are less able to exercise power over those that oppress them. In addition, Indigenous people did not have access to the prevailing media of the day to present their case, to shape images that would place them in a beneficial light. It is for this reason that all authoritarian regimes closely control the medium by which information is disseminated to the masses. It is the medium itself, as Marshall McLuhan (1964) asserted in *Understanding Media*, that is the message.[23]

6. *Was the personnel of the Hudson's Bay Company justified in their killing of Quapakay and his family? If so, on whose authority?*

John McLean (1799–1890) was a long-standing employee of the Hudson's Bay Company and served as manager of several posts. He married his first wife at Norway House and was therefore familiar with the operations of the fur trade in the James Bay area. After the killing of Indigenous people in the McKenzie's River district in 1835, and the killing of eight unarmed Assineboine men by two HBC clerks in the same year, McLean was led to ask, "After this, what protection, or generosity, or justice can the Indians be said to receive from the Hudson's Bay Company (1932: 325)? McLean relates that the two clerks held a court martial "to determine the punishment due to the Indians for having been found near the company's horses, with the *supposed* intention of carrying them off [italics in original] … the whole band, after having given up their arms, and partaken of their hospitality, were condemned to death, and the sentence carried into execution on the spot – all were butchered in cold blood!" (1932: 324). He further indicated that "it may be said that the Company are not answerable for crimes committed by their servants without their knowledge" (ibid., 325). Nonetheless, the perpetrators were allowed "to escape with impunity." When the authorities in the Hudson's Bay Company headquarters were apprised of this incident "the punishment awarded to these murderers was – a reprimand!" (ibid.).

As far as the suspects in the Hannah Bay killings were concerned and considering the acts of violence that the Hudson's Bay Company employees inflicted on Indigenous people, McLean concluded that "both parties exceeded the limits prescribed by law" (ibid., 323). He further comments that aggressors were punished "as the law of God allows, demanding blood for blood," and then sarcastically indicated that "nothing of the kind is done under the *humane* and *gentle* rule of the Hudson's Bay Company." Then McLean asks, "What became of the Hannah Bay murders? They were conveyed to Moose Factory, bound hand and foot, and there shot down by the orders of the Chief Factor" (ibid.). [Actually, the Cree were shot where they were found and not transported to Moose Factory as McLean states, according to the HBC journal reports.] In other words, if the rule of the fur trade country was "an eye for an eye, or blood for blood," then the Hudson's Bay Company should not employ a double standard, an act of hypocrisy, which is to say, letting their own men escape without punishment when they commit murder against Indigenous people, but then exact the strongest revenge when the reverse situation prevailed.[24]

7. *Do the killings at Hannah Bay, by both Indigenous and British people, have a wider theoretical application?*

It is argued in this book that the killings at Hannah Bay are instructive at several empirical and theoretical levels. First, there is the treatment of colonial powers in relations to Indigenous people in the context of capitalistic enterprises and the extent to which these powers are willing to exercise their influence in the pursuit of political and economic gain. Second, there is the question of colonial attitudes towards Indigenous people, including missionary proselytizing and the function that these attitudes serve to justify the colonialists' goals. Third, there is the questionable use of liquor to facilitate the profit motive, and the marriage of Indigenous women who were often abandoned when the trader returned home to Europe, in the context of the colonists' reputed Christian standards of morality. In other words, the Hannah Bay murders are not just about the facts of this particular case but also, and perhaps more importantly, what this case tells us about the wider issues of colonialism, racial attitudes, capitalism, among other concerns.

Scope of the Book

The purpose of this book is to provide contextual information that can be utilized to better comprehend the social, cultural, and historical context in which the Hannah Bay tragedy took place. The book is not meant as a legal enquiry into the culpability of the various parties involved; however, people in whatever time period are accountable for their actions – so possibly one of the issues is, Accountable to whom? In chapter 2, the Cree of the James Bay area are discussed in terms of their historical position when the British fur traders arrived in the 1600s. The British fur traders brought with them a heritage of colonial interaction with Indigenous people from other areas; however, the Cree were quick to adapt to the economic possibilities offered by the fur trade, eventually profiting from a middleman position with other Aboriginal groups in Canada's north country surrounding Hudson Bay. Chapter 3 outlines the consequences of the paucity of subsistence resources (country food) that were available in the Hudson Bay Lowlands and the resultant recurrent references in the Hudson's Bay Company journals of food deprivation and possible starvation. It also traces the journal entries for the 1831–2 period that led up to the murders at the Hannah Bay Post, and the subsequent attempt to locate the guilty parties by an HBC search party.

The focus of chapter 4 is on the resistance of the Cree and other Indigenous groups whose members were involved in the fur trade to the pressures of colonial rule by the Hudson's Bay Company as an arm of British imperialism. The Cree reacted to the various manipulative colonial measures applied to them by devising their own strategies, such as playing different fur-trading posts off against each other to extract a higher return for their furs and ameliorate the divisive effects of "colonial capitalism." The Cree also had to contend with the efforts of Christian missionaries' attempts to undermine their traditional religious beliefs. Chapter 5 extends the discussion of colonialism in the Hudson Bay region by concentrating on the specific details of cultural conflict, such as the development of inland trading posts, country marriages, the liquor trade, and the advent of muzzle-loading rifles.

The main topic of chapter 6 concerns the way that historical discourse is framed in order to lend a sense of entitlement to white privilege and legitimate the legacy of settler colonialism. It also discusses the stereotypical portrayal of Indigenous people in the media in a disparaging or negative manner, laying the basis for racist beliefs, discrimination, and such government policies as President Andrew Jackson's removal act, which lead to the Trail of Tears in 1830, or the later massacre of the Lakota people in 1890 at Wounded Knee. In chapter 7 there is a discussion of the shaking or conjuring tent in northern Canada. The Hudson's Bay Company records of 1832 indicate that Quapakay and his sons were apparently ordered by the spirit of the shaking tent, or the "Spirit Above," as they referred to it, to "spoil the post at Hannah Bay" or their children would not live long enough to see the following summer. Various available sources are consulted, including numerous eyewitness accounts of the shaking tent in order to assess the possible validity or authenticity of Quapakay's claim.

The subject of chapter 8 is about the relative nature of truth and reality, in terms of Cree oral traditions. It also asks the question, Is morality a culturally relative phenomenon? And furthermore, do human rights supersede various cultural norms and values in a cross-cultural perspective? All in all, we are led to the conclusion that the murder of William Corrigal and his family, for whatever reason, was not a humanely acceptable act, in any place and time, except possibly as an act of self-defence. It is recognized, however, that the members of diverse cultures are apt to see the world in sometimes starkly different terms and, as such, understand truth as an imprecise or malleable entity. In the conclusion, chapter 9, an attempt is made to draw together the central themes of this book, to assess the role of tragedy in people's lives, and to contemplate the cultural context that influences the vagaries of human existence.

Chapter Two

The Cree of James Bay

In many ways the Cree are the most important North American Indian group in Canada.

— Anthony D. Fisher, "The Cree of Canada" (1973: 126).

It should be noted from the outset that the Cree are not the only Indigenous people who lived in the James Bay area, or at various times were alone in trading with the Hudson's Bay Company. However, it would be accurate to state that the Cree are the largest group of Indigenous people to live in this area of the Hudson Bay Lowlands. As most anthropologists and ethno-historians will tell you, there are no clear-cut boundaries between the Indigenous groups of northern Ontario and Quebec. As an example, there is a band of perhaps two hundred kilometres wide in which Indigenous people speak a mixture of Cree and Anishinaabe called "Ojib-Cree." It is also important to note that there is a lively debate in the academic literature concerning the location of various Indigenous groups at various points in time. Some even suggests that the area surrounding James Bay, before the Europeans arrived, was hardly populated at all because of its swampy ecological conditions and sparse resource base. Of course, there are others who disagree with this assertion (Clark 1977, 1991; Hanks 1982).

The Cree are members of the Algonquian language family and are closely related to the Montagnais-Naskapi (Innu) of Quebec and Labrador with whom there is some degree of mutual intelligibility. The Cree are also closely related to the Anishinaabe of Ontario (also called Ojibwa or northern Saulteaux) but more distantly related to the Potawatomi, Fox, and Menomini, among others, who form separate languages within the Algonquian family. As far as the original home of the Algonquian speakers is concerned, linguist Frank Siebert (1967: 38–40) suggests that this is in southern Ontario, based on natural history terms that survive in eastern and central Algonquian languages. From here, it is proposed, the Algonquians dispersed in various directions several millennia ago.[1]

The Cree at European Contact

The location of the Cree at the time of European contact in about the mid-seventeenth century is a matter of some uncertainty and controversy in the academic literature. Basically, there are two prominent points of view in contention. On the one side are those adhering to the view that at European contact the Cree were located just north of Lake Superior and no farther north than Lake Nipigon. An opposing view is that the Cree at contact were located well west of Lake Winnipeg. Each side has their own evidence to support their position.

Maintaining the former view is Charles Bishop who has written extensively on the Anishinaabe and the fur trade based on his interpretation of various HBC documents. As he argues, "There is good evidence … that the Cree occupied most of northern Ontario north and west of Lake Superior during the late seventeenth and early eighteenth century" (1974: 5). His accompanying map (on p. 6) shows the Cree residing just north of Lake Superior up to the north shore of Lake Nipigon. An additional map (on p.332) shows the Anishinaabe occupying the territory north of Lakes Superior and Nipigon between 1710–45, with the implication that the Cree then moved farther north, possibly as far north as the Albany River. A further implication, if this scenario is adhered to, is that the area of Ontario north of the Albany was mostly unoccupied territory during the early eighteenth century. The Cree, then, were pushed northward by the advancing Anishinaabe and drawn towards James Bay by the increasing influence of the fur trade. Bishop is willing to admit, however, that the location of the "Cree culture at the time of European contact remains largely conjectural" (1983: 147).

An alternative interpretation is provided by James Smith who argued that the idea that the Cree occupied a territory at European contact no farther than east of Lake Winnipeg is an "anthropological myth" that does not correspond to historical reality. As Smith (1987: 435) explains, "new data provide a basis for re-evaluation of Cree geographical distribution and the depth of their socio-territorial adjustment. The weight of the evidence now indicates that the Cree were as far west as the Peace River long before the advent of the European traders, and that post-contact social organization was not drastically affected by the onset of the fur trade." This "new data" is based on an accumulation of archaeological, ethnological, historical, and linguistic studies, he suggests.

As far as the archaeological evidence is concerned, James Wright (1981: 92) offers the opinion that, "the Nahathaways or Cree were in early contact with Europeans, and it is suggested that due to a reduction in population resulting from exposure to European diseases and a desire to be closer to the European trading locations the more northerly Cree abandoned their lands [just north of Lake Superior?]. However, Wright furthermore appears to support Smith's position that at contact the Cree were located farther west than scholars such as Bishop propose: Archaeological evidence strongly suggests that the Cree had a long period of cultural development in the region under consideration and that they were not easterners who have pushed to the west and northwest in response to the fur trade (Wright 1981: 92).

Additional archaeological evidence is further provided by Ken Dawson, in his *Prehistory of Northern Ontario* (1983) and his extensive excavations in the territory north of Lake Superior. As Dawson postulates, "the homogeneity of the prehistorical cultures and the evidence of continuity of residence in Northern Ontario permits the archaeologist to make firmer interpretations than are possible in the more complex regions to the south" (1983: 1). While much of northern Ontario, that is north of approximately Lake Nipigon, was covered by a continental glacier ice sheet and the huge glacial Lake Ojibwa-Barlow[2] during the Paleo period (7,500–4,500 B.C.), Indigenous populations began to move into the area soon after the retreat of the ice fields by 4,000 B.C. Dawson also suggests that the "initial people of the subsequent cultural period were linear descendants of the earlier population in the north" (1983: 7).

Dawson's important suggestion, then, is that the present occupants of northern Ontario, such as the Cree and Anishinaabe are direct "linear descendants" of previous prehistoric populations who occupied the area and were not transplanted by later peoples entering the area. However, Dawson finds little evidence that the northern Algonquian occupied the swampy Hudson Bay Lowlands during the prehistoric period. During the historical period, with the advent of Europeans, "in every instance, the historical sites are attributed to the Cree. Archaeological evidence indicates that the Cree were not a recent movement of easterners into the northwest, but rather that they have a very long period of cultural development in the region" (1983: 25; see also Wright 1971).

The Arrival of Europeans

With the advent of Europeans, historical records became available. Some of the earliest references to the Cree occur in the *Jesuit Relations* of

Image 2. Dick Butterfly. Butterfly claimed to be the only survivor of the
Hannah Bay Massacre, 1832. Photograph by Walton B. Haydon, 1883.
Source: Smithsonian Institution

the seventeenth century, where they were referred to by various terms,
such as "Kiristinon," "Kilistinon," or "Kinistinon." Bishop (1974: 333–4)
illustrates his study with early maps of 1699 and 1755 in which the Cree
are located just north of Lake Nipigon and are called "Christinaux." In
the *Jesuit Relations* of 1640 it is indicated that the Kilistinons were living
on the shores of the "North Sea" [possibly either James Bay or Lake Su-
perior] and were trading with the Nipissings. Since the Nipissings were
located west of Lake Superior in the area between the Ottawa River
and Georgian Bay, one could surmise that the North Sea refers to Lake
Superior rather than any James Bay locations farther north (see also
Smith 1987, 441).

In summary, the academic dialogue about the location of the Cree at
the time of European contact is a matter in which two opposing points

of view have supporting evidence to back up their claims. However, the one important matter that seems to have been lost in this ongoing discussion concerns whether the Cree were in the Hudson's Bay Lowlands of northern Ontario. There does not appear to be any supporting evidence, either historical or archaeological, that the Cree were located much farther north than the Albany River when European fur traders first made the Cree's acquaintance (Judd 1983; Kenyon 1986).

This is an important point because if one could reasonably assume that the Cree did not inhabit the swampy lowlands of James Bay then the questions arise as to the reasons why they were not located in this area (Macfie 1967). It is true that travel is difficult across the swampy and boggy terrain. However, it is quite possible that the reason the Cree only went into this area in the mid-seventeenth century was in response to a desire to trap beaver for the fur trade. Another important reason could be that the Cree avoided this area in pre-contact times because it was largely devoid of subsistence resources. If this was the case, then right from the very beginning of the fur trade the low level of food resources that could support the Cree meant that living in this area could support only a small population, and inadequately at that. In any event, large numbers of more southerly Indigenous peoples, attracted by the trade goods available at HBC trading posts, rushed into the swampy lowlands, setting the stage for wide-spread starvation and food shortages. In other words, it could be argued that the beginning of the fur trade in Canada was a catastrophe in the making.

The Fur Trade in Canadian History

As far as Canadian history is concerned, there is little doubt that the fur trade dominated the course of developments in northern Canada for well over 300 years. It is also accurate to indicate that the fur trade had significant economic consequences because it was an important feature that conditioned contacts between Europeans and the First Nation inhabitants of this country. The initial period of the history of the fur trade began along the coastal regions of eastern Canada, soon after the initial voyages of Jacques Cartier, beginning in 1534. Carter noted while sailing along the Labrador coast in the Gulf of St. Lawrence that he saw First Nations people, who were probably the Micmac, approaching his ships in two fleets of canoes. They made "frequent signs to us," he noted, "to come ashore, holding up to us some furs on sticks" (Biggar 1924: 49).

It was not long after that French traders made contacts with First Nations trappers, who were probably people who came to be known as the Montagnais and Algonquians. These trappers lived along the shores of the St. Lawrence River while other Indigenous people, such as the Wendat or Huron from the Georgian Bay region, began to act as middlemen in the trade of furs. During this period there were also threats from the Haudenosaunee or Five Nations Iroquois, who lived in the Finger Lakes area of New York state, to disrupt the movement of furs to Quebec City. After this time, the fur trade developed farther down the St. Lawrence to the Ottawa River, which became the main thoroughfare for canoes venturing into the lower reaches of Lake Superior and the Canadian Shield country. In this way trade routes developed through the Nipissing River to Sault Ste. Marie and from there to the northern coast of Lake Superior eventually reaching Lake Nipigon and locations near the present city of Thunder Bay in the Canadian Shield area (Morantz 1980, 1983, 1992).

Within a few years the fur trade developed farther north, during which time important transportation routes were established. Along these routes fur-trading posts were built at such places as Sault Ste. Marie (1668), Fort Kaministikwia (1679) at present-day Thunder Bay, Nipigon (also in 1679) at Lake Superiors most northerly point, and eventually at Nipigon House (1792) on the north shore of Lake Nipigon. With the establishment of these trading outposts European goods were exchanged for beaver pelts, along with other furs such as martin, otter, lynx, and wolf. These manufactured items from Britain and France began to replace those of Native manufacture because they were more durable or offered efficiency in hunting. Copper pots, for example, replaced those made of clay, steel traps were favoured over traps made of wood and leather thongs, and muskets began to become more common than the traditional hunting equipment of bows, arrows, and spears.

One fur trader described this transition in tools and utensils:

> They have abandoned all their own utensils, whether because of the trouble they had as well to make as to use them, or because of the facility of obtaining from us, in exchange for skins which cost them almost nothing, the things which seemed to them invaluable, not so much for their novelty as for the convenience they derived there from. Above everything the kettle has always seemed to them, and seems still, the most valuable article they can obtain from us (quoted in Innis 1970, 18).

Kettles were especially sought after because the traditional methods of cooking using wooden or clay vessels with heated stones was thought to be cumbersome and time consuming. In addition, all tools made of iron were thought to be more durable than those made of flint or wood, so that iron axes and hatchets became a prime item of trade, along with iron needles for sewing which was substituted for awls and needles made of bone. With their new muskets the Indigenous hunter could kill game animals and bird from a much greater distance than was the case with their older weapons (Townsend 1983). Bow and spears might still be used but now they were probably tipped with iron points rather than those made of stone. All in all, Europeans goods replaced those of traditional manufacture because they tended to be more durable and relatively easy to acquire; however, the fur trade also increased the dependence of First Nations people on the fur-trading companies, and this was probably a source of discontent for a people used to their own freedom.

The Hudson's Bay Company

While fur traders working out of Quebec City and Montreal were pushing relentlessly farther north into the Great Lakes and beyond, the English Hudson's Bay Company was expanding its enterprises along the coast and the major rivers emptying into James and Hudson Bay. As an example, fur trading establishments were established at Moose Factory (1677) on the southernmost point of James Bay, Fort Albany (1677) on the Albany River, and Fort Severn (1759) on the Severn River farther north. In addition, further interior expansion by the Hudson's Bay Company followed construction of the coastal posts in order to counteract competition from Quebec, such as Henley House (1720, but destroyed several times) on the Albany River and Osnaburgh House (1786) also on the Albany River near Lake St. Joseph, and Rat Portage (1832) near present-day Kenora in northwestern Ontario.

   While they were probably not aware of it at the time, the fur trade drew the First Nations people in the James Bay area of northern Canada inexorably into an increasingly intricate complex of relationships that ultimately tied them to the centres of world capitalism. Some have called these emerging economic relationships a system of colonial capitalism (Alexander 1986; Brown 2014; Ince 2018; Owen 2014), by which is meant that large imperial powers such as Britain, Spain, and France reaped the wealth of various areas of the world without much regard for the effects, such as food deprivation and impoverished living conditions, on the local people who provided their labour and thereby supported the foreigners' prosperity. There is little doubt that, as far as Canada was concerned, the early fur trade set in motion processes that would eventually have far-reaching effects on the social, economic, and political growth of Canada as a country.

The spread of the fur trade had the most profound effects on those First Nation societies whose members, over increasingly larger and larger geographical areas, abandoned their subsistence-based hunting and fishing ways of life for one based on fur trapping for the purpose of exchange with the European traders. It would be incorrect, however, to think that the First Nations people were hapless victims of the commercial expansion of the fur trade in the Canadian north. "The Indians were not naïve consumers when it came to trading their furs for the white man's goods," suggest Francis and Morantz (1983: 61). "Quite the contrary, they were quick to complain when merchandise was inferior or the price too high ... They often requested better goods or different goods from the post masters and the requests were invariably answered." For the most part the traditional lifestyles of Indigenous people continued with relatively minor changes. Traditional goods were replaced in some instances with tools and utensils of European manufacture; however, the fundamental social and economic foundations of Indigenous societies remained mostly intact.

There was also the matter of the members of Indigenous societies maintaining their autonomy. While there were changes brought on by their relationship with the fur-trading companies, life in the bush shielded many First Nations from overwhelming influences on the core aspects of their societies. Members of First Nations societies were also known to be hard bargainers with the fur-trading companies. This was especially the case when the Hudson's Bay Company was in direct competition with another major trading company called the North West Company, or Nor'westers. For many years the Nor'westers, who were called the "peddlers," sent fur-trading brigades up into northern Ontario and farther west, bartering their goods for furs, then returning to Montreal and Quebec City. The Hudson's Bay Company traders maintained trading posts on the James Bay and Hudson's Bay coasts, attempting to entice the inland Indigenous people to these coastal locations. However, after the amalgamation of the two companies in 1821, the Hudson's Bay Company was able to enjoy a virtual monopoly in the fur-trading business that they had previously enjoyed up until about the 1760s. The net result of this merger was that competition was eliminated, and the First Nations people were in a less advantageous bargaining position than before. This, in turn, increased the dependency of Indigenous people in northern Ontario and Quebec on the Hudson's Bay Company.

Even after the amalgamation of the Nor'westers and the Hudson's Bay Company, however, it has been suggested that the Indigenous Anishinaabe and Cree nonetheless maintained a tactical advantage in the fur trade negotiations. After all, the fur traders were dependent upon the First Nation trappers bringing their furs to them; the fur traders could not force the Indigenous people to trade for their European goods if they were not inclined to do so. For example, as indicated in an historical study of the Anishinaabe of northern Ontario, it was noted that "the traders were more dependent on the Indians for goods and services than the Indians on them." In addition, it was also noted by fur trader Duncan Cameron that the fur traders were seen by Aboriginal peoples "as poor, pitiful creatures who could supply neither themselves nor the Indians" (quoted in Bishop 1974: 229). This sense that the Indigenous people might have had about their ascendency over the fur traders tended to increase as the fur trade continued. The reason for this is that after the First Nations people had acquired their main supply of European goods, such as metal pots, hatchets, muskets, and so on, they had less need to rely on the European traders than was the case in previous decades (Ray and Freeman 1974; Tough 1990).

The British Colonial Heritage

For most people who were taught from Canadian history books, a narrative is often crafted that depicts an Aboriginal population whose members are largely compliant with the Europeans' mercantile interests. First Nations people are portrayed as eager for the benefits that European societies offered, often portrayed as extending their furs in a beseeching, pleading, or otherwise supplicatory manner, subservient to the Imperial powers that have invaded their lands. The image conveyed to Canadian school children is that of an Aboriginal population that is not only subservient to European interests but primeval in their technological and social characteristics, almost childlike in comparison to the superior Europeans. In fact, there were incidents in which the fur traders instructed their Aboriginal trappers to address them as "father." If the First Nations were seen as childlike then the Europeans would feel justified in occupying their lands and in the process enacting paternalistic policies.

Perhaps the most egregious of these policies was to assume that Aboriginal lands were not occupied, or at least mostly vacant, which further provided the justification for the granting of the vast territory of Rupert's Land by the British Crown to the Hudson's Bay Company without any compensation whatsoever being paid to the Indigenous occupants. As Galbraith (1957: 3) writes, Rupert's land was "a vaguely defined territory of approximately 1,400,000 square miles granted to the [HBC] Company by Charles II in the charter of 1670. The validity of the grant was frequently challenged, and the boundaries claimed by the Company under its provisions were often disputed."

This act of presumptive ownership without the consent of the First Nation societies of the area, who were the land's proper owners, involved a grant for which no treaties were ever signed or negotiated. Not only that, when Canadian Confederation occurred in 1867, Rupert's land was later audaciously sold to the Canadian Government by the British Crown. And "when the [British] Colonial office inquired what terms the Company would accept ... as compensation for land and mineral rights, the response indicated that years of attrition had not shrunk the directors' estimate of the value of *their property*" [emphasis mine] (Galbraith 1957: 419). As far as Canadian citizenship is concerned, this was not even granted to the Aboriginal residents of this country, nor were they allowed to vote in federal elections until the 1960s (Hedican 2008: 163). Looking ahead in history, these colonial machinations would have far-reaching consequences for the Cree people.

The British government had assumed control over Aboriginal affairs with the Royal Proclamation of 1763, which stated that the British Crown had the sole responsibility for buying or ceding Native lands under its jurisdiction. Later, in 1860, the British government transferred control of Aboriginal affairs to the Province of Canada. At this time the Crown Lands Department assumed control of Indian matters, and the commissioner was designated as chief superintendent. With the advent of Confederation, Indian lands became the responsibility of Canada's federal government under Section 91 (24) of the British North America Act of 1867. The first federal Indian Act was passed in 1876, which led to the administrative centralization of Indian affairs in Canada. It is difficult to overstate the historical dominance of the Indian Act on the affairs of First Nations peoples in Canada. As Frideres (1988: 25) points out, the Indian Act is the foremost of the legislative Acts that affect Indians in Canada. Its importance cannot be exaggerated, nor can its influence be minimized. It is the principal instrument by which the federal government and, indirectly, the provincial governments have exercised control over the lives of Indian people.

After Confederation the provinces were in no hurry to negotiate treaties with the First Nations in their territories. For example, in Ontario, it took nearly 40 years to negotiate a treaty with the Cree and Anishinaabe people when the province's northern boundary was extended in 1905 from near the north shore of Lake Nipigon, which was the upper limit of the Robinson-Superior Treaty of 1850, to the shore line of Hudson and James Bay, by Treaty No. 9, called the James Bay Treaty.[3] As far as northern Quebec was concerned it was not until the 1970s, at which time most other Aboriginal societies in Canada had signed treaties with either the British or Canadian government, that any provincial attempt was made to negotiate a treaty with the Cree, who were still trying to establish some sort of rights of sovereignty over their traditional territory, which they had occupied for many millennia before the Europeans arrived. However, a treaty was eventually negotiated with the Cree and other Indigenous people of that province in 1975, with the signing of the James Bay Agreement, which comprised some 410,000 square miles of what was termed Nouveau Quebec.[4]

In sum, the colonial heritage in Canada is evidenced by various pieces of legislation that have taken place over the years that have served to undermine Aboriginal autonomy. As mentioned, an important contributing factor in this colonial heritage is that Aboriginal people with status were not even given the right to vote in provincial elections until the 1950s, and federally until 1960. It is evidently difficult to promote any rights whatsoever without the right to vote. Thus, it is also evident that Canada's colonial heritage extends back through many centuries with the establishment of Rupert's Land in 1670.

The primary impetus behind this colonial heritage, as Galbraith (1957: 3) indicates, was that "the expansion of the British Empire has been largely motivated by the energies of the mercantile class." Various authors have furthermore described this expansion as a type of "colonial capitalism," in which the pursuit of wealth and monetary gain was the motivating factor (Owen 2014; Ince 2018). In other words, the British Empire could be described as "a particular kind of empire that is fundamentally characterized by the exploitive relations between an imperial core and a subject periphery" (Subrahmanyam 2006: 220). It is in this context of exploitive economic relationships and colonial capitalism that the murders at Hannah Bay in 1832 are discussed in this book. Such exploitive relationships between the Indigenous people of the James Bay area and the British fur traders are also the basis for one of the book's principal arguments for the violent conflicts that occurred between the Indigenous people of northern Canada and members of the Hudson's Bay Company.

The Cree and the Fur Trade

Most historical studies suggest that the Cree were the first Indigenous people to make the initial contacts with HBC fur traders. As such, their fortuitous position in northern Ontario and Quebec gave them a strategic advantage over others who had to pass through Cree territory to get to the coastal trading posts. Nonetheless, the Cree still had to manage this advantage and develop a strategy that would keep them close to the HBC traders while at the same time using acts of deterrence, or persuasion, to keep others, such as the Anishinaabe, Assiniboine, or other First Nation groups away from the coast.

In this regard, several strategies were developed that showed their ingenuity and determination. One method was to find other services that the Cree could perform for the traders that did not directly involve trapping furs. Some Cree acted as guides, while others hunted geese to fill the larders of the company posts; still others engaged in nominal trapping, and some functioned in all these capacities. Those Cree who kept close to the posts were termed "homeguards," which was a term used to distinguish such people from the "inlanders" who spent the winter hunting and trapping in the interior (Judd 1983). As Francis and Morantz (1983: 41) explain, "The homeguard arrived at Eastmain House earlier than the inlanders did, sometimes as early as the beginning of March, to await the arrival of the geese, which they hunted every spring and fall in the coastal marshes."

Some of the more influential Cree leaders were also designated as "lieutenants," or "captains," who brought in gangs of hunters, and these men were given a special status, which frequently allowed them to move freely about the post when others were restricted in their movements (Morantz 1982a, 1982b). These leading men were also given gifts or presents of tobacco, brandy, and special clothing. In addition, the homeguards also had an earlier access to muskets, which gave them several advantages over more interior groups, such as an ability to secure more geese during the spring hunt or, if necessary, to deter others who might try to bully their way past the Cree to the trading posts. All in all, as Ray (1974: 13) explains, the Cree's "early historic occupation … placed them in a strategically advantageous position to control the trade of the largest and probably most densely populated river system that drained into Hudson Bay."

It also appears from the historical records that the Cree began to trade at York Factory only about a decade after the Hudson's Bay Company became established in 1670. This advantageous position also allowed them to function in an intercalary or middleman role with groups farther into the interior. This strategy in turn benefited both groups since the trappers who lived farther inland did not then have to take the arduous trip to the coast, and the Cree, in turn, could then take the furs that they had just acquired back to the coast and demand higher terms of trade than the interior groups might have gotten if they had traded directly with the company traders. As one would expect, though, the Hudson's Bay Company would want eventually to trade directly with these interior trappers and so they began to build posts inland, beginning in the mid-1700s with the ill-fated Henley House establishment. Other interior posts were eventually built, serving to curtail the strategic trading advantage that the Cree enjoyed for nearly a century.

Cree Social Organization

There are certain difficulties in determining Cree social organization during the fur trade era. One of the problems is that the European traders who might have commented on Cree society probably had little first-hand knowledge of the characteristics of Cree society. Another issue is that there appears to have been a certain degree of flexibility in Cree society such that adjustments could be made depending on the availability of subsistence resources. The general rule would be that in times when country food was relatively abundant then this factor would allow for larger social groups to exist, at least until changes occurred in the amount of food obtainable from the environment.

Based on historical records for the period from about 1815 to 1840, Morantz (1984, 64–7) has identified various levels of social groupings – the family or commensal unit, the co-residential or winter hunting group, the local group or micro-band, and the regional band or macro-group. "The norm," she (ibid., 64) suggests, "was the co-residential group, which consisted of two or three nuclear or extended families, each of which averaged four to five individuals. When resources were scarce, each co-residential group separated into its component familial or commensal units. A local group or band was composed of from two to nine co-residential groups, averaged six hunters, and was both a migrating and, occasionally, economically co-operating group." HBC fur traders suggested that each group was headed by a "principal Indian" who was probably a proficient hunter, acted as a focal person who dealt with outside issues, and attempted to keep to the norm of an equitable distribution of food among the various families. Morantz also is of the opinion that the composition of the co-residential and local groups was determined based on patrilateral kinship ties. In other words, a core group among the Cree would probably consist of an elderly couple, their grown sons, the sons' wives, and children. In this case the marriage patterns could be termed one of patrilocal residence, probably with an initial period in which the newly married couple would spend a year or two residing with the wife's parents before assuming their life with the husband's group.

In another historical study, Rogers and Smith (1981) suggest than among the Cree efforts to establish well-defined territories were inhibited by the people's dependence upon nomadic and migratory big game, however, when game was more localized social groups could be more sedentary for a certain period of time. For example, Honigmann (1961), in describing Cree food habits, suggest that fowling, especially for geese, was of greater importance than most other subsistence activities, and that meat from trapped fur animals may have been quantitatively more important in the diet than that gained by hunting. In their study, Rogers and Smith identify a "set of regional groups, each inhabiting a particular drainage basis or other major cohesive physiographic unit. These regional groups shared a sense of commonality or collectivity based on a common identity, language, and culture. These groups were also united by various ties of kinship and marriage.

As Morantz had also indicated, these regional groups or bands "were the largest entities that might, but not invariably, assemble for seasonal hunting and summer fishing, but were usually dispersed into smaller segments for most of the year, particularly during the winter.... Thus over a period of years or generations, size and composition were fluid as adaptations were made to changing environmental and social conditions" (Rogers and Smith 1981: 143). In all, it could be concluded that the nuclear family rarely operated as an independent residential or economic entity. The most minimal unit of production and consumption consisted of the extended family which, when the availability or resources allowed, might combine for periods of time with other such extended families to form a larger, regional band.

Intergroup ties were also enhanced by marriage patterns, such as bilateral cross-cousin marriage, which served to maintain linkages between the smaller social units. Polygyny was also practised, usually of the sororal variety, when the availability of resourced allowed for larger families and usually by the best hunters or leaders of a group. It would be accurate to conclude, then, that Cree social organization was a flexible arrangement of various groups, the size of which was largely dependent upon the availably of food resources in the surrounding environment. The interrelationships characteristic of Cree social organization was a reflection of their social ethic of generosity towards others, sharing of resources among the members of the group, and practising mutual aid among their social cohorts, all of which was an adaptation to the often severe environmental conditions and which served to promote survival for all the group members.[5]

Cree Society and Their Adaptive Success

While some Indigenous societies in Canada have become extinct, and others greatly diminished in population by disease or a reduced territory, the Cree have been one of the most successfully adaptive of Canadian Indigenous societies. Partly, the Cree's adaptive success can be attributed to the relatively remote geographical locations in which their settlements are located. This relative isolation has acted as a buffer against the deleterious effects of contact with the larger Euro-Canadian society. In their own territories of northern Ontario and Quebec, the Cree have been able to maintain a relative numerical superiority, whereas in other areas of Canada Indigenous people have become submerged by the dominant society into relatively small enclaves, which made survival difficult especially in the face of European influences and exposure to contagious diseases (Morantz 1984: 55–80).

While the Cree have been able to maintain a numerical supremacy, they have also enjoyed certain advantages because of their distance from urban societies. One of these advantages has been the ability to retain the continuing use of their Cree language and traditional cultural practices. For example, according to census reports the Cree language has the largest number of Indigenous language speakers in Canada, with a total of nearly ninety thousand individuals reporting that they are able to carry on a conversation in their native language, while the next most commonly spoken Indigenous language, Anishinaabe, is reported to have only about a third as many speakers as the Cree (Statistics Canada 2018). There is no doubt that the Cree suffered from a population decline because of episodic European diseases during the initial contact period, but they have since recovered substantially and today inhabit a territory beyond their original area of occupation. The Cree have been able to expand into new regions including the Subarctic forests, the eastern woodlands, and the central plains. On this basis it would be fair to conclude that "in many ways the Cree are the most important North American Indian group in Canada. [No other First Nation people] can lay claim to the central historic position, to the geographical extensiveness, or to the contemporary significance of the myriad Cree-speaking bands spread across Canada" (Fisher 1973: 126).

Conclusion

The survival of the Cree today has partly been due to chance, since their settlements are in remote areas of Canada and therefore do not suffer from many of the harmful consequences of more southerly Indigenous groups and their closer contacts with Euro-Canadian society. However, the Cree have also found ways to adapt their culture to the changing economic and social conditions brought on by Europeans and the fur trade. In the process, the Cree have been able to retain a semblance of an independent lifestyle, lending a sense of accomplishment rather than the feeling of demoralization that is frequently felt by some other Indigenous groups. "Cree society," Feit (2005: 191) remarks, "is organized around principles of community, responsible autonomy, and reciprocity." Rather than take on an exploitive attitude to the land they live in, the Cree have attempted to preserve the resources in their environment so that these may be passed on to future generations to come.

The central core of Cree community relationships, which involve sharing and reciprocal social ties, is also a key element in their survival – a characteristic that stands in sharp contrast to the Europeans' attitudes of ecological exploitation and the greedy attainment of wealth, regardless of the human suffering these attitudes have caused. It is small wonder, then, that the Cree of the 1830s could have been so disappointed in the behaviour of the British fur traders who appeared to have so little sense of such common human values as sharing resources, respect for God's creations, and community responsibility.

Chapter Three

"A Starving and Naked State": Responses to Deprivation

Complaints of starvation or near starvation abound in the Hudson's Bay Company journals, and the Cree everywhere had to get used to depleted resources of food and reduced goods in exchange. Food was uppermost in their minds, while dwindling fur returns preoccupied the company traders.
– Toby Morantz, The White Man's Gonna Getcha: The Colonial Challenge to the Cree of Quebec (2002: 27).

Starvation often forced Indians to adopt extreme measures to ensure personal survival.
– Charles Bishop, "Cultural and Biological Adaptations to Deprivation" (1978: 224).

Why do some sociocultural systems variously persist, transmute, or die out at apparently variable rates in comparable ecosystems and in response to similar stimuli? This question is one of the most perplexing in contemporary science.
– Charles Laughlin and Ivan Brady, Extinction and Survival in Human Populations (1978: 2).

There can be little doubt that the North American Subarctic region has long been regarded as a particularly harsh one for people to live in. Governor George Simpson of the Hudson's Bay Company remarked that in the Subarctic "there is more danger to be apprehended of starvation than in any other part of North America" (Rich 1938: 395). Similarly, "Hunger was a constant threat to all inhabitants of the far north" Daschuk (2013: 55) claims. In the spring of 1809, for example, Daniel Harmon reported that a number of Canadians at Great Bear Lake starved to death, and among those who pulled through the ordeal, "some ... ate their dead companions. [Other] instances of cannibalism were reported across the north" (Rich 1959: 120; see also Andrews 1975).

A Complete Picture of Desolation

Fur trader John McLean[1] commented on the conditions of a trading post on the bank of the South River, saying that it was "surrounded by a country that presents as complete a picture of desolation as can be imagined" (1968 [1932]: 201). This opinion was backed by other travellers through the region who remarked on instances of sustained hunger and outright starvation of both whites and Indigenous people (Oliver 1915: 699). Anthropologist Walter Goldschmidt reflected similar sentiments when he suggested that the Subarctic environment is "as difficult and demanding to man as any in the world" (1974: vii). Explorers of the region, such as W. Wentzel, reported extreme privations during the 1810–11 winter, during which three of his employees died from lack of food and "all my Indians have starved more or less" (1889–90: 106). At another fur-trading post (Fort Good Hope) during the 1841–2 winter "most of the Indians ... have died of starvation and the wretched survivors were reduced to the horrible necessity of feeding on the dead bodies of their nearest relatives" (Hudson's Bay Company B.157a/2/; see also Krech 1978: 716).

In another incident reminiscent of the Cree attack on the Hannah Bay post with the intent of stealing food to stave off starvation, on the Crooked Lakes Reserve on the lower Qu'Appelle Valley in Saskatchewan, a group of apparently starving Assiniboine engaged in an armed attack on an Indian Affairs food storage shed. This episode, known as the "Yellow Calf Incident," which occurred in 1884, "arose as a result of the strict enforcement of the policy of the Department of Indian Affairs regarding the issuance of rations" (Andrews 1975: 41). The Assiniboine had been herded onto this reserve several years before and, with the demise of the buffalo, had little means of obtaining food.

The government policy at the time dictated that all but the elderly and sick must work in return for food rations. However, "tools and implements provided at the time the treaties were made," according to Indian Commissioner Edgar Dewdney, "go but small way to keep so many employed" (ibid.). As a group of armed Assiniboine men attempted to take the food from the storage building to alleviate their distressful situation of food deprivation, bloodshed was only narrowly averted between the armed insurgents and the North West Mounted Police. "The farm instructor for the Crooked Lakes Reserve, James Setter, was dismissed in December 1883, for his laxity in carrying out the government policy, which included the issuing of rations" (ibid.). The leader of the Assiniboine's' malcontent group wanted to know the answer to the perfectly reasonable question: "if ... the provisions were not intended to be eaten by the Indians why were they stored on the reserve" (ibid., 46).

Eventually cooler heads prevailed, and a compromise was reached with the result that the charge of an armed insurrection was dropped. Commissioner Reid, in his report on the incident, stated "that the actual rioters were, in conclusion, near starvation, I cannot admit for a moment, their appearance belies the supposition. In turn, the Hudson's Bay Company manager, McKenzie, noted that this winter many of the others who tried to hunt have killed little or nothing, and are going to be hard up before spring" (ibid., 47). And in the same year of 1884, in The Pas, Manitoba, an Anglican cleric lamented that "The times are getting worse, the people are running in all directions hunting for food. Hunger" according to the cleric, "was the main reason for increased sickness in the region" (in Daschuk 2013: 135; and Records of the Church Mission Society, The Pas, 20 February 20, 1884).

Thus, as mentioned by The Pas' Anglican cleric, further problems for the Indigenous people of Canada's north country concern the intertwining of the combined maladies of food deprivation and disease. Cook (1976: 55), for example, has convincingly demonstrated that extended periods of malnutrition makes one susceptible to contracting various diseases. As such, even if the person does not die from starvation, a state of extreme hunger can be the indirect or incipient cause of other fatalities. Similarly, periodic exposure to disease has a tendency to debilitate people to the point where subsistence pursuits become extremely difficult to maintain. As Krech (1978, 717–18) correctly points out, "it is quite likely that as a result of epidemics, more people starved … Starvation may have been a significant cause of mortality principally because diseases have weakened the ability of the band to exploit resources effectively." He also suggests that the fur trade was a complicit factor in food deprivations in the Subarctic because those who were trapping and making excursions to their trading posts needed to change their pre-contact subsistence activities in order to accommodate the varying distribution of fur-bearing animals (ibid., 721).

It was also no secret that during the nineteenth century that most Cree trapping families, and probably any other Indigenous groups who lived in the James Bay area, were practically starving to death during the 1830s. In some areas of northern Ontario, the problem of food shortages among the Anishinaabe could have been happening since the early 1820s – as Bishop reports, "a long period of deprivation involving reduced resource availability" during that decade (1978: 209). Even before this decade, "the valuable beaver supply as well as larger animals were slaughtered in such numbers that they began to grow scarce by 1810" (ibid., 213). It would appear, although there should be more research into the issue of food deprivation, that widespread food shortages were beginning to occur at a much earlier date and over a more extensive geographical area during the fur trade than might have previously been presumed. Food shortages initiated a downward spiral as Indigenous people were required to spend more time hunting, with the result that they were consequently less able to meet their fur trade needs. In turn, as the food supply diminished at an ever-faster pace, the point would be reached when hardly any trapping would occur at all, as hunting and gathering consumed most of the Indigenous people's time. As Bishop reiterated, "survival was balanced precariously between the food quest and trapping. Although both were essential, the immediacy of starvation often necessitated the search for food over furs" (ibid., 219). Of course, the Hudson's Bay Company employees would be well aware of this issue as it hit on their profit margins, but they nonetheless appeared to take no action to ameliorate the problem. As a consequence, "Cases of starvation, even cannibalism, occasioned by the death of large animals, became relatively frequent by the 1820s" (Bishop 1978b: 214).

The Hudson's Bay Company employees reported food deprivation in their journals on virtually a daily basis. So how did the Hudson's Bay Company employees fare in this stressful situation? There were no reports of HBC men going hungry, let alone starving. The reason is that they hired professional Cree hunters to fill their larders which, of course, meant less food for everyone else in the Hudson Bay Lowlands. Why not bring food over from England? The company said that it was "too expensive." Some may say that this was a heartless approach, given the suffering that the traders were experiencing, but the HBC was not a charitable organization – the employees were there to make a profit and for no other reason than economic gain, which is the usual attitude of colonial capitalists.

Physiological Responses to Starvation

One could reasonably assume, given that we are all human beings, that a Cree person from James Bay and an individual from Ireland would have at least similar responses to food deprivation. Lacking such accounts describing the James Bay Cree, there is a plethora of information on the starving Irish during their famine period of 1847–9. Based on a compilation of contemporary newspaper accounts and other reports of the time, Gallagher (1982: 77) provides the following grim account:

> Long before death came from starvation, the victim suffered unquench-
> able thirst, delusions, madness, and a feeling of weakness and fatigue so

complete that it took a concentrated effort to open an eyelid. Whatever strength remained was spent in yearning for life to end, and for some it did with merciful speed. For others, the famine's diseases led to even more horrible varieties of human suffering before death came and rescued them. The youngest and strongest nevertheless clung to survival, and these exerted their will over their ever-diminishing physical resources in the belief that help would come.

When a person has been in a state of starvation for a long period of time there is apparently a general debilitation of the body's organs, so even when food become available the consumption of it could actually increase the danger of death. The starving person's body has great difficulty in absorbing so sudden an intake of nutrients. For example, the heart would have difficulty in withstanding the unexpected workload. "If they get any strong dose at all," observed a member of the Quaker Society of Friends, "they die off at once." He then added "If they get a full meal, it kills them immediately" (ibid., 104). Other calamities that hastened the death of famine victims included severe dysentery and the contraction of various diseases, such as typhus, fever, various infections, dropsy (a disease like scurvy), and gangrene. The lower extremities of starving persons often became swollen with a tumescent condition that rendered them unable to walk, and certainly not able to seek food outside their dwellings.

Lessons from the Irish Famine

The starvation of Cree trappers in the James Bay region during the fur trade era, which was presumably a plight suffered by other Indigenous people also living in the Hudson Bay Lowlands, has hardly been documented, except for the brief, although frequent, mention of food deprivation in the journals of Hudson's Bay Company employees. It would be reasonable to presume that occurrences of food deprivation among the Cree and other Indigenous peoples of the James Bay area would be of concern to the HBC post managers only to the extent that it might impact in a detrimental manner on the supply of furs, rather than out of any humanitarian concern. As such, we seek then to find commonalities with other populations who might have suffered a similar fate, such as the Irish of the late 1840s, who, coincidentally also were impacted by the economic and political policies of the British.[2]

"The Irish Famine," (Butterly and Shepard 2010: 41) suggest, "also remains a popular case study of Malthusian theory." As such, a contributing factor to the famine, therefore, was the high rate of reproduction and large families of the Irish poor, as well as their adherence to Catholicism. More recently, however, Amaryta Sen and others have focused on other possible underlying causes of the famine, such as the poverty of the Irish peasants and their inability to access enough food to feed themselves, even though there was apparently sufficient food available to alleviate their condition in the markets around them. In other words, attention has recently shifted away from the idea that the famine was more of "a tragic ecological accident" to more political and economic factors associated with the colonial situation in which the Irish peasants were embedded. In this regard, the Irish famine could be seen as "an economic and social phenomenon that can occur *when food supplies are adequate to prevent it*" (italics as in orig., Scrimshaw 1987: 2).

The famine, furthermore, is also seen by some as a symbol of the indifference to human suffering under conditions of free-market or laissez-faire economic principles. Even though daily accounts of starvation in nearby Ireland were widely known in Britain, in London imponderable amounts of money were being expended on the Great Exhibition of 1851. Thus, we are forced to ask how such food deprivation as the famine could occur when there existed a situation of relative economic abundance, or why those in power in colonial settings seemed so indifferent to the suffering of those with whom they were engaged. When it comes to assessing the causes of the famine, an apparent multiplicity of factors seemed to have contributed to this catastrophe – the ownership and control of Irish property, an increased dependency of the Irish on a single source of sustenance, and an increased reliance on members of the colonial power structure who were seen not to have taken an interest in the Irish poor. In a curious way, these same factors can be seen to be responsible for modern starvation as well, as in Ukraine (1932–3), India (1943–4), China (1959–60), or Niger and Mali (2005).

Of the various factors that could be seen to contribute to the Irish Famine it is evident that there are both internal (poverty, population growth), and external (economic policies, political relationships) that combine to make the horrific and regrettable situation what it was to become. In other words, as Butterly and Shepard postulate, "No famine stands in isolation" (2010: 47). Nonetheless, laissez-faire economics deserves special attention since it is the one factor that arguably contributed the greatest impact on Irelands struggles. The main tenet of this theory was that it was not the responsibility of government to provide aide for its citizens, much less so for those living in another country, such as Canada or Ireland. At the very least, this economic policy was responsible for making the existing poverty in Ireland worse than it could have been, and subsequently was an important factor in the ensuing starvation of the Irish peasants. In addition, what could be termed "public charity" was thought to only make a bad situation worse because it just delayed the inevitable consequences of the underlying problems themselves.

The situation was analogous to the condition in the James Bay area, where HBC traders employed Indigenous hunters to supply food in support of the post population, thus diminishing the local food supply for Cree trappers. Rather than importing food from Britain, huge quantities of food were exported from Ireland to England throughout the period when the Irish were starving. There is no need to recount these figures for they are well known (Butterly and Shepard 2010: 49); however, it is also important to note that while the potato crop failed, grain in Ireland was still produced in abundance, which some would argue was produced in sufficient quantity to prevent the starvation that eventually occurred.

Deprivation and Survival

[He] brings us the Lamentable news that Many of the Indians are Starving and have eaten their Furs, and that it is firmly believed that one family have actually starved of Starvation.

– W.F. Wenzel, Fort Simpson, 1824 (HBCA B.200/a/4 fo.1)

Prior to the killings at the Hannah Bay fur-trading post, on January 20, 1832, it was reported that about a dozen Cree people had arrived at Rupert House "in a Staving and Naked State" requesting food and other provisions (B.135/a/137:15).[3]

"The man who was there to look after Eastmain [a small outpost of Waskaganish or Rupert House] was named Corston … She [the narrator's grandmother] asked Corston if anyone had seen them [her lost relatives]. Corston told her that nobody had seen them. Then she knew that they had starved. At that time when people were lost, they didn't even think to look for them right away. That's the kind of [Hudson's Bay Company] bosses they were long ago. [The bosses were unconcerned about the perils of starvation or tragedy of death without burial, and the anguish of other Natives to know if people were, in fact, dead, and how they had died]" (Preston 2002: 139).

"By the nineteenth century, the population of food-animals and fur-bearing animals in the James Bay region had been depleted and people were sometimes starving, and the company had long since expanded westward in search of new sources of furs" (Preston 2012: 22).

"There were quite a few people who died of starvation (in the James Bay region around Eastman and Rupert's House). My grandmother, who was very old, told me a lot of stories about people starving. My grandmother's father, mother, and brother starved to death. Many people were searching for them in the spring, fall, and winter. They never did find the bodies. No one was able to find a trace of them" (Preston 2002: 25).

"Up the Eastmain River, this area was hard hit by starvation in the later decades of the nineteenth century, many [people] died on their lands" (Preston 2002:25).

"I moved to Waskaganish from far inland. I did not miss it because many times I was very hungry … After I left, I heard stories about people starving there … I heard people were starving because there were no more caribou or other animals for meat. Two of my cousins starved [to death] there. One of my cousins, his four children also starve with him. My other cousin starved but the other Indians found his wife in time to survive" (Preston 2012: 31–2).

"If a man was hunting far inland, he could not leave his family and return to the post because his family would probably starve by the time he returned" (Preston 2012: 33).

Ellen Smallboy's Story

Ellen Smallboy, a Cree woman from the James Bay of northern Ontario, talks about having to fend for herself and children when her husband went hunting or left for the post; she speaks about the fears she had of starvation during the 1930s. "In lean years," Ellen remarked, "a woman might be left alone in camp for several days to cope as best she could" (Flannery 1995, 38; see also Flannery 1935). Ellen described how, during the winter in 1935, when game was extremely scarce, she and her family of young children had to shift their camp to a different part of their hunting grounds where they hoped to find game. However, they did not find any animals, so her husband had to leave them in order to travel to the post at Moose Factory in an attempt to obtain food. Ellen described this ordeal:

"There was nothing to eat and all that was there was some dried tea. My old man was going off to the Post, leaving me and the children, to be gone five nights. He was very thin and poor, so the night before he left I made him a rabbit-skin blanket. He would never have made it without that. He would lie on the rabbit-skin next to the fire and would be afraid to sleep too long because he might freeze to death" (ibid.).

During the first day after her husband left for Moose Factory, she and her three children had nothing to eat. The following day she took her baby in a cradle board, leaving her two small boys in the camp, to check on their snares. This time there were a few rabbits to eat, but the next day there was nothing there. During the next day, she decided to travel over to one of their old camps because she had left some snares there. Again, she left her two young boys at the camp. When she arrived at her former camp Ellen found only two old beaver oil sacs and some castor which were used to lure beaver in trapping (see Cooper 1938: 10–13). The dried oil sacs provided her with enough sustenance to continue in her search for food.

After roasting the oil sacs Ellen was fortunate enough to find ten rabbits in the snares at this old camp, and two more nearby, after which she started for home. When she arrived, Ellen discovered that her older boy had caught a whiskey jack (Canadian Jay) and had cooked it. She then told her boys to go out to the toboggan and bring in the rabbits so that could make a meal, about which her children were very happy. The next day she travelled out to some beaver traps that her husband had set and was fortunate to have caught a young beaver. Ellen said that this beaver was very fat, which made her sick when she attempted to eat the roasted meat. Eventually her husband returned from Moose Factory with a small amount of food from the post, and so Ellen and her family were able to survive for a while longer and avoid starvation in the bush.

According to Ellen Smallboy's biographer, anthropologist Regina Flannery, even during the 1930s, a full century after the Hannah Bay incident, there were "times of near-starvation when no game at all could be found, and the group was forced to gather lichens to boil and eat. She [Ellen] remarked that this staved off intense hunger for a while, as did caribou dung gathered from the snow and boiled. The availability of food was unpredictable throughout the area. Semi-starvation was not uncommon, and death from starvation was all too frequent" (1995: 17–18). One wonders if any Hudson's Bay Company personnel at any time or place in the James Bay area had to suffer such an ordeal or take such desperate measures to survive as those described by Ellen Smallboy. Ellen further related an account of a family that she knew in which the father and several of the children died of starvation. In this case "the mother and the youngest child were only able to survive by eating the flesh of the deceased" (ibid., 18). Ellen also described that in her own life she and her family suffered from "chronic shortages of food which sometimes reached dire proportions" (ibid., 54). The James Bay region was evidently a harsh environment to live in for the Indigenous people of the area.

The Ecology of the Hudson Bay Lowlands

The James Bay region of which Hannah Bay occupies the southern most part is situated on the Canadian Shield within the Subarctic region of Canada. During the advance of the last ice age the existing soil cover was scoured virtually to the underlying bedrock, which left little earth remaining for possible vegetation to grow. In addition, the melting of the ice sheet resulted in the formation of extensive rivers, lakes, rock outcrops, and marshy swamps. Many scientific studies have found that as a result of these ecological conditions the environment of the James Bay region is one of the most inhospitable territories in North America and one hardly providing a favourable setting for human habitation (Knight 1968; Masty 1991; Peloquin and Berkes 2009; Royer and Herrmann 2011, 2013 have all commented on the paucity of food resources in the southern James Bay region).

Widespread starvation in the James Bay area was first reported from Albany to Eastmain in 1703 (Davies 1965:8; see also Morantz 2002: 105–10; Francis and Morantz 1983: 3), and these accounts provided a stark portrayal of the eastern James Bay region:

"The land is rugged and impenetrable to all but the most resourceful travellers. The rivers drop through thunderous cataracts to a swampy coastal plain, blank, and featureless. The climate is one of extremes, ranging from the hot, mosquito-plagued days of summer to the deadly cold of mid-winter. All in all, it is among the most intimidating country in the Canadian Shield. Human inhabitants have always found it difficult to wrest a living from such a harsh environment" (Francis and Morantz 1983: 3).

Richard Preston, in an essay on the East Main Cree, commented that "trips inland were short and by snowshoe; people remained along the coast and river mouths during the summer months to avoid the soft and soggy muskeg and the biting insects that bred there" (1981: 197–8). With reference to the Shield country south of James Bay, Rogers and Smith comment that "long and severe winters alternated with short and moderately warm summers. It was the winter, especially, that placed its stamp on the inhabitants by limiting their activities and requiring maximal exertions for survival ... during the spring thaw ... human travel was minimal ... With late autumn (September-October) the water again begins to freeze, limiting travel and subsistence activities" (1981: 130).

The major rivers flowing into James Bay, such as the Attawapiskat and the Albany, formed virtually the only access into the interior territory since overland routes were practically impassable because of the swampy conditions. These rivers, for the most part, were characterized by tumultuous rapids or impassible water falls that inhibited travelling and exploration by European explorers. These aquatic conditions tended to keep the fur traders close to the coastal region, and it was only after about a century of operation that the Hudson's Bay Company attempted the construction of any interior trading posts. The first of these interior posts, Henley House built in 1720 along the Albany River, was destroyed on several occasions because of conflicts between fur traders and members of the local Indigenous population, which resulted in several bloody confrontations (Bishop 1976). Thus, another possible reason why exploration of the interior was inhibited, aside from environmental conditions, pertained to the potential resistance on the part of the Cree and Anishinaabe populations to any interior travels by European traders.

Vegetation in the James Bay region consists primarily of stretches of boreal forest, comprising mainly coniferous trees, such as the stunted black spruce, interspersed with cedar, tamarack, and poplar. The forests become less dense as one proceeds northward, eventually giving way to areas of tundra and extensive barren ground. Thus, another important factor that deterred the interior expansion of the Hudson's Bay Company was the scarcity of suitable building materials for the construction of trading posts. As far as the Indigenous Cree were concerned, sparse forested conditions meant that there was a relative shortage of materials to construct their toboggans, canoes, and snowshoes, which were necessary for their survival. A diminished forest habitat furthermore caused a reduction in the available food supplies because of a lower population of animals upon which the Cree depended for food, clothing, and shelter (see Francis and Morantz 1983: 4–6).

In an environment thin on subsistence resources, the Indigenous people did not have the luxury of concentrating their hunting efforts on one species of animals, such as the Plains buffalo or the moose in northern Ontario. Instead, hunters by necessity needed to exploit every possible opportunity to survive. This meant a subsistence strategy by which the population needed to disperse thinly over the land in small families and to adopt an opportunistic approach, sometimes even trapping rabbits and other small game when fish or larger game were not available. This ever-present need to find food often meant that the time for trapping was restricted, or at least subordinated, to the effort devoted to hunting and fishing, much to the disappointment of the fur traders.

In an ecological area of the Subarctic such as the James Bay region, the Cree adopted what could be termed a "maximal foraging strategy" as one of the only means to afford enough time for trapping. According to this strategy, hunters pursued the largest game animals available at any one time of the year, thus attempting to maximize effort by providing the most calories for the work involved. Since caribou were the largest mammals living in this area, opportunities were never lost to hunt this animal. Unfortunately for local hunters, caribou are migratory animals whose movements are usually unpredictable and, therefore, as a hunting resource cannot be counted on with any degree of certainty. The meat of the caribou was prized over that of other animals, and the hides provided a much-needed resource for clothing and tents. Again, when the choice between hunting caribou and trapping for furs presented itself, trapping was not pursued, thus lessening possible income from the Hudson's Bay Company. To be sure, the choices involved – trapping, which yielded steel traps, guns, and ammunition in return for furs, on the one hand, or hunting for food upon which everyone in the family required for survival on the other – were no doubt difficult ones to make.

It is evident, then, from these observations and many more like them that in the James Bay area life for the Indigenous population was a precarious existence. At best this territory barely provided just enough country food for people to survive. A perpetual movement from one area to another was necessary in order avoid overuse of the existing food resources in any single region. At various times of the year travel in search of game became virtually impossible, which risked starvation and threatened the very survival of life itself. Life in the southern James Bay area, one must conclude, involved a continuous pursuit of the necessities of life. As Dunning summarized for the Anishinaabe of northwestern Ontario, and which is no doubt true for the James Bay area as well, "Periodic times of shortage reduced the population to near starvation. But the important point is that there was no mechanism either technological or sociological for building up more than limited surpluses of goods for insurance against times of want and to allow a greater or more diversified economic base" (1959a: 175).

The Easter Subarctic: Comparative Subsistence Areas

The food resources available to the Cree and Anishinaabe of northern Ontario and Quebec vary from one geographical area to another across the region known as the Eastern Subarctic. The Eastern Subarctic is a region north of the Eastern Woodland area, which is to say, the region that could be considered as a rough demarcation zone north of about the Albany River area in Ontario, sweeping several hundred kilometres south of James Bay and then arcing northeastward again to about Chicoutimi near the St. Lawrence River. The distribution of food resources is an important factor as a demographic feature that influences population densities in an area, the size of local groups, and other internal social aspects, such as kinship and family structures.

A study of subsistence resources in the Eastern Subarctic was conducted by Edward Rogers (1966), which he refers to as a preliminary study. His research strategy was to divide the Eastern Subarctic into several zones that are understood to be internally similar in terms of climate, animal populations, and vegetation areas. The assumption is then made that the adaptation of the Cree and Anishinaabe would be similar in each of these areas, which is an idea previously postulated by Alfred Kroeber (1939) according to his "culture area concept."[4]

Kroeber's approach differed from the conventional view of the time, which focused more on the individualistic characteristics of a culture, such as Boas's concept of "historical particularism."[5] Kroeber was to look beyond these individualistic characteristics by examining various ecological relationships that tie humans to their environmental settings. The basic idea behind the cultural area concept is that within certain geographical settings, such as the Great Plains or the Northwest coast, cultures tend to be similar to one another because of the similar adaptive process within these areas.

In addition, when social groups move into a new geographical area, they begin to adapt their social and economic systems to take advantage of the new subsistence opportunities for procuring food in this new environment. The emerging adaptive process, then, for each group entering the area will be more or less the same for each group. Hence, what emerges over time is a similarity in cultural forms regardless of the characteristics of the original cultures. Studying the adaptive process of a social group that enters a new environment allows for the study of the decision-making processes that take place among its members. It also helps to explain why some groups may be more successful, or not, in surviving under new ecological conditions. Thus, in anthropology, Kroeber's culture area concept, with its emphasis on adaptive aspects, provided an explanatory model of culture change that went beyond the Boasian paradigm of historical particularism.

The culture area concept was later modified in the 1950s in an attempt to rectify some obvious deficiencies in anthropology's ecological approach. The problem with Kroeber's all-encompassing approach is that not all aspects of a culture are similarly affected by the ecological adaptive process. Julian Steward (1955) recognized that technological and economic systems are linked to environmental conditions more directly than other aspects of a culture, such as kinship systems, religious beliefs, and rituals. It is for this reason that Steward visualized a culture as forming two important areas – its "core" (techno-economics) and "superstructure" (ideology). Thus, Steward provided a significant refinement on Kroeber's ecological approach by identifying more precisely the sectors of a social and cultural system that are impacted more directly in various ways by changing ecological conditions. If people, for example, changed their subsistence strategy from hunting large game animals to fishing and goose hunting, their religious belief and accompanying rituals will probably remain intact, according to Stewards approach.[6]

These theoretical approaches by Boas, Kroeber, and Steward therefore form the anthropological background for Rogers's (1963, 1966, 1973, 1986; Rogers and Black 1974, 1976; Rogers and Smith 1981) study of the subsistence areas of the Eastern Subarctic among the Cree and Anishinaabe. These studies by Rogers and his colleagues provided a significant refinement on Kroeber's culture area concept because they illustrated the substantial differences that can occur in subsistence strategies over time, and the variations in resource variability that can take place even within one ecological zone. His basic research approach was to map out subsistence areas for three different time periods (1600–1800, 1800–1900, 1900–1960) and then to characterize each of these periods in terms of the subsistence production that was prominent in terms of the changing resource base. For example, the major food categories examined were mammals (big game: moose, caribou; aquatic mammals, such as beaver; small game, particularly hare), birds (especially waterfowl), and fish. It was deemed that the importance of vegetal foods was negligible in this area.

During the first of these periods (1600–1800) conclusions were difficult to arrive at because of limitations in the existing information. However, available data was derived from explorers such as Pierre-Esprit Radisson, who apparently reached James Bay from Lake Superior, and various English and French fur traders who travelled through northern Ontario and Quebec. The *Jesuit Relations* provided additional information, although this is often not derived by direct observation by the missionaries. On this basis two subsistence areas were identified – a moose-fish area for the territory north of Lake Superior up to about the Albany River area, and a caribou-fish area extending north to the southern portion of James Bay.

The area comprising the Hudson Bay Lowlands (directly east of James and Hudson Bay) did not have enough information to arrive at a characterization of this area. Furthermore, as Rogers (1966: 112) points out, "As for the Hudson Bay Lowland ... there even is the question of whether all or even a part of this area was inhabited until after trading posts were established along the coast and the Indians were attracted out of the interior." This observation would therefore support the idea that the Hudson Bay Lowlands were so deficient in subsistence resources that the Cree and Anishinaabe did not live in this area before the fur trade because there were insufficient food resources available to support them.

Further support for this suggestion is derived from a startling report from Fort Albany in 1783, stating that the Indigenous people of the area left the post early that fall because the geese were so scarce, they had a fear of starving. Fort Albany was the Hudson's Bay Company's most important post: "It was the centre of the company's operations," Ray and Freeman (1978, 165) assert. In the lowlands bordering on Hudson and James Bay, "Game and fur-bearing animals were never numerous in the region. Food was in short supply ... thus the lowlands were not a favourable environment for permanent habitation. It is unlikely that many Indians lived in the region throughout the period prior to European contact" (ibid., 39).

A diminished supply of food in this area was further exacerbated by the fact that the HBC personnel brought very little of their own provisions with them. Transporting food supplies from Europe was relatively expensive so, as a cost-cutting measure, every effort was made to secure food from the local area, thus further diminishing game that would otherwise be utilized to support the local Indigenous trappers and their families. HBC men at the posts did not have the skills to hunt themselves or enough knowledge of available game in the area, so local Indigenous people were hired to hunt and fill the posts' larders instead. Consequently, Native trappers were pitted against their kinsmen who were hunting for the HBC for an ever-diminishing supply of subsistence resources. Another result was that some Cree gave up trapping altogether to become virtually permanent HBC employees, who came to be known as the Home Guard Cree, which served to solidify a dependency relationship of certain Cree on HBC resources (ibid., 40–1).

If the initial (1600–1800) period of the fur trade was characterized by such an insufficient subsistence resource base, could one expect an improvement in the food supply during the following centuries? It was becoming evident that the pressure on game resources in the James Bay area was beginning to take its toll. Caribou, for example, which were never abundant in the Eastern Subarctic in any event, by the nineteenth century "became less numerous in the southern part of the area and later farther north. [In addition,] by the beginning of the twentieth century, the 'Caribou-Fish' subsistence area was pretty much confined to the Labrador Peninsular. At present, it hardly exists anywhere" (Rogers 1966: 114).

With a decrease in larger game such as caribou, adjustments in the quest for food were made by relying on smaller game and fish. Such a resource strategy, of course, required a great commitment of time that would probably otherwise be used to trap furs. As Rogers (1966: 102) indicates, "As fur trapping increased in importance, more small game, such as mink, were accordingly taken and consumed by the people." Others have noticed an increased reliance on small game. Burgesse (1940: 35–6), for example, commented that "the staple article of food for the Canadian Indian was decidedly not moose or caribou. Most often it was fish, rabbit, squirrel, and other small fry."

In addition, Skinner (1910: 82–3; see also 1911: 25) stated that "the great mainstay of the Indians of the north in the winter is the vast quantity of rabbits. In the winter these form the staple food." For northern Ontario, referring to his research among the residents of the Pekangekum Band of Anishinaabe, Dunning reports that the meat of the fur-bearing animals that are trapped is a mainstay of the diet, rather than larger game such as moose: "During the winter season beaver and muskrat are relied on for the meat supply, in addition to hares when available.... For a large part of the year, especially the warmer months, fish is relied upon almost entirely as the staple food" (1959a: 24). It must be admitted, though, that there were various factors involved in the reliance on certain food resources over others across the East Subarctic, such as fluctuations in game densities over the years, regional differences in habitats, or variations in food resources that were relied upon because of seasonal variations (Rogers 1966: 92). In addition, as Gillespie (1981: 17) states, "Although the quantity and quality of data on Subarctic animals are not uniformly adequate, there is clear evidence of population fluctuations of all animal types significant in the native subsistence economy. A complex set of variables results in fairly unpredictable oscillations of the Subarctic populations of large game animals." In addition, a major factor in the fluctuations in the numbers of large as well as small animals is the various successions of forest stages, each stage supplying adequate food for only certain species. Thus, as Waisberg (1975: 176) summarizes, "For any species living in an area undergoing succession, the amount of preferred food that can be taken is gradually reduced. Different animal populations will eventually die or migrate out of their area as their food resource base is transmuted into a different one through vegetational successions." The regular successional stages of forestation are furthermore affected by forest fires, which can alter the vegetational food supply in a dramatic manner, causing, in turn, a radical change in the movements and numbers of animals by species (see Feit 1973).[7]

In other words, a diminishing supply of large game required an almost full-time commitment to securing smaller mammals, which drew the Cree away from commodity production. In fact, a tally of beaver and marten returns from Hudson's Bay Company records for the period 1701–63, for Forts Albany, Churchill, Moose, and York showed a relatively steady decline in production after reaching a high point in the middle of this period. At Fort Albany, for example, "whole parchment beaver" reached a high of 12,006 pelts traded in 1731 but was down to 905 pelts by 1755. Eastmain post had a high of 1,274 pelts traded in 1747 but decreased to 903 pelts by 1763. At Fort Churchill, during its second year of existence in 1738, there was a high of 14,320 pelts traded but never again reached this level. York Factory had a high level of beaver pelts traded in its third year of existence (1739) of 20,402 pelts but also never reached this level again. Similar patterns are evident throughout the records – high levels of parchment beaver traded in the early years; then a slow diminishing in returns thereafter (Ray and Freeman 1978:168–74).

Of course, further research would be required to ascertain more precisely the direct relationship between a decline in fur production over time and the relationship to the ever-increasing amount of time required by the Cree and other Indigenous groups to secure an adequate food supply, yet this appears to be the predominant relationship until further data would be produced to the contrary. For example, in a table of fur returns for the East Main District of western James Bay during the period of 1854–68, prime beaver pelts reached a high point of 1,686 pelts in 1858 and then steadily declined year by year to 409 pelts by 1868 (Francis and Morantz 1983: 148).

Certainly, from the perspective of the Hudson's Bay Company, if the Cree and others were relinquishing trapping in order to feed themselves, then this would have been a worrisome situation because it would reduce profits for the company. There are even cases of the Cree eating their own furs because of a lack of food. The Moose Factory Post Journal for 1831–2 (B135/a/137), for example, includes the following entry:

Monday, February 20, 1832 (folio 19)
Cootutig, Apischaupaish and their families Arrived – they inform me that they were driven to the necessity of eating their Skins (8 in number)

... their furs consisted of Beaver, being driven to the necessity of killing those animals for food as Martins were very scarce this Winter. Besides the scarcity of prov's [provisions?] this season, 4 Indians, had been poaching on their Grounds which made them more impoverished than otherwise they might have been.

There were other reports similar to this one.

The destruction of fur and game animals became particularly prevalent in the period between the Treaty of Paris in 1763 and the merger of the Hudson's Bay and Northwest companies in 1821. As Ray (1974: 117) indicates, "this intense competition favoured a ruthless exploitation of the region's fur and game animals." Although this comment refers primarily to the western interior of Manitoba and Saskatchewan there is no reason to believe that a similar situation of "ruthless exploitation" of fur and game animals was not also occurring in the James Bay area because of the frequent reports in the Hudson's Bay Company journals of starvation and declining fur production. For example, James (1987: 442) states with supporting evidence that "the depletion of big game and fur bearers in the area between Hudson Bay and Lake Superior has been well documented." Bishop furthermore commented for the Anishinaabe of northern Ontario that "there is no question that subsistence activities frequently interfered with the fur quest" (1974: 183). In fact, it was reported that the Anishinaabe of the Osnaburgh House area "suffered so much from starvation that 'not an Indian is Making any hunt in furs'" (ibid.). Among the Attawapiskat Cree living on the west coast of James Bay, it was observed that "people don't like to go very far in the bush, for fear of starvation" (Cummins 2004: 30). In other words, by at least the 1820s the resource base in most of Canada's northern territory had seriously eroded. Increasingly, reports were reaching the HBC posts of the Indigenous Assiniboine, Cree, and Anishinaabe resorting to subsisting on small game such as rabbits and squirrels to survive, or worse, eating their own fur catches. As time went on, starvation was becoming an ominous spectre over much of the Hudson and James Bay regions.

Minutes of a Council Held at Michipicoten Southern Department of Ruperts Land, May 17–28, 1830

This document shows minutes of a council held at Michipicoten (probably just north of present-day Wawa on the north shore of Lake

Superior in the vicinity of Sault Ste. Marie) attended by Governor George Simpson, John G. McTavish, George Keith, Alexander Christie, and John McBean, all chief factors. The meeting was called to establish rules and regulations to help conduct proper business for the department and "in order to investigate the result of the trade of last year and determine the Outfits and general arrangements for the trade of the current year comfortably." From the perspective of the importance of the present study is concerned, the summer and winter arrangements for posts are listed, including an arrangement for the Hannah Bay Post to have William Corrigal there as post master (B. 135/k/1 1830 folios 97 and 102).

John George McTavish[8] to HBC London Committee, September 24, 1831

The following is a summary account of a letter that Chief Factor John McTavish, Moose Factory, wrote to his superiors in London describing the conditions of the fur trade around his post before the Hannah Bay murders. The stress is on the positive aspects of the fur trade with some unexpected comments on the dire situation of food deprivation in the James Bay area (the word "starvation" is even used) and the necessity of conservation during this time.

The letter mentions Chief Factor Beioley[9] (of Rupert House) "whose District compared with former years shows an increase of nearly one sixth and thereby causes the Department collectively to show an increase in the value of returns and consequent increase of apparent gain compared with last year of £2000 (folio 11)." It is important to note, however, that McTavish's report indicates a "scarcity of small furs in all of the Districts except Ruperts River [which] added to a dearth of Rabbits their usual resource for food, caused the Natives to look more to beaver than they otherwise would" (folio 12). There are also comments by McTavish pertaining to his views on "nursing the Country." Folio 12 states:

"They [Natives] are fully alive to all that we say on the subject of nursing the Country and appear perfectly sensible that our motives for wishing them to spare the Beaver are solely for their benefit, but plead the cravings of hunger as paramount to all other considerations and I have not the smallest doubt that they are perfectly sincere and will follow our counsel upon all occasions when not pressed by positive [distrefs?] from starvation" (A.11/46 folios 11–13d).

Comments: The Hudson's Bay Company began to show a serious concern for conservation measures after the 1821 amalgamation. However, as McTavish notes, country food was in short supply for the Indigenous population, and beaver was a preferred food source. As Francis and Morantz comment:

"Clearly the Indians were willing enough to abide by the Hudson's Bay Company regulations to help preserve the [beaver] species but unlike the company their prime consideration was not economic. Next to caribou meat beaver was the most preferred food, and they could not be persuaded to go to unnecessary extremes to preserve it. In an attempt to discourage the hunting of summer beaver even for food the company in 1827 reduced the price of its fishing tackle, ammunition, and provisions by one-third" (1983: 129).

Similarly, Arthur Ray suggests that

"Hudson's Bay Company traders and Indians alike began to see the need for conservation. However, the traditional tenure system was not well suited to a situation in which scarcity had become a chronic and widespread problem instead of an occasional localized one. When certain Indian bands attempted to conserve the fur resources in their hunting and trapping ranges by curtailing trapping activities, their neighbours frequently moved in and collected the furs" (1984: 6; see also Ray 1975: 61–2; Krech 1984: 130–1; Bishop 1970: 10–11).

Starvation, Murder, and Retribution in Fur Trade Territory

As a prelude to a discussion of the events that took place at Hannah Bay in 1832, a brief search was conducted of the Moose Factory (B.135/a/137–8) and Rupert House (B.186/a/45/b/22) post journal entries, looking in particular for references to game scarcities and poor hunting and trapping returns. What follows, then, is the exact accounts in the writers' own words as they appear in the HBC journals of James Bay just before and after the Hannah Bay deaths of William Corrigal,[10] his wife, and others as indicated below.

Moose Factory Post Journal, 1831–2

Note: The author is presumably Chief Factor John George McTavish. Also, rather than paraphrase the author's words and risk misinterpretation, with the reader's indulgence, I have quoted the journal entries directly for purposes of accuracy. The purpose here is to use these journal entries as contextual information and as a timeline, for the murders at Hannah Bay.

Friday, October 21, 1831 (folio 1)

Seven Men were sent in a Batteau with supplying for Hannah Bay Post and to bring back the Geese that may have been procured there – one of the Crew Edward Richards was sent to winter there.

Saturday, October 29, 1831 (folio 3)

About 11 am – the Boat at last, returned from Hannah Bay – with 12 Casks of Geese (1257) [?] after discharging their Boat they had the day to rest themselves having been ever since Yesterday morning in the Boat exposed to the inclemency of the Weather.

Sunday, October 30, 1831 (folio 3)

Milder weather than usual – Most all the Indians came from the Marshes, saying it was useless to remain any longer, as all the wild fowl had fled to the Southward – but their principal Motive is to get their Advances, and set off to their Wintering Grounds. Olicketashish received his Advances for the Winter, intending to leave here tomorrow.

Monday, October 31, 1831 (folio 3d)

Mishisckets, Ouskeegee, Uckanakushick, Neepeeckilloe, and Waitchaicpaish were debited with Goods, and they took their departures for there [sic] Wintering Grounds.

Monday, November 14, 1831 (folio 5d)

The Indian Saunders – who came in Saturday – with a Sick Wife – left here for Medical Aid – and went off to his hunting ground.

Thursday, December 1, 1831 (folio 8)

The Indian Saunders brought in 34 trout but only one Martin Skin; complains of the scarcity of them and Rabbits and Partridge are also scarce; supply'd him with provisions that he may be off tomorrow, to resume his hunt.

Thursday, December 15, 1831 (folios 9d-10)

The Indian Sanders [sic] came in with only 7 Martin Skins – and complaints of Poverty.

Monday, December 26, 1831 (folio 11)

The Indian Saunders return'd from visiting his Traps – 7 Martin Skins and 6 Pheasants was all he brought in.

Thursday, December 29, 1831 (folio11)

The people keeping holliday [sic] – The Indian Amutcheway – visited but added little to the Trade – Complains much of the scarcity of Martins, Rabbits and Birds this Winter – 3 Beavers, 13 martins, 5 Musquash and 100 Quill belonging to himself and his Brother Appee.

Image 3. Cree winter camp, James Bay. Some Cree hunting families in the James Bay area were still living in tents up until the 1970s.
Source: Public domain

Friday, December 30, 1831 (folio 11d)

Saunders and Amutcheway were both furnished with some Provisions, and they set off to renew their hunting.

Saturday, January 7, 1832 (folio 12d)

The Indian Saunders paid another visit but brought 6 martin and 1 Fisher Skin only.

Monday, January 16, 1832 (folio 13d)

Old Job and Ouskeegee – visited the former with 5 and the latter with 15 MBeaver – chiefly Beavers – these Indians complain much of hunger and scarcity of Martins, Rabbits, and Partridges this Winter.

Wednesday, January 18, 1832 (folio 14)

Waitchaiepaish brought 10 MBeaver – Chiefly Beaver Skins – complains much of the scarcity of this winter both of animals and Birds.

Thursday, January 19, 1832 (folio 14)

Supplied the Indian of Yesterday with some Provisions – and he returned for his Lodge.

Monday, January 23, 1832 (folio 14d)

The weather mild for most of the day – about 3AM two Indians [Nitaha] and Crooked Dick, 2 Indians who have been resident at Hannah Bay Post, had fled from there, without Mittens, Caps or Snowshoes to [preserve] their lives – They bring the melancholy Account of a Band of Rupert House Indians having taken Possession of the House and had killed an Indian Man and Woman outside the House (ere themselves [yel'd] for their own preservation) and am sorry to say very little hopes of Mr Corrigal or his wife escaping the same fate; as these Indians affirms the Band had shut the door to prevent their Entrance, but they distinctly heard 3 shots inside the House, with the cry of load again; in the Indian language – these 2 Indians were pursued some distance by a couple of the Villains, which obligated Crooked Dick to desert a Brother of his he was leading by the Hand as the last recourse of escaping their pursuers; – about 10AM another Indian Tishewyac, reach'd here. Wounded in the Hand, having had his own Chief shot under his arm, this Indian had done all he could to force the Door, but could not get in to help Mr Corrigal. Although he got one of the Rascals out of the door, they got him drag'd in again; – about 4PM Edward Richards (who was resident at that post) arrived much fatigued and Jaded – But all the light he can throw on this Brutal outrage, is that the band arrived on Friday last in a Starving and naked State; they got Provisions given to them, But on Sunday afternoon, by Stratagem having got all [these] Indians outside the House, they began their Bloody intentions.

Tuesday, January 24, 1832 (folios 15–15d)

From 33 above Zero yesterday, it was 23 below this morning; At 3AM – Mr Swanson accompanied by the following Men – Viz Thos Wigand, John Brown, Geo Moore B, John Richards, J Beads and Philip Turnor – (natives) – and W Linklater & J Goudie (Orkneymen) – Jean Marie Boucher, Paul Germain and Pierre Niveu (Canadians) left here for Hannah Bay Post – If Mr Swanson should not meet with the Murderers at the Post to make an example of – He is to proceed with his party to Ruperts House; and is the Bearer of a Letter to Mr Chief Factor Joseph Beioley to Inform him of the Crimes committed by the Indians belonging to his District.

Wednesday, January 25, 1832 (folio 15d)

Eggaienaishcum and the other Indians returned again, they brought 65 MBr in which quantity there was only 3 Otters and 2 Martins the other Furs being Beavers, they being driven to the necessity of killing these Animals, as there are no Martins – in short the scarcity of the Winter is complaind [*sic*] of by every arrival.

Thursday, January 26, 1832 (folios1b-2a)

[William Swanson[11] and his search party arrived at Hannah Bay]: not one living person was to be found; the Doors were standing open and the Windows destroyed. [Later that day after securing "furs and goods that could be found" [the search party] "went up the River a short distance and encamped."

Friday, January 27th to Sunday, January 29th, 1832 (folios 2b-3a)

[The next day Swanson's search party set out to find the culprits. On January 29, after a couple of days of searching, the party set off to try to find the offenders, with no success. Swanson no longer found it necessary to follow the shore and went on to Ruperts House to deliver a letter to Mr. Beioley that was made] "in case of not finding the Indians at Hannah Bay." [Also ...]

Having now examined so far along the coast without discovering any tracks or vestiges of the Indians whom we are seeking, I [William Swanson] considered it useless to follow the shore towards Nodaway River, therefore crossed the Bay from Black Bear Point and reached Ruperts House about 2 O'Clock in the afternoon. Delivered a Letter/ which I had in charge in case of not finding the Indians at Hannah Bay/ to Mr. Beioley, and acquainted him with the state in which I found things at Hannah Bay.

Wednesday, February 1, 1832 (folio 16d)

The Indians of the 25th Ultime, who have been living on the factory since that date, having finished their Snowshoes got some necessities they absolutely require to enable them to hunt, intending to proceed to their hunting Ground again tomorrow.

Thursday, February 2, 1832 (folio 3a)

[William Swanson's left Ruperts House on January 31st, 1832, for their return to Moose Factory. On February 2nd, 1832, looked and found a boy] who was reported to have accompanied the Indian lads and Edward Richards, in their escape from Hannah Bay on the [January] 22nd of last month; found it about 2 miles from the House; he had been shot, and at so short a distance that his clothes had taken Fire; conveyed the Body to the House, where we arrived at sunset, and found every thing in the same state as when we left here. Slept at the House.

Friday, February 3, 1832 (folio 3b)

At Daylight [Swanson's men] dug a Grave in the Potatoe Vault, the only place where the ground was not frozen. It was necessary to break down the Privy before the Bodies could be taken out ... that of Mr. Corrigal had been stripped of Coat, Waistcoat and Trousers, he was shot and stabbed; and his head wrapped round with a piece of Cloth, his Wife has been dreadfully cut. A coffin being made, Mr. Corrigal and Wife were then buried in as proper a manner as circumstances permitted; the Bodies of the Indians were also put into the Vault, and the door closed up with the Earth and Wood. Search was made for a little Girl, the Daughter of Pierre Robillard, who had been brought up by Mrs. Corrigal, and was with her on the morning of the murder, but in vain; we therefore concluded that the Indians had taken her along with them. The whole number of Individuals ascertained to be killed on this occasion is nine.

As we were making preparations for our departure, a Hannah Bay Indian (Quaquatcheshish) and his son arrived; we communicated to him what had occurred at the Post and amongst the Indians killed were two of his sons; gave the poor fellow a supply of such Provisions as there was remaining, with some ammunition, and he set off again with all speed to rejoin the rest of his family. The Furs and Property as to annexed List having been made up in convenient parcels last night, the Goods we were obliged to leave secured as well as possible, and every part of our painful duty performed, we sett of about 1 O'Clock and stopped at our encampment near the Big Stone for the night.

Saturday, February 4, 1832 (folio 17)

At dusk Mr William Swanson and party return'd without seeing any signs to enable them to track out the Murderers although they searchd (at the usual Places where they used to hunt) all along the Coast – from Hannah Bay Post to Ruperts House.

Yesterday upon their Return – they performed the last Offices to the Corpse of the murdered – viz – Mr Corrigal & wife – 1 Indian man – 2 Women – 1 Infant, and 3 boys – one of these was found (a distance from the House) on the River, supposed to be the Boy left by his Brother vide the 22nd Jany.

Mr Swansons party brought all the Furs at the House, and a few other Articles, but everything like Blankets, or wearing Apparel, together with all the Provisions, the Wretches have got clear off with, – and also a quantity of Provisions they Robbed the dead of part of their Apparel. A few Foxes and a number of Martin skins they have taken away, but no papers being found too [sic] prevents any reference being made to ascertain the exact number of skins – except from the Indians that escaped from there.

Monday, February 6, 1832 (folios17–17d)

The Indian Woman that arrived on Saturday, after getting a gun and Axe repaired, was furnished with some provisions to enable her to Continue her hunting – She set off to return to her Sons.

Saturday, February 11, 1832 (folio 18)

The Indian Waitchaiepaish Wife and five children set off to hunt again – ever since the 3ʳᵈ Instant they have been furnished with Provisions from the Store. The Mother being a feeble Old Woman, and an encumbrance to them this poor Winter has allowed to be left behind – 2 of her sons stays here also – as well as the 3 that escaped with their Lives from Hannah Bay one of whom is still under the Surgeons Care with his wounded hand.

Friday, February 17, 1832 (folio 18d)

At noon Keshickcoainnee arrived and in a starving state – Informs me that [Coteetis] and all his tribe were in a famishing condition and nearly unable to walk – dispatched John Richards, and an Indian immediately with provisions for them.

Saturday, February 18, 1832 (folio 18d)

The hunt of 2 Indians was only 6 pheasants.

Sunday, February 19, 1832 (folio 19)

About 7 this Evening John Richards and his Indian partner returned from [Cooteetig] with a Couple of sleds of Furs – The Indians being weak and fatigued encamped about 7 Miles off.

Monday, February 20, 1832 (folio 19)

[Cootutig], Apischaupaish and their families Arrived – they inform me that they were driven to the Necessity of eating their Skins (8 in number) ... being driven to the necessity of killing those Animals [the eight beaver?] for food ... 4 Indians had been poaching on their Grounds which made them more impoverished than otherwise they might have been.

Wednesday, February 22, 1832 (folio 19)

Ten men got orders to start tomorrow for Ruperts House ... between 10 and 11 AM Mr W Swanson, accompanied by Mr James Anderson[12] with a party of Ten men and four Indians—left here for Ruperts House.

Sunday, February 26, 1832 (folio 20)

An Indian belonging to the Albany District paid a Visit here – says his errand was to see a Relative here (Mr Flett) he acknowledges that he is come from that quarter without the consent or knowledge of Mr Chief Trader Jacob Corrigal. Said a Brother of his would be in tomorrow complains of privations this scarce Winter and says there [are] a number of Indians in at Albany under the same privations and receiving sustenance from Mr Jacob Corrigal.

Comment: Possibly this reference to Jacob Corrigal is in error, and that the author means William Corrigal. However, Jacob Corrigal might well be a post manager in the Albany District. Also, John McLean (1968 [1932], 99) indicated that "The post of Hannah Bay is situated about sixty miles to the north of Moose Factory, and was at this time (year not indicated, but on two pages previous, i.e., page 97, McLean indicates, "in the autumn of 1830."). Then in a footnote on the bottom of page 99 indicates that "Jacob Corrigal, an officer of the Hudson's Bay Company, who became a chief trader under the union of 1821." Quite probably Jacob Corrigal (1772–1844) is the brother of William Corrigal and he [Jacob] could have been the previous post manager of Hannah Bay in 1830. Jennifer Brown mentions that Jacob Corrigal had a country wife (1980: 140), and that "In 1840, Hudson's Bay Chief Factor Jacob Corrigal retired to Coburg (1980, 193)" where various other retired HBC men had taken up residence in the area. In addition, William Corrigal had a son named Jacob whose date of birth is not known; however, he was old enough to be named administrator of his father William's estate after the murder (A.36/5, fos.105–109; A.44/2, fo. 68). The journal comments are also interesting because they suggest that HBC factors exercised control over trapping territories, which should be a matter for further research.

Tuesday, February 28, 1832 (folio 20d)

Cold boisterous Weather – Cootutis, Arischaupaish, and Kishick-coaninnu with their families after a stay here from the 14th Instant recruiting their Strength at the expense of the Provision Store – set off to renew hunting – supplied them with some Provisions to enable them to begin in hopes they may be able to repay their debts which are large … The 2 Albany Indians were sent back they were furnished with provisions enough to enable them to reach their own District.

Friday, March 2, 1832 (folio 21)

Willow Ascare and his Son [Aitongahanban] brought 14 Martin skins their visit was chiefly to crave provisions to enable them to continue their trapping.

Saturday, March 3, 1832 (folio 21)

Thomas Richards was hunting and visited Mr Swansons [*sic*] … the Indian Visitors of Yesterday were furnished with Provisions to assist their own exertions and continue their trappings and they set off to return to their lodge.

Sunday, March 4, 1832 (folios 21–21d)

Wasspashtou and 3 Sons Indians belonging to Albany came in, craving provisions and complaining much of starvation – the above Men

[Brown and Beads] met 2 of them on their Route to Albany – and gave them a little assistance of Provisions and on the 28th Ult'e they were furnished with some from here, but which they consumed on the road without returning to their own quarters at Albany.

Wednesday, March 7, 1832 (folio 22)

the Indian Sanders [Saunders?] who has been absent 9 days looking for [Ground] bro't 5 Martins only – says Birds are scarce through the lands he travelled over, and Martin Tracks but few.

Monday, March 19, 1832 (folio 23d)

[Eggaienaisheum] and his Tribe, who has been here since the 9th Instant and furnished with food from the Factory. At last went off to renew his hunting and see if he can make a living of it this scarce Season – supplied him with some Provisions to enable him to reach his Grounds.

Wednesday, March 21, 1832 (folio 24)

Mr William Swanson and 3 Men set off for Rupert House.

Thursday, March 22, 1832 (folio 24)

3 of the Indians that went off the 13th Instant – came again with nothing but complaints of poverty – furnished 2 of them with a little Provisions that they may go after their Father [Eggaunaischeum] who left here last Monday.

Saturday, March 24, 1832 (folio 24d)

Kishickcoainnu was furnished with Provisions and returned to his hunting ground.

Sunday, March 25, 1832 (folios 5a and 5b)

[This entry details the arrival of Shaintoquaish (lame son of Quapakay) and Bolland (Son-in-law of Quapakay, son of Artawayham) suspects in the murder of William Corrigal and company at Rupert House (now on the Quebec side of James Bay) where they confessed their crime to postmaster Joseph Beioley and indicated that they were in a starving state.]

About 9 am People were observed approaching towards the House [Ruperts House] they proved to be two of the Four Indian men accused of the murder of Mr. Wm Corrigal at Hannah Bay, and of eight or nine other individuals (Male and Female natives of different age) on the 22nd of January last. The names of the two Indians now arrived are Shaintoquaish and Bolland, the first mentioned being the second son of old Quappukay [as in orig.] and the latter the son in Law of the same old man, their family accompanied them. They are said to have plundered Hannah Bay Post of so much Flour, Oatmeal and other Provisions, and of ammunition and Twines to that it would have been supposed they could not have suffered from Famine under almost any circumstances for a long time, they are at present in a more reduced state from starvation than I recollect ever to have seen Indians at any Post in the country.

They had striven hard to get the "Spirit above" not to enforce the task on them, because they had a disinclination to do what they thought to be wrong but that the "Spirit above" threatened and assured them that except they obeyed they should have all their children taken from them, that what was required of them was merely the Life of one "English man," and was trivial in comparison of what the "English" themselves did who fought with ships close to each other and killed great numbers of people (folios 6a and 6b).

Monday, April 2, 1832 (folio 26)

The following Men getting themselves ready to proceed again to Ruperts House quarter for the purpose of securing or making an Example of the rest of the Murderers if they can possibly be found – Viz John Goudie, Wm Johnson, [Andrew] Linklater, Jean Marie Boucher, Pierre Niveau, Jacques Paignant, James Beads, John Brown, [L] Wiegand, Geo Moore B, John Richards, Edward Richards and an Indian – the 3 [latter] had Relatives massacred by these Fiends … the Indian Arrivals of yesterday were all Supplied with Provisions to enable them to continue their hunting and they went off again.

Tuesday, April 3, 1832 (folios 26–26d)

[A search party under the command of William Swanson was sent out with Shaintoquaish to find the other Indians (folio 9a). Shaintoquaish] "promised to act as guide in finding out the rest of the gang" [but then the] "Indian either could not or would not walk" [and was killed after it was put on a sled for while (up until Middleburg) and then was seen to be too much of a burden (folio 9a). Stacemow's (son of Quapakay) wife went with the search party to help find the other Indians who were involved in the Hannah Bay Massacre (folio 9b). In the end, all who plundered the Hannah Bay post on January 23rd, 1832, were killed and the wives and children were given provisions (folios 9b and 10a).]

About 5 AM Mess'rs William Swanson, James Anderson and John Geo McKenzie – Accompanied by the party mentioned yesterday – set off for Ruperts House – the Indian prisoner was released from his irons and went off in Company – but pretending he could not walk in hopes of making his Escape should the party leave him an opportunity, they hauled him away about 4 miles – when he began to [murmur], and the Indians Shot him. Mr Chief Factor. Joseph Beioley and his three men left here for Ruperts House about Noon. In the afternoon sent three 3 [*sic*] Men to dig a hole and Inter the Body of the Murderer.

Comment: Note remark by Francis and Morantz 1983: 158):

Beioley conducted the two men to Moose, and although Bolland escaped enroute, his brother-in-law (Shaintoquaish) agreed in return for his life to lead a pose of Hudson's Bay Company men in search of the other accused (B.135/a/138,7). This party left Moose early in April. Shaintoquaish, who appeared to be lame, was hauled on a sled until he was thought to be too much of a burden on the expedition and was summarily shot. (B.135/a/138, 9).

Question: The HBC journal entry above, presumably written by John McTavish, states that Shaintoquaish was "pretending he could not walk in hopes of making his Escape," would suggest that McTavish believed that Shaintoquaish was not lame at all, only *pretending* to be so, while Francis and Morantz suggest that he was, in fact, lame. An important question here is whether or not the Hudson's Bay Company would condone the killing of an Indigenous man who had volunteered to act as a guide for the Swanson's search party would be summarily shot and killed simply because he *appeared* to be disabled, and as a consequence was unable to keep pace with the rest of Swanson's expeditionary party. Or was he simply killed because he was a suspect in the murder of William Corrigal and party, as his father, Quapakay, was?

Saturday, April 7th, 1832 (folio 40b, Rupert House Journal)

Bolland's (son-in-law of Quapakay) wife, I (probably Joseph Beioley) observed her

preparing to take her departure I told her in the hearing of the Indians, that she must not think of leaving this place, until I receive order to that effect from any superiors and that if she made the attempt to get away, it would surely excuse mischief to be done on the spot (folio 40b).

Comment: This entry could be interpreted to suggest that Post Master Beioley was making a direct threat to the life of Boland's wife. This threat by Beioley in an attempt to force Bolland's wife to remain at the Ruperts House post apparently against her will is in direct contradiction to Governor George Simpson's report to the HBC London Committee of July 1832, in which he states that "the women and children were set at liberty, being furnished with necessary supplies to enable them to provide for themselves" (folio 60).

Note also the Moose Factory journal entry of April 3, 1832, in which it is stated (by John McTavish) that "Stacemow's wife went with the search party to help find the other Indians"; however, there is no mention of Bolland's wife similarly helping out in this task. In addition, there is an entry in the Rupert House Post journal of April 4, 1832, indicating that Bolland escaped from two of the "Moose Men" and he was said to have "arrived at Attawayhaw's [probably his father Artawayham] tent, on last Sunday." As such, Joseph Beioley was apparently keeping Bolland's wife as a hostage in an attempt to entrap her escaped husband.

Sunday, April 8, 1832 (folio 27)

In the Afternoon [Olicketashish] arrived with his Winters hunt amounting to 78 MBeaver – chiefly Beavers – all these Indians complains greatly of scarcity of Martins this Winter, exclusive of being pinched for food this scarce season ... The [kille?] and [Kishickican-innu] with their family, and [Areare] with her 2 Sons came in all craving Alms and complaining much that there is nothing to be got for hunting.

Monday, April 9, 1832 (folio 27)

At 111/2 AM Mess'rs W Swanson, J Anderson, and John Geo McKenzie – with their party returned all safe having found the murders, and inflicted that punishment their Crimes merited, without hurting either Woman or Children – it seems it was their further intention, had there been a small party travelling between here and Ruperts House to have murdered and plundered them.

Journal of an Expedition to Punish the Murderers of Mr. and Mrs. Corrigal and Eight Other Individuals: James Anderson, April 1832

James Anderson's journal begins with entries on Tuesday, April 3, 1832, and concludes on April 9, 1832. The journal begins:

> Started from Moose Factory in company with Mess'rs Swanson, McKenzie, 13 men and Santoquiesh a prisoner (the murderer of Mrs. Corrigal and 2 other women, and was brought here from Ruperts House by Mr. Beioley) we took this man with us as a guide if we could not do without him, but finding he would not walk we hauled him to Middleburgh 4 miles from the factory and there shot him ... Mr. Beioley and 3 men arrived about 9 P.M.

Anderson's journal then describes weather conditions: "Blowing a hurricane, snowing and drifting so much that we could not cross the Bay," and continues with a description of their camping arrangements and details of the terrain that they were travelling over. On April 6, the party came upon some tracks in the woods and after crossing a small swamp noticed smoke about one mile distant, at which point they

commenced a general chase, and after running about 4 miles came up with 2 women and a boy, who proved to be the wife of Stacemow, one of the murderers, her son and the daughter of Quappekay, another of the villains and the father of Stacemow and Santoquie's boy. They informed us that their tent was close at hand and that Stacemow and Quappekay and a younger son were out, that there was no one at the tent but Quappekay's wife the children and Stacemow's eldest son, one of their conjurers and principal instigator of the dreadful crimes they have committed: we told them that if they guided us faithfully and told us no falsehoods their lives should be spared as well as those of the children, but on the contrary if they deceived us in one instance death would be the penalty. Sent the women in the front formed the party and entered the woods we came upon the Tent unobserved and desired the women to enter and inform the rest directly afterwards the Conjurer came running out with some of his apparatus towards a tent which had been formed for his operations before he reached it he was seized, his hands tied behind his back, thrown into his tent and 2 men placed over him, in the mean time the other tent had been entered, the Guns (4), powder, shot &c(?) taken out, and a guard placed over it, we here divided the men Party, leaving 7 men and taking the remaining 8 and Stacemow's wife as a guide along with us in search of Stacemow, Quappekay and a lad of about 15 years of age, whom the wife said had been keeping watch for any small party which might have been passing, we found the place where they had been watching the day before and after proceeding about 1/2 mile further perceived Stacemow walking in the willows, desired the woman to call out to him when he came towards us rushed upon him deprived him of his gun tied his hands behind his back and sent two of the men back with him to the tent not wishing to shoot till we had secured the whole. The women now guided us to Quappekay's Track which we followed through the woods about 3 miles when we came upon the lad whose axe we seized and desired him to lead to the Father, we here agreed directly we got Quappekay to shoot him and the lad as there was now no danger of alarming the rest, after walking about a quarter of a mile we discovered Quappakay in the willows, we closed upon him deprived him of his gun (which was on full cock) and shot him as well as the Lad, returned to the Tent where we found Stacemow and the Conjurer safe in the conjuring tent took off the Tentings and shot them.

Anderson then indicates that while all this shooting was going on, "Jacob Corrigal (one of Mr. B's [Beioley, no doubt] men) had selected all the property which had belonged to his late father" and other various goods. Stacemow's wife was sent back to Ruperts House with Mr. Beioley and, with the other women, given provisions 9 flour, oatmeal, pork and bacon), *"as the women and children were, and had been for some time, in a complete starvation"* [emphasis mine]. He then concludes:

> Thus was happily ended the Expedition without the loss of one life or even one person being wounded a thing which we could hardly expect considering the desperate character of the men with whom we had to deal. The women informed us that it was the intention of the men to attack any party, wither of Indians or Europeans, when they could do it with safety to themselves, or could gain anything by it, for which purpose they kept strict watch on the points.[13]

Governor George Simpson to HBC London Committee, July 1832

Note: The following is a summary of details in a letter that Governor George Simpson wrote to the Hudson's Bay Company's London Committee detailing the Hannah Bay murders and the expedition sent out to apprehend the culprits of the crime. For whatever reason it took Governor Simpson six months to provide his response concerning the incident to his superiors in London.

The letter recounts the following details:

> The small outpost or Goose hunting station of Hannah Bay, about 40 miles distant from Moose, I lament to say was last winter the scene of one of the most horrible massacres ever heard of in that or any other part of this country. It appears by the letters and other documents herewith transmitted that this post, which was occupied by a very respectable old servant named William Corrigal, who had long been a postmaster and was for several years past on the superannuated list, was visited in the month of January last by a family of Ruperts river Indians named Quapakay his sons and sons in law, say four men, with their women and children, a young man of about 19 and a lad of 15 years of age, seventeen in all. They were received with the usual hospitality by Corrigal, and remained there for some days, watching as it since appears a favorable opportunity of

carrying their murderous plan into effect. The inmates of the Establishment were Corrigal, his wife and twelve men, women and children, Indians and half-breeds. Corrigal himself was the only European of the party. A fitting opportunity for their bloody work at length presented itself, while two young men belonging to Corrigal's party were out of doors, and they forth word enacted themselves by attacking the inmates with their Guns, Hatchets and Knives, destroying 10 individuals. The two lads on hearing the work in doors and discovering the causes started off with the intelligence to Moose, and were soon followed by an old Indian who escaped wounded. ... Mr. MacTavish [sic] with great promptitude dispatched an armed party after the murderers ... The bodies of their unfortunate victims were shockingly mangled and concealed in a privy. After the corpses were interred and the remaining properly secured the party preceded to Ruperts River, made their melancholy report to Chief Factor Beioley, and soon afterwards returned to Moose [the letter then outlines details of the ensuing investigations by Chief Factor Beioley and William Swanson, the details of which are not repeated here]. Mr. Beioley soon after proceeded to Moose with one of the murderers, and a party under the direction of W. Swanson, the Sloop Master, was immediately dispatched in search of the rest with this man [probably Shaintoquaish, who had returned to Ruperts River and reported the crime to Chief Factor Beioley] as their guide. They succeeded in securing all, six in number, say 4 men and two young men of 19 and 15 years, and forth with inflicted the punishment of death upon them, the only punishment which could serve the ends of justice and deter others from the like crimes. A great part of the stolen property was recovered, and the women and children were set at liberty, being furnished with necessary supplies to enable them to provide for themselves. (A.12/1 folios 59–60)

Comments: The letter mentions "2 young men of 19 and 15 years" being part of the party of Ruperts River Indians; however, these individuals were not mentioned before in other documents. Notice also that Simpson justifies the violence by asserting that it was the "only punishment which could serve the ends of justice and deter others from like crimes." This implies that Simpson feared possible further acts of violence on the part of the Cree in the James Bay area. Also note that Simpson was reassuring the Committee that "a great part of the stolen property was recovered" indicating the material interests of the London Committee's concern with a possible loss of HBC property.

Records of Food Deprivation: The HBC Journals
(October 1831–April 1832)

Rather than discuss each item in the post journal of Moose Factory as they appear by date, a more prudent strategy would be to discuss central themes emerging from the activities at the post as noted by John McTavish, the chief factor and probable writer of these accounts.

The journal records events from October 21, 1831, when a supply boat was sent to the Hannah Bay Post from Moose Factory, and ends on April 9, 1832, with the news that Mr. Swanson and his party killed the supposed killers of William Corrigal and others at Hannah Bay on January 23, 1832. In other words, these HBC accounts cover virtually the entire winter of events on the southern James Bay coast during 1831–2 period. The three most prominent themes that emerge from these records pertain to (1) the activities of the Cree, who appear to reside near the Moose Factory post, often referred to as the Home Guard Cree; (2) frequent reports of food deprivation; and (3), reprisals for the killings at Hannah Bay Post. It is the assertion here that all three of these variables are linked.

In the first two of these entries, made on October 21 and 29, 1831, men are sent with supplies to the Hannah Bay Post and return with 12 casks of geese. It is difficult to determine the quantities of geese in these casks, but it would appear to represent a sizeable amount of food derived from an area of southern James Bay, well known for its food shortages. However, from information derived from other historical sources it is evident that the Hudson's Bay Company hired professional hunters to secure food for its various posts. Carlson (2008: 79), for example, states that "[game] birds were salted down in barrels and kept for winter use; the HBC early on tapped into this traditional Native resource. A small group of hunters ... worked[ed] seasonally as goose hunters. These 'home guard' Natives, as they were known, fed the traders in an important way."

Ray and Freeman (1978: 41) elaborate further by explaining that securing food supplies from Europe was relatively expensive, so, in order "to cut costs, every effort was made to obtain as much food as possible in the bay area. But, since labour was in short supply and many of the men were not skilled hunters and trappers, the Hudson's Bay Company turned to the Indians for the major portion of the food supplies that were used. They encouraged the Indians to bring in moose and deer meat and geese when they came to the posts to trade. Indeed, some Indians were hired to serve as post hunters, particularly goose hunters in the spring and fall." Preston (1981: 196–7) supports this description by noting that "Home Guard Indians ... were in the steady employ of the Hudson's Bay Company or other white organizations." Thus, from the perspective of the Hudson's Bay Company, and its directors and shareholders who may never have even seen James Bay, it would appear to be a prudent economic measure to secure as much of a fort's supplies locally as a way of reducing costs. But at what cost to the trappers and their families in the James Bay area who did not have the luxury to feed themselves from other sources?

It would be a different matter altogether if there was as much country food in the James Bay area that could be used to adequately feed both the Cree and the Europeans; then no one would have reason for complaint. However, as is patently evident in the almost daily HBC reports the local Indigenous population was suffering from serious food deprivations:

> "Most of the Indians came from the Marshes, saying it was useless to remain any longer, as all the wild fowl had fled" (October 29, 1831); "The Indian Saunders ... complains of the scarcity of them [martins] and Rabbits and Partridges are also scarce" (December 1, 1831).
>
> "The Indian Saunders ... complains of Poverty" (December 15, 1831); "The Indian Amutcheway – visited but added little to the Trade – Complains much of the scarcity of Martins, Rabbits and Birds this winter" (December 29, 1831); "Old Job and Ouskeegee ... these Indians complain much of hunger and scarcity" (January 16, 1832),
>
> "Waitchaiepaish ... complains much of the scarcity of this Winter both of Animals and Birds" (January 18, 1832); "All the light he [Edward Richards] can throw on this Brutal outrage, is that the band [presumably Quapakay and family] arrived on Friday last in a Starving and naked State" (January 23, 1832). "Eggaienaishcum and the other Indians arrived again ... they being driven to the necessity of killing these Animals [five otters and martins, meaning presumably, killing these animals for food] – in short the scarcity of the Winter is complained of by every arrival" (January 25, 1832); "the Indians of the 25th Ultime (?) ... got some necessities they absolutely require to enable them to hunt" (February 1, 1832); "At dusk Mr William Swanson and party return'd [to report that] every thing like Blankets, or wearing Apparel, together with all the Provisions, the Wretches have got clear off with – and also a quantity of Provisions, they Robbed the dead of part of their Apparel" (February 4, 1832). [Note: it was reported that most items of value, such as furs and other trade items were left at the post, indicating one would presume that the intruders were mostly interested in securing warm clothing and provisions as opposed to robbing the post of valuables.]

"The Indian woman that arrived on Saturday ... was furnished with provisions" (February 6, 1832), "The Indian Waitchaiepaish Wife and five children ... [were] furnished with Provisions from the Store" (February 11, 1832); "About noon Keshickcoainnee arrived in a starving state – Informs me that [Coteetis] and all his tribe were in a famishing condition and nearly unable to walk" (February 17, 1832); "This evening John Richards and his Indian partner returned with a Couple of Sleds of Furs – the Indians [who owned the furs] being [too] weak and fatigued [to bring the furs in to the post themselves]"(February 19, 1832); "Apischaupaish and their families Arrived – they inform me that they were driven to the necessity of eating their Skins ... being driven to the necessity of killing those Animals for Food ... besides the scarcity of prov's this season, 4 Indians, had been poaching on their grounds which made them impoverished than otherwise they might have been (February 20, 1832).

"An Indian belonging to [the] Albany District paid a Visit here ... complains much or privations this scarce Winter and says there are a number of Indians in at Albany under the same privations" (February 26, 1832); "Willow Ascare and his Son [arrive] their visit was chiefly to crave Provisions" (March 2, 1832); "Wasspashtou and 3 Sons Indians belonging to Albany came in, craving provisions and complaining much of starvation" (March 4, 1832); "the Indian Saunders ... says birds are scarce through the land he travelled over" (March 7, 1832); "[Eggaienasisheum] and his Tribe ... furnished with food from the Factory" (March 19, 1832); "3 of the Indians that went off the 13th Instant – came again with nothing but complaints of poverty – furnished 2 of them with a little Provisions" (Mach 22, 1832); "Kishickcoainnu was furnished with Provisions" (March 24, 1832), and "In the afternoon [Olicketashish] arrived ... all these Indians complain greatly of the Scarcity of Martins this Winter, exclusive of being pinched for food this scarce season ... [Kishickicaninnu] with his family, and Areare] with her 2 Sons came in all craving alms and complaining much that there is nothing to got for hunting" (April 8, 1832).

The reader's forbearance is requested at this point for having been made to re-read this sorrowful litany of complaints about food shortages, deprivation, and starvation in the James Bay area, but how is it that a human being with any conscience at all could remain unaffected by such testimony? One wonders also how many more of these complaints went unrecorded and the extent of the food shortages that lead to actual starvation; there were even reports of cannibalism from other quarters of the HBC territory.

The main point made here is that the HBC post managers could hardly be oblivious to the extent of the suffering of their Indigenous

clients, and for this reason must hold a certain culpability for the suffering that they were witness to on an almost daily basis. There are no
reports that this author could discover of any ameliorative efforts made
on the part of the factors to alleviate the hunger, except for providing
small amounts of food so that a trapper could return to his hunting territory. Under the circumstances it seems particularly insensitive to hire
professional hunters in the Cree's territory to essentially rob the Cree
trappers of their own food. Of course, the HBC factors controlled the reporting of the situation through their post journals – we have no surviving reports of the Cree themselves except for their persistent complaints
of deprivation. We also have no reports of possible starvation or even
worse, cannibalism, resulting from the food shortages. Nonetheless,
when the HBC personnel hired professional hunters, they in effect stole
food from the mouths of vulnerable women and children and served
to be a self-defeating strategy when the trappers themselves were no
longer able to support the posts with furs because they were too weak
to perform such tasks.

As far as the third variable is concerned, that is, acts of retribution,
one is reminded of Preston's Cree informant John Blackned's comment:
"The reason the Indians did that was because the manager wasn't trying to help them. That's what the boss told the manager. I don't know if
that's right. I heard that those Indians were hard up at the time" (2002,
174). On the subject of the Cree views of the English traders, a Cree
trapper at Great Whale River claimed that "the whites did not readily
share food and the local people thought of them as stingy despite the
teachings of the Bible. In terms of collective behaviour, they also found
the whites 'over emotional and addicted to uncalled for petulance and
anger'" (Morantz (2002).

Despite these Cree views of the English traders, Quapakay and his
sons could have simply stolen food from the Hannah Bay Post, but they
killed Corrigal, his wife, and others as an act of retribution for not helping them in their time of need, when Corrigal had the means to do so.
Then, in turn, Swanson and his party of HBC men shot and killed Quapakay and his sons in a further act of retribution for killing Corrigal and
supposedly to prevent further acts of violence among a starving Cree
population in the area.

John George McTavish to HBC London Committee, September 15, 1832

In his annual report to the HBC London Committee, John McTavish
of the Moose District begins with several of his needs, such as a boat

builder, and comments on the abysmal results of the hunt in most cases, and thus lower monetary returns to the Company shareholders, as well as there being cases of famine reported among the Natives. Of particular interest is the report's details surrounding the murders at Hannah Bay, how the post was plundered, and an account of the results of a party sent out to capture the offenders. As such, in John McTavish's own words:

> The returns of this District have also partially failed, this is partly owing to an unsuccessful hunt for small furs, and mainly to an unfortunate catastrophe which befell the Post of Hannah Bay in the month of January last, when it became the scene of one of the cruelest and most abominably deliberate murders I have ever heard of in the Indian Country – in which Mr. William Corrigal the person in charge, his wife, and seven Indians of the Post lost their lives, and the Post was pillaged of all its goods by a family party of Ruperts House Indians consisting of a father, two sons, two grandsons and a son in law with all their women and children. The only servant Mr. Corrigal had, a boy/Edward Richards/ escaped with two young Indians and a wounded man, from whom and the subsequent observations of our own people we could pick up the following story. On the 20th of January the Party of Ruperts House Indians as enumerated above, with 15 empty [Slidges?], arrived at Hannah Bay House in apparently a wretched condition from starvation and living badly clothed Mr. Corrigal [received] them as was his want with kindness, giving them bountifully to eat, and allowing them shelter under his roof; they thus remained until the fatal 22nd about, noon when watching an opportunity when the Indian lads of the Post who happened to be there allured to the Bank and the [doors] secured, they began the cruel work of death and stopped only when their victims were all destroyed or fled. They then deliberately cleared the house of all the corpses by pushing them into the common privy and passed the night or two preparing and packing up the booty which consisted of provisions, furs, and trading goods they carried off. So soon as this news reached me, I immediately sent out a party of armed men under Mr. Swanson of the union(?), to endeavor to overtake the murderers. Bad weather set in and baffled [his] excursion to find out their [haunt] for some time.

McTavish's report continues to discuss the hunt for the culprits and the fact that two were found visiting Mr. [Joseph] Beioley's post. Consequently, Mr. Swanson was sent out again to capture them, his men coming across and killing all but one man, "who was killed by a Party of Mr. Beioley's men afterwards." As well, McTavish writes that "I am happy to have it in my power to report, the truly guilty met the fate they so richly merited without any of the disagreeable consequences of a [m---not] a woman or child was molested and our own people, thank God, returned without a scratch or even having been in any danger – and this is chiefly owing to the cool masterly manner in which the Party was conducted." Lastly, McTavish asks that Captain Swanson's services be rewarded with a raise in his current salary to help out his large family (A.11/46 folios 15–20).

Comment: In McTavish's report to the London Committee, and other HBC accounts of the capture and killing of Quapakay and his sons, the matter is described in an almost heroic manner, as if ten or fifteen well-armed men would have found any resistance in the arrest of an old man and his apparently starving sons. Another peculiarity is that no-where in these account that one can find is there any assessment of the situation or any thoughts on why this unfortunate situation occurred at all. One would presume that an investigation, even a partial one conducted by the Hudson's Bay Company's own employees, would have some interest in ascertaining the reason why such murders took place. The purpose of such an investigation might be to prevent a similar catastrophe from happening again, but, unfortunately, such reasons seem hardly of any importance the London Committee or anyone else in the fur trade.

Perhaps, and this is possibly the underlying reason that no investigation was ever conducted, the Hudson's Bay personnel knew the reason(s) why such a violent act could take place, and as such had no motivation to scrutinize what everyone already knew. Such an investigation would by necessity delve into the Hudson Bay Company's treatment of the Indigenous people of Northern Canada and, thereby, uncover and possibly be made public, facts that would run counter to the favourable narrative of a "Company of Gentlemen and Adventurers" that the HBC so ardently promoted about themselves. Certainly, the HBC would not want it widely known that the northern fur trade was causing ineffable hardships, a persistent state of food deprivation, and other unutterable sources of misery for the Indigenous people upon whom the Company depended for the inflow of wealth, upon which members of the HBC London Committee used in support of their life of inestimable luxury back in their home country. James Bay was a long way from London; the fate of the Indigenous people of the area and their problems could easily be forgotten over a succulent dinner of roast goose, beef, or pork, imported French wine, and other delicacies served up by a veritable army of cooks, waiters, and other servants of the household.

In addition, back at Hudson's Bay, it is evident that the chief factors such as John McTavish were hardly known to have suffered food deprivation of any sort. Mr. McTavish himself was known for his gross obesity. Governor Simpson, with whom Mr. McTavish had amicable relations, commented in 1832 that he was concerned with McTavish's extravagant living habits and signs of intemperance. In fact, as Van Kirk points out, "By the early 1830s McTavish had become so corpulent that a friend declared he had never seen 'such a stout man'" (2003, 2). One must wonder what might have been going through the minds of his Indigenous clients, starving out on their trap lines, to come into the trading post at Moose Factory and witness the gluttonous sight that McTavish must have presented.

The Sorrowful Semantics of Starvation

The term "starvation" could have any number of meanings, depending on the context in which it is used, and several nuances. As such, a more precise discussion is needed to understand this phenomenon as, for example, in the possible difference between starvation, chronic hunger, deprivation, and so on. In *Hunger: The Biology and Politics of Starvation* (2010), Butterly and Shepard differentiated several of the terms involved. For example, their discussion focuses on two defining theories: those of Thomas Malthus and Amartya Sen, concerning hunger, starvation, and famine.

Thomas Malthus, in his *An Essay on the Principles of Population* ([1798] 1999), suggested that population growth, when left unchecked, will increase at a geometric ratio such that a population will double about every twenty-five years. As such, the level of subsistence will determine the population growth trajectory, or alternatively, population would be controlled as balance in the availability of the food supply. While there are several objections that have been raised by Malthus's approach, the primary one is that his theory was not necessarily borne out by the history of Western Europe. The reasons were that (a) European population growth was not nearly as steep as Malthus predicted, and (b) rapid advances in technology were largely responsible for increased food production.

For Amartya Sen, the Indian economist and philosopher, as set out in *Poverty and Famines* (1982), his main theory is that famines occur not only, or even primarily, from a lack of food, but from inequities built into the mechanisms for distributing food. In a later work entitled, *The Idea of Justice* (2009), Sen further developed his ideas on famine and poverty by focusing on human rights, on human capabilities, and on the importance of public discussion in democracies.

Instead of discussing such an all-encompassing term as "starvation," which by itself has little utility, a more useful approach is to discuss possible variations or nuances to this term, such as to differentiate among chronic hunger, malnutrition, starvation, and famine (Butterly and Shepard 2010: 28–30). In this regard, famine can be understood as a process or as a continuum beginning with hunger and ending with famine with stages of malnutrition and starvation in between. In addition, this process is not an evitable one-way progression since impoverished people can slip back and forth between these various conditions; in other words, one condition may progress to another such that survivors of starvation may slide back into a previous condition, which is usually one of chronic hunger or seasonal malnutrition.

Hunger, for example, can be understood as a "recurrent, involuntary lack of access to food" (ibid., 2010, 28–9). Or, "hunger occurs when people do not have enough to eat for a healthy, active life" (Watts 1983: 3). Quite often this involves seasonal hunger, which occurs before a harvest or in other lean periods in a subsistence cycle.

Chronic hunger is a condition that continues from season to season and does not necessarily end with a harvest. Typically, it is a condition that occurs on a daily basis and over a long period of time extending even into years.

Malnutrition refers to a deficiency or other imbalance of specific nutrients which are deemed necessary for good health and can occur with obesity even when an excess of food is available.

Starvation is a condition where people suffer from long-term, extreme hunger to the point where their lives are at risk.

Famine can be defined as "a shortage of total food so extreme and protracted as to result in widespread persisting hunger, notable emaciation in many of the affected population, and a considerable elevation of community deaths from starvation" (Bennett 1968: 322). In another definition, Fields refers to famine as "*the endpoint* of a lengthy process in which people in increasing numbers lose their access to food [italics in original]" (1993: 4).

It is probable that with each of these preceding conditions there would be associated disorders such as high mortality rates, a breakdown or disintegration of a society, or the occurrence of a variety of various diseases. In an attempt to tie these various conditions together, Scrimshaw suggests the following description of starvation as a societal process:

"The essential element is a relatively sudden collapse in the level of food *consumption* by large numbers of people. Starvation refers to people's going without sufficient food, and during famines people do so on such a large scale that mortality is high … Famine is not just the result of an extreme and protracted shortage of food but is also an economic and social phenomenon that can occur *when food supplies are adequate to prevent it*" [italics in original] (1987, 2).

A Loss of Entitlements

These various definitions are useful in differentiating various gradations or distinctions of hunger-stricken people, but they do not by themselves suggest what the various underlying conditions could be that cause these disorders in the first place. As mentioned previously, one may think of these causes in a Malthusian sense as "acts of God," such that increasing population growth overtakes the existing food supply that would otherwise be available to feed the suffering people. On the other hand, a much more recent approach, by Amartya Sen (1981, 2009) for example, would suggest that starvation is the result of poverty, vulnerability, and a "loss of entitlements."

It would be a mistake, though, to suggest that Malthus or Sen propose diametrically opposed ideas, or that a combination of the two would also not be useful. As an example, an expanding population may be just as important in a causal sense than collapsing food production, but the important point is that a balance needs to be maintained between population and a subsistence economy. A population decline may also be understood as a casual factor when this decline accelerates in a manner that is coincident with an even greater decline in the availability of food.

In his theoretical approach, Sen uses the term "catalytic causes" to suggest that there could be intermediate agents that are prone to tip or "trigger" a vulnerable people over into starvation. There may be a variety of these agents that act together such as corrupt or weak governments that cause food shortages through mismanagement of a region's subsistence resources, or civil conflicts which disrupt agricultural planning, crop planting, or markets. There are other possible environmental conditions, such as droughts, flooding, or crop diseases, that can result in a food crisis. Societies that rely on a single crop for sustenance, such as the potato grown by the Irish poor, place people at risk of starvation in the event of a crop failure. Other contributing factors could include unsafe drinking water and poor sanitation resulting in various diseases such as cholera, dysentery, or typhoid fever causing death long before people actually die of starvation.

Central to Sen's argument is the idea that certain people who suffer from food deprivation lack *entitlements* or enough assets to access food. As the argument goes, there are always people in a society that is undergoing severe food deprivation who have enough food to eat, such as the wealthy, government officials, or military officers. Such people usually have sufficient entitlements to survive periodic food shortages because they are not exposed to the vulnerability characteristic of the poor in society. As such, as Sen writes, "people starve because (1) they have insufficient real income and wealth *and* (2) because there are no other means to acquire food" (1982: 459).

The implications, then, of Sen's approach are rather obvious. Starvation will never be alleviated by short-term or stop-gap measures, such as Hudson's Bay Company post managers doling out small amounts of food on an emergency basis to distraught Indigenous trappers just sufficient to feed them so that they will be able to travel back to their trap lines. In the context of food deprivation in the James Bay area, it is also useful to discuss Mary Black-Rogers's study of the semantics of starvation during the fur-trade era of 1750–1850. Her main conclusion is that "fur trade documents contain a selective view of Indian cultures and a business-biased record of the events they witnessed" (1986: 353). In other words, it was in the financial self-interest of the Hudson's Bay Company to minimize reporting of the deleterious effects of the fur trade on the James Bay environment and its Indigenous population. In turn, this goal was at least partially achieved through a rigorous control of the fur-trade narrative in the post journals and other documents. The result is that "readers of fur-trade documents are likely to get a rather lopsided idea about the trader's Indian customers if they rely solely on that man of business for their knowledge" (1986: 354).[14]

The manner in which the Cree accounts of their situations of food deprivation are portrayed in the post journals is an important facet of the manner in which the fur trade narrative is crafted and governed. As an example, the post journals of Moose Factory do report situations of food deprivation on a fairly regular basis, but no accounts of actual deaths resulting from starvation are reported [as far as this author is able to determine in the selective documents examined]. As Black-Rogers notes, references to starvation or other descriptions of food deprivation "are sprinkled quite generously throughout these writings" (1986: 353). In any event, those Cree suffering from food deprivation are sent off to their trap lines with provisions from the factory's larder, thus apparently solving the problem. Any causes of this deprivation are seen in terms of the vagaries of weather conditions, animal movements, or other external factors beyond the control of the HBC, thus absolving them of any responsibility in the matter.

Varieties of Starving

In terms of the semantics of starvation in the post journals is concerned, "'starving' came in a number of varieties, and that only some of the statements are literal, the others conveying messages of a different sort" (1986: 353). What sort of messages? one might ask. Black-Rogers identifies three sorts of messages: *literal* refers simply to a lack of food, *technical* indicates that fur supplies are low because of a lack of food, and *manipulative* messages that go beyond these first two. For example, when a Cree trapper used the term "starving" in discussions with the post manager he might not mean this in a literal sense as being close to death from lack of sustenance, Black-Rogers suggests, but as a means of indicating that the fur quest has become a matter of secondary importance to the search for food so that the meaning of the message is created in a metaphorical form.

One of the problems of determining the semantics of starvation is that starvation, which is to say actually "starving to death," is a complicated process involving a series of interrelated events. Death, for example, may finally come in the form of freezing during the Subarctic winter. As a process, starvation may be interrupted by short periods when small amounts of food are available but not enough to sustain life. A low supply of food may not actually lead to death in itself but reduce a person's ability to combat disease, create adequate shelter and clothing, trap furs with which to trade for ammunition or have the required energy to hunt for game, even though such game may be available in the vicinity.

There is also the matter of religious ideology in terms of the relationship between the Cree and the animals hunted. As Tanner (2005: 211) explains for the Mistassini Cree, "in times of shortage and starvation the whole exchange relationship with the animals breaks down. This viewpoint can be seen as an ideology which hides the contradiction between the use of a strategy of environmental control, in the form of hunting territories, rotation of land and exchange of hunting privileges, and the continual preparedness for starvation times and the consequent discontinuities in the land use pattern." In this sense, starvation is not so much the fundamental result of food deprivation per se, but of a more fundamental matter such as a breakdown in spiritual or ideological relationships.

Conclusion

A discussion of various forms of deprivation and their effects on social systems is presented by Laughlin and Brady in terms of adaptive responses. The most extreme form they identify as "unremitting deprivation. This form of deprivation results from a dramatic and progressive decrement in the resource base of a given population. It is marked by periods of deprivation that predominate over periods of abundance to the extent that abundance rather than scarcity is perceived by the actors as an environmental aberrancy" (1978: 28). It is suggested that this description best characterized the living conditions of the Cree trappers in the James Bay area.

The suggestion that reports in the HBC journals referring to starvation and food deprivation can be interpreted in various ways – that this reporting is all a matter of semantics – suggests that perhaps Native trappers exaggerated their condition in order to bargain better terms from the fur trader. One might regard the idea that reports of starvation among the northern Indigenous population is not much more than a literary debate about meaning and interpretation as an egregious act of misinterpretation that hardly does justice to the daily life-and-death struggles and seems particularly callous.

The fur traders had no reason whatsoever to parse words or attempt to misconstrue what the Cree were telling them. The idea that the Cree and the Europeans lived in different realms of reality and therefore the traders were not capable of understanding the Cree's intentions in describing their deprivation is also an unconscionable act of casuistry in the face of such human suffering. In fact, one would think that the traders would have every motive for not reporting these instances of deprivation, lest their superiors demand some actions that would reduce the company's profits, such as bringing more food supplies from England rather than employing professional hunters to strip the land of game.

In sum, available research suggests the following conclusions. First, the area around James Bay, often termed the Hudson Bay Lowlands, is, and has been in the past, one of the most inhospitable environmental areas in North America as far as game populations is concerned. The deficient resource base of this area is able to support one of the lowest population densities on the continent. Second, historical studies suggest that the Hudson Bay Lowlands was not inhabited by Indigenous people on any consistent basis until they were lured into the area by the prospect of European goods available through the fur trade. Third, once Indigenous people, principally the Cree and Anishinaabe, began a more permanent habitation of the Hudson Bay Lowlands, the limited resource base of the area resulted in frequent food shortages, periodic starvation, and death.

Fourth, this problem of food deficiencies was exacerbated by an inadequate response by the Hudson Bay Company employees who were apparently averse to dealing with the food shortages aside from small-scale provisioning of trappers so that they could return to their hunting grounds. Fifth, the problem of food shortages was made more difficult by a Hudson Bay Company policy of hiring local hunters to provide food for the trading post employees, which further reduced the overall supply of food in the area. Sixth, the Hudson Bay Company was not willing to supply food to the trading posts from England, despite the quotidian remarks in the trading post journals of food shortages, to reduce costs to shareholders. In other words, for whatever reason, whether it was out of economic concerns or otherwise, the Hudson Bay Company, being well aware of the stress placed on the Indigenous people in the area because of the shortage of subsistence resources, was complicit in a policy that resulted in the death of many Cree, Anishinaabe, and other Indigenous people in the Hudson Bay Lowlands. When there was a conflict between the Hudson Bay Company and the Indigenous people caused by food shortages, the Hudson Bay Company engaged in a policy of minimizing the details, blaming the victims, and otherwise abrogating any sense of responsibility for their role in the tragic consequences of this policy.

Chapter Four

Colonial Resistance and Survival

"It was a horrible atrocity, the rumour of which caused a thrill of shame and indignation throughout the county."

This comment was apparently written by a company employee on the page (1968 [932, 324]) of John McLean's *Notes of Twenty-Five Years' Service in the Hudson's Bay Territory* where there is a description of the murder of a group of unarmed Assiniboine men by HBC traders.

It is evident from the historical records that the Hudson's Bay Company engaged in a continuous policy of suppression in the James Bay area in order to control any dissent from the Cree and other Indigenous peoples in the area. This policy was conducted on several fronts. One of these was an attempt to co-opt Cree leaders by providing them with gifts, called a system of "trading captains." The attempt was to control possible dissent by a system whereby important individuals in Cree society would be deterred from voicing criticism of the HBC out of fear of losing privileges or material concessions.

British missionaries were also engaged in attempt to convert the Cree to Christian churches in an attempt to undermine Indigenous belief systems and destabilize the authority of Indigenous religious leaders. These various attempts to control the Cree were not adopted in any enthusiastic manner; in fact, there were various attempts on the Cree's part to resist these control measures. One could argue that the killings at Hannah Bay could be seen, at least in part, as an attempt to impede or resist the HBC's attempt to control those in Cree society through their religious and political affairs.

Sources of the Cree's Discontent

It is not difficult to envisage the killings at Hannah Bay as an act of resistance initiated by a condition of an ever-diminishing food supply and a recalcitrant fur-trading company whose employees doled out meagre provisions that barely keep the Indigenous trappers and their families alive. In addition, the HBC hired professional hunters who stripped the land of available game animals and fowl, further depleting the country resources upon which the Cree depended to stay alive. As the subsistence resource base in the southern James Bay area continued to diminish, it was necessary to devote an ever-increasing amount of time and effort to mere survival rather than trapping in exchange for European goods. In effect, a downward spiral was created, since lower trapping returns for Indigenous families meant that the necessary ammunition and traps became increasingly difficult to purchase as both game and fur-bearing animals became scarcer.

In such a situation, Indigenous families would no doubt feel a sense of desperation. Hopelessness is moreover apt to breed contempt for those thought responsible for the deprivation that could be seen to increase on an annual basis. The HBC personnel at the various posts could hardly be oblivious to this desperation since recordings in the traders' journals noted on an almost daily basis the complaints of trappers that country provisions were becoming ever scarcer and that this deprivation was inhibiting their ability to trap for furs, which were also diminishing as environmental resources in the James Bay area eroded. Thus, when news reached Moose Factory on January 23, 1832, that the post manager at Hannah Bay had been killed along with several other inhabitants by a "Band of Rupert House Indians [who had arrived] in a Starving and naked State," it would no doubt have crossed the post manager's mind that a general rebellion was taking place in the area by disgruntled Cree who were in a desperate state of mind. It was a "Brutal outrage," the post manager noted (McTavish B135/a/137-8); "they got Provisions given them," as if the underlying reasons responsible for the killings were incomprehensible to him.

Nonetheless, quick action was necessary to prevent the contagion of a possible general uprising. Mr. Swanson and a party of eleven well-armed men were dispatched to the Hannah Bay post the very next day "to make an example of … the Murderers." Mr. Swanson was also to continue to Rupert House bearing a letter for the chief factor "to inform him of the Crimes committed by the Indians belonging to his District [a subtle hint perhaps that he was partially responsible]." A report on February 20, 1832, notes that the general scarcity of provisions has led some Cree to begin poaching on other trapper's grounds, suggesting the possibility of the beginnings of a rupture in the established social order of the area. This report is also accompanied by the unfortunate news that the Cree family who arrived at Moose Factory to report the

Image 4. John McLean (1798–1890). McLean was a long-time employee of the Hudson's Bay Company and one of the few former employees to criticize the "Honourable Company" in print after his employment ended.
Source: Georgina Pioneer Village and Archives, photo dated 1862.

poaching was also "driven to the necessity of eating their Skins ... and driven to the necessity of killing those Animals [beaver] for food." Then, on April 2, 1832, a further party of fifteen men from Moose Factory was given orders to get "themselves ready to proceed again to Ruperts House quarter for the purpose of securing or making an Example of the rest of the Murderers if they can possibly be found." On April 9, 1832, Swanson's party reported to have "found the murderers, and inflicted that punishment their Crimes merited ... It seems it was their (Quapakay and sons) further intention, had their [sic] been a small party travelling between here and Ruperts House to have murdered and plundered them."

In sum, it is apparent that the post manager at Moose Factory was intent on finding Mr. Corrigal's killers as expeditiously as possible so that

Quapakay and his sons could be "made an example of," lest other desperate Cree begin to entertain the idea that they might also raid other posts with impunity and thereby instigate a general uprising of discontent. This certainly was the opinion of John McLean, a former HBC employee stationed at Moose Factory during the time of the Hannah Bay killings.

John McLean's Voice of Dissent

John McLean, born in Scotland in 1798, joined the Hudson's Bay Company in 1821, the date of the union with the Northwest Company. He attained some fame in his time as the first European to discover the Great Falls of Labrador, now known as Churchill Falls, in 1839. In 1845 he had a falling out with the HBC governor, Sir George Simpson, when he was superseded for a promotion by an employee of lesser rank and consequently tendered his resignation. From then on, he was considered as a *persona non grata* as far as the company was concerned, and his opinions were considered not reliable because he was a disgruntled former employee. For example, in *The Honourable Company*, Douglas MacKay noted that "The governor made enemies. Some of the disgruntled wrote books about their fur trade days, and of these John McLean was the most articulate. McLean was perhaps not one of the politically strongest men in the fur trade, but he came to hate Simpson." McLean's book "is a satisfying description of fur trade life in the nineteenth century but marred by a manifestly ill-judged denunciation of Simpson which even McLean's late colleagues felt to be quite unfair."

As a result, McLean was judged to be a "disgruntled ex-employee [who] loses perspective" (MacKay 1966 [1936]: 207). Even the editor of McLean's book, W.S. Wallace, admitted that "The chief defect of the book is no doubt the author's somewhat atrabilious attitude toward the Hudson's Bay Company" (McLean, 1968 [1932]: xxii). It is necessary to mention these opinions of John McLean because they impinge directly on his description of the incident at Hannah Bay, of which he was a contemporary observer and who judged the HBC employees in a negative light in terms of their handling of the matter. In fairness to McLean, however, probably any criticism of the Hudson's Bay Company would generate a certain negative backlash given the prominent role of the Company in Canada's colonial history, the prominence of the British hold on power in the country, and the self-serving characterization of the HBC as an "Honorable Company."

Remember Churchill's comment that the victors write their own history, meaning a history that portrays the victors in a favourable light regardless of the veracity of this portrayal, which is a common ploy by colonial powers to deflect any possible criticism for their use of power and to undermine any possible future reproach by those subjected to this power. Take for example George Simpson's (governor-in-chief of the Hudson's Bay Company) commentary in his address to the London Committee at York Factory, August 20, 1830:

> The Hon'ble Company's affairs in this quarter, I am happy to say, look well: the Trade is in prosperous state and the Natives more orderly and appear better disposed than they have been for some time past. (MacKay1966 [1936], front piece)

Apparently, George Simpson was not in the habit of reading the almost daily journal reports of starving Aboriginal people and the widespread deprivation associated with the posts in his jurisdiction.

John McLean hardly believed that the Hudson's Bay Company was an "honourable" institution, and he had the first-hand, insider's view of how the personnel in this company operated. He would no doubt view Simpson's statement as pure propaganda, and his book was meant to correct such mistaken views. Unless anyone happened to be misled by any misinformation promulgated by HBC's proponents, McLean was determined to set the record straight; the HBC was not in any sense a benevolent society meant to help the downtrodden in their jurisdiction: "The history of commercial rule is well known to the world; the object of that rule, wherever established, or by whomever exercised, is gain. In our intercourse with the natives of America no other object is discernible, no other object is thought of, no other object is allowed" (1968 [1932]: 327–8).

Similarly, "There is no hint of imperialism's civilizing mission ... the human dimension is absent, as profit over people is the unashamedly stated governing logic ... of the colonial mentality" (Kennedy 2017: 61–2).

The sole object of the fur trade in Canada could not be put in starker terms. Furthermore, about whatever "generosity" might have been shown to the Cree and other Indigenous people by the HBC in their territories, McLean (1968 [1932]: 326) vehemently disputes this by saying, "As to our vaunted 'generosity' to the natives, I am at a loss to know in what it consists." He indicates that when a band of Natives arrives at a post a few inches of tobacco is given, along with "a few flints, awls, and hooks, and a trifle of ammunition is given to them ... Some of us would even withhold the awls and hooks, if we could; others, at the risk of being 'hauled up' for extravagance, would add another hook to the number ... the strictest economy is not only recommended, but enforced" (326–7).

Moreover, during the history of the fur trade in Canada, "The native population has decreased at an extraordinary rate." McLean is hesitant about directly blaming the Hudson's Bay Company for this Indigenous depopulation because the Northwest Company shared culpability for this demographic catastrophe, "but, from whatever cause arising, it is quite certain they have greatly decreased. Neither can it be denied, that the natives are no longer the manly, independent race they formerly were. On the contrary, we now find them gloomy and dispirited, unhappy and discontented" (1932: 326). There is furthermore no doubt then that the Indigenous population suffered emotionally, intellectually, and physiologically for the constantly deterioration of their habitat and living conditions during the fur trade era and under the oppressive colonial control to which they had been subjected.

The Cree and other Indigenous people in the James Bay area could hardly make any decisions affecting their lives during this era, when at one time they were a free people, excepting, of course, the exigencies of environmental strictures. Preston (2002: 79) explains the suppression that takes place when people are subjected to the power of "colonial mercantile capitalism," as he terms it. "In Cree culture," Preston observes, "one must be free to control himself. This freedom is of paramount importance to Cree individuals and is very proudly held … it is the locus of the manner, agency, and sequencing of social control." One can only imagine the effects on the once proud, freedom-loving Cree resulting from the control exerted on them by the fur-trading companies. The Cree were involved in a downward cycle of subjugation, despondency, environmental degradation, and deprivation from which there was apparently never going to be any escape.

The classic work of Alfred Bailey (1969) on the conflicts between European and Algonkian cultures concisely details the source of the social and economic tensions that resulted from these emerging dependency relationships. During the initial period of first contact there was a phase of relative equality between the Algonkians and the fur traders, but this was short-lived because of the desire of the Indigenous populations for European trade goods judged to be superior to their own weapons and utensils. The use of metal traps and firearms resulted in a decline in local fur-bearing animals, forcing Indigenous hunters to travel farther afield, sometimes causing inter-tribal conflicts. In addition, firearms were more effective than deadfall traps, spears, and bows and arrows, which caused a drastic decline in local subsistence resources and an increasing dependency on the Europeans for Native food supplies.[1]

Eventually the European traders became more efficient in coping with life in the Canadian wilderness and became less dependent on the

Indigenous population for suitable clothing, transportation, herbs, and medicines. European diseases such as smallpox and tuberculous progressively deceased the size of the Native populations along with the introduction of alcohol as a trade item. Pressure by Christian missionaries to convert to new spiritual creeds caused a decline in Indigenous belief systems and a division between Christian converts and those deemed "pagans." Of course, there are many details that are glossed over here in this summary. Bailey's book has now been updated from its original 1937 publication; however, in the opinion of historian Donald Smith (1972: 89) "Bailey produced what still remains the best account of cultural conflict in early Canadian history. Bailey's book ... is still the soundest study currently available on early cultural conflict in Canadian history."

It is evident, therefore, that John McLean's personal observations of the treatment of Canada's Indigenous population during the fur trade era have been largely vindicated by later historical scholars. It is also small wonder, then, that McLean feared that the killings at Hannah Bay in 1832 were a prelude to a general uprising of Cree in the James Bay area, considering the ever-pressing hardships that they were forced to endure, largely caused by the arrival of the Europeans. As McLean (1968 [1932]: 99–100) explained:

> This man [Quapakay] told his fellows that he had a communication with the Great Spirit, who assured him that he would become the greatest man in Hudson's Bay if he only followed the course prescribed to him, which was, first, to cut off their own trading post, and then with the spoil got there to hire other Indians, who would assist in destroying all the other posts the Company possessed in the country. Accordingly, it was determined to carry their design into execution, whenever a favourable opportunity occurred. This was not long in presenting itself.[2]

No doubt the HBC personnel in the James Bay area were relieved that such an expected resurrection did not occur, however the conditions of deprivation remained, keeping open the continued possibility for one.

While McLean was not critical, in print in any event, of Mr. Swanson's summary killing of the Hannah Bay perpetrators of Corrigal's death, he was certainly disparaging when, a few years later, HBC personnel killed a party of unarmed Assiniboine [McLean's spelling is used here] men in what McLean viewed as "cold blooded" murder. McLean's (1968 [1932]: 324) written account of this event is stated here in his own words:

> In that winter [of 1835–6], a party of men, led by two clerks, was sent to look for some horses that were grazing at a considerable distance from the post.

As they approached the spot they perceived a band of Assiniboine Indians, eight in number (if I remember aright), on an adjacent hill, who immediately joined them, and delivering up their arms, encamped with them for the night. Next morning a *court martial* [italics in original] was held by the two clerks and some of the men, to determine the punishment due to the Indians for having been found near the company's horses, with the *supposed* intention of carrying them off. What was the decision of this mock court martial? I shudder to relate, that the whole band, after haven given up their arms, and partaken of their hospitality, were condemned to death, and the sentence carried into execution on the spot – all were butchered in cold blood.[3]

It was further indicated that one of the individuals mentioned was "an old hand in the country," while the other was "a young man of excellent family, who had arrived from London only the preceding Autumn." Anderson also indicated that he subsequently enquired into this affair, writing that "as far as I could ascertain there was a difficulty as to bringing the culprits to trial so as to enforce conviction, as there were no witnesses unconcerned in the murder save God alone." Along the vein of the biblical saying that "Vengeance is mine, I will repay, saith the Lord" (Romans 12, 17–19), the first man mentioned was shot by Siccany [Sekani?] of McLeod's Lake in the summer of 1844, and the second was dismissed from the Company in 1842 for "dissolute and insubordinate conduct" (McLean 1968 [1932]: 325). In addition, Anderson, a contemporary HBC fur trader, apparently seemed to provide some justification for the killings by saying that "During the night the watch discovered the Assinaboins [sic] (who are noted horse-thieves) prowling round the camp, and there can be no doubt as to their intention. They were seized and, in the morning, slaughtered as I mentioned. The only justification attempted by the murderers was that they had no other means of preserving their horses."

Even John McLean apparently offered an explanation that relinquished the HBC of any responsibility in the case when he said that the "Company are not answerable for crimes committed by their servants without their knowledge." However, McLean does provide an opinion that does not exonerate the Company in such cases:

"True; but when they are made fully acquainted with those misdeeds, and allow the perpetrators to escape with impunity, the guilt is transferred to their own head … The proceedings of this court-martial were reported at head-quarters, and the punishment awarded to these murderers was—a reprimand! After this, what protection, or generosity, or justice, can the Indians be said to receive from the Hudson's Bay Company?" (1968 [1932]: 325)[4]

Coping with Colonialism

Colonialism can be defined as "a policy whereby a nation seeks to establish long-term social, political, and economic domination over another people, usually by the installation of an administrative structure using members of the dominant society to facilitate control" (Hedican 2017: 238). Colonialism may also involve military domination over another people and their lands, "which includes the installation of administrative outposts and enclaves of their own citizens in the territories under control" (Sidky 2004: 420). Edward Said (1979, 1994) further indicates that colonialism is a "process of conquest." In *Racism. Colonialism, and Indigeneity in Canada,* Cannon and Sunseri (2011: 274) state that "European colonialism dates from the fifteenth century onwards and involved the brutal establishment of European sovereignty on stolen non-European territory. Colonialism is not only about material accumulation but requires the production of ideologies that justify the theft and violent practices at its root." In a similar vein, Kennedy (2017: 36) suggests that postcolonial studies suffer from a particular sort of amnesia in which "Indigenous peoples of white-settler colonies [serve to] detract from other zones of European aggression" as characterized by British colonial capitalism.

The Hudson's Bay Company ruled over a vast territory from its amalgamation with the North West Company from 1821 to 1869, when it sold its proprietary rights in Rupert's Land to Canada.[5] At the height of its expansion the Hudson's Bay Company had secured a virtual monopoly on all the fur trade in British North America and beyond. The Company ruled an area of over three million square miles, which is approximately one-fourth of the continent of North America. Rupert's Land was the core of this domain, which comprised a vaguely defined territory of about 1,400,000 square miles that was granted to the company by Charles II in the Charter of 1670 (see Galbraith 1957: 3).

The validity of this grant was frequently challenged. The idea that this territory could be considered as *terra nullius,* or "land without owners," was a cornerstone of the British Imperial policy in Canada during the fur trade era, thus apparently legitimizing the territorial grant by Charles II (Asch 2002). The legal justification for the Hudson's Bay Company's possession of Rupert's Land relied on what Asch (2000: 149–50) has termed the "settlement thesis" as a rationalization of British sovereignty over Aboriginal lands. The British claimed that Rupert's Land was essentially unoccupied territory, or at least not belonging to another political entity, despite the obvious evidence that Indigenous people lived virtually everywhere on the lands over which the British claimed possession. As further justification of the *terra nullius* concept, the British believed that the members of Aboriginal nations lacked a concrete concept of land ownership, which served to justify in the colonists' mind the dispossession of Aboriginal lands. Thus, the grant of Rupert's Land to the Hudson's Bay Company was made on spurious legal grounds since there was no basis for the assumption that there were no Indigenous inhabitants in Canada when the fur traders arrived, nor can it be presumed that a condition of *terra nullius* prevailed for the whole of the territory in the initial grant.

As Knafla (2010: 2) suggests, the term *terra nullius* is at the centre of concepts of imperial sovereignty that denied Native title. Furthermore, one way that colonial powers used to circumvent the obvious difficulties in legally justifying the settlement thesis is to vary the *terra nullius* concept so that a justification for occupying Aboriginal lands was based on the premise that "the original inhabitants did not possess political rights or underlying title that required recognition by the colonizers" (Ash 2000: 150). In addition, another related rationale against the recognition of Aboriginal title derives from the view that since Aboriginal peoples in Canada were not Christians at the time of contact their rights did not require recognition.

These arguments Asch refers to as forms of "artificial" reasoning that "have been used in subsequent periods to justify the unilateral assertion of sovereignty and underlying title by colonists in the face of indigenous sovereignty" (ibid.). Similarly, the *terra nullius* doctrine was used in Australia, another British colony, in the famous 1992 Mabo decision (*Mabo v. Queensland*), in which the suggestion was put forth that since the Aborigines did not practise agriculture, they could not claim sovereignty over their territory (Russell 2005: 191–218, 247–70). In a decision handed down by the High Court of Australia, the *terra nullius* doctrine was discredited because it relied on a "discriminatory denigration of Indigenous inhabitants, their social organization, and customs," and this thesis implied that "the Aboriginal inhabitants of the continent ... [were] a different and lower form of life whose very existence could be ignored for the purpose of determining the legal rights to occupy and use their traditional homelands" (cited in Ash 2000: 156).

As Asch explains further, "The concept of Aboriginal rights has existed since the beginnings of the period of European colonization. It originated in the political and legal system of those who colonized and poses the question of what rights rest with the original population after colonization" (2001: 1). According to the opinion of Voyageur and

Calliou (2011: 210), it should be remembered that "Aboriginal peoples were once distinct and sovereign nations on the land that is now Canada ... Long after contact with Europeans they remained sovereign – so much so that they were not only partners in the fur trade economy but also participated in the wars between the European powers in North America." As far as they are concerned, Voyageur and Calliou place the abrogation of Aboriginal rights clearly on European greed and capricious rationalization, indicating that as "European settlement in North America grew, the European's desire for more land and resources became insatiable ... The Europeans created laws based on racist and religious intolerance to dispossess Aboriginal peoples of their land, resources, and cultures."[6]

Certainly, members of the Hudson's Bay Company must have been aware of the Royal Proclamation of 1763, which became official British policy towards the Aboriginal peoples of North America. Sometimes referred to as the "Indian Bill of Rights," the Royal Proclamation established what could be termed as a "protectionist period" of British colonial policy, stating:

"It is just and reasonable and essential to our interest, and the security of our colonies, that the several nations and Tribes of Indians with whom were are connected, and who live under our protection, should not be molested or disturbed in the Possession of such Parts or our Dominions and Territories as, not having been ceded to or purchased by Us, are reserved to them or any of them as their Hunting Grounds" (in Hedican 2013: 24–5).

This proclamation acted to situate the British Crown between the Aboriginal inhabitants and the colonists. It stipulated that the land inhabited by Aboriginal peoples had to be voluntarily ceded to the crown before non-Aboriginal settlers could occupy it (Hedican 2008: 144–5). The Royal Proclamation of 1763 laid the basis for the treaty period which involved the ceding of very large tracts of land to the British Crown, and later, the government of Canada. The important point here is that the Royal Proclamation of 1763 clearly established Aboriginal sovereignty to the lands that they occupied, which was a matter that the Hudson's Bay Company seems to have ignored with impunity. Rather, the Hudson's Bay Company acted as if it were the sole master of Rupert's Land even though this attitude contradicted official British colonial policy. Instead, the Hudson's Bay Company promulgated their own self-serving ideologies, which they used to justify positions of control over the Indigenous population in the territories in which their fur trading posts were situated.

Honourable Gentlemen?

In the Canadian fur-trade era, an example of the production of colonial ideologies can be found in accounts that promoted the notion that the history of the Hudson's Bay Company was "a daring and heroic tale" of a company of "Honourable" gentlemen whose chronicles involved "adventure as thrilling as man could ever hear by tale or history" (MacKay [1936] 1966, foreword to 1936 edition). Indigenous trappers were encouraged to address Hudson's Bay Company officials with such paternalistic terms as their "fathers," suggesting that the trappers themselves could be children. As might be expected in any 'sanitized' history, such as McKay's *The Honourable Company*, there is never any mention of such awkward moments as the killings at Hannah Bay or the murder of unarmed Assiniboine.

Dissenters such as John McLean are portrayed as "disgruntled" former ex-employees whose accounts are not to be believed because they are tainted with vengeful and biased motivations. However, McLean appeared to be fully aware of these colonial ideologies when he rather sarcastically refers to "the *humane* and *gentle* [emphasis as in the original] rule of the Hudson's Bay Company." "What became of the Hannah Bay murderers?" he asked. "They were conveyed to Moose Factory, bound hand and foot, and there shot down by the orders of the Chief Factor ... The penalty was fully paid in blood for blood."[7] In other words, the Company exercised one version of the law when its servants murdered unarmed Assiniboine men, who McLean says were "executed on the spot – all were butchered in cold blood," (ibid., 324) by virtually turning a blind eye to the matter, but extracting the most severe form of punishment on Aboriginal men who were accused of killing Europeans.

McLean asks, then, where is the *humane* and *gentle* rule in these cases? In other words, McLean in his opinion is referring to the hypocrisy of the Hudson's Bay Company in their dealings with the Aboriginal inhabitants in which the outward persona of the Company as "humane" and "honourable" is not matched by their actions with the Company's actual treatment of Indigenous peoples. In addition, it is not helpful that Gov. Simpson himself refers to Aboriginal people in derogatory terms, describing them in 1831 as a "simple harmless race" which invokes the trope of Indigenous inhabitants as child-like and irresponsible (in Galbraith 1957: 40).

In Taiaiake Alfred's article entitled the "Colonial Stains of Our Existence" he suggests that "The challenge we face is made up of specific patterns of behaviour among Settlers and our own people: choices made to support mentalities that developed in serving the coloniza-tion of our lands as well as the unrestrained greed and selfishness of mainstream society" (2011: 3). His reference to "unrestrained greed" certainly echoes McLean's comment that "the sole object of commercial rule is gain" (1968 [1932]: 328) and hence Preston's (2002: 79) charac-terization of the fur trade as an example of "colonial mercantile cap-italism." It has even been suggested that the Hudson's Bay Company had begun to achieve a reputation among the general Canadian popu-lation "as a greedy, grasping monopoly, incompatible with the higher interests of civilization" (Galbraith 1957: 45). Apparently, as a form of propaganda, the self-promoting characterizations of the Company in such benevolent terms as "gentle and honourable" only go so far in achieving their objectives.[8]

The Politics of Encapsulation

The term "politics of encapsulation" came into prominent use in an-thropology during the mid-1970s to designate how the actions of a colonial power are utilized to manipulate a small society in order to control the internal decision-making processes of its members. Using political processes in the Middle East as an example, Salzman charac-terizes the encapsulation of tribes by the Iranian state:

"First, from an administrative perspective, tribes with an Indige-nous centralized authority structure can be more easily encapsulated than tribes with Indigenous decentralized structures. Second, agents of the encapsulating power would, if possible, make use of Indigenous structures and personnel in a traditionally centralized tribe, whereas a centralized administrative structure would be imposed by the encapsu-lating power upon a traditionally decentralized tribe" (1974: 209).

In another example of the encapsulation process, F.G. Bailey (1969: 1–17) provided the following description. He first explained that polit-ical structures can be recognized at all levels of a society, such as from families and villages to regions and states, and that these can be com-pared to one another. It has been discovered in anthropological studies that there are societies that appear to have no authority structure, yet nonetheless, the people are able to live orderly lives. As he explains further:

Given the anthropologist's strong interest in small communities encapsu-lated within larger societies – in villages, tribes within nations or colonial dependencies, sections of urban populations, and so forth – who seem to operate political structures in spite of the fact that the state authorities are only occasionally involved, he has no choice but to consider these political structures which are partly independent of, and partly regulated by, larger encapsulating political structures. (1969: 12)

This reference to political structures that are "partly independent of, and partly regulated by" these larger encapsulating units would appear to be an excellent starting point in understanding the historically accelerating influence of European institutions over the Indigenous societies of Canada. As Europeans began to exert greater control in their interaction with Indigenous peoples, there was a corresponding adjustment necessary on the Europeans' part. In other words, dependency can be a two-way interaction involving accommodations made by both parties in a shared mutual environment. One can surely make the case that this description of a colonial administrative and economic structure has considerable relevance to the encapsulation of Aboriginal societies in Canada.[9]

It is also evident that leadership and political organization in the traditional cultures of Canada's Aboriginal peoples has demonstrated considerable variation in their socio-political organization, from the hunting bands of the boreal forests to the settled villages of the Haudenosaunee and Wendat of southern Ontario and the highly structured societies of the Pacific coast. Each of these societies, in turn, demonstrated considerable variation in the way their members interacted with the colonial presence in their area. The interest of the English and French in establishing a commercial empire based on the fur trade, for example, necessitated the obvious cooperation of Aboriginal people. In this context the prerequisites for successful economic exchange tended to be based on more amical terms between the two parties, at least in the initial period. However, as Alfred Bailey (1969) suggests, the entire interplay between the Europeans and the Eastern Algonkians passed through phases of initial equality to more increasing dependence. This initial period of equality was short-lived, however, as Aboriginal people became more dependent upon European manufactured goods as a necessity in making a living in the northern forests. Game and fur-bearing animals became more depleted over time, further increasing the dependency relationship.

This does not mean that the Indigenous peoples of these northern areas willingly accepted European domination; there was push-back at times, as various attacks on fur trading posts illustrate. These attacks, such as those of Hannah Bay and Henley House (to be discussed shortly), were certainly a rare occurrence, yet they did happen from time to time, suggesting an acknowledgment that the dependency process was a source of grievance among the northern Aboriginal population who, in former times, were able to exercise much more freedom in their lives. As Price (1979: 85) suggests: "The north has been protected by its isolation. Much of the north is still more colonial than neo-colonial, though Whites try to be economically, politically, and ideologically dominant everywhere over Natives. However, when Natives have a clear majority as in the Northwest Territories, they can usually retain some self-pride, social status, and other defenses against White domination and destruction of their culture."

Thus, certain generalizations, although tentatively made, would suggest a certain correlation between the size and complexity of the Indigenous society and the willingness of its people to tolerate European influences. As an example, the Indigenous people of the Plains, such as the Sioux, fought back against the American army. The Haudenosaunee attacked Quebec City, and the Indigenous groups on the northwest coast occasionally engaged in conflict with European sailors and at times captured them.

Political Domination and Response

In some territories of Canada, the political response to colonialism by Aboriginal peoples could be characterized as confrontational in nature. In the Plains region, the Blackfoot and other tribes had little use for the fur trade. In a military sense, the Plains people were better able to protect themselves and therefore were able to mount a greater resistance to the colonizers. But in the end the domination of the colonizers was realized through non-military means, such as through the spread of small pox epidemics, intentional or otherwise, in the early 1800s and the destruction of the bison herds in the 1880s.In the north, the Indigenous population was more widely dispersed which tended to lessen the destructive effects of the spread of European diseases; however, the depletion of game animals still had deleterious effects because of over population, beyond the carrying capacity of the boreal forest environment, and the more wonton destruction of subsistence resources.

In North America, Europeans have had a long history of attempting to co-opt Aboriginal leadership as a mechanism for manipulating the Indigenous societies in order to make them more compliant with the desires of the colonial administrations. One colonial strategy is to deny that Aboriginal people had any leadership at all, or at least to suggest that Aboriginal societies lacked a recognizable authority structure (Miller 1955). This view – that even if Aboriginal leadership existed at all then, at best, it was weak and ineffectual – could be used as a rationale in an attempt to impose European-style forms of governance that could conform to the political norms and values characteristic of European cultural traditions.

There are many examples that could be used to illustrate these attempts at political manipulation, such as attempting to impose a system of elective leadership to facilitate administrative control which was later codified in Canada's Indian Act. Thus, as Smith (1973: 16) summarizes for the southwestern Ojibwa (Anishinaabe), "In response to the changing circumstances and demands [resulting from contact with European societies], chieftainship had proliferated by the late eighteenth and early nineteenth centuries. Characteristically, different kinds of leadership were usually vested in different kinds of men." Power then became diffused rather than concentrated, as had been the case with the hunting group leaders of the past. There emerged, for example, civil chiefs with relatively generalized roles and specialized roles such as war chiefs, chiefs appointed by fur traders, talking chiefs, and clan chiefs.

The fur trade, specifically, brought about demographic and structural social changes resulting from adaptations to different ecosystems, the most important of which was a period of sustained hostilities with the Dakota Sioux after 1736 (Hickerson 1962: 1–8). Tribal distributions among the Anishinaabe were also modified because of early European contacts and the later developments of the fur trade (Bishop 1970: 1–15). Smith's (1973: 31–3) conclusion is that these European contacts in social, economic, and political organization have been largely detrimental to the Anishinaabek's continuing adaptation to the dominant Euro-American society. The Anishinaabe social system has been greatly affected by Euro-American institutions that the Indigenous population has been largely powerless to influence in turn. The results of these European-American contacts have curtailed solutions found in the traditional ways, which has meant that there are limited alternatives available. In some Anishinaabe communities a "culture of poverty" has taken hold, which is perpetuated from generation to generation (James 1961, 1970).

When Aboriginal leaders were seen in their local communities as too compliant with the directives of European powers and would appear to be unable to take decisive action to improve local economic conditions, they were called "boss-like," or *okima.hka.n* in Anishinaabe, a surrogate for the real thing and a "put-up" job (Landes 1937: 2–3; Ellis 1960: 1; Hedican 1986a: 2–3). The effects of colonial powers on the political structures of Aboriginal societies is a common theme in the ethnographic literature. Rogers (1965: 277) noted that Indigenous leaders suffered a loss of power during the fur trade era when Hudson's Bay Company post managers attempted to influence the decision-making processes in Aboriginal societies. "The factors stationed on the shores of the bay," Ray and Freeman (1978: 249) noted, "developed rather possessive attitudes to their Indian trading partners and jealously guarded against any encroachment on their trade by adjacent company posts." For example, as recorded in the Moose Factory post journal of Sunday, February 26, 1832, it was noted that "An Indian belonging to the Albany District paid a Visit here … he acknowledges that he is come from that quarter without the consent or knowledge of Mr Chief Trader Jacob Corrigal … says there are a number of Indians in at Albany under the same privations and receiving sustenance from Mr Jacob Corrigal."

The implication here is that the fur traders controlled the movements of the Cree in the James Bay area such that a Cree trapper would require the permission of the post manager to which the trapper might be attached. As Rogers (1965: 277) concludes for Cree and Anishinaabe leadership, due to colonial influences, "the chief has lost his former powers and acquired no new ones." One of the most important reasons for the diminished power of traditional Cree and Anishinaabe leaders is that they are no longer the main distributors of goods to band members since the Hudson's Bay Company officials, as the Moose Factory journal reports so aptly reported, began to occupy a significant role in the distribution of food, especially during times of severe deprivation.

There were various methods that Company officials used to circumvent dissent among the local Cree population and to co-opt the important men in the community. One method, as previously mentioned, was to institute a system of Home Guard Cree, who were hired directly by the Hudson's Bay Company to act as professional hunters, to transport supplies and messages between fur trading posts, among other duties. These men were probably the best of the Cree hunters and so would have been important leaders even before the fur trade era, since traditional leadership was based on the personal trait of generosity in distributing the products of the hunt to band members. By employing these important Cree directly, the Company was able to at least mute a possible source of dissent among important Cree individuals.

Trading Captains

Another mechanism for influencing Cree leadership patterns was to institute what was termed the trading "Captain" system. As Francis and Morantz (1983: 41–3) explain for the James Bay area, the Hudson's Bay Company servants

> recognized one man as the leading Indian, or "captain."… Large groups
> included more than one captain, the average being five or six canoes per

captain. By the mid-1760s to the mid-1780s the post master also designated several "lieutenants," but this position was abolished because of the extra expense it entailed. As a reward for bringing in hunters and as encouragement to continue doing so, leading Indians received gifts of brandy, tobacco, and, to distinguish them as leaders, an outfit of quasi-military clothing.

Edward Umfreville who was a Hudson's Bay Company employee at Severn House describes this "uniform" as having

> regimental cuffs, and a waistcoat and breeches of baize [chestnut-coloured course woollen material used for coverings] ... He was also presented with a white or check shirt ... [a hat] bedecked with three ostrich feathers and a worsted sash tied around the crown, a small silk handkerchief is tied around his neck. The lieutenant is also presented with a coat ... he is likewise provided with a shirt and cap (1790: 59).

These trading captains were expected to bring in a profitable trade for the Company. "More importantly," Francis and Morantz (1983: 44) indicate, "he had to be a man of influence among his fellows, and in this respect the Indians might be said to have chosen their own captains." These captains were also recognized "as a spokesperson who would represent their interests to the English ... Trading captains retained their position for life." The Company's motives here appear to be quite clear: the Hudson's Bay Company was actively engaged in recruiting the most influential men among the Cree who held their position of influence at the Company's discretion and could be counted on to side with the fur traders in possible disputes with Cree trappers who might form a body of dissentient complainers and troublemakers.

Of course, all these measures ultimately had an economic motive, which was to increase Company profits. Ray (1974: 138) indicated further that "the fur companies attempted to win the loyalties of the band leaders, and at the same time increase the authority of these leaders in the eyes of the Indians. Presumably, if successful, these chiefs could then have been prevailed upon to bring their respective bands to particular posts on a regular basis." In order to increase the prestige, authority, and status of the band leaders, and presumably also to encourage compliance, such influential men were given gifts of brandy, tobacco, and pipes, among other enticements to further the Company's aims. As Ray indicates further, "Once the Indians had accepted these European symbols of political authority and allegiance, the trading companies attempted to use the symbols to manipulate the Indians" (1974: 139). However, despite these manipulating tactics on the part of the Company, "Ultimately, these various efforts to stabilize and enhance the authority of Indian chiefs failed. Rather, they had the effect of increasing factionalism and tensions within bands, creating a more unstable political and social climate" (Ray 1974: 141; see also Ray 1975: 586–602; Ray and Freeman 1978: 15–17, 67–70).

The problem with leadership roles in band societies, as Hansen points out, is that these roles are not formalized, such that "different kinds of leaders are afforded recognition by group census as circumstances warrant" (1987: 40). In addition, when "traditional roles are affected by prolonged contact with European society, either resulting in changes in existing leadership roles or acting as a catalyst for the appearance of new roles that are contemporaneous to, but distinct from, the traditional ones" the fluidity of these roles made it difficult for the British colonial powers to ascertain which individuals should be sought out (ibid.). In such cases, Lee (1982: 46–50) made a distinction between "inside" leaders and "outside" ones. As far as the "trading chiefs" were concerned, Hansen suggests that "their authority was limited and probably only recognized by their own group" (1987: 45). Nonetheless, the trading chief was someone both skilled as a hunter and an effective spokesperson for his group. In other words, such chiefs needed to be not only good speakers but could produce successful fur hunts, and in this sense, such leaders attempted to satisfy the wants and desires of both the Indigenous group and the British fur trader.

The amalgamation of the Hudson's Bay Company with the North West Company in 1821 resulted in the loss of deferential treatment of such prominent roles as trading chief because of the diminished state of competition between the two companies. By the 1830s, Hudson's Bay Company trader George Keith, who had been employed in a number of different posts in the Lake Superior District, claimed that "Chieftainship has in a manner totally disappeared," and that there were no chiefs "properly speaking" among the Anishinaabe (Ojibwa) north of Lake Superior (in Hansen 1987: 46). As such, Keith's observation that there were no chiefs suggests that traditional leaders were being replaced by trading chiefs in the 1830s, but even these persons of authority were beginning to have a diminished influence among their people in the period after the amalgamation in 1821.

The concept of an "egalitarian society" as applied to northern or Subarctic Algonquians, such as the Cree and Anishinaabe, especially in terms of leadership roles, however, has been the subject of some criticism and reinterpretation (see, for example, Begler 1978; MacNeish 1956; Morrison 1976; Rich 1976). Morantz formed her opinion that the term "egalitarian" is an imprecise term to describe northern Algonkian social organization and leadership. Based on her ethnohistorical research, Morantz found that "a system of leadership leapt from the pages of the traders' journals" (1982: 482). As she explains further, "It is the Indian responses to opportunities provided by the Europeans that has led me to question the accepted views of Northern Algonquian concepts of leadership, authority and status. Unlike their portrayal in the anthropological literature, it was discovered in the archival records that certain men deliberately sought to enhance their status. They were not always reluctant leaders" (1982: 482–3).

Morantz is especially critical of previous research that concluded that northern Algonquian traditional leadership was "weakly developed," as Rogers (1965: 273; 1969: 40) suggested, or simply as "irrelevant," in Leacock's (1978: 249) terms. Similarly, in a previous study, Leacock (1958: 206) concluded that ascribed status among northern Algonquians to be "virtually non-existent." Without delving into this extensive debate in any great detail here, the fur-trading records that Morantz referred to above tell a different story. For example, Hearne (1958: 186) stated that he was impressed by the large number of followers commanded by Algonquian leaders. As he writes, his impression of Algonquian leaders was based on "their own desire of being thought men of great consequence and interest with the English" (1958: 187). Similarly, in 1758, an HBC post manager described Algonquian leaders as "bold, commanding, well-loved and feared" (in Morantz 1982:490).

It was also pointed out that if the Algonquian leaders were as ineffectual as some researchers suggest, then how do we explain the "lavish outlay of presents to [trading] captains ... The English [given their frugal tendencies] would never have made such expenditure needlessly" (ibid., 491). As Morantz (1982: 494) sums up, "it is difficult to avoid the conclusions that they [Algonquian leaders] were individuals who wielded power over the European traders and persuasiveness or influence over their own men," and further on, "men seized opportunities for controlling resources, enabling them to wield influence and position" (ibid., 498).

These are important observations as far as the wider effects of colonialism on such northern Algonquians as the Cree are concerned. There is sufficient evidence that one could marshal to demonstrate that the Cree of James Bay were far from hapless victims of the Hudson's Bay Company and, in the wider sphere, of British colonial policy. The Cree were well able to push back on the powerful outsiders who oppressed them. One could argue that this push-back was too extreme in the case of the murders at Hannah Bay in southern James Bay and Henley House on the Albany River in northern Ontario. Nonetheless, no matter how one views these events, they did occur. The question is, why did these events happen? Certainly, a major part of the answer is that British fur

traders died because of the repressive circumstances of food deprivation and interpersonal relationships which bound both the Indigenous
people and the colonial powers in a catastrophic mutual embrace of
survival and possible death.

Wealth Extraction and Colonial Capitalism

John McLean's comment, previously quoted, that "The history of commercial rule is well known to the world; the object of that rule, wherever
established, or by whomever exercised, is gain." He further states from
his own personal experience in the fur trade that the Hudson's Bay
Company traders would never think of "sacrificing their own interests
to benefit Indians" (1968 [1932]: 327–8). McLean's comments describe
rather accurately what has come to be termed "colonial capitalism."
This form of colonialism is primarily concerned with wealth extraction
and the detrimental effects, such as famines, starvation, and other forms
of deprivation, that are suffered by subjugated peoples under colonial
rule. For example, as Butterly and Shepard (2010: 184) suggest, "Britain
benefited economically at the cost to all its colonies and required them
to trade exclusively with its own companies. Thus, one theory of under
development identifies the wealth – in manpower (slaves), minerals,
natural resources, and agricultural products – of colonies as the fuel
that powered Great Britain's Industrial Revolution."

As far as the distribution of food under the hegemonic power of colonial rule is concerned, there is also the opinion held by some agrarian
economists that famines are "socially produced." As an example, in a
review of Michael Watt's book on Nigeria, entitled *Silent Violence*, Donham commented that "Famines – those crises in which people begin to
starve – resulted under colonial capitalism: grain was often available
in the market; [however], peasants did not have the means to purchase
it" (1985: 944). As such, the argument made here is that colonial capitalism is at the root of the disadvantages that characterize the position of
the colonized because they are unable to compete with their wealthier
overlords for precious resources such as food. The result of this situation is that when food shortages occur, it is the poor in the colonies who
suffer first and the hardest.

More recent work suggests further that colonial capitalism is at odds
with liberal thought. The focus on this work is the idea that a claim to
liberal thought is incompatible with the historical development of colonial capitalism. A country, such as Britain for example, which built one
of the great empires of the world, built its wealth on the development
of economic transformations in other lands and used the population of

these lands to create economic prosperity for themselves. Some may argue, as a self-justification, that the creation of this wealth also benefited the local people involved. Of course, there is some debate about whether or not this was the case, since there are many who would see this claim as an attempt to slant the record in favour of the colonial power. However, there is much evidence that this claim was not the case. In fact, it is indeed a very interesting pedagogical situation that there should still be so much academic interest in this aspect of colonialism, as evidenced by a plethora of recent books and articles on the subject.

Onur Ince (2018), for example, argues that the idea that the British Empire should be extolled as a bastion of liberal thought is acceptable only on the condition that its colonial expropriation, extraction, and exploitation be disavowed. The overall conclusion of this study is that the disavowal of the violence inherent in the capitalist relations in the British colonies is seen as a crucial step in the crafting of a liberal image for Anglophone imperialism. Britain's imperial economy, characterized by colonial capitalism, therefore highlights the dilemmas of liberalism that materialized in the efforts to reconcile the peaceful, commercial self-imagination and the coercive economic practices that the British undertook in their imperial possessions. To sum up this relationship between capitalism and liberal thought, Ince concludes that "Colonial capitalism can offer a theoretical account of the imperial context that is largely absent in the extant analyses of liberalism and empire by bringing into focus the political and economic dynamics that propelled, shaped, and delimited the course of imperial expansion" (2018:18).

A reviewer of Ince's book furthermore added that his study offers "a critique of the continuity of colonial capitalism and imperialism in the present [which] shows the contradictory relationship between liberalism, colonialism, and capitalism" (Snelgrove 2018: 968–70). It was also noted that Ince "succeeds in demonstrating the importance of political economy for political theories imperial turn, preoccupied as it has been with a discursive approach to cultural differences" (ibid., 968). One wonders, however, if this reference to "a discursive approach to cultural differences" is in need of a wider discussion in the context of colonial capitalism. In anthropology, most still regard cultural differences as continuing to be important even in the face of such wide-ranging concepts as colonialism.

The members of different cultures, for example, are apt to have varying responses to colonial pressures – some will resist, even violently, some capitulate, some co-operate with the colonial oppressors. Even within the same culture one can find diversity in terms of their response, such as is evidenced by the James Bay Cree with their co-operative homeguard individuals, and others, such as Quapakay and his sons, who were driven to a violent response to food deprivation and various other pressures to take action against the causes of their dissatisfaction with the Cree-British relationship. One the other hand, there were apparently many other Cree people who seldom made it into the HBC journals because they took a peaceful approach, minded their own business, and tried as best as they could to overcome the challenges that the James Bay environment posed for them.

Authors such as Onur Ince acknowledge that their views of colonial capitalism build on, or at least are similar to, Sanjay Subrahmanyam's definition of "colonial empire" as "a particular kind of empire that is fundamentally characterized by the exploitive relations between an imperial core and a subject periphery" (2006: 220). In this sense, Kennedy (2017: 47) refers to British colonial capitalism in terms of its "rapacious origins and unfair distribution of colonial wealth." As such, the conflicts at Hannah Bay are at least partly understandable in terms of these potential "explosive relations," and "rapacious origins" between the Hudson's Bay Company as the "imperial core" and the Cree of James Bay as the "subject periphery."

It would no doubt be correct, however, to think that the Cree themselves would hardly see themselves as peripheral because they had inhabited the James Bay region for many generations, perhaps even for millennia. As such they would consider themselves the masters of their own destiny, rather than be seen as the willing puppets of colonial masters living out in the hinterland of existence. In addition, the Cree would no doubt be aware that it was through their efforts alone that the source of British wealth emanated from the Hudson's Bay region, and that this wealth was unfairly distributed, especially in times of scarcity when the Cree needed it most in order to survive. In any event, the James Bay area was the centre of their world, their spiritual cosmology, and existed not on the edge of a colonial company's own existential reality. British fur traders would come and go, but the Cree would never leave their home in James Bay.

If we take a wider view of colonial capitalism, we do see similarities that allow for cross-cultural comparisons and differences. As an example, there are a number of studies pertaining to a colonial discourse in southeast Asia that suggest common trends (Alexander 1986; Owen 2014; Raben 2014; and Brown 1997, 2014). Each of these authors has studied various regions in the area, such as Java, Vietnam, or Burma in an attempt to discover in their histories the effects of Subrahmanyam's "colonial empire."

Ian Brown (2014: 155–64) described Burma's economic transformation over the period of about seventy years, from the second Anglo-Burmese war in 1853 to the late 1920s, during which the British seized from the Burmese the lower part of their kingdom, the vast plain and delta called Irrawaddy. In this newly seized territory, there was only a sparse population in the 1850s. For the most part this territory consisted mostly of jungle and swamp. There was nonetheless also a huge agricultural potential for this area, and in the decades that followed under British administration, it was physically and economically transformed as tens, or even hundreds of thousands of Burmese cultivators came into and through the delta, felled the jungle, drained the swamps, and put the land under rice production. The area under rice in Lower Burma rose from around 1.4 million acres in the early 1860s to over 9.5 million acres in the late 1920s. In these circumstances, rice production came to far exceed Burma's own requirements, and the average annual volume of rice exported rose from 0.4 million tons in the late 1860s to 2.7 million tons in the 1920s. By the end of this period, it could be claimed that Burma had become the single most important rice exporter in the world. So, what was the outcome of this vast economic enterprise?

As Brown concludes, "the profits from prosperity had gone overwhelmingly to foreign interests … colonial Southeast Asia was being drained by the foreign interests that dominated the modern sectors of the economy" (2014: 162). Yet, Brown cautions that to view Southeast Asia's economic transformation solely as an achievement of colonial rule is apt to miss the contributions of Asian's initiative. While the Burmese were cultivating rice, the Malays were tapping rubber and the Javanese picking coffee. Brown's point is that it is important to view this engagement in these economic endeavours not as a forced imposition of colonial rule. Rather, the region's economic transformations were the result of Asians' initiative in response to economic opportunities.

In the end, though, it was colonial rule that was the most important inhibiting factor in the failure to foster future economic initiatives. Little attention was ultimately paid to developing a foundation for long-term economic progress, and to provide a transition to self-sustaining growth. In the late twentieth century, for example, when some areas of Southeast Asia were becoming transformed from agriculture to industrial production, other areas lagged behind because much of the Chinese wealth in the region was repatriated as income to China. This factor alone, Brown (2014: 163) suggests "drained Southeast Asia of much of the wealth created through the exploitation of the region's resources."

Thus, in summary, what are the important characteristics of colonial capitalism. This form of colonialism is, first and foremost, concerned with the creation of wealth for colonial powers. As far as this creation of wealth is concerned, the role of the local or Indigenous people is of secondary importance, only in so far as they are capable of performing the extractive processes that create this wealth. Second, local people can withhold their labour, but in this case they will not receive the perceived benefits that the colonial power provides. Initially a dependency relationship is created that eventually binds the local population to the colonial power, which then becomes difficult to sever since the colonial power has a monopoly on the distribution of goods, favours, or other benefits to those who work for them. Third, ultimately in most cases this dependency relationship is broken when the local population no longer serves the needs of the colonial power.

By this time there could be significant ecological damage to the environment in which the local people live, or the people become victims of food deprivation and nutritional stress. As Ince concludes, "The optic of colonial capitalism redefines … the focus from who the colonized *are* to what the colonizers *do*, that is, from the cultural differences of the subject population to the deeds of imperial agents themselves" (2018: 4). The implication of this statement is that a shift has recently taken place in colonial studies that holds the imperial power responsible for the damage caused by a single-minded pursuit of wealth that is one of the primary characteristics of imperial regimes.

Missionaries: "Civilizing Colonialism"

Missionary activity was also an important aspect of British colonial policy in the Canadian north. The ultimate goal, of course, was to convert Aboriginal people to a Christian faith, which ultimately served to undermine traditional spiritual beliefs and rituals. In most cases this activity also served to divide Aboriginal communities into Christians and "traditionalists" or "conservatives," leading to factional disputes among the people (see for example studies by Johnson 1964; Shimony 1961; and Weaver 1972 for the divisive effects of missionary activity among the Haudenosaunee of the Grand River Six Nations).

In Toby Morantz's (2002) most recent work she follows Comaroff and Comaroff (1991) whose subtitle to their book is "Christianity, Colonialism, and Consciousness." In her own subtitle, "The Colonial Challenge to the Crees," Morantz continues a theme developed in an earlier work (Francis and Morantz, 1983), in which she argues that in the pre-twentieth century fur trade in the James Bay area the position of the Cree cannot be understood as a form of colonial domination. As a reviewer of her *The White Man's Gonna Getcha* (2002), Paul Nadasdy (2004: 191) suggests, a central theme of Morantz's work is that "the Cree retained their autonomy throughout the fur trade era and were able to dictate in significant ways the terms of that trade as well as of Cree-White relations generally. ... Morantz refuses to see colonialism as a simple story of subjugation by an expanding and monolithic state."

Missionaries, along with the Hudson's Bay Company traders, and later Canadian government officials, acted as a triumvirate that set a particular set of environmental and historical circumstances, which certainly influenced Cree society but did not ultimately control the people in it, or so Morantz suggests. The missionaries and the Cree formed a complex mix of relationships in which the members of each group had difficulty understanding the motives and objectives of each other. Morantz (2002: 7) attempts to explain the particular type of colonial influences that the missionaries exerted on the Cree which she terms "civilizing colonialism," after the Comaroff's (1991) three models of colonialism: state, settler, and civilizing "The missionaries," she suggests, "had to content themselves with reshaping only the ideological framework of the Crees and ignoring their communal family and economic institutions."

The reason for this situation largely has to do with the fact that the Cree were mostly nomadic hunters and trappers, rather than settled agriculturalists, so that more permanent Cree settlements at the trading post were not possible. In any event, it was not in the interest of the Hudson's Bay Company to have a settled Cree population in their midst because the traders wanted the Cree out on the land trapping for furs. Thus, the missionaries' influence on the Cree was only partial and intermittent. At the trading post the missionaries were able to exert some influence on the Cree, but when they went back to their trap lines they tended to revert to their traditional religious ways of relying on the conjuring tent for a sense of direction in their lives. The result was a form of "syncretism" (Morantz 2002: 88, 95–6) in which Christian beliefs intermingled with Cree traditional spiritual ones.

The Cree were able to show considerable composure when the missionaries flung ridicule and verbal abuse at their traditional beliefs. "Missionaries," Morantz (2002: 88) suggested, "denigrated their heathen practices as savage. They did not target only their religious practices but strove hard to alter their daily habits." The Cree, though, must have found certain aspects of Christian beliefs meaningful. What emerged, then, was a blend of Christianity with the Cree's animistic belief systems, which followed parallel systems.

The Bishopric of Rupert's Land was established as early as 1649 with official record keeping beginning in 1780. Jesuit missionaries began to live in what became Fort Albany between 1686 and 1693. The initial Church of England (Anglican) missionaries were first stationed at York Factory in 1823, although most began arriving in the 1840s. Their mission was described in the Diocese of Moosonee official history in heroic terms: "To live and die for the Indian and the Kingdom" (Peterson 1974: 6). A Wesleyan missionary was active in converting Cree at Moose Factory before Roman Catholic oblates began missionizing in 1847 and later extended their influence northward to Fort Albany. In Attawapiskat and Winisk virtually the entire population "converted" to the Catholic faith, (according to the literature found in Niezen 1994: 463–91; Brown and Brightman 1988; Honigmann 1981: 218; Hedican 2017: 48–52).

One of the important factors in the success of the conversion at Attawapiskat was that the oblate missionaries spoke Cree fluently. The missionaries also played an educational role in the community by operating a day school. They also occasionally dispensed medical assistance by issuing pharmaceuticals that had been provided by the Indian Affairs agent. At Moose Factory, fieldworker John Honigmann reported that the relationship between the Cree and the missionary at times "showed strain," although the priests were able "to maintain a dominant moral role and to be a strong force for social control in the community" (1981a: 225). There was also a "strain" at times between the doctrine of the various faiths with Protestant and Roman Catholic missionaries espousing at times contradictory views of Christian principles. The result of such situations, as John McLean recounts, was that "the poor ignorant natives, hearing such conflicting doctrines, are at a loss what to think or what to believe; and, natural enough, conclude that both are alike imposters, and therefore in many cases decline their instructions. [However], the particular dress ... of the Romanish ministers and their imposing ritual, make a great impression on the senses of a barbarous people" (1968 [1932]: 318–19).

Cree conversion to Christianity was a process that started about 1840, according to Morantz (2002: 74). A Methodist missionary, George Barnley, based at Moose Factory, arrived at Rupert House about that time and began baptismal and marriage rituals (Long 1986, 1988a, 1988b). By the late 1850s the HBC post had a resident missionary who served the Great Whale River area, but by the 1860s the Anglican Church had increasing difficulty in finding resident ministers in the distant places, although missions at Moose Factory, Rupert House, and Fort George appeared to be well established. Rev. John Horden, who was based at

Moose Factory, travelled along the James Bay coast performing minis-
terial duties.

As far as the depth of the Cree's commitment to Christianity is concerned, this is difficult to ascertain; however, there have been a few en-
lightening statements that have survived in the historical literature. For
example, the Anglican minister at Fort George in the mid 1850s, Rev.
E.A. Watkins, was not prone to exaggerate any success he might have
perceived when he commented that the Cree "felt no interest whatever in the sacred truths which it is my duty to proclaim." After four
years he was relieved of his Fort George ministry and resituated at Red
River. Similar comments were also made to those noted by Rev. Watkins among the Anishinaabe of the Rainy River area in northwestern
Ontario (Morantz 2002: 75; Frances and Morantz 1983: 162; Brown 1987,
1996; Niezen 1997).

As far as the Indigenous people (Cree and Anishinaabe) of northern Ontario were concerned they made periodic travels to the James
Bay trading posts so that they were more isolated from missionary
influences by geographic distance. For example, it was noted that the
"early missionaries ... found the Ojibwa [Anishinaabe] religion strong
and resistant to change. The first few Christian converts [were] deserted women, the sick old men, the diseased children, the blind, and
the sexually maladjusted" (Schmalz 1991: 10). With time, however, and
increased incursions of fur traders and missionaries into the interior of
northern Ontario, the Anishinaabe began to experience a loss of their
traditional beliefs along with a diminished food supply, making them
more reliant on interior Hudson's Bay Company posts. This was accompanied by a sense of powerlessness in the face of the overwhelming force of European colonialism through time. Increased missionary
activity began to have success in convincing the Aboriginal inhabitants
to abandon their traditional ceremonies and beliefs, which were called
pagan and primitive by the Europeans. An increase in missionary activities led to a diminished role for traditional leaders who increasingly
seemed incapable of providing spiritual guidance in the face of an on-
slaught of destructive outside forces.

One of the most effective strategies of the European missionaries to
increase their influence was to encourage Aboriginal peoples themselves to join the various Christian religious organizations. These converts had the advantage of knowing the Aboriginal language in all
its nuances and to understand the fears, apprehensions, and desires
of the local Native population much better than the Europeans ever
could (see Graham 1975; Grant 1984). John McLean was clearly aware
of the advantages of employing Aboriginal missionaries when he noted

that "the Church of England, it is true, has done a little, but she might have done more – much more. Had the missionaries exerted themselves, from the time of their first arrival in the country, in educating *natives* [emphasis in the original] as Missionaries, and sent them forth to preach the Word, the pure doctrines of Christianity would, ere now, have been widely disseminated through the land. But nothing of this kind has been attempted" (1968 [1932]: 320).

McLean was wrong, however, since there were efforts made to employ Aboriginal men in the proselytizing efforts of the various Christian churches. The first Native priest of the Anglican church, for example, was Henry Budd of Red River. Thomas Vincent, born in 1835 at Osnaburgh House of parents "who had native blood," was sent to Fort Albany after ordination. It was indicated that Vincent "waged a vigorous and fiercely energetic campaign to win souls for God" (Peterson 1974: 14). Rev. Edward Richards graduated from the school at Moose Factory, was ordained in 1887, and then sent to serve at Rupert's House. John Sanders was born near Flying Post, in the Chapleau area, and eventually sent to Moose Factory where he married a local girl. Sanders was instrumental in translating the Moosonee Hymn and Prayer Book into the Anishinaabe language. Although they lived farther south than James Bay, the names of Rev. Peter Jones (Kahkewaquonaby), Rev. George Copway (Kahgegagahbowh) and Rev. John Sunday had widespread appeal across the continent (Chute 1998; Smith 1987).

What Does "Conversion" Mean?

It has been pointed out, nevertheless, that the term "conversion" has a wide range of meanings. "'Converting' to Christianity," Neylan (2003: 27) warns, "has multiple meanings … the idea that Euro-Canadian missionaries converted First Nations to Christianity without Native participation in the process is as preposterous as it sounds. Missionary work involved complex relations of religious cultures." Perhaps in this regard it would be more prudent not to regard traditional Aboriginal beliefs as subsequently "replaced" by Christian ones, but what probably occurred was a form of amalgamation of the two without the traditional ones disappearing entirely, even for those Indigenous people who apparently "converted" to Christianity.

In a similar vein of thought, it is probably more ethnographically correct to regard the colonization process not as a sort of one-way progression whereby Aboriginal social and cultural aspects are exchanged, one for one, with European ones. Rather, it would be more accurate to view the process as an admixture of the two traditions, European and

Aboriginal, whose eventual contents varied from community to community, depending upon a multiplicity of factors that favour change in one direction or another. For example, in the 1670s when the fur trade began to draw large numbers of Anishinaabe and Cree hunters and trappers away from the territory north of Lake Superior, some Aboriginal people, mainly the Cree, chose to live in close proximity to the fur-trading posts on Hudson and James Bay, while others remained quite distant, trading their fur only infrequently. As such, contacts with Europeans and their economic and religious organizations varied considerably from band to band, or community to community, which in turned resulted in wide variations in the nature and depth of European influences. In this sense, a definition of colonialism such as "the domination of another land and people through economic and political control established by violent or coercive force" (Cannon and Sunseri 2011: 276) needs to take into account the variations in the sorts of "domination" that is experienced from region to region, and from society to society.

One would be remiss for not mentioning the psychological and physical stress that colonialist pressures brought upon the Indigenous inhabitants of northern Canada. Rev. John Horton of Moose Factory made an extensive journey up to Fort Albany on the west coast of James Bay, then to Rupert's House, East Main, and Fort George on the east side of the Bay, then on into the interior. This trip caused him to be "torn by sorrow." A description of his journey recounts the following afflictions among the Cree:

"The hardships and the deaths that he encountered on his visits were almost too harrowing to bear even in the reading of them, as he described them in his letters. Horden would find, in settlement after settlement, that the tribe had been decimated, and at times almost wiped out, by hunger, by cold too severe to be endured in their weakened state, by drowning in canoes, and by accidents of various kinds. Added to these were the ravages of the White Man's diseases" (Peterson 1974: 13).

Remember that this assessment of Cree life in the James Bay area was not based on obscure second-hand reports but founded on first-hand observations by Rev. Horton himself. He notes furthermore that "For the past few years they have suffered greatly from a failure of food, and many have starved ... numbers having died of starvation" (ibid. 13–14). It was also noted that "The bodies of both adults and children, weakened by starvation, would be found frozen to death. [In addition], outbreaks of whooping-cough, diphtheria, and influenza wrought havoc among them" (ibid.,14).

These observations are in direct contradiction to the journals of the Hudson's Bay Company at Moose Factory which consistently reported that while the Cree trappers reported being hungry and in a starving state, none had died. There is also nothing in the journals mentioning the spread of disease at all. It is almost as if the assessment by the company factors was, Yes, there is hunger among the Cree, but we supply them with food when they visit our posts, then they are able to continue their trapping. Also, it is never mentioned that probably the greatest cause of hunger was the widespread deprivation caused by the professional Cree hunters who were hired by the Hudson's Bay Company to feed the fur traders and their contingent of employees at the various trading posts, leaving virtually no country food for the Cree attempting to make a living from the land. Also, as far as the oft-touted Christian benevolence of the Hudson's Bay Company is concerned in supporting the aged, diseased, and infirmed at the company posts, McLean contradicts this directly. Even though, he notes, that "we ourselves depend on the natives for a considerable part of our subsistence … we support neither old nor young, diseased nor infirm – that is the truth" (1968 [1932]: 320). Having been a post manager himself, McLean was in a position to know the facts of the matter.

One can only imagine the emotional and psychological trauma caused by a situation in which Cree parents were forced to watch their children and other family members slowly starve to death without any available recourse. Surely the Cree in their lonely, cold abodes in such a forbidding climate as the James Bay Lowlands would suffer from depression and anxiety over the fate of their families. It could be expected naturally that the Cree would become filled with anger and irritability over their fate. They would no doubt have had trouble sleeping on their empty stomachs, thoughts racing through their minds with constant worry. In such conditions bad or regrettable decisions would no doubt be made.

Comparisons of the Cree case of James Bay with the Irish famine of 1847 cannot be ignored. In the Irish case, a free trade policy with Britain resulted in more food being exported out of Ireland that would have been necessary to feed the starving Irish masses as a result of the Act of Union of 1800. In both case – the British Parliament under Prime Minister William Gladstone in the Irish case and Governor Simpson in the situation of the James Bay Cree – were certainly capable of enacting measures to alleviate the food deprivation if they wished to do so (Woodham-Smith 1962; Gallagher 1982; Hedican 2020).

In both cases the starvation was minimized as a short-term problem, and the aid was not forthcoming, except for minimal handouts at the fur trading posts of James and soup kitchens for the needy among the Irish. Both measures were hardly an adequate response to the hardships that both the Cree and the Irish suffered under the watch of their colonial British overlords. The only real difference between the two catastrophes is that many Irish were able to emigrate out of their country, a luxury not available to the Cree who had no other place to go for relief. In another comparison, the absentee Anglo-Irish landlords were too distant to take benevolent action had they witnessed the famine themselves in much the same way that the various shareholders of the Hudson's Bay Company were much more interested in making a profit from the fur trade to be interested in the plight of the starving Cree. Comparing the famines in both Ireland and James Bay is certainly a topic worth pursuing by other scholars, but one is intrigued by the historical parallels in terms of the effects of British colonialism on local populations under their control and the apparent disinterest in helping solve both problems. Millions of people died as a result; however, the only difference was that the Cree had no place of escape – an option that was available to thousands of fortunate Irish migrants.

In summary, relating the forgoing discussion of missionary activity among the Cree to the murders at Hannah Bay, it is noteworthy that the shaking tent ceremony was still practised at Rupert House and at Waswanipi into the 1960s. Likewise, Adrian Tanner (2005: 88–90, 136–52) noted the continued practice of hunting rituals in the Mistassini area, which indicates a persistence of traditional beliefs in supernatural forces and suggests that the apparent loss of Cree practices and beliefs was probably not widespread. Even twenty years later, Knight (1968) was told by Cree informants that in hunting drum singing was still a powerful force. Although Niezen (1997: 466) suggests that "Missions, medicine and education acted together as complementary institutions to conversion," Morantz (2002: 6) argues strongly that "in James Bay, this is not so."

From the available evidence we can therefore reasonably deduce the following propositions. First, food deprivation in the southern James Bay area had been occurring for at least a century before the Hannah Bay incident. This meant that over the long terms there was a diminishing supply of animals and water fowl to maintain the propagation of these species at the levels of pre-fur trading days. Second, food deprivation and starvation among the Cree was either directly or indirectly the result not only of low subsistence resources in the southern James Bay area but also because HBC traders reduced the volume of these resources by hiring professional hunters to supply food to the trading posts. In addition, even with persistent reports of food deprivation in the area, post managers, presumably for reasons of economy, were reluctant to share their food supplies with the trappers who depended upon an adequate supply of food to maintain their trapping activities. Third, the effect of missionary proselytizing among the Cree, which might have resulted in changing their traditional rituals and beliefs, must have been minimal at best since missionary activity in the James Bay area did not begin to take place until the 1840s, a decade after the Hannah Bay incident.

These three factors acted on one another suggesting that Quapakay and his sons relied on the conjuring tent for guidance, as the Cree had always done in the past and, for the Cree, following the guidance of this ritual was a reasonable and valid course to follow. While not attempting to justify the murder of William Corrigal and others at the Hannah Bay post in any manner, as our primary goal here is one of understanding the causes and pertinent factors leading to the end result, it is nonetheless evident that the Hannah Bay post manager was negligent in ignoring long-held Cree practices of sharing, especially when the English were marrying into Cree society and engaging in social and economic transactions with them. It was also reasonable, therefore, that the Cree would regard the English traders as reneging on mutual expectations of care and support that would normally be extended to kinsmen or at least to those who one would regard as a friend. As long-time ethnographer of the Cree, John Honigmann, points out, "Like human beings everywhere, Indians depended on one another, sharing of food being one form of their mutual dependence. Consequently, people strongly deplored the individualistic trends of later fur-trade times that curtailed sharing" (1981b: 737–8).

Strategies of Resistance

In the fur-trade era, the Indigenous hunters and trappers were far from hapless victims of colonial oppression. As Ray and Freeman (1978) aptly note in their concluding remarks concerning a study of the relationships between the Hudson's Bay Company and Aboriginal peoples in "*Give Us Good Measure*," a phrase often used by Aboriginal leaders in trading speeches, Aboriginal trappers were in the habit of manipulating English and French rivalries. They traded more frequently with the closer French posts in the interior for goods, such as powder and flints, for which they were in constant need, but would only travel to the Hudson's Bay Company posts on James Bay much less frequently, that is only once every year or two, to obtain bulkier items such as kettles and guns (Ray and freeman 1978: 252–3).

This tactic of playing one post against another was a source of jealously and anxiety among the post managers who felt that control of their Aboriginal clients was slipping away from them. "Indeed, this art of playing off one trader against another," Bishop (1974: 242) noted, "became so well developed that it may be posited that considerable prestige was accorded individuals who excelled in it. A band leader who was able to procure goods would also be likely to have a larger following." Another tactic that Aboriginal trappers used to their advantage was to establish accounts at several posts and then taking their furs where they pleased. This strategy caused post managers to attempt to entice trappers with bribes, usually to little avail.

As a counter strategy the Hudson's Bay Company began to build interior posts, such as Henley House on the forks of the Albany and Kenogami Rivers, established in 1743, about 120 miles into the interior. This strategy was built on the premise that providing opportunities closer to the Aboriginal people's trap lines would make it easier for them to trade and would therefore result in higher fur returns for the company. As Ray and Freeman (1978: 189) reiterate, "In this strategic location the post was to operate as a way station for Indians travelling down to the bay. There the Indians could obtain a few trade goods and see the line of merchandise which was available at Fort Albany. Also, the post served to protect the Indians en route from intimidation from the French."

The problem, as far as the Company was concerned, was that such interior posts were much more difficult to provision than those on James Bay because of the distance involved from the coast and the limited carrying capacity of the canoes and York boats. As a result, the interior posts tended not to carry a full range of goods, but only those items that were light weight and easy to carry, such as tobacco, rum, flints, awls, fishhooks, and so on. The disparity of goods carried in interior posts and their coastal counterparts was a source of conflict and dissention between trappers and post managers (Bishop 1976; Francis and Morantz 1983: 99–100). To the company's chagrin, while there was a temporary increase in trade at Fort Albany, there was also a corresponding detrimental effect on the trade at Moose Factory.

Eventually, the French built a trading post in the vicinity of Henley House. As a result, the Aboriginal trappers began to pressure the Hudson's Bay Company to provide a wider array of goods to trade at Henley House, which was a move that the London directors of the Company resisted. Although the dynamics involved are complicated, that is, that the issues involved extended beyond merely trade disputes, in 1755 the Henley House post was pillaged and the Englishmen living there were killed. However, whatever the factors involved in the killings at Henley House, it is nonetheless evident that the Aboriginal trapper in the James Bay area were not adverse in developing strategies that increased the power of their bargaining positions by playing the French against the English and playing one post against another. All these tactics may be called "strategies of resistance," which is to say, that the Aboriginal people were pushing back against the hegemonic control of the Hudson's Bay Company and the economic domination that their traders possessed around the bay and its environs.

We cannot know for sure the reasons that Aboriginal trappers in the James Bay area adapted various forms of behaviour in their trading practices; however, we do have evidence of their thinking in the behaviour that they took in dealing with the Hudson's Bay Company traders and others in the fur trade. For instance, we know from a wide range of studies of colonialism that minority groups tend to find ways to resist the hegemonic powers that seek to control them. Resistance, as is often the case, is an aspect of a small group's attempt to seek autonomy from larger powers (Hedican 2013: 88–97, 2016: 142–50).

There are various forms that resistance can take, such as a refusal to comply with some pressure placed on an individual or group. As such, it can involve providing a hindrance to some activity or acting to impede some action, which often takes place in an economic or political context. Essentially these are what could be termed more passive forms of resistance, but there are other varieties as well. For example, Allahar (1998: 338) notes that when discussing strategies of resistance, the term "resistance" can be defined as "any action, whether physical, verbal or psychological, and whether individual or collective, that seeks to undo the negative consequences of being categorized for racial reasons ... Resistance [can] be seen as a political act ultimately tied to wider cultural forces that frame it." Ultimately, Allahar ties resistance to processes of racial oppression, which is to say, that resistance "can be used or manipulated to resist or mollify the deleterious consequences of racism" (ibid.). At least three strategies of resistance can be identified.

One form of resistance strategy identified by Allahar (1998: 338–52) is *multiculturalism* which involves attempts at accommodation on the part of minority group members to the powers that oppress them. A case could be made to regard the Home Guard Cree in this fashion. The Cree who lived around the trading posts of James Bay learned English, dressed in European-style clothes, and were employed by the Hudson's Bay Company in various capacities. This state of affairs placed the Cree in a "partly in, partly out" situation. They were able to maintain relationships with Cree trappers of the interior who were their cultural counterparts while staying on friendly terms with company people at the trading post.[10]

From this intercalary position the Home Guard Cree were able to continue to use their own language with their cultural counterparts and maintain, if they wished, long-standing traditions of religious beliefs, marriage patterns, and so on. However, as John McLean suggests (1968 [1932]: 99), the Home Guard Cree while "frequently in company with white men and Christians ... still retain many of the barbarous habits, and much of the superstitious belief of their forefathers, aggravated, I regret to say, by some of the vices of the whites." From this position their movements and prospects were not curtailed – they could return to the bush as trappers, if they wished, or integrate further into the Company society. This position is also advantageous because it allowed the Cree who lived and worked around the coastal trading posts to circumvent more direct pressures to assimilate, so that in this form the Home Guard Cree could be seen to enact a passive form of resistance.

Assimilation can be seen as another form of resistance, which involves minority group members willing to accept the value system of the dominant society as a means of passing into the larger society. In some ways this strategy can be interpreted as following the path of least resistance. It can be considered a form of resistance because it seeks to undo the negative consequences of racial or ethnic categorization. Even though this strategy is essentially a rejection of multicultural policies of accommodation, which tends to accentuate the distinctiveness of certain groups, it could nonetheless be regarded as political in nature because it is an attempt to negotiate the terms under which the minority group is accepted into the social structure of the dominant society.[11]

As Aboriginal authors Taiaiake Alfred and Jeff Corntassel (2011: 140) explain, the concept of "'aboriginalism' is a legal, political, and cultural discourse designed to serve an agenda of silent surrender to an inherently unjust relation at the root of the colonial state itself." Their point is that this "agenda of silent surrender" has involved some Aboriginal people giving up on their cultural heritage by succumbing to the political and social agenda of the dominant society (Hedican 2016: 143). Among the Cree and other Aboriginal peoples, those individuals who freely became deacons, canons, priests, and ministers in the various Christian faiths could be classified in this assimilationist category because they abjured their own cultural and religious beliefs in favour of the moral values characteristic of a foreign state. However, total assimilation to a European society would never be available to them because their role, from the perspective of the foreign colonial power, was unidimensional in that it was limited to converting members of their own cultural heritage. Passing into the dominant British society was hardly an option or a possibility outside of the fur trading territory itself.

A third strategy of resistance pertains to neither assimilation nor accommodation but involves instead a *direct confrontation* (or *culture conflict*) with those regarded as oppressing a certain group. As is frequently the case, this form of resistance is usually more spontaneous than well-planned and is often not particularly coordinated. This is especially the case in the initial acts of resistance because during these periods the objectives have probably not been particularly articulated in an effective manner. What is generally lacking is a clearer, more coherently articulated vision of the new social order that the minority group hopes to achieve so that the resistance is really not much more than spontaneous acts of violence against member of the colonial majority, that is, those who represent the colonial power structure and as such become symbols of grievances, malaise, or discontent.[12]

The reason that this form of resistance usually lacks effective coordination is not only due to its predominantly spontaneous nature but also because of the lack of effective leadership capable of controlling the emergent acts of violence. As an example, the killings at Hannah Bay were not particularly well planned and involved very limited objectives, and the perpetrators were apparently unable to entice others into similar violence even though grievances against the Hudson's Bay Company's treatment of the Aboriginal population may have been widespread in the James Bay area. Note, though, that the fur traders were worried that a regional upheaval may begin to take place. As an example of the mounting concern in the fur-trading community that the Hannah Bay killings were possibly the first step in a more regional rebellion against the Company, it was the very next day (January 24, 1832) that a party was sent out at 3 a.m. to "meet with the Murderers at the Post to make an example of ... and thereafter He [William Swanson] is to proceed with his party to Ruperts House; and is the Bearer of a Letter to Mr Chief Factor Joseph Beioley to inform him of the Crimes committed by the Indians belonging to his District" (Chief Factor John McTavish B135/a/137-8).

One can presume with reasonable confidence that the Moose Factory manager urged Mr. Swanson to proceed with haste to Ruperts House because he was at least partly fearful of a spread in attacks on company posts. This generally strategy, while not articulated clearly in the fur trading post journals, was nonetheless voiced by fur trader John McLean who was at the time familiar with the James Bay area and with the killings at Hannah Bay. McLean wrote (1968 [1932]: 99–101):

This man [presumably Quapakay] told his fellows that he had had a communication from the Great Spirit, who assured him that he would become the greatest man in Hudson's Bay if he only followed the course prescribed to him, which was, first, to cut off their own trading post, and then with the spoil got there to hire other Indians, who would assist in destroying all the other posts the Company possessed in the country. Accordingly, it was determined to carry their design into execution, whenever a favourable opportunity occurred ... Measures were immediately adopted to frustrate the further diabolical designs of the Indians, as well as to avenge the innocent blood that had been shed. Messengers were dispatched with all possible haste to Rupert's house, the nearest post, to give the alarm, and a party of men, under an efficient leader, was sent to seize the murderers.

It is beyond the scope of the present writing to speculate on how widespread McLean's theory was shared by others in the fur trade industry of James Bay; however, as Francis and Morantz (1983) summarized concerning the Hannah Bay killings, "whether some form of messianic movement was involved is impossible to tell from the evidence." In addition, John Anderson who was involved in the capture of the guilty party, offered the opinion that the Hannah Bay attack was to be the first step in a program of resistance against the company's posts in eastern James Bay: "From the women it was afterwards ascertained that the Indians intended to have cut off the different small posts in the interior of Rupert's River District ... they expected to be joined by all the E. Main Indians and had even contemplated the possibility of capturing the vessel from Europe and murdering the crew" (Anderson Papers, 7; Francis and Morantz 1983: 160).

One cannot even speculate on what basis Anderson arrived at this apparently far-fetched story; however, it does hint at a combination of religious and economic motives for the Hannah Bay attack. In any event, if a general uprising was planned as McLean and Anderson suggest, it did not take place.

In conclusion, in terms of the various strategies of resistance in the James Bay area, the available evidence suggests that all three of the forms of resistance that are itemized by Allahar – accommodation, assimilation, and direct confrontation – took place among the Cree and other possible Aboriginal groups during the fur trade era. One might also add Frantz Fanon's (1963) influential study, *The Wretched of the Earth* to our present discussion. Fanon argued that colonization is of necessity a violent process because in the early phases of resistance the colonized may be unable to direct their frustration and anger at the colonial power.

Colonization as a Violent Process

Given the ecological situation in the southern James Bay area during the early 1800s it is reasonable to assume that the Cree might blame the fur trade and the Hudson's Bay Company in particular for they dire food shortages that were reported almost daily. Shortages of food make one not only physically weak but resentful of those seen to be the cause of this malady. Furthermore, Fanon (1963: 45) also suggests that the colonized may also direct their frustration and anger at their cultural companions. William Corrigal was part Cree and therefore could be seen as not in the same social and cultural universe as "regular" HBC employees. The expectation then could be that Corrigal would be expected to follow Cree norms and values pertaining to sharing in times of need, unlike the expectations that the Cree might have with HBC personnel. Whether we agree with Fanon or not, he suggests that resistance necessarily involves an association of violence and colonialism as inseparable phenomenon.

In her discussion of "native resistance discourse," Emma LaRocque echoes Fanon's point that there are ironies in the resistance to colonialism especially in terms of the topic of "reinvention." For example, LaRoque indicates that in their attempts to redefine the terms of colonialism, the "new Natives" must negotiate a new path in their relationship with the colonial power that is neither tribal nor Western. As LaRoque (2010: 157) states, European culture should not be the goal for Indigenous societies. Thus, a new road must be found between the past and the future, an idea that Fanon puts forth in his assertion that there is a certain inevitability of reinvention with resistance in terms of a mobilization of human creativity, of finding new ways of dealing with the social and cultural changes that are a response to colonialism, and the forging of new relationships with those holding power in the colonial state. LaRoque (ibid., 158) would appear to agree with Fanon's assertion when she indicates that "we must ... throw off the weight of antiquity," suggesting, one would suppose, that "antiquity" for the contemporary Indigenous person could be more of a burden or hindrance than a grounding upon which to build modernity.[13]

Of course, it would be reading too much into the murders at Hannah Bay in 1832 to suggest that Quapakay and his sons had a grand design, one that might envisage the casting off of colonial oppression, but the suppression of the Hudson's Bay Company and the power that this company held over the Cree people, especially with regards the deleterious effects of the fur trade, would no doubt be seen from an Indigenous perspective as the Europeans' responsibility. Despite numerous complaints about starvation and general food shortages, the Hudson's Bay Company apparently was unwilling to take any responsibility for this situation or to attempt remedial measures to increase the food supply in the southern James Bay area.

Certainly, it was within the power of the Hudson's Bay Company to bring more food from England to feed the HBC personnel at the various posts, a move that would nonetheless have increased local costs. We can infer that the HBC factors decided that this move was not necessary despite the constant complaints from the Cree hunters. From the Cree's perspective, then, they could have viewed HBC intransigence on the issue of a diminishing food supply as evidence of a certain callousness on the fur trader's part. If complaining to the HBC post managers about the food shortages brought no tangible results, then a decision might be made to take the matter into their own hands, to take action of a drastic measure and as a means of sending a message that the present situation – not only of the food shortages but of the general relationships between the two parties – was now in an intolerable impasse.

So, many years later, the colonial mantle passed from the English fur traders to the Canadian government, yet Indigenous responses to colonial oppression did not dissipate. At various times this resistance may take the milder or passive form of non-compliance or emerge at other times through violent confrontation. It is for this reason that La-Roque begins her discussion on resistance by explaining that her work is about "the inevitable Aboriginal contrapuntal reply to Canada's colonial constructs. What will emerge is a resistance born from the contested ground upon which we, the Canadian colonizer-colonist and Native colonized, have built our troubled discourse" (2010: 3). As she suggests, then, the colonizer-colonized complex is at the root of Aboriginal resistance in Canada. This resistance originates in the power that is maintained by the colonizer over the colonized that has deep historical roots in Canada.

In terms of the historical development of Indigenous resistance to the colonial ties in Canada, these can be traced back in time, from the Ipperwash protest of 1995, the Mohawk protest in 1990 at Oka, Quebec, the opposition to the 1969 White Paper proposals, and so on, back to the Battle of Batoche in 1885. These various conflicts are deep-rooted historically in Canada and reveal, according to Bonita Lawrence (2011: 69), "the historical record of how [Aboriginal] land was acquired – the forcible and relentless dispossession of Indigenous peoples, the theft of their territories, and the implementation of legislation and policies designed to affect their total disappearance as people."

Decolonizing History

This history of dispossession was written outside of an Indigenous perspective, a history in which the Hudson's Bay Company and English stockholders were portrayed as adventurers, as honourable men of business, rather than as colonial oppressors, who were not culpable in the death and subjugation of Indigenous people. It is necessary, then, according to Indigenous authors such as Bonita Lawrence (2011: 70) to "decolonize history," in order that the colonization process will no longer be viewed as a benign one, but instead as one in which Indigenous perspectives are considered. There will no doubt be British apologists who would cringe at such a proposal, who would regard the Aboriginal experiences with commercial enterprises such as the Hudson's Bay Company as mutually beneficial, rather than repressive. History would suggest otherwise.

Canadians today see themselves as decent people who are innocent of wrongdoing towards the Indigenous people in their midst. Most Canadians are oblivious to the historical processes underlying their very habitation of this country or of the legislation and policies that Lawrence refers to, which served to silence the Indigenous voices of dissent within the national discourse. It is necessary to see in this national discourse of Canadian nation-building the Indigenous resistance that was suppressed and subverted in the historical past in the interest of creating a myth of peaceful interaction between settlers and Indigenous people. Where in the books of Canada's history are situations such as the Hannah Bay killings even mentioned, let alone discussed?

Academic disciplines today are themselves complicit in promulgating the myths of peaceful cohabitation and settlement in Canada, of silencing Indigenous voices of dissent, and creating an academic discourse which places the practitioners of these disciplines as the experts on Canada's past. As Lawrence articulates (2011), "the 'seminal' works of contemporary non-Native 'experts' is an exercise in alienation. It is impossible for Native people to see themselves in the unknown and unknowable shadowy figures portrayed on the peripheries of the white settlements of colonial Nova Scotia, New France, and Upper Canada whose lives are deduced solely through archaeological evidence or the journals of those who sought to conquer, convert, defraud, or in any other way prosper off them."

This historical record is hardly congruent with the "real" facts of history, which reveal a more accurate account of Canada, or what happened at Hannah Bay, Henley House, and other localities during the colonial period. The first acts of concealment originated in the fur traders' journals, then on through the various historical accounts that dissembled the Indigenous view and therefore presented European settlement as somehow "honourable" or even as beneficial to the Indigenous inhabitants. The Hannah Bay killings were apparently not the only acts of resistance in the James Bay area, and one wonders what other accounts of similar events have since been submerged in these acts of colonial suppression, concealment, and misinformation. As such, as far as Bonita Lawrence is concerned, Canadian history from an Aboriginal perspective is all about European history and the lies, fabrications, and rationalizations that the settler population makes about the Indigenous people of this country.[14]

Conclusion

There can be little doubt that the employees of the Hudson's Bay Company engaged in a consistent policy of suppression and control over the individuals in Cree society in order to prevent or impede possible dissent over the conditions of the fur trade in the James Bay area. One of the methods of control was to ingratiate themselves with Cree leaders, especially influential Cree trappers, by providing them with various gifts and honorary titles in a scheme termed the "trading Captain" system. In addition, traditional Cree religious principles were suppressed by Christian missionaries who denigrated the Cree spiritual beliefs as primitive or pagan and made attempts to convert the Cree to various Christian faiths. It remains unclear, however, whether these various measures were successful in controlling the Cree because evidently various members of the Cree population resisted these external pressures for change. A significant factor in these attempts at resistance pertained to the fact that the Cree remained on their trap lines and were therefore isolated from the English posts for most of the year.

Chapter Five

Violent Conflicts Involving Indigenous People

The Hudson's Bay Company was a law unto itself and slaughtered Indians without legal excuse even for the taking of property.
— B. Farrinto, *American Journal of Legal History* (2000: 489).

The officers of the [HBC] company ... certainly believed in the necessity of retaliation when white men were injured or killed ... Fur traders demanded revenge and often in the heat of the moment demanded it in violent terms.
— Robin Fisher, *Contact and Conflict* (1977: 36).

The obligation for return lies at the heart of the most widespread mechanism of economic distribution, namely reciprocity.
— Morton Fried, *The Evolution of Political Society* (1967: 63).

The Cree and the Hudson's Bay Company employees in the James Bay area were engaged in a serious conflict over the fur trade territory for at least a century, lasting from about 1750 to 1850. There were several important facets to this conflict. One of these concerned the propensity of HBC employees to take Aboriginal women as wives and then to abandon them and their children when the employee left the area. Another serious source of conflict pertained to the so-called liquor trade, which had a demoralizing effect on the Indigenous people and ultimately threatened to undermine the fur trade altogether. A third issue related to a conflict in the cultural perceptions held by the Cree and the English with regards to their individual notions of what could be termed "principles of exchange." The Cree and the British views of exchange and reciprocity were at the very heart of the fur trade itself and were a source of manipulation by both parties as each sought to gain an advantage over the negotiation process that bound the two groups together.

Sharing and Survival

There is a long history in anthropology of studying reciprocal relationships in a variety of different societies. Several classic studies in anthropology point to the same principle of human existence and endurance on this planet. Morton Fried's study entitled *The Evolution of Political Society* (1967) is certainly one of these pivotal writings upon which most of modern social-cultural anthropology is built. Probably the most important point that Fried makes in his study is that "the obligation for return lies at the heart of the most widespread mechanism of economic distribution, namely reciprocity" (1967: 63). Later he further adds that "a general principle of reciprocal economic exchanges ... is that the mechanism for balancing exchanges is vested in set formulas for distribution" (ibid., 64–5).

Fried also suggests that "It is improbable that human families existed as isolated, autonomous units until the bands of which they were part were forced into areas of low natural food potential" (ibid., 67).[1] Therefore, the conclusions that we can draw from Fried's study is that humans living in hunting societies, which amounts to almost all of human existence, would have been incapable of inhabiting the more marginal food resource areas of this planet without engaging in reciprocal sharing patterns. We can therefore also conclude that systems of sharing scarce resources was the single most important factor in our survival. Notice also that Fried uses the phrase "the *obligation* for return [my emphasis]" – sharing was not an optional activity; it was obligatory for our survival.

The second classic study is Richard Lee and Irven DeVore's *Man the Hunter* (1968) which echoes Fried's conclusions about human survival. They assert, for example, that one of their basic assumptions about hunters and gatherers, indeed, the one that is "most important, [is] a pattern of sharing out the collected food resources" (1968: 11). Notice that of the many characteristics of hunters that could be mentioned, the "*most important* [emphasis mine]" is sharing. Notice also that both Lee and DeVore are essentially suggesting the same thing as Fried when he used the term "obligation for return." In another essay in the same volume, Richard Lee explains "how [hunters] make out on scarce resources." In hunting societies, the basis of their food supply, namely game animals "are scarce, mobile, unpredictable, and difficult to catch. A hunter has no guarantee of success and may in fact go for days or weeks without killing a large mammal" (1968: 40). In this regard the !Kung Bushmen of the Kalahari are not unlike the Cree of Hudson's Bay – hunting is an unpredictable enterprise and without sharing very few people ever survive. This was the story of all our ancestors up until the domestication of plants which occurred about five or six thousand years ago.[2]

What anthropological studies have shown is that the give and take of social life is a fundamental aspect of human relationships and is probably one of the principal factors of survival for humanity as a whole. In fact, one might assert that reciprocity is a crucial factor of survival in many cultures, especially in those whose people live in marginal environments where subsistence resources are frequently scare and prone to seasonal fluctuations. A simple fact of nature, then, is that humans must adapt to the availability of food obtainable from their environment or they probably will not survive. As such, one of the mechanisms that humans have used to survive in marginal environments is to engage in reciprocal relationships, such that the availability of food is more evenly distributed.

As Lombardi suggests in his paper, "Reciprocity and Survival," "when the resources available to an economically cooperating unit are scarce, fluctuations in the availability of these resources can have consequences for survival" (1975: 245). In other words, reciprocal exchange is a common strategy adopted in order to reduce fluctuations in resources and thereby enhance their chances of survival; however, "without reciprocity the household will spend some time without the means for survival, while with reciprocity a secure though perhaps meagre survival is ensured" (ibid., 252).

A classic case of the role of sharing as an aspect of cultural survival concerned the various studies of the !Kung San of the Kalahari of South Africa. Even though the !Kung San and the Cree of James Bay are worlds apart in both geography and history, there are some important comparisons that can be made between the two societies. One important aspect is that the members of both societies live in environments that could be described as marginal in that in both areas – the Kalahari Desert and the James Bay Lowlands – food resources are relatively scarce. For people to exist in both areas they must develop methods of food sharing as a strategy of survival. For the Attawapiskat Cree, the existential reality was "the possibility of starvation ... the bush, which had sustained them for uncounted generations, and which could be dealt with on its own terms through traditional skills and cosmology, was to be feared. People *did* die in the bush" [emphasis in the original] (Cummins 2004: 30).[3]

In Flannery's biography of Ellen Smallboy in "A Cree Woman's Life" she describes how the Cree ethic of sharing was so important because "the availability of food was unpredictable throughout the area [of

James Bay]. Semi-starvation was not uncommon and death from starvation was all too frequent" (1995: 17–18). Most of the ethnographies of the Cree contain sections describing practices of sharing food (i.e., Preston 2002: 14–15, 44, 45). Similarly, among the !Kung San, Marshall indicates that "the arduous hunting-gathering life would have been impossible without the co-operation and companionship of a larger group ... the people are sustained by a web of mutual obligation." And furthermore, "one must not refuse a proffered gift and that one must give in return (1961: 231, 236, 244; see also Lee and DeVore 1976, and Sylvain 2015).

This accepted principle among hunters that sharing is a basic requisite of survival that is reinforced by a "web of mutual obligation," (remember Fried's phrase "the obligation for return") is also extended to the realm of marriage as well. As such, basic sharing relationships involving subsistence resources are often extended to other reciprocal forms of exchange, such as the development of marriage patterns in which bonds of solidarity are fashioned. The anthropological approach to marriage changed considerably when Claude Lévi-Strauss (1969 [1949]) suggested that the whole point of marriage was being missed all together. He suggested that marriage in many cultures is not so much about ties between particular individuals, which is more of the emphasis in Western societies, but is all about the alliances that are formed through marriage between family groups.[4]

As a consequence of Lévi-Strauss's thinking on marriage, research began to shift towards what came to be known as the *alliance theory* of marriage. As Edmund Leach (1968: 545) explained, "Marriage, for Lévi-Strauss, is not simply a matter of establishing a legal basis for the domestic family; it is an *alliance* resulting from a contractual exchange between two groups – the group of the husband and the group of the bride." This exchange can take several different forms. One of these may involve *generalized reciprocity* – we will give you a woman now if you give us some cattle; then later we will use the cattle to obtain another woman from elsewhere. In some societies there is a transfer of property that legitimizes the marriage, called "bride wealth" or "progeny price" which implies that the husband's family compensates his wife's family for the children who are now lost to them. In many hunting and gathering societies, ones in which material possessions are not transferred at marriage, the bride's family is compensated by labour performed by the husband for his wife's family, called "bride service." Whether it be through some form of service or an exchange of gifts, marriage created bonds not just between two individuals, but, more importantly, alliances between the families involved as well.

Creating Bonds of Social and Economic Exchange

The first systematic study of the widespread custom of exchange systems in various cultural settings was produced by Marcel Mauss, the nephew of eminent French sociologist, Émile Durkheim, in his *Essai Sur le Don* (The Gift). Mauss studied such diverse practices as the potlatch of the west coast of North America and the Kula ring of the Trobriand Islands north of Australia. He espoused the idea that these customs were examples of an "archaic" form of exchange characterized by a "circulation of objects side by side with the circulation of persons and rights" (1954 [1925]:45). Thus, Mauss promoted the idea that an exchange of gifts was by necessity associated with an obligation to reciprocate (see Hedican 1986a: 12–18, 1986b: 97–8). A central argument in his work is the thesis that "exchanges and contracts take place in the form of presents; in theory these are voluntary, in reality they are given and reciprocated *obligatorily* [italics added]" (1954 [1925]: 3). Anyone with the least familiarity with fur trade transactions will recognize this quote as a central part of the Hudson's Bay Company's protocol in which small gifts and toddies of rum or brandy always proceeded the actual fur-trade transactions with Indigenous trappers. The point of this ceremony – that it obligated the Indigenous trapper to his Company host – could not be lost on anyone involved.[5]

In all, Mauss also suggested that in the larger sphere of human interaction, social life itself is understandable as expressions of the principle of reciprocity. This idea of reciprocity as a basis of human social interaction found a later expression in *The Elementary Structures of Kinship* (1969 [1949]), by Claude Lévi-Strauss, who proposed that human beings have a universal psychological need for giving and receiving gifts. Furthermore, Lévi-Strauss suggested, in order to understand the basic forms of reciprocity and exchange, "one must appeal to certain fundamental structures of the human mind" (1969 [1949]: 108). In this context reciprocity is seen as the resolving mechanism between "self and others." With the resolution of this basic opposition, the individual's psychological security and the solidarity relations of the social group are enhanced.

Later works, after the 1950s, placed exchange systems in the context of political and economic relationships. This new perspective recognized the materialistic conditions of human life and the political struggles that frequently occur within it. The exercise of power, as a dynamic of exchange relationships, was also an important dimension of further studies in this field. Peter Blau (1964) for example, in his book *Exchange and Power in Social Life*, attempted to demonstrate that the nature of power could be demonstrated by the conditions and characteristics of the exchange itself. As an example, Blau asserted that power exists when one party is not able to immediately offer something in return for the benefits received from another. The former party may then offer a "promissory note" or lien on future services in order to gain compliance. This relationship, in effect, is an acceptance of the power held by another, since they may threaten a person with the withdrawal of their (future) services.

As far as the diversity of exchange systems in cross-cultural perspectives is concerned, it can be suggested that such exchanges can be grouped into three basic patterns of reciprocity. For example, "generalized reciprocity" is generally found in the context of family members and friends in which no return of gifts is expected, which is supposed to be the rule used for gift-giving at Christmas time, although apparently this ethic is rarely followed, as much bickering can occur among relatives concerning who gave what to whom and at what price. In a more central position is what is termed "balanced reciprocity," which is to say that exchanges between two parties taking place in the context of "mutuality" or feelings of friendship for each other such that one party does not attempt to take advantage over the other. At the farthest extreme is "negative reciprocity" or "commercial exchange," which occurs among parties who are not friends, in which a material advantage dominates the exchange, and in which each party attempts to get from the other all that he can (see Sahlins 1965; Schneider 1974: 43–56; Ray and Freeman 1978: 242–5).

This discussion of forms of marriage and the establishment of exchange relations is a prelude to the following discussion of marriage between fur traders and Indigenous women – relationships encouraged by Governor Simpson to increase fur trade profits. His motive apparently was to establish bonds between Hudson's Bay Company employees and Indigenous families as a means of creating more effective trading relationships. However, violent conflicts between Indigenous people and fur-trade employees were frequently the result of attempts to use women as a means of establishing exchange relationships.

The main point of this discussion, however, is that from the Cree perspective, since members of the Hudson's Bay Company attempted to establish reciprocal exchange patterns through trade and marriage, this meant that HBC men were thus *obligated* to engage in reciprocal sharing patterns. When the Hudson's Bay Company men resisted these sharing patterns, such as when Cree families had run out of food and were close to starvation, the Cree would probably feel that they were being insulted, that the HBC men were not living up to their end of the sharing-reciprocal bargain that they themselves had initiated. The Cree would also feel, therefore, that under such circumstances they could take matters into their own hands, to take the food that the HBC men were hoarding, against all accepted patterns of reasonable behaviour and mutual reciprocity.

Understanding European-Indigenous Conflict

In Robin Fisher's seminal work, *Contact and Conflict*, he expresses a complaint about the way Canadian history, especially pertaining to the colonial fur-trade period, is portrayed. Fisher's dissatisfaction concerns the way in which the relationship between the Indigenous population and the European immigrants has been depicted in the historical literature. His central point is that Canada's Indigenous people have been portrayed as "peripheral" to the country's history, "rather than a central concern in the study of Canada's past" (1977: xi), or as mere "background." Furthermore, even some of the most influential works, such as Harold Innis's *The Fur Trade in Canada* (1973 [1930]), has a tendency to portray the Indigenous people in somewhat disparaging or ethnocentric terms, as for example in his reference to "the limited cultural background of the North American hunting peoples [compared to] the more elaborate cultural development of Europeans" (ibid., 388), as if the "cultural development" of a people only referred to their technological or materialist sophistication while ignoring other facets, such as spiritual conceptions or kinship patterns. Innis's conclusion was that "The fur trade was the means by which this demand [for European goods] of the peoples of a more limited cultural development was met" (ibid., 389).

In other words, from Fisher's perspective, "Some of the major themes of Canadian historical writing have perpetuated a limited view of the Indigenous Canadian [such that] the fur trade preserved the Indians from extinction" (1977: xi). In other words, the Indigenous people of Canada owe the Europeans a great favour, because of their "limited cultural development" in Innis's terms, by saving them from certain annihilation despite the former's ten thousand years of successful survival in this country without any aid from the Europeans whatsoever. However, Innis was nonetheless willing to admit that European influences were not all beneficial, especially since "The supply of European goods [caused] the rapid destruction of the food supply" (1970: 388). Even so, if blame were to be assessed for this deterioration in the food source, this was apparently the fault of the Indigenous people who were seen to have utilized European technology to destroy the existing subsistence resources, while important facets of this destruction, such as the European traders' utilization of and reliance upon this very food supply as well, remain ignored in historical studies. And then, with the decline in the fur trade, "the Indians drop from view ... having ceased to be an important factor in the European economy" (Fisher 1977: xi). Such views, Fisher asserts, are "confidently ethnocentric" (ibid.).

While some in academia are largely sympathetic to Fisher's views on the role of Indigenous people in Canada's historical writing, some of his perspectives on the interaction of Indigenous people and Europeans are problematic. As an example, he states that "During the fur-trading period Indians and Europeans shared a mutually beneficial economic system. Because the fur traders were involved in an enterprise that required the co-operation of the Indians, they did not try to alter the social systems radically, to undermine their beliefs, or to destroy the means of their livelihood" (ibid., xiv–xv). It is no doubt true that each group benefited from the co-operation of the other; however, the fur-trade journals and other contemporaneous sources suggest an increasing conflict between Indigenous people and traders over such issues as a deterioration in the food supply, the role of liquor in the fur trade, the abandonment of Indigenous women kept as "country wives," contrary views on the role of reciprocity and exchanges, and the denigration of Indigenous religious beliefs by Christian missionaries.

As such, the view that disruption to Indigenous cultural and social practices did not take place during the fur trade but later in the settlement phase is largely mistaken. This chapter discusses the basis for such conflicts and provides a view of fur trader-to-Indigenous interaction that counters a common portrayal in Canadian history of harmonious socio-economic relationships between the two groups. This alternative perspective also suggests that the Indigenous people were hardly subservient to Europeans because of the economic benefits received through the fur trade. As the Henley House conflict in Northern Ontario illustrates, Indigenous people at times were more than willing to counteract European influences and manipulations, sometimes by violent means of their own.

The Henley House Conflict

Henley House had been constructed in 1743 at the confluence of the Albany and Kenogami Rivers, situated about 150 miles from the James Bay coast, in an attempt by the Hudson's Bay Company to circumvent the Cree and Anishinaabeks' trade with French fur traders. As was noted earlier, Henley House was poorly stocked with trade goods, and this was a source of discontent with Aboriginal trappers. There were other sources of discontent, especially owing to a growing resentment among the Indigenous men that their women were being "stolen" from them by European men who were resident at this post. While the causes of this conflict are no doubt complex, European relationships with Aboriginal women were apparently a principal factor underlying the Henley House murders of 1754 (Francis and Morantz 1983 91, 99–100, 159; Bishop 1975: 150–62, 1976: 36–41; Ray and Freeman 1978: 189).

As fur-trade historians Arthur Ray and Donald Freeman explain, "In this strategic location the post was to operate as a way station for Indians travelling down to the bay. There the Indians could obtain a few trade goods and see the line of merchandise that was available at Fort Albany. Also, the post served to protect the Indians en route from intimidation by the French" (1978: 189). This plan may have appeared to be reasonable at the time, but it was not long before the French built their own post close to Henley House so that the Indigenous trappers began to pressure the Hudson's Bay Company to construct a more adequately stocked fur-trading post in the vicinity. This proposal was rejected by the company directors who insisted that the primary trading operations be conducted at the posts of James Bay (Rich 1967: 106).

There is some indication that the Fort Albany trade increased with the establishment of Henley House, but it possibly also had a detrimental effect on other James Bay posts, such as Moose Factory. There has even been a suggestion that inter-post rivalries were developing within the Hudson's Bay Company itself along the James Bay coast during this period, such that "This may have been one of the unspecified trading practices that the Moose Factory traders claimed the Albany factors were pursuing which served to undermine the trade of the former [Albany] post" (Ray and Freeman 1978: 189).[6]

Whatever the case with the economic side of the matter, the more salient aspect concerned the rising tension between the Cree and Anishinaabe on one side, and the European traders on the other. The root cause of this tension cannot be determined with any degree of certainty; however, it would appear that economic conditions did not precipitate the conflict directly. The direct cause from most accounts were interpersonal conflicts between the Indigenous people and the traders. The tensions must have been particularly severe because in December 1754, five Hudson's Bay Company traders who were stationed at Henley House were killed, presumably by Aboriginal men in the area, although this was only a speculative assumption. It took another four years, in 1759, for the post to be re-established, yet the conflicts appeared to continue unabated during this time.[7]

According to the HBC records of the time, as articulated by Francis and Morantz (1983: 91), "Resentment among Indian men at having their women stolen by whites was one of the factors believed responsible for the Henley House murders." As an HBC officer wrote to his superiors in London, "Women has been the destruction of your People, your Goods and Trade" (London Inward Correspondence from Hudson's Bay Company Posts, A.11/2: 174d). Even though there was an official HBC policy against fur traders developing relationships with Aboriginal women, such an injunction was based not so much on moral grounds, but because of a suspicion that the Aboriginals women might steal property from the trading posts if left there unattended or facilitate the entry of Aboriginal men into the posts with maleficent intentions.

According to a report given to Joseph Isbister, the Albany postmaster, by an Aboriginal woman from Richmond Gulf, the raid on Henley House was conducted by a man named Wappisis. Isbister managed to lure Wappisis and his two sons into the Albany post, where they were arrested. Apparently, the culprits confessed to this crime, were condemned for murder, and subsequently hanged on June 21. Three other men were also implicated in the Henley House "massacre," as the Hudson's Bay described the event, but were never apprehended.

Since the Henley House murders resulted in the plundering of the post, it was initially assumed that there was an economic motive behind the crimes. However, speculation continued for some time about the true reasons underlying this tragedy. For example, a surgeon at Fort Albany named George Rushworth speculated that three motives were possible. First, when Isbister originally assumed the position of postmaster at Fort Albany in 1753, he began to restrict Wappisis's access to the post where upon Wappisis, presumably holding a resentment against Isbister, formed a plot to inflict retribution in some way against the company.

A second possible motive, according to Rushworth, was that William Lamb, the post master of Henley House, had held two Aboriginal women in the fort as "bed and board;" women who were wives of men involved in the subsequent murders. Thus, the husbands were thought to have exacted revenge upon the Henley House traders for holding their wives for malevolent purposes against their will.

And third, Rushworth claimed to have conducted an interview with Wappisis before he was hanged, at which time the culprit said that the true motive for plundering the post was that "He tould Me he was hungry; I tould him Mr Lamb had no Victuals, only for ye Englishmen, he tould me I Lyed ye victuals was for them as Well as

Englishmen, as they keeped there Women; they had a Right to their Victuals" (quoted in Francis and Morantz 1983: 99). As such, the implication is that the Henley House post master, Mr. Lamb, had violated a norm of what could be termed "balanced reciprocity," that there had been a reciprocal understanding between Wappisis and Lamb that subsistence would be provided to the former in exchange for the sexual services of the Aboriginal women. When Lamb apparently violated this understanding, Wappisis took matters into his own hands by plundering the post of food that he felt had been wrongly withheld from him (Bishop 1976b).

Unfortunately for the Hudson's Bay Company, the troubles at Henley House did not end with Wappisis's execution. Even though the post was re-established in the summer of 1759 it was attacked again, this time by a party of about 40 Indigenous persons the following September. In this incident one Hudson's Bay Company employee was killed and once again the post was abandoned. There were various rumours circulating at the time that this new incident was encouraged by French traders. Another story was that the Indigenous people of James Bay planned an assault on the post at Eastmain River. This report was given credibility by the Eastmain post master who subsequently, in 1760, removed all the trade goods from the post under his command to a nearby ship, which was prepared for a speedy departure should this post as well come under attack. Eventually, a number of incidents which involved New France caused the French traders to withdraw from the area, and there were no further suggestions of attacks from either the French or the Indigenous population in the James Bay area (A.11/3, B. 59/a/29; Francis and Morantz 1983: 99–100; Bishop 1976b: 37–40).

The Hudson's Bay Company reacted to these upheavals by adopting several new strategies, such as increasing the presents for those arriving at the various posts on the Bay, such as brandy, knives, and tobacco, forgiving the debt accumulated by some trappers, and increasing the prices paid for a variety of furs. As far as the murders at Henley House were concerned, Bishop (1976b: 36) has made an astute observation. Acknowledging that a mere description of the murders would have some historical curiosity, nonetheless "The incident must be understood in the context of the fur trade, the Indian's view of this trade, and their relationship with Europeans at the time." While imputing motives for the Cree and Anishinaabek's actions during the period of the Henley House and the later Hannah Bay murders is virtually an impossible task, from our vantage point today one can nonetheless perceive that from the Indigenous perspective there must have been an intense dissatisfaction on their part resulting in the desperate actions that took place. As Bishop indicates, the answer regarding motives and dissat-isfactions must lie in the larger context of the fur trade as well as the actions of individual Hudson's Bay Company traders and the various policies that directed their actions.

In other words, the incidents at Henley House and Hannah Bay can-not be understood solely from the perspective of either party, or in iso-lation from each other, but as an evolving relationship taking place over time, in which one party, the Indigenous population, became increas-ingly dissatisfied with their socio-economic relationship with the colo-nial power that oppressed them. Remember, Hudson's Bay Company employees killed Indigenous people as well, usually with impunity, so the situation is not as if only one party was committing offences against the other. The British may have called any incidences involving the kill-ing of their people as "massacres," but this self-serving terminology could be applied in both directions.

The following quote gives an idea of the Hudson's Bay Company's attitudes towards the murders, shedding any culpability on their part for what happened. The Indigenous perpetrators were called "Savage Natives," thus perpetuating a trope of the bloodthirsty savage, which continued for centuries beyond this incident alone:

"And we the Said Council, do in behalf and in the Name of the Govr and Hudsons Bay Company And in justice to our unfortunate Country Men pronounce the Sentence of death upon Wappisiss alias Woube the land Pirate. And his two Sons, Sheanapp and Young Snuff the Blanket, to be hanged, untell they are dead, dead, dead, for a terour to all the Savage Natives from ever being guilty of the like barbarity in future, Signed by the Chief officers and Men at Albany Fort, June 12th 1755" (in Bishop 1976: 36).

Thus, this death sentence was seen as an act of justice for the killing of the company men, and as a possible act of deterrence for further such crimes. As far as one can tell, the reasons why this incidence took place, such as the "stealing" of Aboriginal women by company employees, was not taken into consideration as one of several mitigating circum-stances, such as charges of starvation in the area and mistreatment of Indigenous people by HBC personnel. For example, when Joseph Is-bister returned to manage Fort Albany in 1753, he was not well received by the local Indigenous population. It was said that he was more mi-serly in giving out gifts than his predecessor, Mr. Spence. Spence also allowed greater access to the Albany post than Isbister, who enacted a stricter policy. Spence apparently also allowed company employees to sleep in the tents of the Indigenous people, a practice that Isbister sternly prohibited. There was even a charge by the Albany surgeon, George Rushworth, that Isbister himself kept "Woman and young Girles," although out of the Factory, thus engaging in an apparent double standard (Bishop 1976: 39). Isbister kept "young Girles"? How young, one might wonder?

Indeed, even Joseph Isbister appears in the company records because of his abandonment of a "county wife." In May 1800, company records noted the illness and death of "a very old Indian Woman who had long been ailing on the Plantation" who had been the former mate of a factor many years before:

> She certainly must be upwards of one hundred years old. Her voice is still strong, and speaks as well at present as ever I knew her. This woman was for many years a wife to Mr. [Joseph] Isbester [spelling as in original] formerly a Chief Factor in your Honours Service (in Brown 1980: 68).

The attacks on Henley House, then, involve two opposing narratives. On the one side the Hudson' Bay Company has promoted the notion that French traders were the instigators. The HBC traders claimed that the French had made threats against the Cree who traded at English posts and had spread rumours that the posts on the Bay were to be attacked and destroyed.[8] However, contrary to this rationale, Cree trappers continued to make the journey to Fort Albany to trade their furs, thus diminishing the validity of the English accounts that the French were somehow controlling the inland trade. In any event, Cree trappers benefited by a competition between the French and English, which would have the tendency to drive up the prices of their furs. As Bishop (1976: 37) explains, the idea that the Cree were interested in eliminating either of the hated rivals, "is far too facile; the Indians were above all, desirous of keeping alive the competitive trade war of the French and English. In this way they could play off the traders against each other to their own economic advantage."

As a rationalization for the murders at Henley House, then, the English account fails to stand up to scrutiny in the face of the facts involved. This narrative is also self-serving because it blames the French for the conflict and removes any culpability by the English for the attacks on the Henley House post. Such a rationale also then suggests that the Cree were being manipulated by the French and, therefore, the Indigenous people were, in at least some small sense, less to blame for their actions. The obvious explanation for the murders is the one that the English would not admit: that they themselves brought on this situation by their own self-interested actions.

A Countervailing Narrative

The countervailing narrative, that the true source of the conflict pertained to the treatment of Cree women by English traders, would appear to have more credibility as an instigating factor and, as such, places the blame squarely on the English traders themselves, which is what Wappisiss was saying all along. It therefore makes sense that the English would wish to hang him as quickly as possible and thereby prevent him from further spreading this account, which the English would see as detrimental to their own system of self-styled honour.

The Hudson's Bay Company has always taken great pains to present a narrative in which the Indigenous people were treated fairly and without prejudice. For example, accounts of the history of the Hudson's Bay Company promote the idea, as one company history relates: "The complete freedom of opinion I have enjoyed reflects the generous, liberal attitude of the Company today towards the interpretation of its own story. Those who are familiar with the extensive library on fur trade and exploration will probably find here more frank criticism of the Hudson's Bay Company than in the works of many who have written from without rather than within the service" (Mackay, *The Honourable Company*, foreword to the 1936 edition). Yet, if this were the case, one wonders why a search through this volume for "Henley House" yields only the slightest mention of it (only on page 84) as "the only inland post" and no more, and there is no mention whatsoever of the Hannah Bay post or what happened there.

It is obvious that these conflicts were problematic from the perspective of the Hudson's Bay Company's role during Canada's colonial fur-trade period was concerned; as such, conflicts between the company employees and Indigenous people were either minimized or not even mentioned at all. In other words, problematic issues in the Indigenous-European relationship were sanitized in an attempt to convey a relatively peaceful relationship between the two groups, and therefore further an image of the British colonial period as not only beneficial to the Indigenous population, but relatively harmonious and amicable. The reasonable conclusion is that the Hudson's Bay Company has always been interested in promoting a favourable view of its history, as one would of course expect. So, as Bishop (1976: 37) asks, "How then to explain the murders?" In order to answer this question, it is necessary to examine some of the specific underlying issues between the traders and the Indigenous people of the area, such as the relationships between the Hudson Bay Company employees and the Cree and Anishinaabe women.

Country Marriages

"Country marriage' is a somewhat euphemistic term which connotes a relationship, usually sexual in nature, between an Indigenous woman and a European fur trader (Brown 1980: 62–3, 79–80). The use of the term "marriage" in most cases is misplaced, or in error, since few such unions were solemnized by a Christian church. In addition, the children of such unions were at times given the surname of their European father, but this was probably not usually the case. Also, when the fur trader retired and returned to Scotland or England, he seldom brought his "wife" and children of the union with him, but simply abandoned them to their own fate.[9]

There are records, though, of small pensions being given by the more affluent traders to their Indigenous spouse upon termination of the relationship, but this was probably a rare occurrence. It is also important to indicate how necessary women were in the fur-trade economy. Kim Anderson points out that "Men worked outside the community as hunters and warriors and women within ... These divisions accommodated the work required for a land-based lifestyle" (2000: 59). In addition, Olsen comments further that "The divisions of labour were based on practical needs. Because women are reproducers as well as producers, their labour consisted mainly of work at home. It was the men who procured the necessary items which were then turned into food, shelter, or clothing" (1989: 55). The involvement of Indigenous women was therefore an indispensable part of the northern bush lifestyle. As such, life in fur trade country would be inconceivable without the participation of women.

Now, returning to Bishop's question about how to explain the Henley house murders, it is necessary to revisit Wappisiss's claim that the Englishmen "keeped there Women," and then one begins to reveal the underlying issue that stimulated the resentment of the Cree. As Bishop (1976: 39) explains, when Joseph Isbister took charge of the Albany post from his predecessor, George Spence, Isbister suddenly began to terminate access to post privileges to important Cree individuals such as the trading captains, an action which would no doubt serve to demean the status of these individuals in the eyes of the other members of the Cree population. "Yet," as Bishop states, "Indian women continued to be exploited by the very person who had curtailed what he [chief captain Woulbee] perceived to be his rights – rights guaranteed by virtue of his senior status and by the reciprocal bond between traders and Indians involving the exchange of sexual and domestic rights to his women in return for free access to post amenities" (ibid.).

As far as Henley House was concerned, Isbister made it quite clear to William Lamb, the person who Isbister appointed as Henley's post master, that under no circumstance was he to allow local Cree to stay overnight at the post. Yet Lamb apparently ignored these instructions. This led George Rushworth to further reinforce Isbister's edict by warning Lamb "by No means to keep no Women in the House," to which Lamb replied "ye Governour keeps two favorites Will not you Alow me to keep One." [It is not clear if the reference to "Govenour" was meant to identify Isbister, as is probably the case, or alternatively is a reference to Governor George Simpson himself, who is reputed to have kept Native women for sexual purposes. As far as the facts are known, Lamb kept "two favorite [Indigenous] women" at his post. One of these (Nam a Shis) was later given to Woulbee's son (Shenap), and the other was Woulbee's own daughter (Won a Wogen) who was the wife also of another Cree man (Annisset). Lamb kept these women at the Henley House post all winter, thus depriving other Englishmen of the food that they would otherwise have received. The murders were apparently triggered when Lamb suddenly reversed his position and instituted a new policy that prohibited Woulbee and his kin from free access to the post, although it is not clear if Lamb also expelled his "favourites" from Henley House as well (ibid.).

Concepts of Marriage

In the opinion of A.G. Bailey (1969: 102–5) one of the major sources of conflict between Europeans and the eastern Algonkians concerned their divergent concepts of marriage. Basing his assessment on Champlain's observations of the pre-marital behaviour of Montagnais adolescents, who he thought were promiscuous compared to the youths back in France, Bailey felt that this period of sexual licence was "taken advantage of by French traders … [such that] the loose morals of the French served as a bad example to the Indians who were accustomed to daily condemnation of these practices by their missionaries" (Bailey 1969: 102; Denys 1908, 450–1). Bailey (1969: 113) also notes that there was a custom among the French "to sell liquor to these [Indigenous] girls, not only to get them drunk for nefarious purposes, but to make them debtors and, therefore, dependents. If they tried to escape, they were offered violence." In this context it is somewhat ironic that those in power in the Hudson's Bay Company, such as Governor Simpson whose condescending comments on the "nature and character of the Indians [he found] repugnant to our feelings" (i.e., in Newman 1987: 226), who espoused such a moral high ground when it was the Europeans themselves whose "loose morals" were a focus at times of censure by the Indigenous people themselves.

One might also conclude, then, that if Governor Simpson found the "character of the Indians ... repugnant," then his condescending attitudes about Indigenous people would probably be reinforced by other Hudson's Bay Company employees as well, since they would apparently be approved of by the top person in the organization. One might also presume that if Simpson should find the customs of the Indigenous people repugnant then he would hardly be predisposed to view these customs in a positive manner, or seek to understand the behaviour associated with these customs.

Take for example the customs of the Algonkian-speaking peoples (or Algonquian) of northern Canada with regards their kinship patterns and corresponding marriage arrangements., all of which have an impact on the distribution of trapping territories in the Hudson's Bay area. Most Algonkian-speaking people, for example, have a kinship system that divides the category of "cousins" in a manner different from the European usage. Among Algonkians, children of one's father's brother or mother's sister, called "parallel cousins" in anthropology, are usually referred to with terms equivalent to "brother" and "sister." Thus, cousins in this category are treated as if they were born into your own natal family and are not available for marriage as this would constitute incest.

On the other hand, children of one's brother's sister or mother's brother, called "cross-cousins" in anthropology, are not considered related to you and are preferred marriage partners in which a degree of licentious behaviour before marriage is allowed. As A.G. Bailey (1969: 113–14) explained, these conflicting perceptions of kinship and marriage patterns between the Algonkian and the French affected the relations between the two groups in various ways. For example, as A.G. Bailey further illustrates (1969: 114), "Cross-cousin marriage, that is, the usage by which the children of biological brothers and sisters were prospective mates, was affected by European immigration in two ways. First, since the French brought few women with them the surplus of males which resulted was bound to exert a disintegrating influence upon a formerly stabilized community. The French cut into this cross-cousin relationship and left male Indians without mates ... Second, the marriage of cousins was not tolerated by the Roman Catholic church, and with the spread of Christianity the custom would naturally have broken down." Thus, Europeans who did not understand Algonkian kinship relations might see this behaviour as suggesting that these Indigenous people were engaging in dissolute relationships which was not the case at all. Gov. Simpson's suggestion that understanding Aboriginal customs was a "repugnant" task would do the traders a disservice because they would be placed in a situation of misunderstanding the behavioural patterns of the Indigenous people in their area.

In terms of marriage, a further custom was for Algonkian people to live with the husband's relatives, a pattern called "patrilocal residence," after the connubial ceremony takes place. In addition, it was common for a brief period, usually comprising several years or less, for the newly married couple to live with the wife's parents, termed "bride service" as a way of compensating the wife's relatives for the services she would otherwise contribute to her kinship group (Hedican 1991, 2012: 159–68). Thus, if a trapper moved to another area to help his wife's relatives for several years, an HBC post manager might not understand the reason why this has happened. One can also credit Bailey's (1969: 102–5, 113–14) observation that marriage relationships were a source of conflict between Algonkian people and Europeans because of their different cultural concepts, especially as these conflicts relate to the understanding of Algonkian hunting and trapping territories (see Davidson 1928; Honigmann 1953; Rogers 1963; Speck 1915, 1918; Strong 1929).

A further source of conflict with Europeans concerned the fact that the Roman Catholic church never recognized the validity in Indigenous communities of traditional marriage ceremonies which the priests regarded as "worthless and contrary to the laws of God" (Bailey 1969: 103). This problem was exacerbated by a degraded position, which the priests regarded Indigenous women. As Bailey concluded, "There is no doubt that women occupied a more degraded position in the settlements of Christians than among the wandering pagans, where divorce was relatively easy." And furthermore, "of all the Algonkian customs the missionaries found polygyny the most difficult to eradicate, and in spite of all their arguments against it, the Indians could give reasons for the continuance of the practice" (ibid., 104–5). The priests however could not offer a solution to the question pertaining to the fate of a man's additional wives – were they to be abandoned and left to starve in the woods, one might ask? As one Algonkian man at Tadoussac stated: "He loved his wife and had sent the others away, but they continually returned so that to kill them was the only way to get rid of them," he said (ibid., 105). However, as Bailey concluded, "There is reason to believe that polygyny continued long after the Jesuits had left the mission among the eastern Algonkians" (ibid.).

The Desertion of "Country" Wives

Furthermore, the treatment of Indigenous women by Hudson's Bay Company employees has certainly been the subject of criticism and complaint, especially the practice of abandoning "country wives" and their children when fur trade employees returned to their home country, or when they married white women. As far as the maritime fur trade of British Columbia was concerned, Fisher suggests that "there was evidently some concern that Indian women and their children were being deserted by traders, for the Council of the Northern Department passed an order in 1824 requiring all officers and servants to make adequate provision for their Indian women, not only while they were resident in the country but also after their departure" (1977: 40; Flemming 1940: 94–5). However, there was little evidence presented that this order was enforced to any degree, which prompted Fisher to conclude that "there were discrepancies between the ideal of the order, and the reality of its execution" (1977: 40). Of course, there were racist undertones to the country marriage practices such that traders might feel ashamed of their Indigenous wives if they moved to an urban centre, or in the opinion of HBC employee John Work, "it was out of the question for an Indian wife to join 'civilized society'" (1977: 40). Despite this view, some traders did take their Native wives with them when they settled out of the fur trade territory, although how many is unknown (Lamb 1957:194–5; Cox 1932: 311).

One of the most vociferous critics of this practice of taking country wives and subsequently abandoning them to their own fate was Alexander K. Isbister who became a spokesperson in England for Indigenous people in fur trade country, especially in terms of his exploitation of British sensitivity to colonial practices. Isbister, born in 1822, was the grandson of Chief Factor Alexander Kennedy and his Native wife. In 1841 Alexander Isbister left the company because he felt that further advancement was not possible for him. His travels took him to England where he became a teacher, studied medicine, and authored many textbooks on various diverse subjects.

Isbister also maintained an active interest in the affairs of the mixed-blood population and on occasion became their advocate. Isbister, for example, presented evidence for parliamentary investigations and even managed to engage the interest of the Aborigines' Protections Society[10] in the treatment of the Natives by the Hudson's Bay Company (Brown 1980: 184). In particular, Isbister was "shocked by the dissolute character of the Company's officers, living, as he conceived it, in sin with Indian and half-breed women" (Galbraith 1957: 319). He also suggested, based on his personal experience, that what the Hudson's Bay Company offered for the Aboriginal people's furs "was outrageously low [and] none of the profits resulting therefrom were returned to the Indians in the form of services, such as educational facilities" (ibid.). "His petition to Westminster's Colonial Office," Newman (1987: 251) asserted, "remains one of the most eloquent and unanswerable indictments of the Hudson's Bay Company's treatment of the Indian Peoples." Although Isbister's views were largely ignored at the time, his writings were an articulate and persuasive condemnation of the racist attitudes of the British colonial practices in Rupert's Land during his lifetime: "When we assert that they are steeped in ignorance, debased in mind, and crushed in spirit, that by the exercise of an illegal claim over the country of the forefathers, they are deprived of the natural rights and privileges of free born men [as the result of] a barbarous and selfish policy, founded on a love of lucre" (ibid.).

It is evident, then, that the inter-cultural problems caused by Hudson's Bay Company fur traders who kept Aboriginal women as "wives" at their posts at Henley House and Albany Post mirrored in macrocosm the larger issues that the company was forced to deal with on a much broader scale (as detailed in Galbraith 1949: 322–35). The classic work on this topic, Jennifer Brown's *Strangers in Blood* (1980), notes that the lack of English- and Scottish-born women available for marriage to fur traders was one of the reasons that these men took native-born wives. However, another important reason was that Indigenous women were well-suited to life in the rugged country in which the fur trade took place. Imported British wives, on the contrary, according to a statement made by George Simpson in 1848, were unsuitable for the country life: "Imported wives fancy themselves such great women that there is no possibility of pleasing them" (in Brown 1980: xvi). Thus, Governor "Simpson himself became more favourably disposed toward native-born wives (and their children) as the people best adapted to domestic life and work in the fur trade country" (ibid., xv). However, this sentiment was expressed in the late 1840s when the term "native-born" referred principally to women of mixed descent and who had been exposed to the "civilizing" (ie., religious and educational) aspects of European society (see Brown 1976: 92–105).

It would be hypocritical for Governor Simpson to pass an edict against sexual relations with Indigenous women when he himself engaged in this practice. As historian John Galbraith comments in *The Little Emperor*: Governor Simpson's "fastidiousness with regard to interracial sex reflected both an increasing concern for his reputation as governor and a change in his attitude toward non-white women. But Simpson's resolution in these early years often gave way to temptation … There were many opportunities for easy sexual contact with Indian and mixed-blood women, and Simpson often responded to the opportunities" (1976: 68).

Image 5. Gov. George Simpson (seated), 1857. Simpson (1792–1860) was the colonial governor of the Hudson's Bay Company during the period of its greatest power. He was known for his physical stamina in travelling through the Canadian wilderness and in this aspect was respected by the Indigenous trappers who traded at his company stores.
Source: Public domain. Drawing by Arthur Hemming from *The Great Company: Being a History of the Honourable Company of Merchants-Adventurers Trading into Hudson's Bay* by Beckles Willson (Dodd, Mead Company 1900, page 464).

Furthermore, in the section of her book entitled "Simpson and Native Women," Brown (1980: 123–30) notes that prior to his marriage to his eighteen-year-old cousin Francis in 1830, "he had fathered at least five children by four different women [four of whom] were born in fur trade country" (ibid., 123; see also Newman 1987, 260).

While he resided at the Red River colony in 1823–4, Simpson apparently became concerned with remaining an "exemplary bachelor," probably because representatives of both the Catholic Church and Church of England had begun a campaign against fur-trade immorality and customary marriages (Van Kirk 1972: 12). However, Simpson also appreciated the practical value of fur-trade wives because of "the business utility of 'connubial alliances' with newly contacted Indian groups." Thus, in 1821, he recommended that inland fur traders "form connections with the principal families immediately on their arrival" (Brown 1980: 126). Such a sentiment was echoed in Fisher's account of country marriages in British Columbia in which he offered the view that "apart from the personal advantages, such unions were often also good business" (1977: 41). This opinion was evidently shared by Governor Simpson who, in 1821, was said to have conveyed the opinion that "Connubial alliances are the best security we can have of the goodwill of the Natives" (Newman 1987: 262) and, as such, as a "useful link between the traders and the savages" (Fisher 1977: 41). It is evident, then, that Governor Simpson viewed country marriages in terms of their facility in serving the economic interests of the company's commercial benefits. Therefore, as Fisher concluded, "The company's drive for profit even affected the most personal aspects of the lives of its servants and officers" (1977: 42).

It is also evident that Governor Simpson held Indigenous people with a certain degree of condescension. In order to further the interests of the fur trade, in 1822, he suggested that this motive could be facilitated by studying "the nature and character of the Indians ... however repugnant it may be to our feelings." Simpson wrote further that "I am convinced they just be ruled with a rod of iron, to bring and to keep them in proper state of subordination, and the most certain way to effect this is by letting them feel their dependence upon us" (in Newman 1987: 226). There can be no doubt, then, that Simpson's attitudes of condescension towards Indigenous people in general would also be extended to his feelings regarding Native women as well, as evidenced by his sexist and ethnocentric reference to such women as "bits of brown" (Newman 1987: 260).

Simpson's longest lasting country relationship was with Margaret Taylor, whom he left pregnant. He referred to Margaret Taylor as "the commodity" and instructed a fur-trade associate to keep an eye on her "and if she bring forth anything in proper time and of the right colour let them be taken care of" (Newman 1987: 261). In due course Margaret did "bring forth" a son, George Junior (see Galbraith 1976: 108–9). Regardless of Simpson's sentiments towards Margaret Taylor, there was apparently some double entendre to the saying that Simpson was "the father of the fur trade." There is a very unlikely claim by Western Canadian historian Grant MacEwan that Governor Simpson had "fathered seventy sons between the Red River and the Rocky Mountains" (MacEwan 1975: 53; see also Newman 1987: 259).

John McTavish: Chief Factor, Moose Factory

John George McTavish (1778–1847) figures prominently in the narrative of the Hannah Bay murders since he was the chief factor at Moose Factory during the 1830s and wrote the journal accounts of the incident that we rely on today for evidence of the event. In this regard, it would be useful to learn something of the character and behaviour of one of the most influential men of the Hudson's Bay Company's northern fur trade. Sylvia Van Kirk, author of *Many Tender Ties*, a study of fur-trade marriages also wrote a bibliographic account of John McTavish's life for the *Dictionary of Canadian Biography* (1988, Vol. 7, accessed June 11, 2020).

In this account we learn that John McTavish was recruited into the fur trade services of the North West Company in 1798. He was apparently a well-educated young man who first served as a clerk at the company's headquarters in Montreal. A few years later he joined a North West Company expedition that attempted to challenge the Hudson's Bay Company's monopoly of the fur trade in the James Bay region. At that time the NWC built a post on Hayes Island near Moose Factory. Relationships between the two companies were apparently cordial enough during this time, at least sufficiently stable for John McTavish to feel confident enough to take a country wife named Charlotte, a daughter of John Thomas, the HBC's chief factor at Moose Factory, and his Native wife. Eventually, in 1806, the NWC decided to abandon their enterprise at James Bay and McTavish returned to Quebec, leaving a distressed Charlotte behind.

Eventually McTavish was posted to the interior, on the Peace River in 1808–9, and later, in 1812, arrived at Fort Astoria (now called Fort George, Astoria, Oregon). As Van Kirk relates, "It was probably during this period that McTavish took as his second mixed-blood country wife, Nancy McKenzie, who had been entrusted by her father, former Nor'Wester Roderick MacKenzie [*sic*], to the guardianship of trader John Stuart of New Caledonia (British Columbia)." In the spring of 1814 McTavish led an armed expedition up the Columbia River to retaliate against the tribe that had attacked and pillaged two NWC canoes at the Cascades (near Cascade Locks, Oregon). By 1816–17 he became embroiled in further conflicts with the HBC and was captured a year later at Grand Rapids, Manitoba. From there McTavish was transported to York Factory and eventually sent to England for trial. The charges against him were dismissed and so the NWC ordered him to return to Grand Rapids in an effort to retaliate against his arrest. Shortly after, in 1821, the two warring companies amalgamated and McTavish, with his (by now) long service in the northern fur trade was made a chief factor at York Factory.

Governor Simpson of the Hudson's Bay Company seemingly took a liking to him, even though they had been trading rivals for many years; yet it was no doubt a mark of his influence and the esteem in which he was held that he was given such an important posting in HBC's Northern Department. During the 1820s McTavish's family was growing along with his accomplishments in the fur trade; by this time, he and Nancy McTavish had at least five daughters. Eventually, in February 1830, McTavish was on furlough in Scotland when he met and married Catherine Turner, thus taking the unprecedented step of casting aside his mixed-blood wife without first making provisions for her. George Simpson, who supported him in this action, did likewise two days later. Simpson and McTavish eventually returned to North America together, travelling by canoe from Montreal up to Michipicoten. At this point McTavish left the Simpsons and branched off with his bride to his new posting at Moose Factory.

McTavish's actions, that is, his cruel abandonment of his Native family, led to severe attacks on his character, particularly by John Stuart and Donald McKenzie. Simpson, however, staunchly defended him and arranged for Nancy McTavish to be married off. John Galbraith's biography of George Simpson, in *The Little Emperor*, makes particular note of McTavish's desertion of his "country wife" and the censure by his colleagues that followed. In one incident, when the McTavish couple were travelling with the Simpsons, the new Mrs. McTavish, Catherine Turner, found out about her husband's previous marriage(s) at which point she "broke into tears and rushed off to her room. Mrs. Simpson followed to commiserate with her and 'found her in a violent fit of crying'" (Galbraith 1976: 108).

Mrs. Simpson, herself newly wed to George Simpson, apparently "had no idea that she had more encumbrances than Mrs. MacTavish, altho she did say that she was always terrified to lok [*sic*] about her in case of seeing something disagreeable" (ibid). Galbraith, in a sarcastic tone, noted that "Simpson's care for the sensitivities of his wife was not matched by delicacy in his treatment of Margaret Taylor [a previous country wife] or of his mixed-blood offspring." As far as McTavish was concerned, "The summary way in which McTavish had rejected his country wife of so many years had evoked a great deal of hostile comment. Donald McKenzie, Nancy's uncle, was outraged; he had expected to formalize a marriage with his niece" (ibid)." In an act of graciousness, for which George Simpson was not well known, "one concession to humaneness in this commodity transfer [Nancy was to receive £30 per year for the support of herself and her children] was Simpson's promise to Nancy McKenzie that she would not be forced against her wishes to take another mate" (1976: 108). In October 1841, McTavish's wife died, and he remarried, this time to Elizabeth Cameron, a woman many years his junior, a union that produced a pair of daughters. McTavish's career in the fur trade lasted nearly fifty years, when he died after a short illness in 1847.

Country Marriage and Fur-Trade Alliances

When Governor Simpson proposed that fur traders engage in marital relations with the women of Native societies for the purposes of increasing the Hudson's Bay Company's profits, he was in fact utilizing one form of exchange (social) to promote another (economic) type. The implicit motive behind this suggestion was to instill in the Aboriginal people's mind the idea that through marriage fur traders of the Hudson's Bay Company would thereby become in-laws of their Indigenous trapping relatives. However, from the Indigenous perspective, such a marital relationship implied much more than the fur traders might have expected, especially in terms of the reciprocal obligation of helping relatives in need, an idea contrary to the Company's profit-oriented attitude. Indigenous trappers also participated in encouraging these arrangements. "[Hudson's Bay Company] officers faced social pressures from Indian groups," Jennifer Brown remarks. "When Indian traders discovered who was the most important man at a particular post, they sought his favour and friendship by offering him gifts, especially of women" (1980: 62). Thus, one can then understand the Cree's dissatisfaction with the implied marital arrangements of the Henley House traders, or for that matter the Métis fur trader William Corrigal at Hannah Bay, who would appear to have reneged on the implied reciprocal obligations of helping kin during times of want.

It is evident, then, that as far as the fur trade is concerned that all these three forms of exchange were practised at various times and among various people. However, this mix of time periods and cultural backgrounds leads to a complicated combination of situations that tends to inhibit effective analysis. Ray and Freeman, in 'Give Us Good Measure,' suggest that the "trade between people from a commercially oriented, politically complex state society (the Europeans) and those from a traditional and later a transitional band society (the Indians) does not fit neatly into previous theoretical categories of trade and exchange" (1978: xvi). This is an extremely important point that is often overlooked, or perhaps misunderstood, by fur-trade historians. First, it is important to recognize that the people of the Indigenous societies themselves comprise a diversity of institutions, some as diverse as the Europeans are to the Aboriginal peoples. To group all the Indigenous peoples of northern Canada who were involved in the fur trade as "Indians" does not render service to the cultural diversity of the Aboriginal inhabitants. Second, few historians have training in the study of cultural diversity and so are apt, as the fur traders might have been, to see Indigenous people as a homogenous group. This fallacy, in turn, could further lead to the inaccuracy in seeing all Indigenous people as having the same response to the economic, social, and political dimensions of the fur trade.

Ray and Freeman subsequently make another important point concerning exchange relations in the fur trade when they posit that "The present case of the Hudson's Bay Company fur trade comprises a *transition* [italics in original] in which 'traditional' exchange institutions of Indian band societies were modified and adapted to effect cross-cultural exchange with Europeans, who were obliged to modify their exchange procedures" (1978: 242). What is meant by the fur trade comprising a "transitional" situation is that many elements of the Indigenous trading systems were not obliterated by the economic and social change initiated by the fur trade. These traditional elements, however, were changed to the extent that they took on new significance and may have lost some of their original meaning, even though some aspects, such as the pre-trade ceremony, might have appeared to be the same.

This would suggest that gift exchange, for example, as a characteristic feature of the fur trade between Hudson Bay Company employees and the Indigenous trappers began to undergo an alteration or modification as the fur trade developed over the decades. In later decades, special gifts were added to the realm of exchange, such as the military-style clothing given to trading captains. And as Ray and Freeman suggest, "The European motives behind gift-giving, not surprisingly, were almost purely pragmatic" (1978: 242). On the Aboriginal trapper's side, it could be suggested by the fact that Native trappers started to give inferior furs in the preliminary gift-giving ceremony is suggestive of a Native approach which also emphasized that the traditional form of the gift exchange had begun to change into a means to their own economic gain.

Of course, it could be expected that both parties to an exchange, Indigenous and European, would modify their behaviour and expectations to some extent for the fur trade to exist at all. What is needed to corroborate this point though is *concrete* evidence that the changes that Ray and Freeman refer to are fundamental, meaningful changes to the attitudes of persons from both parties. It could be, for example, that both parties were simply pretending to change in order to manipulate the exchange relationship to their advantage or, on the other hand, that both parties were sincerely making attempts to understand each other's perception of the exchange system.

We can find no more tangible evidence that the former situation was the case (i.e., attempts to manipulate the exchange situation predominated the fur trade relationship) than when Governor Simpson suggested that fur traders marry into Indigenous societies. Evidently the purpose of this ploy was initiated in order to create, falsely one could suggest, the mere appearance of a "generalized exchange" relationship that was purely a fictive cover for his true intentions, which was to promote an advantage in the arena of "commercial exchange." As such, Simpson's proposal was simply a subterfuge or act of trickery in order to manipulate his Indigenous partners in trade. Such a ploy would seem beneath the dignity of one in charge of one of the world's largest commercial enterprises. In addition, if the Indigenous people took Simpson at his word, which is to say, that they would understand his actions as an act of friendship or even kinship, how could they be blamed for misunderstanding his malevolent intentions. Also, once they then understood his act of betrayal for what it was, who could then blame them for retaliating in kind as a form of "just retribution."

In summation, Ray and Freeman astutely observed that "the concept of *gift exchange* [italics in original] applies to the Hudson's Bay Company fur trade in a formal or superficial sense only, since there is evidence that the spirit behind the gift exchange waned as the trade developed" (1978: 243). By now it should be rather obvious that as time went on the significance of the gift exchange waned because the Indigenous people saw through the superficial mockery of a ceremony that at one time was intended to secure or signify honesty and even friendship, but later was part of a dubious commercial endeavour stripped of any amical intentions. The realization on the part of the Indigenous people that their "friends" in the Hudson's Bay Company were simply mocking their own traditional friendship behaviour must have led to a bitter disappointment on their behalf and soured any future relationships in which the Europeans simply pretended to be their comrades or trusted associates. In this light, any intentions that European men might have espoused in "marrying" Indigenous women, but then later abandoning them and their children, would simply reaffirm the duplicity of fur traders that was now felt in other areas of meaningful exchange behaviour.

In terms of the Henley House murders, this would appear to be exactly the point that Bishop makes, namely, that the European traders could not be trusted to act in good faith, and that their stated intentions were merely further acts of fraudulence. The European traders only pretended to engage in a marriage relationship, rather than engage in a form of social compact which would eventually lead to a bond of kinship being forged between the two parties. According to fur trader Andrew Graham, among the Cree, this exchange of women created "a reciprocal alliance and a series of good offices ... between friends of both parties; each is ready to assist and protect the other ... [which] involved morally sanctioned rights and obligations" (1976: 40).

However, from the actions of the fur traders, it is evident that they held a quite different view of their relationship with their Indigenous "friends," and would appear then not to care about the sexual exploitation of Indigenous women; that is, they did not care so long as the trade did not suffer as a consequence. Among the Cree, though, they probably thought that the fur traders were willingly engaging in a sort of social compact with them. When the fur traders, such as Isbister at Fort Albany and Lamb at Henley House, subsequently denied or at least restricted the Cree leaders free access to the posts this action would no doubt have been understood by the Cree as an insult, as a breach of Cree etiquette, the termination of a reciprocal arrangement, and as a denigration in the eyes of other Indigenous people. The result, as one would expect from this insulting behaviour on the part of the fur traders, was no doubt a growing hatred of Hudson's Bay Company employees.

As far as the English fur-trading records are concerned, there is no indication that the murders that occurred at Henley House or Hannah Bay had anything to do with a serious disjunction in the HBC-Indigenous relationship. Rather, the execution of Wappisiss and later Quapakay was seen as an act of retribution and deterrence "for a terour to all the Savage Natives from ever being guilty of the like barbarity in future" (in Bishop 1976: 36). It is interesting, though, that when news of the hangings reached London, Joseph Isbister was removed from his post for having taken justice into his own hands. There was an ulterior motive, however, in Isbister's removal because there was fear in London that the hangings would have a detrimental effect on the trade and might prevent other Indigenous groups from visiting Fort Albany. In any event, Henley House was eventually re-established five years later, in 1759, but this post was subsequently attacked again, this time by a larger group of perhaps forty Indigenous men.

The Hudson's Bay Company was not to be deterred and, realizing the strategic position at the confluence of the Kenogami and Albany rivers for the incoming fur trade, rebuilt the Henley fort in 1766. By this time, though, times had changed in fur-trade country. The English had previously conquered Quebec, which resulted in the end of French competition for furs. A new threat to the company's hegemony in James Bay emerged, however, with the Nor'Westers and renewed competition, which did not end until a merger in 1821.

The HBC Trader as a "Marginal Man"

In anthropology, several studies have been conducted on the role of the Hudson's Bay Company agent and his Native "clients." For example, Dunning (1958) discussed the changes in Anishinaabe social structure that stemmed from the economic changes resulting from their involvement in the fur trade. He points out that "A fur-trapping economy ultimately controlled by world fur markets is implicitly directed by the agent of this economic system in the form of the local company trader" (1959a: 20). However, as Dunning (ibid.) further reiterates, as far as the northern Anishinaabe are concerned, in terms of "the nature of these influences [the Indigenous people have] not been overwhelmed by the foreign milieu. Rather the social structure has become adjusted to these changes." In Dunning's opinion, "the northern woodland groups [have not] suffered both economically and socially almost overwhelming and revolutionary cultural contact" (ibid.) at least up to the period of his ethnographic field work in the mid-1950s.

This does not mean that as far as the northern Indigenous groups were concerned contact with the Europeans and the fur-trade economy did not have profound effects, it is just that these effects were not "revolutionary," as Dunning states. The Cree and the Anishinaabe of the James Bay area were able to cope with the resulting changes in their social structure and economy, unlike the more tragic consequences suffered by many southern Indigenous groups. Nonetheless the results of contact with Europeans and their involvement in the fur trade were not inconsequential. Bishop suggests, for example, that up until about 1800 the Anishinaabe were able to maintain large social groups in an era of large game hunting and that "group cohesiveness, although modified under new conditions, was also exhibited in a unified aggressiveness towards traders" (Bishop 1974: 11). However, by about 1805 the beaver began to become scarce in northern Ontario. The previously large social groups began to fragment into smaller family units. As Bishop explains further, "Cases of starvation grew more numerous after 1815 as game dwindled. During winter, hunting groups often splintered into family units to more effectively exploit fur and small game" (1974: 12). As competition between the Northwest Company and the Hudson's Bay Company increased, some less profitable posts were closed. Thus, the "withdrawal of many trading centres with cheap goods and the virtual disappearance of large game animals considerably reduced the mobility of Indians who had to rely on a single post" (Bishop 1974: 12).

While Indigenous trapping groups became more dependent on smaller, more isolated fur-trading posts of the interior, the Hudson's Bay Company agents also tended to become "marginal men," to use Dunning's (1959b) term. The result was a new sort of dependency that went both ways; as Native trappers made less frequent trips to the James Bay coast, the interior HBC agents were forced to rely to a greater degree than previously on the members of local Indigenous communities for food, and in some cases protection from neighbouring hostile groups. In this context, Salisbury (1976) proposed that the transactional or exchange basis of the fur trade began to change in a significant manner. As he explains, "A 'traditional' view of these [fur trade] communities ... was that the advent of the HBC in 1670 rapidly made them highly dependent on the fur trade. The organizing focus of each community was its relations with the HBC agent, who was the main patron and/or broker in any settlement" (1976: 47–8). This so-called traditional view, characterized by such studies as Leacock's (1954) research of Montagnais hunting territories and the manner in which the fur trade shaped new economic responses caused by the fur trade, gave way in later years to a focus on the negotiated aspects of the HBC agent as broker and the Native trapper as agent, in terms of emerging dyadic relationships rather than a focus on larger social systems, which had previously characterized this area of research.

The collection of articles in Paine's (1971) *Patrons and Brokers in the East Arctic* aptly illustrate this approach, with its emphasis on emergent social systems resulting from a series of negotiations, tactics, and strategies. In this regard, the approach builds on related studies in political and economic anthropology, such as F.G. Bailey's (1969) *Stratagems and Spoils* or Schneider's (1989) *Economic Man*. While such studies were no doubt innovative during their time, there were issues with an approach that tended to minimize, or even ignore in some cases, the importance of the wider social and economic contexts in which exchange and transactions take place – a problem discussed at some length in review articles on the topic (i.e., Easton 1972; Evens 1974; Hedican 1986b).[11]

These debates in the theoretical literature on exchange systems have set the context for our understanding today of fur-trade interactions. Obviously, the Indigenous trappers were not mere pawns of the various fur-trading companies. It is certainly true that the various goods that Europeans offered in trade for furs were highly sought after, but not at any price, as Ray and Freeman's (1978) 'Give Us Good Measure' attempts to illustrate. Native trappers were not averse to playing one fur-trading company (the French coureurs de bois, the Nor'westers, and the Hudson's Bay Company) against another to obtain the best deal for themselves. As Eccles perceptively indicates, "The Indians were astute enough to maintain trade relations with both the English and Canadians in order to reap the advantages of competition" (1983: 348).

Although the Hudson's Bay Company saw such acts as disloyalty on the Natives' part, from the Indigenous perspective they were no doubt exercising what they thought made good business sense, a policy that the fur trading companies were also following. What this tells us in historical perspective is that there was indeed a movement by the Indigenous trappers away from a strategy of generalized exchange that one would expect between friends, allies, or kinsmen. They soon learned that while fur traders espoused a norm of exchange based on friendship, ultimately their actions spoke differently. In historical perspective, the irony of these shifting strategies is that the fur traders of the Hudson's Bay Company failed to notice the large-scale transitions that were going on; the traders failed to notice that the Indigenous trappers were no longer, or ever were, simply members of primitive cultures whose people could be manipulated with impunity.

In terms of the "patron and broker" studies of previous decades as these apply to our understanding of the fur trade, one can largely agree with Salisbury's assessment that as far as the academic literature and the ethnohistorians' understanding was concerned, "the focus has changed from a role study to analyzing how the transactions involving the HBC agents and other patrons can be seen as part of a 'game.' The 'game' is one in which ... both patron and client adopt strategies in order to increase the 'values' which they obtain from the other transactor" (1976: 48). However, one can find exception with Paine's (1971: 15) conclusion that "a crucial difference between a patron and client ... is that the patron chooses what values he will provide, while a client must provide what the patron chooses" (Salisbury 1976: 48). Such a perspective gives too much power to the patrons, such as the HBC fur traders, who are as much victims, or at least hostages, of their Indigenous "clients," because if the Native trappers withhold their furs for whatever reason the traders lose the raison d'être for their very existence in North

America. "It is now coming to be recognized," Eccles concludes, "that they [the Indigenous people] were by no means as dependent on European goods as has been claimed" (1983: 350).

The Liquor Trade

There is probably no more reprehensible behaviour on the part of the North American fur-trading companies than the use of alcohol as a trade item. The smallpox epidemics that killed thousands of Aboriginal people would probably rank first in the list of catastrophic encounters between Europeans and Indigenous people; however, culpability in this case is hard to prove. There can be no doubt, though, that the trade in liquor was intentional and that the fur traders must have known that it would cause great harm among Indigenous people. Further, the traders just did not even seem to care what harm their behaviour caused to Indigenous societies.

Here is just one example, narrated by trader John Long in about 1778, concerning a trading party that occurred at Lac la Mort (ironically, as it happened) north of Lake Superior and the debauchery that followed during a bout of drinking:

> The rum [two kegs of rum of eight gallons each] being taken from my house, was carried to their wigwaum, and they began to drink. The frolic lasted four days and nights; and notwithstanding all our precautions (securing their guns, knives, and tomahawks) two boys were killed, and six men wounded by three Indian women; one of the chiefs was also murdered, which reduced me to the necessity of giving several articles to bury with him, to complete the usual ceremony of their internments. These frolics are very prejudicial to all parties, and put the trader to a considerable expense, which nonetheless he cannot with safety refuse. On the fifth day they were all sober, and expressed great sorrow for their conduct, lamenting bitterly the loss of their friends. (1791 [1974]: 56)

"Alcohol was crucial in the fur trade for two reasons," Eccles (1983: 350) explained. "First, the Indians craved it more than anything else; even though they knew that it could destroy them, they could not resist it, and they would go to any lengths to obtain all that was available. Second, from the purely economic aspect of the trade, alcohol was the ideal exchange item. Of other goods – cloth, wearing apparel, pots, knives, axes, muskets – the Indians had a limited need" (See also Martin 1978: 63–4; Ray 1980: 255–71). Most metal goods, such as muskets, would last many years. A few items of clothing for each family member did not amount to a great expense for the trapper. In a couple of good months, a Native trapper, under favourable conditions, could secure enough furs to provide for his family's needs. Local fur traders needed, then, to use a commodity such as liquor to balance their account books.

The use of liquor as a trade item began to have immediate results, since Indigenous trappers became more interested in trading for liquor than they were in trading for European goods. "For many [trappers]," Daschuk (2013, 46) claims, "alcohol became the raison d'être for their participation in the trade." Similarly, Hudson's Bay Company historian Edwin Rich comments that "The insatiable desire for rum turned many from sellers of furs to buyers of liquor" (1959: 228). Among the Assiniboine, it was stated that "guides and hunters often refused to work for their white employees if they were not given a bonus in the form of brandy" (Schilz 1984: 100; see also Dempsey 2002; Kennedy 1997 for similar statements).

Competition between the French and the English also increased the brandy trade. As Ray and Freeman indicate, "The French *coureurs de bois* carried considerable quantities of spirits to the interior in spite of the efforts of colonial officials in New France to curtail this traffic. To counter the influence of the *coureurs de bois* among the Indians, it was necessary for the Hudson's Bay Company to make sure that its factors had adequate stocks of brandy in their warehouses" (1978: 129). Thus, liquor became a political tool, as well as an economic one, in gaining influence over the Indigenous population. However, the French traders who lived among Aboriginal people in their hunting grounds were only too aware of the poisonous effects that liquor had on their customers. Frequently they paid for it with their lives when murderous fights erupted. There were senior French officials who were involved in the fur trade for personal gain and who tried to make light of these terrible effects. The French missionaries who resided in the Native villages knew first hand the injurious consequences brought on by liquor consumption. These missionaries, particularly the Jesuits, fought to have liquor barred completely from the trade and threatened excommunication for any traders who persisted in its use. Others both recognized the horrors caused by the liquor trade, but for political or economic reasons decided not to condemn it (Eccles 1983: 349–51).

Fur traders suggested that brandy was largely used in ceremonial gift exchanges, but the facts do not support this. As the tables of trades goods in Ray and Freeman's (1978: 130–4) study clearly show, more brandy was traded every year than was given away at the various posts. Furthermore, the traders began to cheat their fur trading clients by diluting the rum and brandy with water. At Moose factory in the 1730–40 period, for example, factors diluted their brandy with water by one-quarter to one-third; and at York Factory the dilution ratio was also about one-third. As can be imagined, then, fur traders were undercutting what they paid for the incoming furs by one-third as well, when these furs were traded for brandy. Nonetheless, "By the mid-1720s brandy had become one of the Hudson's Bay Company's most important trade items ... and it would remain so into the next century" (Francis and Morantz 1983:39–40).

As time went on there was a trend towards a greater per-capital consumption of alcohol and tobacco, both addictive commodities. Some Indigenous people began to spend much more of their time hanging about the trading post drinking and smoking, which the traders' termed "the indolent life" (Ray 1974: 142–6). In addition, as the demand for trade goods began to diminish some Indigenous people began to spend less time on their trap lines, which, in turn, tended to diminish the supply of furs entering the trading post. It was evident, then, that an increased trade in alcohol could have detrimental effects on the efficacy of the fur trade industry itself.

The deleterious effects of trading in liquor were probably the main reason that the Hudson's Bay Company attempted to curtail alcohol as a trade item, rather than the result of moral or humanitarian concerns for the Indigenous population. At first the HBC attempted to curtail the supply of liquor by adjusting the prices of its goods to a higher level. In 1822, Governor Simpson informed the company directors that "we have taken steps as well to wean the Indians from their insatiable thirst for Spiritous Liquors by passing a resolution that no more than half the quantity usually allowed be given as presents and that the trade in Furs for that article (which was very limited) be altogether discontinued" (in Ray 1974: 198).

As early as 1826, the temperance policy introduced by Simpson was beginning to take effect in the northerly forested regions. Thus, after a brief transition period, the company was actively pursuing a policy of totally banning alcohol as an item of trade. By 1839, the company prohibited entirely the use of liquor as a trade item. However, this prohibition didn't remain in effect for very long because supplies of rum and brandy were available from "free" traders and the American Fur Company and those not controlled by the HBC monopoly. In 1841, Simpson made concessions by once again allowing the distribution of liquor, but nonetheless, the supply was still drastically reduced. It was not until the 1860s that the HBC discontinued the trade in alcohol and the practice of gifting it altogether (see Galbraith 1957: 58–9).

Further Indigenous-Fur Trader Hostilities

The intent in this study is not to suggest that the fur-trade period was riven with dissention between Indigenous people and the fur traders; however, given the evident fact that the Hudson's Bay Company has sought to minimize such conflicts or even to ignore them, in the pursuit of a portrayal of this relationship as harmonious, consensual, and amicable suggests that a more intermediate position be taken as a sort of balance in the historical record. Nonetheless, exploring various cases of conflict is apt to benefit a more accurate portrayal of Canada's fur trade history in general, especially given the fact that Indigenous peoples themselves have written very little, in the past in any event, from their own perspective concerning conflicts with Europeans.

It is recognized, therefore, that accounts of violent conflict between fur traders and Indigenous people are only sporadically mentioned in the historical literature probably because they were not that frequently mentioned in the historical record. Fisher's account of such conflicts in British Columbia notes that there was a general lack of hostility between the two groups because of their shared interests in maintaining a trading partnership (1977: 35). Even so, "relations between the Chilcotin and the traders were always uneasy … there was constant bickering about prices, and the men in the fort were frequently afraid of an attack" (Fisher 1977: 35) and eventually the post was abandoned in 1844 (HBCA, B-37/a).

Governor Simpson's "rod of iron" approach was evidently not particularly helpful in maintaining friendly relations between the two parties. Simpson's view was that peaceful relations were dependent upon keeping the Indigenous people in a state of dependency where possible and in a "proper state of subordination" (see Merk 1968 [1931]: 179). Apparently, officers in the Hudson Bay Company viewed the punishment of Indigenous people thought to be guilty of certain crimes as a necessary deterrent, because "the honour of the whites was at stake" if offences were left unpunished. Thus, retaliation and punishment were used as a method to discourage further offences, in order that they could be made an example to others that the company would not tolerate such behaviour, and as a method that company employees could use to avoid situations that "would lower us in the opinion of the Indians" (Merk 1968 [1931]: 318; Rich 1956: 2).

In one instance, in 1828, James Douglas, who became governor of British Columbia, on hearing that a trader had been killed by an Aboriginal man who was apparently hiding in a nearby village, rushed into this village and beat the man to death. This action aroused the animosity of the Carrier people, and Douglas's life was subsequently endangered on account of this reprisal on several occasions (see Sage 1930: 48, also Sage 1925: 49–55). Fisher (1977: 37) also notes that "The monotonous and uncouth life led by many traders undoubtedly had a brutalizing effect on them, and there were incidents of individual cruelty towards Indians." Acts of cruelty to Indigenous people included having their ears cut off in one instance, and in Fort Vancouver an Indigenous man was castrated by a trader. When a trader named Alexander McKenzie and four other men were murdered in the vicinity of Port Townsend in 1828, an expedition was organized to take revenge. Perhaps the culprits were not found since only property belonging to Indigenous people of the area was destroyed. In another incident involving several murders that occurred at Fort McLeod in 1823, the chief factor, George McDougall, cautioned against any retaliation because the identity of the culprits was unclear, and in any event the men trading at that post were the best beaver hunters and influential persons in their society (Rich 1941: 227, 185–6).

In the history of the fur trade west of the Rockies, an assertion was made by H.G. Barnett, widely considered an authority on the Coast Salish of Canada, that the inhabitants of fur-trading posts in that area were in a constant state of fear that they would be attacked and that "hostility and avoidance marked the interrelations between whites and Indians" (Barnett 1941: 163–4, also see 1938, 1955). At Fort George several traders were murdered as a result of personal disagreements; in 1841 a trader named Samuel Black was killed, although the motive for the killing was unclear aside from a possible case of personal revenge. There were also instances of fur traders becoming involved in conflicts between Indigenous groups, which could have been the reason for an attack on the fort at Dease Lake in the winter of 1838–9 (Fisher 1977: 38–9).

Murder in Yukon Territory, 1898

"What is so fascinating about murder?" asks Ken Coates and William Morrison (2004: xi) in their book *Strange Things Done*. Their answer is that "Perhaps the essential fascination with murder is that it echoes our own mortality. The victims of killers all have one thing in common, trite as it is to point out the fact: they are all dead, and they have not died in the manner that we would wish to die – peacefully and with dignity" (2004: xii). And so begins their study of murder in the Yukon during the gold rush days of the 1890s.

A prominent part of their book focuses on the Nantuck case, which is one of the rare instances in which Indigenous people committed acts of violence against members of the white settler population and the only instance during the Klondike gold rush in which First Nations people shot whites from ambush. Up until the gold rush, the Yukon was one of the most isolated areas in North America. The Hudson's Bay Company did not arrive there until the 1840s, which was more than a century after the fur trade had become a prominent feature of the northern economy of Canada. In fact, one of the reasons that the authors give for the low incidences of conflict between whites and Indigenous people in the Yukon during this period is that both populations tended to live apart since the Native people were apparently not interested in gold mining, and they were not welcome in the mining communities.

The Dene or Athapaskan people of this area were preoccupied with their lives as hunters and gatherers, following the caribou herds during their fall migration and fishing during other seasons. Even as late as the Second World War the Native people of the Yukon and adjoining Northwest Territories were able to maintain their way of life with little interference from the outside world. The pattern of Native and non-Native interaction until the middle of the twentieth century was essentially one of continuous avoidance.

The very first case of murder that was ever tried in the Yukon courts was one in which four Native people, the Nantuck brothers, were accused of shooting a white man in April 1898. At that time two men, Christian Fox and William Meehan, who were experienced northerners were heading from Juneau, Alaska, to the Klondike. While the men were preparing to go down the Yukon River, they were approached by two Tagish men, Joe and Frank Nantuck, who asked for something to eat. These men, along with their two brothers were relatively young; Frank, the youngest, was probably no more than fifteen, while Jim, the oldest, was about twenty. After Fox and Meeham fed them the Nantuck brothers set up camp nearby. Over the next several weeks the two miners and the Nantuck brothers appeared to have a cordial relationship as visiting occurred frequently between the members of the two camps.

On the morning of May 10, the two prospectors were preparing to leave on their down-river voyage when they noticed that the Nantuck brothers had left the area. Not thinking too much about this the miners departed by boat. Soon after they set off, about an hour before noon, shots rang out from the river's bank, hitting Fox, who survived the attack, and knocking him over in the boat. More shots were fired, and this time Meehan was fatally wounded. But Fox managed to guide the boat to the riverbank and escape through the woods. After a while he succeeded in reaching the miners' camp and the police were subsequently informed of the incident.

Jim Nantuck was arrested by a corporal of the NWMP the next day as he was still in the vicinity of the crime. Not too long after, the other three brothers were also arrested, and Meehan's body was later located in the river weighted down with a pickaxe. The Nantucks were also found with a suitcase with Meehan's name on it and some food belonging to the two men. The four brothers eventually went to trial; a defence counsel was appointed along with two interpreters. When asked to make a statement the Nantucks indicated that they were good friends with the miners, but that several years ago two white men had killed two Indians, an explanation that apparently went virtually unnoticed. Joe admitted to firing at Meehan with the intention of killing him, while Jim Nantuck denied firing any shots. His other brother, Frank, for reasons that were obscure, testified against his three brothers.

Despite conflicting testimony from each of the brothers and their various guilty and non-guilty pleas (Joe indicated that he did not fire a shot and therefore was not guilty), and after a deliberation of only thirty minutes, the jury found three of the brothers guilty. Frank, who testified for the prosecution, was similarly found guilty the next morning, although a recommendation of clemency was registered on his behalf. All four brothers were then sentenced to hang on November 1. In February 1899, two brothers (Frank and Joe) died in jail of tuberculosis, and on August 4, Jim and Dawson Nantuck went to the gallows after an unusual delay in the executions of more than a year. The reason for this delay was that a serious flaw had occurred in the way the trial had been conducted. There was also another problem: the Nantuck brothers had refused to explain their reason(s) for committing this act of murder and apparently showed no remorse for killing two innocent men.

Concerning the first point, about the flaw in the legal proceedings, there was an apparent jurisdictional issue that should have resulted in a new trial of the Native men. Aside from the recorded fact that the judge in the case referred to the Nantucks as "a very low order of humanity," thus possibly prejudicing the case against the brothers and indicating "a depiction of common racism," and "an entirely different level of cultural misunderstanding," (2004: 23), when Meehan was killed, the Yukon was a district of the North-West Territories. At this time, Judge MGuire held his position as a judge of the Supreme Court of the North-West Territories; however, when the actual trial convened the Yukon Territorial Act had just come into effect, meaning that the trial of the Nantucks had taken place in the wrong court, under a judge's authority that had lapsed. In other words, Judge McGuire had no authority to try the Nantucks since the trail was no longer in his proper juris-diction. "Why did this happen?" Coates and Morrison (2004: 27) ask. "Why were the Nantucks not retried when it was clear that there had been a defect in their trial, one that today would unquestionably lead to a retrial?"

There are various possible answers to this question, none of which are entirely satisfactory, such as political manoeuvers on the part of the minister of justice to "political ambition, money, and racism" (ibid.). As far as the other issue is concerned – the apparent lack of remorse and motive for the killings – there was a clue given in the testimony of the Nantucks when they told Judge McGuire that the death had to do with the previous killings of several Native people at the hands of a white men a year earlier. McGuire included this testimony in his writ-ten account but otherwise ignored the brothers' words regarding their motive. It is interesting that many years later the case was still remem-bered by the people of the First Nations of the area, and several elders have attempted to explain the situation.

A narrative is recounted about an elderly lady who lived near Marsh Lake. She found a container from a mining site, which she mistakenly thought was flour but probably contained arsenic, used in refining gold. She used this powder to make bread, which she subsequently gave to an old man and a boy, both of whom died as a result. This old man and young boy were members of the Crow clan, and as such its members had a responsibility to avenge their death. According to the usual procedure of the people in the Tagish society at this time, in these cases it was the responsibility of the clan members to negotiate compensation for the deaths, either in terms of payment of a suitable amount of goods or, failing that, requiring the death of another victim of the offending clan or family. In this regard, the two prospectors were seen to represent the "clan" of the white people. The visit to Fox and Meehan's camp was apparently seen as an opportunity for the men to negotiate the compensatory terms for the death. When these nego-tiations failed, the Nantucks felt a responsibility to exact revenge by killing both white men.

Of course, even if the court had been aware of this narrative, it prob-ably would have had very little difference on the result. As various arti-cles in the *Klondike Nugget* (June 16–27, August 3,1898) indicated, "The questions put to the murderers … showed them to be wholly deficient in the most ordinary morals. Their cunning, also, was of a low order." Public sentiment was decidedly against the Nantuck brothers, regard-less of their motives or any justification that may have come from those that would exculpate them of their acts. Unfortunately, the execution of one of the brothers was botched. As Dawson fell his left hand broke free and he clutched his neck, making gurgling sounds. The hangman then grabbed his body, raised it in the air and dropped him to break Dawson's neck, thereby putting an end to his misery.

This case clearly illustrates how incongruent the value and cultural systems of the white settlers and the First Nations of the area were. From the white person's perspective, the killing of Meeham was quite irrelevant to the possible act of poisoning entirely different people. The Nantuck brothers, on the other hand, expected the miners to provide compensation for their loss, as "just some Indian nonsense hardly deserving mention" (ibid., 24). At this point in the discussion, many people would probably find that the case of the Hannah Bay killings and that of the Nantuck brothers would be quite incommensurate with each other. At running the risk of making invidious comparisons in some people's minds, there is at least the cultural-ideological gap in both cases between the white settler population and that of the Indigenous people.

In the case of the Cree, it could be regarded as an incomprehensible breach of cultural norms or etiquette to reject reciprocal obligations "of kin" (William Corrigal's mother was Cree and so apparently was his wife) when the Quapakay family was quite evidently in such desperate need of provisions. Of course, we can never say for sure; all we can go by is what people said at the time. But it is entirely possible that the Nantuck brothers believed that Fox and Meehan were aware of their attempts at negotiating previous deaths in their clan.

Cruikshank has attempted to illuminate reasons for the different "images in Klondike Gold Rush narratives." As she explains, comparing written accounts of official gold rush literature with oral accounts passed on by Tagish participants can lead to starkly different interpretations: "The narratives contrast sharply because they reflect conflicting ideas about social organization in late nineteenth-century northern frontier society" (1992: 20). In addition, she surmises that "Both written and oral accounts of the Klondike gold rush occur within conventional, culturally specific narrative genres that help members construct, maintain, and pass on understanding of how the world works or should work" (ibid., 35, see also Cruikshank 1988, 1989, 2003). Regarding Cruikshank's interpretation of the events, Coates and Morrison (2003: 23) suggest that her "exploration of the [Nantuck] case goes beyond a depiction of common racism to explore an entirely different level of cultural misunderstanding."

As such, an important legal point when it comes to murders involving the members of two quite distinct societies is the extent to which "culturally specific narratives" should be admissible as evidence in determining the guilt of the offending party. In other words, are the white Euro-Americans who control the judicial system prepared to entertain "culturally specific" interpretations of acts that are considered by the white settlers as criminal in nature, rather than dismiss these alternative interpretations offhand as Judge McGuire did in the Nantuck case when he referred to the brothers as representing "a very low order of humanity" (Coates and Morrison 2004: 23) and that their testimony was "just some Indian nonsense hardly deserving mention" (ibid., 24)? Such an attitude about the testimony given by members of a different culture, even that which does not easily fall into the white's realm of "truth," is nonetheless certainly ethnocentric or even racist in nature. Even when the Mounted Police give testimony in cases involving Indigenous people, their standard police accounts "begin with self-righteous indignation, continue by denigrating the accused, and conclude by wallowing in tristesse about the enormity of the white man's burden" (Cruikshank 1990:166).

A study of the Nantuck murders is also worth considering, therefore, from an interstadial perspective, or between the juxtaposition of European written accounts of history and the oral traditions of the members of Indigenous societies in North America. From Cruikshank's (1989) reflections on this issue, she suggests that we place less of a focus on the "veracity" or "truth value" of the various accounts of historical events. Rather, it would be more useful as a matter of interpretation to focus "on the methodological problems of using different kinds of sources, looking specifically at the narrative genres shaping *both* written and oral accounts" (1989: 25). In this way a more rounded, complete version has the possibility of emerging, one in which both versions of the truth have a chance of forming a comprehensive narrative of events.

The Nantuck case, Cruikshank suggests, is a clear example of "radically conflicting visions of society and ideas about authority and social justices." It is probable that the Nantuck brothers "saw themselves as taking absolutely appropriate action to settle the deaths of their kinsmen" (1989: 30). When people feel that they have been denied justice then violent acts against their oppressors is a distinct possibility. And probably more significant is the fact that when a legal system imposes its values on the members of an alien culture, ambiguity and ambivalence are bound to result, thus circumventing closure for both parties because "the accounts are not complementary, no seamless whole emerges" (ibid., 31).

This idea is similar to that proposed by Vibert in her *Traders' Tales* when she argues that "it makes more sense to look at *reciprocal* contributions to cultural meanings and identities … [rather than] … to highlight Western impositions on the identity of the colonial other" (1997: 14). Thus, in the Nantuck case it is the dominant white settler culture which imposes its version of events on the "weaker" Indigenous one. Such a process is a form of legalistic absorption, or assimilation, because the Indigenous version of what happened is regarded as a sort of "Indian nonsense." Ultimately there is bound to be a resistance to absorption in an attempt to perpetuate their own cultural and social survival. Acts of violent opposition to these assimilative pressures are bound to occur as a result of independent people attempting to assert their autonomy in the face of repressive European settler autocracy. It can be anticipated, therefore, that acts of vengeance will undoubtedly occur as a form of retaliation against foreign rule. In any event, Coates and Morrison conclude their narrative of the trial of the Nantuck brothers with this derisive understatement: "This was not a promising start to the administration of justice in the Yukon … On the whole it was an embarrassment to the Canadian justice system" (2004: 29).

Murder at Pond Inlet, 1920

In her study of *Arctic Justice* (2002), Shelagh Grant details the shooting death of fur trader Robert Janes on Admiralty Inlet, just west of Baffin Island in the early spring of 1920. What is significant about this work is her attempts to portray both sides of the incident, particularly providing justification and nuance to the context of the murder, and to the Inuit, Nuqallaq, who was charged and stood trial for the killing. As one reviewer comments, "newly released trial transcripts provided the author with a superb window into the early administration of justice in the North and a clear view of the clash between Indigenous and Western concepts of social justice" (Schledermann 2003: 303). Similarly, another reviewer comments that "Grant recreates the government and police reaction to Janes's death while, on the other, she draws upon transcripts of Inuit statements in concert with oral history interviews to tease out the ways these events were understood and remembered by the region's original inhabitants. The subsequent image is intriguing for a number of reasons, not the least of which is that while both the official and Inuit version of events shared much common ground, how these same events were understood by the participants and spectators was strikingly dissimilar" (Swainger 2002: 238–9).

The wider setting is of particular interest, especially concerning the Dominion of Canada's belated interest in Arctic sovereignty. By the early 1900s Norwegian explorers had been continuously traversing the Arctic, and by the fall of 1902 had completed four years of scientific exploration and mapping of the High Arctic Islands, culminating in a claim of Norwegian sovereignty over all lands that had been reconnoitred, ignoring Canadian claims and interests. As far as the Inuit were concerned, during this time they probably had little grasp of Canadian citizenship or sovereignty in the Arctic since they regularly pursued polar bears and muskoxen as they traversed the territory between northern Greenland and Ellesmere Island. About the only contact that they had with Europeans were the occasional interactions with fur traders, whalers, or missionaries, but aside from these intermittent visits they had little sustained interaction with the outside world. However, it was this threat of a foreign sovereignty claim that shook the Canadian government out of its somnambulant attitude towards the arctic and the people who lived there.

By 1903 the Canadian government established a lonely outpost at Cape Herschel in the Western Arctic. Also in that year a patrol vessel, *Neptune*, carried six members of the NWMP (North West Mounted Police, forerunner of the Royal Canadian Mounted Police) who established a police detachment at Fullerton Harbour and the implementation of Canadian law and the foundation for the government's claim of Arctic sovereignty. It was only twenty years later that Robert Janes was killed near Cape Crawford (as spelled in the text) in Admiralty Inlet, thus setting the stage for the first murder trial of alleged Inuit murderers, which occurred in August 1923, in Pond Inlet. This trial, then, could be considered one of the foundations that shaped the social and political future of the Artic, and thrust several Inuit personalities, most principally the accused Nuqallaq, into the historic limelight.

As one might expect, there were a number of extenuating circumstances and multi-faceted aspects to the interaction between Robert Janes and Nuqallaq. Janes had ten years previously been the Second Officer of Captain J.E. Bernier, who was leader of the government's Eastern Arctic Patrol during 1910–11. Men such as Bernier and Janes had initially been attracted to northern Baffin Island, seeking potential riches in furs and gold, among other commodities. In 1912 Janes and his assistant, Thomas Holden, established a trading post at Tulukkat. According to the account provided by author Shelagh Grant, Robert Janes was a person whose personality bordered on the edge of emotional stability. Eventually Janes behaviour and angry outbursts resulted in the desperate escape of Thomas Holden who managed to reach Bernier's departing ship, only to die of pneumonia before reaching home. According to Grant, Janes's behaviour in incident after incident revealed a person bordering on madness.

The Inuit response to the murder was pieced together through depositions from the investigation and contemporary recollections that were assembled years later. The Inuit admit that the decision to kill Janes was regrettable; however, they nonetheless regarded Janes's behaviour as a threat to their entire community. Nuqallaq was subsequently tried, found guilty of manslaughter, and sentenced to ten years' imprisonment at Stoney Mountain penitentiary in Manitoba. However, he was sent home after serving less than two years of his sentence, having contracted tuberculosis, apparently during his imprisonment. He subsequently passed the illness on to community members in his home village before succumbing to the disease himself.

Grant should be given credit for placing the Inuit perspective of this murder near the centre of this enquiry, since it raises questions about cross-cultural trials of murder when a "foreign" government is in charge of the proceedings. First, the jury was appointed from among the members of the crew of the *Arctic*; thus, Nuqallaq was not judged by a contingent of his peers in any sense whatsoever. In addition, there is the fact that Janes took a country wife, an Inuk woman named Kalluk who, at various times, lived with both Janes and her husband. As Frank Tester, writing in a review of the book in *Études/Inuit/Studies*, comments, "Ultimately, we are left with the picture of a belligerent and temperamental man using threats of physical violence to express himself; behaviour that ultimately leads to Janes' demise" (2003: 533). The salient issue that Grant raises is whether Nuqallaq's actions constituted murder on that night of March 15, 1920. After all, it was a community decision to dispatch Janes because the Inuit considered him a threat to their overall safety and survival. Such a decision was in accordance with Inuit practices, which were taken previously under similar circumstances in order to protect the community from the potential harm of a deranged person. Does this act really constitute murder, which is the question raised in this case? In a similar manner we might think about the cross-cultural administration of justice in this modern, globalized world.

Comparing Cross-Cultural Homicides

A study of homicide cases involving this country's Indigenous people concludes that "if we compare the homicidal death rates of registered Indians with those of the total population (including Indians), we note that for registered Indians in British Columbia the risk to die from homicidal violence is on the average ten times as great as for the total population of British Columbia and Canada" (Jilek and Roy 1976:

201). By comparison, for Native Americans living in the United States, the Department of Health, Education and Welfare notes that the crude homicide death rate has consistently been about three times as high as the rates for all other races (Ogden 1970: 75–80). In another sample, the age-adjusted homicide death rate per 100,000 persons was 26.6 for Native Americans and 3.9 per 100,000 for white Americans (Hackenberg and Gallagher (1972: 211–26). Jilek and Roy (1976: 204–5, 209) conclude their study itemizing three points:

1. There was no significant difference in their sample between the homicide rates of Canadian and American Indigenous people.
2. Indigenous people tend to kill Indigenous people more readily than whites.
3. If the victim of a homicide is an Indigenous person, this person tends to be female or another person holding a kinship relationship with the offender.

So, how are we to interpret this information as it pertains to the homicides occurring in northern Canada that have been discussed thus far? In the first place, the killings at Henley House, in the Yukon territory, and at Pond Inlet all involved Indigenous men murdering whites. The incident(s) at Henley House would appear to involve acts of vengeance for the perceived maltreatment of Indigenous women, or possibly the fur traders' withholding of expected reciprocal payments of some kind. The Nantuck brothers also appear to have thought the white prospectors were responsible for bargaining some form of blood-money for the death of their kinsmen, and as such this could be interpreted as an act of revenge as well. In the Pond Inlet case the fur trader was apparently killed because he was a threat to the Inuit community – a sort of self-preservation tactic. The killing of white men by Indigenous people is from all accounts a relatively rare phenomenon that should be investigated further. The Hannah Bay case is different from the other three in that (mostly) Indigenous people were the perpetrators as well as the victims, thus conforming more closely to the statistical information provided above. However, this case could also be interpreted as an act of revenge based on the rationale that the HBC post manager, William Corrigal, was (perceived to be) responsible for providing food to needy Cree yet withholding it.

What is clearly needed, then, is a further study that delves more deeply into all recorded cases of homicide during the fur trade period – those involving white men killing white men, Indigenous men killing Indigenous men and women, and Indigenous people killing other non-Indigenous persons. The historical record of Canada's colonial period is certainly in need of such a study, one that takes a more objective stance than the sheer propaganda that the Hudson's Bay Company has taken such great pains to craft, putting the British in a favourable light.

The three cases of cross-cultural homicide that have been discussed thus far – Hannah Bay (1832), Yukon territory (1898), and Pond Inlet (1920) – share certain characteristics, as one would expect, but they differ in major ways as well, especially in terms of their political and legal aspects. As far as the murder of post master William Corrigal of Hannah Bay was concerned, William Swanson and his posse who were sent out to apprehend the culprits had little interest in hearing Cree elder Quapakay's protestations of innocence, or that the "Spirit Above" had ordered his sons to commit the crime, or that his family was in a "starving and naked state."

None of this mattered to the Hudson's Bay Company men; they were only interested in demanding "blood for blood," in exacting vengeance and retaliation in kind, according to fur trader John McLean's account. However, as law professor John Reid explains, such retaliatory measures were somewhat ironic since these "practices [were] more closely resembling the laws of the Indian nations than the common law [that] guided the behavior of Hudson's Bay officials in Rupert's Land … It is not a significant fact that there was no trial, because the Hudson's Bay Company never gave Indians trials" (1993a: 7–8). Or as former HBC post master John McLean explained, "When the blood of their [HBC] servants was shed without cause or provocation … they punished the aggressors as the law of God allows, demanding 'blood for blood'" (1932: 323). Thus, "the Hudson's Bay Company was a law unto itself and slaughtered Indians without legal excuse" (Farrinto 2000: 490).

In the case of the Nantuck brothers of the Yukon, the legal authorities were, apparently, similarly not interested in the protestations of innocence of one of the brothers who was hung just as his other two brothers were. As far as any motive was concerned, which is to say that the brothers killed a prospector because one of their clan members had died as a result of the arsenic poisoning by a white person, the judge made a note and then declared that this was" just some Indian nonsense hardly deserving mention" (Coates and Morrison 2004: 24). The judge also referred to the Nantuck brothers as comprising "a very low order of humanity" (ibid., 23). Such comments are remarkably similar to George Simpson's contemptuous description of the Kutenai when he said that they were "a miserable set of human beings, small decrepit and dirty … [they] hardly bore the semblance of human beings" (1847:

130). Such racist attitudes are a reflection of white privilege. They are also founded on a lexicon of Indigenous disentitlement that "favours people who are, or are presumed to be, white by enabling political and economic systems and corresponding power structures to grant only these people unmerited and simultaneously unacknowledged advantages" (Cousins 2004: 1).

In the case of the killing of trader Robert Janes in 1920 and the trial of Nuqallaq of Pond Inlet, the incident itself is perhaps overshadowed by the Canadian government's newly established interest in claiming Arctic sovereignty. One wonders if there would have been any interest at all in this case without the sovereignty issue as a significant territorial backdrop. In fact, Nuqallaq was charged with manslaughter, not murder, suggesting a degree of ambivalence about the merits of the case against him, given the erratic and dangerous behaviour of the victim. As Jonathan Swainger (2005) also indicates, the trial furthermore brought out into the open the Canadian government's ineptitude regarding appropriate and prudent policies concerning the Inuit and their place in Canadian society, if any.

All three cases point to the legal ambivalence and jurisdictional problems faced by colonial powers when they assume control over Indigenous people in the interests of justice, especially when these people themselves have their own codes of conduct, which may clash precipitously with those of the more powerful society. In the case of the Hudson's Bay Company, its officers may have acted as if they were a power unto themselves, but in fact there were serious concerns over the extent to which their dominion encompassed. As an example, an act passed by the British Parliament in 1803 could be interpreted to suggest a requirement that a person accused of a crime within the vast territory of Rupert's Land was to be conveyed to Lower Canada to be dealt with according to British law.

According to legal expert John Reid, "The act of 1803 could have applied to very little territory except to Rupert's Land, the demesne governed by Hudson's Bay. Nonetheless, 'doubts' were 'entertained' whether the force of the act extended there, doubts probably strengthened by the technicality that Rupert's Land was not mentioned in the legislation" (1993a: 6). As I have searched very thoroughly through the Hudson's Bay Company journal records and other related documents and correspondence of the trading posts involved in the Hannah Bay murders, there was never any suggestion whatsoever to be found to indicate that the men led by Mr. Swanson of the HBC posse did not have the jurisdiction to kill the Quapakay male family members on the spot, regardless of any legislative act passed across the ocean in

England. And, of course, there was the related issue about whether British law even applied to Indigenous people in the first place (see Reid 1993a:7).

The other important matter concerns the Hudson's Bay Company officers presumed right to vengeance and retaliation, a life for a life, which has no basis in English common law. This was an issue that was raised by Byram (2008) in his study of a series of violent conflicts between European fur trappers and Native people at Yaquina Bay on the Oregon coast during the spring of 1832. As Byram (2008: 358) explains, "The growing colonial presence meant that Indigenous principles of justice no longer applied in conflicts with outsiders." The Yaquina society was under threat by European fur trappers because of the intense fur trapping, violence, and the contagious diseases spread by the outsiders. The Yaquina felt that they needed to protect themselves and their territory in order to survive. In April 1832, two European trappers were killed by Indigenous people on the coast. John McLoughlin, who was in charge of the HBC interests in the area, ordered a party under the command of HBC employee Michel Laframboise to lead a party under his command in a retaliatory expedition.

The conflict "for the Yaquina was an initial, wide-scale breakdown of principles of justice regarding international relations – principles that had sustained their sovereignty for untold generations" according to Byram (2008: 363). "You will proceed with the party under your command to the Killimook country for the purpose of punishing the atrocious murders" wrote McLoughlin (ibid., 368). On May 8, he reported that "Michel and his party are returned from their Expedition after having killed 6 of the Murderers" (ibid.). Regarding McLoughlin's accounts of the conflict, "the chief factor pursued a strategy closer to payback vengeance than to British law. He expected the killings to deter these Indians from committing homicides in the future ... European adaptations of Native systems of vengeance, even less of Native laws ... have less to do with law ... and are better thought of as *particular strategies of power*, together with the assumptions of social control lying behind them, broadly derived from Europe but framed in the particular circumstance of the fur trade [author's emphasis]" (ibid., 370).

One conclusion that could be drawn here regarding the various cases of cross-cultural murder is that the officers of the Hudson's Bay Company adapted whatever strategy they felt would serve their purposes at the time. For the most part, however, whatever strategy they adopted had less to do with justice per se than to seek vengeance and retaliation in kind, regardless of the foundation of such a stratagem's existence in English common law.

Vengeance and Retaliation in Fur-Trade Country

Various historians have acted as apologists for the Hudson's Bay Company in particular, and British colonial policy towards Canada's Indigenous population in general. Frederick Merk, as an example, wrote that nineteenth-century British North America was a region "inhabited by a numerous and diverse Indian population, [which] was an area of peace and order" (1968 [1931]: lix–lx). The reason for this "peace and order," Howay et al. wrote, was on account of the fact that it was in the British fur companies' "pecuniary interest to be just and humane in their dealings with the natives" (1942: 38–9). In turn, "certain standards of trade ... preserved order... and assist[ed] and protect[ed] those who lived up to the required standard [yet, the fur companies were also] ready and determined to punish offenders." And, referring specifically to the Hudson's Bay Company, it was said that "their treatment of the natives was humane and protective" (Begg 1894: 119; see also A. Ross 1956).

Speaking of the Oregon region, which comprised parts of the province of British Columbia and the states of Washington and Oregon, a prominent Canadian historian, Arthur Morton, concluded that this region was "managed by the English fur-traders for two generations with no more than a rare clash" (1973: 763). It must be remembered, Reid (1993a: 6) reminds readers of Canadian history, that "[f]or about two centuries, the Indian nations [of Rupert's Land] ... dealt only with the Hudson's Bay Company, not with British governmental or military officials ... The Hudson's Bay Company was no mere business concern, but a European colonial power, a virtual sovereign answerable to no one ... [it had] ... territorial jurisdiction over all the lands drained by the waters flowing into Hudson's Bay. In matters of criminal prosecution, the company's charter made it virtually a law unto itself when dealing with the Indians." However, old ideas have a tendency to perpetuate themselves through repetition, leading some to still believe into the 1930s that even after Canadian Confederation the Indigenous people of this country "would be better off today if the Hudson's Bay Company had continued in force" (Pinkerton 1931: 217).

There has accumulated, at least for the last three decades, a growing body of literature that suggests that previous characterizations of the fur trade as peaceful, cooperative, and congenial (as depicted in Donald MacKay's *The Honourable Company*, for example) have misrepresented the actual history of the relationship between fur trade companies and Indigenous people. On the contrary, the emerging contemporary literature is prone to characterize the North American fur trade as violence ridden, comprising frequent patterns of vengeance and brutality.

At first relatively minor incidences of cross-cultural violence were the norm; however, wrongs tended to accumulate over the years as fur traders and Indigenous people began to engage in spontaneous acts of violence for their own immediate ends. This pattern, in turn, fostered a "feeling of mutual suspicion and insecurity" leading those involved, as the saying goes, to shoot first and ask questions later (Howay 1925: 308). Given these prevailing conditions it is not difficult to envisions a frontier with "little margin for considering circumstances, granting mercy, or weighing mitigation of liability." The Hudson's Bay Company, Reid continues, had the "strength of resources to demand satisfaction, as well as the manpower [to] send out brigades of avengers-of-blood to execute the manslayer or kill random members of his nation" (1994: 49). As such, Reid disputes the "mild, humane policy of the British towards the native Indian population (1993a: 5)

Speaking of the Pacific Northwest coastal region of North America, Douthit provides a dismantling of the Hudson's Bay Company's reputation for peaceful relations, noting that whatever "the HBC's record for maintaining good relations with Indians in other places, their conduct toward the Indians of southern Oregon contributed to a pattern of hostile Indian-white relations." He then reached the following conclusions of Indigenous-to-white contact in the area: first, the "Hudson's Bay Company treatment of the Indians ... was more hostile than peaceful"; and second, HBC personnel "used violence against Indians of the [southern Oregon] region and established a hostile pattern of Indian-white relations" (1992: 26, see also Reid 1993b for a similar conclusion).

Apparently, his point struck a sympathetic chord with other historians since Dean (1997: 292) commented that "Douthit's essay is a well-crafted counterpoint to generations of HBC apologists." Dean also concluded that the Hudson's Bay Company was much less interested in maintaining cordial relationships with the Indigenous trappers who traded at their posts because "In the final analysis, the HBC managed [its] affairs ... in the interests of maintaining British commercial supremacy" (1997: 291). He then concluded that "fur trade studies have frequently emphasized ... the presumption of a fairly constant enmity between Native and non-Native" (ibid., 262). In a similar vein, Brenda Farrinto arrives at a comparable conclusion as one propounded by John Reid, a legal historian, in his *Patterns of Vengeance* (1999), a study of cross-cultural homicide in the North American fur trade. Farrinto comments that British fur traders "were just as brutal and genocidal as American fur men. The Hudson's Bay Company was a law unto itself and slaughtered Indians without legal excuse even for taking property

... It is clear that the British fur men put profit above the norms of English or Scottish law" (2000: 490)

In cases of homicide against fur traders, it is suggested that the "retaliation of the [fur trade] companies was more certain, more successful, and, on occasion, more brutal than was retaliation-in-kind exacted by loosely organized groups of American mountain men" (Reid 1994: 49). Thus, there is apparently some evidence that whites took their vengeance out on Indigenous people in a harsher manner than they did with their fellow Europeans and Americans. This would, therefore, challenge what Marshall has termed "a common assumption in Canadian historiography ... that British policy toward North American Indian populations was substantially more human than the harsh, brutal, and often genocidal policy of Americans." On the contrary, he asserts: "The Hudson's Bay Company (HBC) was just as brutal toward North American Indian peoples as were their American counterparts." Alternatively, Marshal suggests that in comparable terms "the brutal responses of fur-trade companies such as the HBC are understandable within the context of [the] times" (2002: 272; see also Blackhawk 2007; Byram 2008; Wallace 1925).

Modern Native American Homicide

According to many researchers, incidences of Native American homicide in the United States is a very serious social problem. The Native American homicide rate, at the time of Bachman's (1991a: 469) study, stood at 9.6 per 100,000 people which was double that of whites at 4.6 per 100,000 people. Furthermore, some reservation county homicide rates in her survey were close to or more than 100 per 100,000 people (in North Dakota, Nevada, and Oregon).

The literature on Native American homicide cases is ever expanding, yet, as Bachman (1991a: 469) explains, "the etiology of American Indian homicide is virtually unexplored in the literature." Nonetheless, these works discuss a number of significant details that are germane to the main topic of discussion in this book concerning homicide by members of the Indigenous population of North America, whether contemporary or historical in nature. For the most part, this literature focuses on socio-cultural factors, psychological or physiological issues, and various other aspects such as social disintegration, internal colonialism, or economic deprivation. It is nonetheless evident, though, that the subject of Native American homicide cannot be explained by one variable alone, and that the context of the conflict situations during which a homicide takes place are usually complex and situationally oriented.

As Bachman concludes based on extensive interviews, "The majority of homicide victims in this sample were acquaintances of the offenders, and most of the homicides were committed during a conflict situation or argument. The most frequent method used was a knife followed by guns" (1991a: 472). As such, it would therefore be a useful epistemological exercise to examine the various variables, theories and approaches that have been utilized by researchers in their attempts to understand the dynamics of Native American homicide.

Neurological approach: As a starting point, Jonathan Pincus M.D., professor of neurology at Georgetown's University School of Medicine, asks a basic question: "What makes killers kill?" His answer: "Regardless of the classification of the killing," he contends, "I believe most killers kill for the same reason" (2001: 11). And that reason, Dr. Pincus argues, is that violent criminal behaviour is the catastrophic product of a dysfunctional brain coupled with an abusive environment. In other words, such an explanation does not leave much room for explanations based on social, cultural, or economic factors. After examining the life histories of 150 murderers, Dr. Pincus found commonalities in their personalities; they tended to be withdrawn, apathetic, irritable, and unable to control the expression of emotions such as anger (2001: 217). In other words, he says that natural-born killers are made, not born.

In an interview, Dr. Pincus indicated that murderers suffer from a "devil's brew" of afflictions: abuse, mental illness, and neurological impairment (Miller 2001). Can murderers be treated, Miller asks Dr. Pincus? "The most constructive thing that society could do would not treat them but rather to prevent violence from occurring (ibid.). The answer then, is "no, murderers cannot be treated." The implication is that murderers must either be executed or imprisoned for life – a harsh reality. A further study (Shon and Barton-Bellesca 2012) of parricide offenders (those who kill their fathers or other close relatives) concludes that such murderers display anti-social tendencies at an early age that persisted into adulthood. Their research indicates that this pattern has been replicated across "cultural, racial, and national boundaries ... and extends across history" (2012 :66). In addition, there are a number of psychological studies linking Native American mental issues with homicide, as in Bloom (1980); Frederick (1973); Humphrey and Kapferer (1982).

Ronet Bachman (1991a, 1991b, 1992) has examined the "social causes of American Indian homicide" in terms of a multi-variate approach and suggests that the diversity of Native American experiences makes generalization problematic and difficult to make. As the author explains: "Problem of generalizability plague most research; however, it becomes more difficult when one investigates a subset of a population whose historical roots were so heterogeneous and diverse; [however, it is contended] that while American Indians may represent a multitude of cultural and tribal identities, they have also experienced some of the same historical and contemporary conditions regardless of tribal affiliation" (1991a: 489).

Social disorganization: One of the most important of these historical conditions has been social disorganization. In sociology, Émile Durkheim (1933 [1893], 2001 [1915]) has largely been responsible for suggesting that under conditions of rapid social change there is a tendency for crime to increase as a result of the lessoning or breakdown of social controls.[12] A wide-ranging evaluation of the social disorganization theory as applied to criminal behaviour has been conducted by Bursik (1988), who has adopted the following definition: "Social disorganization refers to the inability of local communities to realize the common values of their residents to solve community-experienced problems" (ibid., 525). He points out that the concept of social disorganization developed in the 1920s but had fallen into disuse by the 1980s for a number of reasons.

First, the problem of historical change: theories "of social disorganization were grounded on a basic assumption of stability that was simply not justified by historical evidence" (ibid., 525). In other words, societies are always changing, either in small measure or in great leaps and bounds, but they are nonetheless in a constant state of flux to one degree or another, but this fact does not necessarily mean that societies will become disorganized or dysfunctional simply on the basis of historical change.

Second, the problem of confounding cause and effect: social disorganization theories often "did not clearly differentiate the presumed outcome of social disorganization…from disorganization itself" (ibid., 527). The logical inconsistency associated with false cause tautological arguments (i.e., using an effect to explain a cause) is clearly evident when one uses the effects of social disorganization to explain how a society got that way in the first place.

Third, the problem of normative assumptions: "the inability of a local community to regulate itself in order to attain goals that are agreed to by residents of the community implies that the notion of consensus is a central component of the model … [such that the social disorganization] framework appears to many to be insensitive to the realities of political and social life" (ibid., 535). Most communities have a diversity of opinions concerning the directions in which its members should be heading, or about community goals that should be achieved, however this fact by itself does not necessarily mean that the community is "socially disorganized." For the most part, communities have ways of settling their differences, of choosing leaders who will guide them into the future or settle disputes among its members. Assuming a unified consensus without dissent is hardly the way humans live their lives.

John Honigmann, an anthropologist, studied social disorganization and disintegration in five Native communities (mostly Cree and Anishinaabe) situated along the James Bay coast of northern Canada. As he indicates, "Social disintegration means the fragmentation and malfunctioning of a social system from whatever cause ... Specifically, the disintegrated community possesses a large number of homes in which one or both parents are absent or frequently changed, or in which relations between members are chronically hostile and unstable" (1965: 200). Honigmann's conclusion is that "Each of the relatively disintegrated communities manifests its disorganization rather distinctly, though certain specific signs of disintegration, like illegal drinking and weak leadership, recur .... [Other characteristics include] open hostility towards figures who represent the authority of the larger society, like the police and the [HBC] Company manager ... cultural confusion and widespread secularization ... high level of anxiety." Yet, "Social disintegration in the North is no unitary phenomenon, nor does it hinge entirely on a history of recent, widespread cultural change and uprooted traditional roles" (ibid., 212–15).

The pattern of social disorganization as it specifically related to Native American homicide rates is described by Ronet Bachman (1991a: 475–7). Her definition of social disorganization is "a decrease of the influence of existing social rules of behavior upon individual members of the group. When a society is in a state of social disorganization, people are set free of normative constraints and can drift from conformity into deviance" (ibid., 475). The homicide offenders that she studied shared similar life histories, such as living part of their lives in foster homes, were adopted, or sent to boarding schools at a young age. Bachman notes that the "removal of Indian children from their families occurs at a much higher rate than in non-Indian populations" (ibid., 475–6). In Canada, similar patterns of disassociation from one's natal families are found among Indigenous children, especially among those who spent much of their childhood in residential schools, a situation which Linda Jaine (1993) has called "The Stolen Years."

In a related study, Bachman (1991b) utilizes the influence of social organization and economic deprivation on homicide rates among Native Americans at the county level from 114 US counties with reservations. Both variables, she concludes, are "positively and significantly" related to Native American homicide rates. Bachman further suggests that "if reservations are allowed economic opportunity, both levels of economic deprivation and social disorganization as well as rates of lethal violence may decrease" (1991b: 469).

In a later study Lanier and Huff-Corzine (2006) depart from Bachman's approach by investigating the influence of social disorganization on Native Americans who live *both* on and off the reservation. They begin their analysis by indicating that Native American homicide is double the national rate and is the second leading cause of death for Native Americans in the 25–34 age group. In addition, Native Americans are among the lowest group in socio-economic standing in the US, with median incomes well below the national averages (US Department of Health and Human Services, (1996); see also Baker (2006) on homicide as a public health issue).

Their conclusion is stated in two parts: first, "family disruption appears to be an important predictor of social disorganization especially as it correlates to percentages of American Indian female-headed households"; and second, "contrary to expectations, American Indian poverty was not found to be a significant predictor of homicide in the analysis" (2006: 190). In terms of the latter point, they speculate that while "living in poverty maybe more the norm than the exception for American Indians ... social disorganization significantly affects American Indian homicide" (2006: 190–1).

Cultural approaches: There are also a variety of cultural studies that focus on homicide among Native Americans and Canadians. Some of the research in this area concentrates on violence among the members of specific tribal groups, such as the Eastern Cherokee. French and Hornbuckle, for example, assert that "most violence among the Eastern Cherokee indeed involves both cultural frustration and latent subcultural control mechanisms, that when combined, generate a highly charged atmosphere conducive to spontaneous violence" (1977: 336). It is difficult, as researchers assert, for Native American youth to find their way in the modern world in which living in the "traditional ways" conflicts with the "white man's" way. "Traditional American Indian culture," Hochkirchen and Jilek (1985: 25) state, "clashes with the often changing and contradictory values of white society. No longer is there a natural transmission of values from the older to the younger generation." Similarly, homicide offenders among Native youth in the southern areas of Canada tend to lack exposure to traditional cultural values and associated behaviour, although there are significant variations from region to region, province to province, in this regard (Jilek and Roy 1976).

The difficulty of Native American youth finding their way between 'traditional' and 'white society' is reminiscent of the theory of "cultural dissonance" (Daenekinadt and Roose 2014). In situations of cultural dissonance, "everybody plunged into a plurality of social worlds is subjected to heterogeneous and sometimes contradictory principles of socialization. Heterogeneity of socializing experiences is present within and between different stages of life" (Lahire 2011: 26). The idea of 'heterogeneous socialization' can be traced back to Robert Merton's arguments associated with the concept of social ambivalence. Sociological ambivalence refers to a situation with "incompatible normative expectations of attitudes, beliefs, and behavior" (see Merton [1949] on the "ex post facto explanation," and Merton and Barber 1976: 6; Young and French [1997] on the "status integration hypothesis").[13]

Economic deprivation: "Economic deprivation," Bachman (1991a: 483) suggests, "can cause the likelihood of a number of pathologies such as alcoholism, suicide, and lethal violence .... Poverty engenders hopelessness, apathy, and anger. One form of coping with the alienation and hostility that poverty may produce is through aggression." However, despite the appeal of this approach, not all individuals who grow up in poverty commit violent crimes. Such people may be angry about or resent their condition, but they do not necessarily lash out and murder people. They may, in fact, find other constructive avenues to channel their anger and aggression. The problem is how to sort out those individuals in poverty-stricken environments who will act out violently from those who do not. And to remind the reader, Lanier and Huff-Corzine (2016) did not, contrary to expectations, find that poverty was a significant predictor of homicide.

As such, as Bachman (1991a: 487) concludes, "Most of the homicide offenders interviewed were born into cycle of poverty – blocked from legitimate economic opportunities and forced into dependency. For many, the distress of this situation was compounded by family disruption and disorganization." However, as noted earlier with social disorganization theories, which comes first: the poverty or the aggression? Compounding cause and effect, one might be tempted to explain aggression as a result of poverty, and vice versa. Thus, this logical conundrum leads the author to conclude that "It is true that not all American Indians who are born into conditions of poverty are propelled to commit murder. Many go on to college and make their way into the middle class" (1991a: 487). Whatever the argument that Bachman is mounting concerning the role of poverty and economic deprivation as a causal factor in Native American homicide rates, then, would appear to dissipate with this admission.[14]

Internal Colonialism and Native American Subjugation

The various etiological causal factors and approaches to Native American homicide discussed below are ultimately based on colonialism as an antecedent (presumptive, a priori) factor. As Bachman (1991a: 473) argues, "no model explaining any phenomena with regard to American Indians would be complete without the acknowledgement of the colonization process that our government had subjected this population to."

The term "internal colonialism" is generally meant to suggest "colonialism within" as opposed to "beyond the boundaries" of a country. As such, it is usually used to describe relations within countries. Netzloff (2003), for example, argues that the practices of English colonialism were initially formulated in relation to the realm's own "internal colony," which is to say, the displaced classes and colonized regions of early modern England, Scotland, and Ireland. He also describes the destabilizing consequences of internal colonialism and the resistance and agencies that consequently result from this situation. In addition, Robert Blauner describes various components of the colonization process: "Colonization begins with a forced, involuntary entry … The colonizing power carries out a policy which constrains, transforms, or destroys Indigenous values, orientations, and ways of life … Colonization involves a relationship by which members of the colonized group tend to be administered by representatives of the dominant power. There is an experience of being managed and manipulated by outsiders in terms of ethnic status" (1969: 396).

Similarly, Jacobson (1984: 150) suggests that "internal colonies … are created when one area dominates another to the extent that it channels the flow of resources from the periphery to the dominant core." Hechter (1975) also adds that ethnocentrism[15] plays a role in the underdevelopment of periphery areas. Blauner goes even further when he argues that a fundamental component "of colonization is racism. Racism is a principle of social domination by which a group seen as inferior or different in terms of alleged biological characteristics is exploited, controlled, and oppressed socially and psychically by a superordinate group" (1969: 396). Furthermore, the colonizing body places its own authority figures and administrative structures that incorporate the traditional leaders of the colonized group and establishes various policies that act as control mechanisms serving to inhibit the freedom of the minority group (see Dunning 1962; Rogers 1965; Ervin 1987; Hedican 1982, 2013; Watkins 1977).

The historical developments that have led to such a deplorable plight for North America's Indigenous people have been described as "the ethnics of domestic dependency." As Jorgensen explains, "Since corralling Indians on reservations, the dominant white society has demanded that Indians observe the Protestant Ethic, or as it is known, the work ethic: a narrow, competitive, individualistic code of conduct that has served American capitalism well" (1978: 7). From Jorgensen's perspective, the issue of Native American development is more regional and political than strictly economic. He puts forth the so-called metropolis-satellite concept in which capitalist development is seen to involve expropriation and exploitation, thereby inevitably causing underdevelopment in the satellite-rural area. In this case the metropolis-satellite economy is seen as a single integrated structure in which the former grows at the expense of the latter. In an ironic twist, the relegation to the hinterland actually benefited some Indigenous groups, such as those who found their country barren on the surface but rich in oil, gas, or mineral wealth underneath.

This is the very situation that is happening currently in Canada's northern Ontario region in what has been termed the Ring of Fire, which is a name given to a vast region of mineral deposits. This region, situated about 400 kilometres (250 miles) northeast of Thunder Bay, in the James Bay Lowlands, was named after Johnny Cash's famous country-and-western ballad when Richard Nemis, founder and president of Noront Resources, first made significant mineral finds in the area. However, various First Nations are also contesting their rights to the mineral wealth in this region, as some districts of government are implying that the Indigenous people only have access to surface rights, not underground where the minerals are located.

The Indigenous people of northern Ontario suffer from depressed economic conditions in one way or another, such as high unemployment, low per-capital incomes, or lack of employment possibilities. As Tony Clement, former Treasury Board president acknowledged, the Ring of Fire is home to some of the "most socio-economically disadvantage communities in all of Canada" (Hedican 2017: 143). Clement also stated that "chronic housing shortages, low education outcomes, and lack of access to clean drinking water jeopardize the ability of local First Nations to benefit from significant economic, employment, and business development opportunities associated with the Ring of Fire, which according to Clement, represents a "once-in-a-lifetime opportunity to create jobs and generate growth and long-term prosperity for northern Ontario and the nation" (Ontario Ministry of Natural Resources 2013). The Ring of Fire development, therefore, is seen as a possible significant economic benefit to the area, but there are infrastructural challenges that could blunt the possible benefits that the mining activities could bring to the region. The irony here is that the Indigenous people who live in an area of unimaginable mineral wealth are also inhibited by the very internal colonial structures that have kept them isolated for mainstream society and created significant economic deprivation have also now posed substantial barriers (of education, economic infrastructure, and political organization) to reaping the benefits of this wealth that would be of such immense benefit to their continued living conditions.

Vast land expropriations took place in Canada and the United States in their colonial histories. In Canada's north an enormous territory called Rupert's Land, whose title was transferred to the Hudson's Bay Company without any sort of negotiations with the Indigenous inhabitant, entrenched an economic system that ensured a relatively powerless Native populace. Legislation such as the Royal Proclamation of 1763, long touted as a recognition of Aboriginal title by the British Crown, only served in reality to maintain the ascendency of the external colonial powers. The Rupert's Land expropriation mirrored the huge land grabs of Andrew Jackson's government in the United States during the Great Removal of the 1830s.

As a further example in Canada of internal colonialism, "a contentious issue here is that the Indian Act still accords official status to some Natives, but not to others, thus fragmenting Canada's Aboriginal population into various competing interest groups" (Hedican 2008: 14). The Indian Act ensured that Indigenous peoples would be kept separate from the rest of Canada, and because of the various restrictions concerning private property and the elections of local officials filling the positions of chiefs and councillors of each treaty band, Indigenous people had little hope of breaking out of a situation of dependency and inequality. Peter Carstens explains in *The Queen's People* that "the Okanagan [people] were incorporated into the political arenas of the Province of British Columbia and the dominion of Canada, not as equal partners in confederation, but as people of special status defined in the Indian Act ... The Okanagan and other reserve dwellers occupy socio-economic positions which are not unlike those occupied by many peasants and proletarians" (1991: 103).

Regarding the election of Aboriginal leaders, the whole process is controlled by provisions outlined in the Indian Act. As such, Boldt (1980: 15) has so cogently commented: "The context of Indian leadership ... [is] ... characterized by conditions of cultural marginality and lack of structural definitions." The courts and justice system are another mechanism of social control and suppression in internal colonial practices, usually delving out much higher sentences for the members of the ethnic minority than is common for the population of the colonizers. Speaking of the Arizona territorial court system, for example, Clare Mckanna (1993: 367) notes that this system was "instituted [as] a tyrannical program of social control which was disparate, discriminatory, and predisposed to nineteenth-century versions of scientific racism. The region's educated elite – judges, attorneys, and newspaper editors – set the tone for racial intolerance and sanctioned (countenanced, endorsed, approved, and upheld) the perversion of a system designed to safeguard the rights of Americans, Native Americans as well."

The internal colonial approach also finds expression in Frideres and Gadacz's text, in which they argue that the policies of federal and provincial governments in Canada, much like the BIA in the United States, have been an impediment to self-determination and development. As they explain, "the control exerted over Indians is viewed as the only way Natives will be able to escape their poverty and marginal existence. The resistance of this control by Natives has been interpreted as further evidence that Natives are unable to change by themselves, and has thus enhanced the resolve of the government to increase their control and force change" (1993: 515). Other authors apparently support this opinion, as Wotherspoon and Satzewich explain: "In relation to the internal colonial model we agree that a focus on the state is crucial to understanding the dynamics of aboriginal economic development and underdevelopment" (1993: 252).

Similarly, Snipp (1986) describes the temporal processes of the development of internal colonialism in terms of a three-part process, stressing the progression of control that is involved in the eventual subjugation of Indigenous people through bureaucratic strictures and the undermining of the Aboriginal peoples' leadership structures, co-opted by such government agencies as the BIA. In the first stage, Indigenous people in North America were independent of European powers. In the second stage, the Indigenous people become a "captive nation." "The status of 'captive nation'," Snipp (1986: 154) suggests, "is defined mainly in political terms, Captive nationhood describes the limited amount of self-rule that Indian tribes exercised following their submission to the authority of the Federal Government. [in this stage] the rights of political autonomy and self-government were not completely stripped." Inevitably a third stage follows in which "American Indians were made 'wards' of the State with federal authorities, primarily the BIA, assuming extensive oversight responsibilities for the management of remaining Indian lands" (ibid.).

In the United States, in relation to Native Americans, several authors have suggested that the Bureau of Indian Affairs has historically acted as an internal colonial power. In particular, Palmer and Rundstrom (2013: 1142) claim that "the BIA involves various time-honored colonial practices: creating new forms of dependence, imposing complex bureaucratic procedures, misusing funds, distributing free commodities, developing obligatory points of control, and outsourcing both management and labor to a private sector with long experience exploiting Indian resource economics." This description is also corroborated by Natziger who suggests that "the BIA is merely an instrument of carrying out policies that serve the interests of the dominant culture in general, and industrial capitalism in particular" (1980: 38). Snipp (1986:150) arrives at a similar conclusion: "The Bureau of Indian Affairs (BIA) has been instrumental in perpetuating the subordinate, colonized status of Indian reservations. The BIA is blamed for actively cultivating Indian dependencies and for being a willing accomplice to their economic exploitation."

It would appear that at least since 1945 the BIA went through one turbulent period after another. Officer (1978: 61–72) discussed the BIA support for the government's termination policy during the 1950s as one source of discontent. In the 1970s the BIA was affected by a growing frustration and militancy of the Native population. "By late 1976," Office (1978: 61) explains, "it [the BIA] was also beginning to feel the effects of an expanding white backlash against Indians in many areas, stemming at least in part from more aggressive Indian espousal of the concept of tribal sovereignty ... Internally, the Bureau since the mid-1970s has experienced considerable tension between Indian and non-Indian employees, the former having been favored by federal court decisions confirming their entitlement to preference in hiring, promotion, and lateral transfer within the BIA and the Indian Health Service." Additional problems resulted from the control over natural resources, including deposits of uranium and low sulphur coal, which are on Native lands, with the implication that "the Bureau may find itself again in the old frontier situation where it stood between the Indians and the combine of settlers and soldiers who wished to exterminate them" (1978: 72). It would appear that the BIA constantly finds itself in an unenviable position between conflicting parties.

The BIA has also been described as "the most important colonial institution in American Indian Affairs since its inception" (Palmer and Runstrom 2013: 1144). It is also one of the oldest government agencies in the United States. The BIA, originally the Office of Indian Affairs, was created in 1824 and was initially located in the War Department

(Champagne 1983: 3–28; Bee and Gingerich 1977: 70–93). It has been suggested that the BIA has attempted to assimilate Native Americans, control their lands and resources through a network of military forts, Indian agencies, and Christian missionaries (Cahill 2011: 9). Since at least 1870, the BIA has also been accused of acting in concert with various American corporations, such as occurred when railroad construction was allocated to private corporations which circumvented the wishes of tribal governments (Miner 1989). In any event, leaders of tribal governments at times occupy compromised positions. Even though they are duly elected by tribal members, their positions exist at the pleasure of the BIA (Castile 2006: 9). One conclusion is that "Indian country has long been riven with the governmental and corporate institutions of a settler society pursuing a policy of internal colonialism administered by the BIA" (Palmer and Runstrom 2013: 1144; see also Cahill 2011: 3, 113–14; Ostler 2004: 2–5; Moore 1993; Snipp 1986; and White 1988 for corroborating points of view).

In areas in which tribal governments have been able to circumvent BIA controls there has been a modicum of success. One example concerns the forest allocation programs which have been managed effectively by certain tribal governments. In one study it was found that tribal government officials were better at managing, harvesting, and marketing timber because they had incentives that BIA administrators did not, such as an interest in the well-being of both the forests they lived in and the communities of which they were a part (Krepps and Caves 1994). To cite an example, a decade long study by Stephen Cornell found that the White Mountain Apache timber operation on the Fort Apache Reservation had been one of the most productive timber operations in the Western United States. This operation regularly out-performed those in the private sector because the White Mountain Apache developed a competent bureaucracy that controlled the use of their timber resources, based on traditional, culturally prescribed decision-making practices (Cornell and Kalt 1998).

An important factor regarding resource management by tribal governments that is often overlooked relates to the fact that Native Americans are not just another minority ethnic group in America. Native Americans have a distinct claim to sovereignty based on a legal and political status that stems from agreements between them and the federal government. The broader significance of these various treaties, agreements and other arrangements is seldom recognized by most American citizens who might regard their protests as unworthy or their claims to special treatment unfounded because they go beyond that to which the average American is entitled. However, the historical transitions that have taken place, which Snipp (1986: 145–6) describes from "captive nations" to "internal colonies," have resulted in a steady erosion of the autonomy of tribal governments and the special status to which they are entitled as result of their position as "first Americans."

The fact that the federal government retains authority in matters dealing with Native Americans, which the various states do not, provided a certain measure of insularity against outside pressures that threatened to erode their special status, although this unique position in American society is a matter that is constantly contested and at times compromised (Biolsi 2007: 7, 29–30; Cramer 2005: 37). There is also an issue with the American public's perceptions of Native Americans, especially when they are seen to achieve a certain measure of success. For example, some Native Americans fear that demonstrating competency in their own self-administration can, if too successful, raise the spectre of termination (Castile 2006: 113–14). Thus, the notion of simply abolishing the BIA is closely linked to fears of providing a basis for the initiation of termination policies, which would severely erode the special status that Native American currently are entitled to (see Deloria 1988 [1969]: 132–6).

A related fear is that if Native Americans are perceived as too successful this could be a reason for a lessening of white support for their efforts – support that tends to dwindle when Native Americans are perceived as less impoverished. Obviously, as Castile (2006: 132–6) indicates, there is a certain degree of irony and intractability in this situation regarding the perceived social and political support of the settler population whose members are responsible in large measure for the impoverishment of Native Americans in the first place.

We can therefore conclude that throughout history European powers used the various mechanisms of internal colonialism to achieve their goals of submission and control of the North American Indigenous population. In stark terms, Bachman (1991a: 474) describes this history as one "of brutalization, exploitation, segregation, expulsion, and for some tribes, annihilation." The US government at various times used policies of containment as a means of control, and, as with the infamous Trail of Tears, engaged in the forced removal from traditional Indigenous territories: "Military force was used to displace many tribes and resettle them on wasteland reservations, where they remained unless new settlement plans or the discovery of oil and valuable minerals resulted in further displacement. Virtually all the original tribal nations were separated or absorbed into other groups if not exterminated altogether" (Bachman 1991a: 474).

It is not my intention here to provide an in-depth review of the historical and contemporary relations between Indigenous people and the white settler colonists. Suffice to say that the scholarly research cited in these pages corroborates a distinctive pattern virtually from the very arrival of Europeans on this continent of subjugation, exploitation, and the imposition of numerous hardships on the Indigenous people who are the rightful owners of this continent of North America.

Violent Encounters and Cultural Conflict

Rather than explore the topic of violent encounters between Indigenous people and their colonial oppressors in general terms, it would be instructive to examine the cultural variance of such conflicts in terms of individual cultural or tribal societies. In other words, are there cultural differences in the incidences of homicide between, for example, the Apache and Navajo? If there are differences, how can one account for them? And are these differences a matter of cultural patterns or distinctiveness in learned behaviour, environmental conditions, or relationships with the larger Euro-American society, among other alternative explanations?

The Cherokee. Two research reports explore incidences of homicide among the Eastern Cherokee in two different locations. One of these populations, the Cherokee of North Carolina, managed to resist the Great Removal of the 1830s (Kapferer and Humphrey 1975; Humphrey and Kapferer 1982). There are many people, especially among the elderly, who continue to speak their Native language, which is taught in the local schools, and they are able to maintain traditional cultural patterns. They live on their own reservation and as such are considered a rural people. The Cherokee attempt for the most part to maintain harmonious relationships and avoid situations that might threaten amicable interactions with others. As far as the homicide rate is concerned, data from the 1970s indicates that the Cherokee are above the regional rate but not excessively so.

Also living in North Carolina is another Indigenous society called the Lumbee, who are named after a local river. Their ancestors were early contact survivors of Atlantic Coastal tribes who migrated inland to avoid conflict with European settlers. Their language has become extinct, and the Lumbee have lost contact, for the most part, with their traditional culture. They are thought to have "successfully acculturated without assimilating to the American way of life" (Kapferer and Humphrey 1975: 239). None of the Lumbee have reservation status. Their attitudes towards interpersonal relationships are considered "other-directed," meaning the Lumbee have a strong sense of honour, are quick to take offence and often engage in acts of violence towards others.

As far as the homicide rate is concerned, the Cherokee, as noted, are above the regional average, but only slightly so. The Lumbee are also above the regional homicide rate but are nearly twice as high as the Cherokee. To account for these different rates, the researchers tested two hypotheses based on social structural and cultural explanations of violent behaviour. Their research, which was conducted in the 1970s, suggests that homicide rates among Native Americans tends to rise when traditional social controls weaken. As far as the first explanation is concerned, the researchers have concluded that the social structural differences of the two Indigenous populations tend to reflect characteristics of the county or region as a whole; therefore, "explanations for the differing patterns of violence lie not in the social and demographic components but in the cultural characteristics of the two Indian groups ... The differences between the homicide rates of the two Indian populations stem from differences in cultural patterns" (1975: 243; see also Stewart 1964: 61–6).[16]

In the second report concerning homicide among the Eastern (Qualla) Cherokee (French and Hornbuckle 1977), this population also managed to avoid the Removal of 1838 because of their isolated location in the Appalachian Mountains. According to the researchers, this population of Cherokees "represents one of the most traditional elements of the old Cherokee Nation which once encompassed six Southern states" (ibid., 337). When the research was conducted in the 1970s, about 6,000 Cherokee occupied a reservation of some 60,000 acres in rugged mountain terrain. According to the "Harmony Ethic" of the Cherokee, the main tenets are mutual obligation, avoidance, and a "suppression of any expression of overt hostility in interpersonal relations" (ibid., 340–1). However, in today's life there is a high stress factor associated with the reservation environment and a deterioration of the traditional mechanisms of aggression release.

The high level of stress associated with reservation life is explained in the following terms: "Federal paternalism is an important factor in their [Cherokee] cultural frustration. Federal paternalism is a mode of forced accommodation whereby the superiority of the dominant social order is imposed thorough a rigid legal mechanism of control (ibid., 336). The Bureau of Indians Affairs is singled out as the main factor responsible for this "rigid control system." The authors also claim that the Cherokee are torn between two worlds, Indian and white, with almost no chance of being accepted fully in either.

Regarding homicide rates, a "Crime Index" (assaults, rape, armed robbery, and homicide) for the period of 1974–6 was tabulated, comparing national and regional norms for the US as a whole. For criminal homicide, whites ranked 5/100,000 population, Indians 34/100,000 and US as a whole 8/100,000. The authors conclude that "The only viable explanation is a cultural one ... violence among the Qualla Cherokee is due mainly to intensive in-group tensions generated by the restrictive reservation environment ... violence is a common factor resulting from a spontaneous eruption of frustration" (ibid., 353). They suggest the Cherokee need to reduce tension on the reservation to eliminate aggression, but do not articulate how this goal might be achieved.[17]

The rationale that violence is due to an "eruption of frustration" is also suggested by John Gulick in his study *Cherokees at the Crossroads* (1974 [1960]). He suggests that violence among the Cherokee has at its root in a sense of "cultural dissonance" resulting from conflicts in values with Euro-American society. Frustration among the Cherokee is the result of a "conscious resistance to non-Indian traits [as a result of] a resentment of non-Indians ... beginning with the Removal and continuing with the ever-constant threat of non-Indians taking their land away from them" (ibid., 150–1). This constant threat of being dislocated from their ancestral lands is apt to lead some Cherokee to be beleaguered with feelings of "cultural depression, dysfunction, and traumatization" (ibid., 151). In fact, almost the same conclusion is reached by Kapferer and Humphrey (1975: 236) for the Cherokee of North Carolina when they write that "differences in cultural patterns between the Cherokee [and whites] most adequately account for the extent and direction of individual forms of violence."

The Navajo. In the *Roots of Dependency*, White (1988: 212) explained that with continued white contact, many Native American became subjugated people who were "driven into dependency and deprived of control over much of their own lives and the land. The great exception was the Navajos." The Navajo are a farming and sheep-raising nation that has been able to remain relatively self-sufficient and isolated from white society since they live on such a large reservation that straddles Arizona, New Mexico, and Utah.

The Navajo are also a relatively populace society, comprising a population of about 170,000 people, situated mainly around Window Rock, Arizona, characterized by a social organization in which matrilineal descent is a prominent feature. According to several demographic and epidemiological studies (i.e., Carr and Lee 1978; Broudy and May 1983) the Navajo population was considered to be growing rapidly, when these studies were conducted, primarily due to decreased mortality, which, however, remains twice as high as US rates. Mortality is the result of several conspicuous factors relating to social pathology, such as motor vehicle accidents, alcoholism, suicide, and homicide, which are all considerably higher than the national average of the United States.

Homicide rates for the Navajo were studied longitudinally, that is over several historical periods, up until the time of the study in 1969 (Levy et al. 1969). From this perspective, during the 1883–90 period homicide rates were determined to be about 5.88 per 100,000 persons, which was comparable to the national rate of 5.1 in 1900. For the ten-year period (1937–47), when the Navajo population had increased to over 40,000 individuals, the annual homicide rate was 5.8 per 100,000. These rates are substantially the same as the time of this study, thus the rates do not appear to be on the increase. For the 10-year period of the study (1956–65) the criminal homicide rate was between 4.5 and 5.3 per 100,000 total population, compared to an overall rate of 5.4 for the US nation as a whole (Levy et al. 1969: 127–8).[18]

Having established that homicide rates among the Navajo were relatively stable over a long period of time, and were comparable to the nation as a whole, the authors then began to explore the possibility that certain aspects of personality or social organization may be contributing factors that made the Navajo pattern distinct from other Indigenous societies. They also considered various theoretical approaches common to homicide studies, such as the degree to which an individual is integrated into their society, and levels of frustration and aggression. After isolating individual cases of homicide, the authors determined that there was indeed an overall pattern among the Navajo: "a married male in his late 30s who kills his wife as a result of a domestic quarrel – a high proportion of homicides are followed by suicide" (Levy et al. 1969: 219).

"Outbreaks of violence in general," the authors continue, "and homicide in particular were thought to have been increasing as a result of rising levels of tension generated by the acculturative process" (Levy et al. 1969: 124). Other studies of the Navajo point to "structural weaknesses"[19] in social relationships, such as "not infrequently the demands of a man's family or orientation (his mother's) and family of procreation (his wife's) are conflicting, and this is a deep source of strain in Navaho social organization" (Kluckhohn and Leighton 1962: 104). This tension is especially the case with sexual conflicts in marriage: "One of the principal sources of friction among Navahos is sexual jealousy. Fear of witches at night acts to some slight extent as a deterrent to extra-marital sex relations because nighttime would otherwise provide favourable conditions for secret rendezvous" (1962: 249).

Levy (1962) found several patterns that appear to be specifically Navajo in terms of personality and social organization, especially to the extent that homicide is the result of anomie and social tensions. One of these traits is that the Navajo male appears less able to control urges than does the Navajo female. "It is reasonable to suppose," Levy et al. (1969: 134) suggest, "that the young male is suffering a considerable amount of frustration and that much of his hostility will be aimed at his spouse who is able to maintain her security within the matrilineage." This explanation for Navajo aggression, then, is partly built on personality traits and certain aspects of the matrilineal social organization. In addition, the reference to the frustrated male among the Navajo is a theme commonly found in many studies of Native American homicide, although the causes of this frustration would appear to differ from community to community, depending upon the circumstances involved.

The Apache:

> **Florence will soon have a hanging picnic of five Apaches ...**
> **A Step in the right direction. If the civil authorities had delt [sic]**
> **with these Red Devils all along ... the Apache**
> **troubles would have been quelled long before they were.**
> – *Flagstaff Arizona Champion*, October 26, 1889

"White editors [of Arizona newspapers]," suggests McKanna, in her article entitled *Murders All*, "often portrayed American Indians as villains – real or imagined – who deserved to be destroyed." The quote above reflects "a desire for white vengeance and retribution against Apache murder suspects" (1993: 359).

The Apache belong to a group of culturally related societies in the southwestern United states, which includes, among others, the Chiricahua, Mescalero, and Jicarilla. They are also distant relatives of the Navajo with whom they share the Southern Athabaskan (Dene) languages. Historically, the Apache have lived in secluded locations such as high mountains, sheltered and watered valleys, deep canyons, and deserts. For centuries the Apache fought the Spanish and Mexican peoples, and later, the American armed forces in the nineteenth century. The American army found the Apache to be fierce warriors and skilled strategists. In their terrain, which was difficult for armies to traverse, the Apache engaged in a sort of hit-and-run guerrilla warfare. The fame of the Apaches' fighting skills became widely known, bolstered by the dime novels of the day, especially the fighting prowess of famed Apache Chief Geronimo (Lockwood 1987; Thrapp 1967).

Anthropological evidence suggests that the Apache and their linguistic relatives, the Navajo, lived in similar northern localities before migrating into the Southwest sometime between about 1200 and 1500 A.D., just before the arrival of the Spanish. The Apache maintained a nomadic way of life, while the Navajo settled in relatively permanent settlements, farming and raising sheep. When the Spanish arrived in about 1540, the Apache quickly acquired horses, which improved their ability to conduct quick raids on settlements (Goodwin 1969 [1941]). These raids led to many frequent conflicts between the Apache and the Spanish up until the independence of Mexico in 1821. In 1835, Mexico placed a bounty on Apache scalps. The Apache took their revenge. In the Mexican province of Durango, by 1856, it was claimed that in (mostly) Apache and Comanche raids over 6,000 horses were stolen and 748 people abducted. Also in the 1850s an influx of gold miners into the Santa Rita Mountains led to conflicts with the Apache (Basso and Opler 1971; Delay 2008: 298).

Warfare between the Apache and the Americans led to negative stereotyping of the Apache by the media (novelists, historians and, later, filmmakers) as indicated by anthropologist Keith Basso:

> The popular image of "the Apache" – a brutish, terrifying semi-human bent upon wanton death and destruction – is almost entirely a product of irresponsible caricature and exaggeration. Indeed, there can be little doubt that the Apache has been transformed from a native American into an American legend, the fanciful and fallacious creation of a non-Indian citizenry whose inability to recognize the massive treachery of ethnic and cultural stereotypes has been matched only by its willingness to sustain and inflate them. (1969: 462)

In 1875, United States soldiers forced the removal of about 1,500 Apache from their home on the Rio Verde Reservation, treaty land which had been promised to them by the American government, to walk on foot to the San Carlos Indian Agency, about 180 miles away, resulting in the loss of several hundred Apache lives because of the harsh conditions of their travel. In 1886, the final defeat of the Apache took place when 5,000 United States troops forced Geronimo's band of about 50 people to surrender in Arizona, after which they were sent to military confinement at Fort Sills, Oklahoma (Opler 1969, 1983, 1941; Weaver 1974).

The remaining Apache who still lived in Arizona continued their conflicts with the white settlers: "During the 1880s Arizona experienced an exceptionally high rate of interracial killings. Native Americans killed outside their race more than any other ethnic group; 35 percent of their victims were white … [The] Arizona territorial and US government officials waged a protracted war with various Apache groups. Underhanded dealings by white leaders and atrocities by both sides hardened positions" (McKanna 1993: 360, 365).[20]

As far as the "hanging picnic" was concerned, the residents of Florence, Arizona, apparently felt cheated. The five Apache men accused of murdering white men were all found guilty of homicide and sentenced to hang. On the eve of the executions, three of the Apache defendants committed suicide by hanging themselves in their cells. The next morning, when the authorities prepared to execute the two remaining Apache, a large crowd gathered to watch the hanging. Soon after, the *Florence Arizona Weekly Enterprise* ran the following headline (McKanna 1993: 366):

Good Indians

Five Apache Murderers Gone to Glory

The white population became enraged by the suicides because they felt robbed of their retribution. As McKanna (ibid.) relates, "Some of the more sadistic citizens visited the grave site, severed Gon-shay-ee's head, and carried it away as a souvenir." In another area newspaper, the *Flagstaff Arizona Champion*, an editorial suggested that "If there are any good Indians outside of graveyards, they do not live in Arizona" (June 18, 1887). It is hard to justify such an outpouring of venom, which McKanna (ibid.) wrote "typified white hatred for Apaches in Arizona."[21] She also suggests that the Arizona territorial criminal justice system mirrored the larger US legal system. For the most part the Apache did not know their legal rights and seldom had access to effective legal counsel. The result was that the Apache had very high conviction rates compared with the members of white society under similar circumstances.

The following statistical data on Apache convictions for murder for the period between 1880 and 1912 tends to support this contention. In six Arizona counties selected for analysis, comprising a total of 532 indictments for murder during this period, Native Americans accounted for 13 per cent (69 cases). In most of the counties the conviction rates for Native Americans were twice as high as for white rates. In terms of defendants convicted on a reduced charge of manslaughter, the percentage of Native Americans convicted of the lesser charge (14 per cent) was only half of whites receiving the reduced charges (28 per cent). In terms of the actual charges received on this lesser charge, 16 per cent of whites received a sentence of from one to five years, while only 7 per cent of Native Americans received this lesser sentence. McKanna accounts for these discrepancies in conviction rates and duration of sentence between whites and Native Americans in Arizona by stating that the inconsistencies can be "attributed to white hostility towards American Indians, particularly Apaches, poor defence counsel, all-white juries, and a system culturally insensitive to problems faced by Indians forced to adapt to new societal demands" (1993: 362).[22]

Assessing the Etiology of Indigenous Homicide Rates

One cannot but be impressed by the wide range of disciples and subject areas that have contributed the expertise of its practitioners to the subject of Indigenous homicide – anthropology, sociology, criminology history, geography, demography, psychology, statistics, social justice, medical science, and several others as well have all provided insights into this phenomenon. As such, one is also impressed with the various explanations concerning the etiology or casual factors responsible for various homicide rates, from a wide range of perspectives. Some rely on historical trends as an explanatory mode; others are psychological involving "the way people think"; some are cultural, comprising learned behaviour patterns; some, from sociology, have a "functional" orientation; and then there are explanations involving criminological patterns involving conflict theory, racism, and discrimination, and so on. The list of areas discussed in the literature that are seen as causal factors in homicide cases seems at times interminable in its breath, scope, and temporal duration.

When one considers all the different academic disciplines that have contributed to the subject of Native American homicide, it is apparent that the etiology involved follows disciplinary lines. For example, anthropology, with its emphasis on culture and learned patterns of behaviour, is apt to see homicide as stemming from a "culture of violence" (Gastil 1971), or "cultural dissonance or culture change" (Hackenberg and Gallagher 1972). Similarity, in sociology, consider Durkheim's perspectives on functionalism and social integration. As such, Durkheim offers his explanation in his suicide studies that Protestants had a greater propensity towards suicide than Catholics because they lacked close social bonds due to the looseness of their religious organization (Durkheim 2001[1915]) – or, in another of Durkheim's arguments, he maintains that rapid social change is associated with increases in crime due to a breakdown of social controls (see Bachman 1991a: 475). Homicide, then, becomes an opportunity to see violence in society as the result of a lack of social integration or disorganization (Bachman 1991a. 1991b; Bursik 1988; Honigmann 1966).

Political scientists might have a propensity to see homicide as the result of pressures emanating from colonial manipulation and control (Blauner 1969). Psychologists might see social violence as a result of suppressed antagonisms to parent authority, as with Hamlet; with offenders displaying anti-social tendencies at an early age that persisted into adulthood (Bloom 1980; Hochkirchen and Jilek 1985; Shon and Barton 2012); or, "The psychological consequences of being poor are many. Poverty engenders hopelessness, apathy, and anger ... Many American Indians today find themselves struggling with a psychological identity conflict" (Bachman 1991a: 477, 483).

Poverty and material deprivation could be an explanation favoured by economists (Lanier and Huff-Corzine 2006). Of course, one could add a plethora of other approaches that appear to stem from disciplinary propensities, such as variations in environmental and ecological conditions (White 1988). This does not necessarily mean that generalizations are impossible, as Bachman 1991a: 489) asserts, "It is contended, however, that while American Indians may represent a multitude of cultural and tribal identities, they have also experienced some of the same historical and contemporary conditions regardless of tribal affiliation. These similar experiences [for example] have led to the current Pan-Indian movement."

Finally, there are the largely unsubstantiated claims and speculations concerning causal factors of rates for Native American homicide that should not be allowed to be published in a reputable peer-reviewed academic journal. One of these that is spread around from journal to journal posits that the high frustration levels of life in reservation communities are said to account for high incidences of homicide. One wonders if any of these authors who peddle this etiology have ever lived for any extended period of time in a North American Indigenous community, as I have. Have these authors any personal experience, such as one derives from extended ethnographic fieldwork? While Bachman (1991a: 487) does admit that "It is true that not all American Indians who are born into conditions of poverty are propelled to commit murder," she also concedes that "the etiology of American Indian homicide is virtually unexplored in the literature" (ibid., 470).

Yet, at times, Bachman finds herself reverting to a familiar trope: "It is not surprising that feelings of inadequacy and frustration could

Table 1. Homicide rates per 100,000 (1900–92)

Year	Native American	White	National
1900	5.9 (Navajo)	–	5.1
1965	4.9 (Navajo)	–	5.4
1968	34.0 (unspecified)	5.0	7.8
1972	23.0 (Cherokee)	–	–
1973	23.0 (Cherokee)	–	–
1974	9.5 (Cherokee)	–	2.1
1975	20.0 (Cherokee)	–	2.0
1976	34.0 (Cherokee)	5.0	8.0
1991	9.6 (unspecified)	–	–
1992	10.6 (unspecified)	–	9.3
Average	14.1	5.0	5.7

emerge and perhaps even lead to violent behavior" (ibid., 483), and as she indicates later, "Feelings of frustration and powerlessness emerged early in the lives of these offenders" (ibid., 487). Similarly, French and Hornbuckle argue that "violence is a common factor resulting from a spontaneous eruption of frustration" (1977: 353). What is the empirical evidence for this link between "feelings of inadequacy and frustration" and violent behaviour? Or is it simply a matter of speculative rationalization? There is no doubt that people whose ambitions have been supressed for long periods of time would become frustrated, or that frustration is not uncommon in Native American communities, but one needs to ask: What percentage of frustrated people will eventually commit murder because of this causal factor? And if every frustrated person went out and committed murder how many people would be left in this world? Hardly anyone, we would presume.

The point here is that when serious academics make statements that are not grounded in empirical reality there is the danger that such information would be used in an inappropriate manner by those in society who would use any opportunity to disparage Indigenous people. It is unconscionable that very few of such incidences have been called out in the academic literature. However, there is one incident of note that is worth examining. First, though, it is worth scrutinising rates of Native American homicide as reported in the academic literature.

First, this brief tabulation of homicide rates is by no means meant to be a comprehensive summary, as these figures are only derived from the literature cited thus far. The purpose of this tabulation is to make several points concerning the tabulation of homicide rates for Native Americans compared to the national figures. It is true that there is some basis for comparison since all figures are based on a rate of so many cases per 100,000 total population. However, herein lies the first major problem – nowhere in the literature cited thus far are actual figures given, only rates. Rates of homicides per 100,000 can certainly be distorted by a small number of cases, which is probably the reason for the marked difference in Native American figures.

Second, there are hardly any definitions in the literature about what constitutes a homicide, which of course makes comparisons difficult or nearly impossible. For example, it is true that murder is the killing of another person, but what sort of murder? One can reasonably assume that first degree murder would be considered homicide, but what about second degree murder, what about manslaughter, or what about criminal negligence causing death, or about death by misadventure? The criminal justice system goes to considerable length to distinguish these types of killings and sentences the offender accordingly, yet in the academic literature such distinctions do not seem to matter. It is surprising that more attention is not given to this issue of defining your subject matter. What is also apparent is that it is easy, on the basis of suspect data, to readily jump to conclusions about what causes the data in the first place – the classic example of a tautological argument – since the result (or effect) is part of the cause.

Perceptions of Crime Seriousness

In 2007, Julie Abril published a paper on the "Perceptions of Crime Seriousness" (Abril 2007). Her paper reported on research conducted on the Southern Ute Indian Reservation in Colorado, which focused on a comparison of crime seriousness held by the communities' Indigenous and non-Indigenous peoples. Her conclusion was that cultural differences were responsible for differences in perceptions of crime and, hence, in the greater incidences of homicide among Native Americans. The implication was that Native Americans were involved in more homicides than whites because they did not think of murder in such serious terms. Even before Abril's paper was published, her results were big news in Colorado. *The Rocky Mountain News* (November 28, 2006) headline read "Ute Homicide Rate Soars."

At least one researcher was troubled by Abril's data. Greenberg (2012) conducted a re-analysis of her data and arrived at an entirely different conclusion. In fact, he found "little evidence of these differences" noted in Abril's paper. He elaborated further, "When it comes to violations of the criminal law, however, we do not see evidence of cultural pluralism. Indians and non-Indians remember the seriousness of different crimes quite similarly in both absolute terms, and relative to one another" (2012: 36).[23]

As far as Greenberg was concerned there are wide implications for the etiology of Native American homicide in the Abril publication. The most important point concerns the raw data itself and the resulting conclusions that were derived from it. For example, at the time of Abril's research there were only two homicides on the Ute reservation for a single year. Thus, the total population of the Ute reservation was about 8,000 people, implying a homicide rate of about 25 per 100,000. This contrasts with a murder rate of about 3.1 per 100,000 in the state of Colorado as a whole for that year (2012: 37). Thus, one might reasonably conclude that the Southern Ute Reservation had an exceptionally high homicide rate, when in fact the reported rate was based on an extremely small number of cases, which skewed the results.

This issue of the reporting of Native American homicide rates is symptomatic of a wider problem in the academic crime literature in which various authors make one claim or another, sometimes without any supporting data at all, to either support or refute the high incidences of criminality among the Indigenous residents. Disputes concerning the interpretation of statistical data abound in the literature. As an example, Reasons claimed that Native Americans have the highest crime rate of any racial group in the United States. He suggests that this is due to cultural frustration, stating that "While economic factors are important, anomie and cultural conflict theories provide a more substantive basis of understanding" (1972: 325). His conclusion is based on 1968 data of "criminal homicide" in which Native Americans, based on rates of incidences per 100,000 persons, have a rate of 34.0 compared to the US rate of 7.8 for the nation as a whole (whites were listed as having a rate of 5.0).

On this basis the homicide rate for Native Americans is over four times the national average, or one of the highest rates ever recorded, except for homicide rates for the Lumbee of 66.0 per 100,000, recorded in 1972 by Kapferer and Humphrey [1975: 237]). Peak (1994) subsequently disputed Reasons's data since he found in his study that Native Americans had a murder rate of just 10.6 per 100,000 compared to a rate of

9.3 for the US as a whole. In other words, far from concluding, as Reasons did, that Native Americans have "the highest crime rate in the country," Peak concluded that as far as homicide rates are concerned he could find no appreciable difference between Indigenous people and the national average (see also Peak 1987, and 1989 for further data to justify his position, as well as Harring's 1982 data).

Given the local antipathy in this region that whites felt towards the Ute people, the local news media was quick to pounce on the mistaken fact that the "Ute Homicide Rate Soars," feeding into the prevalent discriminatory perception of Indigenous people in the Colorado area. As far as the casual factors responsible for this apparent high rate of homicide among the Ute is concerned, Greenberg (2012) further suggests that the stereotype of the economically depressed Native American reservation would lead one to suspect that extreme poverty is the relevant structural condition underlying the (supposedly) high homicide rate, *but* the Southern Utes are one of the wealthiest Indian tribes in America. In addition, since the Native American population is generally considered to be carriers of a subculture of violence, a theme reinforced repeatedly in the news media and even in the academic literature, one can attribute the misconception of Ute homicide to be derived from patterns of victimization, promulgated by the white settler population whose people are prone to see Indigenous people in negative terms.

It is unfortunate that serious academic research could be utilized to fuel these discriminatory attitudes. So, Clare McKanna wrote in her article *Murders All* that "It is the thesis of this essay that American Indians suffered discrimination in the courts of Arizona Territory. A statistical comparison of data ... will verify this" (1993: 359).[24] She might also have added that a misuse of the statistical data, which suggests that Native Americans were killers to a much higher degree than white citizens, is also cause for concern as well and deserves closer scrutiny in the academic literature. Other authors echo this sentiment about the treatment of Indigenous people in the criminal justice system. As an example, in a report prepared for the Saskatchewan Law Reform Commission in Canada, Whyte states that "it must be acknowledged that a final source of the high rate of criminal offending can be the bias [or racism] of the criminal justice system. This bias could be the result of laws that criminalize culturally appropriate practices, such as holding ceremonies [such as Potlatches, for example] or harvesting wildlife… In racially mixed urban communities, the sense of police bias is expressed in the charge that police officers are much quicker to detain and charge Aboriginal persons whom they suspect of committing a crime than they are when dealing with non-Aboriginal suspects" (2008: 116).[25]

It could also be suggested that inequities in America's criminal justice system are a result of white privilege, of a discriminatory attitude to the members of minority groups. As such, "these [political and economic] systems and structures disadvantage people who cannot pass as white while simultaneously denying that such institutional disadvantage is occurring and asserting that challenges these people experience as a function of their individual or group [often characterized as cultural] deficiencies" (Cousins 2014: 2).

On this basis a thorough review of incidences and rates of Native American homicides needs to be conducted by serious scholars in the criminal justice journals and elsewhere in order to correct the apparent inequities in reporting, which portrays Indigenous people as killers and murderers of the white settler population. Such reporting as now exists in a number of cases simply reflects the stereotyping of Native Americans in the larger television and movie industry as "wagon burners" who are an inherent threat to the (supposed) advancement of white civilization. Inequities in the manner in which minorities are treated in American society is evidently used to suppress and villainize such people through displays of power and suppression.

Culture and Power Relationships

Conflict can occur between the members of different cultures, or within cultures themselves, for a variety of reasons, suggesting that the relationship between culture and conflict is a topic upon which it is difficult to generalize. In historical terms, one of the most influential works on societal tensions, disputes, and controversies is Lewis Coser's seminal study, *The Functions of Social Conflict* (1956). As a preliminary definition Coser suggests that social conflict can be taken to mean "a struggle over values and claims to scarce status, power, and resources in which the aims of the opponents are to neutralize, injure, or eliminate their rivals" (1956: 8). Coser then sets out a number of functional propositions, one of which (number 15) is that "Conflict Establishes and Maintains Balance of Power." He further explains that "conflicts... always involve power of the contenders before a conflict has settled the issue" (1956: 134). So, we are left with the inevitable, it seems, bottom line of power as a defining aspect of human interaction.

In his clever work, *Culture Meets Power* (2002), Barrett suggests that "the concept of power has soared to the top of the anthropological agenda" (2002 back cover). He further indicates that power and conflict are almost identical twins (Barrett 2002: 40–2; Etzioni 1993: 22; Nicholas 1976: 52). Power and conflict, this argument suggests, are interrelated variables in social life. Reiterating the message on his book cover, Barrett (2002: 42) sums up his central thesis by noting that "Even if power remains at the top of the agenda, we can accommodate it by going about our business as usual, probing social action and structure, poking into the informal pockets of everyday life."

Returning now to one of the central themes of this book, namely, the fur trade of northern Canada, anthropologist R.W. Dunning (1959b) has studied the dimensions of power in the remote Pekangekum First Nation community in the early 1950s. He particularly focusses on the role of the Hudson's Bay Company fur trader, who he refers to as the "marginal man," and the distribution of power in the community. "The first aspect [of his study] is the nature of the power structure in the community," Dunning (1959b: 117) asserts.

It is important to state that Dunning's comments are based on first-hand or direct observations, rather than sanitized accounts written by fur company employees, or British colonial apologists. One of his main points is that "The present high-status positions are held by various non-ethnic external representatives of powerful outside organizations" (ibid.). These external organizations, such as the various Christian churches, Canadian government officials, the members of the Hudson's Bay Company, for example, have few controls placed on them. The result is that leadership in many First Nations communities "is an unresolved power conflict, a continual struggle which is expressed by ad hoc prestige-getting decisions" (ibid.).

Under such circumstances many exchange relationships are unbalanced. If members of the local Indigenous population happen to accept goods or services from members of these external organizations, then the First Nations people "must adjust to the particular person or persons who are representatives of that culture" (ibid.). These unbalanced exchanges, in turn, reinforce "the external contact person's role as one of power" (1959b: 120). Control in the community is exercised in various ways. For example, Indigenous people who prove amenable to the trader's leadership or domination "are rewarded with occasional wage labour jobs around the post" (ibid.). However, trappers who complain (about the fur traders or the missionaries) are apt to be subsequently denied access to the amenities available for the outsiders. In some cases, power is exercised on occasion by teasing "the weaker or unfortunate men publicly" (ibid.).

In sum, according to Dunning's account of the role of the fur trader in a northern First Nation community, European outsiders in general occupy the most high-status positions in the community because of their hold on power and their ability to exercise it through their control over the distribution of valued resources. Whereas First Nations people formerly controlled their own fate and had their own local leaders, it would be understandable if they harboured feelings of resentment towards the representatives of these powerful external organizations who now tried to control their lives. The relationship with the outsiders is not an equitable one. First Nations people are told by the Christian missionaries in a disparaging or demeaning manner that their own religious beliefs were primitive, savage, and untrue. Fur traders somehow manipulated the First Nations people into working for them as trappers, becoming further indebted to them. These outsiders who now controlled their fate also brought disease, alcohol dependency, and starvation. The resentment felt by members of the local Indigenous population towards these powerful peoples must have been deep-seated and long lasting.

Fieldwork conducted by Charles Bishop (1975) several decades later among the Cree and Anishinaabe in the First Nations community of Osnaburgh House and surrounding Boreal Forest region of present-day northern Ontario is a further study of "culture and conflict." According to Bishop's ethno-historical account, conflicts were already emerging between the Cree and Anishinaabe by the 1720s because of the inter-tribal struggles to control fur trade routes to the James Bay coast. As he explains, "Cree living great distances inland from Fort Albany were reluctant to make the journey due to food shortages on the trip, and to threats from the French-incited Ojibwa [Anishinaabe], who were expanding north of Lake Superior by the 1720s. For instance, according to Joseph Adams at Fort Albany, in 1726 some Cristeens [Cree] stated that 'ye Echeepoes [Ojibwa] threated to kill them if they came here" (1975: 155–6). Thus, the fur trade early on was causing population shifts and inter-cultural conflicts among the Indigenous population, which resulted in antagonisms emerging over control of trade routes to the James Bay coast.

Similarly, Bailey (1969: 12–13, 26) noted among the eastern Algonkians that the fur trade was a factor in causing a revival of intertribal warfare, and conflicts emerged over the control of trade routes. He noted that many tribal groups in their attempts to access new trapping grounds and secure routes to the trading posts "acquired a knowledge of the country beyond their own territories, which weakened their distinctive traits, hastened diffusion, and created a general instability of life. The search for furs led to an economic and political pressure on the tribes of the interior and was an important cause of the revival of inter-tribal warfare." Innis (1970: 20) apparently agreed with this assessment as well, noting that "Wars between tribes, which with bows and arrows had not been strenuous, conducted with guns were disastrous." With an ever-increasing competition in the fur trade, smaller tribes sought alliances with larger ones, and population densities increased in some areas. With an increased use of firearms and iron weapons, food supplies in some areas became seriously diminished, resulting in a further reliance on European traders for food supplies. Bailey (1969: 13) also suggested further consequences of these trends, such that "European foods tended to unbalance the diet of the natives, causing and facilitating the spread of disease, which resulted in a decline in the birth rate, and the depopulation of the adult members of eastern Algonkian society."

It was also quite probable that there was emerging a strategy among some groups to control the flow of trade goods and thereby profit through a middleman role between the Hudson's Bay Company and more interior trappers. Certainly, in later years the so-called Home Guard Cree began to fulfill such a role, which was reinforced by their access to superior firearms than were possessed by more interior-living Aboriginal groups. In this regard, as Smith (1987: 442) has noted concerning the role of muskets in inter-groups dynamics: "Possession of trade goods obtained from the English and French gave the Cree an overwhelming technological superiority." The Cree first obtained the smooth-bore, muzzle-loading muskets soon after 1670 when interior groups were using spears, bows, and arrows. Ray (1974: 72–9) also documented the large supply of muskets traded to the Cree by the late seventeenth century. He notes, for example, that "firearms were used primarily as weapons in war by most of the Indians... since they had great shock value when first employed against unarmed groups. Tribes possessing these weapons were thereby able to exert on their less-fortunate enemies pressures that were out of proportion to the actual effectiveness of the guns" (1974: 73).

One wonders furthermore about the moral (Christian?) integrity of the Hudson's Bay Company traders who must have known that the sale of their firearms was utilized to kill other Indigenous people, rather than for hunting purposes. In this regard beaver are trapped, not shot with guns, and there were few big-game animals in the James Bay Lowlands, such as moose and deer. Guns were also not an effective weapon to hunt buffalo in the western areas because it could not be fired rapidly, and the noise of the gun discharge could stampede the herds (Ray 1974: 75). The only reasonable conclusion that one could draw was that guns were purchased to hunt other humans. Thus, the Hudson's Bay Company traders, one could argue, were complicit in the murder of many Indigenous people who were only attempting to bring their furs to the James Bay coast.

The result, as Bishop suggests, was that "By the 1720s, the only Indians who could be relied upon to bring furs to Fort Albany were the local homeguards [Cree living in the Lowlands near the post]" (1975: 155). In addition, as Ray reiterates, "the strategic advantage which the Assiniboine and Cree middlemen would have been maintained by holding a balance of power in their favour cannot be dismissed" (1974: 78). Meanwhile in the interior of Ontario various Indigenous groups contended with each other over control of the trade routes to the James Bay coast, an area apparently guarded and controlled by the heavily armed homeguard Cree.

An increasing conflict between Indigenous groups was not limited to the members of Algonkian societies. In the border country between the Hudson Bay Lowlands and the tundra region to the north, the Cree periodically encountered Inuit hunters, resulting in outbursts of warfare. Bishop and Lytwyn (2007: 30–57) have outlined various phases of this emerging competition as the fur trade, and an increasing necessity to acquire access to European goods to remain competitive in a harsh environment, brought the Cree and Inuit into conflict. As Bishop and Lytwyn illustrate, conflicts between the Cree and the Inuit predate the arrival of Europeans and the advent of the fur trade. In addition, they suggest that territoriality may have been a factor responsible for some conflicts but not in others. In fact, access to Western trade goods may have been responsible for some conflicts, but, alternatively, access to trade goods may have suppressed conflicts because the development of exchange relationships between groups and peaceful relationships could have served the advantages of both parties. However, other factors were important as well in contributing to intertribal conflicts, such as "mutual mistrust attributable to irreconcilable ethnic differences, as well as arising from Lowland Cree misfortunes born of post-contact ecological change attributed to Inuit sorcery" (Chacon and Mendoza 2007: 6).

Inter-tribal conflicts in northern Canada, one could argue, are attributable to a complex mix of factors rather than caused by any one reason or another, such as disputes over trade routes or access to European goods. In fact, the European presence may have exacerbated many existing Indigenous conflicts in North America, rather than being seen as the root cause. This was certainly the case with Huron-Iroquois warfare in which trade routes along the St. Lawrence to Quebec were just another factor in a long history of conflicts in eastern America. However, different points of view could be even suggested by the same author. For example, in the case of Charles Bishop and his studies of the Anishinaabe and Cree of northern Ontario, it has been suggested that "the socio-cultural effects of the fur trade on Indian society [and] upon tribal migration and conflict were as profound as they were upon the wildlife ecology which the fur trade had altered" (Rasporich 1975: 12).

Bishop also reinforced this conclusion by noting that "the expansion of the fur trade changed tribal boundaries and altered the social structure of all Indians. By the early nineteenth century all Indians north of Lake Superior were heavily reliant upon the trading post in a drastically altered environment" (1975: 161). However, some years later, Bishop appears to suggest another interpretation, which is to say, "the underlying factors leading to intergroup violence was not dependent on the European presence. The pre-contact population expansion of the Inuit into or near Cree territory probably precipitated conflict, but fear and mistrust deriving from cultural differences cannot be rule out as a reason for some raids. Mutual hatred continued in the historic period" (Bishop and Lytwyn 2007: 55).

In the post contact period Inuit raids into Cree territory diminished; however, Cree incursions into Inuit lands continued, at least until near the end of the 1700s. Thus, an asymmetrical pattern of conflict developed, which could be attributed largely to the Cree's access to firearms which they acquired from the Hudson's Bay Company. In turn, HBC policy prohibited the sale of guns to the Inuit, further contributing to the inequity in tribal differences and power relationships. Yet, the importance of early firearms as an important contributing factor in tribal conflicts probably has been exaggerated, at least according to some authors. Muskets, it has been suggested, "offered no practical advantage over native weapons in terms of its utility as a projectile weapon" because they took too long to load, could misfire or jam and barrels were susceptible to corrosion (Bishop and Lytwyn 2007: 41).

In summary, it is particularly evident that the expansion of the fur trade had diverse effects on the various cultural groups in the Canadian north. The Inuit were more isolated in their own particular habitat of the Arctic and tundra regions so that their association with traders did not occur until later in the twentieth century. The Cree lived much closer to the coastal areas where the Hudson's Bay Company operated and as such had a readier access to European goods than was the case with the members of more distant Indigenous societies. However, this also made the Cree increasingly dependent upon the trading post. The Anishinaabe, on the other hand, made only periodic trading visits to the coastal HBC posts. More contact with traders occurred when inland posts were established, but this was also a source of violent conflict, as evidenced by the killings at Henley House.

In addition, the Anishinaabe social organization began to change with the advent of the fur trade, as large moose hunting clans gave way to smaller trapping family units. As Bishop concludes for the Anishinaabe of northern Ontario, "By the 1780s, group size has shrunk to about thirty persons per winter settlement due to the immediacy of trading-post competition, and to the fact that the environmental productivity was rapidly declining through the uncontrolled slaughter of beaver and large game for both Indian and trading-post requirements" (1975: 160). It is therefore a precarious task to draw far-reaching conclusions concerning the effects of the fur trade on diverse Indigenous groups who had a multiplicity of historical developments relatively unique from other such groups and who, in turn, had dissimilar relations with the Europeans.

Reassessing the Colonial Model

A typical view of colonialism is that a large society or nation exerts control over a smaller society through political, economic, and sometimes military means to obtain some territorial, strategic, or economic advantage that benefits the larger entity and disadvantages the smaller one. However, as far as the James Bay Cree are concerned, ethno-historian Toby Morantz (2002) in *The White Man's Gonna Getcha* attempts to dispute the proposition that the northern Cree were subjugated by the British in the fur trade era.

This is not to say that Morantz denies that colonialism is an important theme in the northern Crees' political and economic history. As she indicates, "The Crees' acquiescence, voluntary and involuntary, to outside authority is the story of the progressive development of colonialism in their territory" (2002: 5). It is interesting, she notes, that the theme of colonialism has not been very prominent in Canadian historical discourse, as if Canada's past as a colony of Great Britain was virtually invisible. "Where," Morantz asks, "are our own colonial studies of our internal colonies? It is strange that one can count on one hand the number of Canadian or American anthropologists or historians who discuss Indian-white relations in these terms" (ibid.).

Axtell (1985), Hickerson (1973) and Patterson (1971) were about the only scholars for a long time who wrote on North American Indigenous-European relations in a colonial context, although that number has increased since the 1990s. In more recent times several scholars have written about internal colonialism to describe the conditions of Canadian Indigenous people. Various terms have been used by several scholars to describes what has been perceived to describe variations on the colonialism theme, such as Adams's (1995: 145) description of "constitutional colonialism" which also "develops a bureaucracy and judicial system of oppression." In addition, Noel Dyck (1991, 1997: 333) refers to "state tutelage," Satzewich and Wotherspoon (1993: 6) to "internal colonialism," and Satzewich (1997) to situations of "coercive tutelage."

Satzewich and Wotherspoon's study is particularly critical of the "internal colonialism" model as it is applied to Indigenous people in Canada. Among the various issues that they discuss is that the model of internal colonialism "draws on literature developed originally in the context of the debates about the position of Black people in America," and as such "doubts remain about the ability of the model to explain Aboriginal people's experiences in a satisfactory fashion." Among other problems, "the internal colonial model is imprecise on the question of timing. The model is ambiguous as to when the colonization process began ... [and] it is unclear whether there have been shifts in the motives, techniques, and practices of colonization over time" (1993: 8–9).

In an attempt to provide more specific details about the meaning of colonialism, with specific reference to the Indigenous population of British Columbia, Kelm (1998: xviii) defines colonization as a process that "includes geographical incursion, sociocultural dislocation, the establishment of external political control, and economic dispossession, the provision of low-level social services, and, finally, the creation of ideological formulations around race and skin colour, which position the colonizers at a higher evolutionary level than the colonized. Canadian colonization – as an expression of the relationship between the First Nations and the Canadian state, settler societies, missionaries, and others – conforms to this process-driven definition."

Morantz (2002: 8–9, 309–10) herself uses the term "bureaucratic colonialism" to describe the historical situation of the James Bay Cree, however the bureaucracy that she refers to occurred in a period of Canadian government involvement in northern Quebec that was well past the primary fur trade era. Overall, though, she is critical of the historical studies in which "we learn very little about how they [Indigenous people in the Canadian north] confronted the takeover of their lands and resources, [where studies] become far too universalistic" to be of much theoretical and comparative use (ibid.). Morantz is furthermore critical of these "universalistic" studies of colonialism because the "focus must be not global histories but local ones; each society dealt with this usurpation in their own way" (ibid.). The term that Morantz uses to describe the domination of the Cree in the James Bay area, "bureaucratic colonialism," is characterized by church, government, and fur trade companies that were instrumental in impressing upon the Cree their insubordination, which is to say, powerlessness, racism, and cultural degradation in the form of a type of colonialism "having a plurality of forms" (ibid.).

The main point that Morantz endeavours to make is that the historical contours of the James Bay Cree are not typical of either other forms of colonialism in a wider perspective or of other Indigenous societies in the western or southern areas of Canada. As Richard Preston, a long-time ethnographer of the Cree of James Bay, reiterates in his review of Morantz's study, she "aims to show how the academic temptation to generalize the popular categories of colonial expansion of the fur-trade would be a serious misrepresentation of the Quebec Cree case, and would miss the opportunity to fully understand the wide range of colonial experience that could, and did, happen in the Canadian north" (2004: 484). In addition, contrary to a neo-Marxist perspective, "mercantile colonialism did not create a bush proletariat in the James Bay region during the 1700–1850 period" (ibid.).

If a more generalized colonial model does not satisfactorily depict the Cree's position in the fur trade era, what factors then are most important? Morantz itemizes three of the more salient transformative aspects of the Cree experience during the 1700–1850 fur trade period, one, we should note, that covers the Hannah Bay period of 1832. Preston summarizes these factors in a very precise manner: "severe suffering from a debilitating combination of disease and starvation, economic instability in the market economy affecting both prices paid for furs and the costs of goods at the trading posts, and the [HBC] Company's response to hard times" (2004: 485).

The Hudson's Bay Company certainly was not responsible for the severe ecological conditions of the James Bay area, which as most reports indicate, was hardly capable of supporting the burgeoning Indigenous population in the area whose people were drawn to the fur trading posts on the coast. However, as indicated in the fur-trade journals of the period, there were constant complaints of food shortages and in some cases of actual starvation and death. It is apparent that the Hudson's Bay Company factors met this catastrophe in a most minimal fashion, doling out food meagrely or in the most parsimonious manner possible.

The Cree were in a difficult situation. Professional hunters hired by the Hudson Bay Company greatly reduced existing country food supplies so that trappers during difficult times were forced to resort to trading their furs merely to support their families and ward off starving to death. In this context, the Hannah Bay murders were a result, directly or not, of this impoverishing policy of the fur traders and should have been foreseen by them if they were not so preoccupied with saving every cent (or shilling) that they could. In other words, Morantz's conclusion was that the Company's response to hard times was a contributing factor in the dire deprivation of food suffered by the Cree.

Other reviewers of Morantz's volume added further important nuances. Oberholtzer, for example, noted that the title "The White Man's Gonna Getcha" is a parental admonition that "aptly conveys Cree feelings of alienation and intimidation arising from contact with outsiders and from the imposition of foreign agencies upon their society" (2005: 575). Oberholtzer also calls attention to the "paradoxical aspects of Cree resistance" (ibid.), which is to say, the cultural tendency of the Cree to distance themselves from strangers and their institutions while simultaneously accepting these intrusions in order to derive the material benefits (tools, clothing, and, in times of need, food) that this interaction with the members of an alien society provided. In this sense, the theme of colonialism, Oberholtzer suggest, is juxtaposed against that of cultural survival. The nuances that Morantz provides of the colonial model encourages the reader to view the loss of self-determination of Indigenous people within local parameters and that the use of such "internal colonialist" models need to be assessed in terms of that particular experience.

Morantz uses archival and archaeological records to reach her conclusion that the Cree, despite the hardships they faced on a daily basis, were ultimately able to exert considerable influence over how they participated in the fur trade, and that they were able to maintain a continuity in their social structure. She also makes it clear in her analysis that during the fur trade period, the Cree retained the means and the power to define themselves (see the further discussion by Oberholtzer [2005: 575–7] on the Cree's struggle to maintain a sense of cultural integrity). In another review of Morantz's study, Paul Nadasdy also points to the epistemological difficulty of interpreting the Cree's relation with the fur trade as a form of colonial domination. "Rather," he indicates, "the Cree retained their autonomy throughout the fur trade era and were able to dictate in significant ways the terms of that trade as well as of Cree-white relations generally. [However, Cree relations with the powerful outsiders remained] complex and ambivalent [mainly because of] the often-contradictory practices, policies, and agendas of particular Hudson's Bay Company (HBC) traders" (2004: 191–2).

Conclusion

The term "colonialism" is generally meant to indicate a strategy whereby a dominant society, nation, or economic power attempts to establish control of a smaller society through a policy of economic, religious, or socio-political domination over another people. There are various forms of colonialism, such as a capitalistic model, which seeks material gain and wealth, and a religious one, in which attempts are made to change the spiritual beliefs of a subjugated people. In turn, there is often resistance to colonial pressures by the local or Indigenous people to the pressures that they feel are meant to control their actions and beliefs.

In most cases this is a policy adopted by European societies who seek control over smaller Indigenous people for political or economic gain. A key component of this strategy usually involved an attempt to control the decision-making of the smaller society through control of the Indigenous leadership structure, either by co-opting the existing leaders so that they are more compliant with the aims of the larger society, or by directly installing new leaders who are willing to facilitate the promotion of the colonial power's objectives.

In addition, colonialism is often associated with the concept of imperialism, which Indigenous authors such as Cannon and Sunseri (2011: 276) have defined as "the domination of another land and people through economic control established by violent or coercive force." Other Indigenous authors have suggested that policies of colonialism and imperialism as acts of socio-political domination are founded essentially on the ethnocentric attitudes of Europeans towards Indigenous people, which they label "Eurocentrism." Marie Battiste and Sakej Youngblood Henderson, for example, argue that Eurocentric attitudes of those in the dominant society are the main source of oppression of First Nations people. As they further explain, "Eurocentrism postulates the superiority of Europeans over non-Europeans. It is built on a set of assumptions and beliefs that educated and usually unprejudiced Europeans and North Americans accept as true, as supported by 'the facts,' or as 'reality'" (Battiste and Youngblood Henderson 2011: 11; for a more extended discussion on the concept of Eurocentrism see Hedican 2014).

The Hudson's Bay Company, and by extension the British Government, has much to answer for in their dealings with the Indigenous people in the region of North America that they controlled through the fur trade. The liquor trade was a particularly pernicious policy foisted on the Indigenous population, which lead to many unnecessary deaths all for the sake of increased profits for British shareholders. The abandonment of Indigenous women and their children in a particularly hostile country to fend for themselves was a further act of heartless irresponsibility on the part of fur traders. It is surprising that there were not more acts of rebellion on the part of Indigenous people, such as that which occurred at Henley House, in the Yukon territory, at Pond Inlet, and at Hannah Bay.

Chapter Six

Creating History: Narratives of Disentitlement

The truth about stories is that that's all we are.
— Thomas King, *The Truth about Stories: A Native Narrative* (2003: 2)[1]

The modern reader's whole view of the Indians comes via the words of the traders, reflecting the aims and the particular cultural perspectives of the elite minority of the period, the literate English or French speakers.
— Mary Black-Rogers, "Varieties of 'Starving': Semantics and Survival in the Subartic Fur Trade, 1750–1850" (1986: 375)

This sense of entitlement, this expression of white privilege, has a long history, manifesting itself in national narratives …
— A. Hirschfelder and P.F. Molin, "I Is of Ignoble: Stereotyping Native Americans, Ferris State University, Jim Crow Museum of Racist Memorabilia" (2018: 1); C.R. King, *Redskins: Insult and Brand* (2016: 100)

Creating narratives is a way of making sense of the world around us and our place within it. In essence, narratives shape our sense of reality and truth. They also shape our views of other people and serve as vehicles by which negative attitudes of others are passed along from person to person and generation to generation. As such, narratives provide a basis for a shared world view. In addition, as Cruikshank suggests, "All societies have characteristic narrative structures that help members construct and remember knowledge of the world" (1992: 22). They may also provide a basis for collective action towards others and a justification for certain types of behaviour. Furthermore, narratives can serve as a basis for viewing people in a certain manner and create a framework for stereotypical viewpoints. "People reflect on their oral traditions to make sense of the social order that currently exists" (Cruikshank 1994: 406).[2]

The Truth about Stories

Thomas (Tom) King, who many of you might recall from the CBC's *Dead Dog Café* radio series, suggests that "the truth about stories is that that's all we are." He then continues: "The Okanagan storyteller Jeannette Armstrong tells us that 'Through my language I understand I am being spoken to, I'm not the one speaking. The words are coming from many tongues and mouths of Okanagan people and the land around them. I am a listener to the language's stories, and when my words form, I am merely retelling the same stories in different patterns'" (Armstrong 1998: 181; King 2003: 2).

This quote reminds me of Michelangelo's claim that he did not actually create his sculptures because they already existed in their stone encasements; all he was really doing was removing the stone around the images, to reveal them as they existed, as they always were. He was not the sculptures' creator, simply the one who allows them "to escape" from their encumbrances. And so, in Jeannette Armstrong's case she is a vehicle through which the past is able to connect with the present, through the medium of her stories.

As for the matter raised by Tom King – that we are really not much more than the stories of our lives – if that's a correct way to interpret his cryptic saying, then we can say that at first we were a twinkle in our parents' eyes, then we were a material being walking on this earth, then after some time, short or long, we disappeared into the ethereal stardust leaving behind certain objects, some kept, most thrown away, perhaps some photos; then no one who knew us was left to tell the stories of our lives, as if we were never there in the first place. And so it is with all of history. Some people wrote things down as they saw them, at the time, but often there is not much in the way of corroborating evidence – we interpret what we see through the lens of what we know.

Narratives, Authenticity, and Folklore

If narratives can be understood as methods by which people frame their sense of reality, then folklore can be viewed as the "culturally specific, orally transmitted genres of narratives" (Sidky 2004: 426). A related concept is that of a "folk taxonomy," which can be defined as "hierarchically organized cognitive categories by means of which members of a culture classify objects" (ibid.). There was a time when folklore was considered one of the four pillars of anthropology, along with the social/cultural, physical (biological), and archaeological. Several journals were devoted to the subject, such as *Folklore* (started in 1890), *Folklore Record* (1878–82) and *Folk Life* (Society of Folk Life Studies). Folklore's prominence in anthropology has fallen precipitously, as an emphasis in applied/public anthropology has gained in importance in the discipline. In fact, one would be hard pressed to find any mention at all of the subject in contemporary anthropology textbooks.

A quick search of my own library of introductory texts took me back to Paul Bohannan's *Social Anthropology* of the early 1960s for a brief discussion of "folk systems," in which he indicates that "It is the method of social anthropology to reveal folk systems of understanding by the creation of analytical systems of understanding" (1963: 14). Apparently, what he means is that there are two methods of organizing "facts." One of these is "the folk conceptions of exotic peoples" (ibid., 10), and the other is an analytic organization "in order to compare the facts and the folk theories" (ibid., 11). And then Bohannan adds this cautionary note: "The most heinous fault that a work of social anthropology can have is assignment of ideas from an analytic system to people who act merely in terms of a folk system" (ibid., 14). The implication, then, is that there is a body of facts that can be viewed in scientific or analytical terms, and the other category of facts that are more local, more culturally based, more specific to a particular body of people. In other words, this viewpoint is similar to what Abu-Lughod refers to, using the jargon of the day, as the "narrative ethnographies of the particular" (1991: 150–1).[3]

Throughout the history of anthropology there has been a concern with assessing the particular validity of oral traditions especially as these relate to comparable historical records. A debate over this relationship began over a century ago when Robert Lowie, at one-time president of the American Folklore Society, expressed his skepticism about the historical value of a culture's narrative accounts. For example, he indicated that he wished to lodge a protest "against the acceptance of oral traditions as historical records ... Those who attach an historical value to oral traditions are in the position of the circle-squarers and inventors of perpetual-motion machines." Lowie, though, was quick to remind his readers that his statement should not mean that oral traditions were not in any way meaningless to the people who believe in them, since he admitted that he "had misconceived the psychology of the situation." In an attempt to clarify what he meant, he asserted that "it is clear that even the wildest and manifestly impossible tales may be of the utmost importance as revelations of the cultural status of the people who cherish them" (1917: 161).

This admission, for what it is worth, would probably be taken as small comfort to those who believe that oral traditions have more historical validly than just psychological importance to the people who espouse them. As a case in point, in Richard Preston's study *Cree Narrative* he particularly uses the Hannah Bay episode to indicate that not only did Cree oral traditions of the event, which were handed down through successive generations for about 140 years (c. 1832–1970), included not only details on most of the individuals and the murderers, but that significant *additional* information was also included in the narratives that were not recorded in the Hudson's Bay Company journals (2002: 153–6).

This dialogue concerning the historical accuracy of oral traditions has been a recurrent theme throughout anthropology's history, with various authors debating the issue from one side or another. In other anthropological writings, treatments of oral narrative accounts of the past have also paid attention to the ideological, symbolic, and metaphysical meanings of oral testimonies that have provided the social and cultural basis for such interpretations (cf. Cohen 1989; Cronon 1992; Cruikshank 1982; Rosaldo 1980; Vansina 1985). There have also been various theoretical positions taken on the subject and discussions of the relationship between the interpretation of historical accounts and different theories. As an example, Steinhart suggested that the theoretical position of the author, such as those proposing functionalist or structuralist arguments, should make one use such interpretations of historical accounts, both written and oral, with a modicum of caution. His reason is that an overly theoretical approach to deciphering historical records is not likely to establish "an unbroken chain of testimony back to the eyewitness account of some past event" (1989: 3).

Susan Hegeman (1989a, 1989b) has written articles concerning the issue of "authenticity" in Native American narrative traditions. "An important example," she writes, "of the sorts of difficulties to which such emphases on 'authenticity' leads is in the evaluation of translations of Native American material. The traditional works of story tellers, shamans, historians, and healers are often parts of complex performances, recited in obscure languages, and...often strange and difficult to understand for many readers" (1989a: 145). In a sense, then, narrative traditions tend to develop their own sense of style and peculiarities in description as they are retold through the generations. She points out that even Native listeners who can speak the language, at time have difficulty following what is happening, so in this context, how can a Euro-American know any better? As a related issue, according to Fogelson, "The importance of the individual in the rendering of Indian histories [is] highly problematic. We must be careful to distinguish individualism as an ideology from the more psychological concept of individuality, or sense of self" (1989: 140).

Preston, in his work *Cree Narrative* (2002), discusses a similar issue, when he indicates that "Narrations are soliloquies, often eloquent and personally expressive as well as culturally meaningful ... The balance between individual autonomy and social practicality ... is evidence in the balance between variation in the style of individual narratives, and the invariance of events described in their precise narrative context" (2002: 74). What Preston seems to be saying is that Cree narrators are allowed their own particular mannerisms ("personally expressive") while attempting to maintain a certain coherence of events ("precise narrative context") that the members of the listening audience will understand in the same way that a minister of a Christian faith will perhaps be allowed some leeway in describing the life of Jesus, but he must always in the end die on the cross and not elude his preordained fate by escaping in a boat with Mary Magdalen. A characteristic of narrative traditions, then, concerns the cultural variations that are allowed and others that are not.

In a similar vein, other authors have provided their own particular points of view on the issue of authenticity in Native texts. As an example, Fogelson discusses certain epistemological problems, which is to say, "The particular form of historical consciousness in the West normally entails written documents, and such entailment poses special epistemological dilemmas [such as] do we simply dismiss them as cultures lacking historical consciousness" (1989: 34). Authenticity has its place in cultural traditions regardless if they are derived from Indigenous experiences or those of Euro-Americans. In this context, it would be incorrect to assume that because Native traditions are (usually) verbally transmitted to the audience, and from generation to generation, then they are necessarily inaccurate in the specific details that are expressed in them. Thus, Hegeman, in addressing the epistemological matter of authenticity, writes that "However one feels about the issue of 'authenticity' in relation to Native American texts, there is a disconcerting tendency to ascribe amoral dimension to every possible position in the debate [which is to say] not all appeals to 'authenticity' are free from objectionable or even racist aspects" (1989b: 268–9).

Non-Natives are often far too quick to provide objections to the credibility of Native traditions, just because they are Native and for not much more reason than that. This point is similarly made by Fogelson when he indicates that "the lack of an authenticated history for many ... groups begs fundamental questions about the authority of history. Who determines it? Who sets the criteria? Or, in a literal sense, who *possesses* history?" (1989: 142). These questions suggest that Euro-Americans are all too hasty to assume that they have some predetermined right to control a narrative discourse, which is all too prevalent in white settler rationalizations for erasing the historical facts of Indigenous occupation of North America.

This is should not suggest that members of the same Euro-American community would necessarily not have their own interpretations of Native narrations just because they belong to the "same" culture. As such, there are various times when several authors might disagree about the interpretation of the same historical event. As Cronon explains, "As often happens in history ... one wonders how two competent authors looking at identical materials drawn from the same past can reach such divergent conclusions." The problem, as he sees it, pertains to the fact that a multiplicity of scholarly disciplines can be involved in the task of historical interpretation all at the same time. "As an environmental historian who tries to blend the analytic traditions of history with those of ecology, economics, anthropology, and other fields," Cronon suggests, "I cannot help feeling uneasy about the shifting theoretical grounds all now seem to occupy" (1992: 1348–9). Of course, one might hasten to add that there are certain topics that are prone to attract interdisciplinary approaches – narrative traditions, oral testimonies, and historical records being one of them – then academics should become acclimatized to this multi-faceted terrain with all its various theories, methodological approaches, and disciplinary idiosyncratic tendencies (see White 1984; Berg 2004).[4]

Narratives and Cultural Representation[5]

"From the moment they encountered Indigenous people in the Western hemisphere," Krech (2010: online) explains, "Europeans classified them in order to make them sensible. They made the exotic comprehensible with familiar categories. In the process they reduced men and women to stereotypes, to caricatures, noble or ignoble, benign or malignant, rational or irrational, human or cannibal – savages all." Thus, European settlers engaged in demeaning narratives of the Indigenous people they encountered, and since these people were characterized in a negative manner, an opportunity was afforded the Europeans to disenfranchise them and in the process divest them of their lands and heritage.

Cultural encounters involve attempts by members of different societies to understand people not known to each other previously. Understanding the cultural behaviour of the members quite different from our own is a challenging task, especially when there are few clues or guidelines that can be utilized to aide in this task. Similarly, as anthropologist Clifford Geertz (1983: 5) so eloquently phrased it, our task during the course of the cultural encounters is to "somehow understand how it is we understand understandings not our own."[6]

In terms of the fur-trade era, and the attempts by members of the Hudson's Bay Company are concerned, their task was to interpret the behaviour of Indigenous people in northern Canada so that each party could engage in forms of transaction and exchange. In other words, these fur-trade transactions involved British cultural assumptions on representations of Indigenous people. Thus, in *Traders' Tales*, Vibert (1997) endeavours to study British perceptions of colonized people. This study, more specifically, is an attempt to explore the images conceived by European fur traders to describe the Native American societies they encountered during the course of their exploration of the northern part of North America. This research task is accomplished by examining the various journals, log books, trading post records, and published narratives that provide an early written historical record of the Indigenous societies. As such, these documents of the fur trade era are utilized in an attempt to comprehend the early insights into an era of exploration and encounters between the traders and their cultural "Other."

Vibert (1997: xi–xii) further explained that the members of each different group had their own version of the truth and that it was evident to her when she explored these differing perceptions in more depth that "it became clear that one's truth is another's tall tale ... native people undoubtedly had very different understandings of their own motivations and practices." In fact, it was an important point of information that the traders could not apparently "let go of the cultural notions they carried with them – notions about the 'civilized' way of life, the proper economy, appropriate social roles for men and women. The assumptions found a kind of coordinating grid in the travellers' encounters with native people."

Her use of the term "a kind of coordinating grid" is interesting. This term suggests attempts by an historian to describe what in anthropology is commonly understood to mean a person's "worldview," which is to say "the totality of precepts and beliefs, ritual attitudes, and religious ideas concerning the way the world is and the position of people and things in it, shared by members of a society and expressed in their myths, lore, rituals, and values" (Sidky 2004: 444). Vibert furthermore points out that it is language that is the medium that conveys cultural meanings. Language is not a neutral medium since "the language of any cultural or social group in any epoch, reflects and helps to constitute the group's view of the world," which, as such, approximates the anthropological definition just given (Vibert 1992: 5). It should also be pointed out, for those not entirely familiar with anthropology's history, that what became known as the Sapir-Whorf Hypothesis approximates Vibert's "coordinating grid," as well, which is to say, "that language determines thought and perceptions of reality," after the work of linguists Edward Sapir and Benjamin Whorf (ibid., 438). Thus, Vibert's (1997: 5) conclusion is that "'facts' are socially constructed; they are products of the social and cultural forces in place as the [fur traders'] texts are continuously interpreted and reinterpreted."

As one reviews the fur traders' accounts in the various post journals and other forms of reporting and correspondence, it is therefore prudent to realized that these writings may represent the truth as the fur trader saw it in that particular time; however, other interpretations are possible. This is not to suggest that fur trader accounts are necessarily biased towards one particular group or another, or that they should be dismissed or ignored, but to realize that they take place within a particular cultural, social, and temporal context. It is in this sense that Vibert, in her *Traders' Tales*, cautions us to be wary of placing too much credence in the idea that these tales represent in any sense objective or truthful interpretations of reality. Thus, it is no longer acceptable simply to read trader and other eyewitness accounts for content, presuming them to be more or less accurate representations of a moment in time (1997: 31). Of course, and it should by now go without saying, that even Indigenous narratives should be similarly regarded as stemming from a particular cultural tradition with its own norms, values, and vantage points.

What, then, are we to make of George Simpson, governor of the Hudson's Bay Company, and his views of the Indigenous people that he met in his travels? As an example, in Simpson's first tour of the Columbia Department (in the Plateau region of North America's west coast), in 1824–5 he dismissed the Native people living along the Columbia River as "indolent and lazy to an extreme" (Vibert 1997: 3). His views were evidently also shared by other fur traders of the Pacific Northwest when one of them referred to the Indigenous inhabitants of the area as living in a "rude state of nature" (ibid.). However, Simpson's scornful description of the Lower Kutenai in an 1841 journal entry was even more truculent:

"[T]hey were a miserable looking set of beings, small decrepit and dirty ... The fair sex bore a striking resemblance to the famous Chimpanzee which delighted London of late, most especially so when they shut their eyes and scratched their head [and then he added in a later 1847 version] hardly bore the semblance of human beings" (Simpson 1847: 130; see also Vibert 1997: 38).

One cannot say much more than that this viewpoint of one's fellow human beings is the voice of privilege speaking. It is arrogant, disrespectful, and condescending in its self-righteous tone of superiority towards the very people that the Hudson's Bay Company depended upon for their economic sustenance. These disparaging comments emanate from a characteristic of a settler colonial attitude that serves to justify the dispossession of Indigenous lands and heritage, all in the spirit of laissez-faire capitalism.

As Simpson's biographer, John Galbraith, explains in *The Little Emperor*, "[B]y the time he [George Simpson] had spent a few months in North America, he had already developed rigid stereotypes about Indians, which remained substantially unmodified the rest of his life. Essentially these views were those prevailing among most of his fellow fur traders" (1976: 61–2).

Concerning relationships with the Indigenous people themselves, any sense of fairness or favourable views on the part of the Company's officers were simply a matter of maintaining satisfactory business dealings. As Galbraith further explains, "There was little intimacy on a human level. Indian women were a source of sexual gratification ... Their white mates did not treat them as equals ... To the fur traders ... in every case they [Indigenous people] were seen as uncivilized, improvident people whose moral and intellectual development was retarded ... Simpson, by the time he spent a few months in the Athabasca country, was already expressing such judgments" (ibid., 62).

The Arrogance of White Privilege

One can be assured, therefore, that if the governor of such a significant firm as the Hudson's Bay Company was openly expressing such disparaging commentary about the Indigenous people in northern Canada, that assuredly these attitudes would begin to permeate the rest of the organization's work force as well. As such, an attitude of "white privilege" towards those that one regards as inferior to oneself best describes the HBC organizational sentiment towards their Indigenous clientele. "White privilege," Cousins (2014: 1385) asserts, "describes unearned advantages afforded to people who are assumed, based largely on complexion and specific physical features, to be of European, especially western European, ancestry ... It favors people who are, or are presumed to be, white by enabling political and economic systems and corresponding power structures to grant only these people unmerited and simultaneously unacknowledged advantages."

The concept of white privilege is also used to understand the mechanisms of social ascendency and power. "White privilege," Stanley (2017: 149) suggest, "indicates that a person who is recognized as 'white' by the broader society is better positioned to reap advantages *owing to their whiteness* ... [thus] they are more likely to benefit from additional layers of protective cushions [such as personal failings, alcohol, or drug addiction]" (see also Rothenberg 2002). In addition, there are other scholars who link concepts of white privilege with processes of settler colonialism. Bonds and Inwood (2016: 715), for example, state that "We situate white supremacy ... as the foundation for the continuous unfolding of practices of race and racism within settler states." They also distinguish between colonialism, in the larger context, and settler colonialism within the parameters of these larger structures. "Settler colonialism focuses on the *permanent* occupation of a territory and removal of Indigenous people with the express purpose of building an ethically distinct national community."

As such, "settler colonialism is theoretically, politically, and geographically distinct from colonialism, [which is to say] the imperial expansion by militaristic or economic purposes." However, settler colonialism is not conceptually divergent from the larger sphere of colonialism itself because it is essentially concerned with "the exploitation of marginalized peoples in a system of capitalism established by and reinforced through racism" (ibid., 715). However, while these authors conceptually distinguish between the larger sphere of colonialism and its subcategory of settler colonialism, these two processes are nonetheless linked historically. As in the Canadian case, the British government established its grip on northern Canada with the Hudson's Bay Company as an important commercial arm of its imperial expansion, and in time its focus nevertheless moved outward as a centre of population growth.

Further support for the premises that settler colonialism is founded on notions of white privilege and, furthermore, that these processes and attitudes, while originating in the historical past, nonetheless find expression in the modern world. Today, Elkins and Pederson (2005: 1) suggest, the "legacies [of settler colonialism] are everywhere to be seen." As such, then, settler colonialism "is not in the past ... but rather the foundational governing ethic of the 'new world' state" (ibid., 3). This proposition – that settler colonialism continues today as a basis for the modern world – finds further expression in the writings of Patrick Wolfe (1998, 2006), who notes that settler colonialism cannot be seen as an essentially fleeting stage but must be understood as the persistent defining characteristic of this new world settler society. Speaking of Australia, another British colony, he succinctly states that "the determination 'settler-colonial state' is Australian society's primary structural characteristic rather than merely a statement about its origins … Invasion is a structure, not an event" (1998: 163).

It follows, then, according to the proposition that racist attitudes towards Indigenous people begin with the assertion of white privilege, that settler colonial structures are essentially built on discriminatory structures of white entitlement and dispossession. Accordingly, the development of modernity across the world is based historically on "the emergence of white racial identities as an integral component" of the inequitable structures that are found in today's world that form the basis of unequal racial relationships in government, the economy, and social orders. "Indeed, it is my contention," Bonnett (2016: 2) asserts, "that one cannot grasp the development of the modern world, and more especially the notion of what is modern and what is not, without an appreciation of the racialized nature of modernity and, more particularly, of its association with a European identified white race." This would suggest, then, that Canada's issues of white privilege have their origins in a British imperialist colonial strategy that begins initially with the Hudson's Bay Company as the vanguard of colonial capitalism, and then emerges later, as in the case of the Red River Colony, in the form of settler colonialism based on Indigenous territorial dispossession.

Territorial Expansion

As an initial effort in Britain's expansionist efforts in Canada, the Red River Colony was established in 1811 as a colonization project on land granted by the Hudson's Bay Company. This land included portions of Rupert's Land, or the watershed of Hudson Bay, and parts of present-day Manitoba, the Dakota Territories, Minnesota, and northern Ontario, which is an area five times the size of Scotland. The initial plan was that Red River would be an agricultural settlement that would grow wheat for flour and raise beef and pork, among other products. The rationale for the settlement was that manufacturing food in this colony would serve to reduce the costly shipments of food products from Britain, especially in light of the steady decline of the bison due to overhunting (see Morton 1949: 305–21). By July 1811, a ship containing primarily Irish and Scottish settlers set sail for the Hudson's Bay post at York Factory and, by August 1812, an additional 120 settlers arrived, which augmented the growing population at the Red River Colony. In 1841, the Red River Colony provided 200 settlers who travelled westwards in an attempt to regain the Columbia District for Britain; however, this expansionist plan was later relinquished in the Oregon boundary dispute. Later, in 1870, it was American expansionists who became interested in the economic potential that the Red River land possessed, and who attempted to assert their dominance by destabilising the British efforts at colonization. Efforts by the new Canadian government forestalled the American initiative, but not the resistance of a discontented Métis Nation (Bumsted and Smyth 2019; Daschuk 2013; Kaye 1986; Wood 1964).

The point here is that the establishment of the Red River Colony illustrates that in terms of the development of early Canada, there is clearly a concrete link between the commercial arm of the British colonial government, the Hudson's Bay Company as a form of colonial capitalism, and efforts at settler colonization, with the intention of expanding a British population base that would eventually extend outwards across the Canadian territory. Thus, one can posit that processes of colonial capitalism, doctrines of white privilege (possible Indigenous claims to Rupert's Land, for example, were completely ignored), and settler colonialism were linked processes of imperial expansionist policy in Canada.

In fact, it is evident that similar processes linking white privilege and settler expansionist strategies occurred in the United States as well. In Hixson's (2013) *American Settler Colonialism* he explains that settler colonialism "ultimately overwhelmed ambivalence and ambiguity. Indians, who had used and changed the land for centuries, proved willing to share land with the newcomers but not simply to give it up to the settlers. The Euro-Americans, however, were on a mission to take command over colonial space – process that entailed demarcation and control, boundaries, maps, surveys, treaties, seizures, and the commodification of the land" (2013: viii; see also Harris 2004).

These settlers were evidently quite meticulous in their efforts to document their newly acquired territory.

Narratives of Inequality

The term "narratives of inequality" has in recent years joined the works on Indigenous disentitlement, along with such now familiar phrases as "Indigenous erasure," "settler colonialism," "colonial capitalism," laissez-faire racism," "post-colonial criticism," among others. In Melissa Kennedy's study she notes that "the crash [of 2008] challenged the discourses of modernity, progress, and development that were touted as the prerequisites for worldwide improvement in standards of living [and] popular conceptions of wealth and poverty, by revealing at once worrying immiseration in the world's richest countries" (2017: 5–6). One of the primary reasons for this "immiseration" is a recognition that the world's people are economically divided, as in the developing terminology, such as First and Third Worlds, "West and the Rest," the Global North and Global South, and so on.

What is pertinent to the present discussion concerns the methods used by colonial powers to "winnow out the Indigenous and migrant losers from the winners of capitalism" (Kennedy 2017: 17). In other words, poverty and disentitlement are "built into" the mechanisms of colonialism in such a way as to create these "narratives of inequality." It is the structures of inequality that are instituted in new colonies that tend to marginalize the local Indigenous people through resource extraction, land privatization, and the labour exploitation of local populations, in the interest of profit maximization in acts of collusion between resident settlers and the imperial powers. This process of marginalization, or even "erasure" in some terminology, is aided by the narratives created by settler populations, which perpetuates in the colonies such unequal social relations and discriminatory attitudes towards the colonized. In turn, these discriminatory attitudes tend to become ingrained in settler attitudes, expressed as racism, and continue into the present day and in the cultural practices of the colonizers today. "Structures and mechanisms of capitalist inequality," Melissa Kennedy suggests, "instituted in early settlement have long-lasting repercussions, continuing today in the disproportionate poverty of Indigenous peoples within nations states" (2017: 60).[7]

Where Does Racism Begin?

The contempt that the employees of the Hudson's Bay Company have historically shown to the Indigenous peoples in the fur trade, from the very top of the organization in Governor George Simpson to the post managers in the local communities, was palpable and offensive. From the continual references to the Cree, Anishinaabe, and other Aboriginal peoples as "savages" and the use of other derogatory references to the very people upon whose effort their fortunes were built is symptomatic of a colonial sense of superiority. This attitude has laid the foundation for similar pejorative and deprecating references that were used in future years to caste the Aboriginal peoples of North America in a demeaning manner. Even Governor Simpson, the head of one of the largest commercial organizations in the world at one time, referred to Indigenous cultures as "repugnant," which would have sent a derogatory message throughout the HBC organization that it was acceptable to demean the trader's First Nation clients. Such instances serve to contribute to a narrative of disrespect.

Apologists for British colonialism will probably comment that that was all in the past, as if that excuses the racism of former times. The problem is that misanthropic attitudes towards Indigenous peoples has been going on ever since these colonial times, virtually unabated, into the attitudes of those in power today. In other words, the disrespect that members of the Hudson's Bay Company showed towards their Indigenous clients has continued up to this day, inexorable in its intensity. Take, as an example, the relatively recent Ipperwash protest in which an unarmed Aboriginal man, Dudley George, was shot and killed by a sergeant of the Ontario Provincial Police during a nighttime raid. One of the police officers, a member of the OPP Intelligence Team, was caught on tape a day before the shooting making the most racist and derogatory comments imaginable about the Indigenous protesters: "No, there's no one down there. Just a big, fat, fuck Indian. Yeah. We had this plan, you know. We thought if we could ... five or six cases of Labatt's 50, we could bait them. And we'd have this big net at a pit. Works in the south with watermelons" (in Hedican 2013: 168).

Unfortunately, these are the very people who we rely on for the protection of our rights and freedoms today. The OPP officer who made these comments is the very type of person who we expect to be our paragons of virtue, our models of excellence, so it is incredibly disappointing to hear of such intolerance. When the recordings were released (or leaked) to the public, the OPP officer who was identified on the tapes was only "informally disciplined." In three hundred years not much, unfortunately, has apparently changed.

Racism, as a historical process, according to Feagin (2010: 6), "is perpetuated by a broad social reproduction process that generates not only recurring patterns of discrimination within institutions and by individuals but also an alienating racist relationship – on the one hand, the racially oppressed, and on the other, the racial oppressors. These two groups are created by the racist system, and thus have different group interests."

Thus, in the case of the Ipperwash protest, these two groups – the racially oppressed, and the racial oppressors – began to align themselves into two opposing camps around the land claim protest. Various other people then began to join one camp or another, depending upon their inclinations towards racial and ethnic minorities. As an example, the local media began to portray the Indigenous protesters as thugs, troublemakers, and potential criminals. The idea formulated was that the protesters were engaging in a criminal act because they were occupying public provincial property, without recognizing in this portrayal that the Indigenous people were the original owners of the park property.

What was lost in this portrayal was the real story, which was the history of betrayal through which the Indigenous protesters, and the generations of their family members before them, who had been dispossessed of their traditional territory through treaties, unscrupulous Indian agents, and other federal government policies of disenfranchisement (Hedican 2013). The point here is that discrimination against Canada's Indigenous people began early on in the British colonial era with the fur traders of the Hudson's Bay Company and has continued through the decades and centuries, up to the present day.

Challenging Indigenous Erasure

Canada's public history displays tell us much about the way Canadians perceive their past and the people in it. Unfortunately, many public history displays in Canada do not include the Indigenous people of this country; it is almost as if they have been erased from the public's memory.

As an example, Jesse Thistle is an Aboriginal student who attended York University. For one of his courses Jesse decided to write an essay on the public representation of the popular Black Creek Pioneer Village for an anthropology class on tourism. As he walked through the village, he noticed that "the history presented there was problematic on many fronts. It didn't have 1860s Canada West things like gallows, brothels, police or soldiers' barracks, or any Indigenous peoples." As he thought about this further he began to realize that "the mythic fables Canadians tell themselves at public history sites [is used] to justify colonial settlement while delegitimizing Indigenous claims to their own ancestral lands" (Thistle 2017).

This was exactly the kind of thinking – that Canada was an empty land or what has been termed *terra nullius* – that justified the granting of Rupert's Land to the Hudson's Bay Company, which was apparently based on the logic that if there were no people in a territory then it was all right to settle there. Some people refer to this attitude as "settler colonialism." "I was shocked," Thistle indicates, "to see a glaring erasure of Indigenous peoples in virtually all of the village's diorama." About the only place where one could find any Indigenous presence at all was in the gift shops in the form of cheap souvenirs. Later, with the help of several professors and fellow students, Jesse Thistle produced a film about his experience called *Kiskisiwin – Remembering: Challenging Indigenous Erasure in Canada's Public History Displays* (http://activehistory. ca/2017/07/kiskisiwin-remembering-challenging-indigenous-erasure-in-canadas-public-history-displays/ accessed April 11, 2020; see also Peers 2007; Sandberg, Stiegman and Thistle 2017).

In another thought-provoking discussion of "Indigenous Erasure," Mia Furtado (2016) suggests that "Though history classes teach historical events ... what courses do not teach is the continual erasure of Indigenous culture and history that continues to occur in this country today." Furtado furthermore suggest that "the white population of this country that denies the existence of while privilege and white supremacy need to understand how the powers have morphed and though they may look different, the power structures are still very much in existence." (https://www.outfrontmagazine.com/perspectives/dismantling-white-privilege-indigenous-erasure/ accessed April 11, 2020).

One definition of "Indigenous erasure" is the process "whereby settler societies discount and eliminate the presence of American Indian peoples, cultures, and polities. This erasure is part of a larger imperative to diminish the existence of American Indians to access land and resources. One method of erasure is to narrowly define who might be an American Indian" (Orr, Sharratt, and Iqbal 2019: 2,078). In fact, this process of elimination has been occurring in Canada for a very long time. When treaties were signed with the various Indigenous peoples a list was made of the signatories to these treaties. Various disputes arose because some Indigenous people were unable to attend the treaty signing ceremony and were therefore off the band's roll. As time went on other Indigenous people were eliminated, such as Indigenous women who married those not regarded as "treaty Indians." These people then became relegated to a "non-status" population and were denied residence on their original reserves.

Eventually, in 1985, an apparent attempt by the Canadian government to rectify this problem was made with the passage of Bill C-31. However, while some Indigenous people had their Indian status restored, others were denied this status because of various technicalities, such as not knowing the name of one of their grandparents. In all, there were approximately 20,000 women who had lost their status because they married males who did not have status under the terms of the Indian Act. This meant also that their subsequent children and grandchildren would also be denied Indian status.

Under the legal stipulations of Bill C-31 there was a limited period for registration, which some people missed for various reasons. The success rate for applicant was also not very high. There were about 42,000 applications for reinstatement of Indian status by 1985, yet only 1,605 were accepted that year. Over the next five years 75,000 applications for reinstatement were received affecting about 135,000 individuals. By 2001 just over 105,000 persons had been added to the total Indian population, which is only one-seventh of the total registered population.

In addition, in the event that a person had their status restored, this did not automatically mean that they would be welcomed back to their home reserves. In fact, it is estimated that only 2 percent were successful in securing reserve housing between 1985 and 1990. While the original intentions may have been to eliminate sexual discrimination in the Indian Act, Bill C-31 also created many new problems as well because it failed to solve the problem of "Indian erasure" in Canadian federal legislation (see Asch, Borrows, and Tully 2018; Frideres and Gadacz 2008: 31–5; Hedican 2008a: 228–9, 2017a: 135–6; Cairns 2000: 74; Morgensen 2012: 2–22).[8]

Settler Colonialism

The topic of settler colonialism has become an increasingly important discussion point in the literature concerning Indigenous people in the modern world. While various definitions of settler colonialism have been proposed in recent years, several characteristic themes have emerged in the academic literature concerning Indigenous issues in North America. As an example, Alicia Cox (2017) suggests that "settler colonialism is an ongoing system of power that perpetuates the genocide and repression of Indigenous peoples and cultures." She further suggests that settler colonialism "normalizes the continuous settler occupation, exploiting lands and resources to which Indigenous peoples have genealogical relationships." This evolving field of settler colonialism focuses on the spread of Eurocentric values, which suggests that the settlers have a moral superiority as a justification to occupy Indigenous lands. This type of colonialism, it is pointed out, is not a thing of the past because in many countries, such as Canada, the United States, and Australia, Indigenous people continue today to be subjected to ongoing systems of domination.

This process of settlement by colonial occupiers is not simply a system of exploitation but one whereby Indigenous people are displaced from their original territories, usually because of economic interests. As Zahedieh (2010: 392–3) notes, all forms of colonization revolved around the expansion of British trade. Thus, the term "settler colonialism" can be understood to mean a form of colonialism in which the goal is to ultimately displace an Indigenous population of a colonized territory and replace them with a new society of settlers. This strategy is based on a form of exogenous domination that is usually initiated, organized, and supported by an imperial authority. The processes of domination are all-encompassing, such that "different expressions of imperialism cover all forms of colonization, including white settler nations, extractive and commodity colonies, and protectorates of strategic locations" (Kennedy 2017: 6).

In Canada the processes of "Indigenous erasure" and "settler colonialism" have been going on almost from the very foundations of this country. If one examines the history of Toronto, for example, a week-long celebration occurred in 1884 with the commemoration of the city's fiftieth anniversary. In effect, this celebration was in reality a commemoration of Toronto's relationship to British colonialism and imperialism, rather than its Indigenous roots. On the first day of this event a parade displayed Toronto's British heritage; there were speeches by Daniel Wilson, president of University College, and Chief Samson Green of the Tyendinaga Mohawks. Sadly, the event really turned out to be a celebration of the erasure of the area's Indigenous past and celebrated instead its European future.

An idealized portrayal of the Indigenous-settler partnership was on display, which ignored the role of local settlers in the dispossession of the Mississauga. The 1884 commemoration marked the founding of the Toronto settlement in 1793, considered the city's "founding moment." The deed by which the British settlers acquired the territory from the Mississauga in the Toronto Purchase of 1787 was deemed not even relevant enough to be mentioned; however, the 1834 Act of Incorporation became "the symbolic deed to Toronto's modernity." Who were the Mississauga? Where did they go? They were just erased from Toronto's colonial history, as if they never existed in the first place, whereas the British allies, the Mohawks who were late-comers to Ontario and certainly not one of the province's "Indigenous" populations, were given the podium to mark the event (Freeman: 2010).

In another example, in Jeffrey Denis's (2020) *Canada at a Crossroads*, he draws on settler colonial studies to illustrate the various social and psychological barriers that exist in transforming white settler ideology towards decolonization. In particular, he finds one of the main barriers is the settlers' sense of group superiority and entitlement in the ongoing colonial process. In his book Denis illustrates how contemporary Indigenous and settler residents relate to one another and the way they differ or maintain conflicting perspectives on such topics as treaties, history, and cultural issues. However, such commonly proposed solutions – intergroup contact, apologies, and collective action – have their pitfalls as well as promises. Ultimately, Denis contends, genuine reconciliation will only come about with a radical restriction of Canadian society, especially in terms of fulfilling historical treaty responsibilities.

As far as the fulfilment of treaty responsibilities is concerned, one of the main reasons that Indigenous people are speaking out against the erosion of their traditional territories by an ever-expanding Euro-Canadian population is that the settlers have an apparent voracious appetite for land. Many businesses in Canada have begun to post notices recognizing that they are situated on Indigenous land. In Guelph, Ontario, for example, the former Bookshelf Café has recently changed its name to the Miijidaa Café in recognition of the area's Indigenous heritage: *miijidaa* in Anishinaabe means "let's eat," according to the café's website.

In addition, two Indigenous leaders have spoken out as advocates for Aboriginal rights in Canada. In *Unsettling Canada* (2015) Arthur Manuel and Grand Chief Ron Derrikson build on a unique collaboration between two First Nation leaders. Both men have served as chiefs of their bands in the British Columbia interior and in the process have established international reputations. It is interesting that their backgrounds are so diverse. Grand Chief Ron Derrikson is one of the most successful Indigenous businessmen in the country, while Arthur Manuel has been a long-time advocate for Aboriginal title and has spoken forcefully against settler colonial attitudes that are at the root of the dispossession of Indigenous lands because of expropriations and other unjust practices that have taken place throughout Canada's history. In particular, both leaders have attempted to bring fresh perspectives and new ideas to the unfinished business of Canadian Confederation, which is the place of Indigenous peoples in the country's political and economic space. In the final chapters of their book, they set out a plan for a new sustainable Indigenous economy and the various processes that could lead to their goal.

On the topic of the dispossession of Indigenous lands, well-known playwright, and director Tomson Highway, known for his highly acclaimed plays *The Rez Sisters* (1986) and *Dry Lips Oughta Move to Kapuskasing* (1989), suggests that the Aboriginal people of Canada have finally woken up to the fact that their lands are being constantly eroded by commercial interests, and this has had dire social consequences. As he suggests, "Hardly a day goes by that the average Canadian does not read or hear about them [Indigenous people] in the media: poverty on the reserves, invasion of hunting and trapping grounds by corporate interests, inequities in education and justice ... We are witnessing the emergence of a generation of Indian people clearly more vocal, more articulate, and more aggressively unwilling to continue playing victims." He points out, additionally, that Aboriginal people are coming forward with skills in the English language and armed with university degrees in many subjects. Aboriginal people have also become lawyers and businesspeople who are capable of navigating the complexities of the modern corporations and their legal statutes. Such people are becoming a force to be reckoned with in combatting the apparently never-ending attrition of Indigenous lands and property rights (in York 1990: vii–ix).[9]

A Settler's Response to Colonialism

In a rare non-Indigenous response to settler colonialism Denise Nadeau, in *Unsettling Spirit* (2020), examines her own role in the displacement of Indigenous people in Canada. Essentially, Nadeau's account is a spiritual journey into what it means to be a white settler on land taken from peoples who have lived there since time immemorial. The main focus of her book concerns the question: "How could I as a settler live with integrity and responsibility in relationship with the Indigenous peoples of these lands?" (2020: 4). Her journey, then, provides a personal perspective on such areas as reconciliation, Indigenous resurgence, and decolonization, informed by Indigenous traditions and life experiences in order to examine her complicity with colonial structures.

Nadeau's search for answers began with Canada's Truth and Reconciliation Commission (TRC),[10] which took place between 2008 and 2015, in which she quotes a statement in a section entitled "Calls to Action." The commissioners stated that "'reconciliation' is about establishing and maintaining a mutually respectful relationship between Aboriginal and non-Aboriginal people in this country" (2020: 5). However, Nadeau found this approach problematic for reasons not specified very clearly, and as a result, decided to focus more on issues of settler decolonization rather than "reconciliation" because of its variable interpretations between Indigenous and non-Indigenous peoples.

As far as the decolonization approach is concerned, Nadeau sees it as a "process of unlearning a worldview and values and ways of acting and being in the world that have prohibited and continues to prohibit any meaningful and mutually respectful relationships between Indigenous and non-Indigenous people" (2020: 5). She refers to this as "my journey into decolonization … what it means to be a settler in a country in which the land we live on was taken – stolen – from the original peoples who lived here" (ibid.). Nadeau uses the term "settler" to include "all those who benefit from settler privilege" (ibid., 6).

One wonders if settler privilege also extends in some manner to Indigenous people, or those who have a biological heritage in both settler and Indigenous social systems. Kim Anderson, for example, who was born with a mix of white and Indigenous parents admits to using either heritage in situations in which she accrues an advantage.

Image 6. Anishinaabe log cabins in Northern Ontario
Source: Author's fieldwork photographs (1974–5)

"A significant part of my Euro-Canadian heritage that I cannot over-look is the privilege that it affords me," she explains. "My race and class privilege separate me from many Native people in terms of lived experiences. I am a privileged Native person in that I have no lived experiences of violent or *overt* racism, poverty, abuse, and family breakdown" (2000: 31). In Nadeau's case she was a Master of Divinity student and now a professor in a religious studies program at Concordia University. In other words, she is benefiting from the privileges, entitlements, and lifestyle advantages of a white settler society through her education and research, yet apparently objects to the manner (Indigenous lands stolen by her white ancestors) that have resulted in her fortunate position in life. Like Anderson, she has never lived in a log cabin without the amenities of running water, electricity, or central heating that were typical of the Anishinaabe communities in which I have lived and conducted my ethnographic fieldwork in northern Ontario.

Nadeau states that her focus is "on the structures that accompany settler colonialism, structures through which those who arrived from Europe imposed their culture and laws on the Indigenous peoples already living here ... I suggest that it is our relationship with an embodied spirit world that will point the way forward in Indigenous-settler relations" (2020: 6, 11). As I was reading these lines for the first time, I could not help thinking what the Anishinaabe people who live in the bush in log cabins north of Lake Nipigon would think of these words, and whether they might find solace in them. I suspect that they would find these statements just as incomprehensible as any other settler jargon they have always heard, even though its intentions might be well meaning.

This is not to suggest that colonial violence is not a real phenomenon. Aron and Corne (1994) use the term "psychosocial trauma" to describe the effects of routinized violence that Indigenous people experience in their everyday lives (see also Battiste 2000; Culhane 2003; Kleinman and Desjarlais 1995 on social suffering and spiritual loss). This trauma results from dehumanizing social relations; "it affects an entire network of social relations ... it is only changing the social relations between colonizer and colonized that psychosocial trauma can be alleviated," Young and Nadeau (2005: 4) suggest. As such there are multiple forms of colonial violence that have resulted in a "spiritual disjuncture." Similarly, Ronald Niezen, in *Spirit Wars*, describes these lost connections with social and psychological relationships as a "radical instability in the human relationship with the spirit world" (2000: 35). Thus, one of the debilitating aspects of colonialism, especially the missionizing variety, is that it directly attacks the religious identity of Indigenous communities and therefore erodes people's sense of spiritual identity. Kim Anderson also argues that forms of spiritual disjuncture are at the root of a process of sexist and racist colonialism by which Indigenous women have lost their collective status as sacred. As she explains, while previously "our cultures promoted womanhood as a sacred identity, an identity that existed within a complex system of relations of societies that were based on balance," now Indigenous women have lost respect, lost a sense of honour, and as such this colonial violence produces a sense of "de-spiriting" (2000: 57).[11]

How Colonialism Dispossesses

Further to this theme, Cole Harris (2004) asks, "How Did Colonialism Dispossess?" In relation to the dispossession of Indigenous people in British Columbia, he observes that when we see the provincial government "combine capital interests in uncluttered access to land and settlers' interests as livelihood, … the principal momentum of settler colonialism comes in focus" (Harris 2004: 179). Harris primarily discusses various techniques of dispossession into two categories: first, earlier methods, such as direct violence, cultural narratives of dispossession, and acts of settler self-interest; and second, the use of maps, demographics, and a reserve geography of resettlement. In particular, Harris attempts to specify what it means to dispossess Indigenous peoples of their lands and living spaces. One of the principal methods, he claims, is the removal of Indigenous populations from their lands by "reterritorializing," which involves competing jurisdictional claims by various parties involved – Indigenous, provincial, and federal all asserting claims to a particular territory.

This type of dispossession could be seen as a form of "displacement without moving," or what Rob Nixon refers to as "slow violence," which "entails being simultaneously immobilized and moved out of one's living knowledge as one's place loses its life-sustaining features" (2011: 19). Acts of Indigenous dispossession are also explained in terms of what Aileen Moreton-Robinson refers to as "the white possessive." She explains her viewpoint by indicating that colonial powers are heavily invested in the nation being a white "possessive." As a form of property, whiteness accumulates capital and social appreciation. White people are recognized within the law primarily as property-owning subjects, she contends. (See also Rifkin's [2017] *Beyond Settler Time* and Wasase's [2015] *Indigenous Pathways of Action and Freedom* for extended discussions of Indigenous attempts at sovereignty and self-determination.)

Other studies, such as that by Lorenzo Veracini (2010, 2011), suggest that interpretive categories developed in colonial and post-colonial studies are inadequate for appraising settler colonialism. He argues, for example, that "settler colonialism should be seen as structurally distinct from both" colonialism and migration because although "the permanent movement and reproduction of communities and the dominance of an exogenous agency over an Indigenous one are necessarily involved … not all migrants are settler migrations and not all colonialisms are settler colonial" (2010: 3). Veracini also proposes to distinguish settler colonialism from classical colonialism when he asserts that "colonisers and settler colonisers want essentially different things" (2011: 1). The colonizers attempt to make Indigenous people work for them in an economic relationship (such as the fur trade) whereas settler colonisers are more interested in removing Indigenous people from their lands so that they can use the land for agriculture or other resource extraction purposes. According to Veracini settler colonialism is a resilient process that rarely ends.

This last point is similar to Wolfe's (1998, 2006) theory that settler colonialism involves a "logic of elimination." As such, settler colonialism constitutes an ongoing structure of power that systematically erases Indigenous peoples from the land. This can be accomplished by genocide, assimilation or other means. Wolfe also suggests that settler colonialism is a system, rather than an historical event. The erasure of Indigenous peoples is a necessary precondition for settler expropriation of lands and resources; in this regard, it also provides the necessary conditions for establishing the present-day ideology of multicultural neoliberalism This is a similar point that is made by Onur Ince (2018: 4) in his studies of colonial capitalism, which focuses on the British Empire as an example of "colonial expropriation, extraction, and exploitation." Thus, Wolfe's essay link two important contemporary topics – Indigenous erasure and settler colonialism – in one systemic pattern of racial exclusion.

It is beyond the scope of this book to extend this discussion of settler colonialism; however, brief mention should be made of the following avenues of research. In *Unsettled Expectations* (2016), Eva Mackey skilfully discusses various ethnographic cases about land rights and what these local conflicts tell us about Indigenous-settler relationships. In particular, she proposes that the settler attitude of certainty should be re-examined in making the case for "settler privilege to be a doomed fantasy of entitlement." In *Unsettling the Commons* (2017), Craig Fortier conducted over 50 interviews with anti-authoritarian organizers, members of radical left movements, in an attempt to define the meaning of "the commons" within a settler colonial context. The author argues that there are multiple commons or conceptualizations of how land, relationships, and resources are shared, produced, consumed, and distributed in any given society.

In a further extension of this discussion concerning settler colonialism, Shiri Pasternak's (2017) *Grounded Authority* is a study of the Algonquins of Barriere Lake and their struggles against the colonial pressures of the Canadian state, both at the federal and provincial (Quebec) levels. She contradicts the idea that Canada has moved into a post-colonial era and that the relationships between the state and the Indigenous peoples have improved since the Algonquins have not been able to restore full governance over their lands. Pasternak concludes that "to understand settler colonialism, one must engage with Indigenous knowledge systems, and the communities within which they are embedded must be recognized and respected" (2017: 48; see also Hedican [2017b] for a review of Pasternak's study).[12]

The Racist Language of Exclusion

Few people today are likely to believe that an entirely bias-free, objective, or dispassionate writing of past historical events is possible. First, it is important to realize that all writers compose their histories from a certain position, standpoint, or perspective. These perspectives derive in large part from the culture and society in which one lives. As a person grows up, they by necessity are inculcated with the various belief systems, cultural norms, and values, modes of behaviour, and so on, which anthropologists term the "enculturation process." Enculturation can be defined as the process by which the individual learns and assimilates the patterns of a culture: the patterns by which cultural traditions are transmitted from one generation to the next (Hedican 2012a: 268). People are not born to discriminate; they learn these attitudes because of the cultural heritage that they inherit from previous generations and the peer pressure of their social contemporaries. Thus, as Feagin (2010: 4) asserts, "Systemic racism is about everyday experience. People are born, live, and die within the racist system."[13]

Language is also an important factor in discriminatory practices because it identifies individuals – based on their skin colour, cultural heritage, or religious beliefs – who are singled out for negative attitudes or other forms of social exclusion. As an example, when Governor George Simpson compared Indigenous women to chimpanzees, he was effectively relegating them to a non-human category, and thus his language was used to exclude them from the human race. It is not surprising, then, that language is one of the initial targets of those aiming to subjugate Indigenous people. As York (1990: 36) points out, "And so it was the language that was the first target of the residential schools. The school officials were determined to destroy the Indian languages, to ensure that the Indian children would be assimilated into the white culture. In many cases, they were successful." Indigenous people who attended residential schools have found that there is a communication gap in which the leaders speak an Indigenous language and their children the language of the colonial powers. The loss of language disassociates one from their Indigenous past and cultural beliefs because these are difficult to express in a non-Indigenous language. This process of forced assimilation has come to be termed the "residential-school syndrome." In sum, York (1990: 36) states that "A culture cannot survive without its language. The language is an expression of the culture – it is the backbone, the identity of the people."

In addition, individuals grow up and live their lives within the context of a certain social structure, which is to say, the ways in which groups and individuals are organized and relate to one another in terms of the various linkages between social roles in a society. In turn, the various substructures of a society include a society's predominant forms of family, religion, economy, political system, and world view. The term "worldview," as Sidky (2004: 444) explains, includes "the totality of precepts and beliefs, ritual attitudes, and religious ideas concerning the way the world is and the position of people and things in it, shared by members of a society and expressed in their myths, lore, rituals, and values."

This is not to suggest that these various aspects of a society are entirely open to investigation or that they form part of a concrete reality. Social scientists have argued for generations about whether a social system consists of an objective reality that can be studied scientifically (Hedican 1994). Basically, the two polar positions have come to be termed positivism and phenomenology. Positivism is "the doctrine that scientific knowledge pertains only to empirical experience and is built up through the generation of propositional (testable) knowledge (Sidky 2004: 435). As such, positivism is an approach to understanding the social and physical world based on a belief that reality is a concrete phenomenon discernible through observation and discoverable laws; doctrine holding that scientific knowledge is obtained through empirical experience. Phenomenology, on the other hand, is an approach to understanding reality that emphasizes sensory information and multiple points of view and therefore is at odds with the view that reality can be apprehended objectively (Hedican 2012: 276–7). In other words, from phenomenological point of view there are as many views of reality, or "truths," as there are people capable of perceiving this reality. Discussions of these polar positions permeate the academic books and journals in the social sciences, and the debates are not likely to be resolved in the near future.[14]

Another complicating factor concerns the language in which speech, conversation, and the very essence of our views of reality are expressed. For many years there was a debate among linguists, anthropologists, and other academics as to whether language was in fact a part of society or culture at all. The reason for this position is that all languages are fundamentally composed of the same parts, (phonemes and semantics, for example) and that languages seem to follow their own rules of historical processes, independent of the constructs of a particular society or culture. Leaving this argument aside, language nonetheless functions in a fundamental manner in how our reality is understood and expressed. While languages may exhibit fundamentally the same characteristics, they nonetheless differ greatly in the way reality is perceived. Take the colour spectrum for example. The colour spectrum is not really composed of individual colours, but humans' need to classify or separate various categories of phenomena led to fundamentally arbitrary systems of classification of the world around us.

In this sense, that is in terms of an arbitrary process of classification, "language is a two-edged sword: at the same time that it allows people to cut through the morass of sensation and communicate not merely gross impression but the intricacies of ideas and interpretations, it also creates disjointed pieces and characteristic unions of them that imprison the mind within a single mode of perception" (Bohannan 1963: 34). Thus, while the colour spectrum is a continuum of light waves, that part of the continuum that humans can perceive is divided up into various cultural categories that are necessary for people to communicate their perceptions. However, the ways in which people in different cultures organize their perceptions in order to communicate them to others are frequently quite different from one another.[15]

Humans also apply the same process to most other areas of their observable universe. Take the individuals that surround one in a community. Some are considered relatives, and some are not. Relatives can be divided into arbitrary categories, according to the preference in any given society. For example, at times descent through the generations is determined through the male line (patrilineal), sometimes through females (matrilineal), and sometime through both sides (bilateral or ambilineal). We divide people by nations, ethnic groups, minorities, or perceived races. There is no doubt a certain arbitrary manner or ambiguity involved. What, for example, is a "race?" Some hold fervently to the view that you can divide people up biologically into white, Black, Asian, and so on. However, from a scientific point of view, races are only a figment of people's imaginations; they do not exist in reality.

The Anthropological Response to Racist Rhetoric

The American Anthropological Associations published a statement on race, in which it attempted to arrive at a general consensus concerning this important topic in the scientific community (AAA 1999, 2014; Hedican 2016: 85–7). This statement, as indicated by the AAA's executive board, is believed to represent "generally the contemporary thinking and scholarly positions of a majority of anthropologists" (www.aaanet.org/stmts/racepp.htm). This statement emphasizes that all humankind is thought to belong to a single species, and not to various subgroups or races. A second important point is that physical variations of any given human trait, such as hair type or skin colour, tend to occur gradually over geographically areas and not abruptly. These traits also tend to vary independently of each other so that hair texture is not related to nose shape. Since physical traits are then inherited independently of each other, this makes "any attempt to establish lines of division among biological populations both arbitrary and subjective" (AAA 1999). The purpose of AAA's statement was to dispel racist attitudes that would have us believe that there are sub-groups of human beings and that could be used to discriminate certain sectors or physical groups in society.

The main conclusion offered by anthropology is that "physical variations in human species have no meaning except the social ones humans put on them." Race can therefore be regarded as a social mechanism invented during the eighteenth century that referred to the various populations, such as slaves from Africa, conquered Indigenous populations, or European settlers, brought together during the colonial era. What emerged, according to the AAA statement, was a classification system based on a "growing ideology of inequality," which was devised as a mechanism used to rationalize European attitudes and treatment of the enslaved or conquered peoples. For many years this ideology was used as a justification for the retention of slavery and aided in the construction of a rigid hierarchy of social and economic exclusiveness. Such a hierarchy, in turn, was used to justify the disentitlement of subjugated peoples for the economic, social, and political benefit of the dominant majority (Hedican 2016: 85).

The main point that could be made here is that dominant groups profit from the subjugation of minority groups. This is accomplished by keeping the minority groups different, by using language in oppressive ways, and ultimately by discouraging any attempts at assimilation into the dominant society. The language of oppression is an important mechanism that keeps minority groups different and in a subjugated state. Think of these very oppressive and offensive tropes that are used in the English language: "nigger," "wop," "spic," "wagon-burner," or "Paki," all of which are intended to demean and subjugate Indigenous people, people of colour, or the people in other minority groups such as Irish Catholics or Italians.

Harrison (1995: 65) explains that one of the sources of racism towards Indigenous people concerns the "colonial anxieties" felt by their oppressors. As she concludes, "Racism must be understood to be a nexus of material relations within which social and discursive practices perpetuate oppressive power relations between populations presumed to be essentially different." Material cultural artefacts collected by missionaries and government officials in the Victorian era were exhibited in Britain as part of colonial exhibitions. These exhibitions served to construct cultural difference, and the objects on display were used as an index symbolizing racial difference. For example, in one exhibition Red River hoods made by Indigenous women were tagged "Headdress worn by Squaws" (Peers 2016: 123). In this context, "Collecting is a form of conquest and collected artifacts are material signs of victory over their former owners" (Classen and Howes 2006: 209). Thus, in this regard, we can understand Pel's (1997: 164) third view of colonialism, "as a struggle that constantly renegotiates the balance of domination and resistance."[16]

Eurocentric Attitudes as Vehicles of Oppression

As was noted in the previous chapter, many Indigenous people point to the Eurocentric attitudes of those in the dominant society as a major source of the oppression that occurs in colonial relationships in Canada. Similarly, Schwarz, in her study entitled *Fighting Colonialism* (2013), argues that popular images of Indigenous people are an important aspect of the colonial process because these images portray and promote negative stereotypes of Native North Americans. As Schwarz (2013: 1) suggests, "images meant to depict Native Americans have traditionally stood as signs or fetishes for such contradictory concepts as primitiveness, nature, spirituality, unbridled sexuality, violence, nobility, or heathenness, depending on the particular time and agenda of the presenters and the code or codes understood by the various audiences." Her central thesis is that control over the way Native Americans are characterized and defined is a salient aspect of power that colonial powers wield to control Indigenous individuals and communities.

The use of negative stereotypes can also be understood to play a significant role in the colonial process because these stereotypes serve to justify the paternalistic attitudes that have historically informed and articulated the interaction between Indigenous peoples and Euro-Americans. One might conclude, then, that portrayals of Aboriginal peoples in the wider society have historically allowed for the exercise of symbolic power over the oppressed members of society. In this light, Susan Hegeman suggests that "most of the pervasive stereotypes of Indians (as savages, noble or otherwise; as 'vanishing' relics of a past era; as sidekicks and squaws, and so on) … present Indians as distinctly different from, and distinctly like what Euromericans see, or wish themselves, to be" (1989a: 145). However, Indigenous people have been known to push back at such negative stereotypes of themselves. For

Image 7. Moose Factory Post, 1854. The post is located on Moose Factory Island near the mouth of the Moose River at the southern end of James Bay. It was the second Hudson's Bay Company post to be established (1673) in North America after Fort Rupert.
Source: Public domain. Moose Factory, 1854, William Ford and West, lithographers.

example, Indigenous authors Bonita Lawrence and Enakshi Dua have employed the term "decolonizing colonialism" in an attempt to "challenge the ongoing colonization of Aboriginal peoples" (Lawrence and Dua 2011: 20). From their perspective Canada, for example, should be regarded as a colonist state, or as they term it, a "settler society." "Settler states," in their view, "are founded on, and maintained through, policies of direct extermination, displacement, and assimilation" (2011: 20).

Thus, from an Indigenous point of view, the people of First Nations ancestry are apt to view the history of North America quite differently than the one presented in textbooks written by members of the colonial society and taught in the school rooms of North America. Unfortunately, as far as the role of the history of the fur trade is concerned, the British and later Canadian historians have largely ignored any pretences to an Indigenous perspective, preferring instead to promulgate visions of heroic adventure and honourable companies of businessmen and so forth, which are ultimately forged into a false narrative of North American colonial history. In North America there is a long history of using such language to subjugate Indigenous populations (Hedican 2013: 165–9; 207–12).

Writing about Indigenous History

In Canada there was a period in the 1970s when studies of the fur trade and First Nations were prominent, of which Charles Bishop's *The Northern Ojibwa and the Fur Trade* (1974), and Arthur Ray's *Indians and the Fur Trade* (1974) were among some of the most noteworthy studies. Based on the archives of the Hudson's Bay Company, these studies primarily focused on economic interactions between Indigenous people of northern Canada and British merchants. Later, by 1780, the Hudson's Bay Company was forced to establish interior posts because of increased competition emanating from the south.

This led to an increased concern with demographic change among the First Nations and a lively debate ensued in the literature during the 1980s concerning the extent to which trapping territories were an Indigenous institution (see Bishop and Morantz 1986). Another notable contribution concerned the studies by Bruce Trigger (*Natives and Newcomers*, 1985, and *The Children of Aataentsic*, 1987) of the Wendat (Huron), based on the 73 volumes of the *Jesuit Relations*, which were compiled between about 1710 and 1750 (Thwaites 1896–1901). In Trigger's case the *Jesuit Relations* documented the attempts of Jesuit missionaries to convert the Wendat to Christianity and the consequent antagonisms between the two parties. In both cases, whether using the accounts of fur traders or that of Christian missionaries, attempts to document the lifeways of Indigenous peoples were fraught with problems of interpretation. Probably the biggest issue is that "Aboriginal people's views of their own history rarely appear in academic journals" (Cruikshank 1994: 403), suggesting that academic researchers, or ethnohistorians, are only interested in the portrayal of Indigenous people as they appear in the accounts of European fur traders, missionaries, explorers, or other travellers.

In turn, the problem of cultural representation is hampered by the obvious difficulty of cultural translation, filtered first through the frequently ethnocentric accounts of the Europeans, and then delving into the relatively obscure social and cultural habits of an Indigenous population taken many centuries from today. In fact, Trigger (1986: 67), commenting in an essay on cultural relativism, explained that "I found that trying to understand the mentality of seventeenth-century Jesuit missionaries required almost as great an act of anthropological imagination as did understanding the perceptions of the Hurons of that period."

These studies of the fur trade and its involvement with Canada's Indigenous populations are grounded in a relatively long history of anthropological interest in processes of cultural change. Since every society is the result of the historical processes by which it is created, anthropologists by necessity have also had a keen interest in history, almost from the beginning of the discipline. For example, Franz Boas (1858–1942), one of the founders of modern cultural anthropology is associated with the concept of "historical particularism." This is a theoretical perspective that stresses the uniqueness of each individual culture and the historical developments that have led to its cultural characteristics (Hedican 2012a: 70–5). Attempts to combine the disciplines of history and social or cultural anthropology have long been a recurrent theme in anthropology's history. In fact, the relationship between history and anthropology has not only been a matter of intellectual interest, but the subject of a good deal of controversy as well, for at least the last century. F.W. Maitland wrote in 1899, for example, that "Anthropology must choose between being history and being nothing" (in Mair 1965: 36). In this case Maitland was primarily concerned with an evolutionary perspective concerning the supposed stages in human society, from a primitive state to civilization.

Alfred Kroeber was another influential American anthropologist from the first half of the twentieth century, who also understood anthropology as a historical discipline (1935, 1952.) He suggested that to understand human behaviour it was important for one to know the temporal and special contexts in which such behaviour took place. His view contrasted with what could be a more scientific perspective in which human behaviour is construed as a pattern of causal connections. Kroeber (1952: 5) described his historical perspective in the following manner: "The essential quality of the historical approach as a method of science I see as its integration of phenomena into an ever-widening phenomenal context ... The context includes the placing in space and time and therefore, when knowledge allows, in sequence."

Thus, Kroeber insisted that anthropology's subject matter was predicated upon a historical approach. As he explains concerning the historical growth of more general cultural patterns, eventually all these patterns tend "to develop and progress, later to degenerate and die" (1963: 41). Yet, as Sidky (2004: 39) concludes: "The version of Historical Particularism expounded by Kroeber retained the idealist (culture as mental rules) anti-science, no-laws-and-causality-in-culture, interpretive, and particularistic thrust of the Boasian program."

George Stocking (1968, 1985) was another American anthropologist who promoted a research agenda employing historical and archival sources and methods. His view of the use of a historical perspective in anthropology appears similar to that expressed by Kroeber in that Stocking refers to "an understanding of context and of change in time" as essential in comprehending cultural phenomena (1968: 109). However, Stocking also promoted the goals of "historicism" by which he meant a "commitment to the understanding of the past for its own sake (ibid., 4). Historicism is contrasted with the idea of "presentism," which Stocking (ibid., 108) explains as follows: "When the governing interpretive context is rather that of the *present-day* theoretical polemic, historical misinterpretation is the all too frequent result." Misinterpretation, Stocking suggests, results from removing things from their historical context, and then judging them apart from this context, which is to say, "organizing the historical study by a system of direct reference to the present" (ibid., 103).

In Britain, Evans-Pritchard (1961, 1981) was largely responsible for bringing historical perspectives into the field of social anthropology. He boldly declared that anthropology and history shared many common aims and methods despite some of the apparent differences between the two disciplines in their own perspectives and methodological techniques. He also reaffirmed Maitland's century-old assertion about the necessity of anthropology choosing between history and nothing (1961: 20).

Shortly after, Lucy Mair, another British social anthropologist, was led to ask the question, presumably based on Evans-Pritchard's foundational work, "What is anthropology if it is not history?" She notes furthermore that while "Much has been written about the relation of history to anthropology ... contrasts and comparisons between the two studies have implied very different arguments at different times" (1965: 35). The uses of history to anthropology can also mean many different things, such as what anthropologists can find out about the past of the peoples that they study, or about what anthropologists can learn from the writings of historians concerning social institutions that are now beyond contemporary, first-hand study. There is also the issue, as Mair notes (ibid., 36), about whether the methodologies of historical research are amenable or appropriate for studying societies that interest anthropologists for which no written records exist.

History and Anthropology: Are They Compatible?

The journal *History and Anthropology* has now been published for over thirty years, but in the initial issue of 1984 the editors felt the need to lay some groundwork in terms of the journal's scope and their views about the relationship between the two disciplines. The editors do specify that the aim of the journal is not to explore the conditions that would help to bring the two disciplines together, or to retrace the historiography of a long debate that was caused by a mutual lack of understanding. Rather, the editors point out, the journal will explore

> two interesting movements [that] have developed within these two disciplines: an anthropologization of history, and, more recently, a historicization of anthropology.... Studied more closely, from the perspective of sociology of knowledge, these movements are complex and far from uniform. Each has its own chronology, and indeed, its own genealogy, according to disciplinary, institutional, and national traditions ... This journal would like to be *one* proposed answer, not to the question "must we?" but *"how* can we?" work together. Primarily, by allowing anthropologists and historians to come together on a project and pursue what then becomes common research, by confronting their material, and crossing their questionnaires, before publishing together the results of their inquiry. (*History and Anthropology*, editorial comment 1984: i)

A lengthy introductory essay by Silverman and Gulliver (1992: 3–72), in *Approaching the Past: Historical Anthropology through Irish Case Studies*, is particularly instructive in illustrating the possible commonalities of purpose between anthropology and history. For example, an important distinction is made between "historical ethnography" and an "anthropology of history," which serves to clarify part of the subject matter involved. A historical ethnography, for example, "provides a description and analysis of a past era of the people of some particular, identifiable locality, using archival sources and, if relevant, local oral history sources ... It was this kind of ethnography that at last brought anthropologists away from long-established, clumsy devices and assumptions, such as the ethnographic present, autarchic 'communities,' and stable 'tradition'" (ibid., 16). In other words, this perspective focuses on how the past leads to and functions to create the present, which would include both synchronic and diachronic studies of a past time.

An important point in the relationship between anthropology and history, as Charles Tilley (1978: 213) observes, is that "the discipline of anthropology is far broader than ethnography," which points to a common misconception of anthropology among those in other disciplines, which sees it as relatively confined, in an intellectual sense, to problems of local interest only, or with those of our "primitive contemporaries." The idea of a closer relationship between anthropology and history, then, can be grounded in an objection of an epistemological nature.

The objection of a closer working relationship with anthropologists by, say, historians, might be questioned on grounds concerning the appropriateness of a focus on the European past that uses "theories, models, and methods which were developed by anthropologists in order to understand and interpret the non-European worlds" (Cohen 1987: 66). Of course, there are anthropologists who might perhaps dispute this characterization, especially as they have attempted to study European history using methods and theoretical approaches of a more recent and innovative nature, but certainly not grounded in an ethnographic methodology as parochial as some scholars outside the discipline might mistakenly perceive it (see, for example, Wolf 1982, 1990).[17]

Is Anthropology a "Type" of History?

It should also be added, though, that anthropology has evolved its own perspectives on viewing the past, because of long-standing ferment in the discipline, and not as just another type of history. From the historian's perspective the difference between history and anthropology is relatively clear; there exists a fundamental difference between what has been termed "narrative history and a history that uses social concepts around which to frame a study," as Silverman and Gulliver (1992: 52) suggest. Another aspect of research might as well include what could be termed the "anthropology of history," defined as a concern with recording and describing an insider's point of view, including their perceptions and assumptions of their own socio-cultural system in their terms (Silverman and Gulliver 1992: 19–21). The goal here is not to provide an analysis of history in an objective sense, which is to say, history external to the insider's perspective. The interest, rather, is in what people know about their place in life, and what they remember about their past, as they can interpret or make sense of the interrelationships that connect the past to the present.

A reasonable conclusion that could be drawn from the foregoing discussion of history and anthropology – whose literature extends for well over a century of debate and various forms of dialogue – is that both disciplines are identifiable in their own right by separate methodologies and epistemologies. Overall, it would not be accurate to characterize anthropology as another form of history, nor would the obverse of this be true as well. Instead, one could more accurately suggest that both disciplines share a conceptual territory, commonly referred to as the past, although this terrain is viewed from different lenses.

As far as the subject matter of this book is concerned, it is important to indicate that an incident such as the Hannah Bay murders of 1832 is not just a matter of esoteric historical interest but can be viewed from different cultural perspectives. The Europeans who worked for the Hudson's Bay Company had their views, which they documented in their various reports and post journals. The Cree also had their own perspective on the event, which was passed down through the generations in their form of oral history. As an anthropologist who adheres to the concept of cultural relativism (i.e., a perspective stressing the uniqueness and individual characteristics of different cultures), I am predisposed to see the European and Cree perspectives on the events at Hannah Bay as both "correct" in their own terms, and that there is not necessarily any one version of the event that is inherently any more "truthful" than another – it all depends on one's perspective. Of course, this idea that one can entertain multiple versions of the truth at the same time runs counter to the idea that there is only one version of "reality."

For the most part our understanding of historical reality has relied for far too long solely on European interpretations of the past. It is for this reason – that Indigenous interpretations of the past have been largely discounted as whimsical fabrications – that "increasingly, Indigenous peoples are demanding that their oral traditions be taken seriously as legitimate perspectives on history. The issue, for them," Cruikshank (1994: 403) asserts, "centres on who controls the images and the representations of their lives portrayed to the larger world." The suggestion, then, is that Indigenous people are beginning to demand that their words be given credibility in their own right and not filtered through foreign interpreters of the past, such as legal experts, anthropologists, missionaries, or historians.

Negative Stereotypes of Indigenous People

When the governor of the Hudson's Bay Company, Sir George Simpson, referred to the Cree and other Indigenous people in the James Bay area as "child-like," or suggested that Indigenous women look like chimpanzees, he was contributing to an ongoing history of negatively stereotyping Indigenous people. When a person is considered "child-like" the implication is that they are not capable of acting as mature adults, with the further implication that they would by necessity have to depend on their "white fathers" (another unfortunate trope) for the necessities of life. Hidden in all this dialogue is the stark reality that the Cree and other Indigenous people in northern Canada have successfully lived in this area for thousands of years, and that, furthermore, their experiences during the fur trade era of food deprivation and the demoralization of the liquor trade were primarily the result of Britain's colonial policies of subjugation and paternalism.

And so we pose the question again: Where does racism begin? In reality, the origins of racism and negative stereotyping is less important than the fact that it continues today and has had a very long history in North America. The origins of racism are multi-faceted but can be understood in the context of settler colonial attitudes towards Indigenous people, and as a rationalization for the dispossession of Indigenous lands. The Hudson's Bay Company, for example, as an arm of British imperialism, took control of the Crees' traditional territory in northern Canada on the premise that this was unoccupied territory, or *terra nullius*. This rationalization was, of course, entirely self-serving and completely disregarded the obvious presence of Indigenous people in the area. Otherwise, if there were no trappers occupying this territory, how could the fur trade even begin?

There are many myths about Native Americans that stem from people's acceptance of stereotypical depictions derived from the news media, Hollywood movies, and television shows. Many white North Americans have probably never met or even talked to a Native American in person, so they lack first-hand knowledge on which to base their opinions. This lack of information leaves white Americans susceptible to believing in all sorts of faulty information that is just not factual. For this reason, Fleming 2006: 213) suggests, "Stereotyping is a poor substitute for getting to know individuals at a more intimate, meaningful level. By relying on stereotypes to describe Native Americans, whites come to believe that Indians are drunks, get free money from the government, and are made wealthy from casino revenue. Or [on the other hand] they may believe that Indians are one with nature, deeply religious, and wise in the ways of spirituality." Either way, a belief in stereotypes, whether positive or negative, is a poor basis on which to base one's attitudes towards other people.

Hollywood Stereotypes

For over a century North Americans have viewed various Hollywood movies that have served to shape the public's perceptions of Indigenous people, such as the Indian princess (Pocahontas), the loyal sidekick (Tonto), or the wise elder (Little Big Man). While there have been more recent exceptions, such as Canadian Dan George, for many decades Indigenous people were portrayed by members of the white-settler population in red face. The list of white people playing "noble savages" is quite lengthy, such as Burt Lancaster, Anthony Quinn, and Elvis Presley for example, usually in exaggerated feathered headdresses, war paint and other stereotypes based on Hollywood's interpretation of Plain Indians. In fact, even by the 1920s Indigenous people began a protest movement against the use of these white actors in Western films. The War Paint Club, founded in the early 1920s was organized in Los Angeles with the sole objective of protecting Indigenous people's employment in the film industry. It is difficult, however, to ascertain if the members of this club saw such employment as an economic or a cultural issue (see La Potin 1987: 164; Hedican 1988: 384–5).

John Ford's iconic 1939 western, *Stagecoach*, starring a host of well-known movie stars such as John Wayne, Andy Devine, and others, was deemed in 1995 to be "culturally significant" and as such the Library of Congress placed it for preservation in the National Film Registry, a sort of cinematic hall of fame. Others are not so generous in their appraisals, as many see this portrayal of the Apache, specifically, and Indigenous people in general, as blood-thirsty savages, as "wagon burners," or as another obstacle that white people have to overcome in their quest for civilized society. Anishinaabe film critic Jesse Wente called *Stagecoach* "the most damaging movie for native people in history" (October 24, 2017). In addition, in a *Washington Post* article (November 22, 2017), Kevin Gover, who is a member of the Pawnee First Nation of Oklahoma and director of the Smithsonian's National Museum of the American Indian, comments that "movies and television perpetuated old stereotypes or created new ones – particularly ones that cast Indigenous people as obstacles to, rather than actors in, the creating of the modern world."

In other words, television shows and Hollywood movies have a tendency to condition North American viewers to conceptualize Indigenous American people as relics of the past who are no longer relevant participants in today's world. This perception feeds into another myth about Native Americans, that they are a "dying race," or what used to be called "the vanishing Red Men," when in fact census material in both Canada and the United States clearly shows that Indigenous people in both countries are increasing in numbers, in some cases well beyond that of their Euro-American counterparts. In Canada, for example, from 2006 to 2011 the First Nations population increased by 23 per cent (Canada, 2012).

From the 1970s onwards, there was a more (apparently) sympathetic portrayal of Indigenous people, and attempts were made to cast Indigenous people wearing authentic costumes and speaking their languages. Chief Dan George turned in an Oscar-nominated performance in *Little Big Man* and brought some humour to the big screen with his role as an old Cherokee in Clint Eastwood's *The Outlaw Jose Wales*. In the 1990s *Dances with Wolves* included an Oscar-nominated performance by Graham Green (Six Nations Oneida) for his role of Kicking Bird. The film, though, had its critics, such as Russell Means's complaint about the depiction of his Lakota people – the only armed force to defeat the US military on US soil – and the charge that this is really only a film "about a white guy." And then there was the obvious step backwards with Johnny Depp's portrayal of Tonto in the *Lone Ranger* remake. Depp's portrayal of Tonto is an excellent example of what Rayna Green (1988: 30–55) has called the "Tribe called Wannabee," or "playing Indian" by Euro-Americans (see also Deloria 1998: 189–90).[18]

Ward Churchill, well-known Native American activist and author of the controversial *Pacifism as Pathology* (2007) who was at one time fired, then reinstated, by the University of Colorado for his political views, argues that the myths and stereotypes built up around Native American were no accident. He maintains that they served to explain in positive terms the decimation of Native tribes and their ways of life by "advanced" cultures in the name of progress, thereby making it necessary to erase the achievements and very humanity of conquered peoples. "Dehumanization, obliteration or appropriation of identity, political subordination, and material colonization are all elements of a common process of imperialism," Churchill says. "The meaning of Hollywood's stereotyping of American Indian can be truly comprehended only against this backdrop" (in *Media Smarts: Common Portrayals of Aboriginal People*, accessed April 15, 2020; see also Bataille and Silet 1981; Berkhofer 1978; Churchill 2001; O'Connor 2003; and Singer 2001).

As these cultural stereotypes, both positive and negative, begin to become promoted and established in movies and other media, such as television, radio, and the internet, they also in time could become seen as truthful narratives and in the process become more firmly embedded into the group consciousness. It is also possible that Indigenous people themselves begin to believe in these tropes, in these figurative or metaphorical expressions that colonial settlers use as a storytelling device in their attempts to convey Indigenous people in any number of ways, such as HBC Governor George Simpson's description of Indigenous people as "child-like" or their cultures as "repugnant." Such characterizations can be seen by some Indigenous peoples as containing a certain truth value, and so they may become ashamed of their Indigenous language, people, or cultural traits.

In a similar vein, Maureen Schwartz (2013: 2) contends that the "colonized classically begin to believe the stereotypes promulgated by the colonizers." Furthermore, as Gramsci points out, "when ensconced within a full range of institutionalized and governmental structures and activities," such a representational regime often results in a marked "sense of fatalism and passivity" on the part of the oppressed that come to accept their own exploitation. In addition to noting the oppressive effect hegemonic culture can render, Gramsci articulates that hegemony has little meaning unless paired with the notion of domination, which in the case of Native Americans takes form in governmental policies and practices. This reveals the integral relationship between hegemonic culture and force (as in Boggs 1976: 39–40). However, "contemporary American Indians demonstrate power and agency through the production and consumption of these age-old images to battle colonialism at home" (Schwartz 2013: 12). The sorts of "age-old images" that she is referring to include such metaphorical symbols as the Indian Princess (Pocahontas), Mother Earth, and the Ecological Indian.

"Indian Princess" Imagery

The Pocahontas story, which President Trump often made reference to in his campaign rallies concerning Democratic rival Elizabeth Warren, is probably just a popular myth and has no basis in known facts. Certainly, his use of the Pocahontas imagery is said in a demeaning manner, to subjugate the position of Indigenous women in society, and as a divisive tool against his female political opponent.[19] "The imagery is so ingrained in the North American consciousness, " Anderson suggests, "that even Native people have, in dark times, internalized these beliefs about their grandmothers, their aunties, their daughters, and themselves" (2000: 99). Native American women are also frequently sexually objectified and are often portrayed in a stereotypical manner as being promiscuous. Such misconceptions lead to murder, rape, and violence against Native American women and girls by non-Native men. In *Killing the Indian Maiden*, Marubbio explains that Native Americans, when seen at all, are still viewed as one-dimensional forms: "They are America's racial Other and alter ego, rejected to justify the violent treatment of them as part of progress and civilization, yet also desired for the freedom, land, and innocent state they represent" (2006: 4; see also Marubbio and Buffalohead 2018).

In her article "The Pocahontas Perplex," Cherokee scholar Rayna Green describes the manner in which Europeans first portrayed an image of Native women, which mirrored western attitudes towards the earth: "Draped in leaves, feathers, and animal skins, as well as in heavy jewelry, she appeared aggressive, militant, and armed with spears and arrows ... She was the familiar mother-goddess figure – full-bodied, powerful, nurturing, but dangerous – embodying the wealth and danger of the New World" (1984: 19, see also Green 1992).

As the white settlers became more familiar with the land, the Native American queen imagery was reduced. She became less powerful, more like a sexualized girl, and the "Indian Princess" imagery became more prevalent such that she could then be "used for the colonizer's pleasure and profit" (Cook-Lynn 1996: 145). The American movie industry attempted to capitalize on the archetypical Native girl in a voluptuous yet innocent looking image. Thus, some of America's most revered institutions have demonstrated that they are capable of racist tendencies. As an example, consider Walt Disney's production of *Pocahontas* (1995). This film appears to honour or pay tribute to Indigenous women; however, it does little more than exploit them for commercial gain. The heroine absurdly sings with forest animals, evidencing a far too common "one-with-nature" trope, and wears provocative costumes that Pocahontas would never have worn in real life. As for the fate of Pocahontas's people, within twenty years after the period depicted in the movie, the Powhatan Confederacy was practically exterminated at the hands of the surrounding colonists (see Mihesuah 2009: 14). Then there is another Disney favourite, *Peter Pan*, the beloved children's classic, with its descriptions of "redskins" carrying "tomahawks and knives," their naked bodies glistening with oil "strung around them are scalps, of boys as well as pirates" (McLaurin 2019: 2). These are powerful images that impress the minds of growing children that are probably not forgotten in adulthood.

As Emma LaRocque (1997: 75–96) indicates, Disney's *Pocahontas* combines many of the typical stereotypes of Indigenous people – part noble savage, part princess, part loose squaw. It would have been possible to portray Pocahontas as a strong Native leader, but instead her character becomes a sort of sleazy, promiscuous urchin who is "easy, available, and willing" (Kidwell 1992: 97–107, see also Kidwell 1978). Thus, the "good" Native woman who is willing to make herself available to the white male settler is elevated to "princess status" (Green 1984: 20). In a similar vein, Carol Sparks has traced this squaw-to-princess transition in accounts of the Navajo. In the nineteenth century the princess image of Native women was found in the adventurous accounts of explorer's records, but this image eventually was downgraded. In this new personification of the diminished princess imagery, "Not only could the squaw be pitied, but her very existence justified American intrusion into her land and society" (Sparks 1995: 135).

In a similar manner Sarah Carter (1997) demonstrates how both the Canadian state and the national press deliberately promoted "dirty squaw" imagery in the later 1800s; such images seemed to justify the repressive measures used against Indigenous people at the time. She noted for example that "One inspector of the [reserve] agencies noted in 1891 that the women did not have soap, towels, wash basins, or wash pails, nor did they have any means of acquiring them. Similarly, it was frequently noted that the women were short of basic clothing and had no textiles or yarn to work with. Yet in official public statements, the tendency was to ascribe blame to the women rather than drawing attention to conditions that would injure the reputation of government administration" (Carter 1997: 162).

Similar rationales were used to depict Native women as poor parents, a justification that was then used to remove their children from their homes and place them in residential schools or foster homes.

The sorts of negative images of Indigenous women became ingrained in the Canadian consciousness. Janice Acoose described how these negative images affected her own feelings of self-worth when she was attending school: "I shamefully turned away from my history and cultural roots, becoming, to a certain extent, what was encouraged by the ideological collusiveness of textbooks, and the ignorant comments and peer pressure from non-Indigenous students" (1995: 29).

Aboriginal author Kim Anderson sums up the effects of racial stereotypes on Indigenous people, especially women, "who fostered destructive and hateful attitudes towards themselves. This self-hatred is rooted in internalized racism that comes from the negative self-concepts of racist stereotypes, internalized racism spreads like a disease through Native communities. This results in self-destructive behaviours, including addictions and involvement in violent relationships" (2000:106). When one internalizes a negative stereotype of oneself the consequences can be destructive to the individual and the community relationships, which are the very fabric of Indigenous society. (See the results of the 2019 final report of Canada's national enquiry into the missing and murdered Indigenous women and girls, http://www.mmiwg-ffada.ca/ accessed August 30, 2020). [20]

The Ecological Indian

The image of the "Ecological Indian," which conveys the metaphor of the "one-with-nature" symbolism, is particularly problematic because any people today – European and Indigenous – view such topics as environmental degradation and climate change as serious matters to be concerned about. Shepard Krech (1999, 2005, 2010) has written extensively about the Ecological Indian imagery and in the process has become engaged in a controversial imbroglio. As Krech (2010) explains, "The image of North American Indians as first ecologists, conversationalists, and environmentalists, which can be called the Ecological Indian, became dominant in the 1960s. Today, many, including American

Indians, accept it as an accurate representation of Indian behavior through time."

In fact, a conference was organized in 2002 that was composed of both Indigenous people and academics that had the overt purpose of examining this Ecological Indian imagery. This conference, known as "Re-figuring the Ecological Indian," was organized by the University of Wyoming's American Heritage Center [21]. Shepard Krech, the scholar deemed to have initiated the stereotypical controversy, was invited to give the keynote address and to explain his particular views on the subject. The organizers admitted that the conference "invited controversy," and fully expected that Krech's imagery would be "assailed as a problematic political tract." Their angst was described as follows: "We were, to put it mildly, unprepared for the reaction. And fortified by that particular variety of naïveté (cluelessness?) reserved for academics, we resolved to ride out (ignore?) the gathering storm" (Harkin and Lewis 2007: xii). Perhaps a change in political climate had occurred, or that modern concerns for the environmental damage caused by modern industrial society has made people more aware of ongoing ecological deterioration of the planet, but whatever the cause, attendants at the conference, even the Indigenous people themselves, appeared at ease with the idea that Native societies were more respectful of Mother Earth than are today's (non-Native) inhabitants.

As the organizers of the conference admitted, the controversy surrounding the "Ecological Indian" had become a multi-faceted one, with the attendant "fears that challenging the 'trope' of the ecological Indian somehow undermines Native self-image, the reality of Indian cultural distinctiveness, notions of sustainability versus the consequences of modern technological society, or just deeply held ideas about Indians and the environment" (ibid., xiii). In other words, the organizers were fearful that any criticism of the ecological Indian imagery would consequently imply that Indigenous people were not respectful of the environment, or worse, that they were just another exploiter of this planet's resources.

As one would probably expect, the academics who were invited to deliver papers on their areas of expertise relating to the conference's main theme, and who probably had their papers prepared well in advance of the gathering, proved to be taken aback by the controversy, which was reflected in their deliberations. Even so, there appeared to be some agreement with Paul Nadasdy's (1999, 2005) position that environmentalism is a complex and at times contradictory continuum, which is to say, that environmentalism is in most ways more problematic than the ecological practices of Indigenous peoples. Furthermore, an important aspect of this "problematic" situation is that images of Indigenous people are organized around more than a few foci, such as "vanishing," "violent," and "wise" (Berkhofer 1979; Smith 2000). In turn, overriding these characteristics is the more prominent notion that the Indigenous people live (or lived?) in harmony with nature. If this 'trope' of equating Indigenous people with nature is pushed further, the consequences could be that Aboriginal people are, on the one hand, denied their own histories, while on the other hand, even deprived of their place in the modern world (Lewis 1995; Warren 2002).

As far as academic support for one viewpoint or another is concerned, there is the Aboriginal overkill hypothesis, or the Pleistocene extinctions version promoted by Paul Martin (1967). On the other extreme is Vine Deloria's "vehement response" to Krech's ideas that tended to contradict the central thesis of Deloria's *Red Earth, White Lies* (1995), which promoted the idea that Native people developed a scientific position that was superior to that of Western science. As such, the Aboriginal overkill hypothesis is deemed to be just another "white lie."

A more middle ground stance between these two polar positions was presented at the conference by McMaster University's Harvey Feit. Feit, an anthropologist, has conducted long term fieldwork among the Cree of the James Bay region of northern Quebec (2005a, 2005b). His position in the ecological Indian controversy is based on historical documents, personal observation, and Native testimony, rather than on various emotional responses and stereotypical opinions. Feit's (2007: 60–3) main conclusion is that Native hunting and trapping practices in northern Quebec were less environmentally destructive to beaver populations than the "conservation techniques" that were recommended by European fur traders of the Hudson's Bay Company, who did not have the Cree's' experience with beaver populations.

It is a documented fact that northern Algonquians, with an apparent view to the future health of their livelihood, actually attempted certain conservation methods so that they did not deplete the beaver populations by over-trapping. One of these methods was the use of "hunting territories" (Bishop 1970; Leacock 1954; Morantz 1978, 1986; Rogers 1963b). The advantages of this plan, as Feit explains, was that "having a recognized claim to use the same land year after year would allow hunters who left some beaver to reproduce to be more assured that the beavers would not be killed by other trappers in their absence" (2007: 63). In fact, there are reports of hunting territories among Algonquians to the east of James Bay going back to the 1740s (Francis and Morantz 1983: 110–12). In other words, the use of hunting territories by northern Algonquians were instituted decades before any conservation attempts

by the HBC were initiated in the 1820s. As evidence for the early institution of hunting territories, there is this clearly worded commentary
on the subject by post master Thomas Mitchell, which was recorded in
1745 in the Eastman post journal:

> Every Indian hath a River or Part where ya Resorts to ye winter Season &
> in Som are More fish yn others. But ya Count it a Trespass ti kil anything
> in one anothers Leiberty for Last winter one of our Indians did not kill one
> Martin & I asked him ye Rason. He sade another Indian Tould him all ye
> martains Be Longd to him so he sade he lived on dear and Som Rabbits.
> (B.59/a/12:17d; Francis and Morantz 1983: 96)

Feit furthermore reports that George Simpson attempted various
conservation methods after the merger of 1821 with the Northwest
Company, which was a period when the HBC had a virtual monopoly
on the fur trade, except for various rogue "free traders" roaming the
wilderness. For example, Simpson tried to restrict the use of steel traps
or restricting the number of beaver pelts purchased from the Cree (Feit
2005b; Ray 1975b); however, his attempts had little overall effects at
improving beaver populations. As Feit explains, fur traders

> did not reduce their purchases of beaver pelts in areas when there were
> still competing traders for fear that if the HBC bought fewer pelts, trappers
> would simply sell more pelts to those competitors (2007: 60). [Similarly,]
> the new regulations presented certain difficulties for the Indians ... Many
> inland Indians trading at the [James Bay] coast had hunting territories in-
> terwoven with the territories of people who traded at inland posts where
> restrictions were not in force. When the former left a section of their land
> for two or three years to repopulate with beaver, the latter sometimes tres-
> passed on the land and trapped it out. (Francis and Morantz 1983: 130–1;
> B.186/b/43: 14)

Therefore, it is apparent that Governor Simpson's beaver conservation strategy was not particularly thought out, that it was impracticable
to implement, was largely unsuccessful, and was probably intended
more as an act of appeasement to the company shareholders in London, who were hoping for some constructive action to prevent the further decline in profits than they were in taking any effective steps that
would curtail the decline of the beaver. The fact is that if there were
some instances where conservation measures were successfully im-
plemented these were not enough to prevent the decline in company's
profit margins. In other words, the will to forgo short-term losses was

insufficient to prevent the greater propensity to place company profits and gain ahead of the longer-term health of the fur trade industry, which is what one would, of course, expect in the context of Britain's colonial capitalist economic approach.

The Hudson's Bay Company shareholders, ensconced as they were in their comfortable mansions in London, could hardly be expected to harbour any empathetic feelings for the Cree trappers of James Bay who, in light of severe food shortages in their wilderness tents, were struggling just to stay alive. As the beaver population declined, so did their hopes that their prospects would improve. The Indigenous trappers were in a double bind: if they increased trapping beaver this would only hasten their desperate plight; alternatively, if they attempted to practise the conservation methods advised by the Hudson's Bay Company, other similarly distressed people would likely take advantage of the situation and move into their territory. All in all, as Feit contends, Hudson's' Bay Company "policies were destructive and wasteful of beavers and other fur bearers, and they dramatically reduced their numbers" (2007: 60).

Violent Savage Imagery

Those who were alive during the decades between 1950 and 1970 would probably be well aware of the huge popularity of Western movies and television shows. Almost every night after supper families were bonded to their television sets watching *The Rifleman, Bonanza, Gunsmoke,* or *Have Gun Will Travel,* among a host of other screen adventures. One of the most popular of these shows was *Wagon Train* (1957–65), which for a while held the number one spot in the Neilson ratings. The show usually began with the wagon train leader, played by Ward Bond, bellowing out his iconic "Wagons Ho!" Even in my own family, when we were starting out on a journey, someone would inevitably shout the familiar "Wagons Ho." To liven up the production and stimulate fan interest, various well-known stars made their arrival, such as Ronald Reagan in one of his last screen appearances (see also Daniel Francis 1993 for Canadian examples).

So, off went the long, snake-like wagon train, set in the post-Civil War period, travelling on its weekly jaunt, traversing a vast and forbidding territory from Missouri to California, populated by hostile tribes of Sioux Indians. Before long the awaited attack would begin: the wagons would form a prescribed defensive circle, and the raging savages, looking horrific in their painted faces (often played by Italians or dark-faced eastern Europeans), began the expected assault. The white male settlers sought refuge behind wagon wheels, taking pot shots at the encircling warriors, while their women folk and children huddled together in the

Image 8. This poster depicts cowboys rounding up cattle and shows a portrait of Col. W.F. Cody on horseback, c. 1899. The Wild West shows were travelling performances given in the United States and Europe around 1870–1920, often portraying Native Americans in a violent, sensationist manner.
Source: Public domain

wagons above, attempting to endure a dreadful fright. Each episode varied in its intensity – sometimes the warriors were driven off until another show, or the Sioux were victorious. If the latter occurred, the warriors' booty was the screaming white settler women and girls, dragged off by their hair to await their ignominious fate. Sometimes the dead white men were scalped against a piteous backdrop of whoops and war cries. So, off the warriors would go with their captives slung over their horses' backs, the distraught and dishevelled women apparently resigned to the rape and murder that would surely follow (Aleiss 2005).

In chronological terms these Western movies and television shows are a further extension of the wild west shows of previous generations, which depicted Indigenous people in stereotypical terms and conveyed these images to an ever-larger audience. These shows were promoted by such Western heroes as Buffalo Bill Cody, whose everyday life on the Great Plains added a measure of historical authenticity. However, in these shows Native Americans, in particular, were often portrayed in a sensationalistic and exploitive manner. Buffalo Bill's Wild West shows, which ran from 1883 to 1915, tended to romanticize the American frontier and usually consisted of re-enactments of historical events combined with displays of showmanship. Indian War battle re-enactments were an important centrepiece of these shows, such as depictions of the Battle of Little Big Horn. For example, Buffalo Bill, the hero, rides into the battle scene in an attempt to save General Custer; however, Custer had already been killed, so Buffalo Bill attempts to avenge his death by killing and scalping a Sioux chief called Yellowhead (Moses 1996).

Native performers were also a critical part of the Wild West shows. These "show Indians" were largely derived from the Plains Nations, such as the Lakota Sioux, and were used to depict historic battles, especially those appearing in attack scenes of white settlers. These shows "generally presented Native people as exotic savages, prone to bizarre rites and cruel violence" (Stanley 2014: 24). In addition, Native women were dressed in "exploitive," non-traditional clothing combined with immodest attire, such as leather shorts, none of which would have ever been worn in reality.

Another interesting aspect of these shows is that Chief Sitting Bull was a star attraction along with other familiar Native American names who performed in the show, such as Chief Joseph and Geronimo. These personages were presented as friends of Buffalo Bill and were introduced to President Grover Cleveland. In a book on the relationship between Sitting Bull and Buffalo Bill, entitled *Blood Brothers*, Deanne Stillman suggested that this relationship was a sign "that America has embarked on the painful and necessary journey of healing our original sin – the betrayal of the Native American" (2017: xvi–xvii). However, this would hardly seem to be the case since Native Americans continue to be the victims of racist attitudes, policies, and institutions in the United States. It is also possible to interpret the friendship between Sitting Bull and Buffalo Bill in terms of the "noble savage" imagery in that Sitting Bull now appears to have atoned for his struggles, has now become as "pure" in his intentions, and has largely seen the errors of his ways in resisting the assimilative power of American civilization. Ironically, perhaps, Sitting Bull was killed on December 15, 1890, at the hands of the Indian Agency police on the Standing Rock Indian Reservation during an attempt to arrest him when authorities feared that he might join the Ghost Dance movement (see Adams 1973; Utley 1993).

Wagon Train and all those other westerns now seems so long ago, as if in a dream. Yet, we are left to wonder what this was all about – the

murderous Sioux, the beleaguered settlers, and the horrendous indig-
nities that were inflicted upon these poor innocent travellers. In hindsight, and with the benefit of 50 years of reflection in history's rear-view
mirror, we can begin to put Ward Bond, his other intrepid travellers,
and his Indigenous foes in perspective.

One aspect that is rather obvious is that the negative stereotyping of
Indigenous peoples serves a political purpose of the white settler population. When Indigenous peoples are seen by the general Euro-American
population as violent, savage, and an uncontrollable threat to the settlers themselves, then it would seem appropriate to develop policies to
enclose this violence. One method is to institute a reservation system
as a method of containment. Another method is to remove Indigenous
populations from areas of major white settlement centres as in the so-
called Trail of Tears. Further suppressive methods could also be applied
using the full force of the American army, such as the quelling of the
Sioux uprising at Wounded Knee and the imprisonment of recalcitrant
leaders (Churchill, Hill, and Hill 1978).

Indigenous Dispossession and the Trail of Tears

When President Andrew Jackson signed the Indian Removal Act of
1830 his intentions were patently obvious. Jackson wanted to rid himself of the "Indian Problem," which was to say, the impediments to
white settler colonization of the southeastern United States. The fact
that his legislation caused untold hardship to the Indigenous people
involved seemed apparently of little concern to him. [22]

Shortly after the Removal Act was passed into legislation, about
125,000 Native Americans were driven from their lands at gunpoint.
Their land comprised millions of acres in Georgia, Tennessee, Alabama,
North Carolina, and Florida, which had been occupied by their ancestors for untold generations before the white settlers arrived. By the
1840s there was hardly any sign anywhere in the southeastern United
States that Indigenous people had ever lived there. Their lands were
shortly turned over to white settlers who wanted to grow cotton (Ehle
1989; Jahoda 1995).

The Trail of Tears forced members of the so-called Five Civilized
Tribes – Choctaw, Chickasaw, Seminole, Creek, and Cherokee – to
travel a slow journey for thousands of miles from their homeland to a
designated location to the west of the Mississippi River, called "Indian
Territory." The primary reason for this massive removal and the hardships it caused was the result of racist attitudes that white settlers harboured towards the Indigenous people in their midst. Although the

Image 9. The Trail of Tears, or the Indian Removal Act of 1830, involved the forced relocation of approximately 100,000 Indigenous people from their homelands between Michigan and Florida to lands west of the Mississippi River.
Source: Public domain. *The Trail of Tears* (1942), painting by Robert Lindneux.

members of the Five Civilized Tribes were a relatively peaceful people, early settlers often feared and resented them. The settlers coveted their lands and were concerned that the Indigenous people did not appear to want to assimilate into the settler population by adopting the English language, embracing Christian beliefs, or accept European-style economic practices of individual land ownership. White settlers expected the Indigenous people to adopt to their ways of life, rather than the other way around. By 1832 another Indian removal took place in the Northern states as well. After the Black Hawk War, in Illinois and Wisconsin, millions of acres of land belonging to Sauk, Fox, and other Native nations were also made available to white settlement. When the Native people in these areas resisted their forced relocation, white settlers burned and looted their houses, stole their livestock, committed murders, and at times squatted on the lands that did not belong to them.[23]

At the federal level, the US Supreme Court objected to these state practices (in Worchester v. Georgia [1832]), which passed laws limiting Indigenous people's sovereignty and illegally removed them from their traditional territories. In its decision the Supreme Court affirmed that Indigenous people belonged to sovereign nations in which state laws held no jurisdiction; therefore, the state actions and laws were invalid. As president, Andrew Jackson refused to enforce the Supreme Court's ruling, thus allowing the states to continue their practice of taking ownership of Native people's lands.[24]

Under President Jackson the Indian removal process continued. In the winter of 1831, the Choctaw became the first Indigenous nation to be expelled from their lands altogether. Then, in1836, the federal government drove the Creeks from their traditional territory. Of the 15,00 Creeks to make the journey to Oklahoma about 3,500 did not survive the excursion. In 1838, over 16,000 Cherokees were driven from their homeland in Georgia at bayonet point by about 7,000 US soldiers, while nearby white settlers looted their homes and belongings. Typhus, cholera, and starvation plagued the Cherokee along the way, and more than 5,000 individuals died along the route. The federal government had promised that Indian territory across the Mississippi would remain in the possession of the members of the Five Civilized Tribe forever; however, by 1907 Oklahoma became a state, and their Indian Territory lands disappeared along with the American government's dubious promises.

The Massacre at Wounded Knee

Whether you call the incident at Wounded Knee on December 29, 1890, a massacre, as the Lakota Sioux saw it, or a battle, as the US Army termed it, it was nonetheless one of the most horrific events of mass killings of (mostly) unarmed women, men, and children in American history (Brown 1970; Treuer 2019).

On the morning of this tragic event, just after the Christmas holidays, US soldiers gathered on the Pine Ridge Indian Reservation in South Dakota near Wounded Knee Creek. A botched attempt to disarm the Lakota camp had taken place on the previous day. And so, the US 7th Cavalry Regiment, along with a battery of four Hotchkiss Mountain guns, surrounded the encampment. Shortly thereafter the Cavalry entered the camp with the intention of disarming the Lakota. A struggle ensued between one of the cavalry troopers and a deaf tribesman who was reluctant to surrender his rifle.

At one point a rifle belonging to the deaf Lakota man, named Black Coyote, was discharged and almost immediately other cavalry began

Image 10. US soldiers heap Lakota corpses into a common grave, 1890. The Wounded Knee Massacre of 1890 was an attempt by the US Cavalry to disarm the Lakota Sioux who lived on the Pine Ridge Reservation The action resulted in the death or wounding of more than 300 men, women, and children.
Source: Public domain

to shoot indiscriminately at the Lakota people. A general skirmish ensued, but by then most of the Lakota men had surrendered their weapons. The result was that somewhere between 250 and 300 Lakota men, women, and children were killed and about 50 wounded. Among the US cavalry, 25 died and 39 were wounded (six of the wounded died later). Twenty soldiers were awarded the Medal of Honor; however, in 2001 the National Congress of American Indians requested that the American government rescind the medals. One hundred years after the event, in 1990, the US Congress passed a resolution expressing its "deep regret" for the killings, but the medals were never withdrawn.

Conclusion

There can be no doubt that the history of the relationship between the Indigenous people of North America and the European settlers has been violent. As historian Alfred Bailey noted, regarding the advent of

European fur traders and settlers in Canada, conflicts between the Indigenous people and Europeans began almost immediately upon the white people's arrival on the North American continent. Bailey commented that "from the contact of the Europeans and the Indians arose the inevitable conflict of their cultures, which resulted in most cases in the obliteration of those of the Indian. Often the latter failed to survive the shock of the conflict, whereas in other cases he adapted himself to the new conditions, which were imposed by the immigration of an alien race" (1969 ix). And furthermore, "as the United States grew," Hirschfelder and Molin (2018: 2) conclude, "it developed a mythology that helped provide Americans with a laudable national heritage while serving to rationalize the dispossession and conquest of Indigenous people." In other words, the Europeans were in the process of constantly crafting narratives, such as Douglas MacKay's history of the Hudson's Bay Company in *The Honourable Company*, which portrayed the British exploitation of Canada's Indigenous people in a benevolent manner. In essence, this was crass self-serving propaganda designed to mitigate any difficulties in the process of commercial and settler colonization

As such, national narratives were composed to justify the supposed inherent privileges of the white settler population who, in turn, used these self-justifying narratives to dispossess the Indigenous people of their lands and resources, as in the case of Andrew Jackson's Indian Removal Act of 1830, and even to rationalize such acts of genocide that occurred at Wounded Knee in 1890. Even today, violence against Native Americans continues unabated. In a recent study by the US Department of Justice, it was indicated that "American Indian and Alaskan Native women and men suffer violence at alarmingly high rates" (Rosay, May 2016).

Several other points, by way of conclusion, need to be made. Perhaps the most important of these is that this "alien race" was relentless in its pursuit of wealth and property, caring little for the destruction of Indigenous populations that stood in its way. The white settlers portrayed the Indigenous people as bloodthirsty savages. These racist attitudes were continuously played out in Wild West shows of the later 1800s, and then in early movie theatres and on television that portrayed Indigenous people as "wagon burners," or as violent savages. These stereotypical depictions set in the white public's minds a negative image of Indigenous people as deceitful, untrustworthy, and ultimately ferocious. By way of a contrasting narrative, white settlers are depicted as innocent victims of Native barbarism, as defenseless against the preying savages. In turn, self-serving narratives used pejorative labels that have become weaponized over time, such as President Donald Trump's mocking use of the name "Pocahontas" as a racial slur against Democratic Senator Elizabeth Warren and her claim to Cherokee ancestry.

All in all, these negative depictions, reinforced across the generations of white settlers, appeared to justify their racist attitudes, and to validate the removal of such people from their lands. Since most Indigenous people lacked a facility in a European language or, for that matter, access to publishing houses, their side of the story was never told. In fact, the historical record clearly shows that it was the members of the European settler population who were much more conniving, violent, and murderous than their Indigenous neighbours.

The truth of the matter is that negative stereotyping of Indigenous people is a knife that cuts both ways: it causes harm to both the victims and the perpetrators. "Stereotyping American Indians," Mihesuah (2009: 118) asserts, "is a form of racism that causes numerous problems, not only for those who are stigmatized, but also for those who perpetuate the myths." For the victims they are apt to suffer from emotional stress caused by anger, frustration, and insecurity. For the ones who stereotype other people they are cheated because they cannot appreciate what Indigenous people have to offer. They speak from ignorance and lack a well-rounded view of American or Canadian history. Their knowledge comes from imagery and hearsay rather from facts.

It is true that there were attacks on white settlers by Indigenous people, but one lacks an understanding as to the reasons for such occurrences. Partly, one suspects that retaliation could have been a prime motive, as a sort of push-back against the relentless force of white colonization that left the Indigenous people on the least favourable lands, on lands where they suffered from a constant state of food deprivation or even starvation because of the paucity of resources in the territories to which they were relegated by the white settlers and forced to reside.[25]

Chapter Seven

The Shaking Tent: Abiding the "Spirit Above"

This was the Chief Spirit, the TURTLE, the spirit that never lied!
— Alexander Henry (the elder), Sault Ste. Marie, 1763

How durst thou doubt anything I say... doubt then no more, and never hereafter call our Power to question.
— Spirit of the Shaking Tent, Lac la Ronge, 1823

Joseph Beioley (1785–1859), who was a chief factor of the Rupert House district, reported that Shantoquaish, son of the elder Quapakay, and his son-in-law Boland, appeared at Rupert House in late March of 1832 in a starving condition and confessed to their part in the killings at Hannah Bay two month previous. According to Beioley's account of this meeting, Shantoquaish and Boland gave a religious justification for killing the residents of the Hannah Bay post. His family, Shantoquaish claimed, had been

> ordered by the "Spirit above"[1] to do what they had done; that they had striven hard to get the "Spirit above" not to enforce the task on them, because they had a disinclination to do what they thought to be wrong but that the "Spirit above" threatened and assured them that except they obeyed they should have all their children taken from them ... He then said that they had conjured, or practised divination repeatedly and separately, that is to say, his father, his brother, and Bolland and himself in order to have the task of executing the orders of the "Spirit above" taken from them. (B 135/a/138: 6–6d; see also Francis and Morantz [1983: 159] for contextual information)

Sault Ste. Marie, 1763

Alexander Henry (the elder) describes what is evidently the first eye-witness account of the shaking tent among the Anishinaabe at Sault Ste. Marie

Image 11. *Shaking Tent* by Norval Morrisseau. This depiction by Aninishinaabe artist Morrisseau illustrates a ceremony in which Indigenous people attempt to contact supernatural or spiritual entities who may provide helpful tips for hunting, healing, or other purposes.
Source: Private collection

before embarking on a further journey to Fort Niagara. Henry indicated that "in setting forward on the voyage, the occasion was of too much magnitude and discretion; and preparations were accordingly made for solemnly invoking and consulting the GREAT TURTLE" (Henry 1969 [1809]: 158). A description then follows in his notes of a tent or lodge constructed of five poles of ten feet in height set in a circle about four feet in diameter. This structure was then covered with moose skins and the top of the poles, or "pillars" as he describes them, were bound together with circular hoops. Henry further indicates that "among the guardian spirits of the Ojibwas, the first place was occupied by the Tortoise or Turtle" (p. 159 fn.).

The ceremony did not begin until the approach of night. Several fires were kindled around the tent, and the "priest" then proceeded to crawl, nearly naked, on his hands and knees into the small opening at the bottom of the structure. Almost immediately the tent began to shake and the sounds of numerous voices were heard beneath them [the moose skins]; some yelling; some barking as dogs; some howling like wolves; and in this horrible concert were mingled the screams and sobs, as in despair, anguish and the sharpest pain. Articulate speech was also uttered, as if from human lips; but in a tongue unknown to any of the audience (1969: 160).

He then describes a "low and feeble voice, resembling the cry of a young puppy [at which time] all the Indians clapped their hands for joy, exclaiming, that this was the Chief Spirit, the TURTLE, *the spirit that never lied!*" [emphasis mine].

Over the next half-hour various other sounds were heard emanating from the tent, some belonging to evil or lying spirits, then a succession of songs was heard from a diversity of voices. Then there was a short period of silence, after which the priest addressed the multitude, declaring the presence of the Great Turtle who was apparently ready to answer questions. The first enquiry came from the chief of the village who wanted to know whether the English were preparing to make war upon the local Indian population. A quarter of an hour then elapsed in silence. In reply, the language of the Great Turtle was not intelligible to the audience, which required the priest to provide an interpretation. The Great Turtle, according to the priest, had gone on a sort of reconnaissance mission during the period of silence travelling across Lakes Huron and Ontario and finally to Montreal. The Great Turtle evidently did not see large numbers of soldiers on his journey but, descending the Saint Lawrence River, saw this river covered with boats that were filled with soldiers "like the leaves on the trees" (ibid., 162).[2]

Individuals were then allowed to take the opportunity to ask about the fate of their absent friends or the condition of their sick relatives. The Great Turtle continued to be consulted until nearly midnight, at which point the crowd began to disperse to their respective lodges. Then, as Henry explained, he attempted "to detect the particular contrivances by which the fraud was carried on; but such was the skill displayed in the performance, or such was my deficiency of penetration, that I made no discoveries, but came away as I went, with no more than those general surmises which will naturally be entertained by every reader" (ibid., 163). Henry then embarked on his journey to Fort Niagara making no further commentary on his observations of the shaking tent performance he witnessed the previous evening.

Lac la Ronge, 1823

George Nelson was an early nineteenth-century fur trader whose interest in Cree and Anishinaabe culture was unusual for his time. Most fur traders were only interested in the economic side of Indigenous life and usually showed little interest in the social and cultural character-istics of the Cree and Anishinaabe people. Nelson served in various fur trading capacities, starting with the XY Company (1802–4), the Northwest Company (1804–21) and then with the Hudson's Bay Company (1821–3). As indicated by Brown and Brighton who complied his various written documents, "His manuscripts are an invaluable and scarcely tapped resource on all parties involved in the fur trade social sphere – and particularly on the Indians" (1988: 3).

Nelson had a particular interest in Cree and Anishinaabe spiritual and religious life, especially with the role of conjuring and the shaking tent among the northern Algonquians. At various points in his man-uscript he described the manner in which the shaking tent was con-structed, the ceremony involved, the spirits who attended the lodge, and the role of the conjurer. At times Nelson and his men participated in the conjuring session in which "the Northern Algonquian practice of conjuring as a means of seeking information and securing game ... [was] found so common in more northerly areas [and] as good and useful a coping strategy as any" (ibid., 8).

The shaking or conjuring tent was found particularly useful in find-ing food and preventing starvation. At Lac la Ronge in 1804, in early February, Nelson described in vivid detail a situation in which both the traders and the Cree were both in great need of food. An old man named "Le Commis," after engaging in some conjuring, indicated that

> you will find a large Bear, after much trouble, in that wind fall, on the opposite Side of this creek. You, young man, to the Commis' Son, you will follow your father's track till you have passed the two Small Lakes – you will see a Fir tree thrown down by the wind, beyond this another wind fallen tree, by the root of which you will find a young one, his first year alone. I also have one up this river ... This is so strange [says Nelson], and so out of the way that I will ask no one to believe it ... We had a Splendid feast at night, for they were very fat. (ibid., 9)

In Nelson's description of the shaking tent (or lodge, which is the term he uses) the diviner or conjurer began to drum and sing in order to summon spirits into the lodge (ibid., 146–56). Sometimes the conjurer is tied hand and foot, but he is soon freed; his release being attributed to the spirits. The shaking of the structure from side to side signals the arrival of the spirit beings. Conjuring with the shaking tent is called *Kosapahcikewin* in Cree. Thus far, Nelson's first-hand observations of the shaking tent among the Cree and Anishinaabe are probably one of the most detailed, along with Alexander Henry's account at Sault Ste. Marie, of any pre-twentieth century source.

As far as the purpose of conjuring is concerned, Nelson believed that the main motivating factor for engaging in this activity concerned prophecy. As an example, a primary purpose of conjuring was to obtain information that was otherwise inaccessible to the diviner, such as knowledge about persons or events in some distant time. Other important motivations pertained to the location of game animals, when game could be killed, the treatment of illness, or the arrival of visitors. The diagnosis of sickness was a particular concern of the typical questions addressed to the spirits since illness was often thought to result from sorcery or at times misdeeds committed by the sufferer of a disorder. At times a sufferer was asked by the spirits to publicly confess to their transgressions for a cure to become effective (see also Hallowell 1942: 53–64; Dunning 1959a: 180 for further examples of sorcery as a cause of illness).

A public confession of misdeeds is an example of the spirits requiring that petitioners also take practical steps to alleviate their troubling conditions. Thus, the spirits indicate that they are not only willing to provide information but also that their human dependents need to do their part in reaching a solution to the problems that life brings. The spirits provide suggestions that the petitioners are expected to act upon, as each has a role to play. The knowledge of the spirits who enter the shaking tent is especially respected: spirits have the ability to travel immense distances by flying, and thereby they have experiences much greater than the average human being. The spirits accomplish this feat by occupying elevated spheres by which they can observe terrestrial events. In this sense the spirits are regarded as omniscient.

As Nelson reported while at Lac la Ronge in 1823, the spirits provided the following admonition for a disbeliever in a spirit's efficacy (as quoted in Brown and Brightman 1988: 151): "How durst thou doubt anything I say – knowest thou not how clearly and distinctly objects are discovered and seen in a plain, from an eminence; and my abode is in the regions above – I see every object as distinctly as you see at your feet, doubt then no more, and never hereafter call our Power to question."

A stern warning indeed, for any supplicant who would doubt the word and advice of the spirits called into the shaking tent. Who knows what harm the spirits of the shaking tent could bring to those contravening the wishes of these spiritual entities?

According to various sources (i.e., Hallowell 1942: 51 fn; Mason 1967: 63; Brown and Brightman 1988: 152) the spirits entering the conjuring tent do not appear as a physical entity but as small spots of light that drift near the top entrance to the lodge. As Richard Preston recorded while witnessing a shaking tent ceremony among the Cree of Rupert House, the spirits "don't come in like the body, just like a spirit" (1975: 79). In one unusual instance noted by Nelson, the conjurer of a shaking tent held out a two-inch-long figure of the Turtle *Mininahk* which astonished the audience. Nelson also witnessed another Cree performance in which the trickster *Wisahkecahk* entered the lodge and dismissed the other spiritual entities, which caused the structure to increase its agitation (Brown and Brightman 1988: 152). This incident is reminiscent of Hallowell's (1942: 49) description of a spirit referred to as the "master of conjuring" which suggests a hierarchical ordering of the spirits of the shaking tent in terms of power and influence. Furthermore, according to Nelson's descriptions, each of the spirits entering the conjuring lodge has their own speech patterns, which include distinctive grammatical and intonational styles. This information, as such, obviates any suggestions that the conjurer himself is responsible for the voices, that he is acting as a charlatan in any way, or that the spirits in the tent are "speaking through" his voice.

In this scenario the spirits interact with the audience and the conjurer and back and forth. At times, however, the operator serves to facilitate interaction between members of the audience and the spirits, but in a passive role rather than in any direct manner. In other instances, the conjurer acts as a translator or facilitator if a particular spirit appears not to comprehend a question or comment from a member of the audience. The spirits, in turn, are able to direct comments to an audience as a whole or to specific individuals, depending on the circumstance involved. Members of the audience are also able to direct their questions to the sprits of the tent collectively, all of which suggests that the conjurer does not in any way direct the proceedings but acts more as a "master of ceremonies" of the event. In terms of the language or languages used by the spirits, Nelson recorded an instance in which spirits spoke in French, English or an unknown language. At Oxford House, Manitoba, during a Cree performance the spirits spoke in Cree, Anishinaabe, English, and Chipewyan (Mason 1967: 64). In addition, Preston (1975: 73) noted that even if a language used by a spirit was recognizable, the message might not be understood because of the use of archaic terminology, or esoteric intonational effects that distorted the communication or other idiosyncratic phenomenon, inhibiting an audience's ability to comprehend the spirit's intent. Nelson reported furthermore that various animals, such as bear, moose, or buffalo, had their own individual languages that were comprehensible to the conjurer alone.

In some instances, such as that recorded by Mason (1967: 63) for the Cree of Oxford House, Manitoba, an animal spirit enters the lodge while making sounds familiar to that species, such as the mating call of the moose, or the "Caw-Caw" of the crow, which gradually became more intelligible to the Cree in their own language. The loon, too, also entered the tent uttering its distinctive call, which resembled aspects of the Cree or Anishinaabe language, with the conjurer, in turn, interpreting the meaning of these sounds for the audience. In one unusual instance, during a performance among the Woods Cree of Alberta, the conjuror's wife listened to the performance inside the shaking tent and proceeded to translate the activity inside for the benefit of the audience nearby (Honigmann 1956: 74). In a further occurrence, in this case among the Eastmain Cree of Quebec, a spirit (in this case called *Mistapew*) acted as an interpreter for the conjuror while functioning as a translator of events inside the tent (see Flannery 1939; Tanner 1979: 114). In other words, as far as variations in the performance of the shaking tent is concerned, a rather wide variety or assortment of instances apparently were possible on any one particular occasion.

Cross Lake, 1930

In the summer of 1930, nearly a century after the Hannah Bay tragedy, anthropologist Irving (Pete) Hallowell arrived at Norway House, a Hudson's Bay Company post situated in northern Manitoba. At this time Norway House was still functioning as an important trading post, although well past the prime standing it had once been to the company when HBC Governor Sir George Simpson had maintained a residence there. Later that summer Hallowell made an 80-mile canoe trip to the Cross Lake Cree, and it was here that he saw the shaking tent performance for the first time, thus providing an important new eyewitness account in the ethnographic literature of this ceremony. Hallowell's description of the shaking tent, especially in *The Role of Conjuring in Saulteaux Society* (1942, rev. 1971 and further updated in 1992 edited by Jennifer Brown after his death), are generally accepted as the most authoritative sources on the conjuring tent among the Cree and Anishinaabe.

In northern Ontario and Quebec, the Cree and their near neighbours, the Anishinaabe (Ojibwa), had at one time (it has not been observed now for many years) engaged in the shaking tent ceremony to divine information not otherwise available to them. The shaking tent is a structure roughly barrel shaped and erected by driving a series of poles into the ground in a circular fashion which are then lashed together with several hoops up and down its length. The top of the structure is open which is said to allow various spirits to enter the tent. The outer portion of the structure is then covered with skins, birch bark or canvas which is draped over the framework.

The diviner then enters this tent through a small opening at the base of the structure with an audience gathered outside around the periphery. The diviner begins by singing songs and drumming as a way of calling the spirits into the tent. The arrival of the spirits is observed by the movement of the tent as it shakes from side to side; first, the movement is slight but can become ever more violent as more spirits enter the tent. In due course, members of the audience are allowed to approach the opening in the tent and ask questions. Most often these questions concern the well-being of relatives who live far away, a treatment for certain illnesses, or the location of animals that are usually hunted in the area.

Members of the audience can also hear different voices in the tent, which signals the arrival of various spirits, some singing their own songs. Many of the spirits have their own distinct voices, such as *Mikinac* (the Great Turtle), who is usually the first to enter the tent. He is recognized by his high-pitched, falsetto-like voice. Other voices may be those of departed souls who often console living persons by saying that they are safe and comfortable in the spirit world and that the living should not worry about them. It is believed that these various voices are those of the spirits directly talking to members of the audience and not "channeled" through the diviner. Sometimes when the voices are not intelligible the diviner will interpret the meaning of the messages for those outside the tent (Brown and Brightman 1988).

When Hallowell observed the shaking tent performance at Cross Lake in 1930 the diviner or conjurer "made a prediction about some difficulties I would experience on the return trip, which proved to be true. I was also given eyewitness accounts by his sons of the miracles performed by a notorious 'medicine man' of a previous generation, who had stoutly clung to his Indian world view [and resisted Christianization]" (1992: 4). Hallowell also took advantage of the ceremony to ask about the health of his father who was ill at the time.

The shaking tent is one example of a meeting place between humans and the other than human entities. "The shaking tent," as Hallowell (1992: 68) extrapolates, "is one of the most familiar situations in which this level of social interaction is perceptually realized. This institution channels direct contact with other than human persons of all kinds. Its purpose is to secure help from these entities by invoking their presence and communicating human desires to them."

The spirits who enter into the shaking tent are considered the conjurer's "guardian spirits" or *pawaganak*. When the spirits arrive, the tent begins to shake because of the Winds who are seen to be responsible for the agitation of the lodge; human hands never shake the tent. In the past a conjurer might even be tied with ropes before entering it. There is even a case in which a conjurer named Yellow Legs (as noted in Hallowell 1992: 68) had four structures built on one occasion. Before entering one of the tents, he placed articles of his clothing in the other three. Evidently all four tents began shaking as soon as he went inside.

Each of the other-than-human persons entering the shaking tent has their own distinctive voice, which is easily recognized by the members of the audience who are positioned outside. At times there is direct communication with the other-than-human spirits and the members of the audience. At times people will call out for *Mikinak*, who is willing to answer questions and always has a witty answer ready, sometimes making jokes about a situation, which would serve to temper what might be another wise serious matter.[3]

Other examples could be given of the other-than-human entities that are apt to enter the shaking tent. The main point to be made, however, is that these spiritual personages are considered part of the Cree and Anishinabek's "real world" who one interacts with on an almost daily basis. These beings, it should be added, are trusted for their wisdom and advice especially as their voices emanate from the shaking tent. To question the veracity of these other-than-human creatures' advice would be inconceivable. As Hallowell (1992: 82) sums up, "all the values implicit in a life free from hunger, illness, and misfortune are in part contingent upon help that in various forms comes indirectly or directly form other than human persons." It is reasonable, then, when misfortune strikes, that humans would feel compelled to appeal to the spirits for assistance, since to achieve the good life and to alleviate life's difficulties "the help of other-than-human persons cannot be omitted."

Spiritual Metamorphosis

Metamorphosis of form, reminiscent of a Franz Kafka novel, is an important theme in the Cree and Anishinaabe spiritual belief systems. As Hallowell explains, "*Wisekedjak,* whose primary characteristics are anthropomorphic, becomes transformed and flies with the geese in one story, assumes the form of a snake in another, and once turned himself into a stump … *Mikinak* marries a human being. It is only by breaking a taboo that his wife discovers that she is married to a being who is able to assume the form of a handsome young man … Persons are capable [in these myths] of metamorphosis by their very nature" (1992: 67).

He also adds that such "myths are considered to be true stories, not fiction" (1992: 65).

As an individual grows up in Cree and Anishinaabe society they become familiar with all the personal characteristics of the "other than human persons." From listening to the myths as told by their parents and other elders, children learn about the Thunder Birds who do not live on earth but in another world above it. In another myth one learns about the four Winds who are brothers – children of the same mother. They come to know that the North Wind is cruel to human beings, whereas the South Wind is kind. Some of these creatures are able to act like human beings, such as the Thunder Birds who acts, hunts, and dances, as humans do, but some, such as the Big Snakes are their prey and act like smaller snakes. Thunder Birds have the capacity to assume anthropomorphic characteristics since they are conceptualized as human beings who can live on this earth.

This theme of metamorphosis occurs in Cree and Anishinaabe myth with considerable frequency and, as such, interactions between human beings and other-than-human persons is considered in a different category than humans' interaction with "ordinary" plants and animals in the physical environment. It is also recognized that from time to time humans have the need of the other-than-persons' help, as when humans have trouble making a living. Hallowell concludes that these other-than-human or spiritual entities share a behavioural environment with humans and, as such, both entities can be seen to be part of a "larger cosmic society" (1992: 68). This relationship between humans and other entities is a particularly salient aspect of the shaking tent ceremony in which humans and various spirits interact.

Pekangekum, 1955

"Pekangekum" is the name of a fur-trading post that was established in 1946 in northwestern Ontario, close to the Manitoba border. When Treaty Number No. 5 was signed in this area in 1876, the Pekangekum band members were then listed in the treaty records along with the members of two other bands as the "Berens River Ojibwa." In his early ethnographic research, A. Irving Hallowell commented how extremely isolated these inland bands were compared to other First Nations, with the result that "these groups of Ojibwa Indians were able to conserve a great deal of the aboriginal culture during a period when armed conflicts with an expanding white population, the effects of the fur trade, and Christianization led to more rapid culture changes among the Ojibwa elsewhere" (1967 [1955]: 112).

Although Hallowell discussed the shaking tent in the Berens River area in 1930, a later anthropologist, R.W. Dunning, conducted fieldwork among the Anishinaabe of the Manitoba-Ontario border region on the Pekangekum Reserve during the 1954–5 period (Dunning 1955). The belief system of these northeast Algonquians is based on a Supreme Being or Great Spirit (*Kitchi Manitou*) who ruled over a world comprising various animate beings, each represented by a *Manitou* who was leader of each particular species. Various authors have commented on the Great Spirit concept, with Hallowell (1934: 403) suggesting that it is an Aboriginal belief, that predates the arrival of Europeans; and Jenness (1934: 23), who argues that the Great Spirit concept is the source of all power. As he further explains, "To the Ojibwa ... all objects have life, and life is synonymous with power, which may be directed for the Indian's good or ill. Just as man's power comes from his intelligence, his soul, so does the power of the animal, tree, and stone" (ibid., 21).

Concerning Cree spiritual beliefs, "When a spirit appeared to an individual in a vision," Mandelbaum indicates, "it became the person's '*pawakan*,' his supernatural guardian, or better, his spirit helper. The power did not guard and protect a man against all contingencies, but rather aided him in definite prescribed situations" (1940: 251). Similarly, Hallowell (1934: 392) suggests that a spiritual owner's powers were accessed through professional leaders or through puberty dreaming. It was usually at puberty, according to Dunning (1959a: 176), that these leaders procured their powers through dreams and visions. In addition, based on her fieldwork among the Anishinaabe near Kenora, Ontario, Ruth Landes (1937: 117–20) said that it was a universal ideal that males sought visions at adolescence concerning names, war powers and doctoring. Among the northern Cree, Rossignol (1938: 69–70) quotes an informant who says that "I also fasted. The spirits came, and I bound myself to several. There were good ones who helped me in hunting. There also maleficent ones, two in particular, who would come, at my call, only if I wanted to do some evil. If someone had offended me, I would make use of these two to avenge myself." Is this what happened at Hannah Bay when William Corrigal would not provide further gifts of food to Quapakay and his family? Although there is no evidence that this was the case, it is possible that Quapakay and his sons enlisted the aid of a malevolent spirit to exact revenge on Corrigal for his apparent lack of generosity. This is a suggestion that has not previously been mentioned in the literature and is worthy of further investigation.

It was on this basis of anthropology's understanding of the northern Algonquian belief system that Dunning was able to witness first-hand the shaking tent (*kosapanchegun*) ceremony among the Pekangekum people in the mid-1950s. He describes (1959a: 177–80) the usual construction of a cylindrical lodge in which the conjuror (*kosabandan*) called in his spirits to divine the cause of illness and to foresee the future. The tent itself was covered with moose hides, and some caribou toe bones were suspended from the top on the outside of the structure, apparently used to more effectively announce the arrival of spirts when the tent began to shake. Before entering the lodge, the conjurer made a little joke to the audience, saying that since he was getting older, he wondered if he would still have the strength to shake the tent. This caused members of the audience to break out in laughter, and it was explained to the ethnologist that since it was the spirits who shook the tent, then the physical capabilities of the conjurer had no bearing on the matter. During most of the time the conjurer conversed with the spirits in the tent, all of whom were audible to the surrounding spectators. The performance continued for about three hours, during which time the tent sometimes shook violently and at other times more gently.

When *Mikenak* (the turtle) entered the tent members of the audience began to laugh especially at the turtle spirit's familiar squeaky voice. However, in a significant departure from the other accounts of the shaking tent discussed above, in which a wide variety of issues usually surfaced when members of the audience posed questions for the spirits in the tent, in the Pekangekum case the performance was focused almost exclusively on matters of retributive justice. For example, several people offered confessions of wrongdoing, which would have been thought almost inconceivable in more private settings. An elderly woman in one instance complained about rheumatism in her hands, which was attributed to a sexual indiscretion with an age mate when she was a pre-adolescent girl. In another case a middle-aged man had lost two daughters, which was thought to be more than a coincidence. A discussion then ensued between the husband and wife concerning details about past misdemeanours that were thought to have precipitated this misfortune.

The Anishinaabe at Pekangekum tended to believe that misfortune in the form of illness and death was the result of a transgression of their society's mores. Therefore, when a person became ill or died under unusual circumstances an underlying cause was sought. A performance of the shaking tent, which was held only occasionally, tended to initiate an investigation through the spirits in the tent into a person's misfortunes and their behaviour that might have instigated this certain calamity. In the case of a public confession, a person might be expected to recover from an illness caused by a wrongdoing, and in this manner the social norms of the group were reinforced and sustained.

Rupert's House (Waskaganish), 1965

Richard Preston was a first-hand witness to a Cree shaking tent (*kwashapshigan*) ceremony at Waskaganish, formerly known as Rupert's House, in 1965. In his ethnography, *Cree Narrative* (2nd ed.), Preston (2002: 80–3, 112–15, in passim) gives a fairly detailed account of the spirits (called *Mistabeo)* who go into the tent, the conjurer's role in the performance, skepticism about conjuring, and a variety of other related matters.

As one might expect, the construction of the tent or lodge does not differ appreciably from that described in the ethnographic literature among other Anishinaabe and Cree groups. The anthropologist in this case asked if he could record the proceedings using a tape recorder, which is a research method that I have never seen in any other description of the conjuring tent in the literature. Permission was granted, and the performance began shortly after dark.

As far as the performance itself is concerned Preston provided little information since, as he explained, "I understood little of the sequence of actions and none of the language used. I was able to observe only that there were apparently several different voices singing at various times, all coming from within the tent ... My eager anticipation was offset by an almost total lack of comprehension of the dramatic proceedings" (2002: 85). We learn very little, then, about the interaction of the conjurer and the audience, or the spirts and the audience. Did members of the audience ask questions of the spirits, and if so, what was the focus of these enquiries?

We are left, then, with a transcript of the tape recording, which was later transcribed and translated. The transcripts indicate that up to seven Mistabeos engaged with the conjurer at various times but usually not more than two at one time. The interaction indicates a sort of easy-going banter between the conjurer and the spirits, such as "Very glad to see you again, I just came in to visit you, just to cheer you up" (ibid., 86). Such pleasantries take up much of the conversations, with little taking place of a dramatic or serious nature. There was a concern, for example, by one of the spirits that the lodge poles were too young, implying that the tent's construction might not be adequate enough to induce other spirits to enter. As Preston indicates, "The poor quality of construction is somehow related to how many spirits will come into the tent, and how these spirits who enter will perform" (ibid., 87). For the most part, though, the proceedings took on an amicable tone as there "is reciprocation by the Mistabeo of the expressions of easy intimacy given by JC's [the conjurer] teasing, above. The message is one of mutual good-will and intimacy and set the mood for the whole performance" (ibid., 86–7).

In several instances members of the audience asked if they would be permitted to give gifts of tobacco to the spirits or the conjurer himself but, on the whole, interaction with members of the audience appeared quite limited. Certainly, there was nothing recorded concerning public confessions, searches for lost relatives, or possible explanations for various illnesses that were the usual topics of shaking tent performances in other locations and times. In fact, one wonders why this performance was held at all, given the limited audience participation with the conjurer and the Mistabeos inside the tent. It would appear that this performance was held to satisfy the curiosity of the anthropologist, as indicated in the statement: "One woman commented to me that she thought that maybe JC [the conjurer] had been waiting until I [Preston] came" (ibid., 81). The virtual lack of audience participation raises the question of why the performance was held in the first place with such little interaction with other members of the community.

This point is only brought up because if one were conducting a comparative study of shaking tent performances in the Canadian Subarctic, then this one held at Waskaganish would appear uncharacteristic of such performances and therefore could unduly skew or distort any comparative conclusions that might be arrived at. All in all, it would have been advisable to have a Cree-speaking informant observing the performance along with the ethnographer, especially when he admittedly "understood little of the sequence of actions and none of the language used [and] an almost total lack of comprehension of the dramatic proceedings" (ibid., 85). The use of a knowledgeable informant would have been especially useful given that "few of the people in the audience were able to fully understand the old, ritual manner of speaking and singing" (ibid.). It is quite possible that members of the audience had comprehension difficulties with the language used in the performance because the shaking tent ceremony in this area of James Bay was either not held on a frequent basis or even not for many years.

Starvation Caused by Conjuring

John Blackned, a Cree informant for Richard Preston at Waskaganish (Rupert's House), narrated a story concerning the evil use of conjuring, when two men sought to do each other harm using the shaking tent. The two men were Meskino and an old man, P. One of Meskino's daughters had a bad leg (it was locked in a flexed position) and she married one of P's sons. Later, the lame daughter got pregnant, and P's son then wanted to change the girl for another daughter. Old Meskino didn't like this proposal and told his son-in-law to keep the woman he wanted first, "after you have made her pregnant." So, this was the basis of the conflict between the two men.

Not long after the old man P returned Meskino's pregnant daughter back to him. This event precipitated a duel between the two men, using the conjuring tent. "This was the time that they started to go in to the *kwashapshigan* to fight each other" (Preston 2002: 134). The conjuring duel went back and forth for some time between the two men. Eventually, Meskino's more powerful conjuring began to weaken the power of old man P because of his morally wrong intentions (i.e., treating Meskino's daughter as he did). When P's family went up the Eastmain River, they had a bad time hunting as they couldn't kill any kind of animal to eat. When they found a good place to fish, they were unable to catch any, and they couldn't get enough to eat. When winter came their situation became worse, and the family was forced to split up. As their situation became worse the old man P quit playing with the conjuring tent. They now realized that Meskino was trying to kill them all. At last, one of P's sons starved while out looking for partridge, and some in the family were unable to walk because of their food shortage. Three days passed without anyone finding food to eat.

As John Blackned related, "When those two families went out from here [to different areas] they were always making the conjuring tent. When one man made the conjuring tent, he could hear the other one making his conjuring tent. It was just like talking to each other" (Preston 2002: 134). This incident, according to Preston (2002: 145) illustrates "the sorcery side of conjuring [which] begins in a particular and focused case of animosity, and it ends in the more powerful and pervasive setting of almost total adversity that renders further attempts at conjuring quite futile, in either its expressive or its instrumental aspects. The power of sorcery is, then, susceptible to being rendered weak or unreliable."

This narrative situates the role of conjuring power as an integral part of the world of the Eastern Cree as it influences the relationships of Cree people among themselves and their relationship with the natural world around them. The conjuring contest between Meskino and old man P demonstrates the way conjuring can be utilized to bring about the downfall of certain people and the use of conjuring for malevolent intentions.

Hannah Bay: A Mistabeo's Betrayal?

Richard Preston explained that the Mistabeo concept "has proven difficult to define, partly because of the private and intimate nature of men's relationships with their Mistabeo. Also, different individuals may have different perceptions of the Mistabeo" (2002: 116). According to Preston's informant, the Mistabeo is not connected to the soul (*achak*) as there is a clear separation between the two. With some apparent hesitation, Preston (ibid., 126) includes the Mistabeo concept in the class of North American "guardian spirits" (i.e., Benedict 1929). Also included in the literature is Flannery's (1939: 12) suggestion that the Mistabeo is a sort of "master of ceremonies" at the conjuring tent. In addition, Lips (1947: 480) indicates that the Mistabeo is the conjurer's "own spirit." In summarizing the Mistabeo concept in the literature, Preston indicates that "probably the idea of an 'attending spirit' will serve best ... not only does the Mistabeo have an autonomy and personality of his own but also that a man does not always have direct communication with the Mistabeo" (ibid., 126).

This idea that the Mistabeo is an entity possessing a separate autonomy from the conjurer himself is a salient point because the Mistabeo may be in a position to have knowledge of certain events that are not known to the conjurer. In other words, the conjurer himself may not know all the facts about a particular situation and may also not have access to the knowledge that the Mistabeo itself possesses. Within the context of the Hannah Bay killings, and given the ostensible role that Quapakay's Mistabeo played in directing these killings (i.e., threatening that the group's children would not see the summer if Corrigal's trading post was not "spoiled"), one cannot only understand Quapakay's reluctance to follow the Mistabeo's instructions, but also his hesitancy in disobeying these instructions because of the distinct possibility that the Mistabeo understood more about the situation than Quapakay and his sons did under the circumstances. Furthermore, as Preston explains (ibid., 127), any spiritual commitment that the conjurer may have with a Mistabeo has its drawbacks since "it involves some sacrifice of the man's freedom and autonomy, and it puts one in a more or less obligated status with respect to the wishes of the Mistabeo" (ibid.). The presumption, then, is that if the Mistabeo wishes the conjurer to perform some act that the conjurer is reticent to conduct, he nonetheless is obligated to do it anyway, lest he offend the Mistabeo who may retaliate in some way for not following through with the Mistabeo's demands.

If a belief in the Mistabeo concept involves some sacrifice of a conjurer's freedom and autonomy, as Preston (ibid.) suggests, then the wishes of the Mistabeo could impose an obligation over the conjurer. As such, a conjurer could suffer a certain degree of loss in his self-control because of the power that a Mistabeo holds over him, resulting also in a possible loss of self-respect. Such a situation could lead to certain conjurers abjuring the shaking tent performance, or only performing it in desperate circumstances, such as that in which Quapakay and his sons were placed because of possible impending starvation.

The old expression on finding oneself between a rock and a hard place perfectly describes Quapakay's predicament. In his case there was no favourable choice, no matter which course of action he took. If he chose to contravene the wishes, or should we say orders, of his Mistabeo, he and his family could be subject to the wrath of this Mistabeo. Alternatively, if he followed the Mistabeo's instructions to "spoil" the post at Hannah Bay, there would certainly be dire consequences inflicted upon his family by the agents of the Hudson's Bay Company. The course of action that Quapakay finally chose – to "spoil" the Hannah Bay post – reinforced by his sons' conjuring, brought about the anticipated results. There is no way of ascertaining the possible consequences of disobeying the Mistabeo and not "spoiling" the post, but there certainly existed in Cree cultural beliefs examples of the unfortunate persons who followed this course of action as well.

This, then, is the context in which Preston's Cree informant John Blackned narrated an historical account, nearly 140 years ago, of the killings at Hannah Bay and the present-day Cree's aversion to using the conjuring tent (Preston 2002: 153–6). In this case Preston preceded the narrative with a summary note: "In the story of the Hannah Bay Massacre … we see what happens when a Mistabeo gives morally and tactically poor advice and the people are foolish enough to accept it" (ibid., 153).

One could only suggest that this judgment of Quapakay's actions is possibly too harsh, given the dilemmas discussed above and the possible retaliation involved in contravening a Mistapeo's orders. Is it an act of foolishness to follow time-held cultural beliefs, a judgment especially troublesome coming from an anthropologist who apparently holds to the concept of cultural relativism? Remember that the Mistabeo in this case warned that the family's children would die if the Hannah Bay post was not spoiled. Faced with the death of one's children, it is easy to say how one would act in a hypothetical situation, but this was hardly the circumstances faced by Quapakay and his sons. If Quapakay and his family were "foolish enough," it was because they were starving to death and desperate to survive, and not because they were credulous enough to follow the misguided instructions of an incompetent or possibly malevolent spirit.

The account of the killings at Hannah Bay narrated by John Blackned generally holds to the view that Quapakay was misled by the spirits of the conjuring tent, and for this reason the James Bay Cree were henceforth reluctant to ever perform this rite again. What is remarkable about Blackned's account is the precision in the detail that he relates, considering that about 140 years had passed since the incident. This attests not only to the impact that this incident had on the cultural memory of the Cree but also on the veracity of oral traditions, which are often seen as unreliable in comparison to literary accounts.

First, Blackned points to the power that a Mistabeo holds over one in the conjuring tent. For example, Blackned provides the following account: "The oldest brother's [i.e., the eldest son of Quapakay, probably Stacemow] Mistabeo told him that to attack the Hannah Bay store was the only way they could live. As soon as they heard that, they were going to do the thing that the Mistabeo said. They didn't even think that if they spoiled a thing (killed the boss) like that, they would get killed. They would sooner listen to what the Mistabeo said" (Preston 2002: 154).

This account, then, illustrates the near absolute power that one's Mistabeo holds over a conjurer. One does not think of the consequences of what the Mistabeo suggests, which in this case meant the certain retaliation by the agents of the Hudson's Bay Company and quite possibly their own death if they carried out the attack on the Hannah Bay store.

The second time the conjuring tent was performed, the Mistabeo was even more emphatic, reiterating that they must kill the [HBC] boss, otherwise "That was the only way they were going to see the summer" (ibid., 154). When the sons asked their father what they should do, Quapakay said "that they could do what the Mistabeo said." Notice the word "could," rather than "should," implying that Quapakay was giving his sons permission to carry out the Mistabeo's orders. The Mistabeo also gave more explicit instructions to the elder brother, for example, indicating that when the group went near the Hannah Bay store they should leave their wives behind, "and then go and fight from there."

From then on in Blackned's narrative the details of the incident bear a close resemblance to the contemporaneous report made by Joseph Beioley, the HBC post master at Rupert House. The killings were carried out using old-fashioned muskets and occurred when the post master was preparing to have his dinner. A servant ran out of the store and was hit in the hand by gun fire. The brothers did not pursue this servant because he was bleeding, and they thought he would never make it to Moose Factory because he would be dead before he got there, thinking that he was hit in the body not the hand. Additionally, they thought that this servant would probably freeze to death because the travel was at least 30 miles to Hannah Bay, and he was not dressed for winter travel, having no mittens or snowshoes. However, this servant slept on the ice and did make it the next day.

After the killings, the oldest brother, in a bizarre twist of the plot, started to wipe away some of the blood and, sitting in Corrigal's spot at the table, began to eat his final meal. Quapakay's family then took what they could carry; what they could use to hunt and for the time being did not stay very far from the store. They just pulled the victims out of the store and left them lying in the snow.

Blackned then related that the HBC reconnaissance party from Moose Factory stayed close to the shoreline because they were afraid of Quapakay and his sons. Upon arriving at Quapakay's tent the search party discovered that none of the men were there, as they had gone out hunting. Soon they followed the trail of the old man who was setting snares. Apparently when asked why he killed the post manager, Quapakay said that his sons had done it. Members of the HBC party then shot old Quapakay right there, and then they set out to follow the trails of his sons. When they encountered the eldest son, who had performed the conjuring tent, his wife hid behind him. The party told her that they weren't going to kill her, so she pushed herself away, and then they shot her husband. In due course they went after the other men and shot them also. In later years the women related that "the reason they did that was because they listened to the conjuring tent, to what the Mistabeo said" (ibid., 156). The women were then taken to Moose Factory where they gave their accounts of the incident.

John Blackned's account sums up several points concerning the Hannah Bay incident. First, one of these was that the HBC post managers suffered repercussions from their superiors: They took the women right to Moose Factory. And they sent a letter way outside to a boss, telling them what the Indians did at Hannah Bay. Then, what we heard, the manager at Waskaganish and at Moose, too, they got trouble from outside (ibid., 156).

Implications: Hudson's Bay Company personnel from Rupert House and Moose Factory acted more like a vigilante mob than representatives of a country whose members supposedly respected the rule of law. This topic needs to be investigated further: To what extent does a global economic power such as the Hudson's Bay Company ignore longstanding legal venues when dealing with the Indigenous residents of their colonial territories? Were there any sanctions, legal or otherwise, applied to those HBC employees who decided to summarily shoot and kill Quapakay and his sons (i.e., to what extent did the managers of the Rupert House and Moose posts get "trouble from outside")?

Second, in addition, there is an implication that the Hannah Bay post manager, William Corrigal, could have done more to help Quapakay and his family because of their dire situation of food shortages during this lean month of January:

The reason the Indians acted as they did was because the manager wasn't trying to help them. That's what the big boss told the manager. I don't know if that's right. I heard that those Indians were hard up at the time (ibid., 156).

Implications: Blackned's statement implies that William Corrigal, who was half Cree, did not follow customary principles of reciprocity when approached by Quapakay and his family. There are reciprocal obligations that should be investigated in this case, such that those in power are expected to help those in need. Hudson's Bay Company post managers hold the power of life and death over the Cree trading at their posts; the relationship between the Cree and HBC employees was more than just a mercantile one.

Lastly, there is the role of the conjuring tent and the Mistabeo in bringing about this incident: "After that, those Moose Indians never used to play with that anymore, that *kwashapshigan* … They had always been thinking that the conjuring tent was a pretty true thing. The Moose Indians never played with it after that" (ibid., 156).

Implication: The conjuring tent and the Mistabeos in it have customarily provided good advice (i.e., "a pretty true thing"), so it would be expected that the Cree would follow the advice of the conjuring spirits without question, as they had always done in the past. The Cree probably thought that they were not in a position to pick and choose from among the various bits of advice offered by the conjuring tent spirits, otherwise there would be no point in conducting a conjuring performance at all. Here again, life and death matters are at stake, which is to say, if the Mistabeos of the conjuring tent directed people to a particular area to find game they had better follow this advice or risk starvation in the future.

It is evident, therefore, from the foregoing account of the Hannah Bay incident provided by John Blackned that the Cree people of the James Bay area attempted to ameliorate or cope with their physical hardships by resorting to spiritual means. An appeal to spiritual entities as a way of alleviating the Cree's physical distress caused by malnutrition and frequent food shortages was essentially a request for guidance by spirits who had served them well in the past. On this basis, these spirits could be expected, based on their past performance, to be counted on in the present circumstances. However, the reader should be aware that this dichotomy between the spiritual and physical world, such as the connection between a Mistabeo and a person, is based on a Westerner's interpretation; there is no assurance that the Cree themselves think in this manner at all.

Remember that informant John Blackned's account was spoken in the Cree language and later translated by another Cree person. There are so many nuances that are possibly lost in the translation process, such as what Mistabeo means to a Cree person, as well as the various possible interpretations that individual Cree people could hold concerning the Mistabeo concept itself. Not everyone had a Mistabeo, and even those who had one might possibly see their connection to this spiritual entity in ways that are different from other Cree people. In sum, the whole matter is not as easy as one might think to unravel. Facile interpretations are easy to make but difficult to demonstrate or prove scientifically.

Nemaska, Quebec: Conjuring Tent Remains a Source of Controversy in 2016

In a CBC news report (September 3, 2016) Celina Wapachee reports that at a cultural gathering in Nemaska, Quebec, use of the shaking tent became a source of controversy among the Indigenous residents. According to former Grand Chief Matthew Mukash, "There is a reason why the shaking tent wasn't used for a long time. People would use it in a negative way. They would kill each other. It was like that everywhere."

Mukash also wanted people to remember the benefits of the shaking tent ceremony as well as the negative aspects; the custom, he says, was part of the Cree people's survival. "People used it long ago to find out about things. When a person lived off hunting, they used it to look for game," Mukash said. "Also, when a person was sick, it would tell what needs to be used to get healed."

Charles Cheezo, caretaker of the land where Nemaska is built, said that he saw how a shaking tent was made by watching his late grandfather. "I heard an elder say to me that there was some sort of presence around their family, "he said, "It's as if someone had put a curse on them, and that had affected their hunting." Cheezo was just one of the residents who spoke about his concerns during a local assembly in Nemaska, a community of 800 people about 12 hours north of Montreal. He is among some residents who were concerned about bringing the shaking tent ceremony, a way of communicating with the spirit realm, into the community during a gathering. This Nishiiyuu cultural gathering is an opportunity for Cree elders to transfer traditional knowledge to young people, to share traditional healing practices, and to strengthen Cree culture and language. According to the Cree elders, the shaking tent was performed so that people could contact the spirits to receive helpful tips for hunting, healing, and even locating someone who was lost.

Concerns that the ceremony was not always used for good finally outweighed the beneficial educational aspects of the shaking tent ceremony. In the end, Nemaska's Cree residents decided that the shaking tent could be part of the cultural gathering, but it would have to be conducted outside the community.

Conclusion

From a wide variety of historical and ethnographic accounts, the conjuring or shaking tent ceremony was evidently an important cultural factor in the life of the Cree and Anishinaabe people of the eastern Subarctic region. While there were certainly variations from region to region, it is possible on the basis of available literature to draw several conclusions. The first is that the conjuring tent performance was primarily an avenue into the unseen world of spiritual entities. The Cree and Anishinaabe sought to find out where game animals were located, where lost items might be found, and where missing relatives might be located. There was at times a certain entertainment value to the performance, as the spiritual entities joked among themselves and with the audience. The high-pitched nasal tones of *Mikanac*, the flying turtle, often brought hails of laughter from the crowd as he teased members of the gathering by revealing little known sexual secrets or other hidden aspects of local gossip.

Although rare, there was also at times a more sinister aspect to the conjuring performance. Certain people who felt aggrieved by another party might seek to revenge their disagreement through the conjuring tent by bring injury, starvation, or other misfortunes to another party. In such cases the conjuring tent is used as a mechanism of sorcery in which two parties focused their animosity on each other. Such was the case with old man P and Meskino who had an ongoing argument over the return of Meskino's crippled daughter. In this case old man P and his family began to suffer from starvation, which the local people attributed to the moral superiority of Meskino's case.

The whole purpose of this exploration into variations in the conjuring tent performance has been to ascertain a certain social or spiritual context for the killings at Hannah Bay. It was claimed by Quapakay and his sons that the "Spirit above" ordered the men to conduct the killing of William Corrigal (i.e., "spoil the post at Hannah Bay") and if they did not do this act the family would never see the summer. Although, as noted above, that use of the conjuring tent for malevolent purposes would appear to have a very rare occurrence we are compelled to take Quapakay's account of the events at face value. Unfortunately, there was no independent witness to the conjuring performance(s) so we have no idea of the veracity of this version of events. It is, of course, entirely possible that Quapakay and his sons manufactured the story of the Mistabeo ordering the killings in order to assuage their guilt for their acts.

If we attempt to determine Quapakay and his sons' motives for the killings, certainly the threat of starvation is a very real one. There is also, of course, the possibility that the killings were motivated by avarice on the part of the men. Another contributing factor could have been retribution for Corrigal's possible slighting of cultural norms of reciprocity. In today's Western society if a person says that they killed someone else because they were ordered to do so by a spiritual entity one would question their mental state of mind. Was this the case with Quapakay, and is it appropriate in a cross-cultural perspective to even broach such questions without risking a charge of ethnocentrism?

We are also confronted with the issue of Quapakay's Mistabeo ordering the killings. A central question concerns extent to which the Cree were compelled to follow a spirit's orders. There certainly is enough confusion about the Mistabeo concept itself to cast doubt on Quapakay's rationale for his actions, which, in any event, when confronted by HBC personnel, he blamed on his sons and not himself.

Chapter Eight

The Relative Nature of Truth and Reality

Should we resign to the fact that everything, after all, is interpretation, that reality is culturally constructed, and efforts to apprehend reality are misplaced?
– H. Sidky, *Perspectives on Culture* (2004: 18)

Probably everyone at some point in their lives asks why they were placed on this earth. Is it simply to procreate and pass their genes on to the next generation, in some sort of meaningless perpetual cycle? Also, how are we to ever know that our own personal perceptions of reality are those shared by our fellow human beings? And more to the point, what is "reality" anyway? There is the possibility that it could all be just a grand illusion, a sort of Rod Serling plot in *Night Gallery*.[1] But then, for what purpose? Whether for better or worse, we are simply here for such a short period of time that we can hardly ever make a start on the answers to these questions before we are gone, and others then take our place, destined to make the same queries into the purpose of life and how it is perceived.

There is a certain point of view in anthropology that has been called the "cultural constructionist" view of reality, which holds that "thought and reality are really one and the same" (Williams 2001: 138). The basic idea is that something can only become real when someone assigns meaning to it. The argument is that things do not exist apart from the "discourse that constitutes them" (Sidky 2004: 422). Taken to its logical conclusion, we come to the assumption that it is impossible for us to acquire any reliable knowledge about the external world. Yet, knowledge can be based on a number of foundations, such as logic, authority, popular consensus, or faith and revelation. These different foundations generate their own forms of understanding and knowledge. There are many people, for example, who believe that first-hand knowledge gained from our senses is the most reliable manner of knowing. From this way of thinking emanates the adage "seeing is believing."[2]

This is a simplistic view of knowledge accumulation since just relying on our senses can lead to faulty assumptions about the world (Brook and Stainton 2000: 15–31). Most people realize that our observations can be influenced (or prejudiced?) by cultural filters, a person's individual personality, as well as political and historical exigencies. All these aspects, and even more of them, have an effect on what we see, where we might look for answers to life's difficulties, and even what we are predisposed to ignore. In other words, even though our sensory experiences can have a profound influence on the manner in which we accumulate knowledge, we can also be led into error from the information derived from our senses, as Thomas Gilovich (1991: 2) suggests:

Just as we are subject to perceptual illusions despite, and largely because of, our extraordinary perceptual capacities, so too are many of our cognitive shortcomings closely related to, or even an unavoidable cost of, our greatest strengths.

People invented science as a "self-correcting mode" in an attempt to overcome these perceptual-sensory issues about the world (Lett 1987: 21). While science attempts to produce objective knowledge, this does not mean that such knowledge is "value-free," as some might assert (see, for example, discussions in Abu-Lughod 1991: 150–1; and Rosaldo 1991: 21). Rather, we are prone to accept Wagner's (1999:88) suggestion that "a value-free social scientist has a fool for a philosopher." In anthropology, most do not espouse the idea of a value-free knowledge because, among many factors, individual languages and cultural perspectives condition the way people perceive the world. As such, one attempts to achieve objective knowledge through various epistemological operations, such as testability and verification (for a continuation of this discussion, consult Berger and Luckmann 1966; Truzzi 1974).[3]

Who Decides What's Real?

It would save human beings a lot of trouble, although it might put innumerable philosophers out of a job, if there was some sort of "Supreme Court of Knowledge." The idea would be that a committee of eminent scholars would take case by case and rule: "Yes, this is real; no, not this one, this is not real," and so on. That way there would be no arguments about the nature of truth and reality. Whether it is unfortunate or not, humans have to decide for themselves about these issues. Certainly, I for one am not willing to go along with the idea that just because we think something is real that this would make it so. It is hard to imagine a world where this proposition would constitute acceptable logic; anyway, where is the evidence for such an idea? Here is the problem: "While we cannot really be sure that we are not in the midst of a grand illusion, not with absolute certainty, neither can we reasonably doubt that there is a real knowable world out there of people, cultures, objects, things, processes, forces, and so forth" (Sidky 2004: 19; see also Sosa 1999: 145).

It might be also all right to just say, who cares what is real and what is not? After all, we are surviving well enough with our own conceptions of reality, we are apparently capable of operating with some measure of success, although not always, so we can proceed, based on the assumption that some sort of objective reality exists. We depend on our senses to guide us and so far, so good. Furthermore, it can be assumed that for the long history of *Homo sapiens* on this earth, others have been doing pretty much the same thing as us, with some measure of success. In other words, there are certain pragmatic grounds that allow us to get on with our lives, suggesting that certain epistemological positions are more useful for us than others when we are trying to figure out how the world works. As such, "The universe forces those who live in it to understand it ... The universe belongs to those who, at least to some degree, have figured it out" Sagan (1993: 19).

However, we would not be human if our senses did not let us down periodically. We are not infallible creatures, yet we need not abandon what our senses are telling us. What we need is a more critical way of assessing what our senses tell us, and then, what we think we know. True, there are no hard and fast rules, and nature allows us to make mistakes at times which are not too life threatening.[4]

Understanding "Truth" in Quapakay's World

It is a curious matter that an interest in the Hannah Bay killings of 1832 continues to hold our interest nearly two centuries after the event. I first heard about the Hanna Bay incident while attending Richard Preston's class at McMaster University when I was a graduate student there in about 1972–3. One of the students in Preston's class even drove up to Nipigon, in northwestern Ontario, in an attempt to locate archival information at the local museum pertaining to James Anderson (1812–67), who at the time of the Hannah Bay murders was posted at Moose Factory and played a leading role in apprehending and executing Quapakay and his family. Later, in 1847, Anderson was promoted to chief trader at the Hudson's Bay Company post at Nipigon (Anderson 1961).

I have been thinking about the Hannah Bay murders on and off for nearly 50 years, trying to untangle why such an act could have occurred; why some Cree people would have become so psychologically unsettled (or deranged?) that they would murder their post manager, his wife, and child and a few others. There is undoubtedly a very human element here that we can relate to: What would you do to save your starving children whose cries would become unbearable as hunger gnawed at their empty stomachs? As a person of Irish descent whose family fled the famine in that country at the end of the 1840s, I can relate on that level as well.[5]

Oral accounts of the tragedy at Hannah Bay were subsequently passed down from generation to generation by the Cree in the James Bay area. Finally, in the mid-1960s, John Blackned, a Cree elder who was living at Waskaganish (Rupert's House), narrated to anthropologist Richard Preston the Cree's account of the 1832 Hannah Bay killings. To condense what has already been discussed, as Mr. Blackned related:

> I'll tell you about the story of the Indians who killed their boss at Hannah Bay. The way I heard it, some time ago ... And then one old man there, he had four sons and himself – five men altogether. And the old man had a Mistabeo [achak, soul, guardian spirit] but now his son had it. When the old man had gone into the conjuring tent. It didn't work very well, but he used to think a lot of it ... This oldest brother's Mistabeo told him that to attack the Hannah Bay store was the only way they could live ... The first time the Mistabeo told them to spoil the Hannah Bay store, they didn't do it right away. Then, the second time they made the conjuring tent, the Mistabeo told them to kill the boss. The Mistabeo said, "That was the only way they were going to see the summer" ... And the old man said that they could do what the Mistabeo said.

As far as Mr. Blackned's assessment of the Hannah Bay killings is concerned, he summarizes the event in the following manner:

> They told people that the reason they did that [went ahead with the killings] was because they listened to that conjuring tent, to what the Mistabeo said. [And later he continues,]
> Then, what we heard, the manager at Waskaganish [Rupert House] and at Moose, too, they got trouble from outside.
> The reason the Indians did that was because the manager wasn't trying to help them. That's what the big boss [Gov. Simpson?] told the manager [John McTavish, Moose Factory postmaster, or Joseph Beioley, Rupert House postmaster?]. I don't know if that's right. I heard that those Indians were hard up at the time.
> After that, those Moose Indians never used to play with that anymore, that kwashapshigan. Those people there who used to play with it, they knew then that it was not a very good thing (Preston 2002: 153–6).

Similarly, Morantz (2002: 14) concludes that "the Cree oral traditions tell us that messages received through conjuring was the motive for the killings, as well as the hardships the hunters were facing due to the stinginess of this outpost's manager." In addition, The Cree Way Project of 1975, which is a collection of oral history accounts collected at Rupert House, indicated that "the oral accounts do not judge these punitive actions" by the Hudson's Bay Company personnel (Morantz 2002: 235; Preston 1975).

The "truth value" of Cree oral traditions is situated somewhere between the reality that one can see with one's own eyes, the tactile connection with the real world, and the manner in which these are combined in the perceptions of the mind. As Preston (2002: 157–8) summarizes about truth in Cree society, one's truth value or confidence level may taper gradually with the directness of one's perceptual information, until it reaches a state where one is not sure of the truth of something and diminishes finally into doubt and disbelief. As one follows the oral testimony of Cree elder John Blackned it is evident that in his description of the Hannah Bay killings and what caused them, he is veering away from the Mistabeo in the conjuring tent as the determining factor, and placing more "truth" on the physical deprivation experienced by Quapakay and his family, in conjunction with the neglect of post master William Corrigal in perceiving the depth of the Cree's physical needs. In other words, the spiritual aspects of Blackned's oral testimony in the form of the spirits of the conjuring tent begin to diminish in importance compared to the corporal needs and existence of the body.

As Preston further discusses the matter of Cree reality, the more he places a primacy on what he terms "the inherent nature of a contingent existence" (ibid., 158). All of nature is conditional, in other words, depending upon certain factors relating to one's survival. Ultimately every person's life is of a limited duration, whether it be long or short, and, as Preston reminds us, "men have only a partial grasp of their situation" (ibid.). As much as we may examine, explore, and analyze as social scientists engaged in the rational and empirical pursuit of truth our perceptions of events will always only be incomplete and lacking in a multiplicity of perspectives. The spirit or spirits in Quapakay's conjuring tent may have been real to him, or at least partially real since they lacked a corporal existence. And we can understand Preston's (2002: 171) statement that "if the conjuring is real to the conjurer, then we must assess his ability to gauge reality, and in fairness to him, assess our own ability ... I think we should be relativists, and say that the conjurer's world is as valid for him as ours is for us. Many anthropologists will not find this statement satisfactory."[6]

However, whatever the perceptions of reality were in this case the cold fact of reality is that 16 people eventually died as a result of Quapakay's actions and that is a fact that cannot be denied or written off as an alternate view of reality. A relativist view of reality may be a tidy philosophical compromise between the reality perceived in cross-cultural situations, but it is nonetheless cold comfort for those who lost loved ones as a result of the Hannah Bay killings.

If we condense Mr. Blackned's account even further, as Preston (2002: 156) summarizes, "The events of the preceding narratives repeatedly indicate physical hardship with spiritual attempts at coping, followed by physical consequences of spiritual efforts and guidance." Ultimately, as Preston concludes, "The really fundamental question that I face, as an ethnographer, is: What is the *psychologically real* [emphasis in the original] perspective in Cree culture?" (2002: 158). This question harkens back to the 1960s, appropriately enough since this is the time of Preston's interviews with John Blackned, to the period of anthropology called "cognitive anthropology" (Tyler 1969). However, there were anthropologists during this time who doubted if we would ever know what was "psychologically real," such as Wallace's (1965) essay on "The Problem of the Psychological Validity" of "native cognitive worlds." However, Wallace concludes his analysis with the somewhat ambiguous statement that "it is necessary to take the position that psychologically real propositions may be held by an individual without ... being psychologically real in any sense to him, although these equivalents and implications may be structurally real and apparent to the ethnographer" (1965: 246). So, is Wallace saying that anthropologists know what is in the minds of their informants even though the informants themselves may not realize it?

If Wallace's statement does not clear the issue of "psychologically real phenomenon," then there is Robbins Burling's (1964) article on "God's Truth or Hocus-Pocus." As Burling asks: "When an anthropologist undertakes semantic analysis, is he discovering some 'psychological reality' which speakers are presumed to have, or is he simply working out a set of rules which somehow take account of the observed phenomena? The attitude taken in this paper is far over on the 'hocus-pocus' side" (1964: 27). Apparently, many other anthropologists during this time felt the same way as Burling, and the so-called cognitive anthropology period dwindled to a halt as new, and presumably more effective approaches took over in the disciple. So, returning to Preston's "fundamental question" concerning the "psychologically real" perspective in Cree culture, we can now say with a fair degree of certainty some 50 years after the cognitive phase in anthropology that "getting into the heads of the natives" is not a fundamentally productive task?[7]

If we look specifically at Mr. Blackned's testimony, without subjecting what he says to any test of psychological validity, we can say that Quapakay and his family made a terrible mistake. We can no doubt understand that food deprivation may spur people to undertake unspeakable actions, but in the end killing other people in order to relieve yourself of a temporal difficulty is not excusable. By the same principle, then, it is also not excusable for the Hudson's Bay Company employees to summarily execute those they deemed had committed murder, especially if they are presumably following Christian principles of morality.

Thou Shalt Not Kill

> Vengeance is Mine, and recompense;
> Their foot shall slip in *due* time;
> For the day of their calamity *is* at hand,
> And the things to come hasten upon them.
> Deuteronomy 32:35, KJV
> Repay no one evil for evil. Have regard for good
> things in the sight of all men.
> If it is possible, as much as depends on you, live
> peaceably with all men.
> Beloved, do not avenge yourselves, but *rather* give
> place to wrath; for it is written,
> "Vengeance *is* Mine, I will repay," says the Lord.
> Romans 12:17–19, KJV
> O Lord God, to whom vengeance belongeth;
> O God, to whom vengeance belongeth, shew
> thyself.
> Psalms 94:1, KJV

In other words: Don't worry about taking revenge in this lifetime: two wrongs *will* never make a right.

In most cultures the killing of another human being is allowed under certain circumstances, such as war or self-defence. The killing of other human beings is thus never an unequivocal affair. No matter which code of behaviour or set of commandments one wishes to abide by, there are always various exceptions to the rule. The question, then, posed by the killings at Hannah Bay is this: In what context should we view this incident, keeping in mind, of course, that there were killings on both (European and Indigenous) sides?

Is Morality a Culturally Relative Phenomenon?

First, as a matter of disciplinary importance, given that the discussions in this book are essentially an anthropological exploration of an historical incident involving the members of two cultures, each of whom killed members of the other culture, we are led to ask about the relevance of a central theoretical pillar of anthropology – namely, that of cultural relativism. In its most elemental form cultural relativism promotes the idea that a society's ideas and customs should be viewed in the context of that society's opportunities, problems, culture, environment, norms and values. Now this idea obviously covers a lot of conceptual space, and it is recognized in anthropology that most people in the world are apt to regard their own culture as superior to others, and that they take pride in their own beliefs and traditions. It is also recognized in anthropology that the enculturative process in society tends to predispose people in that society to regard not only the superiority of their own traditions, but to see the traditions of other people in a less than objective manner.[8]

However, anthropologists also recognize that if they were to view the behaviour of people in other cultures in an ethnocentric manner then it would be entirely impossible to understand other's point of view or to engage in any type of cross-cultural understanding. In this regard, cultural relativism as a theoretical underpinning of cultural anthropology is believed to provide an intellectual antidote to ethnocentric opinions and to promote an objective, inside view of other cultures. There is no doubt, though, that cultural relativism, despite its apparent merits as an attempt to promote cross-cultural understanding and perhaps empathy, is not without its difficulties as a guiding principle in anthropological research.

For example, there is considerable debate today in anthropology about the merits of a relativist orientation that stresses the particularity and uniqueness of each culture. Sidky (2004) refers to the relativist or subjective fallacy, which is to say, "the logical fallacy that truth is relative to a particular culture, time, or individual" (2004: 437). He explains further: "Take, for example, the assertion that for the members of culture X the earth is flat. For those who commit the relativist fallacy, this does not mean simply that beliefs are relative to cultures, but rather that truth is relative. Hence the members of culture X live in a world that is ontologically different from the one occupied by the rest of humankind. Such assertions frequently appear in the discourse of cultural constructionist, antiscience anthropologists" (2004: 14).

Furthermore, Sidky explains that the "cultural construction of reality" theory is "based on the ultra-idealist doctrine that 'thought and reality are in actuality one and the same,' that something becomes real only when it is assigned meaning because things do not exist apart from 'the discourse that constitutes them'" (2004: 422).

In his study *Culture Meets Power*, Stanley Barrett suggests that cultural relativism is no longer "the moral and epistemological core of the disciple" because the culture concept itself has come under attack. He explains that "Abu-Lughod [1990, 1991] and company scored a direct hit on the culture concept, contending that difference was exaggerated, and inequality ingrained" (2002: 45). Others, such as Yengoyan, propose that hardly any other social science accepts cultural relativism, which he contends is dismissed "as a game that pervades anthropology as a means of maintaining cultural differences" (1986: 371). The opinion is even offered that cultural relativism has become a bankrupt position in the wake of the Nazi regime, and that culture sometimes is a "divisive and destructive force in human affairs" (Bennett 1987: 50).

So, in the context of the killings at Hannah Bay, how are we to reconcile important theoretical underpinnings in the discipline that have themselves become a divisive force in the discipline and in the search for cultural understandings of how and why certain behaviours occur? It would certainly be useful to examine the cultural basis for European versus Indigenous moral concepts of killing humans to see what convergence or disparities might exist. It is possible, of course, that one might conclude that this exercise is largely irrelevant because human rights take precedence over a search for the cultural basis of behaviour.

Cultural Relativism versus Human Rights

The philosophy of cultural relativism encourages anthropologists to avoid making ethnical judgments about the behaviour in cultures different from one's own. In other words, the anthropological curiosity that is the foundation of the discipline is based to a large degree on an attitude of tolerance towards the behaviour of others and, even more so, on a belief that the patterns in other cultures have an intrinsic worth. However, it is undeniable that certain conditions or behaviours, such a sexual abuse, discrimination, or poverty, could be seen as being essentially detrimental to humans' well-being. It would be virtually impossible, one could suggest, to conduct an objective study of genocide or that this topic be accorded the same relativistic status as, say, a more benign topic such as the family in cross-cultural perspective, matrilineal kinship, and so on. As such, most people would agree that the two topics, genocide and kinship, are hardly comparable on moral or ethical grounds.

Cultural relativism, then, is not a specifically bound topic such that one area or another of culture either applies or it doesn't. In fact, we can regard the topic of relativism as existing on a sliding scale of applicability. This is the point at which the topic of universal human rights enters the discussion. At the state level, in some countries, such as Pakistan, one can be put to death for blasphemy, while in other countries, such as Canada, state-level capital punishment is prohibited under any circumstance. Obviously, each country has a rationale for their own particular laws in each instance.

It is these sorts of situations that presents a moral dilemma for anthropologists and have led some to argue that it is not possible to possess a truly neutral or objective research agenda. In this case, it is suggested, anthropology should abandon its long-held relativist stance. The alternative is to discourage certain cultural practices, such as genital mutilation (i.e., Daly 2000), and promote others. The result, if this suggestion is followed, would result in an anthropology with an avowed political agenda. As Barak (1988: 10) has expressed the issue: "the self-determination and emancipation of anthropology's subject peoples is as much (if not more) contingent upon the recognition of their common experiences as of their differences."

These "commonalities of experience" are particularly relevant with regards to responses to colonialism. The World Council of Indigenous Peoples, for example, is an organization with a strong presence among Canada's Indigenous societies (see Manuel and Poslums 1974). It was founded largely on the commonalities of shared colonial experiences rather than a recognition of cultural differences or similarities. Some anthropologists have become activists in buttressing colonial pressures by adopting various advocacy or activist roles, thus largely eschewing a relativist prospective (i.e., Hedican 2008a: 69–81, 2016: 3–18; Heyman 2010; Doughty 2011; Maskovsky 2013).

The Concept of Historical Relativism

Admittedly, the terminology in anthropology starts to get confusing. We have cultural relativism as well as George Stocking's distinction between presentism and historicism. To refresh the reader's memory, Stocking proposed that a distinction be made viewing history between the concepts of "presentism" and "historicism." Presentism implies studying "the past for the sake of the present" (1968: 11), whereas historicism involves a "commitment to the understanding of the past for its own sake" (ibid., 4) which is to say, "to understand the past for the sake of the past" (ibid., 9). However, Stocking is ultimately dissatisfied with both approaches. A history, for example, written for the sake of the present is apt to lead to conceptual errors such as "anachronism, distortion, misinterpretation, misleading analogy, neglect of context, [and] oversimplification of process" (ibid., 8). In turn, as far as presentism is concerned, "When the governing interpretive context is that of a *present-day* theoretical polemic, historical misinterpretation is the all too frequent result" (ibid., 108).

Based on his studies of the Huron of Southern Ontario, Trigger (1986) suggests the use of the term "historical relativism," which proposes that past cultures should be understood in the context of certain historical periods and should be studied in a holistic manner. A holistic approach recognizes that social and cultural institutions do not exist in a vacuum but are intimately related to wider economic, political, religious, and other contexts that influence these institutions in certain fundamental ways in an overall system of behaviour. However, as far as the Huron are concerned, such a perspective as that proposed by Professor Trigger poses particular fundamental difficulties because of the distance of many centuries and also the problem of the limited and cultural biased documentary evidence provided by *The Jesuit Relations*. In other words, our view of the Huron is largely based on a perspective written by Jesuit missionaries who were not necessarily interested in providing an unbiased account of the Huron but on their own interests and objectives.

We are, therefore, left with a few largely unsatisfactory proposals for viewing the past as well as contradictory theoretical perspectives from anthropologists themselves. Ultimately, we are left with some very troubling dilemmas. For example, the Spanish Inquisition was established in 1478, with the aim of preserving Catholic orthodoxy. Estimates of how many people were executed at the behest of the Spanish Inquisition are unclear; however, between 1478 and 1490 about 2,000 people were burned at the stake. Overall, in the range of 30,000 to 50,000 people were burnt at the stake (alive or not) during its 300 years of activity. Similarly, the Salem witch trials were a series of hearings and prosecutions of people accused of witchcraft in colonial Massachusetts between February 1692 and May 1693. More than 200 people were accused, 19 of whom were found guilty and executed by hanging.

How are we to view these atrocities? How are we to view the state-sponsored killing of innocent men, women, and children in such a horrific manner? Is it all right, or does it satisfy the conscience, to say, oh well, this all happened in the past? The authorities had their reasons for burning people at the stake within the religious and political context of their time. This is not to suggest that the Hannah Bay killings were comparable in scale, but there is an underlying principle involved that is similar, which raises the question: What is the moral justification for killing people on the basis of some form of retribution? A conceptual explanation that is based on historical relativism seems hardly satisfactory.

Killing a Witiko

During the 1960s the Cree people of Waskaganish (or Rupert's House) relate a story about an elderly woman who was killed because the people feared that she had turned into a witiko (or windigo among the Anishinaabe, meaning a cannibal spirit). In this case the men feared leaving their camp to go hunting because of a "terribly distressed and out-of-control woman." The people were afraid that this woman would cause harm to the children and other woman in the camp if the men left them alone. They thought that this woman was becoming progressively stronger or ever more threatening, which is a sign of spirit possession by an evil cannibal spirit. The solution arrived at was to deprive her of food and then of water, until she died. When she succumbed to this deprivation the people of the camp wanted to burn her body which was what people did with the remains of a monstrous person thought to be a threatening non-human creature such as a witiko. Eventually, there was some disagreement among the members of the group about whether the woman deserved such treatment and eventually she was buried in the normal manner (Preston 2002: 61).

Killing the Shaman

Among the Cree who lived in the upper Severn River area, near the present Sandy Lake community in northern Ontario, lived two brothers named Jack and Joseph Fiddler (the details of this case are found in Fiddler and Stevens, 1985). In the fall of 1907, Jack Fiddler, a shaman, and his younger brother, Joseph, were charged with killing a woman who the Fiddlers thought was possessed with a cannibalistic spirit, the dreaded Windigo. The Canadian press at the time relished in the exotic details of the case, with headlines such as "Chief and Medicine Men Chocked Out the Evil Spirit," "Devilish Indian Cruelty," and "Barbarian Custom among Indians."

At the urging of a local missionary, officers of the Royal North West Mounted Police (forerunner of the Royal Canadian Mounted Police) arrested the Fiddler brothers who were subsequently charged with murder and transported to Winnipeg to stand trial. This trial, which only lasted one day, found the Fiddler brothers guilty as charged. As far as the Canadian public was concerned, the press moulded a narrative depicting Jack Fiddler as a devilish shaman. Joseph Fiddler, whose role in the case was an ambiguous one, was left to languish in Stony Mountain Penitentiary.

The arrest of the Fiddler brothers and the subsequent trial was preceded by several hard winters that led to the death of 20 to 30 Cree people living near Sandy Lake, according to Reverend Frederick Stevens. The *Manitoba Free Press* subsequently carried the following headline in 1900: "Indians Starved to Death: Members of Saulteaux Tribe in Northern Keewatin Perished Last Winter Owing to Failure of Game." The story was based on Rev. Stevens's report, which was sent to the newspaper. It was curious that the HBC post manger at nearby Island Lake and the Indian agent at Berens River both indicated that they had no news of starving people. As a result, there was a move to have Rev. Stevens removed from the area because of his "contrived falsehood." Another missionary stationed at Norway House reported in 1901: "It is a matter of serious question why these people should be in a condition of chronic want ... It is true that the normal condition of the Indian of this portion of Keewatin is one of hardship and privation ... It is claimed that these people are so reduced that they eat bark from the trees and lichen from the rocks" (Fiddler and Stevens 1985: 67).

During the investigation of the murder case against the Fiddler brothers a preliminary hearing was held at Norway House into the death of an elderly woman who, judged by members of the Sucker clan, had turned into a windigo. Agnus Rae testified that the windigo died at the hands of Jack and Joseph Fiddler: "I saw the woman, the sick woman in her wigwam; she had very little life left in her; she could not speak; she yelled in pain. I saw Jack Fiddler hold the woman down when she was out of her mind" (Fiddler and Stevens 1985: 78).

Another witness, a European man who was associated with the Island Lake post, testified that "the old man did not do anything wrong in strangling the woman. Of one thing is certain, the Indians are not guilty of blood-lust in their relationships to members of their own tribe" (ibid., 79).

Also, the former chief factor at Norway House, who knew Jack Fiddler as his guide in 1898, wrote to the *Manitoba Free Press* that "A moment's reflection will, I think, show anyone the position, the trying position, of those living in an Indian tent where an insane or delirious person is. There is a fire in the centre; kettles of boiling water hanging over it;

young children and helpless infants lying round … with these Indians they have but one way of disposing of the matter (ibid., 79–80).

Author James Stevens comments: "It seems the men from beyond the forests are told that not all killing is murder. It is strange that Westerners in settled areas build huge wooden scaffolds; with nooses of heavy rope; hang healthy men and women before an enraptured audience; and this is not considered murder because it represents their view" (ibid., 80).

After the prisoners had been held for ten weeks and a trial had not been arranged, Superintendent Saunders wrote to a commissioner in Regina: "I would strongly recommend that if possible, the prosecution be dropped. The Indians sent back to their homes. It appears the evidence will not warrant a conviction" (ibid., 80).[9] In the meantime Jack and Joseph Fiddler waited for the outcome of their fate at Norway House. After over a hundred days of captivity, Jack Fiddler, who normally had breakfast down by the riverbank at Norway House, disappeared from the view of Constable Wilkins, who guarded the prisoner. A search was conducted, and Jack Fiddler was finally located at half-past three that afternoon back in the bush. According to the Sergeant's report: "He was lying on a rock with his sash tied in a large slip-knot 'round his neck … He was dead. Suicide by strangulation" (ibid., 82).

On October 7, 1907, Joseph Fiddler went on trial at Norway House. He was found guilty of murder but with a recommendation for mercy. He declined to testify on his own behalf. Commissioner Perry, who was the judge in the case, wrote to the Minister of Justice in Ottawa: "The accused knew that it was wrong to take life under ordinary circumstances. He believed, however, that insane persons were dangerous to the well-being of his tribe and that unless they were strangled, they would turn into cannibals" (ibid., 109).

On July 26, 1909, Joseph Fiddler, pleading for his life, wrote a letter to the Minister of Justice:

Dear Sir – I desire to lay my case before you and ask that a pardon be granted me … I desire to ask you not to look upon me as a common murderer. I was the Chief of my tribe, we had much sickness, and the sick ones were getting bad spirits and their friends were afraid of them and sent for me to strangle them. This was *not* common killing, for we never strangle a well person, neither would we dare to shoot, or stab a sick person. It has always been the rule of our people to strangle sick ones who went mad. (ibid., 115)

Based on Perry's recommendation, Joseph Fiddler's sentence was commuted to life imprisonment. However, Joseph Fiddler became ill and was subsequently placed in the infirmary at Stoney Mountain prison. On September 4, 1909, the governor general of Manitoba authorized the immediate release of Joseph Fiddler. However, the warden replied that Joseph Fiddler had died of consumption three days earlier, on September 1, after being in the penitentiary hospital for 18 months.

The Windigo Psychosis

It is obvious from his written account that Joseph Fiddler did not believe that he had committed murder by killing a woman who had gone insane, presumably by becoming a windigo, or cannibal spirit. Known in the ethnological literature as the "windigo psychosis," an extensive literature has developed since the 1930s concerning the characteristics of this presumably psychological phenomenon. "Cannibalism," Morantz (2002: 52) explains, "is one aspect of the Cree/Algonquian complex witiko phenomenon. The witiko (or windigo in Ojbwa dialect) is a monster-like creature that may eat humans or possess them spiritually so that they become cannibals. Writers distinguish witiko from starvation cannibalism, the difference being that witikos crave human flesh when there is other food available. The killing of such a person, so possessed, was considered justifiable."

This justification for killing a witiko (or windigo) in order to protect people from cannibalistic attacks has been reported extensively in the historical and anthropological literature (Smith 1976: 18; Brightman 1988: 337, 351; Flannery et al. 1982: 59).

In general terms, the literature on this phenomenon falls into two broad categories, or theoretical orientations. First, there are scholars who consider the windigo phenomenon as a folk illness or culturally specific mental disorder; and second, there are those who were critical of this position suggesting that there are no well-authenticated cases of this supposed ailment (Honigmann 1981: 737). Richard Preston (1980: 124), for example, a long-time ethnographer of the James Bay Cree, suggested in his 1960s research that the witiko is more akin to the Christian notion of the devil, which is to say, a non-specific character.

On the other hand, Regina Flannery (1982: 58–9), who collected information on the witiko in the 1930s from the Cree who lived in the western area of James Bay, garnered a dozen accounts of this phenomena including one concerning a man who had apparently killed a person inflicted with cannibalistic cravings. Her informants were therefore reticent about sharing this information because he was still alive and could still be subject to legal repercussions. For Flannery there is a clear relationship between a belief in a cannibalistic spirit and the fearful dread of food deprivation and possible starvation. The witiko complex, according to Flannery, functions as a symbolic expression of the inherent dangers of Indigenous life in the Canadian Subarctic, especially in wintertime when food resources are scarce. A belief in the witiko serves to link various dangers, such as the isolation of Subarctic life, a way to rationalize one's fears around food deprivation, and the possibility of deviant behaviour.

Father John Cooper, an anthropologist and Catholic priest who conducted fieldwork in the eastern Subarctic during the 1925–45 period and who one might think would not be sympathetic to Cree and Anishinaabe traditional religious beliefs, states with a tone of sympathy for the hardships of northern Canadian life among the Cree and other Indigenous people in the area, that "it seems fairly clear that this particular craving in the psychosis is directly traceable to prevalent environmental and cultural conditions in the northeastern Canadian woodlands, where death by starvation has been relatively very common, and where the native culture includes both a rigid taboo on and a profound horror of cannibalism" (1933b: 21). And then he posits the justification for killing those afflicted with this psychosis: "Human witikos were dangerous, as they were apt to kill or to be suspected of desiring to kill living adults or children in order to satisfy their psychotic craving for human flesh. Hence, human man-eaters who had become witikos were often put to death" (ibid., 21–2).

It should be noted that Father Cooper does not admonish those engaged in such a practice, suggesting by his silence on the matter or his apparent reticence to condemn the killing of witikos, that he feels that there was some justification for it as a means of preserving human life under extremely difficult environmental conditions.

Interest in this phenomenon continued into the 1960s, when Parker (1960) suggested a psychoanalytic interpretation of the psychosis. The proposal here is that the condition represents a breakdown of the ego's defences and an expression of dependency and aggression needs. Teicher, on the other hand, focused on the northern Algonquians' belief system and how it influences the "conscious content of the illness, the symbols used, the delusional mold, the distortions of reality and the character of the compulsions" (1960: 113).

Nearly a decade later, into the 1970s, the debate about the windigo psychosis shifted from environmental influences as a causal factor to other determinants. Rohl (1970), for example, focused on nutritional or biological factors, which she refers to as "extracultural dimensions," as an important contributing factor in this psychosis. Her study builds on Fogelson's (1964) previous work on possible organic influences in the etiology of the windigo psychosis. The suggestion in these articles is that there is a positive relationship between nutrition and mental health. For example, "It has been demonstrated that a drop in the blood sugar level can lead to many psychic phenomena, including depressive states, anxiety, and other symptoms that have been lumped together as 'neuroses'" (Rohrl 1970: 100). However, such a hypothesis has yielded inconclusive results, since, as Rohrl (ibid., 101) notes, "dietary deficiencies have different behavioural manifestations in different cultures, depending on the total cultural pattern."

It is not surprising, then, that such a tentative approach, which emphasizes possible nutritional aspects of the windigo psychosis, or which sees this disorder as simply a "folk illness," should attract criticism. J.S.H. Brown, for example, questions the nutritional approach, or other biological and psychiatric theories that are founded on sparse evidence: "I question the validity of the idea that the Indians collectively, at some level of thought, connected deprivation of animal fats with windigo psychosis and formulated a cure on sound nutritional practice" (1971: 20). She also points out that "Malnutrition may have been endemic in these northern populations, but our evidence does not now prove that it was the primary or precipitating factor in the majority of windigo cases" (ibid.). Brown then quotes from the archival records of Norway House (July 28, 1871) in which it is recorded that a fifteen-year-old boy "went crazy, and in his ravings kept asking to eat flesh. At last, he said, 'I will surely kill somebody, and eat them if I can!' One day he attacked his father and tried hard to bite him. The father and an elder brother of the crazy one then deliberately strangled him and burnt his body to ashes." The Rev. Egerton Young, who recorded this event in a letter, then noted: "Poor boy, he was only a lunatic, and perhaps a few months in an asylum would have restored reason to its throne" (in Brown 1971: 21).

Interest in the windigo psychosis continued unabated up until recent times, finding commentary in various academic disciplines such as English literature. Cynthia Sugars, for one, suggests that "If the story of the windigo was originally intended as an ethical warning against giving in to libidinous impulses, it has also been widely used as a metaphor for the violence of imperialism and the sickness at the heart of the modern capitalist world" (2004: 79). Debora Root, in *Cannibal Culture*, then explores the manner in which contemporary Western society "has aestheticized wetiko sickness and we ourselves have become cannibals" (1996: 13). Diana Brydon then suggests that Root's notion of "white Cannibal culture" shows "non-Indigenous Canadians their own rapacious desire imaged as the consumer other" (2003: 53). Sugars then even suggests that Freud's *Totem and Taboo* (1913) "gives a disturbingly

Eurocentric account of the links between aboriginal ('primitive') and European ('civilized') instances of taboo and savagery" (2004: 81). She elaborates further on this analogy by noting that the windigo psychosis is an "ideal metaphor ... windigo can be construed as an embodiment for the greed of contemporary consumer culture and as a type of serial killer" (2004: 88).

In all this literature one wonders if there is any limit to which the windigo psychosis is capable of inspiring the human imagination. As a final word on the subject one can refer to the recent *Dictionary of Cultural Anthropology*, (Vivanco 2018), which states:

"Windigo psychosis: A psychological affliction reported historically among Northern Algonquian societies in which an individual is possessed by a cannibalistic monster called a 'windigo' and desires to eat the flesh of those around them. Anthropologists have long argued that it is an expression of *folk illness* rooted in particular notions of *personhood*, expectations of appropriate social behaviour, and responses to stress." In the late 1980s a debate was sparked by Marano et al. (1982), who argued that no reliable evidence exists than any individual ever suffered a psychosis; rather they were better thought of as accusations made due to social disapproval for certain behaviours.

Perhaps it is prudent at this point to give the last word to Charles Bishop, long-time ethnohistorian of the Cree and Anishinaabe of northern Ontario and Quebec, for no other reason than at least a temporary cessation of this debate needs to occur sometime:

"I also agree fully that the idea of a culture-specific psychotic syndrome labelled windigo psychosis should be rejected. Further, I concur that the examples of killings of persons assumed by Indians to have been windigos were the result of collective witch fear generated by stress-inducing infrastructural degradation. This is as far as I am willing to go" (Bishop 1982: 398)

It is a wise person who knows when to stop![10]

The Truth about Reality

There are times when it appears that academic debates are interminable. Certainly, after 70 years the deliberation over the windigo psychosis it is difficult to argue differently, especially after all this time, as there does not seem to be any reasonable resolution to the matter. Probably the reason for this endless back and forth is that each side has its adherent who, on philosophical grounds at least, appear entrenched in their positions. Another reason is that there are so many facets to a discussion of something like the windigo psychosis that one is hard-pressed to decided which side is right, which is wrong, and where the truth lies. In the end, the discussions are almost always about the nature of reality.[11]

Probably it would be more accurate to say the *understanding* of the nature of reality. Is reality in the end only just in the eye of the beholder? The positivists would argue otherwise claiming that, for example, the law of gravity applies equally to every human being, regardless of their language, perceptions of reality, or cultural backgrounds. In the other camp are those, the epistemologists, who argue that there can be as many versions of reality as there are persons capable of perceiving it. So, who is right? Perhaps, one version of reality applies to one set of circumstances, such as scientific laws of the universe, and another version of reality applies to one's personal perceptions, such as what objects you might see in a Rorschach Test.

Imagine, for an instance, if it were the Cree who were the dominant colonial power, and that the Euro-Canadians were in a minority and relatively powerless. It is possible in this case that they would be channelling their resources into investigations into the causes, treatment, and so on of the windigo phenomenon. In this case the Cree might regard Euro-Canadian perceptions of mental illness, such as schizophrenia, bipolar, or depression as not much more than witchcraft or hocus-pocus. They might even recommend that the Euro-Canadian propensity to incarcerate the more extreme cases, such as the criminally insane, a useless waste of resources and order the doors of mental institutions opened up and the patients released as a cost-saving measure. As one can readily see, much depends upon which side of the cultural-social fence one sits. Of course, all this eventually brings us back to how we perceive the nature of reality. Why, one might ask, is any of this philosophizing important?

Conclusion

There has never been a society ever known that did not have some form of religious or spiritual belief system. Of course, in human history there have been a multiplicity of such belief systems, from the highly structured state organizations with their hierarchical ordering and diverse roles, to societies – commonly found with hunting and gathering economic systems – with more diffuse systems of belief, with an array of spiritual entities. Whatever the case, there is a fundamental principle that applies to all these systems, which is that spiritual entities are more powerful than human beings and that these entities should command respect and authority. Religions are also powerful entities. Wars have been fought over them, as in the Crusades in the Middle Ages, and many lives lost, as in the Spanish Inquisition, often in the most hideous manner. In other words, religion and loss of life seem to be coexistent with human societies.

As far as Hannah Bay is concerned, the HBC journal entries indicate that the reason for the killing was because Quapakay and his sons were ordered by the "Spirit above" to "spoil" the post managed by William Corrigal. We have no contemporaneous Cree translation for the word "spoil," but one can reasonably assume that it did not mean "kill" or "murder." In all probability, given the circumstances surrounding the event, which is to say that the "Spirit above" indicated that their children would not survive the winter, and the general condition of food deprivation in the area, that the intention was more simply to rob the post of food. There were also the social expectations that the Hudson's Bay Company would return reciprocal favours in time of need so there could have been a breach of social etiquette involved as well.

There was no need for Quapakay and his sons to kill the post manger and all the other inhabitants simply to obtain food. A simple robbery would suffice. If this were the case then a reasonable scenario of events would be that Quapakay and his sons approached the post demanding food, and that this request was denied. Then the living quarters of William Corrigal were breached, and an armed conflict ensued. Shots were fired, resulting in the wounding or killing of Mr. Corrigal. At this point, because of a fear of detection, other witnesses to the event were subsequently shot. However, several men escaped to inform the post master at Moose Factory. In other words, this could possibly be the case of an armed robbery gone astray, and as all too frequently happens in such cases, a case of robbery turns into a case of murder.

Chapter Nine

Conclusions

The principal conclusions of this study are that the killings at Hannah Bay in 1832 were the result of a "a catastrophe in the making" caused by (1) a subsistence base in the Hudson's Bay Lowlands that was ultimately insufficient to support the combined population of Indigenous people and the British fur traders; (2) breaches of reciprocal obligations regarding food sharing in times of need by the Hudson's Bay Company personnel; (3) capitalist colonial attitudes which placed the pursuit of wealth above human survival; (4) discriminatory attitudes of white privilege on the part of the British colonial powers, which saw the Indigenous population in North America as a "lower form of human life"; and (5) religious beliefs of the Indigenous population, which placed their own survival above the lives of other human beings.

The killings were not the result of any single causal factor but a combination of these working in conjunction with each other. In addition, it is difficult in this case to ascertain the independent (cause) from the dependent (effect) variables.[1] The British fur traders brought with them discriminatory attitudes towards North America's Indigenous people, along with a capitalistic attitude that placed wealth creation above human suffering, but these in themselves must be considered contributing factors – these attitudes did not cause the murders. The Hudson's Bay Company fur traders wrote in their journals on an almost daily basis about the severe food deprivation suffered by the Indigenous people of the James Bay area. If the traders had had more empathetic attitudes towards the Cree trappers, they might have alleviated this suffering by arranging for more food to be imported from Europe, but it is difficult to ascertain if such measures would have prevented the catastrophe that took place.

In the end, one can only say that Quapakay and his sons were ultimately responsible for their own actions. To pass the blame for their behaviour on to the "Spirit above" is an unacceptable motive for the killing of other human beings. One is therefore prone to agree with

Preston's (2002: 153) assertion that "In the story of the Hannah Bay Massacre ... we see what happens when a Mistabeo[2] gives morally and tactically poor advice and the people are foolish enough to accept it." The fact that the other Cree people in the James Bay area did not follow Quapekay's lead and initiate a general resurrection would seem to indicate that they did not agree with the killing of William Corrigal and the others as well. Nonetheless, we are left with a nagging question, posed in the beginning of this book, to wit: To what length would you go to save your children? This is another matter for debate.

This book began with Winston Churchill's famous dictum that "history is written by the victors." If we continue the analogy just presented in which the Cree are the colonial power, if for no other reason than as a heuristic exercise, we might ask how the Hannah Bay killings might have turned out. Almost certainly, the Cree would have begun to craft their own narrative of the events as a counterpoint to whatever the minority Euro-Canadian might be saying.

The main question that this book has been attempting to answer is: How did the Cree people of James Bay become so desperate that they saw no other alternative in their attempts to save themselves that they eventually killed occupants of the Hannah Bay trading post in 1832? Of course, as has been said at various times in this book, the position taken by this author is that the killings were not justified, but this caveat does not also mean that we should not attempt to understand the various extenuating or mitigating factors and conditions – social, economic, political, or religious – in which this tragedy was situated. We might also ask: Could the killing have been prevented? If so, by whom and in what manner?

It is certainly not possible at this time, nearly two centuries later, to interview Quapakay and his sons about the reasons for the killings. And even if we could conduct such interviews, it is not at all certain that these men would have been able to articulate reasonable answers for such a perverse act. As the old saying goes, "Desperate people do desperate things." Having said this, were the killings attributable to (a) a shortage of food in the area, (b) a feeling among the Cree people that they were losing control over their lives because of the British foreigners in their territory, (c) a sense of social disintegration, or (d) an understanding that the spiritual powers that had guided their people from time immemorial had now become irrational? Probably the reader can supply additional factors that would appear relevant to our understanding of this case, but the fact of the matter is that we will never have a definitive answer.

It is also important to indicate what the present study is not. It is not, for example, a work of psychology in which one searches in the hidden recesses of the human mind for mysterious motives that might be seen to justify, or at least account for, this gruesome act. It is also not a legal treatise in which one searches for broken laws in which justice in one form or another is administered. What this study comprises is a work in anthropology in which the interactions of people from diverse cultural backgrounds engage in forms of exchange so that each transaction is embedded in traditions, mores, and expectations. In this context there is a great possibility, even a probability, of confusion in terms of what is happening by each party. In large part, it is contended in this book that the killings at Hannah Bay resulted from this confusion, or cultural misunderstanding, about what is appropriate behaviour and how people should behave towards one another. In other words, for the members of each cultural tradition, the English and the Cree, their view of what happened at Hannah Bay forms a narrative that "makes sense" in their own particular cultural context.

It is a fact of life that all human behaviour takes place in a complicated matrix of inter-relationships. There is not that much that we can control in life except some of our own actions. For the most part we are embedded in the traditions that we inherit from all those yesterdays long ago. Or, to quote Marx, "Men make their own history, but they do not make it just as they please ... [they do so] under circumstances directly encountered and inherited from the past" (1978 [1852]: 9). Another basic principle of life, as the adage goes, is that there are two sides to every story.

As far as the inhabitants of the James Bay area in the early 1800s are concerned, The Hudson's Bay Company employees had every reason to believe that a general uprising would take place among the Indigenous inhabitants of the region. After all, all they had to do was read the post journals to see how evident it was that there was a general dissatisfaction with the conditions of life, especially with the shortages of food and the harsh environment in which they lived. The HBC employees not only had to deal with the complaints of the Cree but there was always the pressure from bosses and shareholders back in England to pare costs and increase profits. As for the Cree and other Indigenous inhabitants, there must have been a feeling of dismay that even the spirits appeared to be abandoning them, that their previous life of independence that they enjoyed for so many centuries was becoming increasingly controlled by an apparently uncaring and money-driven foreign population.

John McLean, it almost appears, had a prescient knowledge of how these counter narratives might be portrayed. In the case of Hannah Bay, Quapakay and his sons "were conveyed to Moose Factory, bound hand and foot, and there shot down by the orders of the Chief Factor" (1968 [1932]: 323–5). No ostensible enquiry or further investigation was deemed necessary as the facts of the case were apparently so clearly evident. However, shortly after the events of 1832, in 1835, a party of Hudson's Bay Company men approached a band of eight Assiniboine men who had previously delivered up their arms and, as John McLean related,

> A *court martial* was held by the two clerks and some of the men, to determine the punishment due to the Indians for having been found near the company's horses, with the *supposed* intention of carrying them off. What was the decision of this mock court martial? I shudder to relate, that the whole band, after having given up their arms, and partaken of their hospitality, were condemned to death, and their sentence carried into execution on the spot—all were butchered in cold blood! (1968 [1932]: 324)

Obviously, this was a case of murder in the first degree, premeditated and, as MacLean indicates, "in cold blood". In a handwritten note in a volume of McLean's book, a Mr. A.C. Anderson, presumably with knowledge of the case, writes that "It was a horrible atrocity, the rumour of which caused a thrill of shame and indignation throughout the country." However, this "thrill of shame" was apparently not enough to apprehend the Hudson's Bay Company men who were not arrested and tried for their crime because "there was a difficulty as to bringing the culprits to trial so as to enforce conviction, as there were no witnesses unconcerned in the murder save God alone" (in McLean 1832: 324).

These two cases stand in sharp contrast to one another. In the one case, Hannah Bay, the Cree are summarily executed; in the killing of eight unarmed Assiniboine men, there is hardly any investigation conducted by the employees of the Hudson's Bay Company, and "the perpetrators [were allowed] to escape with impunity ... The punishment awarded to these murderers was – a reprimand! After this, what protection, or generosity, or justice, can the Indians be said to receive from the Hudson's Bay Company?" (McLean 1932: 325)

We can only speculate of course, but if the Cree were in power and the incidents reversed, so to speak, they might have been busy crafting their own narrative for history, one in which the Cree were the victims of "savage white avarice." But the Cree never had the chance to tell their own version of the Hannah Bay events, so the version that has passed down through history is certainly one-sided, and probably a biased account disfavouring the Cree. Other versions are also certainly possible.

It is also possible, for instance, that Quapakay and his sons visited Corrigal's post with friendly purposes in mind and were fired upon, for whatever reason, by a fearful person suspecting malevolent intentions inside the post. A wild exchange of gunfire could then have broken out. There is at least a modicum of reason to believe that the Cree did not see themselves as the culpable party, since even in the weeks and months to follow Quapakay and his family never ventured far from the Hannah Bay post. This is hardly the actions of a guilty party. Possibly they were waiting for the Hudson's Bay Company to come and investigate so that they could tell their version of the events, but we will never know now, because the HBC factors quickly shaped a narrative in which the Cree were obviously the guilty party and therefore deserved summary execution.

Not Hapless Victims

The Hudson's Bay Company, as the undisputed colonial power in the area, acted as judge, jury, and executioner. In addition, the other Cree in the area were hardly in a position to complain that justice had not been served since they were constantly on the verge of starvation and so heavily dependent upon the Company for the bare necessities of life. This is one opinion set out by ethnohistorians of James Bay, Daniel Francis and Toby Morantz, who summarize this point of view: "Because of their abject dependence on European goods, the Indians lost all freedom of action and control over their own destinies" (1983: 168). This opinion is mirrored by fur-trade historian E.E. Rich who notes that "European supplies were necessities, not luxuries, for the Indian who traded at the Bay, and to many times that number of Indians living inland … The Indian starved if he did not own a serviceable gun, powder, and shot" (1967: 102). It is fair to note, though, that not all ethnohistorians share this point of view, in particular Ray (1974) and Bishop (1974), who write of a "partnership" between Indigenous trappers and fur traders.

Nonetheless, the English fur trader could always go back to Britain on the next out-bound ship as a means of escaping hardship, while the Cree and other Indigenous people had nowhere else to go. As such, they had to make the best of whatever resources were available in their homeland. Contrary to the opinion expressed by E.E. Rich (1967) as reiterated above, Francis and Morantz concluded that "the Indians did not surrender their freedom of action to the trader. The records are full of examples of their refusing to bend to the will to the Hudson's Bay Company. On the contrary, as long as competition existed among traders, the Indians were able to manipulate trade practices to their own advantage … [The Cree were] not hapless victims" (1983: 168).

It is apparent, then, that there is some disagreement in the ethnohistorical literature concerning how dependent the Cree were on the fur trade companies. Why is this an important issue? Well, for one thing, if the Cree were as dependent upon the fur traders for their very lives as Rich and others imply, then it is unlikely that they would jeopardize their life-giving relationship with the English. The fact that the killings at Hannah Bay occurred at all would suggest that some of the Cree were willing to assert themselves in order to save their lives when they came upon desperate times. This would further suggest that the later generation of ethnohistorians, such as Francis, Morantz, Ray, and Bishop, were more correct in their assessment of the Indigenous-trader relationship than their predecessors. It is interesting, though, that not much has been said on the topic of possible dependencies in the fur-trade era over the last 50 years, since the 1970s, Morantz's (2002) study excepted.

After viewing the Hannah Bay killings from various perspectives – food deprivation, the shaking tent and extant religious beliefs, racial bias, all in the context of colonial pressures and resistance – one can provide only tentative conclusions to be followed up by further study. Probably the main observation that one could make was that the southern James Bay area was a disastrous area for the Indigenous people during the fur-trade era, which resulted in constant food deprivation and periodic starvation. These unfavourable ecological conditions would have placed the Cree under near constant psychological stress, leading at times to desperate actions to survive. It is surprising that there were not more raids on trading posts to secure food. Possibly the fear of retaliation by the Hudson's Bay Company meant that many people simply starved to death in their quiet back woods seclusion, as the Irish did during their famine, with their futile lives not recorded for posterity.

Fateful Decisions

On January 20, 1832, Cree elder Quapakay and his sons made a fateful decision to rob the fur trading post at Hannah Bay and shoot the post manager, William Corrigal, and other inhabitants. Their justification for doing so, they claimed, was that the spirit of the shaking tent told them that if they did not "spoil" the post at Hannah Bay their children would not survive the winter. They also suggested that William Corrigal should have been more generous in distributing food from the post's larder on the basis that the Cree and Europeans were "partners," meaning that each party was obligated to help the other in times of need.

This situation from the perspective of anthropology, and other social sciences, is a classic case of the dilemmas that researchers face when dealing with cross-cultural issues – two salient philosophical principles are pitted against each other, each one with its own merits and weaknesses. Each position is more or less diametrically opposed to the other, so that a middle ground between the two positions is difficult to achieve.

On the one hand is the tried-and-true position in anthropology of cultural relativism, derived from the days of Frans Boas and his attempts to see cultures as independent entities and free from the constraining principles of unilinear evolution. From this perspective it is suggested that each culture must be evaluated on its own terms, on the values that are specific to that culture and not in terms of the standards and values of the anthropologists' own society.

Under the "normal" conditions of ethnographic research such a principle is of great value in avoiding invidious comparisons with other cultures and as such avoiding a misrepresentation of people's behaviour. This philosophy lasted for several decades until the atrocities of the Second World War were revealed, especially the concentration camps of Nazi Germany. How, one might ask, could any social scientist reasonably take a relativist perspective with such horrific behaviour in which human beings were slaughtered simply based on their religion or ethnicity.

The result of internal deliberations in the discipline did not totally lead to the abandonment of the cultural relativism philosophy, but it did bring to the forefront the idea that anthropologists need to pay more attention to human rights. So, the question is posed: Do human right supersede the cultural relativist philosophy? While there was much debate about this matter, with different scholars choosing different positions and answers to this basic question, the end result was that the American Anthropological Association voted in 1999 to adopt a Human Rights Declaration. In essence, anthropologists were persuaded to adopt this declaration and acknowledge that they have a responsibility, indeed, and obligation, to uphold international human rights through their research.

There are those, however, who see the human rights declaration as limiting tolerance, suggesting that human rights and cultural understanding can be antithetical to each other. As Engle suggests in an article in the *Human Rights Quarterly*, "To support an acceptance of conflicting cultural practices would be to oppose human rights" (2001: 536). "In particular," Engle (2001: 537) summarizes, "the question of how one might be a cultural relativist and still make overt political judgments guides today's [American Anthropological Association] Human Right Committee." In the 1999 AAA Declaration, it is asserted that "People and groups have a generic right to realize their capacity for culture, and to produce and change the conditions and forms of their physical, personal and social existence, *so long as such activities do not diminish the same capacities of others* [emphasis mine]."

In the discipline of history, a similar dilemma is posed in understanding past societies and behaviours. In his seminal chapter, "On the Limits of 'Presentism' and 'Historicism' in the Historiography of the Behavior Sciences," George Stocking (1968: 1–12) deftly navigates the philosophical issues with each of these polar positions as a guide to research: "historicism," he suggests, is an "attempt to understand the past for the sake of the past"; while the second term, "presentism," seeks to characterize the study of "the past for the sake of the present" (1968: 3). While one can readily understand the epistemological difficulties in attempting to understand the past by utilizing the norms and values of the present, one is nonetheless forced to ask that if the concept of human rights transcends cultural boundaries, does it not then transcend in a similar fashion historical boundaries as well? In other words, while the concept of human right is a phenomenon specific to our own time, why should we not be allowed to adopt a critical eye on past behaviours? If it is all right for us to criticize Nazi concentration camps during the Second World War, why can we not also then disparage the tortuous deaths of the Spanish Inquisition (1478–1834), the Irish famine (1847–9), or the Rwanda genocide (1994). Should such horrors evade our present-day scrutiny simply because they occurred in the past, and today we see ourselves as more humane? Just because we may have a Human Rights Declaration in anthropology or at the United Nations does not mean that these principles will be carried out.

All this background information, both contemporary and historical, leads us inevitably in this book to make a number of pronouncements regarding the killings at Hannah Bay in 1832. I hasten to point out that these opinions expressed are mine alone and do not necessarily represent any anthropological society or association. This disclaimer notwithstanding, debate about these issues is certainly in order. I begin with Richard Preston's assessment in his *Cree Narrative*: "In the story of the Hannah Bay massacre ... we see what happens when a Mistabeo gives morally and tactically poor advice and the people are foolish enough to accept it" (2002: 153). In this case Preston is undeterred in calling Quapakay and his sons "foolish." They should have known, he says, that a Mistabeo is at times unreliable and can give misleading or incorrect information in the conjuring tent. In conclusion, if it's blame you're looking for, Preston clearly places it on the shoulders of the Cree themselves. However, as history has shown time and time again, faced with a despairing situation, people have been willing to take desperate measures to save themselves and their loved ones, regardless of the moralistic debates involved.

Postscript

It appears that the Hannah Bay incident is still a topic of discussion in Moose Factory even into modern times. In Joseph Boyden's novel *Through Black Spruce*, he describes the following narrative:

> Sometimes I'd look south toward Hannah Bay, and it always made me think of Annie and Suzanne's father. And that, in turn, made me think of his relations. His people from long ago. The consensus around here is that his ancestors were crazy. Me, I believe they were simply tired of the Hudson's Bay Company stealing from the *Anishnaabe*. So, Lisette's husband's people killed a few of them to make a statement and stuffed their bodies down a hole cut in the ice to try and get rid of the evidence. But ice becomes water, and water likes to carry its anger to the surface. (2008: 404–5)

So the white men were to blame after all. Perhaps in the spirit world old Quapakay and William Corrigal are still wrestling with each other, after all these years, trying to determine who was right and who was wrong. Yet that was so many years in the past one would think that these murders, by both the Cree and the white men, would have been forgotten long ago in the mist of history.

And so, one final thought before we go. The Spirit above told them that their children would not see the spring if they didn't spoil the post at Hannah Bay, and so they spoiled the post at Hannah Bay and their children lived. The Spirit above did not lie after all.

Notes

1 Introduction

1 For further details on the Indian Act see Kelm and Smith, *Talking Back to the Indian Act* (2018), Joseph, *21 Things You May Not Know about the Indian Act* (2018), and *Indigenous Relations: Insights, Tips and Suggestions to Make Reconciliation a Reality* (2019). On issues pertaining to the debate over Indian status, problems with status reinstatement, especially as it related to Bill C-31(1985), and in particular the Lynn Gehl court challenge, see Hedican (2017: 132–6) and Palmater (2014)

2 In the United States, see Elder (2018) for a discussion of, "Indian" as a political classification."

3 King George III issued the Royal Proclamation of 1763, sometimes referred to as the "Indian Bill of Rights." The proclamation established what could be denoted as the protectionist period of British colonial policy, in which it stated:

"It is just and reasonable, and essential to our interest, and the security of our colonies, that several nations or Tribes of Indians with whom we are connected, and who live under our protection, should not be molested or disturbed in the Possession of such Parts of our Dominions and Territories as, not having been ceded to or purchased by US, are reserved to them or any of them as their Hunting Grounds" (quoted in Hedican 2013: 24–5).

A main point of the proclamation was that it stipulated that the British Crown had the sole responsibility for buying or ceding Indian lands. Thus, the proclamation prevented (or tried to prevent) the sale of Indian lands to unscrupulous land developers. It also laid the foundation for the treaty period in Canada, which involved the ceding of very large tracts of land to the British Crown, and later the government of Canada. The proclamation also laid the foundation for the Indian Act of 1876, which was a cobbling together of various pieces of legislation from the colonial era of Canada (see Surtees 1969, 1982; Hedican 2008a: 12, 135, 144).

4 Bronislaw Malinowski (1884–1942) was born in Poland but became one of the most influential British anthropologists of the early twentieth century. He is primarily known for his theory of functionalism, which was based on the idea that human societies "function" to provide for the basic needs of the individual. Malinowski is also known for his fieldwork among the Trobriand Islands and their ceremonies involving the Kula Ring, a widespread system of exchange involving numerous islands linked in patterns of reciprocal relationships. This ring served furthermore to reduce the hostilities of the people living on these various South Pacific islands. Another important aspect of Malinowski's career involved his commitment to using anthropology for addressing significant public issues of his time, such as the rise of Nazism in Germany during the Second World War.

5 What Marvin Harris probably meant by Lowie's "peculiar methods of research" is no doubt a reference to "historical particularism," as postulated by Franz Boas (1858–1942), which stressed the uniqueness of each individual culture and the historical developments that led to particular cultural characteristics. As such, in Robert Lowie's case, his research became preoccupied with a focus on elder Crow individuals, their bravery in battle, and other themes pertaining to certain individuals in the Crow society, rather than a more well-rounded description of Crow social and economic organization (see Hedican 2012a: 31–5, 70–5).

6 Salzman describes "balanced opposition" in the following manner:

"[It] is an ingenious way to organize security. It is decentralized, in that no central officials or organizers are required. It is democratic, in that decision-making is collective and everyone has a say. It is egalitarian, in that there is no ascribed status rank, or hierarchy into which people are born, and all groups and individuals are equal in principle. It is also to a substantial degree effective, in that balanced opposition often successfully deters attack by threatening reprisal." (2008: 11)

It is obvious, then, that the relationship between the Cree and the members of the Hudson's Bay Company are hardly set against each other in any sort of balanced opposition. The HBC had a preponderance of wealth and power on its side and could use these advantages over the Cree to manipulate and control them in various ways, which was probably at the root of the problem in their asymmetrical relationships.

7 In a preface to Goldschmidt's article, the editor, only identified as G.H., comments:

"The question of peace and war has always been an important question in anthropology. But anthropological concern with this question has changed and somewhat widened in scope over the last decade [i.e., 1976–86]: from a concern with situations of feud and acts of negative reciprocity 'out there,' it is now posed as a question more directly relevant to anthropologists as members of their own respective societies. With the introduction of such subjective issues, has the anthropologist thereby thrown off the cloak of the objective scholar?" (See Goldschmidt 1986: 12.)

8 One of the goals of this study is to encourage the reader to assess their own viewpoints regarding such topics as violence in society (is there ever a place for it?), or the ultimate nature of truth and reality (granted, we will probably never have a definitive answer, but the issues are nonetheless worth contemplating).

9 Even though Schmidt and Schröder (2001: 1) focus their analysis on "conscious actors," they nonetheless point out that the study of violence in anthropology, from their perspective, has begun to undergo a fragmentation resulting in three main approaches. The reader is encouraged to consult the original source for more complete details, but it is sufficient to say here that these are (1) an operational approach, with a focus on the material and political causes of conflict; (2) a cognitive approach, focusing on the emic features of the cultural construction of conflict in a given society; and (3) the experimental approach in which one regards violence as not necessarily confined to situations of intergroup conflict but something that structures people's everyday life. They also point out that these approaches are nonetheless ideal types that "pull away in a different direction from the [current] consensus on the social nature of violence" (ibid.).

10 It is far too easy to discount the views of people in other societies, especially when they are less powerful. As this book shows time and again, the authorities in the colonial regimes probably never cared to learn about the rationale behind Indigenous person's behaviour. To do so would then require a much broader understanding of the Indigenous culture as a whole. As Hickerson (1973: 28) argues, the fur traders usually held little sympathy for the Indigenous trappers on an individual level; they "commonly exploited Indian peoples and depleted their resources in the most ruthless way." If one believes that attitudes in an organization emanate from the top, then we should be cognizant of Gov. George Simpson's opinion concerning the Indigenous people upon whom the HBC depended for their livelihood: "I have made it my study to examine the nature and character of the Indians," Simpson states, "[and] I am convinced they must be ruled with a rod of iron to bring and keep them in a proper state of subordination, and the most certain way to effect this is by letting them feel their dependence upon us" (in Innis 1973: 287).

11 Obviously none of these authors have read much of the ethno-historical literature. The following description of the Wendat (Huron) capture of victims during raids hardly describes a modern football game:

"Women and children who were captured were usually tortured and killed on the spot ... As soon as the Huron had an enemy in their power, they tore out his fingernails, cut or bit off his fingers, and slit his back and shoulders with a knife. These injuries made it difficult for him to escape from the leather thong with which his arms were then bound. At the same time, the Huron reminded him of the cruelties he and his people had practised on them, saying that he must now be prepared to suffer likewise" (Trigger 1987: 70, 72).

12 There are various themes running through the academic literature that encourages anthropologists to become more accountable for the effects that their studies have on Indigenous people. Montijo, for example, comments that "a continuous monologue has persisted and will persist if anthropologists do not accommodate themselves to the politics of the native communities they study ... We must challenge those distorted images imposed upon our people by others" (1993: 16). Similarly, Chacon and Mendoza (2007: 225) state that "we believe that various scholars ... are essentially justified in claiming that many anthropologists have fundamentally fallen short in the valuation of the human rights of Indigenous people." And then there is Deloria's (1995: 65) now famous comment that for Native Americans, "the struggle of this century has been to emerge from the heavy burden of anthropological definitions." There are also criticisms of anthropologists within their own ranks as well, as some feel that ethnography is fine, but anthropologists need to become more politically engaged so that they do not become part of the problem, or as Hickerson suggested: "Often, as individuals sympathetic to Indians, they have nonetheless ignored the very historical relationships which have led to the marginal position held by most Indians today" (1973: 40).

13 There has been a heated debate among scholars in the ethno-historical field for several decades (ca. 1965–85), which has now mostly subsided, concerning the identification of various Indigenous groups in northern Ontario and the Hudson Bay area. Edward Rogers (1969: 36) has noted, for example, the confusing array of nomenclature relating to Indigenous peoples in the historical literature of explorers, missionaries, and fur traders. Some appear to be territorial group names, others Indigenous clan designations, while others are descriptions of broad European or Indigenous origin. Pertaining to differences between the Cree and the Anishinaabe of northern Ontario, Rogers suggests that "the distinction between Cree and Ojibwa [Anishinaabe], in this area [Round Lake] at least, is one based on such minute linguistic details that early travellers and later residents would not have been able consistently to distinguish between the two groups" (1963: 65). In addition, Wright, an archaeologist, indicates that he has avoided the issue by using a general ethnic designation such as "Ojibwa," now commonly known as "Anishinaabe," to apply to a variety of groups in the historical records (1965: 190–1). On the other hand, Hickerson (1967: 45)

asserts that many of these "Ojibwa groups" were probably all Cree, with names such as Kilistinon, Monsoni, and Muskegoes.

14 The first firearms available to the Cree were acquired from the English at the southern end of James Bay after 1670, and at York Fort after 1682. The French posts on the Great Lakes also made muskets available, beginning about 1670 at Sault Ste. Marie. The guns that the Cree first used were a smooth-bore, muzzle-loading trade musket (Smith 1987: 442).

There appears in the ethnohistorical literature a fairly general agreement on the effectiveness of early firearms in influencing fur-trade relationships. Ray (1974: 19–23) notes that the Cree's "territorial expansion [into the Chipewyan area near the head of the Churchill River] was accompanied with a great deal of bloodshed, especially in the northern and southwestern frontiers." James Knight, who was in charge of York Factory, reported that "as many as 6,000 men had been killed along the Cree-Chipewyan border. Most of these losses had been borne by the Chipewyan, which Knight said would not have been the case had they been armed earlier … The opening of Fort Churchill in 1717 made it possible for Indians living in this area to arm themselves, and the Cree no longer had any military advantage over them." It was also noted that the "Cree were said to have become so accustomed to using them [firearms] that they had forgotten how to use bows and arrows as early as 1716" (ibid., 73). At York Factory alone, between 1720–74, nearly 10,000 guns were traded (ibid., 87). HBC records at York indicate that the supply of muskets to the Cree was highest in the late seventeenth century at the beginning of the fur trade, which Ray (1974: 78) attributes to "the initially high demand which was associated with their use in warfare would have been met fairly early," after which there was a downward trend in sales as inter-tribal conflicts subsided (ibid., 78). The lower sales volumes in later years were also the result of older guns being refurbished with new parts.

An opposing view concerning the effectiveness of firearms in the fur trade era is suggested by Joan Townsend, who does not accept the argument that European arms were necessarily superior to Indigenous weapons, at least until about 1850. She states her case succinctly:

"In no case, until after about 1850, can it be assumed that the possession of firearms gave one group an overwhelming advantage over another group with native weaponry. Firearms cannot be used as a primary reason for the successful conquest or domination of one group over another … Technological arguments are on the whole inadequate as explanations of social dynamics" (1983: 1).

One can readily accept the argument that early flintlocks were cumbersome weapons to use. They took an inordinate amount of time to reload and often misfired because of damp powder or any number of other reasons. However, Townsend appears to be missing the point altogether regarding the effectiveness of muskets as a weapon of war – they were very intimidating, made a loud noise, and looked fierce with all this billowing of smoke, especially to anyone not familiar with them. In any event, the evidence that she marshals to support her opinions – a few attacks on Russian vessels by Natives of Alaska – is hardly convincing. However, the larger question is this: if bows and arrows had such a distinctive advantage over early firearms, why did the Cree and other Indigenous people trade for the guns in such large numbers? In addition, if the firearms used by the northern Indigenous populations were so ineffective, as Townsend contends, then how is it that 6,000 men were killed in the Cree-Chipewyan border country around York Factory?

15 In F.G. Bailey's classic work *Stratagems and Spoils*, he describes the various methods by which middlemen attempt to solidify their hold on their position and possibly profit by it: "A middleman is well positioned to build himself a team by transactional means, if, for whatever reason, he has some degree of monopoly of resources which are available from the outside world. [However] there are special conditions ... which inhibit the evolution of their middleman position into a leader." One of these conditions is an inability to "effectively tap those [outside] resources." In effect, then, this is a situation of indirect rule which can nonetheless break down when the subjects who were at once dependent upon the middleman learn to make their own connections, or the controlling power may decide that the existence of the middleman role can no longer be tolerated (1969:174–5).

Similarly, Salzman's (1974, 2008) studies of the politics of encapsulation in the Middle East suggest that colonial powers will attempt to install local leaders who are sympathetic to their agenda of control in cases, such as that of the Cree, in societies that lack a centralized leadership structure. The problem with this approach is that many people in the local society may not regard such leaders as having legitimate authority and therefore will not heed their directives. Furthermore, in the case of the Cree, one could regard the trading captains as a "single-purpose" form of leadership since his authority did not extend beyond dealings concerning the fur trade. In any event, the HBC eventually discontinued this practice because they regarded the provision of presents as too expensive in light of the possible benefits accruing to the company.

16 Eventually the Cree lost their position of importance with the Hudson's Bay Company and were reduced to trapping furs and attempting to subsist in a mostly depleted environment. As such, their reduced position as marginal trappers led to a downward spiral characterized by a near-starvation existence.

17 This saying, today commonly quoted as "discretion is the better part of valour," essentially indicates that "caution is preferable to rash bravery." It is said by Falstaff in William Shakespeare's *King Henry the Fourth, Part I*.

18 In an earlier publication Feagin asks, "What are the distinctive social worlds that have been created by racial oppression over several centuries?" He answers this question by arguing that because racism is more than "racial prejudice and individual bigotry … [it is also a] material, social, and ideological reality that is well-established in major [social, economic, and political] institutions." It is therefore systemic to society as a whole (2006: 2). In turn, what he refers to as "racial profiling processes" are also responsible for generating the "recurring and habitual discriminatory actions" that are manifested in the routine activities of social institutions (2006: 25).

19 What is sorely missing in all these accounts of the Hannah Bay incident is the Cree version of the events, especially a version written in the Cree language. It is impossible to know, for example, the term used by the Cree for the "Spirit above" in reference to the shaking tent. Which spirit ordered Quapakay and his sons to commit such a heinous act? There are many accounts of the shaking or conjuring tent ceremony recorded in the literature, and quite a few by eyewitnesses, mostly anthropologists. In most of these accounts an array of spirits enters the tent, but usually in an ordered procession. The so-called Great Turtle or *Mikinak* is usually the first to enter, known for his peculiar squeaky voice and humorous tone, or as Hallowell records (1942 [1971]: 46), "when smoking he [Mikinak] has the peculiar habit of emitting a long uninterrupted whistle." It is inconceivable that Mikinak would order anyone on the shaking tent to kill anyone. There is so much we do not know, from the Cree perspective. All the accounts that have survived were written by white men who were not likely to see the shaking tent ceremony in a favourable light.

20 For details of this 1827 Huron Tract Treaty see, Canada, 1891, *Indian Treaties and Surrenders*, Vol. 1: 65–78.

21 Premiere Mike Harris's use of this expletive in reference to the Ipperwash protesters was apparently made during a meeting at the Ontario Legislature in a dining room next to the premier's office. The meeting was attended by Premier Harris, various ministers, and their support staff. Ontario's Attorney General Harnick testified during the Ipperwash Inquiry under oath that while he was taking his seat for the meeting, he heard Premier Harris say in a loud voice, "I want the fucking Indians out of the park." Harnick further testified at the inquiry that he was "stunned" by Premier Harris's "insensitive and inappropriate" remark. In a later CBC interview (*CBC News*, Feb. 14, 2006 [ironic that this statement should be made on Valentine's Day]) Mike Harris denied that he had uttered the words reported by Harnick and that he considered such words to be a racist statement. He also said that he had no idea why the Attorney General would fabricate or concoct such a statement (see Hedican 2013, 162).

22 Given Premier Harris's stern statement, OPP officers marched in a hubristic posture into Ipperwash Park the next day, as evening was setting. They

were protected by body armour and shields and had guns at the ready. From all accounts the Indigenous protesters numbered from ten to forty people, including many women and children. At the sight of the advancing police, women began to huddle over their children in an attempt to protect them. Some of the protesters began to hurl stones at the officers in defiance.

Unknown to the police officers, a recording device had been accidently left on that produced a 17-minute tape, which was played during the Linden Inquiry. Inspector Ronald Fox, who had attended the dining-room meeting at Queen's Park, is heard quoting Premier Harris assertion that the government has "tried to pacify and pander to these people far too long," and that the use of "swift affirmative action" was required to remove the protesters from the park. Inspector Fox is then heard to comment to a fellow officer that "we're dealing with a real redneck government … They are just in love with guns." In another tape recording made the day before Dudley George was killed, several OPP officers are heard making disparaging comments about the Indigenous protesters. OPP Sergeant Stan Korosec, who was in charge of the OPP's Emergency Response Team, is heard saying: "We want to amass a fucking army. A real fucking army and do this. Do these fuckers big time" (orig. quoted in Linden 2007: 27, also Hedican 2013: 161–5). As such, not only did Premier Mike Harris, but several OPP officers as well, by their comments, evidenced a hardened racist disposition regarding the Indigenous protesters.

23 McLuhan's main point is that it is the medium that controls and shapes "the scale and form of human association and action" (1964: 9). The media, as in movies, manipulates our conceptions of time and speed. The so-called content is what we concentrate on, but what we are apt to miss is the way this content is delivered to us, and thereby our senses are manipulated during the whole process. A good example is the way history is presented, as if it was all about factual events and not about the manner in which various individuals, societies, and cultures are portrayed. In time, one may begin to accept an (unfounded and unproven) assumption that Indigenous people are lazy, untrustworthy, and otherwise deserving of their fate as disadvantaged people in a settler state. What is never mentioned in the history books that children read are the unscrupulous actions, policies, treaties, and laws that were promulgated by the settlers themselves, which are responsible for this disadvantaged position of Indigenous people in the first place. What is evident, then, is that the way history is presented, and the characteristics of the medium through which the information is channelled, is perhaps every bit as important as the so-called facts themselves.

24 The Hudson's Bay Company does not take kindly to any criticism, especially by former employees. Donald MacKay, in his semi-official HBC history entitled *The Honourable Company*, goes to a considerable length to disparage John McLean's autobiographical account of his life as an HBC

employee in *Notes of a Twenty-Five Years' Service in the Hudson's Bay Territory* (McLean 1968 [1932]). As MacKay relates, "The governor [George Simpson] made enemies. Some of the disgruntled wrote books about their fur trade days, and of these John McLean was the most articulate. McLean was perhaps not one of the politically strongest men in the fur trade, but he came to hate Simpson" (MacKay 1966 [1936]: 207).

McLean's criticism is written off as one holding a grudge: "He [McLean] resigned in 1845, protesting bitterly that Simpson had not given him [a] promised promotion" (ibid.). McLean does indeed disparage Governor Simpson in his book, wondering how the governor "could treat so ungenerously one whom he admitted to be a faithful and meritorious servant, and whom he had acknowledged to be deserving of preferment: and that not on the present day only, but on several former occasions" (1968 [1932]: 333). McLean goes on to say that he regards Governor Simpson as a "despot" and wonders how he "could possibly have the interests of the Company at heart; even supposing for a moment there were no *injustice* in the case" [italics in orig.] (ibid.). He also says that he was "completely disgusted with a service where such acts could be tolerated" and with the governor's decision not to promote him, which McLean regarded as a case of nepotism, since one of Simpson's relatives was promoted instead of McLean. Also, "Clothed with a power so unlimited, it is not to be wondered that [Simpson could] play the tyrant" (ibid., 334). Another fur trader who had served in the company with McLean, A.C. Anderson, is reputed to have said of McLean that:

"I feel assured that on reconsideration he would at this day wish much of what has evidently been written under feelings of anger and disappointment were unwritten. As regards his individual affairs with the Company, I will only say that he was considered in the wrong by all his colleagues in the country who were cognizant of the circumstances" (in McKay 1966: 208).

In another more objective account, John Galbraith's *The Little Emperor* – a title that apparently delighted Simpson since "he was an admirer of Napoleon and read all that he could about his hero" (1976: 121) – Galbraith indicated that John McLean "hated Simpson for what he considered to be bad judgement ... McLean's allegation of Simpson's arbitrariness was exaggerated but, again, not entirely untrue" (ibid., 122). In Peter Newman's account of the Hudson's Bay Company, in *Caesars of the Wilderness*, he also recounts McLean's complaints noting that "the source was suspect because the Governor had refused its author a promotion" (1987: 223). Newman also accused McLean of fabricating the story that the governor wrote up the minutes of council meetings even before they happened (ibid., 244). In McLean's defence, if one reads his account of this story, he was simply relating what another HBC employee had told him about the governor, probably in jest. In sum, there was apparently much fur-trade gossip drifting around in the heads of old men to last for many years, so important when they were young, but now all but forgotten except in the pages of history.

2 The Cree of James Bay

1 As a rule, in anthropological linguistics, there is an assumption that all languages belong to a family of languages and that these languages are related to each other either more closely or more distantly depending upon the departure of the people who spoke these languages from the proto-language or ancestral homeland. One can therefore envisage various people departing from this ancestral homeland at various times. Linguists are often successful in determining also the original words or vocabulary of the proto-language, and the various permutations of these words that took place over time.

A method devised in the 1950s to determine the age of the separation of languages is termed "lexico-statistical dating," or "glottochronology." This dating method is based on vocabulary changes of words assumed to be descended from the same source, or what are termed "cognates." The Grimm brothers of fairy tale fame were largely considered to be the first linguistics to suggest that linguistic change involves a systematic process rather than a haphazard set of events. The task, then, is to determine these various rules by which cognates evolved over time, using their method termed "the law of phonetic change." As an example, "pater" in Latin becomes "father" in English because /p/ changes to /f/ and /t/ changes to /th/ according to the regular changes in phonemes, which are the basic units of sound in a language. As far as the Cree are concerned, they belong to the Algonquian (or Algonkian) family, which comprised about 13 languages. In turn, another related linguistic family of the Algonquians includes the Muskogean family, comprising the Choctaw, Creek, Seminole, among others. There are also various language isolates, meaning that wider language connections have not been determined, such as the Yurok and Wiyot of California. All these languages belong to the Macro-Algonquian Phylum. As one could imagine, there is a great, but yet undetermined, time depth involved, and linguistic studies are determining more language connections as time goes on.

2 Quimby notes that "By the beginning of this period [i.e., the Terminal Glacial Period, 8,000 to 5,000 B.P.] the ice front had retreated to a point near Cochrane, Ontario. Between the ice front and the height of land there was a tremendous glacial lake called Ojibwa-Barlow. It lay east of Lake Agassiz [in present-day Manitoba] and north of the Lake Huron basin, and drained southward either into the Huron basin or into the Ottawa River" (1960: 24).

3 Treaty No. 9, often referred to as the James Bay Treaty, signed between 1905 and 1906, extended Ontario's northern boundary from the Height of Land

(just north of Lake Nipigon) to its present northern boundary of Hudson and James Bay. The treaty comprised some 130,000 square miles of territory whose rivers mostly flowed northward. Various adhesions were made to the treaty in 1929–30, covering an additional 128,000 square miles. Over the years there have been numerous disputes over what the Cree and Anishinaabe claimed they heard the treaty commissioners say when the treaty was negotiated and what eventually was written down in the treaty's provisions. As Macklem (1997: 98) points out, "an examination of the nature, scope, and status of Treaty 9 raises complex questions regarding the relationship between oral and written understandings of the treaty's terms." When Aboriginal people claim that their oral traditions indicate that certain promises made by government representatives were not included in the written text, or that their traditions indicate a different interpretation of the government promises, it is generally the rule that the written account takes precedence over the oral one (see also Hedican 2013: 67).

4 The James Bay Agreement (1975) is often referred to as the first "modern" treaty. In previous treaties the text might comprise several pages of often vague references to the Crown. In the James Bay Agreement there was considerable financial compensation and territorial provisions, at least in comparison to previous treaties. In return for their Aboriginal sovereignty over some 410,000 square miles of northern Quebec, the Cree, Inuit, and (later) the Montagnais-Naskapi received a financial settlement of $225 million, most of which was paid out over a twenty-year period. For example, $75 million was to be paid out over this twenty-year period (1975–95), $75 million when the Quebec hydro project was complete, and $75 million in Quebec bonds (which had a maturity date of 1995). Under this agreement the Cree, and other Indigenous groups in the northern Quebec territory had certain exclusive hunting and fishing rights, as well as a role in the supervision of wildlife harvesting (see Hedican 2008: 173–7 for further details).

5 For those who might be unfamiliar with the anthropological terminology of kinship and marriage, here are some definitions (Hedican 2012: 263–81):

Band: A territorial-based social group, usually relatively small-scale, who live by hunting and gathering.

Bilateral descent: The system of kinship structure in which an individual belongs equally to the kindred of both parents.

Clan: A unilineal kin group in which its members regard themselves as descended from a common ancestor, usually legendary or mythological. *Unilineal descent* means tracing one's relatives through one parent only; through males, *patrilineal descent*, through females, *matrilineal descent*.

Cross-Cousins: Cousins whose related parents are siblings of unlike sex. Offspring of a person's mother's brother or father's sister.

Descent group: A social unit in which members claim descent from a common ancestor.

Exogamy: Marriage outside of a specific social group of which a person is a member, as required by custom or law; contrasts with *Endogamy*, which requires people to marry within a social group.

Kinship system: The customary complex of statuses and roles governing the behaviour of relatives.

Kinship terminology: The set of names applied to the various statuses in kinship system; the linguistic labels used in the classification of kin in particular categories that are used to designate certain genealogical connections between individuals.

Matrilineal: Pertaining to descent through the mother or female line; serves to define groups membership and inheritance rights.

Matrilocal residence: Describes the practice whereby a newly married couple settles in the domicile of the wife's family. Contrasts with *patrilocal residence* in which the married couple reside with the husband's relatives.

Nuclear family: A social group comprising married parents and their children, usually living in the same residence.

Parallel cousins: A cousin whose related parents are of like sex. The offspring of a person's mother's sister or father's brother. Contrasts with *cross-cousins*.

Polygyny: The marriage of a man to two or more women simultaneously; if the women are sisters, then this is called *sororal polygyny*.

3 "A Starving and Naked State": Responses to Deprivation

1 John McLean (1798–1890) was a Hudson's Bay Company fur trader, author, explorer and bank manager. Born in Scotland, he married Margaret Charles at Norway House, Manitoba, in 1837, and they had one child. He married his second wife, Clarissa Evans, in 1845 at Rossville, Manitoba, and they had five children. Her father, Rev. James Evans invented a syllabic writing system for the Cree of James Bay so that the Bible might be translated into their language. McLean first entered the services of the North West Company in Montreal in 1820, and when the Nor'Westers amalgamated with the HBC a year later he was given a posting in British Columbia. Eventually McLean was transferred to the Northern Department at Norway House. With sixteen years of service McLean thought he was eligible for the position of Chief Trader, but he was rejected in his application for promotion, which he thought was the result of the HBC Governor George Simpson. McLean was then given a posting in the Ungava District in 1830 and began exploring present-day Labrador, during which he became the first European to view Grand Falls (now named Churchill

Falls). He eventually returned to the British Isles in 1843 but returned to service a year later. He eventually retired in 1846, partly out of a resentment towards Gov. Simpson and partly due to ill health. McLean is known for his fur trade biography, *Notes of a Twenty-Five Years' Service in the Hudson's Bay Territory* (1968 [1932]), first published in 1849 (Wells 2003).

2 There are some rather startling similarities between the Irish famine and the starvation of the Cree in the Hudson's Bay Lowlands. First, there is the rather obvious fact that both food deprivation situations happened under British colonial rule. Second, in both situations the Irish and the Cree were not able to make their own decisions concerning the distribution of food supplies. In Ireland, the Act of Union of 1800 effectively removed decision-making from Irish hands. As Gallagher (1982: 87–8) explains, "France, Belgium, Holland, German, and Russia all suffered a potato blight in 1846–7. But unlike British-ruled Ireland, they stopped all other food exports to make up for the loss. With virtually its whole population starving, Ireland under self-rule would have done the same thing." And later he notes, during the Irish Famine "The Wheat, barley, oats, and live cattle, sheep, and pigs continued to flow in only one direction – from Ireland to England" (1982: 89). Similarly, in the Hudson Bay region, the Cree were powerless to prevent the British fur traders from hiring professional hunters to virtually deplete the region of existing food sources. It would be interesting to calculate the amount of country food that was consumed by the Hudson's Bay Company employees and their dependents during the 1830s, and subsequently determine the number of Indigenous lives that this food might have saved had it been consumed by the Cree and other Aboriginal people rather than by the British traders who were quite capable of bringing food from England to feed the HBC personnel.

3 A note on transcriptions. Readers need to be aware that the journal records, letters, and other forms of correspondence from the Hudson's Bay Company archives were written almost two hundred years ago. At that time, mostly around the decades from about the 1830s, the English used in the records had certain individual idiosyncrasies, manners of expression, or word usage that might not be familiar to the modern reader. In addition, all the records were handwritten such that the clarity of some surviving records are better, or worse, than others.

The transcriptions used in this book are intended to reflect the spelling and grammatical structures of the original journal entries with the greatest possible accuracy. As a result, verbs written in the past tense often omitted the letter "e," instead opting for an apostrophe, or simply adding "d" as a suffix to the verb. The authors of the journal entries seldom used periods, preferring instead to use hyphens at times. Some passages contain unrecognizable symbols that seem to serve the role of ellipses, which I have often omitted since in most transcriptions ellipses are used to indicate places where words could not be made out. In places where the spelling of certain words, most often names, could not be determined satisfactorily, square parenthesises are used, such as [i.e., Cootutis?]. Remember also that in those times the names for Indigenous people were not recorded other than as a phonetic transcription, which means that the records might contain many different references to the same person, each reference spelled differently depending on what the fur trader heard in that instance. And finally, as indicated, some records are clearer than others, such that a full record could be transcribed with some confidence, but in others, a paraphrasing of the journal entry was used.

4 Kroeber's culture area concept has been the subject of several criticisms. As Sidky (2004: 135–6) points out: "Despite considerable effort invested in the culture area perspective for over two decades, in the end such studies proved sterile because of numerous inherent problems ... First, there was the problem of scale, which entailed continents and subcontinents and environmental complexity on the ground that could not possibly be taken into account theoretically ... Second, the variables employed in such research posed problems [as] there was a lack of consensus as to what constituted a typical cultural trait with which culture areas were to be defined."

5 "Historical particularism" has been defined as follows: "the anti-scientific relativistic, idiographic anthropological perspective associated with Franz Boas, which stressed the uniqueness of each culture thought to be the outcome of chance historical development" (Sidky 2004: 428). In another opinion, Barrett suggests that while Boas has been criticized as being un-scientific, "this is quite unfair ... in fact, it could be argued that in his own way Boas was exceptionally scientific-oriented. The standards that he demanded for fieldwork were rigorous" (2009: 57).

6 Julian Steward was a student of Alfred Kroeber who, in turn, was taught by Franz Boas, so that there is a continuity of sorts through the historical development of anthropological theory. Kroeber added an environmental aspect to Boas's culture concept with this "culture area" concept. Steward then further refined the environmental approach in anthropology by focusing on those areas of a culture that were more clearly influenced by ecological factors, such as technology and economic systems, as opposed from those farther removed, such as religion and art. Then, in taking this approach a step further, Steward welded his core-periphery idea to develop a connection between ecology and evolutionism. In Steward's words, "particular cultures diverge significantly from one another and do not pass through unilinear stages" (1955: 28) As such, he attempted to differentiate his approach from the early evolutionists in anthropology, such as Tyler and Morgan, by coining the term "multi-linear evolutionism."

7 Based on his fieldwork among the Waswanipi Cree of northern Quebec, Feit placed a considerable emphasis on the role of chance in a hunter's success. As he explains:

"Among the game hunters the very scarcity, mobility, unpredictability, and difficulty of capture of the animals leave the hunter with little hope for, except that he kills the animals he needs and adjusts himself to the results. It has been repeated again and again, that there can be little planning, and little foresight because so much of the outcome of the hunt is chance" (1973: 115). [However], "for each animal species the Waswanipi harvest, they attempt, like for the moose, to utilize it at times when chances of success are highest and the efficiency of capture maximized" (ibid., 120).

8 John George McTavish (c. 1778–1847) was born in Scotland and entered the service of the North West Company in 1798 (A.36/A; A.44/3). During his twenty-three years of service with the NWC he started as a company clerk, at one time travelled with famed explorer David Thomson, and, at the time of the amalgamation, was in charge of the company headquarters at Fort William. With the Hudson's Bay Company, he was made a chief factor at York Factory (1821–8), Moose Factory (1830–5), Lake of the Two Mountains (1836–46) and then retired from service in 1847, the year of his death. He was married four times, first to Charlotte Thomas (daughter of John Thomas), Nancy McKenzie (daughter of Roderick McKenzie, having five daughters). His next wife was Catherine Turner (two daughters), and finally Elizabeth Cameron (two daughters). See also David Thompson, *Narrative of Explorations in Western North America* (1916).

9 Joseph Beioley (1785–1859) entered the service of the Hudson's Bay Company in 1800 where he first began to serve as an apprentice and clerk at Fort Albany (1800–10, A.1/48 fo.19d). From there he served as an accountant at four different postings in the Red River and Osnaburgh (northern Ontario) Districts (1808–15). From then on he served as chief factor of Moose Factory and Rupert's River (1821–41), after which he retired in 1843 after a brief furlough in Europe. He was married to Isabella McKay, daughter of John McKay, of Albany River, having one son, Richard William Fletcher (his "natural, lawful and only child"), who went to England in 1819 (A.44/4/p.7).

10 William Corrigal (1774–1832) was born in Kirkwall, Orkney, and died in the Hannah Bay murders of January 22, 1832 (see B.135/a/137 for description of event). He entered the Hudson's Bay Company service in 1794, starting as a labourer in the Albany District and eventually promoted to post master at Eagle Lake (1794–1810). Corrigal spent a year in Montreal as a witness in the murder trial of John Mowat who had killed Aeneas McDonnell in Eagle Lake in 1809. William Corrigal was also implicated in the murder, along with Mowat, was imprisoned but later tried and acquitted. In 1812 he received some compensation from the HBC. He had a brother,

Jacob Corrigal (possibly John, 1772–1884), and a son, Jacob Corrigal, who was named administrator of William's estate (A.36/5, fos. 105–9).

11 William Swanson (1794–1865) was the leader of the search party that was recruited to find the culprits of the Hannah Bay murders and ascertain the situation at the Hannah Bay post. Swanson entered the services of the Hudson's Bay Company in 1812 at age 18 and served at various times as a sailor, sloop master, and postmaster spending most of his career in and around the Moose Factory post where he was eventually buried. During his service he had numerous wives and children. Swanson first wife was Anne Brown (daughter of Joseph Brown) with whom he had eight children (four daughters and four sons born between 1816 and 1832), followed by Betsy Hister (one son born in 1837), and Frances Robinson, daughter of John Robinson of Michipicoten, with whom he had eleven children (seven sons and four daughters born between 1841 and 1858), for a total of twenty children. Source: Anglican Church of Canada B.135/g/48; B.135/g/12 fo.21).

12 James Anderson (1812–67) was born in Calcutta, India, where his father was a military officer and later ran a plantation. Anderson joined the Hudson's Bay Company in 1831 and was first posted at Moose Factory where he played a leading role in apprehending and summarily executing the offenders in the 1832 murders at Hannah Bay. He was promoted to chief factor in 1847 while serving at Nipigon post. In 1850 he was transferred to the Northern Department and put in charge of the Athabasca District for one year. For the next eight years he headed the more distant Mackenzie River District at Fort Simpson, its headquarters, where he was promoted to chief factor in 1855.

Anderson also played a significant role in the search for the Arctic expedition of Sir John Franklin when the British Admiralty asked the HBC to send an expedition down the Great Fish (Black) River in 1855 to verify a report that the remains of Franklin's crew had been found there. Upon reaching his destination Anderson found scattered tools and wood fragments, one bearing the name *Terror*, thus confirming the previous report. He suffered health issues on this excursion, first permanently losing his voice, and later his death from tuberculosis. When Anderson died in 1867, he was survived by his wife Margaret, daughter of Roderick McKenzie, also an HBC chief factor, six sons and one daughter (Mackinnon 2003).

13 The front page of Anderson's journal has the following notation: "Transcribed by G.H. Gunn, Provincial Archives of Manitoba, MG 9 A 78–2 Box 5 File #49, fos.4–6." At the end of the journal is the following notation:

"The above journal was copied by me this day from the original MS journal kept by Jas. Anderson, who was on the punative [*sic*] party, and loaned to me by his son, James Anderson of Ainslie Hill Farm, Sutton West, and is hereby certified by me as a correct copy of the original, which was all in the hand-writing of James Anderson, Sr. Sutton West, Ont., July 1st, 1931, G.H. Gunn" [his signature].

14 As an example, a search was conducted through the index to MacKay's 1966 [1936] *The Honourable Company* for such terms as "hunger," "food," "deprivation," or "starvation," and there were no entries for these. Similarly, a search was further conducted through Harold Innis's *The Fur Trade in Canada* (1970) with a similar result, as well as Galbraith's *The Hudson's Bay Company* (1957), leading to the conclusion that such a condition did not exist or was of no interest to historians of the fur trade. What is even more interesting is the virtual lack of any mention of Indigenous people themselves and their role in the fur trade, which are decidedly Euro-centric accounts.

4 Colonial Resistance and Survival

1 Of course one could argue against any of these claims. It probably matters little if a bear is shot or killed in a deadfall since the result is the same in any event. There must have been a reason, though, why Indigenous people sought European goods over those of their own manufacture, even if this reason had to do with matters of prestige, economic efficiency, political relationships, or some other cause. What matters is that Indigenous people sought European goods and were willing to go to a considerable length and effort to obtain them. As far as the reputed European dependency on Indigenous people is concerned, this also is a contentious issue. Few would doubt that Indigenous people possessed superior skill in the bush environment in which they were raised, but Europeans could purchase the food they needed without actually hunting it themselves, so the argument that could be made on both sides of this issue are in some ways hardly worth making.

2 It is difficult to determine where McLean might have obtained such information and, furthermore, to gauge the extent to which this idea of a general rebellion in the James Bay area might have been shared by other fur traders. It is possible, of course, that the fur traders were aware of a general dissention among the Indigenous people because of the lack of food in the Hudson Bay Lowlands, and as such linked the Hannah Bay murders to this pervasive situation of malcontent. However, given the fact that such a rebellion did not take place would indicate that such feelings were not widely shared by the Indigenous people. Remember also that Boland, Quapakay's son-in-law, was eventually turned in by his own father when he sought refuge among his biological family. This possibly meant that the Cree feared reprisals from the HBC for anyone who aided the murderers, that they didn't agree with the killings, or a combination of both reasons.

3 The editor of this volume, W.S. Wallace (ibid.), indicated in a footnote that there were some marginal comments on this passage in the handwriting of A.C. Anderson, written in a copy of McLean's *Notes* in the Legislative Library at Victoria, British Columbia, as follows:

"It was a horrible atrocity, the rumour of which caused a thrill of shame and indignation throughout the county."

4 What McLean is apparently indicating was that the HBC was not interested in justice, but mere retaliation, for attacks on their own personnel. However, when it came to attacks by HBC employees on Indigenous people, this was a matter of little interest, suggesting the hypocritical nature of British colonial standards of democracy and fair play.

5 The Hudson's Bay Company was prepared to sell to the Americans who would pay top dollar, but the British government made it clear it wanted the territory to be sold to Canada. On March 20, 1869, the Hudson's Bay Company reluctantly, under pressure from Great Britain, sold Rupert's Land to the Government of Canada for $1.5 million. The sale involved roughly a quarter of the continent, a staggering amount of land, but it failed to take into account the existing Indigenous residents (see "Canada Buys Rupert's Land," https://www.cbc.ca/history /EPCONTENTSE1EP9CH1PA3LE.html, accessed July 28, 2020).

6 In addition, Voyageur and Calliou explain that "The newcomers justified taking First Nations' land by characterizing Aboriginal peoples – their former benefactors and allies – as being less than human ... Over time, Aboriginal peoples' numbers were depleted by disease and epidemics. Non-Aboriginals saw them as a dying race. The First Nations increasingly came under the control of the state and its institutions and were subjugated by law." (2011: 210).

7 However, as the editor of McLean's volume, W.S. Wallace, indicates, "This statement is not strictly accurate," since Quapakay and his sons were apparently, that is according to the post records at the time, shot by William Swanson and his posse near the Hannah Bay post, he asserts (1968 [1932]: 323–4).

8 For example, in an article on "Public Relations and Propaganda Techniques," at the Graduate School of Political Management at George Washington University, it is stated that

"Propaganda has been an effective tool to shape public opinion and action for centuries. Since propaganda and public relations both share the goal of using mass communication to influence public perception, it can be easy to conflate the two. Propaganda, however, traffics in lies, misinformation, inflammatory language, and other negative communication to achieve an objective related to a cause, goal, or political agenda. Though propaganda techniques can be employed by bad actors on the world stage, these same concepts can be utilized by individuals in their interpersonal relationships. Regardless of how propaganda is employed, these common techniques are used to manipulate others to act or respond in the way that the propagandist desires."

(See https://gspm.online.gwu.edu/blog/public-relations-and-propaganda-techniques/ accessed July 30, 2020).

9 The conventional view is that at the beginning of the colonial encounter Europeans were dependent upon Indigenous people for food, shelter, and other necessities of life, but with time this relationship began to change such that it was the Indigenous people who became dependent upon the Europeans. However, this is simply the European point of view. What is lacking are the Indigenous perspectives on this cultural interaction. As A.G. Bailey pointed out:

"It is difficult, if not impossible, to form an idea of what the Indian thought of the European during the first period of encounter. It is difficult because, as we cannot transcend our own traditional processes, we are bound to read into the actual Indian view one that has been especially conditioned by our peculiar cultural background. That is, the subjective standpoint cannot be eliminated (1969: 6)."

It goes without saying that this condition, in which Indigenous perspectives are either not known or ignored all together, not only relates to this "first period of encounter" but throughout most of Canadian history.

10 Sociologist Jennifer Eagan suggests the following definition of "multiculturalism":

"*Multiculturalism*: the view that cultures, races, and ethnicities, particularly those of minority groups, deserve special acknowledgment of their differences within a dominant political culture. That acknowledgment can take the forms of recognition of contributions to the cultural life of the political community as a whole, a demand for special protection under the law for certain cultural groups, or autonomous rights of governance for certain cultures. Multiculturalism is both a response to the fact of cultural pluralism in modern democracies and a way of compensating cultural groups for past exclusion, discrimination, and oppression. Most modern democracies comprise members with diverse cultural viewpoints, practices, and contributions. Many minority cultural groups have experienced exclusion or the denigration of their contributions and identities in the past. Multiculturalism seeks the inclusion of the views and contributions of diverse members of society while maintaining respect for their differences and withholding the demand for their assimilation into the dominant culture." (https://www.britannica.com/topic/multiculturalism#info-article-history, accessed August 3, 2020).

11 Anthropologist Elizabeth Pauls defines "assimilation," from a social and cultural perspective, in the following way:

"*Assimilation*: In anthropology and sociology, the process whereby individuals or groups of differing ethnic heritage are absorbed into the dominant culture of a society. The process of assimilating involves taking on the
traits of the dominant culture to such a degree that the assimilating group
becomes socially indistinguishable from other members of the society. As
such, assimilation is the most extreme form of acculturation. Although
assimilation may be compelled through force or undertaken voluntarily, it
is rare for a minority group to replace its previous cultural practices completely; religion, food preferences, or proxemics" (https://www.britannica
.com/topic/assimilation-society, accessed, August 3, 2020).

12 The Merriam-Webster dictionary defines "culture conflict" as
"The conflict of behaviour patterns and values that results when different cultures are incompletely assimilated" (https://www.merriam
-webster.com/dictionary/culture%20conflict, access August 3, 2020).

13 Fanon further explains that while the colonized may be unable, initially, to direct their anger at the colonizers and their institutions, this
anger may instead be directed inwards, against their fellows. In time,
however, as the struggle builds, there is the realization that the settler
is not any more inherently superior to the Native, and this "discovery shakes the world in a very necessary manner" (1963: 45). Thus, in
Fanon's resistance scenario, violence and colonization are inseparable
phenomenon. In this manner he poignantly captures the ironies of the
resistance to colonialization in terms of reinvention. The "new Natives"
are forced to find their own way along a path that is neither tribal nor
Western since, as Emma Larocque (2010: 157) states, "We cannot accept
that human progress begins and ends with European culture. Because it
does not." There is a certain inevitability of reinvention with resistance,
as far as Fanon is concerned, in a mobilization of human creativity.
Larocque, however, counters with a statement which echoes one made
by Fanon when she states that, "I believe we must reinvent ourselves ...
our country, our Americas, our world. By reinvention, I do not mean
prefabrication or mythmaking, I mean, among other things, throwing
off the weight of antiquity, and, by doing so, offering new possibilities
for reconstruction" (ibid., 158).

14 The colonial relationship between the Indigenous people and the settler
population in Canada is described by Asch (2000: 148) in the following
manner:
"While Canada, like many other settler states where the former colonists
have now become the majority of the population, may have achieved its
formal independence from its former 'parent' state, at a most basic level
it finds itself nonetheless a creature of the very colonial institutions and
values that formed the fabric of the political culture of the colonizers. It is

therefore not so much postcolonial as it is 'colonial in its own political ideology and composition.'"

5 Violent Conflicts Involving Indigenous People

1 This sentence is completed with "or – what amounts to the same thing –
were not able to leave areas that, through desiccation or other geoclimato-
logical processes, were becoming low in natural food potential." This latter
part of Freid's sentence further describes the difficult ecological situation
of the Cree, who, because of their attachment to particular trapping territories, were in effect forced to remain in a deteriorating environmental area
with declining potential for food production.

2 It is a general tenet in anthropology that before the advent of horticulture
(small scale agriculture usually dependent upon a single dominant crop)
hunters lived in the most propitious ecological areas of the earth, such as
the Pacific Northwest coast, where the actual subsistence activities took up
relatively small amounts of time. Even the Kalahari Desert, described by
Richard Lee as having a "drought every second or third year, [is] by any
account, a marginal environment for human habitation" (1968: 30). In sum,
"the fact emerges that !Kung Bushmen of Dobe, despite the harsh environment, devote from twelve to nineteen hours a week to getting food …
The level of work observed is an accurate reflection of the effort required
to meet the immediate caloric needs of the group … [In other words] food
getting occupies … a small proportion of a Bushman's waking hours"
(ibid., 37). It is reasonable to assume, then, that people living in more
favourable environments would devote considerably less time to basic
subsistence activities. Unfortunately, comparable ethnographic reporting
for the Cree in the James Bay area is difficult to determine, since the meat
secured by trapping is eaten along with other birds, fish, and game. Given
the near constant reporting in the HBC journals of food deprivation among
the Cree one might assume that the Hudson Bay Lowlands might be an
even less favourable area for human habitation than the Kalahari Desert, as
remarkable and disconcerting as this might appear.

3 For those who live in contemporary North America, with its abundance
of food and millions of obese people, it is hard to imagine anyone having
a fear of starvation, which was the essential ongoing dread of the Cree
in northern Ontario and Quebec. In Cummins's (2004: 30–1) study of the
Attawapiskat Cree even in the 1940s it is noted that "Today, there are people in Attawapiskat who either remember themselves, or who remember
being told by their parents of being afraid to leave the post out of fear of
'dying in the bush.' As a general rule people did not want to go too far
into the bush because they might get lost and starve to death." At the

local fur trading post, in an entry dated on March 21, 1920, it was noted that "arrived today from his camp starving and also sick ... his family ... had nothing to eat when he left them" (HBC B.243/a/1). A decade later, on March 13, 1930, conditions appear not have improved, according to the following HBC entry: "David Ookiitigoo's wife arrived at the post and reported that her husband was sick and that they were entirely out of 'grub' " (HBC B.243/a/1). Cummins' conclusion was that the Church and fur-trading companies did make attempts to aid the poor and destitute, since there are numerous references in the post journals to "the issuing of rations." "Nonetheless, we must regard the response of the fur companies to the Attawapiskat Cree's plight as ambiguous at best ... [It is apparent] that the profits of the stores was a priority." As far as the generosity of the Church was concerned, "while not denying the undoubted decency of intent through the giving of food, we must examine the underlying message of this benevolence. It is rather clear: life as the Cree knew it was evil and dangerous; the more desirable ideology was that offered by the Church ... As was plainly visible, the missionaries and the traders were not subject to disease and starvation. Indeed, they had surplus goods to share – if they wanted to" (ibid., 31). What is also eminently obvious is that the situation of the Cree at Hannah Bay during the previous century, that is, during the 1830s, remained virtually the same over this time as that experienced by their Attawapiskat neighbours in a much earlier period. In both periods, the English colonialists had access to an abundance of food but seemed rather oblivious, despite their Christian upbringing, to the impoverished plight of the Indigenous people in their midst.

4 For those readers who might be unfamiliar with all the nuances of anthropological theory, it is important to indicate that Lévi-Strauss's so-called structural approach has been the target of criticism from several points of view. Sidky (2004: 273–6), for example, in an assessment of this approach indicates that "as a research strategy it has numerous shortcomings ... Its methodological procedures are impossible to replicate ... Lévi-Strauss's program dismisses empirical reality as irrelevant. He totally glosses over intercultural and intracultural variations ... The structures that Lévis-Strauss talks about are fictional and unreal and exist only in his own mind." Despite these criticisms, Lévis-Strauss has had his defenders. Barrett (2009: 150) notes, for example, that "Lévis-Strauss threw fresh light on a number of classical topics, from kinship to social structure, totemism, and the logic of pre-industrial thought."

5 It is important to note, however, that after the merger of 1821 with the virtual elimination of competition from "free" traders, the Hudson's Bay Company mostly discontinued the practice of gift-giving as a prelude to trade, based on the rationale that it was "too expensive" and no longer

necessary to curry the favour of the Indigenous trappers who might otherwise trade with the HBC's competitors.

6 Rivalries among the various fur-trading companies has been well documented in the historical literature; however, scant attention has been paid to the internal conflicts within the Hudson's Bay Company itself. In addition, it would be interesting to find out more concerning the various post managers' remuneration: Were they paid strictly a wage, or were they offered incentives to increase the volume of trade, which potentially could increase tensions between the various trading posts? There are also the issues of post managers attempting to secure the loyalty of Indigenous trappers in a particular region. A volume dealing with these matters would provide interesting insights into fur trade operations.

7 One can search in vain for any mention of the Henley House incident. Just as the Hannah Bay murders are not even mentioned in MacKay's *The Honourable Company* (1966), Henley House is only given this scant note: "Henley House was the only inland post, and it was barely one hundred and fifty miles up the Albany" (ibid., 84). Unfortunately, no further details are given.

8 Any fears that the English traders had concerning French attacks on their posts were certainly well founded. During 1682–3, for example, Pierre Radisson and Médard des Groseilliers deserted the Hudson's Bay Company with the intention of establishing a trading post at the Nelson River. On August 20, they captured Benjamin Gillam, his ship and crew and the Hudson's Bay Company servants. They then travelled to the mouth of the Hayes River and established Fort Bourbon. In 1683 some of the Hudson's Bay Company prisoners were allowed to leave on a ship, *Ste Anne*, to James Bay. Eventually the English, in 1684, captured Fort Bourbon, at that time occupied by Radisson's nephew, Jean-Baptiste Chouart (Rich 1958: 135).

In another incident, which occurred in 1686, Pierre de Troyes led a French overland expedition from Montreal from March 20 to early October with the intention of capturing Hudson's Bay Company posts in James Bay in retaliation for the loss of Fort Bourbon. A detachment of 100 men in 35 canoes travelled by the Ottawa River and Lakes Timiskaming and Abitibi, reaching James Bay on June 20. This party successfully captured Moose Fort, Rupert House, and Fort Albany all by surprise attacks. Fifty-two Englishmen were sent to York Factory and the rest kept prisoner in James Bay over the winter (Kenyon and Turnbull 1971; Rich 1958: 212–27).

9 In anthropology, developing a definition of marriage has historically posed numerable issues. Human beings have a propensity for taking what would appear to some as a relatively simple relationship and complicating it beyond reason, or using every possible permutations as if they were conducting an experiment beyond all practical necessity. As an example, there is the case of several women married to one man (polygyny), several

men married to one woman (polyandry), or the marriage of one woman to one man (monogamy). The older definition in anthropology – that is, marriage is a socially approved sexual and economic union between a man and a woman – has all sorts of problems inherent in it, especially in today's world of same-sex marriage and trans-gender relationships. In addition, in some societies a distinction is made between a *"pater,"* who is the father with legal rights over a child, and a *"genitor,"* who is the biological father but who does not have legal rights. There are even cases of women "standing in, or as a surrogate" for a father, which means that one does not necessarily even have to be a male to be a "father," or even a "husband" (see Hedican [2012a: 122–5] for further discussion of these issues).

10 The Aborigines' Protection Society (APS) was an international human rights organization, founded in 1837, to ensure the health and well-being of Indigenous peoples along with their sovereign, legal, and religious rights while also promoting the civilization of the Indigenous people who were subjected under colonial powers. (https://en.wikipedia.org/wiki /Aborigines%27_Protection_Society, accessed August 11, 2020).

11 The point that is made here is that the relationships between patrons and their clients do not take place in a vacuum; they take place within certain historical, cultural, political, and economic settings that influence the "shape" of these relationships. As an example, if the patron is distributing resources to clients, then the source of these resources is an important factor in the success that a patron is able to achieve in influencing the behaviour of clients.

12 Durkheim was quite opposed to reducing explanations of social life to basic psychological explanations. As Barrett (2009: 35) explains, Durkheim "declared that when any psychological explanation is provided for a social phenomenon we may be certain that it is wrong." On this basis, social anthropologists "take the personality system as a constant, and look for variations in the social structure as the basis for their investigations; psychologists accept the social structure as a constant, and look for variations in the personality system as the basis for their analysis" (ibid.).

13 Robert Merton, a renowned sociologist in his time, was a great critic of what he termed the "ex post facto explanation," which essentially means crafting an explanation of an event or situation when it is over, which he regarded as the weakest form of theorizing. As an example, one could say that Native American youth had a troubled upbringing and use this information to explain the reasons why they might be more prone to homicide than other youths with a more "normal" upbringing. There are several problems here: For example, how then does one explain incidents of homicide among youth who did not experience the trauma of a troubled upbringing? Second, to be convincing one would need a control group, say

Native American youth with so-called normal upbringings and then see if those regarded as the troubled youth differed in a significant way from the control group with regards to the variable(s) under study. Since this deductive approach (logical reasoning from the general to the particular) is almost never carried out, one is simply explaining so-called facts that account in a reasonable manner for the phenomenon under study, whether the crafted explanation is valid or not. Think about the explanations that have been offered for incidences of Native American homicide and see which ones fit this pattern of ex post facto explanations. (See Merton 1949; Merton and Barber 1976.)

14 Economic explanations are commonly employed in the social sciences. There is an obvious appeal for this perspective in that economic studies often employ "hard" data, such a census reports, employment incomes, or other numerical information that appears valid simply because of its less subjective use than, say, assessing one's feelings or opinions, which are seen as less concrete. However, there are times when economic explanations are also seen to be at the root of most sociological phenomenon, sometimes referred to as "economic determinism." Obviously, there are a multiplicity of explanations possible for any number of situations – social, cultural, psychological, economic, religious, and so on, depending upon the researcher's perspective, training, and propensity towards understanding social phenomenon.

15 "Ethnocentrism" is commonly understood to mean "the making of value judgments concerning other people or their culture on the basis of a belief in the superiority of one's own way of life or cultural standards" (Hedican 2012a: 268).

16 Cultural comparisons have been a long-standing problem in the history of anthropology. Principal among these issues is the matter of the commensurability of different cultural aspects and the methodology used to accomplish this task. In an attempt to deal with this problem the "comparative method" was developed. As Sidky (2004: 44) explains, "The rationale behind [the comparative method] was the idea that traits and customs that are similar to one another have evolutionary connections and similar points of origin that could be revealed through systematic comparisons." Later approaches attempted to refine this method, conducting what were termed "controlled comparisons" and "statistical cross-cultural comparisons." The main idea behind both approaches involve the comparison of particular cases that share certain factors in common. Statistical methods are used in cross-cultural comparisons to test the validity of hypotheses against data drawn from various cultures around the world. A common data base used for these comparisons is the *Human Relations Area Files*, which are used to examine correlations between such variables as kinship

types, marriage patterns, leadership roles, religious beliefs, and a wide variety of other characteristics.

17 As is evident in many of these studies of homicide, the result (a certain level of homicide in a community) is stipulated and then a probable cause (such as interpersonal aggression) is deemed to be the factor most responsible. In some cases, this end result, such as interpersonal aggression, is then used to explain the initial cause of such a homicide. Thus, there is evidence of tautological explanations in many of these reports. In addition, there is almost complete lack of explanation that links the variables together, other than to stipulate that one leads to another and so on without tangible evidence presented. Even so, in the case of attributing homicide to interpersonal aggression, it is not at all clear why certain aggressive individuals do not commit homicide if their aggressiveness is the determining factor.

18 The authors (Levy et. al. 1969: 124) were careful to distinguish between "criminal homicide," that is, murder in the first and second degree, and manslaughter or accidental homicide. This is a distinction that I found was not commonly made in the literature concerning homicide among Native Americans, with the result that the homicide figures that were reported in some studies may be considerably higher than in those studies in which only criminal homicide is taken into consideration.

19 All kinship systems have their particular problems and inconsistencies. The reference here to "structural weaknesses" in the matrilineal kinship system requires further explanation, which those who follow a bilateral (kinship reckoning from both the father's and mother's side of a family) might not appreciate. When a couple married using a matrilineal kinship system, generally the man went to live with the wife's relatives in her village, a practice referred to as matrilocal residence (Hedican 2017: 82–4). The village social structure was therefore solidified by the kinship ties between related women and children. Children were considered to belong to their mother's kinship group, rather than the father's family. In the case of a matrilineal system, male children do not belong to the same kinship group as one's father, so male relatives on the mother's side of the family tend to be just as important, or more so, than one's actual biological father (Labelle 2013: 178–80). There are good reasons why divorce in a matrilineal system might not be initiated by males, since in such societies they are in a particularly vulnerable position. If a man divorced, for example, he would no longer be allowed to live in the same village as his wife, as he would have no kinsmen there. Alternatively, if he returned to his natal village, he could be regarded as a matter of disgrace. In this case, the husband would be "reduced to a wretched life, seeing that it is the women in our country who sow, plant, and cultivate the land, and prepare food for the husbands" (Tooker 1964: 126).

In matrilineal systems, men were frequently involved in various inter-tribal conflicts. "Among the Huron [Wendat]," Trigger (1987: 69) explains, "every man was a warrior and the virtues of man and warrior were identical … Men sought every opportunity to test their courage." Conflict between the Wendat (Huron) of Ontario and the Haudenosaunee (Iroquois) of New York State became a prevalent pattern of tribal relations during the 1600s (Hunt 1940). Raids, usually of a retaliatory nature, were carried out on a relatively small scale for many decades; however, the number of such skirmishes increased dramatically during the 1640s. There have been various reasons proposed for this warfare. Hunt (1940), in *The Wars of the Iroquois*, suggested that the conflict between the Wendat and the Haudenosaunee was the result of economic competition in an attempt to control the fur trade. There are other explanations proposed, mainly of a psychological nature, such as Ot-terbein's (1964) suggestion that because of the matrilocal marriage-residence pattern, men lacked methods of asserting their prowess. As such, warfare provided an outlet for male aggression and a method of gaining prestige.

20 McKanna (1993: 366) notes further that "Native Americans received inferior legal representation and experienced intense plea-bargaining coercion. Their convictions rates were higher, and they were more likely to receive death sentences than whites. "With intense racial prejudice and numerous interracial homicides," she asks, "is it any wonder that Indian defendants were treated so harshly?"

21 It has also been suggested that Arizona territorial authorities in the nineteenth century failed to provide methods whereby Native Americans could be incorporated into an American justice system, which was a "foreign and distinct legal structure" from that of the Indigenous population of the country. Furthermore, it was her conclusion that "historical data illuminate two standards of justice: treatment of American Indian defendants within the Arizona territorial criminal justice systems was disparate, discriminatory, and unfairly severe compared to white defendants" (ibid., 366).

22 There is also another serious issue pertaining to the number of persons convicted of homicide who subsequently die in prison, especially among Native American inmates. Mortality statistics for Yuma Territorial Prison show that Native American death rates were much higher than those for either whites or Hispanics. Within the first four years of incarceration, 37 percent of Native Americans sentenced to prison for murder or manslaughter died. By comparison, just 4 percent of whites, and 10 percent of Hispanics, died in prison during this period. In addition, at San Quentin Prison in California, 43 percent of Native Americans convicted of homicide or manslaughter died within the first four years of their sentence (ibid., 365).

23 The discussion of a comparison in the assessment of crime seriousness is based on the previous writings of Wolfgang and Ferrucuti (1967), who

postulated that there should be a close correspondence between homicide rates and cultural assessments of homicide. See also Perry's (2004) statistical reporting on murder victims. He notes that between 1976 and 2001, Native Americans were just .07 per cent of all murder victims in the US, and of all those arrested for violent crimes (such as homicide and aggravated assault) about 1 per cent were Indigenous people, which is in line with the overall population percentages. In other words, Native Americans are no more prone to commit violent crimes than anyone else in America, although for whatever reasons there is a distinct attempt to prove otherwise in the academic literature.

24 The statistical data that Mckanna (1993: 359) refers to is derived from court records of Cochise, Coconino, Gila, Pima, Pinal, and Yavapai counties for the period 1880–1912. In addition, as she indicates, "County registers of criminal action provide the main source of comparative aggregate data, but will be supplemented by Yuma Territorial Registers, and federal district court records." For crime research techniques pertinent to Native American homicide cases, see also McKanna's articles in the *Journal of Social History* (March 1985) and *Pacific Historian* (Spring 1987).

25 For further discussion of issues relating to the Canadian Justice system see Carol La Prairie (2002). There is also a considerable discussion in the Canadian literature concerning the wrongful convictions of Indigenous people, such as the Donald Marshal decision (Coates 2000), the rule of law issues in the Caledonia dispute (DeVries 2011), and the shooting of an Aboriginal protester such as occurred in the Ipperwash protest (Hedican 2012b, 2013).

6 Creating History: Narratives of Disentitlement

1 Thomas (Tom) King is the first Massey lecturer (2003 CBC Massey Lectures) of Indigenous descent. In his Massey lectures he asserts that "Stories are wondrous things. And they are dangerous" (2003: 9). What is meant by this statement is that "Stories assert tremendous control over our lives, informing who we are and how we treat one another as friends, family, and citizens" (King 2003, back cover). King is also known for his popular CBC Radio series, *The Dead Dog Café Comedy Hour*. His book *The Truth about Stories: A Native Narrative* was broadcast in November 2003 as part of CBC radio's *Ideas* series.

2 In anthropology, with the merging of linguistic and cultural studies, it is now generally accepted that the language one uses controls, shapes, or otherwise conditions the world view of the participant. More specifically, this is what has come to be called the *Sapir-Whorf Hypothesis*, which Sidky (2004: 438) describes as "the principle that language determines thought and perceptions of reality, after work of the linguistic anthropologists

Edward Sapir and Benjamin Whorf." An alternative phrasing of this supposition is that of *Linguistic Relativity*, "the view that holds that language
and culture are interrelated and that people's thoughts and perceptions
of reality are powerfully influenced by the language they speak" (Lucy
1997: 291–312). What both formulations suggest is that an entirely accurate
cross-cultural translation of ideas is virtually impossible.

3 Abu-Lughod has also written about the relationship between culture,
power, narrative representations, and the portrayal of "the Other" (which
generally refers to people in non-Western societies). For example, in her
words, "Culture is the essential tool for making other. As a professional
discourse that elaborates on the meaning of culture in order to account for,
explain, and understand cultural difference, anthropology also helps construct, produce, and maintain it. Anthropological discourse gives cultural
difference (and the separation between groups of people it implies) the air
of the self-evident" (1991: 143). She also tends to equate culture with race,
when she indicates that "Despite its anti-essentialist intent … the culture
concept retains some of the tendencies to freeze difference possessed by
concepts like race" (ibid., 144). Thus, as a concluding thought on the subject of cultural representation, Whittaker suggests that "Culture is the very
epitome of othering. It depends for its existence on the subjective ordering
of a world full of Others" (1992: 113).

4 One methodological technique used in qualitative research to deal with
the problem of multiple viewpoints is referred to as "triangulation." As
explained in one text, "Every method is a different line of sight directed
toward the same point, observing social and symbolic reality. By combining
several lines of sight, researchers obtain a better, more substantive picture
of reality; a richer, more complete array of symbols and theoretical concepts; and a means of verifying many of these elements" (Berg 2004: 4–5).
Triangulation can involve the use of a multiplicity of data-gathering techniques (interviewing, document analysis, or participant observation) that
are used to investigate the same phenomenon, a variety of theoretical approaches (functional, structural), as well as a diversity of subjects who have
viewed the same phenomenon and are capable of describing their experience. Another important aspect of research used to verify the authenticity of
different points of view concerns replication. As Sidky (2004: 438) explains,
"Replication [is] the scientific requirement that results must be tested by
different researchers in order to establish the validity of propositions."

5 In anthropology the term "cultural representation" is primarily associated
with a school of thought called "postmodernism." While there are various
interpretations available in the literature on what constitutes postmodernist anthropology, Sidky (2004: 436) describes it as an "antiscience, subjective, literature perspective, which rejects the idea of universally valid

objective knowledge and focuses upon culture as open-ended negotiated meanings and stresses the examination of how ethnographies are written." The origins of the postmodernist approach in anthropology can be traced to a single publication, *Writing Culture* (1986) by James Clifford and George Marcus, one of the principal themes of which is a focus on interpretation and meaning, as opposed to causality. As Barrett (2009: 157) explains, "Culture is regarded as a system of signs and symbols, a complex of meanings, a language – indeed, a text in its own right … A text in the postmodernist sense need not be a written document. Oral tradition, folk tales, culture – indeed, anything infused with meaning and requiring interpretation – qualify as a text." Thus, as far as the present discussion is concerned, the normal view of "texts" needs to be extended to include oral traditions, whether they are written or spoken.

6 Clifford Geertz (1926–2006) was an America cultural anthropologist known for attempting to establish a new perspective called "interpretive anthropology" (see Hedican 2012: 49, 60–1.) He was also known for his rather cryptic insights, such as in his book *Local Knowledge* (1983: 9) in which he suggests that "Our consciousness is shaped at least as much by how things supposedly look to others, somewhere else in the lifeline of the world, as by how they look here, where we are, now to us."

Someone might then exclaim, "Now, that explains it!"

7 As Knafla (2010: 23) explains, "Contemporary Aboriginal problems were born in the early colonial era … Both the Roman and the common law of property were used to extinguish Indigenous title in a discriminatory manner." However, just as early colonists to North America needed Indigenous allies against continental European imperial rivals, they also were required to accommodate the wishes of Indigenous people, just as the Hudson's Bay Company did in their commercial enterprises.

8 The federal government's attempts to deal with the issue of Indian status reinstatement through the Bill C-31 amendment to Canada's Indian Act appeared to create more problems than originally anticipated. One significant issue is that Bill C-31 in effect created two classes of legal "Indian." As an example, under Section 6 (1) of the Indian Act were those individuals who had their Indian status taken away from them, such as women who married non-status males. On the other hand, there were individuals who were classified under Section 6 (2), that is, those who obtained Indian status through a parent who had originally lost it. Thus, different categories of reinstatement were possible, and the ability to pass on status to subsequent generations was different for both Section 6 (1) and 6 (2) groups. As an example, if a person obtained status through Section 6 (2) and subsequently married a non-Indian, then their children would consequently be considered non-Indians and would not be able to be registered under the Indian

Act. For some people, this differentiation of status Indians indicates an attempt by the federal government to reduce the status Indian population in Canada – in other words, an attempt to "erase" a portion of the registered Indian population. In addition, as a general rule those whose status had been reinstated were not welcomed back to their reserves (see Cairns 2000 74; Hedican 2017a: 133–5).

In a highly publicized case, a member of the Algonquin-Anishinaabe First Nations, Lynn Gehl, challenged the federal government in court because her application for status reinstatement under Bill C-31 had been rejected because she did not know the identity of one of her grandfathers (CBC News 2014). Lynn Gehl claimed that the federal government made an arbitrary decision that her unknown grandfather was a non-Indian man without evidence. In her defence, Pamela Palmeter, a First Nations lawyer claimed that the Gehl case was a clear act of discrimination against Indian women. "Imagine," Palmeter (2014) asks, "if Canadians had to worry about losing their Canadian citizenship or the right to live in their home province based on who they married or their gender." Furthermore, Gehl claimed that Canada's federal government was engaged in acts of "Indian erasure," stating that "it's obvious that Canada wants to get out of making status Indians and they want to get out of treaty responsibilities that they have to provide for status Indians." Eventually, in a decision of Ontario's Court of Appeal, Lynn Gehl was granted Indian status under the provisions of the Indian Act on April 20, 2017.

9 In a short story entitled "Hearts and Flowers," Tomson Highway writes about Canada's Indigenous people finally gaining the right to vote in federal elections in 1960. As further evidence of Canada's attempts at Indian erasure, up until 1960 Indigenous people with status under the Indian Act were not even considered Canadian citizens – it took Canada 93 years to extend voting rights to its Indigenous residents, even though many Indigenous soldiers lost their lives fighting for Canada's freedom in two world wars; ironically, a freedom which they themselves were not even granted by Canadian society. As Highway explains, he wanted to write about an event that was "universally transformative." As he says, "It had to be an event that changed *all* our lives, clean across the country, in a manner that was significant, powerful, and permanent, and 'all' meaning, of course, the Native people of Canada. and that event, I came to decide, was the day – the 31st of March 1960 – when we, as a 'nation,' as a people, as human beings, got the right to vote" (2004: 180). Thus, the extension of the federal right to vote to Indigenous people in Canada was a step in the direction of reversing the government policies of Indian erasure, in this country.

10 The Indian Residential Schools Truth and Reconciliation Commission (TRC) was officially established on June 2, 2008 (www.trc-cvr.ca). The

residential school system is often considered the most outstanding act of cultural genocide ever inflicted on Aboriginal peoples in Canada. Starting in the later 1800s, the Department of Indian affairs and various churches took approximately 24,000 Indigenous children from their homes to attend residential schools. The desired government outcome was for them to become self-sustaining members of the non-Aboriginal community. However, nearly 50 per cent of the students that attended these residential schools never returned home, according to a statement made by the Grand Chief's office of the Ontario Grand Treaty #3 (www.gc3.ca/administrative -departments/indian-residential-school-i-r-s/). The students who did not return home either died at the residential schools from diseases, neglect, or corporal punishment and abuse, or they no longer were able to function in their home communities because of the loss of language and cultural skills as a result of the enforced policy of assimilation to non-Aboriginal society that was prevalent at the time (see Henderson and Wakeham 2013; Niezen 2013).

11 Needless to say, it is becoming more and more difficult to describe the state of research in the social sciences to people with whom one is conducting this research. The term "settler colonialism," is probably not so difficult to explain; however, where does one begin to unravel the intricacies of such inscrutable phrases as "unlearning a world view," "a journey into decolonization," or "an embodied spirit world" (Nadeau 2020: 5, 11), "psychosocial trauma" (Aron and Corne 1994), and a state of "de-spiriting" (Anderson 2002: 57).

12 The topic of settler colonialism has branched out into a number of diverse areas in recent years. As such, there is an obvious need for a discussion of the commonalities of this approach and ways in which different authors may perceive this concept. Such a volume could draw together the various characteristics of settler colonialism and explain how this concept differs from other forms of colonialism. For example, is settler colonialism a form of internal colonialism, or are there sufficient reasons to regard this concept as distinct in its own right. There is also an analytic need to set out clearly the various defining characteristics of this form of colonialism and how it provides a guiding principle for understanding colonial studies in the broader sense.

13 The implications of Feagin's remark are that people are largely unaware of their racist tendencies and, as such, would not be cognizant that their racist attitudes are doing harm to others. An opposing view would be that people see themselves as benefitting in certain ways by their racist attitudes and behaviour, and this advantage propels them to consciously engage in racist acts. There are also those who believe that racial groups were created by God and this idea provides a justification for racist acts. As an example, in Barrett's study of the right wing in Canada (Is God a Racist?

1987), he suggests that "The more benign members of the right wing ... are concerned about unsettling changes in society, and dream of a bygone age when life was simpler and the moral order was intact" (1987: vii). As far as the religious element of racism is concerned, Barrett suggests that "from the point of view of these [racist] people, their protest has an essential religious component. This view is reflected specifically in the belief of extreme racists religion – the Christian religion[s] – condemns blacks and other colo[u]red peoples to an inferior, subhuman level, and identifies Jews as the children of the Devil" (1987: 5).

14 The problem with a positivistic view of society and the reason that this epistemological perspective has not been more successful in the social sciences is that human social systems are "messy" and not necessarily compatible with the more rigorous canons of science. "Positivism was severely restricted from the outset," Barrett (1984: 3) explains. "It was assumed that the social world was highly structured, and that it was amenable to measurement by techniques comparable to those used in the hard sciences. But man is a contradictory, manipulating, choosing creature."

15 Paul Bohannan (1963: 35) explains, "That part of the continuum of [light] waves is called the spectrum. The longer waves we see as violet, the shorter ones as red; all the other colors of the spectrum fall between them. The perception of light, broken into colors, seems to be the same for all human beings except the color blind, and even they have the same range. But the ways different cultures organize these sensations for communication show some strange differences." See also Berlin and Kay (1969) for an anthropological treatment of the ways in which the people in various cultures interpret the colour spectrum in apparently arbitrary ways.

16 A classic example of the manner in which Indigenous cultures are portrayed in a stereotypical manner, and represented in a stagnant, "primitive" mode is the Chicago World's Fair of 1893, in which anthropology played a prominent role. The Fair was designed as a tribute to Christopher Columbus's discovery of American in 1492 (see Green 2017; Di Cola and D. Stone 2012). There was an Anthropology Building at the World's Fair. Nearby, "The Cliff Dwellers" featured a rock and timber structure that was painted to recreate Battle Rock Mountain in Colorado, a stylized recreation of an American Indian cliff dwelling, with pottery, weapons, and other relics on display. There was also an Eskimo display. In addition, there were birch bark wigwams of the Penobscot tribe. Nearby was a working model Indian school, organized by the Office of Indian Affairs, that housed delegations of Native American students and their teachers from schools around the country for weeks at a time. According to University of Notre Dame history professor Gail Bederman, an exposition called "White City" sparked considerable controversy. In her 1996 text *Manliness and*

Civilization, she writes, "The White City, with its vision of future perfection and of the advanced racial power of manly commerce and technology, constructed civilization as an ideal of white male power." According to Bederman, people of colour were barred entirely from participating in the organization of the White City and were instead given access only to the Midway exhibit, "which specialized in spectacles of barbarous races – 'authentic' villages of Samoans, Egyptians, Dahomans, Turks, and other exotic peoples, populated by actual imported 'natives'" (1996: 35, 40).

17 This discussion suggests that a useful study could focus on the interrelationship between anthropology and history as academic disciplines, and not just on the overlaps between the two as a result of their shared interest in past events. It is also evident that historians have not shown a great deal of understanding of anthropology. Possibly historians do not think that anthropological approaches would be useful for their own research and, similarly, anthropologists have not exerted a great deal of effort in attempting to understand how historians go about their research. Both disciplines share a common interest in the historical past, but this has not necessarily led to shared understandings concerning the way the members of each discipline conduct their investigations. Such a study would be a valuable contribution to an interdisciplinary comprehension of past events.

18 Notice that Native American are at time nominated for Oscars and other significant awards, but all too frequently they do not win these awards. This suggests that those on the nominating committees do not see Indigenous people as truly deserving of these awards but, by placing them in second place, offer Indigenous people a sort of back-handed compliment or consolation prize – good, but not good enough, an appeasement prize.

19 Before and after his election, President Donald Trump has sneeringly referred to Massachusetts Senator Elizabeth Warren as "Pocahontas" as a way of mocking her claim to some sliver of Native American heritage. At an earlier rally in Montana, he called on her to take a DNA test (something former GOP Massachusetts Senator Scott Brown, defeated and unseated by Warren in 2012, suggested in 2016) and even made her a memorable offer. "I will give you a million dollars to your favourite charity, paid for by Trump, if you take the test and it shows you're an Indian," Trump said. "I have a feeling she will say no but hold it for the debates." Later, Warren revealed that an analysis of genetic testing confirmed her distant Native American ancestry. Trump shrugged off the news and denied he made the big dollar wager. (https://www.cnn.com/2016/06/29/politics/elizabeth-warren-native-american-pocahontas/index.html. Accessed August 30, 2020).

20 Responding to repeated calls from Indigenous groups, and other activists, the government of Canada under Prime Minister Justin Trudeau established the National Inquiry into Missing and Murdered Indigenous

Women and Girls in September 2016. According to the April 22, 2016, background of the inquiry, between the years 1980 and 2012, Indigenous women and girls represented 16 per cent of all female homicides in Canada, while constituting only 4 per cent of the female population. A 2011 Statistics Canada report estimated that between 1997 and 2000, the rate of homicides for Aboriginal women and girls was almost seven times higher than that for other females. Compared to non-Indigenous women and girls, they were also "disproportionately affected by all forms of violence." They are also significantly over-represented among female Canadian homicide victims and are far more likely than other women to go missing.

Throughout this report, and as witnesses shared, we convey truths about state actions and inactions rooted in colonialism and colonial ideologies, built on the presumption of superiority, and utilized to maintain power and control over the land and the people by oppression and, in many cases, by eliminating them.

Canada, *Reclaiming Power and Place: The Final Report of the National Inquiry into Missing and Murdered Indigenous Women and Girls* (June 3, 2019, page 54).

21 The American Heritage Center is the University of Wyoming's repository of manuscripts and rare books, and houses the university archives. Its collections focus on Wyoming and the Rocky Mountain West (including politics, settlement, and western trails) and a select handful of national topics: environment and conservation, the mining and petroleum industries, air and rail transportation, popular entertainment (particularly radio, television, film, and popular music), journalism, and US military history. The rare book centre has book history (see http://www.uwyo.edu/ahc/, accessed August 30, 2020).

22 The Trail of Tears continues to be the subject of academic and public interest. As an example, a documentary film was produced by History Television in 1996 as part of the "Real West" series which was distributed by A&E Television Networks (New York: Films Media Group). A fictionalized account by B.M. Hausman (2011) is described as "a surrealistic revisiting of the Cherokee Removal. *Riding the Trail of Tears* takes us to north Georgia in the near future, into a virtual-reality tourist compound where customers ride the Trail of Tears, and into the world of Tallulah Wilson, a Cherokee woman who works there. When several tourists lose consciousness inside the ride, employees and customers at the compound come to believe, naturally, that a terrorist attack is imminent. Little does Tallulah know that Cherokee Little People have taken up residence in the virtual world and fully intend to change the ride's programming to suit their own point of view" (from the book's back cover). In a more recent account (Riley 2016) it is contended that the destructive American government policies of today towards Native

Americans are a continuation of such past legislation as the Indian Removal Act: "If you want to know why American Indians have the highest rates of poverty of any racial group, why suicide is the leading cause of death among Indian men, why native women are two and a half times more likely to be raped than the national average and why gang violence affects American Indian youth more than any other group, do not look to history. There is no doubt that white settlers devastated Indian communities in the 19th and early 20th centuries. But it is our policies today – denying Indians ownership of their land, refusing them access to the free market and failing to provide the police and legal protections due to them as American citizens – that have turned reservations into small third-world countries in the middle of the richest and freest nation on earth" (in the preface). Other works of interest include Jahoda (1975), McLoughlin (1993), and Rozema (2003).

23 The Black Hawk War was a brief but bloody war, lasting from April to August 1832, between the United States and Native Americans led by Black Hawk (Ma-ka-tai-me-she-kia-kiak), a 65-year-old Sauk warrior who in early April led some 1,000 Sauk, Fox, and Kickapoo men, women, and children, including about 500 warriors, across the Mississippi River to reclaim land in Illinois that tribal spokesmen had surrendered to the US in 1804. The band's crossing back into Illinois spurred fear and anger among white settlers, and eventually a force of some 7,000 mobilized against them – including members of the US Army, state militias, and warriors from various other Indian peoples. Some 450–600 Indians and 70 soldiers and settlers were killed during the war. By 1837 all surrounding tribes had fled to the West, leaving most of the former Northwest Territory to white settlement.

This new, mostly white population viewed the Native American population with great concern. Some, including Presidents George Washington and Thomas Jefferson, believed that Native Americans would adopt the culture of white Americans (in their thinking, become "civilized") and merge into white society, but, like the majority of western settlers, most Illinoisans rejected this belief and saw Indians as not only permanently inferior but dangerous. Settlers of isolated farms and villages worried about Native American raids, and their fears were not entirely unjustified. It had not been long since Illinois tribes had attacked frontier settlements and federal forts during the War of 1812. Moreover, personal violence between natives and whites (as well as among natives and among whites) was common at the time.

(James Lewis, https://www.britannica.com/event/Black -Hawk-War#info-article-history, accessed August 30, 2020).

24 Worcester v. Georgia (1832), was a landmark case in which the United States Supreme Court vacated the conviction of Samuel Worcester (a missionary to the Cherokee) and held that the Georgia criminal statute that prohibited non-Native Americans from being present on Native American

lands without a licence from the state was unconstitutional. During this period, the westward push of European-American settlers from coastal areas was continually encroaching on Cherokee territory, even after they had made some land cessions to the US government. With the help of Worcester, they made a plan to fight the encroachment by using the courts. They wanted to take a case to the US Supreme Court to define the relationship between the federal and state governments and establish the sovereignty of the Cherokee nation (see Banner 2005; Beyer 2000).

25 The reader is encouraged to read further into the literature of white privilege, Eurocentric attitudes as vehicles of oppression, and the creation of negative stereotypes of Indigenous people. While there is certainly a large literature that could be consulted, Robert Jarvenpa's (2018) recent book *Declared Defective* is recommended for an historical approach to the subject of eugenics, which suggests that human abilities are largely inherited. As indicated in the introduction, "the dire consequences of eugenicists' racial purity arguments confused the distinction between culture and biology and functioned to preserve existing white power structures" (2018: xi). Other writings of interest would include Lee Baker's (2010) *Anthropology and the Racial Politics of Cultures*, as well as Keith Basso's (1996) study of the Western Apache in *Wisdom Sits in Places*.

7 The Shaking Tent: Abiding the "Spirit Above"

1 The "Spirit above," as far as I can ascertain, is never identified in any of the HBC journal entries, nor is there a Cree translation for this ethereal personage. Usually – in terms of the many descriptions of the conjuring or shaking tent – it is Mikinak or the Great Turtle who is the first to appear, identified by his wheezing voice and jocular expressions. I, personally, have never seen the term "Spirit above" used in the extant literature to identify such an entity in the shaking tent, although Preston's informant uses the problematic term "Mistabeo." The idea that this spirit should order someone to kill another person is also a matter that I have never heard about in the literature; however, others may be aware of this sort of instruction. Remember, also, that Richard Preston makes several connections with regards to the conjuring tent: "The events of the preceding narratives [concerning the Hannah Bay Massacre] repeatedly indicate physical hardship with spiritual attempts at coping, followed by physical consequences of spiritual efforts and guidance. There appears, for the outsider, to be some unexplained connection between the spiritual domain and the physical domain, between Mistabeo and man, that demands explanation" (2002: 156–7). This "unexplained connection," it appears to me, is at the crux of the problem in attempting to understand, or explain, what happened at Hannah Bay.

2 It is interesting that the Great Turtle should perceive so many boats and soldiers on the St. Lawrence since, as most will probably know, the year 1763 is so significant in North American and European history. This is the year of the Treaty of Paris and the Seven Years' War (1756–1763) which embroiled the French and English colonies. With the Treaty of Paris, France ceded Canada to Great Britain and so in the previous years it could be expected that the St. Lawrence River should be the sight of much military traffic (see Morton [1939] 1973: 257–8; Rich 1967: 130–4). Evidently the Great Turtle was a very perceptive spirit.

3 In my own fieldwork among the Anishinaabe of northern Ontario I found that little clever jokes were always appreciated, especially when such witticisms served to diffuse social tensions. For example, I devised this little linguistic leger-de-main. If someone posed a question for me in the Anishinaabe language, I would respond "*Kaween, Anishinaabemose,*" which literally means that "I do not speak Aninishinaabe." At first the other person usually had a confused look on their face, because I said that I don't speak the language but was in fact doing so. Soon, they caught on and invariably laughed at the little trick. They always appreciated these little bits of humour. Sometimes, in response, I would say, "*Kaween nindekanduse Anishinaabe*" literally meaning that "I don't understand Anishinaabe" which, if this was the case, then how did I know how to answer? In another instance, while sitting in a train station at Armstrong, I found myself beside an Indigenous woman who evidently knew very little Anishinaabe. An elderly gentleman sat on the other side of her began to talk to her in Anishinaabe, presuming, I suppose, that she could speak his language. I quietly translated for her, and she replied in English. Soon the elderly man caught on and began laughing.

8 The Relative Nature of Truth and Reality

1 There is one episode of *Night Gallery* that still haunts my teenage imagination. In this show a spaceship crashes on an alien planet. One of the crew members is having comforting dreams of his family back on Earth. The camera pulls way, revealing the broken remains of the ship entangled with vines. In a long row are a set of cocoons, each encompassing a crew member. A huge spider then approaches, salivating at the prospect of enjoying its next meal, after apparently injecting its victims with some sort of hallucinogenic preservative. The message was obvious: reality is just in our heads, while we could be enjoying the comfort of our illusions, we could also be some creatures next meal – how would we know otherwise?

2 Of course, while "seeing may be believing," this does not necessarily mean that we are seeing reality, since there are many forms of seeing that are not

all paths to perception of the real world. Take hallucinations for example. They may be real to the beholder, but not to others. This situation is somewhat like having people identify what they see in the clouds, or in the inkblot test known as the Rorschach Test. People see many things depending on their psychological or emotional state. One person's butterfly may be another's brain scan. The question I imagine is: Why are people's perceptions so variable when they are looking at the same thing?

3 The idea of "value-free knowledge," as the reader probably suspects, is a matter of some debate. As Sidky (2004: 27) indicates, "Science generates objective knowledge. Objectivity has a specific meaning here. It does not mean absolute transcendental or 'value-free' knowledge (the straw man argument), as opponents of scientific approaches erroneously assert." Rather, science "claims provisional certainty based upon a process of unrelenting skeptical inquiry in which no premise or assumption is ever considered to be beyond question" (Lett 1997: 42).

4 There is this old saying that "hindsight is 20–20," meaning that looking back we can perceive the error of our ways. If only this were true. Evidently, people are not that introspective. We continue to make the same mistakes over and over again, expecting different results, which some people claim is one definition of insanity.

5 When one reaches the age of 70, as I have, you begin to realize that certain events begin to stand out in your life as significant memories, such as the senseless murders of John Lennon, Robert and John Kennedy, or Martin Luther King. As a beginning graduate student in the 1970s I was impressed with the curious murder of Hudson's Bay people by relatively peaceful Indigenous people. As a youngster viewing one western movie after another in which the Indigenous people were portrayed as savage killers of white settlers, I later wanted to know how accurate these events were that Hollywood portrayed on the movie screen. Later, as an anthropology graduate student I was taught to be objective in my views, that there were two sides to every story. In the Hannah Bay story, I wondered what the Cree's side of this tragedy could be. I also realized that the 1830s were still several decades away from Canadian Confederation, but nonetheless the role of Indigenous people did not seem to be portrayed in the history books as participating in the early history of Canada in any meaningful way except as background material. The arrival of Europeans was the real beginning of Canada; this was the message that I was taught in school.

6 Preston's statement that "the conjurer's world is as valid for him as ours is for us" is one of the key observations in this whole book. The idea that we cannot understand the murders at Hannah Bay without taking a relativist position is a salient observation in comprehending the Cree's side of this dreadful scenario. While many social scientists evoke a relativist

philosophy in their research, in the end they can hardly do so because of their acculturation into a settler society, which ultimately predisposes one to think of Indigenous peoples in a lesser light than Europeans.

7 The period of anthropology known as "cognitive anthropology," (after the book edited by Stephen Tyler [1969] of the same name, also variously known as the new ethnography, ethno-semantics, formal analysis, componential analysis, sociolinguistics, as well as a few other monikers) roughly encompasses a two-decade period, from about 1955–75. In all, a search for what is termed "psychological reality" is at the core of this research. The foci of this research primarily centred on folk taxonomies, semantic structures, and formal accounts of kinship terminologies. This period was considered, in theoretical terms, to constitute a distinct break with past approaches in anthropology, or as Tyler (1969: 2) explains, "These new formulations contrast sharply with many of the aims, assumptions, goals, and methods of an earlier anthropology [such as the evolutionist, diffusionist, and functionalist periods of the discipline] ... Contrary to expectations, anthropology became more and more particularistic rather than more general and universal." Thus, the cognitive anthropological period, however, gave way to more comprehensive approaches, such as Marvin Harris's cultural materialist position. Despite lofty and in many ways valid goals, it slipped into disuse and, later, heavy criticism. Sidky (2004: 303), for example, points to the problem of "ill-informed and uninformed informants ... [and] insurmountable problem[s] for perspectives that focus on the native's point of view. Geertz (1973: 11–12) referred to "merely clever simulations...and other ingenuities." All in all, we are still left with the issue of understanding what people think in cultures other than that of the anthropologist specifically, or the European in general. Such an approach, which would focus on Cree cognition, would, however, be of considerable use in the present study in an attempt to understand why the members of a Cree family would find no other recourse to their food shortage problem than to kill the people associated with the Hannah Bay post.

8 One hastens to add that the so-called enculturative process, which is usually defined as the means by which cultural traditions are transmitted from one generation to the next, does not necessarily mean that all the members of a particular culture will automatically think the same. It is true that there are commonalities of thought, but this is more of a distribution issue. In addition, cultures change over time and so do people's attitudes and behaviour patterns.

9 The reader is never informed in this work about the reason(s) why Superintendent Saunders's letter to the commissioner in Regina did not result in an acquittal of the Fiddler brothers. Even more perplexing is the guilty verdict of Joseph Fiddler in the absence of any testimony of eyewitness

accounts or other corroborating evidence that he in fact was the person who committed the murder. The court also apparently did not take into consideration the possible threat that the deranged woman posed to the safety of the group, especially young children, or of the cultural antecedents for the killing of windigos in Cree and Anishinaabe society.

10 It is rather remarkable the number of different theories that have been proposed for a supposedly psychological phenomenon that no European has ever witnessed. As far as the killing of a windigo is concerned, the main issue from a legal or criminal matter is that those deemed to suffer from the windigo psychosis only *posed a threat* to members of their community. It is rare that a cannibalistic attack on another person was actually witnessed. Thus, in the case of the Fiddler brothers, they killed a woman who they thought *might* actually harm someone, rather than catching a person in the actual act of causing harm to another person. If everyone who ever had malevolent intent towards others was executed, there would be few remaining members of society.

11 While there are many facets to the debate about the windigo psychosis, it should be noted that A.F.C. Wallace is one of the few scholars to suggest that a biological context is the best explanation for this phenomenon. As Wallace argues (1996) in his study of anthropological views on religion, the future shaman is a person who is often suffering from various mental and physical ailments caused by a profound identity crisis. Also of note is Robert Hahn's (1978) review of "Aboriginal American Psychiatric Theories," as well as Mitrani's (1992) "Psychiatric Approaches to Shamanism."

9 Conclusions

1 The independent variable is the variable the experimenter changes or controls and is assumed to have a direct effect on the dependent variable. Two examples of common independent variables are gender and educational level. The dependent variable is the variable being tested and measured in an experiment and is dependent on the independent variable. An example of a dependent variable is depression symptoms, which depends on the independent variable such as the type of therapy in psychology (see S. McLeod, 2019 https://www.simplypsychology.org/variables.html, accessed August 17, 2020).

Similarly, Northey et al. (2012: 17) indicate that "An *independent variable* is a causal or explanatory variable: a condition or characteristic that we presume to be the cause of change in a dependent variable. A *dependent variable* is a characteristic or condition that is altered or affected by changes in another variable: we assume that it is the effect of an independent variable. For example, participation in campus politics is the dependent variable we are hoping to explain through reference to three independent variables: gender, grades, and socio-economic background [italics in original]."

2 As Tanner (2005: 113) explains, "the first spirit to enter the shaking tent is said to be *Mistaapew*, who is the host of the ceremony. According to some informants, *Mistaapew* is the only spirit who speaks in human language, and he translates what other spirits say … Most informants describe *Mistaapew* as a great joker when he is in the shaking tent. He is said to be particularly fond of making women laugh." It is not clear if the reference to the "Spirit above" is *Mistaapew* (in Tanner's reference) or *Mistabeo* (in Preston's usage).

References

A&E Television Networks. 1996. *The Trail of Tears*, produced by History Television. New York: Films Media Group.

Abril, J.C. 2007. "Perceptions of Crime Seriousness, Cultural Values, and Collective Efficacy among Native American Indians and Non-Indians within the Same Reservation Community." *Applied Psychology in Criminal Justice* 3, no. 2: 172–96. http://dev.cjcenter.org/_files/apcj/3_2_perceptionsofcrime.pdf

Abu-Lughod, L. 1990. "The Romance of Resistance: Tracing Transformations of Power through Bedouin Women." *American* Ethnologist 17: 41–55. https://doi.org/10.1525/ae.1990.17.1.02a00030

– 1991. "Writing Against Culture." In *Recapturing Anthropology*, edited by R.G. Fox, 37–62. Santa Fe, NM: School of American Research, University of Washington Press.

Acoose, J. 1995. *Iskwewak.Kah'Ki Yah Ni Wahkomakanak: Neither Indian Princess nor Easy Squaw*. Toronto: Women's Press.

Adams, A.B. 1973. *Sitting Bull: An Epic of the Plains*. New York: G.P. Putnam's Sons.

Adams, H. 1995. *A Tortured People: The Politics of Colonization*. New York: Oxford University Press.

Adelson, N. 2000. *"Being Alive Well": Health and the Politics of Cree Well-Being*. Toronto: University of Toronto Press.

Aleiss, A. 2005. *Making the White Man's Indians: Native Americans and Hollywood Movies*. Westport, Conn.: Praeger.

Alexander, P. 1986. "Colonial Capitalism in Java." *Mankind* 16, no. 1: 49–54. https://doi.org/10.1111/j.1835-9310.1986.tb01278.x

Alfred, T. 2011. "Colonial Stains on Our Existence." In *Racism, Colonialism, and Indigeneity in Canada*, edited by M.J. Cannon and L. Sunseri, 3–11. Don Mills ON: Oxford University Press.

Alfred, T., and J. Corntassell. 2011. "Being Indigenous: Resurgence against Contemporary Colonialism." In *Racism, Colonialism, and Indigeneity in*

Canada, edited by M.J. Cannon and L. Sunseri, 139–44. Don Mills, ON: Oxford University Press.

Allahar, A. 1998. "Race and Racism: Strategies of Resistance." In *Racism and Social Inequality in Canada: Concepts, Controversies and Strategies of Resistance*, edited by V. Satzewich, 335–54. Toronto, ON: Thompson Educational Publishing.

American Anthropological Association. 1999. "Declaration on Anthropology and Human Rights." Retrieved from http://humanrights.americananthro .org/1999-statement-on-human-rights/, October 7, 2019.

Anderson, D. 1985. *The Net in the Bay, or the Journal of a Visit to Moose and Albany*. London: Hatchards, Piccadilly.

Anderson, J. 1961. *A Fur Trader's Story*. Toronto: Ryerson Press (PAC Transcripts 1849–63, MG 19, A29).

Anderson, K. 2000. *A Recognition of Being: Reconstructing Native Womanhood*. Toronto: Sumach Press.

Andrews, I. 1975. "Indian Protest against Starvation: The Yellow Calf Incident of 1884." *Saskatchewan History* 28, no. 2: 41–51. http://sakimayarchives.ca /wp-content/uploads/2015/05/Andrews-Yellow-Calf-Incident-of-1884 -Sask-History-1975.pdf

Appadurai, A. 1991."Global Ethnoscapes: Notes and Queries for a Transnational Anthropology." In *Recapturing Anthropology*, edited by R.G. Fox, 191–210. Santa Fe, NM: School of American Research Press.

– 1998. "Dead Certainty: Ethnic Violence in the Era of Globalization." *Public Culture* 10: 225–47. https://doi.org/10.1215/08992363-10-2-225

Armstrong, J. 1998. *Speaking for the Generations: Native Writers on Writing*. Tucson: University of Arizona Press.

Aron, A., and S. Corne, eds. 1994. *Writings for a Liberation Psychology*. Cambridge, Mass.: Harvard University Press.

Asad, T., ed. 1973. *Anthropology and the Colonial Encounter*. Atlantic Highlands, NJ: Humanity Press. NJ: Humanity Press.

Asch, M. 2000. "First Nations and the Derivation of Canada's Underlying Title: Comparing Perspectives on Legal Ideology." In *Aboriginal Rights and Self-Government: The Canadian and Mexican Experience in North American Perspective*, edited by C. Cook and J.D. Lindau, 148–67. Montreal: McGill-Queen's University Press.

– 2001. "Indigenous Self-Determination and Applied Anthropology in Canada: Finding a Place to Stand." *Anthropologica* 43, no. 2: 201–9. https:// doi.org/10.2307/25606035

– 2002. "From Terra Nullius to Affirmation: Reconciling Aboriginal Rights with the Canadian Constitution." *Canadian Journal of Law and Society* 17, no. 2: 23–9. https://doi.org/10.1017/S0829320100007237

– 2014. *On Being Here to Stay: Treaties and Aboriginal Rights in Canada*. Toronto: University of Toronto Press.

Asch, M., J. Borrows, and J. Tully. 2018. *Resurgence and Reconciliation: Indigenous-Settler Relations and Earth Teachings*. Toronto: University of Toronto Press.

Axtell, J. 1985. *The Invasion Within: The Contest of Cultures in Colonial North America*. New York: Oxford University Press.

Bachman, R. 1991a. "The Social Causes of American Indian Homicide as Revealed by the Life Experiences of Thirty Offenders." *American Indian Quarterly* 15, no. 4: 469–92. https://doi.org/10.2307/1185365

– 1991b. "An Analysis of American Indian Homicide: A Test of Social Disorganization and Economic Deprivation at the Reservation County Level." *Journal of Research in Crime and Delinquency* 28, no. 4: 456–71. https://doi.org/10.1177/0022427891028004006

– 1992. *Death and Violence on the Reservation: Family Violence and Suicide in American Indian Populations*. New York: Auburn House.

Bailey, A.G. 1969. *The Conflict of European and Eastern Algonkian Cultures, 1504–1700: A Study in Canadian Civilization*. 2nd ed. Toronto: University of Toronto Press.

Bailey, F.G. 1969. *Stratagems and Spoils: A Social Anthropology of Politics*. Toronto: Copp Clark Publishing.

Baker, L.D. 2010. *Anthropology and the Racial Politics of Culture*. Durham: Duke University Press.

Baker, T. 2006. "Homicide and Native Americans." *American Journal of Public Health* 96, no. 1: 8– 9. https://doi.org/10.2105/AJPH.2005.076497

Balikci, A. 1970. *The Netsilik Eskimo*. Prospect Heights, Illinois: Waveland Press.

Ball, T. 1983. "The Migration of Geese as an Indicator of Climate Change in the Southern Hudson Bay Region Between 1715–1851." *Climatic Change* 5, no. 1: 85–93. https://doi.org/10.1007/BF02423429

Banner, S. 2005. *How the Indians Lost Their Land: Law and Power on the Frontier*. Cambridge, MA: Harvard University Press.

Barak, V. 1988. Review of *Anthropology as Cultural Critique*, by G.E. Marcus and M.J. Fischer. *Culture* 8, no. 2: 100–1. https://doi.org/10.7202/1085919ar

Barnett, H.G. 1938. "The Coast Salish of Canada." *American Anthropologist* 40, (January–March, 1938): 118–41. https://doi.org/10.1525/aa.1938.40.1.02a00120

– 1941. "Social Forces, Personal Conflicts, and Cultural Change." *Social Forces* 20: 160–71. https://doi.org/10.2307/2571335

– 1955. *The Coast Salish of British Columbia*. Eugene: University of Oregon Press.

Barrett, S.R. 1984. *The Rebirth of Anthropological Theory*. Toronto: University of Toronto Press.

– 1987. *Is God a Racist? The Right Wing in Canada*. Toronto: University of Toronto Press.

– 2002. *Culture Meets Power*. Westport, CT: Praeger Publishers.

– 2009. *Anthropology: A Guide to Theory and Method*. 2nd ed. Toronto: University of Toronto Press.

Basso, K.H. 1969. *Western Apache Witchcraft*. Series: Anthropological Papers of the University of Arizona (No. 15). Tucson: University of Arizona Press. https://doi.org/10.2307/j.ctv1jf2cx6

– 1996. *Wisdom Sits in Places: Landscape and Language Among the Western Apache*. Albuquerque, NM: University of New Mexico Press.

Basso, K.H., and M.E. Opler. 1971. *Apachean Culture History and Ethnology*. Series: Anthropological Papers of the University of Arizona (No. 21). Tucson: University of Arizona Press.

Bataille, G., and C. Silet. 1981. *The Pretend Indians: Images of Native Americans in the Movies*. Iowa City: The University of Iowa Press.

Battiste, M., ed. 2000. *Reclaiming Indigenous Voices and Vision*. Vancouver: University of British Columbia Press.

Battiste, M., and S. Youngblood Henderson. 2011. "Eurocentrism and the European Ethnographic Tradition." In *Racism, Colonialism, and Indigeneity in Canada*, edited by J. Cannon and L. Sunseri, 11–19. Don Mills, ON: Oxford University Press.

Bauer, G.W. 1971. *Cree Tales and Beliefs*. Vol. 12 of *Northeast Folklore*. Orono, ME: Northeast Folklore Society.

Beardy, F., and R. Coutts. 1996. *Voices from Hudson Bay: Cree Stories from York Factory*. Montreal: McGill-Queen's University Press.

Bedermann, G. 1996. *Manliness and Civilization: A Cultural History of Gender and Race in the United States, 1880–1917*. Chicago: University of Chicago Press.

Bee, R., and R. Gingerich. 1977. "Colonialism, Causes, and Ethnic Identity: Native Americans and the National Political Economy." *Studies in Comparative International Development* 12: 70–93. https://doi.org/10.1007/BF02686484

Begg, A. 1894. *The History of British Columbia from Its Earliest Discovery to the Present Time*. Toronto: William Briggs Publishing.

Begler, E.B. 1978. "Sex, Status and Authority in Egalitarian Societies." *American Anthropologist* 80, no. 3: 571–88. https://doi.org/10.1525/aa.1978.80.3.02a00030

Benedict, R. 1929. *The Concept of the Guardian Spirit in North America*. Series: Memoirs of the American Anthropological Association, Vol. 29. Menasha Wis.: American Anthropological Association.

Bennett, J.W. 1987. "Anthropology and the Emerging World Order: The Paradigm of Culture in an Age of Interdependence." In *Waymarks*, edited by K. Moore, 43–69. Notre Dame, IN: University of Notre Dame Press.

Bennett, M.K. 1968. "Famine." In *International Encyclopedia of the Social Sciences*, Vol. E, edited by D.L. Sills, 322. New York: Macmillan and Free Press.

Berg, B.L. 2004. *Qualitative Research Methods for the Social Sciences*. Boston: Pearson.

Berger, P., and T. Luckmann. 1966. *The Social Construction of Reality*. New York: Anchor Books.

Berkhofer, R. 1978. *The White Man's Indian: Images of the American Indian from Columbus to the Present*. New York: Knopf.

Berlin, B., and P. Kay. 1969. *Basic Color Terms: Their Universality and Evolution*. Berkeley: University of California Pres.

Bettinger, R.L. 1983. Review of *Strategies for Survival: Cultural Behavior in an Ecological Context*, by M.A. Jochim, 1981. *American Anthropologist* 85, no. 3: 720–1. https://doi.org/10.1525/aa.1983.85.3.02a00560

Beyer, S. 2000. "The Cherokee Indians and the Supreme Court." *The Journal of Supreme Court History* 23, *no.* 3: 215–27. https://doi.org/10.1111/1059 -4329.00009

Biggar, H.P. 1924. *The Voyages of Jacque Cartier*. Ottawa: Publications of the Public Archives of Canada, no. 11.

Biolsi, T. 2007. *Deadliest Enemies: Law and Race Relations on and off Rosebud Reservation*. Minneapolis, Minn.: University of Minnesota Press.

Biolsi, T., and L. Zimmerman. 1997. *Indians and Anthropologists: Vine Deloria and the Critique of Anthropology*. Tucson: University of Arizona Press.

Bishop, C.A. 1970. "The Emergence of Hunting Territories among the Northern Ojibwa." *Ethnology* 9 :1–15. https://doi.org/10.2307/3772698

– 1974. *The Northern Ojibwa and the Fur Trade: An Historical and Ecological Study*. Toronto: Holt, Rinehart and Winston.

– 1975. "Ojibwa, Cree and the Hudson's Bay Company in Northern Ontario: Culture and Conflict in the Eighteenth Century." In *Western Canada Past and Present*, edited by A.W. Rasporich, 150–62. Calgary: McClelland and Stewart West.

– 1976a."The Emergence of the Northern Ojibwa: Social and Economic Consequences." *American Ethnologist* 3: 39–54. https://doi.org/10.1525 /ae.1976.3.1.02a00030

– 1976b. Henley House Massacres. *The Beaver* 307 (Autumn): 36–41.

– 1978. "Cultural and Biological Adaptations to Deprivation: The Northern Ojibwa Case." In *Extinction and Survival in Human Populations*, edited by C.D. Laughlin Jr. and I.A. Brady, 209–30. New York: Columbia University Press.

– 1981. "Territorial Groups Before 1821: Cree and Ojibwa." In *Handbook of North American Indians: Subarctic*, Vol. 6, edited by J. Helm, 158–60. Washington, DC: Smithsonian Institution.

– 1982. Comment on "Marano, L. et al.1982. Windigo Psychosis: The Anatomy of an Emic-Etic Confusion." *Current Anthropology* 23, no. 4: 385–97, 398. https://doi.org/10.1086/202868

– 1983. "The Western James Bay Cree: Aboriginal and Early Historical Adaptations." *Prairie Forum* 8, no. 2: 147–55. https://ourspace.uregina.ca /handle/10294/237.

Bishop, C.A., and V.P. Lytwyn. 2007. "Barbarism and Ardour of War from the Tenderest Years: Cree-Inuit Warfare in the Hudson Bay Region." In *North American Indigenous Warfare and Ritual Violence*, edited by R. J. Chacon and R. G. Mendoza, 30–57. Tucson: University of Arizona Press.

Bishop, C.A., and T. Morantz, eds. 1986. *Who Owns the Beaver? Northern Algonquin Land Tenure Reconsidered. Anthropologica* Vol. 18, nos. 1–2. Sudbury: Laurentian University.

Blackhawk, N. 2007. *Violence Over the Land: Indians and Empires in the Early American West*. Cambridge, Mass.: Harvard University Press.

Black-Rogers, M. 1986. "Varieties of 'Starving': Semantics and Survival in the Subarctic Fur Trade, 1750–1850." *Ethnohistory* 33 (4): 353–83. https:// doi.org/10.2307/482039

Blau, P.M. 1964. *Exchange and Power in Social Life*. New York: John Wiley.

Blauner, R. 1969. "Internal Colonialism and the Ghetto Revolt." *Social Problems* 16: 393–408. https://doi.org/10.2307/799949

Bloom, J.D. 1980. "Forensic Psychiatric Evaluation of Alaska Native Homicide Offenders." *International Journal of Law and Psychiatry* 3, no. 2: 163–71. https://doi.org/10.1016/0160-2527(80)90037-0

Boas, F. 1888. *The Central Eskimo*. Report of the Bureau of Ethnology, 1884– 1885. Washington, DC: Smithsonian Institution.

Boggs, C. 1976. *Gamsci's Marxism*. London: Pluto Press.

Bohannan, P. 1963. *Social Anthropology*. New York: Holt, Rinehart and Winston.

Boldt, M. 1980. "Canadian Native Leadership: Context and Composition." *Canadian Ethnic Studies* 12, no. 1: 15–33. https://www.proquest.com /openview/a169946e1ced12983f9570a8d24d41ae/1?pq-origsite =gscholar&cbl=1817720

– 1993. *Surviving as Indians: The Challenge of Self-Government*. Toronto: University of Toronto Press.

Bonds, A., and J. Inwood. 2016. "Beyond White Privilege: Geographies of White Supremacy and Settler Colonialism." *Progress in Human Geography* 40, no. 6: 715–33. https://doi.org/10.1177/0309132515613166

Bonnett, A. 2016.*White Identities: An Historical and International Introduction*. London: Prentice-Hall.

Boyden, J. 2008. *Through Black Spruce*. Toronto: Penguin Group.

Brightman, R. 1988. "The Windigo in the Material World." *Ethnohistory* 35, no. 4: 337–79. https://doi.org/10.2307/482140

Brook, A., and R. Stainton. 2000. *Knowledge and Mind: A Philosophical Introduction*. Cambridge, MA: MIT Press.

Broudy, D.W., and P.A. May. 1983. "Demographic and Epidemiologic Transition among the Navajo Indians." *Social Biology* 30, no. 1:1–6. https://doi.org/10.1080/19485565.1983.9988511

Brown, D. 1970. *Bury My Heart at Wounded Knee: An Indian History of the American West* New York: Holt, Rinehart & Winston.

Brown, I. 1997. *Economic Change in South-East Asia, c. 1830–1980, Kuala Lumpur.* Oxford: Oxford University Press.

– 2014. "Colonial Capitalism and Economic Transformation." In *Colonial Capitalism and Economic Transformation: Routledge Handbook of Southeast Asian History*, edited by N.G. Owen, 155–64. New York: Routledge.

Brown, J.S.H. 1971. "The Cure and Feeding of Windigos: A Critique." *American Anthropologist* 73, no. 1: 20–2. https://doi.org/10.1525/aa.1971.73.1.02a00020

– 1976. "Changing Views of Fur Trade Marriage and Domesticity: James Hargrave, His Colleagues, and the "Sex." *Western Canadian Journal of Anthropology* 6, no. 3: 92– 105. https://www.researchgate.net/publication/284268656_Changing_Views_of_Fur_Trade_Marriage_and_Domesticity_James_Hargrave_His_Colleagues_and_'the_Sex'

– 1980. *Strangers in Blood: Fur Trade Company Families in Indian Country.* Vancouver: University of British Columbia Press.

– 1987. "I Wish to Be as I See You": An Ojibwa-Methodist Encounter in Fur Trade Country, Rainy River, 1854–1855. *Arctic Anthropology* 24, no. 1: 19–31. http://www.jstor.org/stable/40316130.

– 1996. "Reading Beyond the Missionaries, Dissecting Responses." *Ethnohistory* 43 (4): 713– 19. https://doi.org/10.2307/483252

Brown, J.S.H., and R. Brightman. 1988. *"The Orders of the Dreamed": George Nelson on Cree and Northern Ojibwa Religion and Myth, 1823.*Winnipeg: University of Manitoba Press, St. Paul: Minnesota Historical Society.

Brydon, D. 2003. "Canada and Postcolonialism: Questions, Inventories, and Futures." In *Is Canada Postcolonial? Unsettling Canadian Literature*, edited by L. Moss, 49–77. Waterloo: Wilfrid Laurier University Press.

Bumsted, J.M., and J. Smyth. 2019. Red River Colony. In *Canadian Encyclopedia.* Toronto: Historica Canada (https://search-proquest-com.subzero.lib.uoguelph.ca/docview/2316370537?pq-origsite=primo, accessed April 28, 2020).

Burgesse, J.A. 1940. "Our Abused Aborigines." *The Beaver* 271: 31–8. https://www.canadashistoryarchive.ca/canadas-history/the-beaver-december-1940/flipbook/34/

Burling, R. 1964. "Cognition and Componential Analysis: God's Truth or Hocus-Pocus?" *American Anthropologist* 66 (1): 20–8. https://doi.org/10.1525/aa.1964.66.1.02a00020

Burnett, S. 2006. Ute Homicide Rate Soars. *Rocky Mountain News* (November 25, 2006), www.rockymountainnews.com/com/news/2006/Nov/25/Ute-homicide.

Bursik, R.J. 1988. "Social Disorganization and Theories of Crime and Delinquency: Problems and Prospects." *Criminology* 26, no. 4: 519–52. https://doi.org/10.1111/j.1745-9125.1988.tb00854.x

Butterly, J.R., and J. Shepard. 2010. *Hunger: The Biology and Politics of Starvation.* Lebanon, NH: University Press of New England.

Byram, R.S. 2008. "Colonial Power and Indigenous Justice: Fur Trade Violence and its Aftermath in Yaquina Narrative." *Oregon Historical Quarterly* 109 (3): 357–87. https://doi.org/10.1353/ohq.2008.0040

Cahill, C. 2011. *Federal Fathers and Mothers: A Social History of the United States Indian Service, 1869–1933.* Chapel Hill, NC: University of North Carolina Press.

Cairns, A.C. 2000. *Citizens Plus: Aboriginal Peoples and the Canadian State.* Vancouver, BC: University of British Columbia Press.

Canada, 1891. *Indian Treaties and Surrenders, From 1680–1890.* Vol. 1. Ottawa: Queen's Printer (Coles Canadiana Collection, 1971. Toronto: Coles Publishing.)

– 2012. *Aboriginal Peoples Survey (APS).* Ottawa: Statistics Canada. https://www150.statcan.gc.ca/n1/en/catalogue/89-653-X, accessed April 23, 2020.

– 2019. *Reclaiming Power and Place: The Final Report of the National Inquiry into Missing and Murdered Indigenous Women and Girls. June 3, 2019.* http://www.mmiwg-ffada.ca/, accessed August 30, 2020.

Cannon, M.J., and L. Suneri, eds. 2011. *Racism, Colonialism, and Indigeneity in Canada.* Oxford: Oxford University Press.

Cardinal, H. 1969. *The Unjust Society: The Tragedy of Canada's Indians.* Edmonton: Hurtig.

Carlson, H.M. 2008. *Home Is the Hunter: The James Bay Cree and Their Land.* Vancouver: UBC Press.

Carr, B., and E.S. Lee. 1978. "Navajo Tribal Mortality: A Life Table Analysis of the Leading Causes of Death." *Social Biology* 25, no. 4: 279–87. https://doi.org/10.1080/19485565.1978.9988349

Carstens, P. *The Queen's People.* Toronto: University of Toronto Press.

Carter, S. 1997. *Capturing Women: The Manipulation of Cultural Imagery in Canada's Prairie West.* Montreal: McGill-Queen's University Press.

Castile, G. 2006. *Taking Charge: Native American Self-Determination and Federal Indian Policy, 1975–1993.* Tucson: University of Arizona Press.

CBC News. 2006. "Harris Denies Using Profanity over Native Protest." February 14, 2006.

– 2014. "Lynn Gehl Challenges Indian Status Denial in Ontario Court." October 20, 2014.

Chabot, C. 2010. "Reconciling Amerindian and Euroamerican (Mis) understandings of a Shared Past: Cross-Cultural Conflict Historiography and the 1832 Hannah Bay "Massacre." *The Canadian Journal of Native Studies* 30, no. 2: 229–65. https://cjns.brandonu.ca/wp-content/uploads/30-2 -02chabot.pdf

Chacon, R.J., and R.G. Mendoza, eds. 2007a. "Introduction." In *North American Indigenous Warfare and Ritual Violence*, edited by R.J. Chacon and R. G. Mendoza, 3–9. Tucson: University of Arizona Press.

Chacon, R.J., and R.G. Mendoza, eds. 2007b. "Ethical Considerations and Conclusions Regarding Indigenous Warfare and Violence in North America." In *North American Indigenous Warfare and Ritual Violence*, R.J. Chacon and R.G. Mendoza, 222–32. Tucson: University of Arizona Press.

Chagnon, N. 1968. *Yanomamö: The Fierce People*. New York: Holt, Rinehart and Winston.

– 1988. "Life Histories, Blood Revenge, and Warfare in a Tribal Population." *Science* 239: 985–92. https://doi.org/10.1126/science.239.4843.985

Champagne, D. 1983. "Organizational Change and Conflict: A Case Study of the Bureau of Indian Affairs." *American Indian Culture and Research Journal* 7 (3): 3–28. https://doi.org/10.17953/aicr.07.3.bpp1631722t91459

Chance, N.A., ed. 1968. *Conflict in Culture: Problems of Developmental Change among the Cree*. Ottawa: Canadian Research Centre for Anthropology, Saint Paul University.

Churchill, W. 2001. *Fantasies of the Master Race: Literature, Cinema, and the Colonization of American Indians*. Monroe, Main: Common Courage Press.

– 2007. *Pacifism as Pathology: Reflections on the Role of Armed Struggle in North America*. Oakland, CA: Arbeiter Ring Publishers (AK Press).

– 2020. Comments in *"Media Smarts: Common Portrayals of Aboriginal People."* https://mediasmarts.ca/diversity-media/aboriginal-people/common -portrayals-aboriginal-people?gclid=EAIaIQobChMIiIfN--jq6AIVr __jBx0UQAudEAAYASAAEgIRnPD_BwE. Accessed April 15, 2020.

Churchill, W., N. Hill, and M.A. Hill. 1978. "Media Stereotyping and the Native Response: An Historical Overview." *The Indian Historian* 11, no. 4: 46–56.

Chute, J. 1998. Shingwaukonse: A Nineteenth-Century Innovative Ojibwa Leader. *Ethnohistory* 45 (1): 65–101. https://doi.org/10.2307/483172

Clark, D.W. 1977. "Arctic and Subarctic America: Current Early Man Research." In *Early Man News*, Volume 2. 24–33.

– 1991. *Western Subarctic Prehistory*. Archaeological Survey of Canada. Ottawa: Canadian Museum of Civilization.

Classen, C., and D. Howes. 2006. "The Museum as Sensescape: Western Sensibilities and Indigenous Artifacts." In *Sensible Objects: Colonialism, Museums and Material Culture*, edited by E. Edwards, C. Gosden, and R. Philips, 199–222. Oxford: Berg.

Clifford, J., and G.E. Marcus, eds. 1986. *Writing Culture*. Berkeley: University of California Press.

Clifton, J.A. 1989. *Being and Becoming Indian: Biographical Studies of North American Frontiers*. Chicago: Dorsey Press.

Coates, K.S. 2000. *The Marshal Decision and Native Rights*. Montreal: McGill-Queen's University Press.

Coates, K.S., and W.R. Morrison. 2004. *Strange Things Done: Murder in Yukon History*. Montreal: McGill-Queen's University Press.

Cohen, B.S. 1987. "History and Anthropology: The State of Play." In *An Anthropologist among the Historians and other Essays*, edited by B.S. Cohen, 18–49. Oxford: Oxford University Press.

Cohen, D.W. 1989. "The Undefining of Oral Traditions." *Ethnohistory* 36 (1): 9–18. https://doi.org/10.2307/482738

Comaroff, J., and J.L. Comaroff. 1991. *Of Revelation and Revolution: Christianity, Colonialism and Consciousness in South Africa*. Chicago: University of Chicago Press.

Conklin, B. 2003. "Speaking Truth to Power." *Anthropology News* 44 (7): 5. https://doi.org/10.1111/an.2003.44.7.5

Cook, S.F. 1976. *The Conflict between California Indian and White Civilization*. Berkeley: University of California Pres.

Cook-Lynn, E. 1996. *Why I Can't Read Wallace Stegner and Other Essays*. Madison, Wisc.: University of Wisconsin Press.

Cooper, J.M. 1933a. "The Northern Algonquian Supreme Being." *Primitive Man* 6 (3–4): 41–111. https://doi.org/10.2307/3316465

– 1933b. "The Cree Witiko Psychosis." *Primitive Man* 6 (1): 20–4. https://doi.org/10.2307/3316222

– 1938. *Snares, Deadfalls and Other Traps of the Northern Algonquians and Northern Athabascans*. Washington, DC: Catholic University of America, Anthropological Series, No. 5.

– 1944. "The Shaking Tent Among Plains and Forest Algonquians." *Primitive Man* 17 (3–4): 60–84. https://doi.org/10.2307/3316315

Cornell, S., and J. Kalt. 1998. "Sovereignty and Nation-Building: The Developmental Challenge in Indian Country Today." *American Indian Culture and Research Journal* 22 (3): 187–214. https://doi.org/10.17953/aicr.22.3.lv45536553vn7j78

Coser, L. 1956. *The Functions of Social Conflict*. New York: Macmillan Publishing Co.

Cousins, L.H., ed. 2014. "White Privilege." In *Encyclopedia of Human Services and Diversity*. Western Michigan University, Thousand, Oaks, CA: Sage Publications.

Cox, A. 2017. "Settler Colonialism." *Oxford Bibliographies* (https://www.oxfordbibliographies.com/view/document/obo-9780190221911/obo-9780190221911-0029.xml, accessed April 11, 2020).

Cox, R. 1932. *Adventures on the Columbia River…*" New York: J. & J. Harper.

Cramer, R. 2005. *Cash, Color, and Colonialism: The Politics of Tribal Acknowledgement*. Norman: University of Oklahoma Press.

Cronon, W. 1992. "A Place for Stories: Nature, History, and Narrative." *Journal of American History* 78, no. 4: 1347–76. https://doi.org/10.2307/2079346

Cruikshank, J. 1982. "Legend and Landscape: Convergence of Oral and Scientific Traditions in the Yukon Territory." *Arctic Anthropology* 18, no. 2: 66–93. https://www.jstor.org/stable/40316002

– 1988. "Myth and Tradition as Narrative Framework: Oral Histories from Northern Canada." *International Journal of Oral History* 9: 198–214.

– 1989. Oral Traditions and Written Accounts: An Incident from the Klondike Gold Rush. *Culture* 9 no. 2: 25–34. https://doi.org/10.7202/1079363ar

– 1990. *Life Lived Like a Story: Life Stories of Three Native Yukon Elders*. Vancouver: University of British Columbia Press.

– 1992. Images of Society in Klondike Gold Rush Narratives: Skookum Jim and the Discovery of Gold. *Ethnohistory* 39 (1): 20–41. https://doi.org/10.2307/482563

– 1994. "Oral Traditions and Oral History: Reviewing Some Issues." *The Canadian Historical Review* 75, no. 3: 403–18. muse.jhu.edu/article/574633.

– 2003. Discovering Gold in the Klondike: Perspectives from Oral Tradition. In *Reading Beyond Words: Contexts for Native History*, edited by J.S.H. Brown and E. Vibert, 433–59. Peterborough, ON: Broadview Press.

Culhane, D. 2003. "Their Spirits Live with Us." *American Indian Quarterly* 27, no. 3: 593–606. https://doi.org/10.1353/aiq.2004.0073

Cummins, B.D. 2004. *"Only God Can Own the Land": The Attawapiskat Cree*. Canadian Ethnography Series Vol. 1. Toronto: Pearson Education Canada.

Daenekindt, S., and H. Roose. 2014. "Social Mobility and Cultural Dissonance." *Poetics* 42: 82–97. https://doi.org/10.1016/j.poetic.2013.11.002

Daly, M. 2000. African Genital Mutilation: The Unspeakable Atrocities. In *The Gender Reader*, edited by G.A. Olson and M.G. Perry, 1–17. Needham Heights: Allyn and Bacon.

Daschuk, J. 2013. *Clearing the Land: Disease, Politics of Starvation and the Loss of Aboriginal Life*. Regina, SK: University of Regina Press.

Davidson, D.S. 1928. "Family Hunting Territories of the Waswanipi Indians of Quebec." In *Indian Notes*, volume 5. 42–59. New York: Museum of the American Indian, Heye Foundation.

Davies, K.G., ed. 1965. *Letters from Hudson's Bay, 1703–1740*. London: Hudson's Bay Record Society, No. 25.

Dawson, K.C.A. 1983. *Prehistory of Northern Ontario*. Thunder Bay, ON: Historical Museum Society.

Dean, J.R. 1997. "The Hudson's Bay Company and Its Use of Force, 1828–1829." *Oregon Historical Quarterly* 98, no. 3: 262–95. https://www.jstor.org/stable/20614826

Delay, B. 2008. *The War of a Thousand Deserts*. New Haven: Yale University Press.

Deloria, P.J. 1998. *Playing Indian*. New Haven, CT: Yale University Press.

Deloria, V. Jr. 1988 [1969]. *Custer Died for Your Sins: An Indian Manifesto*. Norman: University of Oklahoma Press.

– 1995. *Red Earth, White Lies: Native Americans and the Myth of Scientific Fact*. New York: Scribner.

Dempsey, H. 2002. *Firewater: The Impact of the Whiskey Trade on the Blackfoot Nation*. Calgary: Fifth House.

Denis, J.S. 2020. *Canada at a Crossroads: Boundaries, Bridges, and Laissez-Faire Racism in Indigenous-Settler Relations*. Toronto: University of Toronto Press.

Dentan, R.K. 1968. *The Semai: A Non-Violent People of Malaya*. New York: Holt, Rinehart and Winston.

DeVries, L. 2011. *Conflict in Caledonia: Aboriginal Land Rights and the Rule of Law*. Vancouver: University of British Columbia Press.

Di Cola, J.M., and D. Stone. 2012. *Chicago's 1893 World's Fair*. Chicago: Arcadia Press.

Dignard, N., R. Lalumiere, and A. Reed. 1991. *Habitats of the Northeast Coast of James Bay*. Occasional Paper, No. 70. Ottawa: Canadian Wildlife Service.

Dixon, R.B. 1909. "The Mythology of the Central and Eastern Algonquians." *Journal of Folklore* 22: 1–9. https://doi.org/10.2307/534304

Donham, D.L. 1985. Review of *Silent Violence: Food, Famine and Peasantry in Northern Nigeria*, by Michael Watts, 1983. *American Anthropologist* 87, no. 4: 943–4. https://doi.org/10.1525/aa.1985.87.4.02a00400

Doughty, P.L. 2011. "Mary Lindsay Elmendorf: Citizen Activist to Applied Anthropologist." *American Anthropologist* 113, no. 3: 498–502. https://doi.org/10.1111/j.1548-1433.2011.01358.x

Douthit, N. 1992. "The Hudson's Bay Company and the Indians of Southern Oregon." *Oregon Historical Quarterly* 93, no. 1. 25–64. https://www.jstor.org/stable/20614432

Driben, P., and R.S. Trudeau. 1983. *When Freedom Is Lost: The Dark Side of the Relationship between Government and the Fort Hope Band*. Toronto: University of Toronto Press.

Dunning, R.W. 1958. "Some Implications of Economic Change in Northern Ojibwas Social Structure." *Canadian Journal of Economics and Political Science* 24, no. 4. https://doi.org/10.2307/139092

– 1959a. *Social and Economic Change Among the Northern Ojibwa*. Toronto: University of Toronto Press.

– 1959b. "Ethnic Relations and the Marginal Man in Canada." *Human Organization* 18, no. 3. 117–22. https://doi.org/10.17730/humo.18.3.7582628001559333

– 1962. "Some Aspects of Governmental Indian Policy and Administration." *Anthropologica* 4: 209–31. https://doi.org/10.2307/25604539

– 1964. "Some Problems of Reserve Indian Communities: A Case Study." *Anthropologica* 6: 3–38. https://doi.org/10.2307/25604598

Durkheim, E.1933 [1893]. *Division of Labor in Society*. New York: Macmillan.
- 2001 [1915]. *The Elementary Forms of Religious Life*. Oxford: Oxford University Press.
Dyck, N.D. 1985. *Indigenous People in Nation States: Fourth World Politics*. St. John's: Memorial University of Newfoundland.
- 1991. *What Is the Indian "Problem": Tutelage and Resistance in Canadian Indian Administration*. Social and Economic Studies No. 46, Institute of Social and Economic Research. St. John's, NL: Memorial University of Newfoundland.
- 1997. "Tutelage, Resistance and Co-Optation in Canadian Indian Administration." *Canadian Review of Sociology and Anthropology* 34, no. 3: 333–48. https://doi.org/10.1111/j.1755-618X.1997.tb00212.x
Easton, D. 1972. "Some Limits of Exchange Theory in Politics." *Sociological Inquiry* 42 (3–4): 129–48. https://doi.org/10.1111/j.1475-682X.1972.tb00233.x
Eccles, W.J. 1983. "The Fur Trade and Eighteenth-Century Imperialism." *The William and Mary Quarterly* 40, no. 3: 341–62. https://doi.org/10.2307/1917202
Ehle, J. 1989. *Trail of Tears: The Rise and Fall of the Cherokee Nation*. New York: Anchor Books.
Elder, A.K. 2018. "'Indian' as a Political Classification: Reading the Tribe Back into the Indian Child Welfare Act." *Northwestern Journal of Law and Social Policy* 13, no. 4: 417–38. https://scholarlycommons.law.northwestern.edu/njlsp/vol13/iss4/3
Elkins, C., and S. Pederson, eds. 2005. *Settler Colonialism in the Twentieth Century: Projects, Practices and Legacies*. New York: Routledge.
Ellis, C.D. 1960. A Note on Okima.hka.n. *Anthropological Linguistics* 2:1.
Engle, K. 2001. "From Skepticism to Embrace: Human Rights and the American Anthropological Association from 1947–1999." *Human Rights Quarterly* 23: 536–59. https://doi.org/10.1353/hrq.2001.0034
Ervin, A.M. 1987. "Styles and Strategies of Leadership During the Alaskan Native Land Claims Movement: 1959–71." *Anthropologica* 29, no. 1: 21–38. https://doi.org/10.2307/25605207
Etzioni, A. 1993. "Power as a Social Force." In *Power in Modern Societies*, edited by M.E. Olsen and M.N. Margers, 18–28. Boulder, CO: Westview Press
Evans-Pritchard, E.E. 1961. *Anthropology and History*. Manchester: Manchester University Press.
- 1981. *A History of Anthropological Thought*. New York: Basic Books.
Evens, T.M.S. 1977. "The Predication of the Individual in Anthropological Interactionism." *American Anthropologist* 79, no. 3: 579–97. https://doi.org/10.1525/aa.1977.79.3.02a00030
Fanon, F. 1963. *The Wretched of the Earth*. New York: Grove Press.

Farrinto, B. 2000. "Review of *Patterns of Vengeance: Crosscultural Homicide in the North American Fur Trade*, 1999, by J.P. Reid." *The American Journal of Legal History* 44: 489–1. https://doi.org/10.2307/3113825

Feagin, J.R. 2006. *Systemic Racism: A Theory of Oppression.* New York: Routledge.

– 2010. *Racist American: Roots, Current Realities, and Future Reparations.* 2nd ed. New York: Rutledge.

Feit, H.A. 1973. "The Ethno-Ecology of the Waswanipi Cree; or How Hunters Can Manage their Resources." In *Cultural Ecology*, edited by B. Cox, 115–25. Toronto: McClelland and Stewart.

– 1982. "The Future of Hunters within Nation-States: Anthropology and the James Bay Cree." In *Politics and History in Band Societies*, edited by E. Leacock and R.B. Lee, eds. 373– 414. Cambridge: Cambridge University Press.

– 2005a. "Hunting and the Quest for Power: The James Bay Cree and Whitemen in the Twentieth Century." In *Native Peoples: The Canadian Experience*, edited by R.B. Morrison and C.R. Wilson, 181–223. Toronto: McClelland and Stewart.

– 2005b. "Re-Cognizing Co-Management as Co-Governance: Histories and Visions of Conservation at James Bay." *Anthropologica* 47, no. 2: 267–88. http://www.jstor.org/stable/25606240

– 2007. "Histories, Science, and Rights in North American-Native American Relations." In *Native Americans and the Environment: Perspectives on the Ecological Indian*, edited by M.E. Harkin and D.R. Lewis, 52–92. Lincoln: University of Nebraska Press.

Fiddler, Chief T., and J.R. Stevens. 1985. *Killing the Shamen.* Moonbeam, ON: Penumbra Press.

Fields, J. 1993. *The Challenge of Famine.* Boston: Kumarian Press.

Fisher, A.D. 1973. "The Cree of Canada: Some Ecological and Evolutionary Considerations." In *Cultural Ecology*, edited by B. Cox, 126–39. Toronto: McClelland and Stewart [orig. 1969. *Western Canadian Journal of Canada* 1, no. 1: 7–19].

Fisher, R. 1977. *Contact and Conflict: Indian-European Relations in British Columbia, 1774–1890.* Vancouver: University of British Columbia Press.

Flannery, R. 1935. "The Position of Women among the Eastern Cree." *Primitive Man* 8: 81–6. https://doi.org/10.2307/3316438

– 1939. "The Shaking-Tent Rite among the Montagnais of James Bay." *Primitive Man* 12, no. 1: 11–16. https://doi.org/10.2307/3316273

– 1995. *Ellen Smallboy: Glimpses of a Cree Woman's Life.* Montreal: McGill-Queen's University Press.

Flannery, R., M.E. Chambers, and P. Jehle. 1982. "Witiko Accounts from the James Bay Cree." *Arctic Anthropology* 18, no. 1: 57–77. https://www.jstor.org/stable/40315990

Flannery, R., and M.E. Chambers. 1985. "Each Man Has His Own Friends: The Role of Dream Visitors in Traditional East Cree Belief and Practice." *Arctic Anthropology* 22, no. 1: 1–22. https://www.jstor.org/stable/40316077

Fleming, W.C. 2006. "Myths and Stereotypes about Native Americans." *Phi Delta Kappan* 88, no. 3: 213–17. https://doi.org/10.1177/003172170608800319

Flemming, R.H., ed. 1940. *Minutes of Council, Northern Department of Rupert Land, 1821–1831*. Toronto: Hudson's Bay Record Society.

Fogelson, R. 1965. "Psychological Theories of Windigo "Psychosis" and a Preliminary Application of a Model Approach." In *Context and Meaning in Cultural Anthropology*, edited by M.E. Spiro, 74–99. New York: The Free Press.

– 1989. "The Ethnohistory of Events and Non-Events." *Ethnohistory* 36, no. 2: 133–47. https://doi.org/10.2307/482275

Fortier, C. 2017. *Unsettling the Commons: Social Movements Within, Against, and Beyond Settler Colonialism*. Winnipeg, Man.: Arbeiter Ring Publishing (ARP Books).

Francis, D. 1979. "Les relations entre Indiens et Inuit dans l'est de la baie d'Hudson, 1700–1840." *Étude/Inuit Studies* 3, no. 2: 73–83. https://www.jstor.org/stable/42869459

– 1993. *The Imaginary Indian: The Image of the Indian in Canadian Cultures*. Vancouver, BC: Arsenal Pulp Press.

Francis, D., and T. Morantz. 1983. *Partners in Fur: A History of the Fur Trade in Eastern James Bay, 1600–1870*. Montreal: McGill-Queen's University Press.

Frederick, C.J. 1973. *Suicide, Homicide, and Alcoholism Among American Indians: Guidelines for Help*. Rockville, MD: National Institute of Mental Health.

Free, M. 2018. "Settler Colonialism." *Victorian Literature and Culture* 46 (3–4): 876–82. https://doi.org/10.1017/S1060150318001080

Freeman, V. 2010. "'Toronto Has No History!' Indigeneity, Settler Colonialism, and Historical Memory in Canada's Largest City." *Urban History Review* 38 (2): 21–35. https://doi.org/10.7202/039672ar

French, L., and J. Hornbuckle. 1977. "An Analysis of Indian Violence: The Cherokee Example." *American Indian Quarterly* 3 (4): 335–56. https://doi.org/10.2307/1183859

Freud, S. 1913. *Totem and Taboo: Some Points of Agreement between the Mental Lives of Savages and Neurotics*. A.A. Brill, trans. New York: Moffat, Yard.

Frideres, J.S. 1988. *Aboriginal Peoples in Canada: Contemporary Conflicts*. Scarborough, ON: Prentice-Hall.

– 1996. "The Royal Commission on Aboriginal Peoples: The Route to Self-Government?" *Canadian Journal of Native Studies* 16, no. 2: 247–66. https://cjns.brandonu.ca/wp-content/uploads/16-2-frideres.pdf

Frideres, J.S., and R. Gadacz. 2008. *Aboriginal Peoples in Canada: Contemporary Conflicts*. 8th ed. Scarborough, ON: Prentice-Hall.

Fried, M.H. 1967. *The Evolution of Political Society: An Essay in Political Economy*. New York: Random House.

Furtado, M. 2016. "Dismantling White Privilege: Indigenous Erasure." *Out Front Magazine*, July 18, 2016. https://www.outfrontmagazine.com /perspectives/dismantling-white-privilege-indigenous-erasure. Accessed April 11, 2020.

Galbraith, J. 1949. "The Hudson's Bay Company Under Fire, 1847–1962." *Canadian Historical Review* 30, no. 4: 322–35. https://doi.org/10.3138 /chr-030-04-02

– 1957.*The Hudson's Bay Company as an Imperial Factor, 1821–69*. Berkeley: University of California Press.

– 1976. *The Little Emperor: Governor Simpson of the Hudson's Bay Company*. Toronto: Macmillan of Canada.

Gallagher, T. 1982. *Paddy's Lament, Ireland 1846–1847: Prelude to Hatred*. New York: Harcourt Brace and Company.

Gastil, R.P. 1971. "Homicide and Regional Culture of Violence." *American Sociological Review* 36: 412–27. https://doi.org/10.2307/2093082

Geertz, C. 1973. *The Interpretation of Cultures: Selected Essays*. New York: Basic Books.

– 1983. *Local Knowledge: Further Essays in Interpretive Anthropology*. New York: Basic Books.

George, P.J., and R.J. Preston. 1987. "'Going in Between': The Impact of European Technology on the Work Patterns of the West Main Cree of Northern Ontario." *Journal of Economic History* 47, no. 2: 447–60. https:// doi.org/10.1017/S002205070004818X

George, P.J., F. Berkes, and R.J. Preston. 1995. "Aboriginal Harvesting in the Moose River Basin: A Historical and Contemporary Analysis." *Canadian Review of Sociology and Anthropology* 32, no. 1: 69–90. https://doi.org/10.1111 /j.1755-618X.1995.tb00835.x

– 1996. "Envisioning Cultural, Ecological and Economic Sustainability: The Cree Communities of the Hudson and James Bay Lowland, Ontario." *Canadian Journal of Economics* 29 (special issue): S356–60. https://doi.org /10.2307/136016

Gillespie, B.C. 1981. "Major Fauna in the Traditional Economy." In *Subarctic: Handbook of North American Indians*, Vol. 6, edited by J. Helm, 15–18. Washington, DC: Smithsonian Institution.

Gilovich, T. 1991. *How We Know What Isn't So: The Fallibility of Human Reason in Everyday Life*. New York: The Free Press.

Glen, E.N. 2015. "Settler Colonialism as Structure: A Framework for Comparative Studies of U.S. Race and Gender Formation." *Sociology of Race and Ethnicity* 1 (1): 57–72. https://doi.org/10.1177/2332649214560440

Goldschmidt, W. 1974. "Forward." In *Athapaskan Adaptations: Hunters and Fishermen of the Subarctic Forests*, edited by J. W. Vanstone, vii–viii. Chicago: Aldine.

– 1986. "Anthropology and Conflict: Why Men Fight." *Anthropology Today* 2 (1): 1213. https://doi.org/10.2307/3032902

Goodwin, G. 1969 [1941]. *The Social Organization of the Western Apache*. Tucson: University of Arizona Press.

Gover, K. 2017. "Five Myths about American Indians." *The Washington Post*, November 22, 2017. (https://www.washingtonpost.com/outlook/five -myths/five-myths-about-american-indians/2017/11/21/41081cb6-ce4f -11e7-a1a3-0d1e45a6de3d_story.html. Accessed April 23, 2020).

Graburn, N.H.H. 1969. *Eskimos Without Igloos: Social and Economic Development in Sugluk*. Boston: Little Brown.

Graham, E. 1975. *Medicine Man to Missionary: Missionaries as Agents of Change among the Indians of Southern Ontario, 1784–1867*. Toronto: Perter Martin Associates.

Grant, J.W. 1984. *Moon of Wintertime: Missionaries and the Indians of Canada in Encounter Since 1534*. Toronto: University of Toronto Press.

Grant, S.D. 2002. *Arctic Justice: On Trial for Murder, Pond Inlet, 1923*.Montreal: McGill-Queen's University Press.

Gree, R. 1988. "The Tribe Called Wannabee: Playing Indian in America and Europe." *Folklore* 99 (1): 30–55. https://doi.org/10.1080/0015587X .1988.9716423

Green, C.T. 2017. "A Stage Set for Assimilation: The Model Indian School at the World's Columbian Exposition." *Winterthur Portfolio* (The University of Chicago Press Journals) 51, no. 2/3: 95–133. https://www.journals .uchicago.edu/doi/10.1086/694225. Accessed August 24, 2020.

Green, R. 1984. "The Pocahontas Perplex: The Image of the American Indian Woman in American Culture." *The Massachusetts Review* 16, no. 4 (Autumn 1975): 698–714. https://www.jstor.org/stable/25088595

– 1992. *Women in American Indian Society*. New York: Chelsea House.

Greenberg, A.M., and J. Morrison. 1982. "Group Identities in the Boreal Forest. The Origin of the Northern Ojibwa." *Ethnohistory* 29 (2): 75–102. https:// doi.org/10.2307/481370

Greenberg, D.F. 2012. "Assessment of Crime Seriousness on an American Indian Reservation: A Reanalysis of Abril (2007)." *Race and Justice* 2, no. 1: 29–41. https://doi.org/10.1177/2153368711436013

Griffiths, R. ed. 2004. *Our Story: Aboriginal Voices on Canada's Past*. Toronto: Doubleday Canada.

Gulick, J. 1973 [1960]. *Cherokees at the Crossroads*. Chapel Hill: Institute for Research in Social Science, University of North Carolina Press.

Hackenberg, R.A., and M.M. Gallagher. 1972. "The Costs of Culture Change: Accidental Injury and Modernization among the Papago Indians." *Human Organization* 31: 211–26. https://doi.org/10.17730/humo.31.2 .212n472561217815

Hahn, R.A. 1978. "Aboriginal American Psychiatric Theories." *Transculture and Psychiatry*15, no. 1: 29–58. https://doi.org/10.1177/136346157801500102

Hallowell, A.I. 1934. "Some Empirical Aspects of Northern Saulteaux Religion." *American Anthropologist* 26: 389–404. https://doi.org/10.1525/aa.1934.36.3.02a00060

– 1942 (rev. 1971). *The Role of Conjuring in Saulteaux Society*. Philadelphia: University of Pennsylvania Press, vol 2.

– 1967 [1955]. *Culture and Experience*. Philadelphia: University of Pennsylvania Press.

– 1992. *The Ojibwa of Berens River, Manitoba: Ethnography into History*, edited by J.S.H. Brown. Case Studies in Cultural Anthropology. Fort Worth, Texas: Harcourt Brace Jovanovich.

Hanks, C. 1982. "The Swampy Cree and the Hudson's Bay Company at Oxford House." *Ethnohistory* 29, no. 2: 103–15. https://doi.org/10.2307/481371

Hansen, L.C. 1987. "Chiefs and Principal Men: A Question of Leadership in Treaty Negotiations." *Anthropologica* 29, no. 1: 39–60. https://doi.org/10.2307/25605208

Harkin, M.E., and D.R. Lewis, eds. 2007. *Native Americans and the Environment: Perspectives on the Ecological Indian*. Lincoln: University of Nebraska Press.

Harring, S. 1982. "Native American Crime in the United States." In *Indians and Criminal Justice*, edited by L. French, 93–108. Totawa, NJ: Allanheld, Osmun.

Harris, C. 2004. "How Did Colonialism Dispossess? Comments from the Edge of Empire." *Annals of the Association of American Geographers* 94, no. 1: 165–82. https://doi.org/10.1111/j.1467-8306.2004.09401009.x

Harris. M.1968. *The Rise of Anthropological Theory: A History of Theories of Culture*. New York: Thomas Y. Crowell.

Harrison, F. 1995. "The Persistent Power of 'Race' in the Cultural and Political Economy of Racism." *Annual Review of Anthropology* 24: 47–74. https://doi.org/10.1146/annurev.an.24.100195.000403

Hausman, B.M. 2011. *Riding the Trail of Tears*. Lincoln: University of Nebraska Press.

Hawthorn, H.B., ed. 1966–7. *A Survey of the Contemporary Indians of Canada: Economic, Political, and Educational Needs and Policies*. Ottawa: Indian Affairs Branch, Queen's Printer.

Hearne, S. 1958. *A Journey from Prince of Wales's Fort in Hudson's Bay to the Northern Ocean, 1769, 1770, 1771, 1772*, edited by R. Glover. Toronto: Macmillan.

Hechter, M. 1975. *Internal Colonialism*. Berkeley: University of California Press.

Hedican, E.J. 1976. "Ecological and Patron-Client Relationships: Algonkians of Eastern Subarctic Canada." *Man in the Northeast* 12 (Fall): 41–50.

– 1982a. "Governmental Indian Policy, Administration, and Economic Planning in the Eastern Subarctic." *Culture* 2, no. 3: 25–36. https://doi.org/10.7202/1078110ar

- 1982b. "The Whitesand Ojibwa: Land Claims and the Societal Mediator." In *Indian SIA: The Social Impact Assessment of Rapid Resource Development on Native Peoples*, edited by C. Geisler et al. 258–73. Ann Arbor: University of Michigan Press.
- 1986a. *The Ogoki River Guides: Emergent Leadership among the Northern Ojibwa.* Waterloo: Wilfrid Laurier University Press.
- 1986b. "Some Issues in the Anthropology of Transaction and Exchange." *The Canadian Review of Sociology and Anthropology* 23, no. 1: 97–117. https:// doi.org/10.1111/j.1755-618X.1986.tb00397.x
- 1988. "Review of *Native American Voluntary Organizations. Rural Sociology.* 53, no. 3: 384–5. https://doi.org/10.1177/034003528801400415
- 1990. "Algonquian Kinship Terminology: Some Problems of Interpretation." *Man in the Northeast* 40 (Fall): 1–15.
- 1994. "Epistemological Implications of Anthropological Fieldwork, with Notes from Northern Ontario." *Anthropologica* 36: 205–24. https:// doi.org/10.2307/25605771
- 2001. *Up in Nipigon Country: Anthropology as a Personal Experience.* Halifax: Fernwood Publishing.
- 2008a. *Applied Anthropology in Canada: Understanding Aboriginal Issues.* 2nd ed. Toronto: University of Toronto Press.
- 2008b. "The Ipperwash Inquiry and the Tragic Death of Dudley George." *The Canadian Journal of Native Studies* 28, no. 1: 159–73. https:// cjns.brandonu.ca/wp-content/uploads/28-1-07Hedican.pdf
- 2012a. *Social Anthropology: Canadian Perspectives on Culture and Society.* Toronto: Canadian Scholars' Press.
- 2012b. "Policing Aboriginal Protests and Confrontations: Some Policy Recommendations." *The International Indigenous Policy Journal* 3, no. 2: 1–17. https://doi.org/10.18584/iipj.2012.3.2.1
- 2013. *Ipperwash: The Tragic Failure of Canada's Aboriginal Policy.* Toronto: University of Toronto Press.
- 2014. "Eurocentrism in Aboriginal Studies: A Review of Issues and Conceptual Problems." *Canadian Journal of Native Studies* 34, no. 1: 87–109. https://www.proquest.com/openview/32bd3fa292dd4de3e4dad1e3139b6c 4a/1?pq-origsite=gscholar&cbl=44018
- 2016. *Public Anthropology: Engaging Social Issues in the Modern World.* Toronto: University of Toronto Press.
- 2017a. *The First Nations of Ontario: Social and Historical Transitions.* Toronto: Canadian Scholars' Press.
- 2017b. "Review of *Grounded Authority: The Algonquins of Barriere Lake Against the State.*" *Canadian Journal of Native Studies* 37, no. 2: 211–13.
- 2020. *After the Famine: The Irish Family Farm in Eastern Ontario, 1851–1881.* Toronto: University of Toronto Press.

Hegeman, S. 1989a. "History, Ethnography, Myth: Some Notes on the 'Indian-Centered' Narrative." *Social Text* 23: 144–60. https://doi.org/10.2307/466425

– 1989b. "Native American 'Texts' and the Problem of Authenticity." *American Quarterly* 41 (2): 265–83. https://doi.org/10.2307/2713025

Helm, J. ed. 1981. *Subarctic. Handbook of North American Indians*, vol. 6. Washington, DC: Smithsonian Institution.

Henderson, J., and P. Wakeham, eds. 2013. *Reconciling Canada: Critical Perspectives on the Culture of Redress*. Toronto: University of Toronto Press.

Henry, A. (the elder). 1969 [1809]. *Travels and Adventures in Canada and the Indian Territories Between the Years 1760 and 1776*. Edmonton: M.G. Hurtig.

Heyman, J. 2010. "Activism in Anthropology: Exploring the Present Through Eric R. Wolf's Vietnam-Era Work." *Dialectical* Anthropology 34: 287–93. https://doi.org/10.1007/s10624-010-9186-6

Hickerson, H. 1961. *The Southwestern Chippewa: An Ethnohistorical Study*. Washington, DC: American Anthropological Association, Memoir 92.

– 1967. "Land Tenure of the Rainy Lake Chippewa at the Beginning of the Nineteenth Century." *Smithsonian Contributions to Anthropology* 2: 37–63. https://doi.org/10.5479/si.00810223.2.4

– 1973. "Fur Trade Colonialism and the North American Indian." *Journal of Ethnic Studies* 1, no. 2: 15–44. https://www.proquest.com/openview/d107d05f52c003a2ac385fb884ba436a/1?pq-origsite=gscholar&cbl=1821393

Highway, T. 2004. "Hearts and Flowers." In *Our Story: Aboriginal Voices on Canada's Past*, edited by R. Griffiths, 179–99. Toronto: Random House Canada

Hirschfelder, A., and P.F. Molin. 2018. "I Is of Ignoble: Stereotyping Native Americans, Ferris State University, Jim Crow Museum of Racist Memorabilia." Accessed April 22, 2020. https://www.ferris.edu/HTMLS/news/jimcrow/native/homepage.htm.

Hixson, W.L. 2013. *American Settler Colonialism*. New York: Palgrave: Macmillan.

Hochkirchen, B., and W. Jilek. 1985. "Psychosocial Dimensions of Suicide and Parasuicide in Amerindians of the Pacific Northwest." *Journal of Operational Psychiatry* 16, no. 2: 24–8.

Hoffmann, H. 1960. "Culture Change and Personality Modification among the James Bay Cree." *Anthropological Papers of the University of Alaska* 9 no. 2: 81–91. https://www.uaf.edu/apua/files/Hoffman1961.pdf

Honigmann, J.J. 1953. "Social Organization of the Attawapiskat Cree Indians." *Anthropos* 48 (5–6): 809–16. https://www.jstor.org/stable/40449802

– 1956. "The Attawapiskat Swampy Cree: An Ethnographic Reconstruction." *Anthropological Papers of the University of Alaska* 5, no. 1: 23–82. https://www.uaf.edu/apua/files/Honigmann1956.pdf

– 1958. "Attawapiskat – Blend of Traditions." *Anthropologica* 6: 57–67. https://www.jstor.org/stable/25604413

– 1961. *Foodways in a Muskeg Community: An Anthropological Report on the Attawapiskat Indians.* Ottawa: Northern Co-ordination and Research Centre, Department of Northern Affairs and National Resources

– 1965. "Social Disintegration in Five Northern Communities." *The Canadian Review of Sociology and Anthropology* 2, no. 4: 199–214. https://doi.org/10.1111/j.1755-618X.1965.tb01338.x

– 1981a. "West Main Cree." In *Handbook of North American Indians*, Volume 6: *Subarctic*, edited by J. Helm, 217–30. Washington, DC: Smithsonian Institution.

– 1981b. "Expressive Aspects of Subarctic Indian Culture." In *Handbook of North American Indians*, Volume 6: *Subarctic*, edited by J. Helm, 718–38. Washington, DC: Smithsonian Institution.

Howay, F.W., W.N. Sage, and H.F. Angus, eds. 1942. *British Columbia and the United States: The North Pacific Slope from Fur Trade to Aviation.* Toronto: The Ryerson Press.

Howay, W. 1925. "Indian Attacks Upon Maritime Traders of the Northwest Coast, 1785–1805." *Canadians Historical Review* 6, no. 4: 287–309. https://doi.org/10.3138/chr-06-04-01

Hudson's Bay Company Archives. Public Archives of Canada, Ottawa, Ontario; Provincial Archives of Manitoba, Winnipeg, Manitoba.

– *Various Correspondence, Letters and Reports*

– 11/2,3 *London Inward Correspondence*

– 1/58 HBC Governor and Committee Minutes, January 3, 1833.

– 11/46 folios 11–13d., John George McTavish to HBC London Committee, September 24, 1831.

– 11/46 folios 15–20, John George McTavish to HBC London Committee, September 15, 1832.

– 12/1/ folios 59–60, Governor George Simpson to HBC London Committee, July 1832.

– *Post Records*

– B. 37/a Fort Chilcotin Post Journal, December 23, 1838–January 2, 1839

– B. 59/a/29 Eastmain Post Journals, 1736–1837

– B. 135/a Moose Factory Post Journals, 1730–1833

– B. 135/k Minutes of Council, Southern HBC Department, 1822–1875

– B. 186/a Rupert House Post Journals, 1777–1871

– B. 186/b Rupert House Correspondence Books, 1820–1870

– B. 200/a Fort Simpson Journals

Humphrey, J.A., and H.J. Kupferer. 1982. "Homicide and Suicide among the Cherokee and Lumbee Indians of North Carolina." The *International Journal of Social Psychiatry* 28, no. 2: 121–8. https://doi.org/10.1177/002076408202800210

Hunt, G.T. 1940. *The Wars of the Iroquois: A Study of Intertribal Trade Relations.* Madison: University of Wisconsin Press.

Ince, O.U. 2018. *Colonial Capitalism and the Dilemmas of Liberalism.* Oxford: Oxford University Press.

Innis, H.A. 1973 [1930]. *The Fur Trade in Canada: An Introduction to Canadian Economic History.* Toronto: University of Toronto Press.

Jacobson, C.K. 1984. "Internal Colonialism and Native Americans: Indian Labor in the United States from 1871 to World War II." *Social Science Quarterly* 65: 158–71. https://www.proquest.com/openview/2d2031106ab8 6daf227b09e912db5fe7/1?pq-origsite=gscholar&cbl=1816420

Jahoda, G. 1975. *The Trail of Tears: The Story of the American Indian Removal, 1813–1855.*New York: Random House.

Jaine, L. 1993. *Residential Schools: The Stolen Years.* Saskatoon, SK: University Extension Press.

James, B.J. 1961. "Social-Psychological Dimensions of Ojibwa Acculturation." *American Anthropologist* 63: 283–6. https://doi.org/10.1525/aa.1961 .63.4.02a00040

– 1970. "Continuity and Emergence in Indian Poverty Culture." *Current Anthropology* 11, no. 4/5: 435–42. https://doi.org/10.1086/201145

Jarvenpa, R. 1982. "Intergroup Behavior and Imagery: The Case of Chipewyan and Cree." *Ethnohistory* 21, no. 2 (October): 283–99. https://doi.org/10.2307 /3773760

– 2018. *Declared Defective: Native Americans, Eugenics, and the Myth of Nam Hollow.* Lincoln, NE: University of Nebraska Press.

Jenness, D. 1935. *The Ojibwa Indians of Parry Island: Their Social and Religious Life.* Bulletin 78. Ottawa: National Museum of Canada.

Jeremie, N. 1926. *Twenty Years of York Factory, 1694–1714: Jeremie's Account of Hudson Strait and Bay*, edited by R. Douglas and J.N. Wallace. Ottawa: Thornburn and Abbott.

Jesuit Relations. 1896–1901. *The Jesuit Relations and Allied Documents: Travel and Explorations of the Jesuit missionaries in New France, 1610–1791.* 73 vols. Cleveland: Burroughs Brothers.

Jilek, W., and C. Roy. 1976. ªHomicide Committed by Canadian Indians and Non-Indians." *International Journal of Offender Therapy and Comparative Criminology* 20, no. 3: 201–16. https://doi.org/10.1177/0306624X7602000301

Jochim, M.A. 1981. *Strategies for Survival: Cultural Behavior in an Ecological Context.* New York: Academic Press.

Johnston, C.M. 1964. *The Valley of the Six Nations.* Toronto: University of Toronto Press.

Jones, W. 1905. The Algonkin Manitu. *Journal of American Folklore* 18: 183–90. https://doi.org/10.2307/533138

Jorgensen, J.G. 1978. "A Century of Political Economic Effects on American Indian Society, 1880–1980." *The Journal of Ethnic Studies* 6, no. 3 (Fall 1978): 1–82. https://www.proquest.com/openview/bdc67b8e8281e7cfefcb82f1224 1ac34/1?pq-origsite=gscholar&cbl=1821393

Joseph, R.P.C. 2018. *21 Things You May Not Know about the Indian Act: Helping Canadians Make Reconciliation with Indigenous Peoples a Reality*. Port Coquitlam, BC: Indigenous Relations Press.

Joseph, R.P.C., and C.F. Joseph. 2019. *Indigenous Relations: Insights, Tips, and Suggestions to Make Reconciliation a Reality*. Port Coquitlam, BC: Indigenous Relations Press.

Judd, C. 1983. Housing the Homeguard at Moose Factory, 1730 –1982. *The Canadian Journal of Native Studies* 3, no. 1: 23–37. https://cjns.brandonu.ca /wp-content/uploads/3-1-judd.pdf

Kapferer, H.J., and J.A. Humphrey. 1975. Fatal Indian Violence in North Carolina. *Anthropological Quarterly* 48 (4): 236–44. https://doi.org/10 .2307/3316634

Kaye, B. 1986. "The Red River Settlement: Lord Selkirk's Colony in the Wilderness." *Prairie Forum* 11, no. 1: 1–20. http://hdl.handle.net/10294/245

Keeley, L. 1996. *War Before Civilization: The Myth of the Peaceful Savage*. New York: Oxford University Press.

Kelm, M-E. 1998. *Colonizing Bodies: Aboriginal Health and Healing in British Columbia, 1900–1950*. Vancouver, BC: UBC Press.

Kelm, M.-E., and K.D. Smith, eds.2018. *Talking Back to the Indian Act: Critical Readings in Settler Colonial Histories*. Toronto: University of Toronto Press.

Kennedy, M. 2017. *Narratives of Inequality: Postcolonial Literary Economics*. Cham, Switzerland: Palgrave Macmillan.

Kennedy, M.A. 1997. *The Whiskey Trade of the Northwestern Plains: A Multidisciplinary Study*. New York: P. Lang.

Kenyon, W.A. 1986. *The History of James Bay, 1610 – 1686: A Study in Historical Archaeology*. Archaeology Monograph No. 10. Toronto: Royal Ontario Museum.

Kenyon, W.A., and J.R. Turnbull. 1971. *The Battle for James Bay 1686*.Toronto: Macmillan Co.

Kidwell, C.S. 1978. "The Power of Women in Three American Indian Societies." *Journal of Ethnic Studies* 5 no. 3 (Fall 1978): 113–21. https:// www.proquest.com/openview/9a0534eba01b7f70f78582dd0d09ca81/1 ?pq-origsite=gscholar&cbl=1821393

– 1992. "Indian Women as Cultural Mediators." *Ethnohistory* 39, no. 2: 97–107. https://doi.org/10.2307/482389

King, C.R. 2016. *Redskins: Insult and Brand*. Lincoln: University of Nebraska Press.

King, D.H., and E.R. Evans. 1978. "The Trail of Tears: Preliminary Documents of the Cherokee Removal." In *The Journal of Cherokee Studies* Volume 3, 130–87. Museum of the Cherokee Indian in Cooperation with the Cherokee Historical Association.

King, T. 2003. *The Truth about Stories: A Native Narrative.* Toronto: House of Anansi Press.

Kleinman, A., and R. Desjariais. 1995. "Violence, Culture, and the Politics of Trauma." In *Writing at the Margin: Discourse Between Anthropology and Medicine,* edited by A. Kleinman, 173–89. Berkeley, Calif.: University of California Press.

Kluckhohn, C., and D. Leighton. 1964. *The Navaho.* The National Museum of Natural History, Garden City, NY: Doubleday and Co.

Knafla, L.A. 2010. "'This is Our Land': Aboriginal Title and Indigenous Peoples." In *Aboriginal Title and Indigenous Peoples: Canada, Australia and New Zealand,* edited by L.A. Knafla and H. Westra, 1–34, Vancouver: University of British Columbia Press.

Knight, R. 1968. *Ecological Factors in Changing Economy and Social Organization Among the Rupert House Cree.* Anthropological Paper 15. Ottawa: National Museum of Canada.

Krech, S. 1978. "Disease, Starvation, and Northern Athapaskan Social Organization." *American Ethnologist* 5, no. 4: 710–32. https://doi.org/10.1525/ae.1978.5.4.02a00050

– 1984. The Trade of the Slavey and Dogrib at Fort Simpson in the Early Nineteenth Century. In *The Subarctic Fur Trade: Native Social and Economic Adaptations,* edited by S. Krech, 130–1. Vancouver: University of British Columbia Press.

– 1993. *Native Canadian Anthropology and History.* Norman: University of Oklahoma Press.

– 1999. *The Ecological Indian: Myths and History.* New York: Norton.

– 2005. "Reflections on Conservation, Sustainability, and Environmentalism in Indigenous North America." *American Anthropologist* 107: 78–86. https://doi.org/10.1525/aa.2005.107.1.078

– 2010. "American Indians as the 'First Ecologists.'" *The Encyclopedia of Religion and Nature.* Accessed April 17, 2020. https://www-oxfordreference-com.subzero.lib.uoguelph.ca/view/10.1093/acref/9780199754670.001.0001/acref-9780199754670-e-25?rskey=d6F9q9&result=3.

Krepps, M., and R. Caves. 1994. "Bureaucrats and Indians: Principal-Agent Relations and Efficient Management of Tribal Forest Resources." *Journal of Economic Behavior and Organization* 24, no. 2: 133–51. https://doi.org/10.1016/0167-2681(94)90022-1

Krieg, G. 2018. "Here's the Deal with Elizabeth Warren's Native American Heritage." Accessed August 30, 2020. https://www.cnn.com/2016/06/29/politics/elizabeth-warren-native-american-pocahontas/index.html.

Kroeber, A. 1935. "History and Science in Anthropology." *American Anthropologist* 37: 539–69. https://doi.org/10.1525/aa.1935.37.4.02a00020

– 1939. *Cultural and Natural Areas of Native North America*. University of California Publications in American Archaeology and Ethnology, Volume 38. Berkeley: University of California Press.

– 1963. *An Anthropologist Looks at History*. Berkeley: University of California Press.

Krohn-Hansen, C. 1994. "The Anthropology of Violent Interaction." *Journal of Anthropological Research* 50: 367–81. https://doi.org/10.1086/jar.50.4.3630559

Kupferer, H. 1966. "Impotency and Power: A Cross-Cultural Comparison of the Effect of Alien Rule." In *Political Anthropology*, edited by M.J. Swartz, V.W. Turner, and A. Tuden, 61–71. Chicago: Aldine.

– 2002. *Muskekwowuck Athinuwick: Original People of the Great Swampy Land*. Winnipeg: University of Manitoba Press.

Labelle, K.M. 2013. *Dispersed but Not Destroyed: A History of the Seventeenth-Century Wendat People*. Vancouver. University of British Columbia Press.

Lahire, B. 2011. *The Plural Actor*. Cambridge, UK: The Polity Press.

Lamb, W.K., ed. 1957. *Sixteen Years in Indian Country: The Journal of Daniel Williams Harmon, 1800–1816*.Toronto: Macmillan.

Landes, R. 1937. *Ojibwa Sociology*. New York: Columbia University Press.

Lanier, C., and L. Huff-Corzine. 2006. "American Indian Homicide: A Country-Level Analysis Utilizing Social Disorganization Theory." *Homicide Studies* 10, no. 3: 181–94. https://doi.org/10.1177/1088767906288573

La Potin, A.S., ed. 1987. *Native American Voluntary Organizations*. New York: Greenwood Press.

La Prairie, C. 2002. "Aboriginal Over-Representation in the Criminal Justice System: A Tale of Nine Cities." *Canadian Journal of Criminology and Criminal Justice* 44, no. 2: 181–208. https://doi.org/10.3138/cjcrim.44.2.181

LaRocque, E. 1997. Re-examining Culturally Appropriate Modes in Criminal Justice Applications. In *Aboriginal Treaty Rights in Canada: Essays in Law, Equality, and Respect for Difference*, edited by M. Ash, 75–96. Vancouver: University of British Columbia Press.

– 2010. *When the Other Is Me: Native Resistance Discourse 1850–1990*. Winnipeg: University of Manitoba Press.

Laughlin, C.D., and I.V. Brady. 1978. "Introduction: Diaphasis and Change in Human Populations." In *Extinction and Survival in Human Populations*, edited by C.D. Laughlin and I.V. Brady, 1–48. New York: Columbia University Press.

LaViolette, F.E. 1973. *The Struggle for Survival: Indian Cultures and the Protestant Ethic in British Columbia*. Toronto: University of Toronto Press.

Lawrence, B. 2011. "Rewriting Histories of the Land: Colonization and Indigenous Resistance in Canada." In *Racism, Colonialism, and Indigeneity in Canada*, edited by M.J. Cannon and L. Sunseri, 68–80. Don Mill, ON: Oxford University Press.

Lawrence, B., and E. Dua. 2011. "Decolonizing Antiracism." In *Racism, Colonialism, and Indigeneity in Canada*, edited by M.J. Cannon and L. Sunseri, 19–27. Don Mill, ON: Oxford University Press.

Leach, E.R., ed. 1968. *The Structural Study of Myth and Totemism*. London: Tavistock Publications.

Leacock, E. 1958. "Status among the Montagnais-Naskapi of Labrador." *Ethnohistory* 5, no. 3: 200–9. https://doi.org/10.2307/480663

– 1954. *The Montagnais "Hunting Territory" and the Fur Trade*. American Anthropological Association, Memoir 78, Washington DC.

– 1978. "Women's Status in Egalitarian Society: Implications for Social Evolution." *Current Anthropology* 19, no. 2: 247–75. [Reprinted: *Current Anthropology* 1992, 19, no. 2: 247– 75]. https://doi.org/10.1086/202074

Lee, R.B. 1968. "What Hunters Do for a Living, or, How to Make Out on Scarce Resources." In *Man the Hunter*, edited by R.B. Lee and I. DeVore, 30–48. Chicago: Aldine Publishing.

– 1982. "Politics, Sexual and Non-Sexual, in Egalitarian Societies." In *Politics and History in Band Societies*, edited by E. Leacock and R.B. Lee, 37–59. Cambridge: Cambridge University Press.

Lee, R.B., and I. DeVore. 1968. "Problems in the Study of Hunters and Gatherers." In *Man the Hunter*, edited by R.B. Lee and I. DeVore, 3–12. Chicago: Aldine Publishing.

Lee, R.B., and I. DeVore, eds. 1976. *Kalahari Hunter-Gatherers: Studies of the !Kung San and Their Neighbors*. Cambridge: Harvard University Press.

Lett, J. 1987. *The Human Enterprise: A Critical Introduction to Anthropological Theory*. Boulder, CO: Westview.

– 1997. *Science, Reason, and Anthropology: The Principles of Rational Inquiry*. Lanham, MD: Rowman and Littlefield.

Lévi-Strauss, C. (1969 [1949]). *The Elementary Structures of Kinship*. Boston: Beacon Press.

Levy, J.E. 1962. "Community Organization of the Western Navajo." *American Anthropologist* 64: 781–801. https://doi.org/10.1525/aa.1962.64.4.02a00080

Levy, J.E., S.J. Kunitz, and M. Everett. 1969. "Navajo Criminal Homicide." *Southwestern Journal of Anthropology* 25, no. 2: 124–52. https://doi.org/10.1086/soutjanth.25.2.3629198

Lewis, D.R. 1995. "Native Americans and the Environment: A Survey of Twentieth-Century Issues." *American Indian Quarterly* 19, no. 3: 423–50. https://doi.org/10.2307/1185599

Liebow, E., and J. Trudeau. 1962. "A Preliminary Study of Acculturation Among the Cree Indians of Winisk, Ontario." *Arctic* 15, no. 3: 191–204. https://doi.org/10.14430/arctic3573

Linden, Hon. Sidney B. 2007. *Report of the Ipperwash Inquiry*. Toronto: Publications Ontario.

Lips, J.E. 1947. "Naskapi Law: Law and Order in a Hunting Society." *Transactions of the American Philosophical Society*, N.S., Vol. 37, no 4: 377–492.

Lockwood, F.C. 1987. *The Apache Indians*. Lincoln: University of Nebraska Press.

Lombardi, J.R. 1975. "Reciprocity and Survival." *Anthropological Quarterly* 48, no. 4: 245–54. https://doi.org/10.2307/3316635

Long, J. 1791 [1974]. *Voyages and Travels of an Indian Interpreter and Trader*. Reprinted by Coles Publishing Company, Toronto.

Long, J.S. 1986. "The Reverend George Barnley and the James Bay Cree." *Canadian Journal of Native Studies* 6, no. 2: 13–31. https://www.researchgate.net/publication/242151630

– 1988a. "The Rev. G. Barnley, Wesleyan Methodism and the Fur Trade Company Families of James Bay." *Ontario History* 77, no.1: 43–64.

– 1988b. Narratives of Early Encounters between Europeans and the Cree of Western James Bay. *Ontario History* 80, no. 3: 227–45.

– 2006. "How the Commissioners Explained Treaty Number 9 to the Ojibway and Cree in 1905." *Ontario History* 98, no. 1: 1–29. https://doi.org/10.7202/1065838ar

– 2010. *Treaty No. 9: Making the Agreement to Share the Land in Far Northern Ontario in 1905*. Montreal: McGill-Queen's University Press.

Long, J.S., and J.S.H. Brown, eds. 2016. *Together We Survive: Ethnographic Intuitions, Friendships, and Conversations*. Montreal: McGill-Queen's University Press.

Lowie, R. 1912. "Social Life of the Crow Indians." In *Anthropological Papers of the American Museum of Natural History* Vol. 9, no. 2: 145–248. http://hdl.handle.net/2246/159

– 1917. "Oral Tradition and History." *Journal of American Folklore* 30, no. 116: 161–7. https://doi.org/10.2307/534336

– 1920. *Primitive Society*. New York: Boni and Liveright.

Lucy, J.A. 1997. "Linguistic Relativity." *Annual Review of Anthropology* 26: 291–312. https://doi.org/10.1146/annurev.anthro.26.1.291

Lytwyn, V.P. 1986. *The Fur Trade in the Little North: Indians, Peddlers, and Englishmen East of Lake Winnipeg, 1760–1821*.Winnipeg: Rupert's Land Research Centre, University of Winnipeg.

– 2002. *Muskekowuck Athinuwick: Original People of the Great Swampy Land*. Winnipeg: University of Manitoba Press.

MacEwan, G. 1975. *Fifty Mighty Men*. Saskatoon: Western Producer Prairie Books.

Macfie, J. 1967. "The Coast Crees." *The Beaver* 47 no. 1: 13–15. https://www.canadashistoryarchive.ca/canadas-history/the-beaver-winter-1967/flipbook/12/

MacKay, D. 1966 [1936]. *The Honourable Company: A History of the Hudson's Bay Company*. Toronto: McClelland and Stewart.

Mackey, E. 2016. *Unsettled Expectations: Uncertainty, Land and Settler Decolonization*. Halifax, NS: Fernwood Publishers.

Mackinnon, C.S. 2003. Anderson, James. *Dictionary of Canadian Biography* Vol. 9. Toronto: University of Toronto Press. Accessed June 16, 2020. http://www.biogaphi.ca/en/bio/Anderson_james_9E.html).

Macklem, P. 1997. "The Impact of Treaty 9 on Natural Resource Development in Northern Ontario." In *Aboriginal and Treaty Rights in Canada*, edited by M. Asch, 97–134. Vancouver: University of British Columbia Press.

MacNeish, J.H. 1956. "Leadership among the Northeastern Athabascans." *Anthropologica* 2 (1956): 131– 63. https://www.jstor.org/stable/25604376

Mair, L. 1965. *An Introduction to Social Anthropology*. Oxford: Clarendon Press.

Malinowski, B. 1941. "An Anthropological Analysis of War." *American Journal of Sociology* 46, no. 4: 521–50. https://doi.org/10.1086/218697

Malthus, T. 1999 [1798]. *An Essay on the Principle of Population*. Oxford: Oxford University Press.

Mandelbaum, D.G. 1940. "The Plains Cree." *Anthropological Papers of the American Museum of Natural History* Volume 37, pt. 2: 155–316. http://hdl.handle.net/2246/136

Manuel, A., and Grand Chief R.M. Derrikson. 2015.*Unsettling Canada*: A *National Wake-Up Call*. Toronto: Between the lines.

Manuel, G., and M. Posluns. 1974. *The Fourth World: An Indian Reality*. Don Mills, ON: Collier-Macmillan.

Marano, L., et al. 1982. "Windigo Psychosis: The Anatomy of an Emic-Etic Confusion." *Current Anthropology* 23, no. 4: 385–97. https://doi.org/10.1086/202868

Marshall, D.P. 2002. Review of *Patterns of Vengeance: Crosscultural Homicide in the North American Fur Trade*, 1999, by J.P. Reid. *Oregon Historical Quarterly* 103, no. 2: 272–4. https://www.jstor.org/stable/20615238

Marshall, L. 1961. "Sharing, Talking, and Giving: Relief of Social Tensions among !Kung Bushmen." *Africa: Journal of the International African Institute* 31, no. 3: 231–49. https://doi.org/10.2307/1157263

Martin, C. 1978. *Keepers of the Game: Indian-Animal Relationships and the Fur Trade*. Berkeley, Calif.: University of California Press.

Martin, P.S. 1967. "Prehistoric Overkill." In *Pleistocene Extinctions: The Search for a Cause*, edited by P.S. Martin and H.E. Wright, 75–120. New Haven, Conn.: Yale University Press.

Marubbio, M.E. 2006. *Killing the Indian Maiden: Images of Native American Women in Film*. Lexington, KY: The University Press of Kentucky.

Marrubio, M.E., and E.L. Buffalohead, eds. 2018. *Native Americans on Film: Conversations, Teaching, and Theory*. Lexington, KY: The University Press of Kentucky

Marx, K. 1978 [1852]. *The Eighteenth Brumaire of Louis Bonaparte*. Peking: Foreign Language Press.

Maskovsky, J. 2013. "Protest Anthropology in a Moment of Global Unrest." *American Anthropologist* 115, no. 1: 126–9. https://doi.org/10.1111/j.1548-1433.2012.01541.x

Mason, L. 1967. *The Swampy Cree: A Study in Acculturation*. Anthropological Papers 13, Department of the Secretary of State.Ottawa: National Museum of Canada,

Masty, D. 1991. "Traditional Use of Fish and Other Resources of the Great Whale River Region." *Northeast Indian Quarterly* 8, no. 4 (Winter 1991): 12–14.

Mauss, M. 1954 [1925]. *The Gift: The Form and Reason for Exchange in Archaic Societies*. New York: W.W. Norton.

McIlwraith, T.F. 1948. *The Bella Coola Indians*. Toronto: University of Toronto Press.

McKanna, C.V. 1985. "Ethnics and San Quentin Prison Registers: A Comment on Methodology." *Journal of Social History* 18 (March): 477–82. https://doi.org/10.1353/jsh/18.3.477

– 1987. "The Nameless Ones: The Ethnic Experience in San Quentin." *Pacific Historian* 31, no. 1 (Spring 1987): 21–33. https://www.jstor.org/stable/community.28380849

– 1993. "Murders All: The Treatment of Indian Defendants in Arizona Territory, 1880–1912." *American Indian Quarterly* 17, no. 3: 359–69. https://doi.org/10.2307/1184879

McLaurin, V. 2019. "Native American Stereotypes in Popular Media: Why the Myth of the 'Savage Indian' Persists." *Sapiens*, February 27, 2019. Accessed April 24, 2020. https://www.sapiens.org/culture/native-american-stereotypes/ https://www.sapiens.org/culture/native-american-stereotypes/.

McLean, J. 1968 [1932]. *John McLean's Notes of a Twenty-Five Years' Service in the Hudson's Bay Territory*, edited by W.S. Wallace. Toronto: The Champlain Society.

McLeod, S. 2019. "What Are Independent and Dependent Variables?" Accessed August 17, 2020. https://www.simplypsychology.org/variables.html.

McLoughlin, W.G. 1993. *After the Trail of Tears: The Cherokees' Struggle for Sovereignty, 1839–1880*. Chapel Hill: University of North Carolina Press.

McLuhan, M. 1964. *Understanding Media: The Extensions of Man*. Toronto, ON: McGraw-Hill.

Means, R., and M.J. Wolf. 1995. *Where White Men Fear to Tread: The Autobiography of Russell Means*. New York: St. Martin's Press.

Merk, F. 1968 [1931]. *Fur Trade and Empire: George Simpson's Journal and Remarks Connected with the Fur Trade in the Course of a Voyage from York Factory to Fort George, 1824–1825*. Cambridge, Mass.: Harvard University Press.

Merton, R.K. 1949. *Social Theory and Social Structure*. New York: Free Press.

Merton, R.K., and E. Barber. 1976. Sociological Ambivalence. In *Sociological Ambivalence and Other Essays*, edited by R.K. Merton, 3–31. New York: Free Press.

Mihesuah, D.A. 2009. *American Indians: Stereotypes and Realities*. Atlanta, GA: Clarity Press.

Miller, D.W. 2001. "Neurologist Explains What Makes a Killer." *Chronicle of Higher Education* 48, no. 3 (September 14, 2001). https://www.chronicle.com/article/neurologist-explains-what-makes-a-killer/

Miller W. 1955. "Two Concepts of Authority." *American Anthropologist* 57: 271–89. https://doi.org/10.1525/aa.1955.57.2.02a00060

Miner, H.C. 1989. *The Corporation and the Indian: Tribal Sovereignty and Industrial Civilization in Indian Territory, 1865–1907*. Norman: University of Oklahoma Press.

Mitrani, P. 1992. "A Critical Overview of Psychiatric Approaches to Shamanism." *Diogenes* 40, no. 158: 145–64. https://doi.org/10.1177/039219219204015813

Moore, J. 1993. *Political Economy of North American Indians*. Norman: University of Oklahoma Press.

Montijo, V. 1993. "In the Name of the Pot, the Sun, the Broken Spear, the Rock, the Stick, the Idol, Ad Infinitum, Ad Nauseam: An Expose of Anglo Anthropologists Obsessions with and Invention of Mayan Gods." *Wicazo SA Review* 9, no.1: 12–16. https://doi.org/10.2307/1409250

Morantz, T. 1978. "The Probability of Family Hunting Territories in Eighteenth Century James Bay: Old Evidence Newly Presented." In *Papers of the Ninth Algonquian Conference*, edited by W. Cowan, 224–36. Ottawa: Carleton University.

– 1980. "The Fur Trade and the Cree of James Bay." In *Old Trails and New Directions: Paper of the Third North American Fur Trade Conference*, edited by C.M. Judd and A. J. Ray, 39–58. Toronto: University of Toronto Press.

– 1982a. "Northern Algonquian Concepts of Status and Leadership Reviewed: A Case Study of the Eighteenth-Century Trading Captain System." *Canadian Review of Sociology and Anthropology* 19, no. 4: 482–501. https://doi.org/10.1111/j.1755-618X.1982.tb00876.x

– 1982b. "A Reconstruction of Early Nineteenth Century Social Organization in Eastern James Bay." In *Papers of the Thirteenth Algonquian Conference*, edited by W. Cowan, 261–73. Ottawa: Carleton University.

– 1983. *An Ethnohistoric Study of Eastern James Bay Social Organization, 1700–1850*. Canadian Ethnology Service Paper, No. 88. National Museum of Man, Mercury Series. Ottawa: National Museums of Canada.

– 1984. "Economic and Social Accommodations of the James Bay Inlanders to the Fur Trade." In *The Subarctic Fur Trade: Native Social and Economic Adaptations*, edited by S. Kretch, 55–80. Vancouver: University of British Columbia Press.

– 1986. "Historical Perspectives on Family Hunting Territories in Eastern James Bay." *Anthropologica* 28 (1–2): 64–91. https://doi.org/10.2307/25605193

– 1992. "Old Texts, Old Questions: Another Look at the Issue of Continuity and the Early Fur Trade Period." *Canadian Historical Review* 73: 167–93. https://doi.org/10.3138/CHR-073-02-02

– 2002. *The White Man's Gonna Getcha: The Colonial Challenge to the Cree of Quebec*. Montreal: McGill-Queen's University Press.

Moreton-Robinson, A. 2015. *The White Possessive: Property, Power, and Indigenous Sovereignty*. Minneapolis, Minn.: University of Minnesota Press.

Morgensen, S.L. 2012. "Theorising Gender, Sexuality and Settler Colonialism: An Introduction." *Settler Colonial Studies* 2, no. 2: 2–22. https://doi.org/10.1080/2201473X.2012.10648839

Morrison, A.H. 1976. "Dawnland Directors: Status and Role of Seventeenth Century Wabanaki Sagamores." In *Papers of the Seventh Algonquian Conference, 1975*, edited by W. Cowan, 1–19. Ottawa: Carleton University.

Morton, A.S. [1939]1973. *A History of the Canadian West to 1870–71 Being a History of Rupert's Land (the Hudson's Bay Company's Territory)*. Toronto: University of Toronto Press [orig. London: Thomas Nelson].

Morton, W.L. 1949. "Agriculture in the Red River Colony." *The Canadian Historical Review* 30, no. 4: 305–21. https://doi.org/10.3138/chr-030-04-01

Moses, L.G. 1996. *Wild West Shows and the Images of American Indians, 1883–1933*. Albuquerque, NM: University of New Mexico Press.

Nadasdy, P. 1999. "The Politics of TEK: Power and the 'Integration' of Knowledge." *Arctic Anthropology* 36, no. 1/2 (1999): 1–18. https://www.jstor.org/stable/40316502

– 2004. Review of *The White Man's Gonna Getcha: The Colonial Challenge to the Crees of Quebec*, (2002) by T. Morantz. *Ethnohistory* 51, no. 1: 191–2. https://doi.org/10.1215/00141801-51-1-191

– 2005. "Transcending the Debate over the Ecologically Noble Indian: Indigenous Peoples and Environmentalism." *Ethnology* 52, no. 2: 291–337. https://doi.org/10.1215/00141801-52-2-291

Nadeau, D.M. 2020. *Unsettling Spirit: A Journey into Decolonization*. Montreal: McGill-Queen's University Press.

Natziger, R. 1980. "Transnational Corporations and American Indian Development." In *American Indian Energy Studies, Resources and Development*, edited by R. Ortiz, 9–38. Santa Fe, NM: University of New Mexico Press.

Netzloff, M. 2003. *England's Internal Colonies: Class, Capital, and the Literature or Early Modern English Colonialism* New York: Palgrave Macmillan.

Newman, P.C. 1987. *Caesars of the Wilderness: Company of Adventurers, Vol. II.* Markham, ON: Penguin Books.

Neyland, S. 2003. *The Heavens Are Changing*. Montreal: McGill-Queen's University Press.

Nicholas, R.W. 1976. "Segmentary Factional Political Systems." In *Political Anthropology*, edited by M.J. Swartz, et al., 49–59. Chicago: Aldine Publishing Company.

Niezen, R. 1994. "Healing and Conversion: Medicine Evangelism in James Bay Cree Society." *Ethnohistory* 44, no. 3: 463–89. https://doi.org/10.2307/483032

– 2000. *Spirit Wars: Native North American Religions in the Age of Nation Building*. Berkeley, Calif.: University of California Press.

– 2013. *Truth and Indignation: Canada's Truth and Reconciliation Commission on Indian Residential Schools*. Toronto: University of Toronto Press.

Nixon, R. 2011. *Slow Violence and the Environmentalism of the Poor*. Cambridge: Harvard University Press.

Northey, M., L. Tepperman, and P. Albanese. 2012. *Making Sense: A Guide to Research and Writing*. Don Mill, ON: Oxford University Press.

Oberholtzer, C. 2005. Review of *The White Man's Gonna Getcha: The Colonial Challenge to the Crees in Quebec* (2002), by T. Morantz. *American Review of Canadian Studies* 35, no. 2: 575–7.

O'Connor, J. 2003. *Hollywood's Indian: The Portrayal of the Native American in Film*. Lexington: The University Press of Kentucky.

Ogden, M., M.I. Spector, and C.A. Hill. 1970. "Suicides and Homicides Among Indians." Washington, DC: United States Department of Health, Education and Welfare, Public Health Report, 85, no. 1: 75–80. https://www.ncbi.nlm.nih.gov/pmc/articles/PMC2031630/pdf/pubhealthreporig01049-0079.pdf

Officer, J.E. 1978. "The Bureau of Indian Affairs Since 1945: An Assessment." *The Annals of the American Academy of Political and Social Science* 436 (March): 61–72. https://doi.org/10.1177/000271627843600107

Oliver, E.H. 1914–1915. *The Canadian North West, Its Early Development and Legislstive Records*. No. 9. Ottawa: Publications of the Canadian Archives, Government Printing Bureau.

Olsen, K. 1989. "Native Women and the Fur Industry." *Canadian Women's Studies* 10, no. 2–3: 55–6. https://cws.journals.yorku.ca/index.php/cws/article/view/11171

Ontario, Ministry of Natural Resources. 2013. "Far North Ontario: Community-Based Land Use Planning in the Far North Ontario." Retrieved from www.mnr.gov.on.ca/en/Business/Fa/North.

Opler, M.E. 1941. *An Apache Life-Way: The Economic, Social, and Religious Institutions of the Chiricahua Indians*. Chicago: University of Chicago Press.

– 1969. *Apache Odyssey*. New York: Holt, Rinehart and Winston.

– 1983. "The Apachean Culture Pattern and Its Origins." In *Handbook of North American Indians: Southwest*, Vol. 10, edited by A. Ortiz, 182–92. Washington, DC: Smithsonian Institution

Orr, R., K. Sharratt, and M. Iqbal 2019. "American Indian Erasure and the Logic of Elimination: An Experimental Study of Depiction and Support for Resources and Rights for Tribes." *Journal of Ethnic and Migration Studies* 45, no. 11: 2078–99. https://doi.org/10.1080/1369183X.2017.1421061

Ostler, J. 2004. *The Plains Sioux and U.S. Colonialism from Lewis and Clark to Wounded Knee*. Cambridge, UK: Cambridge University Press.

Otterbein, K.F. 1964. "Why the Iroquois Won: An Analysis of Iroquois Military Tactics." *Ethnohistory* 11, no. 1: 56–63. https://doi.org/10.2307/480537

– 1997. "The Origins of War." *Critical Review* 11: 251–77. https://doi.org/10.1080/08913819708443456

– 1999a. "Crime." In *The Encyclopedia of Cultural Anthropology*, Vol. 1, edited by D. Levinson and M. Ember, 254–7. New York: Henry Holt.

– 1999b. "Feuding." In *The Encyclopedia of Cultural Anthropology*, Vol. 2, edited by D. Levinson and M. Ember, 493–6. New York: Henry Holt.

– 2000. "The Doves Have Been Heard From: Where Are the Hawks?" *American Anthropologist* 102, no. 4: 841–4. https://doi.org/10.1525/aa.2000.102.4.841

Owen, N.G., ed. 2014. *Routledge Handbook of Southeast Asian History*. New York: Routledge.

Paine, R. 1971. "A Theory of Patronage and Brokerage." In *Patrons and Brokers in the East Arctic*, edited by R. Paine, 8–21. Institute of Social and Economic Research, Newfoundland Social and Economic Papers No. 2. St. John's, NL: Memorial University of Newfoundland.

Palmater, P. 2014. "Indian Status: Why Lyn Gehl's Court Challenge Matters." *CBC News*, October 20, 2014.

Palmer, M., and R. Rundstrom. 2013. "GIS [Geographic Information Systems], Internal Colonialism and the U.S. Bureau of Indian Affairs." *Annals of the Association of American Geographers* 103, no. 5: 1142–59. https://doi.org/10.1080/00045608.2012.720233

Pasternak, S. 2017. *Grounded Authority: The Algonquins of Barriere Lake Against the State*. Minneapolis, Minn.: University of Minnesota Press.

Parker, S. 1960. "The Witiko Psychosis in the Context of Ojibwa Personality and Culture." *American Anthropologist* 62: 603–23. https://doi.org/10.1525/aa.1960.62.4.02a00050

Pate, J. 1974. "Indians on Trial in a White Man's Court." *Great Plains Journal* 14, no. 1: 56–71.

Patterson, P. 1971. "The Colonial Parallel: A View of Indian History." *Ethnohistory* 18, no. 1: 1–17. https://doi.org/10.2307/481590

Peak, K. 1987. "Crime in Indian Country: Another Trail of Tears." *Journal of Criminal Justice* 15: 485–94. https://doi.org/10.1016/0047-2352(87)90004-3

– 1989. "Criminal Justice, Law, and Policy in Indian Country: A Historical Perspective." *Journal of Criminal Justice* 17: 393–407. https://doi.org/10.1016/0047-2352(89)90049-4

– 1994. "Policing and Crime in Indian Country: History, Issues and Challenges." *Journal of Contemporary Criminal Justice* 10, no. 2: 79–94. https://doi.org/10.1177/104398629401000202

Peers, L. 2007. *Playing Ourselves: Interpreting Native Histories at Historic Reconstructions.* New York: Altamira Press.

– 2016. "A Token of Remembrance: The Gift of a Cree Hood, Red River Settlement, 1844." In *Together We Survive: Ethnographic Intuitions, Friendships, and Conversations*, edited by J.S. Long and J.S.H. Brown, 107–29. Montreal: McGill-Queen's University Press.

Peloquin, C., and F. Berkes. 2009. "Local Knowledge, Subsistence Harvest and Socio-Ecological Complexity in James Bay." *Human Ecology* 37: 533–45. https://doi.org/10.1007/s10745-009-9255-0

Pels, P. 1997. "The Anthropology of Colonialism: Culture, History, and the Emergence of Western Governmentality." *Annual Review of Anthropology* 26: 163–213. https://doi.org/10.1146/annurev.anthro.26.1.163

Pentland, D.H., and H.C. Wolfart. 1982. *Bibliography of Algonquian Linguistics.* Winnipeg, Man: University of Manitoba Press.

Perry, S.W. 2004. *American Indians and Crime.* ABJS Statistical Profile, 1992–2002. Washington, DC: U.S. Department of Justice, Office of Justice programs, Bureau of Justice Statistics.

Peterson, O.M. 1974. *The Land of Moosoneek.* The Diocese of Moosonee: The Bryant Press.

Pincus, J. 2001. *Base Instincts: What Makes Killers Kill?* New York: W.W. Norton.

Pinkerton, R.E. 1931. *The Hudson's Bay Company.* New York: Henry Holt and Co.

Preston, R.J. 1979. "The Cree Way Project: An Experiment in Grass-Roots Curriculum Development." *Journals at Carleton University* 92–101. Accessed Sept 28, 2019. https://ojs.library.carleton.ca.

– 1980. "The Witiko: Algonkian Knowledge and Whiteman Knowledge." In *Manlike Monsters on Trial. Early Records and Modern Evidence*, edited by M. Halpin and M. Ames, 111–31. Vancouver: University of British Columbia Press.

– 1981. "East Main Cree." In *Handbook of North American Indians: Subarctic*, Vol. 6, edited by J. Helm, 196–207. Washington, DC: Smithsonian Institution.

– 1982. "Towards a General Statement on the Eastern Cree Structure of Knowledge." In *Papers of the Thirteenth Algonquian Conference*, edited by W. Cowan, 299–306. Ottawa: Carleton University.

– 2002 [1975]. *Cree Narrative: Expressing the Personal Meanings of Events*. 2nd ed. Montreal: McGill-Queen's University Press.

– 2004. Review of *The White Man's Gonna Getcha: The Colonial Challenge to the Crees in Quebec* (2002), by T. Morantz. *The Canadian Journal of Sociology* 29, no. 3: 484–5. https://doi.org/10.1353/cjs.2004.0046

Price, J. 1979. *Indians of Canada: Cultural Dynamics*. Scarborough, ON: Prentice-Hall.

Purich, D. 1992. *The Inuit and Their Land: The Story of Nunavut*. Toronto: James Lorimer.

Quimby, G.I. 1960. *Indian Life in the Upper Great Lakes: 11,000 B.C. to A.D. 1800*. Field Museum of Natural History, Chicago: The University of Chicago Pres.

Rabin, R. 2014. "The Colonial Intrusions: Boundaries and Structures." In *Colonial Capitalism and Economic Transformation. Handbook of Southeast Asian History*, edited by N.G. Owen, 25–35. New York: Routledge.

Rasporich, A.W. 1975. "Introduction." In *Western Canada Past and Present*, edited by A.W. Rasporich, 9–13. Calgary: McClelland and Stewart West.

Ray, A.J. 1974. *Indians in the Fur Trade: Their Role as Hunters, Trappers, and Middlemen in the Lands Southwest of Hudson Bay, 1660–1870*. Toronto: University of Toronto Press.

– 1975a. "The Factor and the Trading Captain in the Hudson's Bay Company Fur Trade before 1763." In *Proceedings of the Second Congress, Canadian Ethnology Society*, edited by J. Freedman and J. Barkow, 586–602. Mercury Series, paper 28. Ottawa: National Museum of Man

– 1975b. "Some Conservation Schemes of the Hudson's Bay Company, 1821–50: An Examination of the Problems of Resource Management in the Fur Trade." *Journal of Historical Geography* 1, no. 1: 49–68. https://doi.org/10.1016/0305-7488(75)90075-4

– 1980. "Indians as Consumers in the Eighteenth Century." In *Old Trails and New Directions: Papers of the Third North American Fur Trade Conference*, edited by C.M. Judd and A.J. Ray, 255–71. Toronto: University of Toronto Press.

– 1984. "Periodic Shortages, Native Welfare, and the Hudson's Bay Company, 1670–1930." In *The Subarctic Fur Trade: Native Social and Economic Adaptations*, edited by S. Krech, 1–20. Vancouver: University of British Columbia Press.

Ray, A.J., and D.B. Freeman. 1978. *"Give Us Good Measure": An Economic Analysis of Relations Between the Indians and the Hudson's Bay Company before 1763*. Toronto: University of Toronto Press.

Reasons, C. 1972. "Crime and the American Indian." In *Native Americans Today*, edited by H.M. Bahr, B.A. Chadwick, and R.C. Days, 325. New York: Harper and Row.

Redbird, D. 1980. *We Are Métis: A Métis View of the Development of Native Canadian People*. Toronto: Ontario Métis and Non-Status Indian Association.

Reed, A. 1996. *Duck Use of the Coastal Habitats of Northeastern James Bay*. Occasional paper, No. 92. Ottawa: Canadian Wildlife Service.

Reid, J.P. 1993a. "Certainty of Vengeance: The Hudson's Bay Company and Retaliation in Kind against Indian Offenders in New Caledonia." *Montana: The Magazine of Western History* 43, no. 1 (Winter 1993): 4–17. https://www.jstor.org/stable/4519545

– 1993b. Principles of Vengeance: Fur Trappers, Indians, and Retaliation for Homicide in the Transboundary North American West. *Western Historical Quarterly* 24, no. 1: 21–43. https://doi.org/10.2307/970006

– 1994. "Restraints on Vengeance: Retaliation-in-Kind and the Use of Indian Law in the Old Oregon Country." *Oregon Historical Quarterly* 95, no. 1 (Spring): 48–92. https://www.jstor.org/stable/20614559

– 1999. *Patterns of Vengeance: Cross-Cultural Homicide in the North American Fur Trade.* Pasadena, Calif.: Ninth Judicial Circuit Historical Society.

Reyna, S.P. 1994. "A Mode of Domination Approach to Organized Violence." In *Studying War: anthropological Perspectives*, edited by S.P. Reyna and R.E. Downs, 29–65. Langhorne, Penn.: Gordon and Breach.

Rhodes, R., and E. Todd. 1981. "Subarctic Algonquian Languages." In *The Handbook of North American Indians, Vol. 6, Subarctic*, edited by J. Helm, 52–66. Washington, DC: Smithsonian Institution.

Rich, E.E., ed. 1938. *Journal of Occurrences in the Athapaskan Department by George Simpson, 1820 and 1821.* Toronto: The Champlain Society.

– ed. 1941. *The Letters of John McLoughlin from Fort Vancouver to the Governor and Committee, First Series,1825–1838*, Vol. 5. London: Hudson's Bay Record Society.

– ed. 1956. *London Correspondence Inward from Eden Colvile, 1849–1852.* Vol. 19. London: Hudson's Bay Record Society.

– 1958. *The History of the Hudson's Bay Company, 1670–1870.* Vol. 1, (1670–1763), Publication 21. London: Hudson's Bay Record Society.

– 1959. *The History of the Hudson's Bay Company, 1670–1870.* Vol. 2, (1763–1870), Publication 22. London: Hudson's Bay Record Society.

– 1960. "Trade Habits and Economic Motivation among the Indians of North America. *Canadian Journal of Economics and Political Science* 26: 35–53. https://doi.org/10.2307/138817

– 1967. *The Fur Trade and the Northwest to 1857.* Volume 11 in *The Canadian Centenary Series.* Toronto: McClelland and Stewart.

Richardson, B. 1972. *James Bay.* Toronto: Clarke, Irwin and Co.

– 1975. *Strangers Devour the Land.* Toronto: Macmillan Co.

Rifkin, M. 2017. *Beyond Settler Time: Temporal Sovereignty and Indigenous Self-Determination.* Durham: Duke University Press.

Riley, N.S. 2016. *The New Trail of Tears: How Washington is Destroying American Indians.* San Francisco: Encounter Books.

Rogers, E.S. 1963a. "Changing Settlement Patterns of the Cree-Ojibwa of Northern Ontario." *Southwestern Journal of Anthropology* 19, no. 1: 64–88. https://doi.org/10.1086/soutjanth.19.1.3628923

– 1963b. *The Hunting Group-Hunting Territory Complex among the Mistassini Indians*. Bulletin 195. Ottawa: National Museum of Man.
– 1965. "Leadership among the Indians of Eastern Subarctic Canada." *Anthropologica* 7: 263–84. https://doi.org/10.2307/25604661
– 1967. *Subsistence Areas of the Cree-Ojibwa of the Eastern Subarctic: A Preliminary Study*. Bulletin 204: 59–99 in Anthropological Series 70. Ottawa: National Museum of Canada.
– 1969. "Band Organization among the Indians of Subarctic Canada." In *Contributions to Anthropology: Band Societies*, edited by D. Damas, 21–55. Bulletin 228 in Anthropological Series 84. Ottawa: National Museum of Canada.
– 1973. *The Quest for Food and Furs: The Mistassini Cree, 1953–1954*. Publications in Ethnology No 5. Ottawa: National Museum of Canada.
– 1986. "Epilogue: Re-evaluations and Future Considerations." *Anthropologica* 28, no. 1–2: 203–16. https://doi.org/10.2307/25605200
Rogers, E.S., and M.B. Black 1974. "Cultural Ecology in the Subarctic. Review article of *Hunters of the Northern Forest: Designs for Survival among the Alaskan Kutchin*, by R.K. Nelson." *Reviews in Anthropology* 1, no. 3: 343–8. https://doi.org/10.1080/00988157.1974.9977094
– 1976. "Subsistence Strategy in the Fish and Hare Period, Northern Ontario: The Weagamow Ojibwa, 1880–1920." *Journal of Anthropological Research* 32, no. 1: 1–43. https://doi.org/10.1086/jar.32.1.3629990
Rogers, E.S., and J.G.E. Smith. 1981. "Environmental and Culture in the Shield and Mackenzie Borderlands." In *Handbook of North American Indians: Subarctic*, Vol. 6, edited by J. Helm, 130–45. Washington, DC: Smithsonian Institution.
Rohrl. V.J. 1970. "A Nutritional Factor in Windigo Psychosis." *American Anthropologist* 72, no. 1: 97–101. https://doi.org/10.1525/aa.1970.72.1.02a00120
Root, D. 1996. *Cannibal Culture: Art, Appropriation, and the Commodification of Difference*. Boulder: Westview Press.
Rosaldo, R. 1980. "Doing Oral History." *Social Analysis: The International Journal of Anthropology* No. 4: 89–99. https://www.jstor.org/stable/23160313
– 1991. *Culture and Truth: The Remaking of Social Analysis*. Boston: Beacon Press.
Rosay, A.B. 2016. *Violence against American Indian and Alaska Native Women and Men*. National Institute of Justice Research Report. Washington, DC: U.S. Department of Justice, Office of Justice Programs, May 2016. Accessed April 22, 2020. https://www.ncjrs.gov/pdffiles1/nij/249736.pdf.
Ross, A. 1956. *The Fur Hunters of the Far West: A Narrative of the Oregon and Rocky Mountains*, edited by K.A. Spaulding. Norman, OK: University of Oklahoma Press.
Rossignol, M. 1938. "Cross-Cousin Marriage among the Saskatchewan Cree." *Primitive Man* 11, no. 1/2: 26–8. https://doi.org/10.2307/3316200

Rothenberg, P.S., ed. 2002. *White Privilege: Essential Readings on the Other Side of Racism*. New York: Worth Publisher.

Royer, M.-J.S., and T.M. Herrmann. 2011. "Socio-Environmental Changes to Two Traditional Food Species of the Cree First Nation of the Subarctic James Bay." *Cahiers de Geographie du Québec* Vol. 55, no. 156: 575–601. https://doi.org/10.7202/1008895ar

– 2013. "Cree Hunters' Observations on Resources in the Landscape in the Context of Socio-Environmental Change in the Eastern James Bay." *Landscape Research* 38, no. 4: 443–60. https://doi.org/10.1080/01426397.2012.722612

Rozema, V. 2003. *Voices from the Trail of Tears*. Winston-Salem, NC: T.F. Blair Publisher.

Russell, P.H. 2005. *Recognizing Aboriginal Title: The Mabo Case and Indigenous Resistance to English-Settler Colonization*. Toronto: University of Toronto Press.

Sagan, C. 1993. *Broca's Brain: Reflections on the Romance of Science*. New York: Ballentine Books.

Sage, W.N. 1925. "Sir James Douglas: Fur Trader and Governor." Report of the Annual Meeting, *Canadian Historical Association* vol. 4, no. 1: 49–55. https://doi.org/10.7202/300529arCopied

– 1930. *Sir James Douglas and British Columbia*. Toronto: University of Toronto Press.

Sahlins, M.D. 1965. "On the Sociology of Primitive Exchange." In *The Relevance of Models for Social Anthropology*, edited by M. Banton, 139–227. ASA Monographs, No. 1. London: Tavistock.

Said, E. 1979. *Orientalism*. New York: Vintage Books.

– 1994. *Culture and Imperialism*. New York: Vintage Books.

Salisbury, R.F. 1976. "Transactions or Transactors? An Economic Anthropologist's View." In *Transaction and Meaning: Directions in the Anthropology of Exchange and Symbolic Behavior*, edited by B. Kapferer, 41–59. Philadelphia: Institute for the Study of Human Issues.

– 1986. *A Homeland for the Cree: Regional Development in James Bay, 1971–1981*. Montreal: McGill-Queen's University Press.

Salzman, P.C. 1974. "Tribal Chiefs as Middlemen: The Politics of Encapsulation in the Middle East." *Anthropological Quarterly* 47, no. 2: 203–10. https://doi.org/10.2307/3316580

– 2008. *Culture and Conflict in the Middle East*. New York: Humanity Books.

Sanberg, L.A., M. Stiegman, and J. Thistle. 2017. "'But Where Am I?' Reflections on Digital Activism Promoting Indigenous People's Presence in a Canadian Heritage Village." In *Methodological Challenges in Nature-Culture and Environmental History Research*, edited by J. Thorpe, S. Rutherford, and L.A. Sandberg. New York: Routledge.

Satzewich, V. 1997. "Indian Agent and the 'Indian Problem' in Canada in 1946: Reconsidering the Theory of Coercive Tutelage." *Canadian Journal of Native Studies* 17, no. 2: 227–57. https://cjns.brandonu.ca/wp-content/uploads /17-2-cjnsv17no2_pg227-258.pdf

Satzewich, V., and T. Wotherspoon. 1993. *First Nations: Race, Class and Gender Relations*. Scarborough, ON: Nelson Canada.

Sawchuk, J. 1978. *The Métis of Manitoba: Reformulation of an Ethnic Identity*. Toronto: Peter Martin Associates.

Schilz, T.F. 1984. "Brandy and Beaver Pelts: Assiniboine-European Trading Patterns, 1695–1805." *Saskatchewan History* 37, no. 3: 95–102. https:// doi.org/10.1111/j.1468-0289.1984.tb00320.x

Schledermann, P. 2003. Review of *Arctic Justice: On Trial for Murder, Pond Inlet, 1923*, by S.D. Grant. *Arctic* 56, no. 3: 302–4. https://doi.org/10.14430/arctic670

Schmalz, P. S. 1991. *The Ojibwa of Southern Ontario*. Toronto: University of Toronto Press.

Schmidt, B.E., and I.W. Schröder. 2001. "Introduction: Violent Imaginaries and Violent Practices." In *Anthropology of Violence and Conflict*, edited by B.E. Schmidt and I.W. Schröder, 1– 24. New York: Routledge.

Schneider, H.K. 1974. *Economic Man: The Anthropology of Economics*. Salem, Wisc.: Sheffield Publishing.

Schwarz, M.T. 2013. *Fighting Colonialism with Hegemonic Culture: Native American Appropriation of Indian Stereotypes*. Albany, NY: State University of New York Press.

Scrimshaw, N.S. 1987. "The Phenomenon of Famine." *Annual Review of Nutrition* 71, no. 1: 1–22. https://doi.org/10.1146/annurev.nu.07 .070187.000245

Sen, A.1982. *Poverty and Famines: An Essay on Entitlement and Deprivation*. Oxford: Clarendon Press.

– 2009. *The Idea of Justice*. London: Penguin Books.

Shaeffer, C.E. 1969. *Blackfoot Shaking Tent*. Occasional Paper 5. Calgary: Glenbow-Alberta Institute.

Shepard, J. 1974. *The Politics of Starvation*. Washington, DC: The Carnegie Endowment.

Shimony, A.A. 1961. "*Conservatism among the Iroquois at the Six Nations Reserve*." Yale University Publications in Anthropology, No. 65. New Haven: Yale University Press.

Shon, P.C., and S.M. Barton-Bellessa. 2012. "Pre-Offense Characteristics of Nineteenth-Century American Parricide Offenders: An Archival Exploration." *Journal of Criminal Psychology* 2, no. 1: 51–66. https:// doi.org/10.1108/20093821211210495

Sidky, H. 2004. *Perspectives on Culture: A Critical Introduction to Theory in Cultural Anthropology*. Upper Saddle River, NJ: Pearson Prentice Hall.

Siebert, F.T. 1967. "The Original Home of the Proto-Algonquian People." *Contributions to Anthropology: Linguistics I*. Bulletin 214, Vol. 1: 13–47. Ottawa: National Museum of Canada.

Sillitoe, P. 1985. "War, Primitive." In *The Social Science Encyclopedia*, edited by A. Kuper and J. Kuper, 890–1. London: Routledge and Kegan Paul.

Silverman, M., and P.H. Gulliver, eds. 1992. *Approaching the Past: Historical Anthropology through Irish Case Studies*. New York: Columbia University Press.

Simpson, G. 1847. *Narrative of a Journey Around the World*, vol. 1. London: Henry Colburn.

Singer, B. 2001. *Wiping the War Paint off the Lens: Native American Film and Video*. Minneapolis, Minn.: University of Minnesota Press.

Skinner, A.1910. "A Visit to the Ojibway and Cree of Central Canada." *American Museum Journal* 10: 9–18.

– 1911. "Notes on the Eastern Cree and Northern Saulteaux." *Anthropological Papers of the American Museum of Natural History* 9, no. 1: 1–179.

Slobodin, R. 1966. *Métis of the Mackenzie District*. Ottawa: Canadian Research Centre for Anthropology.

Smith, D. 1972. Review of *The Conflict of European and Eastern Algonkian Cultures, 1504–1700: A Study in Canadian Civilization*, by A.G. Bailey. *Ethnohistory* 19, no. 1: 88–9. https://doi.org/10.2307/481357

Smith, D.B. 1987. *Sacred Feathers: The Reverend Peter Jones (Kahewaquonaby) and the Mississauga Indians*. Toronto: University of Toronto Press.

– 1985. *Objects and Others: Essays on Museums and Material Culture*. History of Anthropology Series, vol. 3. Madison: University of Wisconsin Press.

Smith, J.G.E. 1973. *Leadership among the Southwestern Ojibwa*. Publications in Ethnology, no. 7. Ottawa: National Museum of Man

– 1976. Notes on Witiko. In *Papers of the Seventh Algonquian Conference*, edited by W. Cowan, 18–38. Ottawa: Carleton University.

– 1981. "Chipewyan, Cree, and Inuit Relations West of Hudson Bay, 1714–1955." *Ethnohistory* 28, no. 2: 133–56. https://doi.org/10.2307/481115

– 1987. "The Western Woods Cree: Anthropological Myths and Historical Reality." *American Ethnologist* 14, no. 3: 434–48. https://doi.org/10.1525/ae.1987.14.3.02a00020

Smith, S.L. 2000. *Reimagining Indians: Native Americans Through Anglo Eyes, 1880–1940*. New York: Oxford University Press.

Snelgrove, C. 2018. "Review of *Colonial Capitalism and the Dilemmas of Liberalism* (2018), by O.U. Ince." *Canadian Journal of Political Science* 51, no. 4: 968–70. https://doi.org/10.1017/S0008423918000562

Snipp, C.M. 1986. "The Changing Political and Economic Status of the American Indians: From Captive Nations to Internal Colonies." *American*

Journal of Economics and Sociology 45, no. 2: 145–57. https://doi.org /10.1111/j.1536-7150.1986.tb01915.x

Sosa, E. 1999. Skepticism and the Internal/External Divide. In *The Blackwell Guide to Epistemology*, edited by J. Greco and E. Sosa, 145–57. Malden, MA: Blackwell.

Sparks, C.D. 1995. "The Land Incarnate: Navajo Women and the Dialogue of Colonialism." In *Negotiators of Change: Historical Perspectives on Native American Women*, edited by N. Shoemaker, 135–56. New York: Routledge.

Speck, F.G. 1915. "The Family Hunting Band as the Basis of Algonkian Social Organization." *American Anthropologist* 20, no. 2: 143–61. https:// doi.org/10.1525/aa.1918.20.2.02a00010

– 1918. "Kinship Terms and the Family Band Among the Northeastern Algonkian." *American Anthropologist* 20, no. 2 (April–June 1918): 143–61. https://www.jstor.org/stable/660081

Sponsel, L.E. 1996. "The Natural History of Peace: A Positive View of Human Nature and Its Potential." In *A Natural History of Peace*, edited by T. Gregor, 95–128. Nashville: Vanderbilt University Press.

– 1998. "Yanomamo: An Arena of Conflict and Aggression in the Amazon." *Aggressive Behavior* 24, no. 2: 97–122. https://doi.org/10.1002/(SICI)1098 -2337(1998)24:2<97::AID-AB2>3.0.CO;2-P

Stanley, D. 2014. "Native Performers in Wild West Shows: From Buffalo Bill to Euro-Disney." *Journal of Folklore Research* 51 (1): 24–31.

Stanley, S.E., ed. 2017. *Confronting White Privilege*. New York: Oxford University Press.

Statistics Canada. 2018. *Aboriginal Peoples of Canada, 2016 Census*. Ottawa: Statistics Canada.

Steinhart, E.J. 1989. Introduction. *Ethnohistory* 36, no. 1: 1–8. https:// www.jstor.org/stable/482737

Stevens, J.R. 1971. *Sacred Legends of the Sandy Lake Cree*. Toronto: McClelland and Stewart.

Steward, J. 1955. *Theory of Culture Change*. Urbana: University of Illinois Press.

Stewart, O. 1964. "Questions Regarding American Indian Criminality." *Human Organization* 23: 61–66. https://doi.org/10.17730/humo.23.1 .dj81823750261m60

Stillman, D. 2017. *The Story of the Strange Relationship Between Sitting Bull and Buffalo Bill*. New York: Simon and Schuster.

Stocking, G.W. 1968. *Race, Culture, and Evolution: Essays in the History of Anthropology*. New York: The Free Press.

Stone, D. 2003. "Nazism as Modern Magic: Bronislaw Malinowski's Political Anthropology." *History and Anthropology* 14, no. 3: 203–18. https://doi.org /10.1080/0275720032000143356

Strong, W.D. 1929. "Cross-Cousin Marriage and the Culture of the Northeastern Algonkian." *American Anthropologist* 31, no. 2: 277–88. https://doi.org/10.1525/aa.1929.31.2.02a00050

Subrahmanyam, S. 2006. "Imperial and Colonial Encounters: Some Comparative Reflections." In *Lessons of Empire: Imperial Histories and American Power*, edited by C. Calhoun, F. Cooper, and K.W. Moore, 220. New York: The New Press.

Sugars, C. 2004. "Strategic Abjection: Windigo Psychosis and the 'Postindian' Subject in Eden Robinson's 'Dogs of Winter.'" *Canadian Literature* 181 (Summer): 78–91. https://canlit.ca/article/strategic-abjection/

Surtees, R.T. 1969. "The Development of an Indian Reserve Policy in Canada." *Ontario History* 61: 87–98.

– 1982. *Canadian Indian Policy*. Bloomington: Indiana University Press.

Swainger, J. 2005. Review of *Arctic Justice: On Trial for Murder, Pond Inlet, 1923*, by S.D. Grant. *Northern Review* 25–6: 38–240.

Sylvain, R. 2015. "Foragers and Fictions in the Kalahari: Indigenous Identities and the Politics of Deconstruction." *Anthropological Theory* 15, no. 2: 158–78. https://doi.org/10.1177/1463499614564750

Tanner, A. 2005 [1979]. *Bringing Home Animals: Religious Ideology and Mode of Production of Mistassini Cree Hunters*. St. John's, NL: Institute of Social and Economic Research, Memorial University of Newfoundland.

Teicher, M.I. 1960. *Windigo Psychosis: A Study of a Relationship between Belief and Behavior among the Indians of Northeastern Canada*. Seattle: University of Washington Press.

Tester, F. 2003 [2002]. Review of *Arctic Justice: On Trial for Murder, Pond Inlet, 1923*, by S.D. Grant. *Études Inuit Studies* 27, no. 1–2: 532–5. https://doi.org/10.7202/010820ar

Thistle, J. 2017. *Kiskisiwin – Remembering: Challenging Indigenous Erasure in Canada's Public History Displays*. Accessed April 11, 2020. http://activehistory.ca/2017/07/kiskisiwin-remembering-challenging-indigenous-erasure-in-canadas-public-history-displays/.

Thompson, D. 1916. *Narrative of Exploration in Western America*. Toronto: Champlain Society.

Thrapp, D.L. 1967. *Conquest of Apacheria*. Norman: University of Oklahoma Press.

Thwaites, R.G., ed. 1896–1901. *The Jesuit Relations and Allied Documents: Travels and Explorations of the Jesuit Missionaries in New France, 1610–1791*. 73 vols. Cleveland (Reprinted: Pageant, New York, 1959).

Tilly, C. 1978. Anthropology, History, and the Annales. *Review* 1, no. 3/4 (Winter–Spring, 1978): 207–13. https://www.jstor.org/stable/40240781

Tooker, E. 1964. *An Ethnography of the Huron Indians, 1615–1649*. Washington, DC: Smithsonian Institution, Bureau of American Ethnology.

Tough, F. 1990. "Indian Economic Behaviour, Exchange, and Profits in Northern Manitoba during the Decline of Monopoly, 1870–1930." *Journal of Historical Geography* 16, no. 4: 385–401. https://doi.org/10.1016/0305-7488(90)90142-X

Townsend, J.B. 1983. "Firearms against Native Arms: A Study in Comparative Efficiencies with an Alaskan Example." *Arctic Anthropology* 20, no. 2: 1–33. https://www.jstor.org/stable/40316044

Trigger, B.G. 1985. *Natives and Newcomers: Canada's "Heroic Age" Reconsidered.* Montreal: McGill-Queen's University Press.

– 1986. "Evolutionism, Relativism and Putting Native People into Historical Context." *Culture* 6, no. 2: 65–79. https://doi.org/10.7202/1078737ar

– 1987 [1976]. *The Children of Aataentsic. A History of the Huron People to 1660.* Montreal: McGill-Queen's University Press.

Treuer, D. 2019. *The Heartbeat of Wounded Knee: Native America from 1890 to the Present.* New York: Riverhead Books.

Truzzi, M. 1974. *Verstehen: Subjective Understanding in the Social Sciences.* Menlo Park, Calif.: Addison-Wesley Publishing Co.

Tyler, S.A., ed. 1969. *Cognitive Anthropology.* New York: Holt. Rinehart and Winston.

Umfreville, E. 1790. *The Present State of Hudson's Bay.* London: C. Stalker.

United States. 1996. *Homicide and Suicide among Native Americans, 1979–1992.* Washington, DC: Department of Health and Human Services.

Utley, R.M. 1993. *The Lance and the Shield: The Life and Times of Sitting Bull.* New York: Simon and Schuster.

Vandersteene, R. 1969. "Some Woodland Cree Traditions and Legends." *Western Canadian Journal of Anthropology* 1, no. 1: 40–64.

Van Kirk, S. 1972. "Women and the Fur Trade." *The Beaver* (Winter): 4–21.

– 1980. *"Many Tender Ties": Women in Fur Trade Society, 1670–1870.* Norman, OK: University of Oklahoma Press.

– 1988. McTavish, John George. *Dictionary of Canadian Biography*, Vol. 7. Toronto: University of Toronto Press (http://www.biographi.ca/en/bio/mctavish_john_george_7E.html. accessed June 11, 2020).

Vansina, J. 1985. *Oral Tradition as History.* Madison, Wis.: University of Madison Press.

Veracini, L. 2010. *Settler Colonialism: A Theoretical Overview.* Palgrave: Macmillan.

– 2011. "Introducing Settler Colonial Studies." In *Special Issue: A Global Phenomenon. Settler Colonial Studies* 1, no. 1:1–12. https://doi.org/10.1080/2201473X.2011.10648799

Vibert, E. 1997. *Traders' Tails: Narratives of Cultural Encounters in the Columbia Plateau, 1807–1846.* Norman: University of Oklahoma Press.

Vivanco, L.A. 2018. *Windigo* Psychosis. *A Dictionary of Cultural Anthropology*. Oxford: Oxford University Press. Accessed online October 5, 2019. https://www-oxfordreference-com.subzero.lib.uoguelph.ca/view/10.1093/acref/9780191836688.001.0001/acref-9780191836688-e-398?rskey=TmqGlk&result=394.

Voyageur, C., and B. Calliou. 2011. "Aboriginal Economic Development and the Struggle for Self-Government." In *Racism, Colonialism, and Indigeneity in Canada*, edited by M.J. Cannon and L. Sunseri, 203–12. Don Mills, ON: Oxford University Press.

Wagner, M. 1999. "The Study of Religion in American Society." In *Anthropology of Religion: A Handbook*, edited by S. Glazier, 85–101. Westport, CT: Praeger.

Waisberg, L.G. 1975. "Boreal Forest Subsistence and the Windigo: Fluctuation of Animal Populations." *Anthropologica* 17, no. 2: 169–85. https://doi.org/10.2307/25604943

Wallace, A.F.C. 1965. "The Problem of the Psychological Validity of Componential Analysis." *American Anthropologist* 67, no. 5: 229–48. https://doi.org/10.1525/aa.1965.67.5.02a00800

– 1966. *Religion: An Anthropological View*. New York: Random House.

Wallace, W.S. 1925. "The Beginnings of British Rule in Canada." *Canadian Historical Review* 6, no. 3: 208–21. https://doi.org/10.3138/chr-06-03-02

Wapachee, C. 2016. "Concerns Move Indigenous Ceremony Meant to Contact 'Spirit Realm' Outside Quebec Community." *CBC News*. September 3, 2016.

Warren, L. 2002. "The Nature of Conquests: Indians, Americans, and Environmental Histories." In *A Companion to American Indian History*, edited by P.J. Deloria and N. Salisbury, 278–306. Malden, MA: Blackwell.

Wasase, T.A. 2015. *Indigenous Pathways of Action and Freedom*. Toronto: University of Toronto Press.

Watkins, M., ed. 1977. *Dene Nation: The Colony Within*. Toronto: University of Toronto Press.

Watts, M. 1983. *Silent Violence: Food, Famine, and Peasantry in Northern Nigeria*. Berkeley: University of California Press.

Weaver, S.M. 1972. *Medicine and Politics among the Grand River Iroquois: A Study of the Non-Conservatives*. Publications in Ethnology, No. 4. Ottawa: National Museums of Canada.

– 1981. *Making Canadian Indian Policy: The Hidden Agenda 1968–1970*. Toronto: University of Toronto Press.

Wells, G. 2003. "McLean, John (d. 1890)." *Dictionary of Canadian Biography*, vol. 11. Toronto: University of Toronto Press. (http://www.biographi.ca/en/bio/mclean_john_1828_86_11E.html).

Wente, J. 2017. Comments in *The Evolution of Native American Representation in Westerns*, October 24, 2017. Accessed April 15, 2020. https://www.sbs.com

.au/guide/article/2017/10/11/evolution-native-american-representation
-westerns.

Wentzel, W.F. 1889–1890. "Letters to the Hon. Roderick McKenzie." In *Les Bourgeois de la Companie du Nord-Ouest*, edited by L.F. Masson. Première Série. Quebec: A. Cote.

White, H. 1984. "The Question of Narrative in Contemporary Historical Theory." *History and Theory* 23, no. 1: 1–33. https://doi.org/10.2307/2504969

White, R. 1988. *The Roots of Dependency: Subsistence, Environment, and Social Change Among the Choctaws, Pawnees, and Navahos*. Lincoln, NB: University of Nebraska Press.

Whittaker, E. 1992. "Culture: The Reification Under Siege." *Studies in Symbolic Interaction* 13: 107–17.

Whyte, J.D. 2008. "Developmental and Legal Perspectives on Aboriginal Justice Administration." In *Moving Toward Justice: Legal Traditions and Aboriginal Justice*, edited by J.D. Whyte, 107–28. Regina, SK: Saskatchewan Institute of Public Policy.

Williams, M. 2001. *Problems of Knowledge: A Critical Introduction to Epistemology*. New York: Oxford University Press.

Wolfe, P. 1998. *Settler Colonialism and the Transformation of Anthropology: The Politics and Poetics of an Ethnographic Event*. London: Cassell.

– 2006. "Settler Colonialism and the Elimination of the Native." *Journal of Genocide Research* 8, no. 4: 387–409. https://doi.org/10.1080/14623520601056240

Wolfgang, M.E., and F. Ferrucuti. 1967. *The Subculture of Violence: Towards an Integrated Theory*. Beverly Hills, CA: Sage Publications.

Wood, L.A. 1964. *The Red River Colony: A Chronicle of the Beginnings of Manitoba*. Toronto: University of Toronto Press.

Woodham-Smith, C. 1962. *The Great Hunger*. New York: Penguin Books.

Wotherspoon, T, and V. Satzewich. 1993. *First Nations: Race, Class, and Gender Relations*. Scarborough, ON: Nelson Canada.

Wright, J.V. 1965. "A Regional Examination of Ojibwa Culture History." *Anthropologica* 7: 189–227. https://doi.org/10.2307/25604657

– 1971. "Cree Culture History in the Southern Indian Lake Region." Bulletin 232, *Contributions to Anthropology*. Ottawa: National Museum of Man.

– 1981. "Prehistory of the Canadian Shield." In *Handbook of North American Indians: Subarctic*, Vol. 6, edited by J. Helm, 86–96. Washington, DC: Smithsonian Institution.

Yengoyan, A.A. 1986. "Theory in Anthropology: On the Demise of the Concept of Culture." *Comparative Studies in Society and History* 28, no. 2: 368–74. https://doi.org/10.1017/S0010417500013906

Yerbury, J.C. *The Subarctic Indians and the Fur Trade, 1680–1860*. Vancouver, BC: University of British Columbia Press.

York, G. 1990. *The Dispossessed: Life and Death in Native Canada*. Foreword by Tomson Highway. London: Vintage U.K.

Young, A.E., and D. Nadeau. 2005. "Decolonizing the Body: Restoring Sacred Vitality." *Atlantis* 29, no. 2: 1–13. https://doi.org/10.1089/eco.2009.0043

Young, T.J., and L.A. French. 1997. "Homicide Rates among Native American Children: The Status Integration Hypothesis." *Adolescence* 32, no. 125: 57–9.

Zahedieh, N. 2010. *The Capital and the Colonies: London and the Atlantic Economy, 1660–1700*. Cambridge: Cambridge University Press.

Index

Ingram Content Group UK Ltd.
Milton Keynes UK
UKHW011535250423
420753UK00021B/193